CONGRESS
RECONSIDERED

ch 18

CONGRESS RECONSIDERED

Fifth Edition

✧ ✱ ✧

Edited by

LAWRENCE C. DODD
University of Colorado

BRUCE I. OPPENHEIMER
University of Houston

A Division of Congressional Quarterly Inc.
Washington, D.C.

Cover and book design: Paula Anderson

Copyright 1993 © Congressional Quarterly Inc.
1414 22nd Street, N.W., Washington, D.C. 20037

Printed in the United States of America

Library of Congress Cataloging-in-Publication Data

Congress reconsidered / edited by Lawrence C. Dodd,
Bruce I. Oppenheimer. --5th ed.
p.   cm.
Includes bibliographical references and index.
ISBN 0-87187-712-0
1. United States. Congress.   I. Dodd, Lawrence C., 1946-
II. Oppenheimer, Bruce Ian.
JK1061.C5871993
328.73--dc20   92-43242
                                                          CIP

Contents

✦✦✦

Prologue

Part I: Patterns and Dynamics of Congressional Change

Part II: Elections and Constituencies

Part III: Committee and Subcommittee Politics

Part IV: Congressional Leadership and Party Politics

Part V: Congress, the Executive, and Public Policy

Part VI: Congress and Political Change

Tables and Figures

Tables

Figures

Preface

✦ ✦ ✦

As we bring together the collection of essays that constitute the fifth edition of *Congress Reconsidered*, we are more convinced than ever of the correctness of the basic rationale that guided our work on the first and subsequent editions. Put simply, it is that the institution of Congress is ever changing. Although the shifts have rarely been abrupt—and one is well advised not to lose sight of the continuities—Congress does not remain the same. Like other political institutions, it responds to the broader social and political environment in which it exists as well as to internal forces. Congress today is in many ways very different from the way it was when the first edition of *Congress Reconsidered* was published. It is important that we, as students and scholars of Congress, remain current in our understanding of its workings and be able to comprehend recent alterations in the larger context of the historical development of the House of Representatives and the Senate. Conveying these ideas was our primary purpose when we edited the first edition, and our purpose remains the same with the fifth edition.

Most of the nineteen essays in this edition are new. They are not reprinted from other sources but have been written specifically for this collection. Five essays have been substantially revised from versions that appeared in the fourth edition. It may, in fact, be more appropriate to consider this the fifth volume of *Congress Reconsidered* rather than the fifth edition.

A number of themes run through the essays. The most striking, however, addresses how the changes that have occurred in Congress will affect and be affected by the movement from divided party government to unified party control. Clearly, it is too soon to provide any certain answers. But more than in any previous edition, the essays in this edition focus on the capacity of our political parties to function effectively in Congress and consider the general capacity of Congress itself to govern.

Again, we have attempted to make the materials here accessible to a broad readership of students and scholars and to ensure that the essays are of the highest quality of scholarship. In addition, we wanted the work to be as current as possible. Accordingly, the collection begins with a prologue that analyzes the 1992 congressional elections and their implications for governing in the 103d Congress.

Following the prologue, the book is divided into six parts. The first, "Patterns and Dynamics of Congressional Change," contains an overview of the Senate, a new essay on the House of Representatives, and an extensive essay on career patterns in Congress. Part II, "Elections and Constituencies," includes a major update of an essay on voters and elections, an analysis of resource allocation in House campaigns, and an extensive, historical analysis of congressional incumbency. The third section, "Committee and Subcommittee Politics," covers representation and participation in congressional committees, the power of committee leadership on the House Ways and Means Committee, and the growing strategic implications in the use of multiple referrals.

The essays in Part IV, "Congressional Leadership and Party Politics," include an examination of House and Senate leadership, both developmentally and in their present state; an extended essay on the Republican party in the House and Senate; and a historical study of how changes in workload and time constraints affect House deliberation. Part V, "Congress, the Executive, and Public Policy," contains three essays analyzing congressional activity in foreign, domestic, and budgetary policy. The two contributions in the final section of the book, "Congress and Political Change," consider respectively the prospects for citizen control of Congress and the possibility for the renewal of Congress as a democratic policymaking institution.

There are many individuals to whom we are indebted in the preparation of this edition. Our contributors, as in the previous editions, are the ones who make this book possible. Any value this collection has to its readers rests in the fine research of these scholars. In addition, we would like to thank our colleagues at our respective institutions who are a regular source of ideas and encouragement.

The staff of CQ Press once again was invaluable in preparing this book. Dave Tarr provides these editions with important continuity. Brenda Carter maintains the fine relationship that we previously enjoyed with Joanne Daniels and Jean Woy. CQ has a knack for attracting the finest of professionals. Working with Shana Wagger and Ann Davies has eased considerably the demanding tasks of editing and producing this book. The process has been smooth and even enjoyable. In addition, Nola Healy Lynch was most helpful in editing a number of the manuscripts. We are also appreciative of Kathryn Suarez and Kate Quinlin in marketing *Congress Reconsidered*.

More important than the professional support have been the personal relationships that sustain us. Leslie, Susan, Meredith, and Cris have tolerated our moods and enlivened our spirits. Unlike Congress and the president, Dodd and Oppenheimer rarely struggle over issues of responsibility. This undertaking remains a joint effort for which we are both willing to assume blame and willingly credit each other for any success. Although we are sometimes surprised that *Congress Reconsidered* has lasted through five editions, we never have had any doubts about our friendship.

Contributors

John R. Alford is associate professor of political science at Rice University. He received his Ph.D. from the University of Iowa in 1981 and is the author of numerous articles on congressional elections.

R. Douglas Arnold is professor of politics and public affairs at Princeton University, where he chairs the Department of Politics. He received his Ph.D. from Yale University. He has written two books, *Congress and the Bureaucracy: A Theory of Influence* (1979) and *The Logic of Congressional Action* (1990), as well as articles on legislatures, bureaucracy, and public policy. He has been a Research Fellow at the Brookings Institution, a Guggenheim Fellow, and the recipient of the Richard F. Fenno prize in legislative studies.

John B. Bader is a Ph.D. candidate in political science at the University of Wisconsin at Madison. He has been a Fulbright scholar to India and worked for the political unit at ABC News. He is now a Governmental Studies Research Fellow at the Brookings Institution, studying congressional party leadership and policy agenda setting.

David W. Brady is the Bowen H. and Janice Arthur McCoy Professor of Political Science, Business, and Environment in the Graduate School of Business and professor of political science, School of Humanities and Sciences, Stanford University. He received his Ph.D. from the University of Iowa in 1970. His publications include *Congressional Voting in a Partisan Era: A Study of the McKinley Houses* (1973), *Public Policy and Politics in America*, 2d ed. (1984), *Public Policy in the Eighties* (1983) and numerous articles in professional journals. His most recent book is *Congressional Elections and Congressional Policy Making* (1988).

Eileen Burgin is assistant professor of political science at the University of Vermont. She received her Ph.D. from Harvard University and writes in the general area of Congress and foreign policy.

George E. Connor, assistant professor of political science at Southwest Missouri State University, received his Ph.D. from the University of Houston in 1989. His major area of interest is American political thought. He has published a comparative analysis of the Shays', Whiskey, and Fries' rebellions and is currently reexamining the influence of the Book of Deuteronomy on the American founding.

Joseph Cooper is provost and professor of political science at Johns Hopkins University. He has served as Autrey Professor of Social Sciences at Rice University, staff director of the House Commission on Administrative Review, and program chair for the 1985 American Political Science Association meeting. He is the author of several works on the development of the committee system and numerous articles on congressional structures, processes, and politics.

Lawrence C. Dodd is professor of political science and director of the Center for the Study of American Politics at the University of Colorado, Boulder. He received his Ph.D. from the University of Minnesota. He is the author of *Coalitions in Parliamentary Government* (1976), coauthor of *Congress and the Administrative State* (1979), and coeditor of *Congress and Policy Change* (1986) and *Governmental Processes and Political Change* (forthcoming). He has served as president of the Southwestern Political Science Association (1979-1980), as a Congressional Fellow (1974-1975), and as a Hoover National Fellow (1984-1985).

Samantha L. Durst is a Ph.D. candidate in political science at American University. Her publications include articles on the U.S. civil service and the congressional budget process. Her research interests are federal personnel issues, legislative voting behavior, and congressional activity in the area of social welfare policy.

Robert S. Erikson, distinguished professor of political science at the University of Houston, has written numerous articles on congressional elections. He received his Ph.D. from the University of Illinois. He is the coauthor of *American Public Opinion: Its Origins, Content, and Impact,* 3d ed. (1988), and coauthor of *Statehouse Democracy: Public Opinion and Policy in the American States* (forthcoming).

Richard L. Hall is associate professor of political science and public policy studies at the University of Michigan. He received his Ph.D. from the University of North Carolina at Chapel Hill in 1986 and served as a Congressional Fellow (1987-1988). He has written numerous articles on congressional decision making and is the author of *Participation in Congress* (forthcoming).

John R. Hibbing is professor and chair of the Department of Political Science at the University of Nebraska at Lincoln. His Ph.D. is from the University of Iowa (1981), and his primary research interests include congressional careers, congressional elections, and comparative legislative studies. He has been a NATO Fellow in Science at the University of Essex in Great Britain and a Visiting Fellow at the Institute for Regional Studies in Budapest. He is the author of *Congressional Careers: Contours of Life in the U.S. House of Representatives* (1991).

Gary C. Jacobson, professor of political science at the University of California, San Diego, received his Ph.D. from Yale in 1972. He is the author of *Money in Congressional Elections* (1980), *The Electoral Origins of Divided Government* (1990), and *The Politics of Congressional Elections*, 3d ed. (1992), and coauthor of *Strategy and Choice in Congressional Elections*, 2d ed. (1983).

Charles O. Jones is Hawkins Professor of Political Science at the University of Wisconsin at Madison and Nonresident Senior Fellow at the Brookings Institution. He was managing editor of the *American Political Science Review* (1977-1981) and president of the Midwest Political Science Association (1991-1992). He is president-elect of the American Political Science Association. He has written books and articles on Congress, the presidency, political parties, elections, and public policy.

Bruce I. Oppenheimer is professor of political science at the University of Houston. He received his Ph.D. from the University of Wisconsin. He has been a Brookings Fellow (1970-1971) and a Congressional Fellow (1974-1975). He served as coeditor of *Legislative Studies Quarterly* (1988-1992). In addition to writing numerous articles, he is the author of *Oil and the Congressional Process* (1974) and primary author of *A History of the Committee on Rules* (1983).

Norman J. Ornstein is resident scholar at the American Enterprise Institute for Public Policy Research and election analyst for CBS News. His books include *Groups, Lobbying, and Policymaking* (1978), *The New Congress* (1981), and *Vital Statistics on Congress, 1991-1992* (1991).

Robert L. Peabody is professor of political science at Johns Hopkins University. He served as associate director of the American Political Science Association's Study of Congress project. He is the author of numerous books on Congress, including *Leadership in Congress* (1976). He is the coauthor of *Congress: Two Decades of Analysis* (1969) and *To Enact a Law: Congress and Campaign Finance* (1972), editor of *Education of a Congressman* (1972), and coeditor of *New Perspectives on the House of Representatives*, 4th ed. (1992).

David W. Rohde is University Distinguished Professor of Political Science at Michigan State University. He received his Ph.D. from the University of Rochester and has written numerous articles and books about internal congressional politics and congressional elections. He is the author of *Parties and Leaders in the Postreform House* (1991) and coauthor of *Change and Continuity in the 1988 Elections*, rev. ed. (1991). He is former editor of the *American Journal of Political Science*, chairman of the Legislative Studies Section of the American Political Science Association, and APSA Congressional Fellow.

Catherine E. Rudder, executive director of the American Political Science Association, received her Ph.D. from Ohio State University. She has worked for two members of the House Committee on Ways and Means and has written about tax policy since serving as a Congressional Fellow (1974-1975).

Barbara Sinclair is professor of political science at the University of California, Riverside. She received her Ph.D. from the University of Rochester and served as an APSA Congressional Fellow (1978-1979). Her writings on Congress include *Congressional Realignment* (1982), *Majority Leadership in the U.S. House* (1983), and *Transformation of the U.S. Senate* (1989), winner of the Richard F. Fenno Prize and the D. B. Hardeman Prize. She spent 1987-1988 in the House Speaker's office researching party leadership.

Steven S. Smith is professor of political science at the University of Minnesota and associate staff member of the Brookings Institution. He served as a Congressional Fellow (1980-1981). His writing on Congress includes *Call to Order: Floor Politics in the House and Senate* (1989), *Committees in Congress,* 2d ed. (1990), and *Managing Uncertainty in the House of Representatives* (1988). Material for his essay is drawn from *Leading the Senate* (forthcoming).

Randall Strahan is associate professor of political science at Emory University and Fulbright professor of American studies at Odense University in Denmark for 1992-1993. He received his Ph.D. from the University of Virginia in 1986. He is the author of *New Ways and Means: Reform and Change in a Congressional Committee* (1990) and is currently working on a study of congressional leadership.

James A. Thurber is professor of government and director of the Center for Congressional and Presidential Studies at American University. He was legislative assistant to the late senator Hubert H. Humphrey, D-Minn., and to Rep. James G. O'Hara, D-Mich. He has published extensively on Congress, interest group politics, congressional budgeting, and U.S. nuclear power policy and is editor of *Divided Democracy* (1991) and coauthor of *Setting Course: Congress in Transition,* 4th ed. (1992).

Gerald C. Wright is professor of political science at Indiana University and was formerly the political science program director at the National Science Foundation. He received his Ph.D. from the University of North Carolina at Chapel Hill. His publications include *Electoral Choice in America* (1974) and numerous articles in professional journals. He coedited *Congress and Policy Change* (1986) and is coauthor of *Statehouse Democracy: Public Opinion and Policy in the American States* (forthcoming).

Garry Young is a Ph.D candidate in political science at Rice University. His research interests include legislative organization and decision making, interest group and party behavior, and foreign policy.

Perspectives on the 1992
Congressional Elections

Lawrence C. Dodd and Bruce I. Oppenheimer

The anti-incumbency mood of 1992, like the fabled month of March, came in like a lion and went out like a lamb. In the spring and summer of 1992, in the wake of scandals, frustration, disaffection, and House redistricting, the number of legislators leaving Congress through retirement or defeat in primaries set post-World War II records. These early departures fostered the belief that turnover in the House and Senate would reach proportions not witnessed since the 1930s. In the general election the voters surprised everyone, perhaps including themselves, by reelecting 93 percent (325) of the 349 House incumbents and more than 84 percent (22) of the 26 Senate incumbents. They reelected Democratic majorities in both chambers and again deflected Republican hopes for sizable gains in congressional representation.

The dramatic incumbency turnover of 1992 comes not in the Congress but in the presidency. In the general election 62 percent of the voters cast ballots against President George Bush, one of the most stunning rebukes to a sitting president in modern history, while a plurality of 43 percent voted to elect Gov. Bill Clinton of Arkansas, making him president by one of the smallest vote percentages of the century. In a warning to both major parties, 19 percent of the voters cast ballots for independent candidate Ross Perot.

Clinton's election ends, at least for the time being, divided party control in Washington and creates the possibility of a reinvigorated national government. Unlike Jimmy Carter, the last president to have his party in the majority in both the House and the Senate, Clinton has the advantage of a Democratic party in Congress that during the Reagan and Bush presidencies developed the highest level of cohesiveness since the early 1930s. The election, however, left Clinton with fewer Democrats in Congress than was the case for any Democratic president at the beginning of his term since FDR's reelection in 1944. The 103d Congress, as a combined result of retirements, deaths, primary losses, and general election defeats, will have one of the largest groups of new members in the past fifty years. It remains to be seen whether President Clinton can overcome his status as a plurality president and persuade members of Congress—Democratic and Republican, new and old—to join with him in breaking the gridlock of national government. His success undoubtedly will be shaped by the outcomes of the 1992 congressional elections.

Senate Elections

The story of the 1992 Senate elections is one of lost opportunity for the Republican party. Of the thirty-five seats contested in the November election, Democrats had held twenty in the 102d Congress and Republicans had held only fifteen. Had there been an anti-incumbency vote in the general election, the Democrats were situated to suffer the greater consequence because of the disproportionate number of Democratic seats subject to contest. In addition, this class of senators had been elected in 1986, a year in which the partisan forces favored the Democrats. Republicans who survived the 1986 election thus could be considered strong incumbents who would be particularly difficult to defeat in 1992, whereas some of the Democrats could be considered weak incumbents who survived in 1986 because of national partisan forces rather than their own political savvy. Finally, with President Bush's extraordinary popularity in 1991 after the Persian Gulf war, the 1992 elections had seemed to favor Republican challengers, particularly in light of the vote of most congressional Democrats against the war. For all of these reasons, the 1992 election was an opportunity for the Republicans to position their party to retake control of the Senate in 1994.

In the end, however, the Republican party was fortunate to break even. Of eight Senate contests decided by a margin of 5 percent or less of the vote, Republicans won six and Democrats won two. Perhaps because of the nation's growing economic troubles, the Republicans failed to attract the strongest challengers in some races and were shortsighted in their failure to select women candidates who could have taken advantage of the widespread national desire to diversify gender representation in the Senate. Most critically, the Republican senatorial candidates suffered from a weak presidential campaign and from the public's unhappiness with the economy. As a result, Senate Republicans will still have only forty-three seats in the 103d Congress. Republicans would need a sizable victory in the 1994 Senate contests to achieve a majority. Because the class up for election in 1994 is overwhelmingly Democratic, the Republicans do have opportunities to make inroads. Since the early to mid-1980s Democrats have been able to increase their Senate numbers in the East, Midwest, and West. Only in the South do Republicans maintain Senate strength comparable to the level they enjoyed during the early Reagan years. (See Table 1.) One problem the Republicans face in 1994 is that a third of the Senate seats to be contested are in the East, the region of the country in which the Democrats are the strongest.

Despite the Democratic success in retaining control of the Senate, and the 80 percent reelection rate of incumbents running in the general election, it would be misleading to overemphasize the safety of Senate incumbents. Of the eight open-seat contests, one was created when an incumbent, Alan Dixon, D-Ill., was defeated in a primary. Two others involved retirements of scandal-plagued incumbents, Alan Cranston, D-Calif., and Brock Adams, D-Wash., who likely would have been defeated had they run for reelection. In addition, of the twenty-six incumbents who were reelected, ten received less than 60 percent of

Table 1   Partisan Distribution of Senate Seats, 1981-1993, and Contested Seats, 1994

Congress	East	Midwest	South	West	Total
97th (all seats)					
Democrats	13	10	15	9	47
Republicans	11	14	11	17	53
99th (all seats)					
Democrats	13	12	14	8	47
Republicans	11	12	12	18	53
101st (all seats)					
Democrats	15	13	17	10	55
Republicans	9	11	9	16	45
103d (all seats)					
Democrats	16	15	15	11	57
Republicans	8	9	11	15	43
104th					
Democrats	8	5	4[a]	5	22
Republicans	3	3	2	4	12

Note: East: Conn., Del., Maine, Md., Mass., N.H., N.J., N.Y., Pa., R.I., Vt., W.Va. *Midwest:* Ill., Ind., Iowa, Kan., Mich., Minn., Mo., Neb., N.D., Ohio, S.D., Wis. *South:* Ala., Ark., Fla., Ga., Ky., La., Miss., N.C., Okla., S.C., Tenn., Texas, Va. *West:* Alaska, Ariz., Calif., Colo., Hawaii, Idaho, Mont., Nev., N.M., Ore., Utah, Wash., Wyo.

[a] Included in this number is the seat vacated by Sen. Al Gore when he became vice president. Gov. Ned McWherter, D-Tenn., is expected to appoint a Democratic successor, who will face a special election in 1994. The winner of that race will face reelection in 1996.

the two-party vote and could be described as having been vulnerable.

With the election of twelve new senators in 1992, and another coming when a replacement for Al Gore is made, the composition of the Senate will change substantially. The group will include four women—among them Carol Moseley Braun, the first African American woman to serve in the Senate—thus increasing the number of women elected to the Senate from two to six. In the "year of the woman" five of the eleven women running in thirty-five Senate contests were elected. In addition, Ben Nighthorse Campbell, D-Colo., becomes the first native American to serve in the Senate since 1929.

Although we might expect these changes in the composition of the Senate to have some policy implications, the new senators cannot be considered outsiders prepared to mount dramatic attacks on the political establishment. All but two of them previously held elective office, and those two held appointive positions. Among the new senators are three House members, a governor, two mayors, two state senators, a county official, and the son of a former U.S. senator. And despite the influx of newcomers, the institution is likely to retain about the same ideological balance. At the outside, the new senators may make the body slightly more liberal than it was during the 102d Congress.

House Elections

The 1992 elections brought 110 new members into the House—the largest turnover since 1948. Most of the turnover occurred before the general election through retirements and primary defeats. Unlike other years of high turnover, such as 1964 and 1974, few incumbents were ousted in the general election, and the new members caused little change in the partisan composition of the House. In contests during the general election, however, incumbents received only about 63 percent of the vote, considerably below the 68 percent average in the presidential election year of 1988 and slightly below the average for the 1990 election (which was itself a period of citizens' unhappiness with Congress).

In part, the success of House incumbents in the general election is a direct result of the retirements and primary defeats of members who would have been vulnerable in the fall if they had run. For example, of the members who bounced more than one hundred checks in the House "bank," eight were defeated in primaries and eleven retired and did not run for another office.

Of the twenty-four incumbents defeated in the general election, seventeen losses could be attributed to redistricting or to scandal. Five members had each bounced more than a hundred checks, and bounced checks played a role in the defeat of two others. Five incumbents lost contests when redistricting forced them to run against other incumbents. Four others lost in large part because redistricting created far less favorable districts in which to run. And one defeated incumbent was under criminal indictment.

Despite the wholesale reelection of incumbents and the election of a Democratic president, the majority party Democrats suffered a small loss in the number of House seats. At the beginning of the 103d Congress the House will have 258 Democrats, 10 fewer than in the previous Congress. The Democratic losses were short of what had been anticipated by leaders of both parties. It was thought that the Democrats would suffer disproportionately from the anti-incumbency mood and would be blamed for mismanagement of the House bank and post office. Furthermore, it was expected that Democrats would suffer from efforts under the Voting Rights Act to create black and Hispanic districts. (With minority voters concentrated in certain areas, Republicans would have increased opportunities in normally Democratic districts that had lost supportive voting blocs to the new minority districts.) Finally, the Democrats were expected to suffer from the reapportionment by the shift of congressional seats away from their strongest area of support, the Northeast, and toward the Republican areas of strength in Florida, the Southwest, and the West. In many estimates, Democrats were expected to lose from 25 to 30 seats.

Those estimates proved wrong for several reasons. First, as noted above, retirements and primary defeats removed many of the weak incumbents, especially Democrats. Second, the effects of redistricting and reapportionment are usually overstated. Because Democrats may control redistricting in some states and Republicans in others, the effects of redistricting can cancel each other out. (The creation of minority districts may have cost the Democrats some seat advantage, particularly in the South.) Furthermore, the movement of seats from the Frost Belt to the Sun Belt has been followed by a determined effort of Democrats to improve their competitiveness in the West. Their membership has increased in the West more than in any other region. Finally, the short-term forces that are normally thought to affect the partisan outcome of House elections, particularly the economy and the public's approval of the incumbent president, were both working against the Republicans. These forces may have offset the ones thought to be favoring the Republicans. In these circumstances the long-term, normal seat split between the parties again proved to be the best estimator of the election outcome, with the Democrats doing just slightly better than the average of their seat strength since 1938.

In the new House, Democrats maintain a majority of members from each of the four regions. (See Table 2.) Since the Reagan years, Republican gains have come primarily in the South. The picture in other regions is a discouraging one for the Republicans. Perhaps most disheartening is their continued lack of success in open-seat contests. In 1992 Democrats won fifty-seven of the ninety-one open-seat races (63 percent). This number, which is consistent with data from elections since the late 1970s, suggests that it is not incumbency advantage that keeps the Democrats the majority party in the House. Republicans fare about the same in open-seat contests as in those in which incumbents are running. This finding runs contrary to the assumptions of Republicans, who see the term-limit movement as the path to improving their fortunes in House elections.

One of the ironies of the 1992 elections is that as term-limit initiatives were being passed by the voters in fourteen states more than 93 percent of the incumbents running in the general election were reelected. It remains to be seen whether the initiatives will pass the test of constitutionality or whether a constitutional amendment limiting congressional terms will be pursued. What is clear is that voters remain reluctant to retire their own House members.

Although there was little change in the partisan makeup of the House, the 1992 elections produced big increases in the representation of women and minorities among the membership. The number of women in the House increased from twenty-nine to forty-eight. The number of African American members rose from twenty-six to thirty-nine, and Hispanics increased from twelve to nineteen. Except for two women and two Hispanics, all of the changes in the representation of women and minorities are in the Democratic party. The Democrats' disproportionate share of minority members is not new and is consistent with the party's strength among minority voters. As in the Senate, however, the gender gap in the partisan composition of women representatives is new. In the 103d Congress, 75 percent of the women House members will be Democrats.

Although the number of women in the House (and in the Senate) may increase substantially, the immediate future gains for Hispanics and especially for African Americans will be limited. In part, both ethnic groups benefited from

Table 2   Partisan Distribution of Senate Seats, 1981-1993 (by region)

Congress	East	Midwest	South	West	Total
97th					
Democrats	68	58	78	39	243
Republicans	49	63	43	37	192
99th					
Democrats	65	62	82	44	253
Republicans	43	51	47	41	182
101st					
Democrats	66	64	85	45	260
Republicans	42	49	44	40	175
103d					
Democrats	57	61	85	55	258
Republicans	42	44	52	38	176
Other	1				1

Note: The regional categories are the same as those in Table 1.

the redistricting that resulted from application of the Voting Rights Act. As Hispanic registration increases, more Hispanics will be elected to the House. But African Americans will increase their numbers only as they win more seats in districts in which whites make up a majority of the population.

Finally, it is worth noting that the 110 new members of the class of 1992 are quite different from the 92 members of the Watergate class of 1974, who were mobilized to support a broad range of House reforms. First, the 1974 class contained a high concentration of members with little previous political experience. The 1992 class is more experienced, with nearly 72 percent previously having held elective office. Second, the House reform agenda is not as well defined as it was in 1974, although reform activities are being considered in the House party organizations and in a new joint committee. Third, the freshmen in 1974 were overwhelmingly Democrats, and the current crop is more evenly divided between the parties. Because new House Republicans are likely to have different partisan perspectives on reform from those of the Democratic cohort, a united effect of the freshman class is less likely than it was in 1974. Although the freshman class will have a strong presence in the new House, it may be less inclined to divert the House into preoccupation with reform and thus it may allow legislators to focus on issues of governance and policy change.

Governing in the 103d Congress

After twelve years of attributing the nation's problems to a Republican president and divided party government, the Democrats now control the Senate, the House, and the executive branch. With united control they face the daunting task of proving that they can redress the nation's domestic ills—including an economic recession, a massive deficit, a national health care crisis, and urban decay—while maintaining the international movement toward democratization and the downsizing of nuclear arsenals that gained momentum during the Bush presidency. How well they do may influence the party's fate in future elections and quite possibly the public's faith in Congress and national government.

The Democrats begin this period of united government with some distinctive strengths and substantial challenges. Perhaps their greatest single strength originates from a subtle irony of the election year itself. The election of the new president, combined with the large congressional turnover, has created a sense of political rejuvenation in Washington that may energize the government and dampen the public's frustration with entrenched incumbency. And because much of the anti-incumbency sentiment played itself out through "forced" congressional retirements and primary defeats, the congressional Democrats as a group were able to avoid becoming the object of public hostility and thereby to retain power. Thus there is a chance for substantial continuity and stability in the governing processes of congressional Democrats, despite a volatile political year that could have generated a chaotic upheaval on Capitol Hill.

The 1992 elections also provide the Democrats with strength in a second sense. Clinton's victory, though narrow as a percentage of the popular vote, was a broad-based plurality win that crossed all regions of the country and virtually all sectors of the voting public. Likewise, the congressional party sustained or expanded its support in virtually all regions and amidst a diverse set of voting groups. As the party approaches its governing tasks, it has a sense of a mandate that, if narrow in vote terms, is broad in its political inclusiveness.

The Democrats also face significant obstacles. One concern must be the differences between President Clinton and his congressional counterparts. Clinton was elected as an outsider with no experience in Congress or in national government (though he was a congressional staff assistant as a college student), whereas in the near term Congress will almost certainly continue to be led by stalwart party leaders who are part of the Washington establishment. Clinton was elected as a "new kind of Democrat," with a moderate agenda and governing style, whereas the congressional Democrats emerge from the 1992 elections perhaps as slightly more liberal than in past years and with numerous legislative programs they are eager to pursue after years of obstruction by Republican presidents. Finally, Clinton and the congressional Democrats necessarily respond to some very different political incentives. Clinton is most concerned about the nation's economy in the 1996 presidential election, whereas most members of Congress are concerned about the 1994 elections and the interests and economic well being of their individual districts. Clinton and congressional Democrats thus may set priorities for economic and social recovery programs in very different ways and according to very different political timetables. These differences could produce tensions between Congress and the president despite united party government.

A second concern for congressional Democrats must be the large number of new members entering the 103d Congress, 58 percent of whom are Democrats. Although most new members cannot be seen as political outsiders, they generally campaigned as nonincumbents wanting to change "politics as usual." To reach out to new members and ease their inclusion into the politics of the House, Speaker Thomas S. Foley, D-Wash., and other House Democratic leaders took the unprecedented step of meeting with the sixty-four freshmen Democrats in three separate sessions across the nation within a week of the general election. Nevertheless, a large number of new members could become so preoccupied with reform and with distancing themselves from traditional congressional politics that they would obstruct the ability of the new president and Congress to focus on critical policy issues.

A third obstacle facing the Democrats will be the loyal opposition, the Republicans. The minority party knows that Clinton won only 43 percent of the popular vote and thus has a limited claim to a governing mandate. Although 1992 may have been a lost presidential opportunity for the Republicans, it was not a congressional defeat. The party gained seats in the House, and it has a larger number of senators and representatives than at the beginning of either the Carter or Kennedy presidency. This strength will allow them to play critical roles on close votes and will give them a chance to engage more aggressively in Senate filibusters (Senate Democrats lack the sixty votes necessary to invoke cloture through straight party voting). How well the Democrats respond to such challenges depends heavily on the quality of Senate and House leadership within both parties and on the distinctive politics of the two chambers.

In the Senate, Majority Leader George Mitchell of Maine and Minority Leader Robert Dole of Kansas will again face off against each other and provide the chamber with experienced and stable leadership. Mitchell has indicated concern about the inefficiency of the Senate and a strong desire to address this issue. Any actions probably would arise from recommendations for change by the Joint Committee on the Organization of Congress, which was authorized by Congress in August 1992. This committee is expected to issue its reports in early 1993. Aside from any such reform, the Senate's leadership will probably remain stable in the new Congress, with few major leadership changes in Senate committees unless President Clinton nominates a leading senator to a Cabinet post.

The most visible change in the Senate likely will be an effort to rectify the institution's image as a white male club. The Senate leadership undoubtedly will seek to place at least one of the new women senators on the Senate Judiciary Committee to redress the all-male image of Senate justice that it generated in 1991 during its hearings into the sexual harassment allegations against Supreme Court nominee Clarence Thomas. Senate leaders might consider appointing Carol Moseley Braun to the Judiciary Committee and thereby provide racial as well as gender diversification. They might also want to place Ben Nighthorse Campbell on the Interior Committee, where he could address issues related to native Americans and symbolize the institution's commitment to represent ethnic and underclass Americans.

Relations between the Senate and the executive should be considerably better with Clinton than they were with the outgoing administration. Clinton probably will submit judicial and executive nominees who are more acceptable to the Democratic Senate than those submitted by Bush or Reagan. In any case, members of the Senate majority should be less inclined to haggle with a president of their own party over nominations early in his term. Senate Democrats, who were consumed by anxiety over their general opposition to the war in the Persian Gulf early in the 102d Congress, would expect to have a less tense relationship on foreign policy with the new president. Moreover, the new president of the Senate, Vice President Al Gore, gained wide respect among colleagues during his Senate years, and he should ease Senate relations with the White House.

In the House, Thomas Foley and Richard Gephardt, D-Mo., appear to have solidified their grip on the speakership and majority leadership as the result of effective legislative leadership late in the 1992 congressional session. On the Republican side, Robert Michel of Illinois and Newt Gingrich of Georgia will continue as minority leader and minority whip. Should leadership upheavals come, either in the 103d or 104th Congress, it will likely be among Republicans, and probably on the House side, with disgruntled members responding to the national election by seeking new leadership styles. Even without party leadership changes, the institution can expect significant organizational change.

The 110 members who left at the end of the 102d Congress opened a number of positions in top committees, including nineteen on Appropriations, thirteen on Ways and Means, and twelve on Commerce. The parties will be under considerable pressure to appoint some new House members to fill these positions; in any case, they must infuse considerable new blood into the major authorization and money committees, thereby upsetting established committee behavior.

The opportunity for serious reform could come as the House Democratic Caucus reviews the proposals of House rules changes being prepared by its Committee on Organization, Study, and Review, chaired by Rep. Louise M. Slaughter, D-N.Y. The Slaughter committee proposes some far-reaching alterations in party and House rules. It recommends the creation of a Democratic policy council designed to set the party's agenda and play a major role in seeking its enactment. The Slaughter committee also proposes substantial reductions in the number of House subcommittees and streamlined measures for the unseating of committee and subcommittee chairs. These and similar proposals would continue the shifting of House power toward a party and committee oligarchy that has been underway for almost a decade, while seeking to make that oligarchy more responsive to the membership.

Although none of the changes are likely to constitute major restructurings of congressional politics akin to the reforms of the early to mid-1970s, they demonstrate that members continue to be concerned about the effects of rules and organizational arrangements on the policy process. During periods of national policy gridlock, as occurred during the Bush presidency, politicians and the public alike embrace congressional reform as a solution to policy immobilism. Yet a major concern must also be whether preoccupation with reform may not divert members of Congress from confronting difficult policy issues and engage them in personal power machinations that have only limited relationship to policy deliberation. The success of the congressional Democratic party in its governing tasks, and of the Clinton administration, requires that members act rapidly to implement those reforms that are truly essential to policy activism and then move on to grapple directly with the problems confronting the nation.

Conclusion

The 1992 election creates an opportunity for coherent party governance that Congress and the nation have not experienced for twelve years. The immediate task for the new president and Congress is to resuscitate the nation's economy. If they are successful in this endeavor, particularly if they find a strategy that could ignite the stalled economy and reverse the long-term decline in economic productivity, they might dramatically change the dynamics of American politics over the coming decade. Such developments could lay the foundations for a resurgence in support of Congress and the national government, a period of united national government, and a resolidification of Democratic dominance of national politics. This scenario would prove particularly compelling were Clinton to avoid major failure in foreign policy. On the other hand, the Clinton administration faces structural problems in the nation's economy and an unstable international scene, particularly in the new republics of the former Soviet Union. The Democrats thus confront many hazards that could derail their governing efforts.

Should the Democrats falter in their domestic or international responsibilities, the possibility would then exist for Republican resurgence. Much depends on the ability of the Republican party to rebound from the electoral disappointments of 1992, revitalize their party at the grassroots level, and generate quality congressional candidates who could effectively challenge the Democrats in 1994 and thereafter. If the Democratic party should flounder in 1994, as a result of poor economic performance, international crisis, or domestic scandal, many of the advantages that the Republican party appeared to enjoy in congressional races in 1992 might reappear. One could imagine considerable Republican success in the new and redrawn southern, southwestern, and western districts that went Democratic in 1992.

Much rests on the early success of the Democrats in demonstrating that they can govern in a cooperative and effective manner and can address the nation's immediate economic problems. If the Democrats fail, the 1994 or 1996 congressional elections might yet demonstrate the full force of the public's anti-incumbency fury that threatened early in 1992. The Republicans then could challenge Democratic control of Congress. Democratic success in governing, by contrast, could possibly defuse the electorate's unhappiness with Washington, at least for a time, and give Congress and the president an opportunity to address the fundamental economic dislocations and international alterations that will continue to confront the nation into the twenty-first century.

Part I

...

Patterns and Dynamics of Congressional Change

1

The U.S. Senate in an Era of Change

Norman J. Ornstein, Robert L. Peabody, and David W. Rohde

The 102d Congress brought two radically different images of the U.S. Senate to the American public. The first, in January 1991, was the dramatic and moving debate on the Senate floor over whether to give the president authority to use military force in the Persian Gulf to force Iraq out of Kuwait. The televised debate, which lasted three days, riveted public attention, underscoring the time-honored image of the Senate as the world's greatest deliberative body, known for its stirring debate.

The second image came a few months later, with the Senate Judiciary Committee hearings on Anita Hill's allegations about Supreme Court nominee Clarence Thomas. These hearings were also televised nationally but—unlike the Gulf debate, covered largely by C-SPAN and public television—were broadcast live on network television, preempting soap operas and game shows. What Americans saw was a very different Senate, one almost universally vilified for its stumbling ineptitude, insensitivity, and incompetence. The Hill-Thomas hearings amplified a different image of the Senate, one of an aloof and out-of-touch chamber filled with bumblers, blowhards, charlatans, and chauvinists.

As the Senate moved into the 1990s, it struggled with the contradictions and cross-pressures caused by these conflicting images. The proud traditions of the institution have been ingrained, at least in general terms, by such classic movies as *Mr. Smith Goes to Washington* and *Advise and Consent,* but so have the classic cynical images of politicians and the political process. In the 1990s the high points, like the Gulf war debate, have been few, while the low points have included not just the Thomas-Hill hearings but the congressional pay-raise controversy, the Keating Five scandal, the catastrophic health insurance debacle, and, more broadly, the failure of government to come to grips with the budget deficit and other major domestic problems.

For the contemporary Senate, pushed and pulled by internal change and changes in its external environment, identity crises are everywhere. Finding a role as both a deliberative body and a policymaking body has always been a difficult balancing act for the institution, but rarely to the degree it was in the early 1990s. Maintaining a sense of institutional dignity became even more difficult in an era of deep cynicism about politics and even deeper cynicism about Congress, especially during a time in which individual senators and the entire institution came under frequent attack for ethical lapses. The Senate of the 1960s was the prime breeding ground for presidential candidates; in 1992 only two senators competed for the Democratic presidential nomination, and their status as senators did not keep them from becoming the first two candidates forced to drop out of the race.

That the Senate faced internal conflicts, external pressures, and substantial change in the 1990s is itself not surprising news. The Senate has been characterized by change for most of its history, particularly in the post-World War II era. It has continued to change in recent years, in the nature of its membership, in its formal and informal leadership, in its internal processes and structures, in its policy directions, and in its role in the American political system. In this essay we will look at some of the recent changes in the Senate and its environment, trying to sort out the changes and their meaning.

The Membership

With six-year terms for its members, the Senate does not always change its membership abruptly or regularly. But membership change is a staple of Senate life. Some of the change has come gradually; some of it has occurred in large jolts—for example, the elections of 1980 and 1986 brought the only changes in partisan control of the Senate since the early 1950s.

The public's image of the Senate is an institution filled with thirty-year, gray-maned veterans of the seniority system. But that image is anything but accurate. The aggregate effect of membership change since Donald R. Matthews and Ralph K. Huitt wrote their brilliant portraits of the Senate of the 1950s has been substantial.[1] When the 102d Congress convened in January 1991, only three senators who had served before John Kennedy became president in 1961 remained in the Senate. Indeed, forty-nine of the hundred members were new to the chamber since Ronald Reagan's election to the presidency in 1980.

Membership change is more than just a matter of substituting one senator for another. With respect to a variety of attributes, different kinds of senators have replaced those who served earlier, and this turnover has substantially affected the operation of the Senate and the policies it has produced. We will consider three particular attributes related to these changes: partisan division, sectional party affiliation, and ideology.

The most obvious change has been in the party affiliation of the membership. From the end of World War II through most of the 1950s, the partisan division of the Senate was very close; neither party ever controlled the body by more than a few votes. In the election of 1958, however, the Democratic membership of the Senate jumped from forty-nine seats to sixty-four. Through the 1970s the number of Democrats was usually greater than sixty. But 1981 brought a stunning reversal: Democrats saw their two decades of dominance transformed into a narrow Republican majority that retained control of the Senate through 1986. After nearly two decades of being in the majority, Senate Democrats suddenly were thrust into the foreign condition of minority status, while Senate Republicans, long accustomed to being in the minority, gained the power—and the responsibilities—of the majority. The election of 1986 reversed fortunes again, restoring a narrow Democratic majority, which has expanded by a couple of votes in subsequent years. The Democrats' margin gives them a cushion to work with in their effort to retain control, but it is not large enough to make that control certain for the near future.

A second aspect of change involves the regional character of the two parties. Through the 1950s Democratic membership was concentrated in the South and West, while Republicans came primarily from the East and Midwest. In 1957, for example, the Democrats held every Senate seat from the South and thirteen of the twenty-two seats from the West, but they controlled only five of twenty eastern seats and three of the twenty-two midwestern seats. By the 1970s, however, these regional patterns had changed. In 1979 the Democrats held majorities in every region except the West (where Republicans held fourteen of twenty-six seats), including thirteen of twenty-two seats in the Midwest. These dramatic gains by Democrats were offset somewhat by losses in the South. In the early 1980s the Republicans built their majority on significant gains in the South and Midwest, but 1986 restored the distribution of seats to a pattern very similar to that of 1979. Again, the only region where Republicans held a majority was the West. This distribution persisted with little change through 1992.

The partisan and regional changes in the Senate contributed to changes in the ideological character of the membership. Table 1-1 shows the proportions of liberals, moderates, and conservatives among various groups of senators in the 85th Congress (1957-1959) and in the first sessions of the 94th (1975), 96th (1979), 98th (1983), 100th (1987), and 102d (1991) Congresses.

Democrats in the 85th Congress were divided almost evenly between liberals and conservatives, whereas the Republicans were overwhelmingly conservative. This ideological makeup produced a conservative majority in the Senate in 1957-1959. The subsequent steep increase in the number of Democrats and almost matching decline in the number of Republicans produced a liberal plurality by 1975.

Not all of the ideological change was due to these numerical shifts, however. The makeup of various subgroups in the Senate also was different, as Table 1-1 indicates. In the 85th Congress, for example, northern Democrats and southern Democrats had distinct ideological characters, but there was also heterogeneity within each group. By the 94th Congress this mixture no longer existed; there were no northern conservatives and no southern liberals, and the proportion of moderates in each group also had declined. On the other hand, over the same period the Republicans in the Senate became considerably more heterogeneous.

In the 94th Congress these trends began to reverse. In the late 1970s and 1980s the Republicans became more homogeneous and the Democrats more diverse. As the years passed, moderates represented a larger share of the Democratic coalition in the Senate. For all the partisan change that occurred, there has been relatively little change in the past decade in the overall ideological makeup of the Senate.

Yet this analysis tells only part of the story, for it applies only to aspects of

Table 1-1   Ideological Divisions in the Senate, 85th Congress and the First
Sessions of the 94th, 96th, 98th, 100th, and 102d Congresses
(in percentages)

	Northern Democrats	Southern Democrats	All Democrats	Repub- licans	All members
85th Congress (1957-1959)	(27)	(22)	(49)	(47)	(96)
Liberals	67	9	41	2	22
Moderates	19	27	22	26	24
Conservatives	15	64	37	72	54
94th Congress (1975)	(46)	(16)	(62)	(38)	(100)
Liberals	85	—	63	16	45
Moderates	15	19	16	26	20
Conservatives	—	81	21	58	35
96th Congress (1979)	(43)	(16)	(59)	(41)	(100)
Liberals	58	—	42	7	28
Moderates	37	31	36	32	34
Conservatives	5	69	22	61	38
98th Congress (1983)	(35)	(11)	(46)	(54)	(100)
Liberals	47	—	39	—	20
Moderates	47	55	39	30	34
Conservatives	6	45	22	70	46
100th Congress (1987)	(38)	(16)	(54)	(46)	(100)
Liberals	53	—	37	—	20
Moderates	39	50	43	24	34
Conservatives	8	50	20	76	46
102d Congress (1991)	(40)	(17)	(57)	(43)	(100)
Liberals	55	—	39	—	22
Moderates	38	47	40	12	28
Conservatives	8	53	21	88	50

Sources: The scores for 1957-1959 were calculated from the appropriate roll calls listed in the *Congressional Quarterly Almanac* for those years. The scores for 1975 were taken from *Congressional Quarterly Weekly Report*, Jan. 24, 1976, 174; and the 1979 scores from *Congressional Quarterly Weekly Report*, Jan. 26, 1980, 198. The 1983 scores are from *Vital Statistics on Congress, 1984-1985,* ed. Norman J. Ornstein et al. (Washington, D.C.: American Enterprise Institute, 1984). The 1987 scores are taken from *Congressional Quarterly Weekly Report*, Jan. 16, 1988, 107, and the 1991 scores are from *Congressional Quarterly Weekly Report,* Dec. 28, 1991, 3795.

Note: The classification is based on a variation of the conservative coalition support score published annually by Congressional Quarterly. The support score of a member was divided by the sum of his or her support and opposition scores, which removes the effect of absences. Members whose scores were 0-30 were classified as liberals, 31-70 as moderates, and 71-100 as conservatives. The number of persons used to compute each percentage is shown in parentheses.

liberalism-conservatism that are captured by the conservative coalition support scores employed in Table 1-1. This measure has its origins in the 1950s, when southern Democrats and Republicans shared conservative attitudes on a wide range of issues. The conservative coalition was defined to exist on any vote on which a majority of northern Democrats voted in opposition to a majority of southern Democrats and a majority of Republicans. This coalition used to form quite often. In most years from the mid-1960s through the early 1980s, it existed on between 20 percent and 30 percent of the roll call votes in the Senate.[2] This is, however, no longer true.

One of the most consequential changes in the character of the Senate's membership in the 1980s was the election of a large contingent of southern Democrats who respond to a wide range of issues in ways similar to their northern colleagues. This change has had a dual effect. First, the conservative coalition is much less likely to form because there have been fewer issues on which southern Democrats were inclined to agree with the Republicans. In 1987 the coalition appeared on only 8 percent of the Senate votes, an all-time low. In 1991 the comparable figure was still only 14 percent. Second, on votes that divided the parties from one another (which had become *more* frequent), southern Democrats were substantially more loyal to their party than in the past. In the 92d Congress (1971-1973), for example, southern Democrats supported their party's position only 46 percent of the time on average, while the support level for northern Democrats was 82 percent—a difference of 36 percentage points. By contrast, in 1991 the average support for southern Democrats was 73 percent and for northerners 87 percent. The difference between the two groups had declined to only 14 points. Meanwhile, the Republicans have also exhibited greater homogeneity on partisan issues, with average party loyalty increasing from 73 percent in the 92d Congress to 83 percent in 1991.[3] Thus on issues that divide Democrats from Republicans, both parties in the Senate have become more internally homogeneous and more different from one another.

These changes have resulted in Democratic solidarity across regional lines on many issues that certainly would have produced conservative coalitions in the past. In 1991, for example, majorities of both northern and southern Democrats supported a common position in opposition to the GOP on authorizing force against Iraq, instituting a waiting period for handgun purchases, granting most-favored-nation status to China, legislating family and medical leave, and confirming Clarence Thomas to the Supreme Court.

In addition to affecting voting patterns on the Senate floor, the intensification of partisan divisions has affected the internal politics of the parties. Although individual senators are still free to vote their conscience or constituency, consistent deviation from party positions can result in negative consequences. For example, Sen. Charles S. Robb, D-Va., was dropped from the Budget Committee in 1991, a move which many observers saw as a consequence of his fiscal conservatism and his support for authorizing President Bush to use force in the Persian Gulf crisis.[4] A clearer example involved the Senate Republican Confer-

ence's 1990 decision to dump its chairman, moderate senator John H. Chafee of
Rhode Island, in favor of Sen. Thad Cochran of Mississippi, who was much more
conservative. Chafee had worked with Democrats on a number of legislative
matters, had voted to override Bush's veto of the 1990 civil rights bill, and was
only one of three Republicans to support cutting off a filibuster against a campaign finance bill. Conservative senator Daniel R. Coats, R-Ind., said that the
leadership election "may reflect the fact that there is a sense that business as
usual is not going to serve us in 1992. We need an aggressiveness in defining
differences between the two parties." [5] If the increased partisanship between the
parties and the increased homogeneity within them continues, the patterns of
policymaking in the Senate will be significantly different from the pattern of the
postwar period.

Norms and Rules

One vivid part of the public's image of the Senate comes from *Mr. Smith
Goes to Washington:* the lone senator filibustering until he drops on the Senate
floor highlights the unique role of the individual in the Senate, an institution
without the tight limitations for debate placed on members of the House. But, of
course, the Senate is a decision-making institution, and as such it has an extensive set of formal rules that regulate its operations. It is also a group of individuals, and "just as any other group of human beings, it has its unwritten rules of
the game, its norms of conduct, its approved manner of behavior." [6] The Senate,
therefore, has both formal and informal rules, and, although there has been
continuity in both categories for more than three decades, significant changes
have also occurred.

The unwritten rules, or norms, of the Senate are patterns of behavior senators think they and other senators should follow. In an institution that leaves
great leeway for its members' behavior and actions, these norms can be important. Most members share similar expectations about how a senator ought or
ought not to behave. In his study of the Senate in the mid-1950s, Matthews
cited six norms, or "folkways": legislative work, specialization, courtesy, reciprocity, institutional patriotism, and apprenticeship.

The first norm required that senators devote a major portion of their time
to their legislative duties in committee and on the floor and not seek personal
publicity at the expense of these legislative obligations. Under the second
norm, specialization, each senator was expected to concentrate on matters pertaining to committee business or directly affecting constituents. The third
norm, courtesy, required that political conflicts within the Senate should not
become personal conflicts. References to colleagues in legislative situations
should be formal and indirect, and personal attacks were deemed unacceptable. Reciprocity, the fourth folkway, meant that senators were expected to
help colleagues whenever possible and to avoid pressing their formal powers
too far (for example, systematically objecting to unanimous consent agreements). A senator was to understand and appreciate the problems of colleagues

and to keep bargains once they were struck. The fifth norm of institutional patriotism required that a member protect the Senate as an institution, avoiding behavior that would bring it or its members into disrepute. Finally, new senators were expected to serve a period of apprenticeship. A freshman senator, it was felt, should wait a substantial amount of time before participating fully in the work of the Senate. During this time freshmen were expected to learn about the Senate and seek the advice of senior members.

Many of these folkways benefited the collective membership, and it is not surprising that some of them are still recognized in the Senate today. But, as patterns of power and ambition inside and outside the Senate have changed, both normative expectations and the degree to which they are observed underwent change as well. During the 1960s and 1970s the frequency of behavior that seemed to violate the norms increased, and by the 1980s a number of them had disappeared as expectations or had became significantly altered. As Barbara Sinclair concluded from her analysis, "Both in terms of expectations and behavior, the norms of apprenticeship, specialization, and legislative work are defunct; reciprocity and institutional patriotism have undergone major changes; courtesy is still a Senate norm but is more frequently breached in practice." [7]

As the scope of federal government activity increased and the degree of regional and interstate differences declined, more and more senators were induced by electoral incentives and by their own policy interests to become involved in a wide range of issues. This undermined the norm of specialization. Both Sinclair and Steven S. Smith have shown that the percentage of floor amendments coming from senators who were not members of the committee of jurisdiction increased somewhat over time.[8] It is important to note that this increase has occurred during the time that the committee responsibilities of senators have broadened. Moreover, in terms of expectations, Sinclair draws the following conclusion from her interview data: "That a senator will be broadly involved in a number of issues, some of which do not fall within the jurisdiction of his committees, is taken as a matter of course." [9]

Even before the specialization norm disappeared, senators had ceased to expect junior members to serve a period of apprenticeship. This norm had provided the general Senate membership with little benefit. By the 1950s the only groups that could be seen to benefit from the observance of this norm were the senior conservatives in both parties who dominated the Senate's positions of power. Beginning with the 1958 election, liberal northern Democrats entered the Senate in greater numbers, and the conservative dominance began to break down.[10] Consequently, junior members had less incentive to observe the norm. Gradually, as those junior senators of the early 1960s became senior members, the expectations regarding the norm became less widely shared than they had been formerly.

As the Senate returned to conservatism in the late 1970s and early 1980s, the continuing influx of junior members who made the ideological reversion possible had no interest whatsoever in restoring the norm that their earlier liberal brethren had helped to abolish. Junior members across the board neither want nor feel the need to serve an apprenticeship; furthermore, no senior members expect them to do so, as these statements from senators indicate:

> All the communications suggest "get involved, offer amendments, make speeches. The Senate has changed, we're all equals, you should act accordingly." [A junior Democrat]
>
> Well, that [apprenticeship] doesn't exist at all in the Senate. The senior senators have made that very clear, both Democrats and Republicans. [A junior Republican]
>
> We now hope and expect and encourage the younger guys to dive right into the middle of it. [A senior conservative Republican][11]

Thus the Senate of the 1980s, when considered along seniority lines, is a more egalitarian institution than it used to be. Junior members now play important roles, and this change in the informal rule structure of the body has contributed to several changes in the formal rules. In 1970, for example, a rule was adopted that limited members to service on only one of the Senate's four most prestigious committees: Appropriations, Armed Services, Finance, and Foreign Relations. This rule prevented senior members from monopolizing these important committee posts and facilitated the appointment of relatively junior senators much earlier in their career than had previously been possible. In addition, both parties adopted rules limiting the role of seniority in the selection of committee chairmen.

As junior members became more active, they began to feel more intensely the disparity of resources between themselves and senior senators, particularly with regard to staff. The junior members therefore sponsored and aggressively pushed a resolution that permitted them to hire additional legislative staff members to assist in their committee duties. The Senate adopted the resolution in 1975.

These changes in the amount and the distribution of resources among members also helped to undermine another folkway: legislative work. In the Senate of the 1950s, when members had relatively little staff, the institution had to depend on members to do the "great bulk of the Senate's work [that] is highly detailed, dull, and politically unrewarding." [12] The wide dispersion of substantial staff resources made this no longer necessary; senators could devote their time and attention to other pursuits, including the increasing demands of electoral competition and its accompanying demand of fund raising. In addition, many members pursued active candidacies for the presidency or sought the media attention that would, they hoped, make such a candidacy possible. These pursuits further reduced the time available for detailed legislative work.

Regarding institutional patriotism, senators continue to have an interest in protecting the reputation and integrity of their institution. This interest is intensified by the recurrence of partisan division (and, therefore, of institutional competition) between the Senate and the presidency. On the other hand, partisan divisions between the House and the Senate and the substantial public disapproval of Congress have made it easier for senators to criticize the Senate with impunity.

The courtesy norm also continues to serve the interest of members, but it too is violated more frequently than in the past. Courtesy permits political conflict to remain depersonalized, allowing yesterday's opponent to be tomorrow's ally. (As one Republican senator said, "It's the catalyst that maintains a semblance of order.") The ideological divisions in the contemporary Senate, however, frequently have pitted one or more of the staunch liberals (such as Democrat Howard M. Metzenbaum of Ohio) or, more often, the extreme conservatives (such as Republican Jesse Helms of North Carolina) against their colleagues in public and often bitter exchanges. These personal conflicts also occur within partisan and ideological groups. For example, William S. Cohen, R-Maine, reported that Lowell P. Weicker, Jr., of Connecticut responded to a statement by John Heinz of Pennsylvania by saying, "Anyone who would make such a statement is either devious or an idiot. The gentleman from Pennsylvania qualifies on both counts." [13] It also used to be almost unheard of for one senator to campaign against another, but in 1990 Sen. Wendell H. Ford, D-Ky., campaigned for the Democratic challenger to Sen. Larry Pressler, R-S.D. Ford said of Pressler's service on the Senate committee on which they both served, "He comes in late, makes a quick press statement and leaves. . . . He doesn't sit there and have any input or do any of the actual work." [14]

Under the final norm, reciprocity, it was expected that members would not press their individual prerogatives too far. During the past two decades the Senate has seen increasingly frequent violations of this folkway as well. The Senate's expanding workload and the increase in amending activity have led to substantial pressures on floor time. [15] This altered context, in turn, created strategic opportunities for opponents of legislation to use filibusters to extract concessions from supporters, especially late in a session when the press of legislation is greatest. More frequent use of the filibuster in the early 1970s resulted in a change in the procedure for formally ending debate (called "cloture"); the number of votes needed for cloture was reduced from two-thirds of those present and voting (sixty-seven votes for the full Senate) to three-fifths of the entire membership (sixty votes). In the years immediately after the rules change, cloture was more frequently sought and more often successful than in the past. [16]

During the 1980s, however, the advent of a Republican majority and growing partisanship within the institution increased the inclination of members to employ filibusters, and the tactic frequently was successful. Sinclair analyzed the thirty-seven filibusters waged between 1981 and 1986. She found that fifteen "ultimately rendered the Senate's decision on the measure at issue more favorable to the filibusterers than it would have been otherwise. When the chance of having such an impact is 40 percent, the incentives to engage in extended debate are obvious." [17] Moreover, the frequency and substantial success of filibusters made even the threat of one an important bargaining chip in the legislative process. To keep the schedule of legislation on track, Senate leaders were usually compelled to seek a unanimous consent agreement among the members before bringing a major bill to the floor. Such agreements usually specify the length of time for debate, the time of a final vote, and the amendments that may be considered. Since the agreements must be unanimous, leaders often have to make concessions to bill opponents to secure them.[18]

The restoration of a Democratic Senate majority in 1986 increased the Republican conservatives' incentives to use their individual prerogatives to block liberal initiatives. As Christopher Bailey has noted, "a small group of 'new Right' senators believed that obstructionism was not only a right, but a duty. Senator Jake Garn (R-Utah) summed up this attitude when he stated: 'If I'm against a bill in committee, I try to keep it there. If I can slow down a mark-up, or find some tactic to keep it off the floor, I'll do it. . . . I don't particularly have a loyalty to tradition.' " [19]

To counter GOP efforts to obstruct Democratic bills, Majority Leader George J. Mitchell, D-Maine, and his predecessor Robert C. Byrd, D-W.Va., frequently had to resort to early imposition of cloture and other tactics, which further fueled partisan and interpersonal conflict. In July 1990, for example, the Senate imposed cloture on a civil rights bill opposed by President Bush, limiting debate to only thirty hours. Minority Leader Bob Dole, R-Kan., heatedly responded:

> If we're going to shove it down the throats of the minority, things are going to get tough around here. . . . If we're going to be treated like a bunch of bums on this side of the aisle, then say so. . . . There's not going to be any time agreements, any agreements on anything at all, until we have some understanding this place is going to be run in a civil manner.[20]

One result of these changes in Senate norms and behaviors has been frequent calls to alter the institution's rules to deal with their consequences. Sen. Lloyd Bentsen, D-Texas, has said, "The protection of individual prerogatives has advanced to the point that it weakens the Senate as an institution. We have become more skilled at avoiding decisions than at making tough policy choices." [21] David L. Boren, D-Okla., and Pete V. Domenici, R-N.M., for example, pushed to create a joint Senate-House committee that will systematically consider the entire legislative process. The committee's charge is to propose reform measures in 1993 modeled on the Legislative Reorganization Act of 1946. Others have called for more limited, specific changes, such as reducing further the number of votes required for cloture or requiring that floor amendments be germane to the subject of the bill to which they are attached. Whether the Senate will adopt such changes depends on whether members calculate that the gain to them from institutional efficiency would compensate for the loss of individual prerogatives—and whether proponents could muster the two-thirds votes necessary to shut off the filibuster that would likely seek to block them.

Before closing this section it is worth noting one significant rules change that the Senate did adopt not long ago: the decision in 1986 to permit televising floor sessions.[22] Although the House had permitted televised sessions seven years earlier, the Senate delayed because of widespread concerns about the effect on the legislative process. Some believed that speech making would increase and thereby would intensify the legislative backlog. Others were concerned that senators would find compromises more difficult than formerly. Still others feared that viewers would misunderstand the Senate's complex procedures and would bring pressure to change the rules that protected minority rights but slowed the process. The feared consequences appear not to have materialized. An analysis of the six-week test period in 1986 showed a modest increase in debate time and no change in amending activity. Most of the original opponents seem to have concluded, with Sen. William Proxmire, D-Wis., that "TV has had virtually no impact on the Senate. . . . Most senators, including myself, go for days taking an active part in floor discussion and completely forgetting that television is in fact covering the body." [23]

Thus the Senate's norms and rules, and the patterns of behavior they relate to, continue to evolve as the individual incentives and preferences of members also change. The Senate is a more egalitarian and open institution than it was—and a more partisan and conflictive one.

Leadership

The Senate's formal leadership often determines the policy directions the institution takes. The leadership can shape the degree of partisan conflict or consensus, the success or failure a president has in relating to the Senate, and the efficiency or slowness with which the nation's agenda is considered. The top party leaders, especially the majority and minority leaders, are selected in secret-ballot votes by their party colleagues. Who they are and why they are selected can tell us a great deal about the nature of the Senate at the time.

Matthews's classic analysis of senators provides a historical baseline for analyzing Senate party leadership in the post-World War II era. "Democratic party leadership," he argued, "is highly personalized, informal, centralized in the hands of the floor leader." In contrast, "even when compared to a Democratic party under a relatively weak leader, the Republican leadership is more formalized, institutionalized and decentralized." [24] These generalizations about the differences between the two Senate party leadership structures held up remarkably well through the 1970s and 1980s and into the 1990s, although exceptions occurred from time to time.

Both parties use secret ballots in party conferences to elect a floor leader (whether majority or minority), an assistant floor leader (or whip), and a conference secretary. But the Democratic floor leader, until George Mitchell was elected in December 1988, presided over committee assignments as chairman of the Democratic Steering Committee and also directed party strategy and the scheduling of legislation as chairman of the Democratic Policy Committee.

After Mitchell decisively won a three-way contest for majority leader, he reached out to his rivals and rewarded his followers by spreading the action. He appointed Daniel K. Inouye of Hawaii, his most senior rival, as chairman of the Steering Committee. He also appointed freshman senator Tom Daschle of South Dakota as co-chairman of the Democratic Policy Committee. The Democratic floor leader continues to serve as chairman of his party's conference, which comprises all senators elected under the Democratic label in state-by-state elections. Mitchell also anointed Wyche Fowler, Jr., of Georgia as deputy floor leader; this appointment, together with that of Daschle, demonstrated Mitchell's willingness to share party leadership with junior members, many of whom had been crucial to his election.

But Mitchell's willingness to share leadership with his colleagues did not signal a weakness or lack of desire to assert his power as majority leader. In keeping with the desire of Senate Democrats to show an assertive and partisan presence in the face of continued Republican dominance of the White House, Mitchell became a major spokesman for the Democratic party as a counterpoint to President Bush. He used his role as leader to help shape a policy agenda as well.

Mitchell, appointed to the Senate to replace Democrat Edmund Muskie in May 1980, was selected by Majority Leader Byrd to head the Democratic Senatorial Campaign Committee in 1985. In 1986 Democrats regained control of the Senate. Mitchell's efforts had helped to finance and elect eleven new Democrats, including both Daschle and Fowler. His efforts in their behalf, as well as his telegenic appearance and rhetorical abilities, served as his springboard to the majority leadership two years later.

Senate Republicans, whether in the majority, as they were from 1981 until the election of 1986, or in the minority, as in all other Senates since 1955, divide their leadership into seven offices: floor leader, assistant floor leader (or whip), chairman of the Republican Policy Committee, chairman of the Republican Conference, secretary of the conference, chairman of the Republican Senatorial Campaign Committee, and chairman of the Republican Committee on Committees. The winners are elected, often in spirited contests. The one exception is the chairman of the Committee on Committees, who is appointed by the chairman of the Republican Conference after consultation with the floor leader.

Thus, despite minor changes in leadership positions and performance into the 1990s, Senate Democrats have greater potential for strong, concentrated leadership than do Senate Republicans. Democrat Mike Mansfield of Montana, who served longer as majority leader (1961-1977) than anyone in the history of the Senate, was among the least assertive of Senate floor leaders, whereas strong GOP leaders such as Robert A. Taft of Ohio (1953), Everett McKinley Dirksen of Illinois (1959-1969), and the current incumbent, Bob Dole of Kansas (1985-), have been able to centralize power and transform the obligations of lesser party officers into mainly supportive roles.[25]

Two other formal Senate leadership positions, both constitutionally designated, require brief mention. First, the vice president of the United States is also president of the Senate but has "no vote unless [the Senate] be equally divided"(Article I, Section 3 [4]). In the absence of the vice president, the Senate selects a president pro tempore. By long tradition, this position is held by the most senior member of the majority party. Recent incumbents have been Dan Quayle, former Indiana senator and vice president, and Robert C. Byrd, former Democratic floor leader and powerful also as chairman of the Senate Appropriations Committee.

From the early 1950s through the early 1990s only four men—Lyndon Johnson (1953-1961), Mike Mansfield (1961-1977), Robert Byrd (1977-1989), and George Mitchell (1989-) served as Democratic floor leaders in the Senate. Except for Johnson in his first two years and Byrd, who had a midcareer minority stint, they all served as majority leader. In contrast, the six Republican floor leaders—Robert Taft of Ohio (1953), William Knowland of California (1953-1959), Everett Dirksen of Illinois (1959-1969), Hugh Scott of Pennsylvania (1969-1977), Howard Baker of Tennessee (1977-1985), and Bob Dole of Kansas (1985-)—almost invariably had to compensate for minority status and the inability to move their legislation unless they could persuade Democratic senators to cross over. This prolonged minority status—all but the 83d Congress (1953-1955) and the 97th through 99th Congresses (1981-1987)—has been substantially offset, however, by Republican control of the White House—under Presidents Eisenhower, Nixon, Ford, Reagan, and Bush.

Historical Patterns

The mid- to late 1950s are remembered as an era of strong, individual leadership in the Senate—Johnson, especially, in the majority, and Knowland and Dirksen in the minority. As White, Matthews, Huitt, Evans and Novak, and others have observed, their floor leadership helped to centralize what was a much "flatter" hierarchy compared with that of the House.[26] But with the election results of 1958, which brought in large Democratic majorities, Johnson's ability to persuade, if not to "strong-arm" his fellow Democrats, suffered. Harry McPherson, a Johnson Senate staffer (and later White House staffer), made this observation:

> He did his best as leader when he had a narrow majority, when he had forty-nine to forty-seven. When the tremendous majority was elected in 1958, including a lot of liberals, he was confronted with much more of an issue-oriented Senate.... It extremized, polarized the two parties, and the Southerners, being unable to go along with their Northern Democratic brothers, would go over and join the Republicans more frequently. It also made the acts of legerdemain less spectacular because you had a much larger [Democratic] vote [on other issues].[27]

Democrats Mike Mansfield and Robert Byrd

In 1960, after Sens. John F. Kennedy and Lyndon B. Johnson were elected president and vice president, respectively, they tabbed Majority Whip Mike Mansfield of Montana to succeed Johnson as floor leader. Austere, highly intelligent, a conciliator by temperament, Mansfield found it difficult to be unpleasant to any of his colleagues. He was much more interested in influencing foreign policy (from a continuing position on the Foreign Relations Committee) than in establishing a tight rein over the Kennedy-Johnson legislative programs. As Bryce Harlow, chief congressional liaison officer in the Eisenhower and Nixon administrations commented, "He led the Senate by letting the Senate do what it wanted to do, and the senators found that fun." [28] In general, Mansfield backed off from exercising the power he had inherited until, from 1966 to 1968, he began to take issue with President Johnson's Vietnam War policies. His style of leadership also reflected the independent and decentralized trends that increasingly characterized the Senate of the 1960s. Mansfield's gentle reins of leadership were complemented by the equally gentlemanly, somewhat aloof style of Minority Leader Hugh Scott. In 1976 both leaders announced their plans to retire from the Senate.

Even before this, something of a counterrevolution in Senate norms was underway. Increasingly, in the early 1970s senators on both sides of the aisle began to complain of a lack of formal direction. Byrd, who had won the whip position by upsetting Chappaquiddick-plagued Ted Kennedy of Massachusetts in 1971, succeeded Mansfield as floor leader in 1977. Almost immediately, he set out to restore the floor leader's traditional position of dominance. Still, there would be no return to the concentrated leadership style of Johnson. As Byrd commented in a 1979 interview:

> I could not lead the Senate as Johnson did. . . . Johnson could not lead this Senate [the 96th]. These are different times.
> He had cohesive blocs, he had the southern senators. When Johnson was the majority leader, both senators from Texas were Democrats; both senators from Virginia, from South Carolina, and so on. Now you have a lot of Republican senators from the South.
> The members are younger now; they tend to be more independent. We are living in different times now.[29]

If Byrd lacked Johnson's overwhelming techniques of personal persuasion and his dominating physical traits (Johnson was 6'4"; Byrd less than 5'10"), he was nevertheless a master of parliamentary procedure and indefatigable in attending to legislative detail and looking after the needs of other senators, Republicans as well as Democrats. As Byrd gained in experience, his overall legislative achievements mounted. He was especially successful at steering complex legislation through the Senate, less impressive perhaps as an external spokesman. Byrd was quick to acknowledge that other senators might be more successful in presenting Democratic views to the media and a broader public. "Television was not my forte." [30]

Republican Howard Baker

While Byrd was ascending to the floor leadership in January 1977 (an ailing former vice president Hubert Humphrey dropped out just before the vote), minority Republicans had their own leadership change. Robert Griffin of Michigan, the incumbent whip since 1959, was considered the favorite (and probably would not have been challenged had President Gerald Ford, his close friend and former House colleague, defeated Jimmy Carter in 1976). At the last minute, however, Howard Baker of Tennessee, who had challenged Scott, unsuccessfully, for the minority leadership in 1969 and 1972, decided to take on Griffin. Baker won by a vote of 19 to 18. (One Republican senator remained out of the country, advised that his committed vote to Griffin would not be needed.) Most observers concluded that Baker won, not because of any ideological differences between the two men—they were both moderately right of center—but because of the support of a majority of incoming Republican freshmen. Most were convinced that Baker would be a stronger external spokesman than Griffin, a skill increasingly important with Republicans no longer in control of the White House. Four years later, in 1980, Republican senatorial candidates rode the Reagan electoral crest as the Republicans won control of the Senate for the first time since 1954.

Sidestepping a possible challenge from the right after the 1980 Republican surge, Baker and Assistant Floor Leader Ted Stevens of Alaska were advanced to majority status in their respective posts without challenge. In the 97th and 98th Congresses (1981-1985), Baker demonstrated considerable legislative acumen working closely with President Reagan and his White House staff. Still, for all Baker's skills of persuasion, it became increasingly difficult for him to maintain winning coalitions of Republican senators from the ideological right and left or to attract Democrats from across the aisle. Baker found himself buffeted by the demands of conservatives, such as Jesse Helms, and the filibustering delays of liberal Republican Lowell Weicker and Democrat Howard Metzenbaum. In January 1983, after sixteen years in the Senate, the last six as Republican floor leader, Baker announced his plans to retire from the Senate. He would serve out his term, join a law firm, and consider running for the presidency himself. His possible bid for the Republican nomination for the presidency in 1988 was set aside, though, when a troubled President Reagan selected Baker to become chief of staff in place of Donald Regan.

Republican Bob Dole

In the elections of 1984, despite Reagan's landslide victory over former vice president Walter Mondale, Senate Republicans suffered a net loss of two seats. They returned to Washington in November to organize and select a replacement for Baker. The campaign to succeed him had gone on for nearly two years, since Baker had first announced his impending retirement. Ted Stevens of Alaska, sixty-one years of age, the assistant majority leader who had served under Baker since 1977, and Bob Dole of Kansas, also sixty-one, a former vice presidential candidate on the Ford ticket in 1976 and chairman of the powerful Senate Finance Committee since 1981, would emerge as front-runners. Three other senators with less seniority also declared their candidacies: Energy and Natural Resources Chairman James A. McClure of Idaho, age fifty-nine; Budget Committee Chairman Pete V. Domenici of New Mexico, age fifty-two; and Richard G. Lugar of Indiana, chairman of the National Republican Senatorial Committee, age fifty-two.

On November 28, 1984, Senate Republicans, fifty-three members strong, elected Dole as their majority leader for the 99th Congress (1985-1987). Dole won on the fourth and final secret ballot, 28-25, over Stevens. On earlier votes, first McClure, then Domenici, and finally Lugar were eliminated on a "low-man out" procedure. Never before in the history of the Senate had five candidates competed for floor leadership in either party.

As is true for all party leadership contests, Senate or House, Dole won for a combination of reasons; chief among them were his national prominence and his media connections. Clearly, in narrowing the contest to Dole and Stevens, Senate Republicans were looking for a more assertive and independent leadership style, freer from White House influence and less conciliatory than that which Baker had provided. Senate Republicans knew that the 1986 elections would be the major test of their majority status, when their class of 1980, the Reagan landslide class, would be up for reelection. They wanted a leader who would protect their interests first and who would be both an attractive public spokesman and an aggressive party leader. The voluble, hot-tempered Stevens was the latter, but Dole was seen by a majority of his colleagues as having a better combination of desirable traits.

In this same November 1984 conference, Senate Republicans elected a slate of lesser party officials headed by Alan K. Simpson of Wyoming as assistant majority leader (whip) and John H. Chafee of Rhode Island as chairman of the Republican Conference. All positions but one were hotly contested. The Senate Republicans' uneasiness as Reagan's second term began was matched on the minority side. Many Democrats privately questioned whether their floor leader, Robert Byrd, had the "outside" skills, including a telegenic appearance, to compete with Reagan and Dole. But unseating an incumbent leader in the Senate is an extraordinary and unusual occurrence. Byrd did face a challenge, from Florida senator Lawton Chiles, in early December 1984, but he withstood the belated challenge and retained his position by a 36-11 vote.

Throughout the 99th Congress, Dole had the delicate task of demonstrating his assertiveness without excessively antagonizing the White House or plunging Senate Republicans into further disarray. In May 1985, for example, he won a dramatic late-night, one-vote victory on the budget by having Sen. Pete Wilson, R-Calif., brought from the hospital and wheeled onto the floor, intravenous hookup and all, to gain a tie vote. Wilson's presence gave Vice President George Bush the opportunity to cast the winning vote for the Republican plan. Picking his issues carefully, usually siding with the president, but sometimes opposing his programs or seeking modifications, Dole won a series of legislative battles. Despite taking every opportunity to put Republican freshmen forward, Dole's intensive campaign efforts in behalf of his colleagues fell short of the mark in the 1986 elections. Democratic challengers picked up nine of the twenty-two contested seats previously held by Republicans and lost only one of their own— Missouri. After six uneasy years in the minority, Democrats again controlled the Senate, this time by a 55-45 margin.[31]

Marked by intense partisanship and increasing legislative stalemate, the

100th Congress was also characterized by enhanced speculation about its future Senate leaders. Minority Leader Dole gave little indication that he would resign from his leadership position in the Senate, even as his bid for the GOP presidential nomination entered its most intensive and critical phases in early 1988. When his presidential bid foundered in the New Hampshire primary, Dole returned to his Senate leadership post.

Meanwhile, Byrd, who had served as Democratic floor leader (majority or minority) since 1977, announced in April 1988 that, although he would seek his sixth Senate term in 1988, he would not seek reelection as majority leader. Instead, at the urgings of his West Virginia constituents, he would opt for the chairmanship of the Senate Appropriations Committee and assume the position of president pro tempore (presiding officer) of the Senate. His decision would set in motion an intense three-way competition for the majority position.

Democrat George Mitchell

Three Senate Democrats sought to replace Byrd as majority leader: Daniel K. Inouye of Hawaii, age sixty-four, first elected to the Senate in 1962; J. Bennett Johnston of Louisiana, age fifty-six, first elected in 1972; and a relative newcomer, George J. Mitchell of Maine, age fifty-five, appointed to the Senate in May 1980 to take the seat of Edmund Muskie.

Fifty-five Democrats entered the Democratic Conference in mid-December 1988 before the 101st Congress convened. A majority of twenty-eight would secure election. Mitchell won handily, with twenty-seven votes on the first ballot to fourteen each for his two opponents. Johnston immediately moved to make the election unanimous, a motion seconded by Inouye. As already indicated, Mitchell set about sharing power by making a number of appointments, including the selection of Inouye as chairman of the Democratic Steering Committee (which was responsible for making Democratic committee assignments).

Why did Mitchell, with only eight years of Senate experience, win so handily? First of all, his opponents probably split the vote of more senior Democrats. Second, Mitchell, as chair of the Democratic Senatorial Campaign Committee, had led his party to impressive victories in the 1986 elections. According to two senators in the Mitchell camp, as many as nine of the eleven incoming freshmen voted for Mitchell. The new majority leader, a former state party chairman and federal judge, had carved out a fine legislative record in his eight years in the Senate. A strong theme of his campaign was "reforms" to improve the quality of life of Senate members. But as important as anything else was the sense that Mitchell would be the strongest public spokesman for the Democratic majority. As the party out of the White House, Democrats wanted an individual who could be an attractive and persuasive counterweight to the Republican president. At the same time, they wanted a leader who would personify an image of the Senate and its Democratic majority as judicious, reasonable, and forward looking. The "inside" skills that mattered most in selecting earlier leaders such as Lyndon Johnson and Robert Byrd were less significant in an era of divided government and television coverage. Despite his junior status, Mitchell fit these requirements best, in the eyes of a majority of his colleagues.

How successful has Mitchell been as Senate majority leader? Most observers would give him excellent marks: first, for acting as external spokesman for his party; second, for demonstrating strong skills in advancing his party legislative agenda in the Senate; and third, for being an effective countervoice to President Bush and the Republican administration. In 1989 Mitchell almost single-handedly blocked passage of a capital-gains tax cut, a top initiative of President Bush that had sailed through the House of Representatives and seemed unstoppable. One of his most impressive legislative accomplishments was steering through the exceedingly complex Clean Air Act of 1991. Day after day, Mitchell, other senators, and spokesmen for the Republican administration hammered out the compromises necessary to get the legislation passed.

The Senate cannot operate without reasonable comity and cooperation. The two floor leaders, Mitchell and Dole, although occasionally partisan, generally worked well together. The civil rights bills of 1990 and 1991 were two dramatic examples of where comity broke down. For most of the 101st and 102d Congresses the two men got along better and with more positive results than any recent senatorial leadership tandem. But the approach of the 1992 presidential election brought more partisanship and more tension to the Senate, and thereby to its party leaders, than had been evident in the previous two years.

Committees

From its earliest days, the U.S. Senate, like the House of Representatives, has used a division of labor in a committee system to organize its work. The committee system is the single most important feature affecting legislative outcomes in the Senate; not surprisingly, it has changed as other aspects of the Senate—workload, membership, power—have changed.

Committee Assignments

Shortly after being sworn in, each senator is given committee assignments. When vacancies occur on an attractive committee, senators can and do switch assignments. The assignment process and the selection of committee and subcommittee chairmen are crucial to the Senate, because they can determine the policy orientation and activity of the committees. The Democratic and Republican parties handle their members' assignments differently. Democrats use a twenty-five-member Steering Committee (nearly half their total members), chaired since 1988, as we noted above, by Senator Inouye, who was appointed by the majority leader. Republicans have a five-member Committee on Committees, with an elected leader (Trent Lott of Mississippi in the 102d Congress). In many ways, committee assignments exhibit important aspects of the broader institution. In the 1940s and early 1950s committee assignments reflected the apprenticeship norm; freshmen were assigned only to minor committees, and senior members dominated prestigious committees such as Appropriations, Armed Services, Finance, and Foreign Relations.

When Lyndon Johnson became majority leader in 1955, he changed these procedures by instituting the "Johnson Rule," which guaranteed every Democrat, no matter how junior, a major committee assignment. As has been shown, however, Johnson ran the Steering Committee as a one-man show, and he handed out truly choice assignments very selectively. Senior, more conservative members continued to dominate the most prestigious panels.

After Johnson, the process became more democratic, especially under Mansfield. Assignments to all committees became more open to junior and liberal Democrats, in part because there were more of them. But because of the importance members attach to committee slots, the process frequently has generated controversy. Soon after Byrd's election as majority leader in 1977, junior liberal Democrats, led by Iowa's John Culver, forced an acrimonious debate in the Democratic Caucus to protest Byrd's choices to fill Steering Committee vacancies. These senators feared that the power to make committee assignments would be controlled by an unrepresentative group insensitive to their needs. They won an agreement, still in effect, that future Steering Committee choices would be submitted in advance to the party membership.

Another controversy arose over the additional clout the party leader had as chairman of the Steering Committee. After Byrd announced in April 1988 that he would step down as Democratic leader before the 101st Congress convened, the contenders for the post began to discuss the option of separating the party leader position from the chairmanships of the Steering and Policy committees, as the Republicans do. Mitchell achieved this reform in December 1988. The Republicans employ a different assignment process, relying on a more automatic process based on seniority. Still, in the 1970s and 1980s, as important committees were enlarged, limits were imposed on the ability of senior members to "stockpile" all the good assignments, and junior Republicans, increased in number, changed the GOP makeup of many important committees. Junior Republicans were a particularly striking force after the 1980 election, with their huge freshman class (sixteen in number) that rivaled the 1958 Democratic group; but the change in party ratios on committees after the Democrats lost the Senate did not allow for many vacancies on the blue-chip committees such as Finance and Armed Services.

These changes combined to swing the Senate committees in a more junior and liberal direction in the mid- to late 1970s, but after 1980 they swung back in a more conservative direction. The Democrats' recapture of the Senate majority in 1986 changed the committee system makeup once again. The entry of eleven freshman Democrats, in many instances replacing conservative Republicans, moved many committees in a more liberal direction. Three of the freshmen Democrats won seats on Budget, two on Appropriations, two on Armed Services, two on Foreign Relations, and one on Finance. This record of success would not have satisfied many of the more aggressive freshmen of the mid-1970s, but it was perfectly acceptable to the class of 1986. Small Senate classes in 1988 and 1990 brought no fundamental changes and no serious controversies over assignments, except for the aforementioned flap over Senator Robb's seat on the Senate Budget Committee.

Chairmanships

For many decades Senate committee chairmanships and ranking minority memberships have been selected through the process of seniority, even though there are no formal requirements for seniority to rule. The process is not entirely clean and consistent, however. Because some senators with longevity become senior on more than one committee, they can choose which one to chair, creating an occasional pattern of musical chairs. In the 100th Congress, for example, Edward Kennedy chose the Labor and Human Resources Committee chairmanship over that of the Judiciary Committee, which he had chaired in the late 1970s. Kennedy's move enabled Joseph R. Biden, Jr., D-Del., to take over Judiciary—but blocked Howard Metzenbaum from chairing Labor. Kennedy did not make his choice to help Biden or to hinder Metzenbaum, but he did end up shaping the agendas and directions of the two committees. In 1981 conservative Republicans persuaded Strom Thurmond, R-S.C., to choose the Judiciary Committee chairmanship over that of Armed Services, where he was also senior, specifically to keep liberal Charles Mathias, R-Md., from assuming the Judiciary reins.

The seniority process became controversial for Republicans after the 1986 election. Jesse Helms, the ultraconservative senior Republican on both Agriculture and Foreign Relations, had chosen for constituency reasons to chair Agriculture in the 99th Congress, leaving Foreign Relations to the more junior and more moderate Richard Lugar. But after the Republicans lost the Senate in 1986, Helms decided to assert his seniority rights and make the switch to become the ranking Republican on Foreign Relations. Lugar, who had been an effective and well-respected chairman, vigorously contested Helms. Despite the sharp ideological differences between the two, the overriding issue became the sanctity of the seniority system. Liberal Republican Lowell Weicker, afraid of what breaking the seniority precedent would do to his own future chances of chairing the Appropriations Committee, came out publicly for his archfoe Helms, as did several other senior Republicans, both moderates and liberals. Helms won, solidifying the seniority principle in the GOP.

When Weicker and his colleagues voted for Helms, they voted to preserve a seniority process that has dampened the overall trends in ideology and region that have affected the Senate as a whole and the committee rosters in particular. This preference for seniority over ideology held true for Democrats in the 1970s, for Republicans during their majority status in the Senate from 1981 through 1986, and for the Democrats again in the 100th through the 102d Congresses. In the House, by contrast, during the 1989-1991 period, several chairmen were forced out of their positions for being too old, conservative, or passive. The decentralization of the power structure in the Senate—in the 102d Congress 89 percent of majority senators chaired at least one sub-committee or committee—contributed to the friendly attitude toward the seniority process.

Thanks to the stable seniority process, the decline in the number of southern Democratic senators in the 1970s was reflected only somewhat in committee chairmanships. In 1975 southerners accounted for only 26 percent of Senate Democrats, but they held 39 percent of the chairmanships, heading powerful panels such as Appropriations, Armed Services, Finance, Foreign Relations, and Judiciary.

Seniority also limited the effect of the conservative trend in American politics and in the Senate in the late 1970s and early 1980s. The senior majority members in the Republican Senate in 1981 were more moderate than their colleagues. The top quartile in 1981 had an average conservative coalition score of seventy-two, compared with an average of eighty-eight for the more junior three-fourths of Republicans. As a result, nearly half the major committee chairmen in the Republican Senate, including the chairmen of Appropriations and Foreign Relations, were more liberal than their committee colleagues.

By the time the Democrats regained control of the chamber in 1987, a number of post-1958 northern liberals had departed, through defeat or retirement, while several post-1970s vintage southerners had moved steadily up the seniority ladder, joining a few of their senior, die-hard colleagues. Therefore, in the 100th Congress, southern Democrats once again had a disproportionate share of the chairmanships, holding seven of the sixteen standing committees, or 44 percent, while making up only 29 percent of the party membership. Included among the seven chairmanships were some of the most significant committees: Appropriations, Armed Services, Budget, Commerce, and Finance. In 1991, the 102d Congress, southerners accounted for 27 percent of Senate Democrats, but they held 38 percent of the chairmanships, including several of the most powerful.

Workload

With its small membership, the Senate is profoundly affected by its workload.[32] The 1960s and 1970s saw that workload burgeon, leading to calls for reform, some of them successful. Although the workload stabilized and in some ways even declined in the 1980s, senators' level of satisfaction with their output and lifestyle deteriorated—leading to more calls for reform. Work activity took particularly sharp increases in the early 1970s. There were five times as many roll call votes on the Senate floor in the 95th Congress as there were in the 84th (1,151 compared with 224); the huge number of votes were accompanied by increases in the number of bills introduced and hearings held.

Responding to the number and complexity of decisions senators had to make, the Senate expanded the committee system. In 1957 there were 15 standing committees with 118 subcommittees; by 1975 there were 18 standing committees with 140 subcommittees. If special, select, and joint committees were included in the tally, the number would rise to 31 committees and 174 subcommittees.

More important, perhaps, the sizes of the panels also increased. Because the Senate had increased by only four members since the mid-1950s (with the admission of Alaska and Hawaii in 1959), this meant more assignments per member. In 1957 each senator averaged 2.8 committees and 6.3 subcommittees. But by 1976 senators on the average served on 4 committees and 14 subcommittees. Junior members in particular objected to the fragmentation and frenetic scheduling that flowed from this process. At their urging, the Senate early in 1976 created a twelve-member, bipartisan committee chaired by Adlai E. Stevenson III, D-Ill., to revamp the committee system. Called the Temporary Select Committee to Study the Senate Committee System, the panel recommended substantial reductions in the number of committees and subcommittees and even greater reductions in the number of assignments allowed senators.

S. Res. 4, which passed the Senate early in 1977, eliminated 3 standing committees and 5 select and joint committees, rearranged several others, and resulted in a dramatic drop in the number of subcommittees (from an overall total of 174 to 110) and in the number of assignments for each senator (from an average of 4 committees and 14 subcommittees to 3 committees and 7.5 subcommittees). In a trend typical for an individualized, democratized institution, however, the assignments immediately began to escalate again, well beyond the limits set by S. Res. 4. By the 98th Congress the average number of assignments had risen nearly to 12, and forty senators had violated, in one way or another, the chamber's rules on assignment limitations. In frustration, the Senate created yet another Select Committee to Study the Committee System, chaired by Dan Quayle. The Quayle committee essentially recommended that the Senate simply enforce the assignment limitations already in the rules, but to little avail. In the 100th Congress the average number of assignments was 11, and forty-nine senators continued to violate the assignment rules; no change occurred in the succeeding four years.

The system is more compact than it was in the mid-1970s, but member satisfaction is, if anything, lower. Multiple assignments and fragmented responsibilities, added to frustration over erratic and unpredictable Senate scheduling that made normal family life impossible, led to increased grumbling among senators. In 1987 junior and midseniority senators, led by Democrat David Pryor of Arkansas, began to meet as an informal task force to recommend change. In part due to their efforts, the Senate regularized its schedule, moving to a three-weeks-on, one-week-off pattern. The premature, voluntary retirements in 1988 of Lawton Chiles, D-Fla., Paul Trible, R-Va., and Dan Evans, R-Wash., raised further concerns about the Senate and and its members.

In 1991 two highly respected senators, Democrat David Boren and Republican Pete Domenici, joined by two equally respected House members, Democrat Lee H. Hamilton of Indiana and Republican Bill Gradison of Ohio, called for the creation of a joint committee on Congress to take a comprehensive look at the institution, including its committee system. By mid-1992, battered by allegations of scandal and sharp public and press criticism, the House and Senate moved toward passage of their resolutions and toward the likelihood of more substantial reform in 1993.

To cope with the workload, the Senate enlarged its professional staffs, both committee and personal. Committee staff grew from roughly 300 in the 85th Congress to well over 1,200 (including permanent and investigative staff) by the 95th. The numbers stabilized and even declined thereafter, settling to just under 1,100 in the 100th Congress. The large staffs in the modern Senate have had several effects. Senators have been able to cope better with their heavy workloads and responsibilities—but entrepreneurial, active, and ambitious staff also have created more work in promoting ideas, writing amendments, and drafting bills and speeches. Large staffs also have contributed to the democratization and decentralization of the Senate. In recent years staffs have been allocated increasingly through subcommittees rather than through full committees. This change has accentuated the spread of power to junior senators and has correspondingly reduced the power of committee chairmen.

Along with the expansion of subcommittee chairmanships and staffs, committee deliberations have become more open than they were in the past. Together, these changes have loosened the control that committee leaders once maintained over their committee rank and file. Junior senators now have subcommittee bases from which to challenge the policy recommendations of committee chairmen. Moreover, senators who do not serve on a particular committee have enough access to information to enable them to offer successful amendments to the committee's bills on the floor. Thus, committees have become less cohesive internally, and their bills have become more vulnerable to challenge on the Senate floor. To combat these trends and to gain more control over the Senate's legislative process, some savvy chairmen have begun to use closed meetings and sessions, along with attempts to restrict debate through unanimous consent agreements. The 1982 tax bill and 1986 tax reform are good examples. But these efforts are few and far between.

During the 1970s the legislative struggle shifted from the committee rooms to the Senate floor, while the functions of agenda setting and legislative oversight moved from the committees to the subcommittees. During the 1980s, in both Democratic-controlled and Republican-controlled Senates, legislative activity declined somewhat; the Senate considered fewer bills, took fewer roll call votes, and passed fewer laws than it had in the preceding several years. Nevertheless, the patterns of legislative initiation and the relative importance of Senate institutions remain the same. Committees continue to be highly important; all legislation is referred to them, as are all executive and judicial nominations, and they retain the authority either to kill or to report out bills and nominations. But the present-day Senate is a more open, fluid, and decentralized body than it was in the 1950s. Power, resources, and decision-making authority have become more diffuse. The combined effects of changes in membership, norms, leadership, workload, committees, and, as we shall see, television coverage have produced a markedly different Senate.

The Senate and the Political System

The Senate does not operate in a vacuum. It has been and is affected by trends in society and in the broader political system, and it has, in turn, affected American politics. Nowhere is this effect felt more strongly than in presidential nominations. The Senate has been a major breeding ground for presidential candidates for many decades, but in the period from 1960 to 1972, it was dominant. Since then the Senate has lost some luster, but it continues to turn out many presidential contenders and to attract many who aspire to the Oval Office.

During the "golden era" of 1960 to 1972 the two parties nominated either senators (John Kennedy, Barry Goldwater, and George McGovern) or former senators who had become vice presidents (Richard Nixon, Lyndon Johnson, and Hubert Humphrey). Why this importance for the Senate? The near-revolutionary growth in media influence over politics, particularly through television, focused public attention on Washington and especially on the Senate. Television contributed to, and was affected by, the increasing nationalization of party politics. A national attentiveness to foreign affairs heightened the importance of the Senate, with its well-defined constitutional role in foreign policy.

Many of these trends and conditions remained, of course, beyond 1972. But after the Watergate scandal, a turn in public attitudes about government enabled Jimmy Carter, a young former governor with no Washington experience, to capture the Democratic nomination in 1976 and to run successfully for president by campaigning against Washington politics. Despite the continuing role of senators and former senators as candidates in 1980 (Howard Baker, Bob Dole, and Edward Kennedy) and in 1984 (Gary Hart, John Glenn, Alan Cranston, and Ernest Hollings), another former governor, Ronald Reagan, won the GOP nod in 1980, while former vice president (and senator) Walter Mondale beat out the more contemporary Senate contingent for the Democratic nomination in 1984.

There are several reasons for the decline in presidential competitiveness of senators. Among them are the emergence of a number of attractive governors from important states and the increased national attention paid to the House after 1979, when it began to televise its floor sessions over cable television's C-SPAN. In 1986, frustrated by their comparative decline in national attention, senators finally brought gavel-to-gavel television coverage to their own proceedings.

In 1988 several more senators entered the presidential sweepstakes, including Bob Dole, who, as floor leader, could benefit from the television coverage, and Democrats Paul Simon of Illinois and Al Gore of Tennessee. From his vantage point in the leadership, Dole showed early success, winning a large victory in the Iowa caucuses. Gore managed to stay in the race after several others had faltered. But the party nominations once again went to nonsenators— Vice President George Bush and Gov. Michael Dukakis of Massachusetts (although both Bush and Dukakis did pick senators for their running mates).

In 1992 some of the most prominent senators mentioned as presidential prospects chose not to run, including Al Gore, Bill Bradley, George Mitchell, and 1988 vice presidential nominee Lloyd Bentsen. Two other senators did run—Democrats Tom Harkin of Iowa and Bob Kerrey of Nebraska—along with former senator Paul Tsongas of Massachusetts. But continuing the recent record of senatorial futility in the presidential selection process, they all faltered and dropped out by March. Gore, of course, later became Bill Clinton's vice presidential choice.

Despite the recent lack of presidential successes, the Senate remains an institution that receives national and international attention and produces numerous serious presidential contenders. Many senators consider themselves presidential possibilities, or they are mentioned as such on television networks and in the polls. Senators tailor their behavior accordingly, spreading their legislative interests, increasing their activity and media visibility. The preoccupation with presidential aspirations has contributed to violations of the norms of specialization and legislative work. It has also increased the pressure within the Senate to distribute resources and power to junior members.

The advent of gavel-to-gavel television has brought the Senate back to its previous high share of public attention, compared with the House of Representatives, without any of the dire consequences to the quality, balance, and depth of debate predicted by television's opponents. Television has brought a side benefit as well: Not wishing to be embarrassed on national television, senators take more care with preparing their floor speeches.

But coverage on C-SPAN has not insulated the Senate from the broader unhappiness the American public has sometimes felt about the Senate, nor has it kept the Senate from individual or institutional scandal. And television coverage has not enabled the Senate to move more expeditiously or with more unity toward resolving serious problems such as the budget deficit and national health policy.

Conclusion

The Senate has changed in many ways since the 1950s. The nature of its membership, its internal norms and rules, its leadership styles and effects, its committees, and its role as a breeding ground for presidential candidates have all evolved to make the Senate of the 1990s an institution quite different from its postwar incarnation—and to make the Senate of today different from that of a decade ago.

The composition of the Senate has gone from a close partisan balance during the Truman and Eisenhower presidencies in the 1950s to dominant Democratic party control in the 1960s and 1970s to a narrow Republican majority in the early and mid-1980s and back to narrow Democratic control after 1986. A powerful southern Democratic wing, which had maintained great power through the seniority system and a coalition with like-minded Republicans, diminished in size and influence and made a comeback of sorts by the time the Democrats recaptured the Senate. At the same time, another group of Democrats, elected in the 1970s and mostly in their forties, began to move into positions of influence; among them were such senators as Joe Biden, chairman of the Judiciary Committee, Sam Nunn of Georgia, chairman of the Armed Services Committee, Bennett Johnston, chairman of the Energy Committee, and Donald Riegle of Michigan, chairman of the Banking Committee.

With these shifts of power, the Senate, overall, has become a more open, more fluid, more decentralized, and more democratized chamber than it was before. Individual senators, from the most senior to the most junior, have benefited—but have also become frustrated with the institutional consequences of these trends. Although the overall work burden has decreased in the past few years, declining roughly to the levels of the mid-1970s, the Senate has become more preoccupied for extended periods of time with a small number of issues, especially the budget, which seem never to be resolved satisfactorily. Filibusters, once rare and reserved for the weightiest of issues, are now employed routinely on even trivial matters, tying up the institution even more, requiring sixty votes on minor as well as major matters to move ahead, and causing lengthy delays in debate even after cloture has been invoked.

The lack of progress on many issues and the preoccupation with talk over action have not brought a return to the leisurely, "clublike" atmosphere of the past, nor have they greatly increased the role or level or quality of debate. Although televised sessions have improved floor attendance and show promise for improving the quality of floor speeches, the evidence is spotty at best. Today's Senate shows no clear institutional direction or identity. Neither a great deliberative body nor an efficient processor of laws, the Senate, after years of dramatic change, is an institution in search of an identity.

This identity crisis has been accompanied, in the early 1990s, by the public's growing discontent with the Senate and by the press's vilification of individual members and the institution. "In two decades here, I have never seen such unhappiness among my colleagues, across the board," lamented one senior senator in mid-1992. Undoubtedly, more change, through institutional reform and turnover in membership and leadership, will characterize the Senate through the rest of the decade.

Notes

1. See Huitt's collection of essays in *Congress: Two Decades of Analysis*, ed. Ralph K. Huitt and Robert L. Peabody (New York: Harper and Row, 1969); and Donald R. Matthews, *U.S. Senators and Their World* (Chapel Hill: University of North Carolina Press, 1960).
2. These figures on the frequency of conservative coalition votes are taken from Norman J. Ornstein, Thomas E. Mann, and Michael J. Malbin, eds., *Vital Statistics on Congress, 1991-1992* (Washington, D.C.: Congressional Quarterly, 1992), 201. These data were in turn derived from figures published by Congressional Quarterly. Congressional Quarterly uses a slightly different definition of the South from the classification we have used in our previous analysis of the Senate, which serves as the basis for Table 1-1. We included only the eleven states of the Confederacy, while CQ adds Kentucky and Oklahoma. Because other analyses we wish to draw on here also used

the Congressional Quarterly definition, we will ensure maximum comparability by employing solely that classification from this point on. We should note that the alternative chosen would not significantly affect any of our conclusions.

3. The data for the 92d Congress are taken from David W. Rohde, "Electoral Forces, Political Agendas, and Partisanship in the House and Senate," in *The Postreform Congress,* ed. Roger H. Davidson (New York: St. Martin's, 1992), 27-47. The 1991 data are from *Congressional Quarterly Weekly Report,* Dec. 28, 1991, 3788-3792.

4. See Helen Dewar and Kent Jenkins, Jr., "Party Squalls Pose Test for Robb," *Washington Post,* March 26, 1991, A4.

5. Quoted in Janet Hook, "Senate Republican Conference Takes a Step to the Right," *Congressional Quarterly Weekly Report,* Nov. 17, 1990, 3871.

6. Matthews, *U.S. Senators and Their World,* 92.

7. Barbara Sinclair, *The Transformation of the U.S. Senate* (Baltimore: Johns Hopkins University Press, 1989), 101.

8. Ibid., 82; Steven S. Smith, *Call to Order: Floor Politics in the House and Senate* (Washington, D.C.: Brookings Institution, 1989), 143.

9. Sinclair, *Transformation of the U.S. Senate,* 101.

10. For a discussion of the changes during the 1960s, see Randall B. Ripley, *Power in the Senate* (New York: St. Martin's, 1969).

11. These quotations, and other unattributed ones in this essay, are taken from semistructured, taped interviews, conducted between 1973 and 1979, with more than sixty sitting or former senators. The interviews were part of a broader study of the Senate conducted by the authors with the help of a grant from the Russell Sage Foundation.

12. Matthews, *U.S. Senators and Their World,* 94.

13. William S. Cohen, *Roll Call: One Year in the United States Senate* (New York: Simon and Schuster, 1981), 238.

14. Quoted in *Washington Post,* Sept. 16, 1990, A16.

15. See Bruce I. Oppenheimer, "Changing Time Constraints on Congress: Historical Perspectives on the Use of Cloture," in *Congress Reconsidered,* 3d ed., ed. Lawrence C. Dodd and Bruce I. Oppenheimer (Washington, D.C.: CQ Press, 1985), 393-413.

16. Ibid., 398. Under the new cloture rule, efforts to change the Senate's rules are still governed by the old two-thirds requirement.

17. Sinclair, *Transformation of the U.S. Senate,* 136.

18. See Smith, *Call to Order,* 94-119, for a discussion of cloture and the use of unanimous consent agreements.

19. Christopher J. Bailey, "The United States Senate: The New Individualism and the New Right," *Parliamentary Affairs* 39 (July 1986): 357-358.

20. For a more detailed discussion of changes in Senate norms through the 1970s, see David W. Rohde, Norman J. Ornstein, and Robert L. Peabody, "Political Change and Legislative Norms in the U.S. Senate, 1957-1974," in *Studies of Congress,* ed. Glenn R. Parker (Washington, D.C.: CQ Press, 1985), 147-188.

21. Lloyd Bentsen, "Our Senate 'Club' Should Change Its Rules," *Washington Post,* Oct. 20, 1991, C4.

22. This discussion is drawn primarily from Smith, *Call to Order,* 125-127, 242-243.

23. Quoted in Helen Dewar, "Senate on TV: Cool Under the Lights," *Washington Post,* June 3, 1987, A17.

24. Matthews, *U.S. Senators and Their World,* 123-124.

25. Robert L. Peabody, *Leadership in Congress* (Boston: Little, Brown, 1976), 332-333; Robert L. Peabody, "Senate Party Leadership: From the 1950s to the 1980s," in *Understanding Congressional Leadership,* ed. Frank H. Mackaman (Washington, D.C.: CQ Press, 1981), 56; Sinclair, *Transformation of the U.S. Senate,* 45.

26. See William S. White, *Citadel: The Story of the U.S. Senate* (New York: Harper, 1967); Matthews, *U.S. Senators and Their World;* Huitt and Peabody, *Congress: Two Decades of*

Analysis; and Rowland Evans and Robert Novak, *Lyndon B. Johnson: The Exercise of Power* (New York: New American Library, 1966).

27. Harry McPherson, Oral History Interview, Dec. 5, 1968, Tape I, 25-26, Lyndon B. Johnson Library, Austin, Texas.
28. Bryce Harlow, Oral History Interview, May 6, 1979, Tape II, 36, Lyndon B. Johnson Library, Austin, Texas.
29. Majority Leader Robert C. Byrd, interview with authors, July 13, 1979.
30. Robert C. Byrd, *The Senate, 1789-1989,* II (Washington, D.C.: U.S. Government Printing Office, 1991), 608.
31. Robert L. Peabody, "The Selection of a Senate Majority Leader, 1983-1984," unpublished manuscript, 1986.
32. Figures within this section come from Ornstein, Mann, and Malbin, *Vital Statistics on Congress, 1991-1992.*

2

Maintaining Order in the House: The Struggle for Institutional Equilibrium

Lawrence C. Dodd and Bruce I. Oppenheimer

The 1990s are posing a serious challenge to the organizational equilibrium of the House of Representatives. In the four years since the 101st Congress was sworn in, the House has experienced the first forced resignation of a Speaker and the resignation of its first elected majority whip, both leaving office under a cloud of financial impropriety; scandals in the House "bank" and House post office produced the most widespread public disaffection with Congress in modern times; bitter conflict between the House's majority and minority parties is at a level perhaps not seen since the nineteenth century; policy gridlock has become so severe that the government was forced to close down, not just for an afternoon but for days at a time; and a national anti-incumbency movement threatens to make the constitutional imposition of congressional term limits a major focus of the mid-1990s. These developments have left the House shaken—unsure of its capacity to maintain an orderly and constructive role in national governance, fearful that the influx of a large number of new members in 1993 might further destabilize the institution, and apprehensive that the demands for policy action by the new president might overwhelm the institution and throw it into an even greater period of disarray.

Whether the House can soon recover its sense of institutional balance and reassert its policymaking capacities remains to be seen. The nature of the challenge is best grasped, perhaps, by examining the factors that led to institutional destabilization. Chief among these factors, we suggest, is the conflict between the House parties during the twelve years of divided government from 1981 through 1992 and the role that party conflict played in fueling the congressional scandals and policy immobilism of the 1990s. Before we can fully grasp the difficulties facing the House, however, we must first acknowledge the significant reversal that occurred in the patterns of House turnover with the 1992 election.

Membership Change

Much has been written about the potential for House membership turnover in 1992. Even before the election, sixty-six incumbents announced that they would not seek reelection (thirteen of those were running for other offices); nineteen others were defeated for renomination. With the redistricting that took place after the 1990 census meaning that many incumbents would have sizable new constituencies, with some incumbents having to explain large numbers of overdrafts at the House bank, and with high levels of public dissatisfaction with government, many of those seeking reelection found that incumbency has burdens as well as advantages.[1] Some analysts believed that the 103d House would have more new members than any House since the end of World War II. Turnover, however, was short of that record.[2]

This membership turnover must be viewed in context. Although redistricting, scandal, and voter discontent are given primary credit for high turnover, low turnover in each of the preceding four House elections is also a consideration. The elections from 1984 through 1990 produced an average of only 40.5 new House members. By contrast, the elections of 1972 through 1982 resulted in an average of 75 new members. Membership turnover comes from two major sources: retirements and reelection defeats. The 1984-1990 elections brought relatively small average turnovers in both of these categories, averaging only approximately 28 retirements and 12.5 reelection defeats. Thus the high turnover in 1992 is to some degree making up for the very low turnover that occurred during most of a decade.[3]

The low turnover affected the composition of the House in terms of its junior and senior members. The number of junior House members, those with three or fewer terms, after rising to a post-World War II high of 214 at the beginning of the 96th Congress in 1979, dropped to 120 members at the beginning of the 101st Congress in 1989, the lowest point since the House has had 435 members. (See Figure 2-1.) Correspondingly, the percentage of House "careerists," those members serving in their tenth term or greater, had declined from 20 percent before the 1972 election to a low of 11 percent after the 1980 election. By the beginning of the 102d Congress in 1991, the number of careerists had increased to more than 17 percent of the membership.[4] Clearly, the turnover in 1992 will bring a significant increase in the number of junior members and a decline in the number of careerists. It will be interesting to see whether this high turnover will undercut the movement for term limitations.

Party Control Remains Democratic

Despite three overwhelming Republican victories in the 1980, 1984, and 1988 presidential elections, Democratic control of the House has not been seriously threatened. With only 40 percent of the House of his own party upon his election to the presidency, George Bush and the Republicans set a record low. (It is no wonder that Republican losses in the 1990 midterm election were so low—8 seats—when the party had only 174 seats entering the election.) At the beginning of the 102d Congress, the Democrats held 267 seats, 13 more than the mean number of seats they have held since the era of Democratic House control stabilized in the 1930s.[5]

For several reasons the prospects for Republicans in the House are not as encouraging as they have been for Republicans in the Senate. Popular conceptions that the advantages of incumbency and redistricting efforts have kept Democrats from being threatened for control of the House are not well founded. First,

Figure 2-1 House Service: New Members (Three or Fewer Terms) and Careerists (Ten or More Terms), 1911-1991

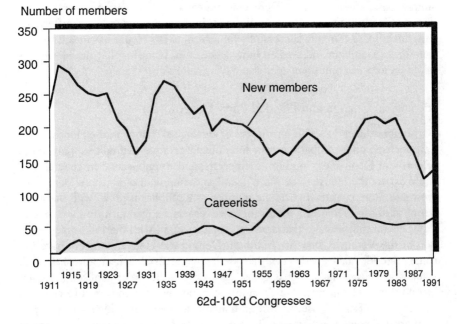

Number of members

62d-102d Congresses

Republicans have been faring only slightly better in open-seat House contests than in ones in which incumbents are running. There are some indications that Republicans lack the "farm system" for producing quality House candidates.[6] Second, although anecdotal material about partisan redistricting is common, there is no evidence that it has produced a significant effect on the partisan composition of the House. The same party does not control redistricting in every state, and in most states neither party has total control. Even when a party controls redistricting, it does not always try to maximize seats. That party's House incumbents may fight against making their seats more marginal in order to improve the chances of the party winning more seats. And even when a party does try to maximize seats, it is not always successful. For example, a Republican redistricting plan put into effect in Indiana in 1982 was designed to improve on the 7-4 advantage the party held in congressional seats. After the 1990 election, however, Democrats held all but two of the seats.[7]

Aside from the difficulty of finding good candidates, a major problem Republicans face in competing for House control arises from the fact that the House is apportioned on the basis of population, not voters. Each district elects one House member regardless of how many people vote. Yet there are often great differences in the number of votes cast in different districts. Districts that cast more votes have a bigger effect on Senate and presidential races than do districts that cast fewer votes. For a number of reasons, low-vote districts tend to be heavily Democratic and high-vote districts tend to be heavily Republican. This means that the Republicans tend to fare relatively better in Senate and presidential contests and that the Democrats tend to fare better in House contests. Put simply, populations are more Democratic in composition than are voters.[8]

As Charles O. Jones and John B. Bader indicate in Chapter 12, the Republicans' inability to compete successfully for control of the House has meant frustration for its members and tension in its leadership. It means that the House has taken on a more contentious partisan flavor than has the Senate.

Ideological Change and Divided Party Government

Before the early 1980s an analysis of ideological change in the House would have focused on a comparison over time of conservative coalition support scores of northern Democrats, southern Democrats, and Republicans.[9] In general, one could expect the House to be more liberal as the number of northern Democrats grew and more conservative as the number of Republicans grew, with the number of southern Democrats remaining relatively unchanged historically.

Several things make that analysis obsolete. First, with the full implementation of the Voting Rights Act, southern Democratic House members have become more ideologically diverse; they are by no means all conservatives. Second, when Republicans make House gains, they come at the expense of southern, not just northern, Democrats. Third, and most important, the conservative coalition appears less often. Conservative coalition votes—those on which a majority of northern Democrats are opposed by a majority of Republicans and a majority of southern Democrats—comprised a fifth to a quarter of the roll call votes in Congress until the 1980s. They have dropped markedly and since 1987 have remained about 10 percent.[10]

As the conservative coalition declined, interparty conflict grew. Party votes—those on which a majority of Democrats opposed a majority of Republicans—comprised over half of all roll call votes in the House in every Congress since the 98th (1983-1985), reaching a high of 64 percent in 1987. This change has been accompanied by an increase in intraparty cohesion. The average party-unity score for House members has risen to record levels, with House Democrats averaging 85 percent or higher every year since 1985.[11]

The combination of a Democratic House majority and higher levels of party unity created difficulties for Ronald Reagan and George Bush in their dealings with the House. Previous Republican presidents who had worked with Democratic congressional majorities always could depend on winning the support of enough conservative Democrats to pass many of their legislative programs. During years of Democratic Congresses, Eisenhower, Nixon, and Ford won averages of 54.3 percent, 53.4 percent, and 41.3 percent, respectively, of the House roll call votes on which they took a position. By comparison, Reagan averaged only 33.3 percent during his presidency, and Bush averaged 32 percent in the two years of the 101st Congress. Some of these figures may have resulted from polarizing presidential administrations. But whatever the cause, clearly, stronger congressional parties have had major implications for divided party government.

Divided party government in the 1950s, 1960s, and 1970s did not result in as much stalemate as has recently been the case.

Membership Diversity

The low membership turnover since 1984 has limited the trend toward greater diversity of House members. By the beginning of the 102d Congress, there were twenty-nine women House members, a modest increase from twenty-two in the 99th Congress, and the number of African American members reached twenty-six, up from twenty in the 99th Congress. In addition, the 102d Congress had twelve Hispanic members, including the nonvoting delegates from Puerto Rico and the Virgin Islands. The large number of retirements, the redistricting after the 1990 census (and the Voting Rights Act requirement against diluting minority populations in new districts), and the active recruitment by various groups of women and minority candidates greatly increased these underrepresented groups in the 103d Congress. The number of women, African Americans, and Hispanics elected in 1992, respectively, increased by 50 percent or more. The new House will include forty-eight women, thirty-nine African Americans, and nineteen Hispanics.[12]

In addition, fifteen of the retiring members and two of those defeated for renomination in 1992 were more than 70 years old. The House membership, whose members averaged 52.1 years at the beginning of the 102d Congress, will be a bit younger than this when the new House is sworn in.[13]

Because of an increase in the diversity of the House membership, together with the great influx of new members after the 1992 elections, the House of Representatives in the 103d Congress will continue to face considerable internal tensions. The diversity of the membership helps to ensure that a broad range of policy issues and perspectives will be introduced to House deliberations and that a wide range of membership factions will press for inclusion in House decision-making structures. The newness of the membership will help to lessen members' commitment to preexisting power arrangements and induce sensitivity to calls for reform of the House. With the demise of the conservative coalition, these developments raise the possibility that a primary dividing line in the 103d Congress will be between the more diverse group of newer members and the more senior and established members of the House. The primary issue dividing the members may well be the reform of rules and procedures in the House.

Rules and Procedures

Because the House is a much larger institution than the Senate, it must rely more heavily on formal rules and explicit procedures than on norms. Norms such as reciprocity, courtesy, hard work, expertise, and seniority exist in the House.[14] But the rules of party caucuses, of committees, and of the House itself are primary guides to member behavior and have become the centers of contention in power struggles. In the early to mid-1970s, the period of increased turnover, the rules were subjected to their most extensive restructuring in sixty years, altering the formal power structure of the House in dramatic ways.

House Reforms

The reform movement of the 1970s really began in the late 1950s with the creation of the Democratic Study Group (DSG), an organization committed to liberal legislation and liberal control of the House.[15] Throughout the 1960s the group pushed for changes in House procedures and party practice. Liberals' efforts in the 1960s resulted in the Reorganization Act of 1970. That measure, passed by a coalition of Republicans and liberal Democrats, liberalized and formalized parliamentary procedure in House committees and on the floor.

In the late 1960s liberal Democrats developed a second strategy. They shifted their attention to reform of the House Democratic party. In January 1969 the Democratic Caucus, which had been dormant for most of the century, was revitalized with a rule allowing for a monthly meeting if fifty members demanded it in writing. Liberals then used the caucus throughout the early 1970s to create committees to study the House and propose structural and procedural reforms.

Three reform committees, each chaired by Julia Butler Hansen, D-Wash., proposed reforms in 1971, 1973, and 1974.[16] In addition, Speaker Carl Albert, D-Okla., initiated the creation of a Select Committee on Committees headed by Richard Bolling, D-Mo. The Bolling committee introduced its proposals in 1974, but they were defeated by the House, which chose instead to adopt the more limited jurisdictional changes of the last Hansen committee.[17]

These reform efforts had five particularly important consequences. First, they established a clear procedure for the Democratic Caucus to select committee chairs by secret ballot. This change provided members with a way to defeat renominations of incumbent chairs and bypass the norm of committee seniority. Second, the reforms increased the number and strength of subcommittees. Third, the House moved to open to the public virtually all committee and subcommittee meetings. Fourth, the reforms increased the power of the Speaker by giving the post considerable control over the referral of legislation. A fifth change, which was not actually part of these caucus reforms but stemmed from the overall reform movement, was the creation in 1974 of a new congressional budget process, including the creation of a House Budget Committee. But the defeat of the Bolling committee provisions that attempted to restructure committee jurisdictions left the maze of overlapping committee and subcommittee jurisdictions relatively untouched.

Other reforms of the post-1973 period also were adopted. In the 94th Congress, House Democrats refined the procedures for nominating committee chairs and voted down several incumbents. The caucus also adopted a rule requiring nominees for Appropriations subcommittee chairs to be approved by similar procedures. This change seemed in order because these subcommittees are more powerful than some standing committees. Although two incumbent chairs were displaced at the beginning of the 102d Congress, rarely have incumbent chairs (or the senior member when a vacancy exists) not been elected. The vote on occasion has been used to warn a chair who has gotten out of line. This occurred at the beginning of the 101st Congress, when Les Aspin, D-Wis., nearly was deposed from his Armed Services Committee chair (a position he had gained in the previous Congress when he defeated the aging incumbent chair).

Ethical Concerns

In August 1992 the House and Senate agreed to create a Joint Committee on the Organization of Congress. In part, it was created in response to members' dissatisfaction and frustration with the operations of Congress and in part in response to the low levels of public support for Congress in the wake of much-publicized ethical misconduct and perquisite abuse in the House and Senate. The resolution creating the committee identifies the committee system, leadership responsibilities and powers, and relationships between the House and the Senate and between Congress and the executive branch as matters to be studied. The agenda for the joint committee is not as well defined as the reform efforts of the 1970s.[18]

The recent scandals involving the operation of the House bank and the House post office have generated widespread media attention and significant public outrage. The House has had to respond with alterations in ethical standards and internal management, as it has had to do with other ethical and management scandals in the twenty-five years since the creation of the Committee on Standards of Official Conduct (hereafter, the Ethics Committee). One problem for the House has been that no sooner does it act to deal with one set of ethical violations than another appears.

In 1976-1977, in the wake of sex and payroll scandals and the probe of South Korean influence peddling on Capitol Hill, the bipartisan House Commission on Administrative Review, chaired by David Obey, D-Wis., led to the adoption of a new ethics code. The new code provided for annual financial disclosure by House members, officers, and professional staff; it prohibited gifts totaling $100 or more from a lobbyist or a foreign national; it prohibited unofficial office accounts; it placed restrictions on the use of the franking privilege; and it limited the amount of outside income members could earn. The House, however, refused to pass other Obey commission recommendations that would have established an administrator to oversee the operation of internal management services.

In 1980 six House members were caught in an FBI sting operation in which agents posing as wealthy Arabs offered them bribes. Two of the six were defeated for reelection before they were convicted, three resigned from the House rather than risk likely expulsion, and one—Michael "Ozzie" Myers, D-Pa.—was expelled from the House after his conviction and upon recommendation of the Ethics Committee. Throughout the 1980s a series of cases involving money and the ethical, and sometimes criminal, behavior of House members occurred. Some, such as those involving Reps. Mario Biaggi and Robert Garcia, both

D-N.Y., and Wedtech, a defense contractor, resulted in criminal convictions that preempted House ethics sanctions.

In the ten years from 1982 through 1991 the Ethics Committee investigated more than twenty members charged with violations. None of them received more attention than House Speaker Jim Wright, D-Texas, who was charged with violations that eventually led to his resignation. In this unusual situation, Newt Gingrich, R-Ga., was joined by Common Cause in demanding an investigation of allegations against Wright. After a ten-month inquiry by the Ethics Committee and its outside attorney, Wright was charged with violating ethics provisions by accepting gifts from a business associate and using bulk sales of his book as a means of evading the limits on House members' outside incomes.[19] Because of Wright's strong, and highly partisan, speakership, some Democrats believed the investigation was politically motivated. The investigation did illustrate, however, that no House member was immune from the new ethics standards.

Shortly after Wright announced his intention to resign, Tony Coelho, D-Calif., the majority whip, resigned his House seat. Charges had surfaced that Coelho had received certain advantages in a "junk bond" transaction.

These resignations and the rise of Thomas S. Foley, D-Wash., to the speakership seemed to put to rest the uproar over ethics. Foley's reputation for fairness and for honesty were viewed as important assets. Moreover, the Ethics Reform Act of 1989 was passed and appeared to tighten previous provisions. Among other things, the new law prohibited House members from keeping honoraria from speeches.

During the 102d Congress scandals involving the House bank and the House post office reawakened the public's concern about congressional ethics and privilege and the overall management of the institution. Whether or not the House bank was a bank in the traditional sense was unimportant. Unlike more isolated ethics violations, this one involved a large number of House members and had some impact during the 1992 primary season. Of the nineteen members defeated for renomination, eight had made more than a hundred overdrafts. In the case of the House post office, an investigation that originally involved drug dealing and embezzlement by employees widened to include charges that some House offices had obtained cash through phony stamp purchases and that campaign checks were cashed there.

Claims that Speaker Foley was slow to address these practices and that he inadequately defended the House and its members against the charges seemed to threaten his effectiveness as Speaker.[20] More important, the scandals had the potential to undermine the power that had accrued to the party leadership since the late 1970s. In the short term, the House closed the bank, abolished other perks, and removed much of the administration of the House from political control. The long-term effect of these actions, the results of the investigations of charges, and the influx of new members on the operations of the House may well affect public trust in the institution and membership confidence in the leadership.

In the maze of scandals, the struggle over campaign finance legislation was nearly overlooked. Yet it is the financing of campaigns that often is seen as the root of ethics problems in Congress. The 102d Congress passed a major, Democratic-sponsored campaign finance bill. It provided for some public financing of congressional campaigns in the form of matching funds (up to $200,000 total) for small contributions and set a spending limit of $600,000 for candidates who accepted federal money. In addition, limits were set on contributions from political action committees, individuals, and parties. Other provisions allowed for subsidized mailings and for low-broadcast advertising rates. President Bush, who opposed public financing, vetoed the bill, claiming it would continue to protect incumbents.[21] Yet it is clear that this bill would have given the overwhelming majority of House challengers a far more competitive opportunity than they currently enjoy. Campaign financing, though not in the jurisdiction of the new Joint Committee on the Organization of Congress, is likely to be revisited in the 103d Congress.

Of equal concern in the 103d Congress will be the capacity of the institution to govern through its existing committee and party systems. Scandals in the House in recent years have taken on particular salience to the public because of widespread dissatisfaction with the policy performance of Congress. Although some of this dissatisfaction is caused by the policy gridlock produced by divided party government, it also is a result of the problems that the House has experienced in sustaining internal policy leadership. These problems reflect the difficulty that the modern House has faced in developing stable committee and party arrangements that can ensure broad-based support within the House for policy solutions to the nation's pressing policy dilemmas. This difficulty is rooted in part in the reform movement of the 1970s and in part in the emergence of a new policy environment during the 1980s that the earlier reformers failed to foresee.

Committees

The reforms of the 1970s sought to decentralize power in House committees and to weaken the power of committee chairs. These reforms, which sought to democratize the House and make it more responsive to policy innovations, immediately proved successful and, beginning in the mid-1970s, produced a period of subcommittee government, weak committee chairs, and inclusive policy entrepreneurship. By the mid-1980s, however, a new kind of committee politics was emerging, a centralized committee oligarchy that reversed the decentralization of the 1970s. This new committee oligarchy arose from the Reagan presidency; in particular, it was a consequence of the effect of large deficits and tight spending. In committee politics, an environment of scarcity tends to produce centralized dominance by party leaders and the committees that control the nation's purse strings. Ironically, the move toward oligarchical dominance was facilitated by the procedural weakness of the chairs of most authorization committees, who, as a result of the reforms of the 1970s, could not protect their committees' decision-making prerogatives. By the 1990s these developments had weakened the role of most House members, produced a less democratic decision process, and engendered policy conflict between the House oligarchy and the rank-and-file members.

Committee Decentralization

The effort to decentralize committees grew out of the historic domination of the House by approximately twenty committee chairs. The era of committee government had begun in the 1920s and was characterized by brokerage politics: committee chairs, usually conservative, attempted through bargaining and compromise to aggregate the numerous competing policy interests within their committees' jurisdictions.[22] As liberals began to dominate the Democratic party in the House, opposition to the existing structure of committee government escalated.

Aside from ideology, the opposition was fueled by other pressures. In particular, the increase in the number and complexity of federal concerns increased the committee workload and created the need for higher levels of legislative specialization than the standing committees could handle. As reformers looked for ways to deal with the workload, they strengthened the subcommittees. Their efforts brought about the reforms of the 1970s; these reforms had two major dimensions: the rise of subcommittee government and the decline of committee chairs.

Subcommittee government means that the basic responsibility for most legislative activity (hearings, debates, legislative markups) occurs not at a meeting of an entire standing committee but at a meeting of a smaller subcommittee of the standing committee.[23] The decisions of the subcommittee are viewed as authoritative, altered by the standing committee only when the subcommittee is seriously divided or when its decisions are considered unrepresentative of the full committee. The growth of subcommittee authority from the 1950s to the late 1970s is indicated by the sheer increase in their number; they grew from 83 standing subcommittees at the beginning of the 84th Congress (1955-1957) to 135 standing subcommittees in the 98th Congress (1983-1985).

With the rise of subcommittee government in the 1970s, basic responsibility shifted from approximately 20 standing committees to approximately 160 committees and subcommittees.[24] In the process, the power of committee chairs declined. Formal change in the power of committee chairs came in 1973, when the caucus passed rules implementing the election of chairs, removing their invulnerability. When this development was combined with the other reforms of the early 1970s, and with the removal of three sitting chairmen in 1975, it clearly altered the status and authority of the chairs. They lost the right to determine the number, size, and majority party memberships of subcommittees. They lost the power to appoint subcommittee chairs, to control referral of legislation to subcommittees, and to prevent their committees from meeting. Finally, as a result of the growth of subcommittee activity, many were forced to defer to their subcommittee chairs in managing legislation on the House floor.

The emergence of subcommittee government, together with the decline of committee chairs, altered considerably the character of House decision making.[25] It brought more members into the policy process, opened the possibility of policy innovation to a wider range of members, and probably increased legislative expertise in the House. But subcommittee government had its cost as well.

Most significantly, subcommittee government created a crisis of interest aggregation. It largely removed committees as arenas in which interests could be compromised, brokered, and mediated. And it led to increased dominance of committee decision making by clientele groups, to narrowly focused policy leadership, and to confusion in policy jurisdictions. These problems were not necessarily unmanageable; strong party leadership, for example, could have militated against them. But by the early 1980s it was clear that the committee reforms of the 1970s had generated their own problems that would eventually need to be rectified.[26] Just as these problems were becoming clear, however, the structure of committee decision making again began to change, not as a result of conscious planning and rules reform by House members but as a result of contextual change.

The Rise of a New Committee Oligarchy

Committee decentralization and subcommittee government grew out of the vast expansion of governmental services that occurred in the 1950s and 1960s. An activist government required many specialized working groups to investigate, legislate, and oversee new and expanded programs. This need, together with the career ambitions of junior legislators and the desire to break the power of conservative chairs, fueled the committee reforms of the 1970s. Just as subcommittee government was becoming firmly entrenched, the nation elected Ronald Reagan. The president pushed through giant tax cuts without a concomitant reduction in spending, and the country suddenly faced massive federal deficits, which blocked new programs and new spending. Seemingly overnight, the rationale for subcommittee government was gone: without money to spend, there was less need for a highly specialized system of subcommittees.

Instead of the extensive legislative agenda of the past, the House moved to what many members refer to as the "four bill" system.[27] In an average year there may be only four important domestic legislative vehicles: the budget resolution, continuing appropriations, supplemental appropriations, and the reconciliation package of spending cuts dictated by the budget. A fifth bill, to raise the federal debt limit, is sometimes needed. Members who can influence one of these "must-pass" bills are important players in the House; the rest are more nearly spectators. The result is a new committee oligarchy different from the committee government of the early part of the century. In the earlier system, power was vested in seniority, and the chairs of the standing committees were the oligarchs. In the new system, power is concentrated in the membership of a few elite committees, primarily those dealing with money.

The elite committees certainly include the Appropriations Committee. Its power derives from its role in drafting the continuing resolution, the bill that funds all programs for which regular appropriations bills have not passed when the new fiscal year begins October 1. Because so few money bills clear Congress by the deadline, the continuing resolution is essentially a budget. It is all but certain of presidential approval and is so massive that there is little chance to question any item placed on it by Appropriations members. Members of less fortunate committees, even very senior members, must persuade Appropriations members of whatever rank to help them out. In this sense, being a junior Appropriations Committee member can be more significant than being a subcommittee chair on an authorization committee.

Ways and Means is also an elite committee in the new oligarchy, in part because of its role in writing tax bills and in part because of its jurisdiction over must-pass legislation concerning the federal debt ceiling; this legislation becomes a vehicle for scores of legislative initiatives that might not pass on their own. Ways and Means also plays a significant role in the reconciliation process because of its jurisdiction over hundreds of billions of dollars in spending for health, Social Security, and other social need categories. This jurisdiction gives Ways and Means leverage in the reconciliation process over reductions in these areas; in making the cuts, it can reshape the programs.

Another important House committee is Energy and Commerce, the one authorization committee that continues to play a strong policy role in the 1980s. Its influence is a testament to its broad jurisdiction, which touches major regulatory agencies and covers nuclear energy, toxic waste, health research, Medicare and Medicaid, railroad retirement, telecommunications, tourism, and commerce. Also part of the new oligarchy is the Budget Committee, which oversees the preparation of the congressional budget resolutions and the reconciliation process. The power that membership on this committee bestows comes from the potential for its members to influence the debate over the nation's long-term policy agenda. The final member of the oligarchy is the Rules Committee, which reviews every major bill before the bill reaches the House floor and drafts the ground rules for floor debate on bills.[28]

The remaining committees—the authorizing committees concerned with substantive areas of policymaking such as agriculture, banking, education, and labor—play a more peripheral role in the contemporary House. In principle, these committees should be the heart of the policy process in Congress, drafting and creating programs in a vast array of problem areas. Yet, according to a report by House Republicans, these committees "are rapidly approaching irrelevance—squeezed out by the budget and appropriations processes, and caught up in jurisdictional infighting and subcommittee strangulation." [29] The problems associated with committee decentralization and with budget limitations have crippled the authorizing committees: little discretionary money is available for them to fund new programs, and any authorization, particularly liberal ones, faced veto threat under President Bush. The new oligarchy, ironically, addresses some of the problems of interest aggregation that arose with committee decentralization, providing fairly centralized consideration of a broad range of policy concerns. But for average members, the system is frustrating, greatly limiting their influence on legislative policymaking.

Both the importance of the oligarchy in the policy process and the frustrations of members with that influence were vividly demonstrated in the 1990 negotiations over the nation's budget.[30] Faced with a continuing fiscal crisis and the possibility of across-the-board cuts in federal spending, President Bush and the congressional leaders agreed in May 1990 to a summit that would create a new budget strategy that Congress and the president could support. For six months the president's negotiators, the Senate, and the House met in grueling discussions that bypassed normal committee processes in Congress. The House was represented in the discussions by members of the party leadership, the Ways and Means Committee, the Appropriations Committee, and the Budget Committee. In the end, the budget strategy produced by the negotiators and passed by Congress included new taxes that President Bush during the 1988 elections had promised to avoid. Almost certainly, this final bill would not have been produced and passed through normal congressional processes, involving as it did a complex set of tax increases and spending cuts that had detrimental effects on most congressional constituencies. Final passage of the bill came on October 27, only after rank-and-file members had rejected the original and more distasteful budget package on October 5 by a vote of 179-254. The initial rejection demonstrated members' great frustration with the increasing reliance on a centralized policymaking process that overrides their disparate policy concerns and committee roles. It also indicated that in the end the power of the new oligarchy comes more from the necessity of centralized decision making to address the nation's fiscal problems than from members' fear of the institutional power of the new oligarchy.

Because members feel a sense of independence from the committee oligarchs—and will vote independently on major legislation—the continued authority of the committee oligarchs probably depends on the nation's continued fiscal crisis. It also depends on the existence of an effective majority party leadership in the House that can mediate between the powerful committees, maintain a cooperative relationship with the minority party, and generate vote support from the rank-and-file members.

Consolidating Majority Party Leadership

The rise of a new oligarchy in the House means the consolidation of considerable power in the majority party leadership. Unlike the emergence of a powerful committee oligarchy, the expanding power of the leadership is grounded solidly in the rules reforms of the 1970s. Ironically, it took fiscal austerity and the Reagan presidency for the majority party leaders to use fully the powers given them by the reforms. Although the Reagan revolution undercut the subcommittee reforms, it breathed life into the powers of the Speaker and the party leadership.[31]

The Democratic Party Caucus

Among other things, the reform process of the early 1970s expanded the powers of the House Democratic Caucus, the organization of all House Democrats. Democrats began to use the caucus to debate policy positions and to nurture personal careers. The activism of the caucus led to cries from some Republicans and conservative Democrats that "King Caucus" was running the House and overriding the wishes of its total membership. Hoping to cripple its effectiveness, these dissidents called for opening meetings of the caucus.

The eventual opening of the caucus, together with the election of a Democratic president in 1976, reduced its effectiveness in the mid to late 1970s. The election of Ronald Reagan further defused the activism of the caucus, by confronting House Democrats with a Republican president and a conservative legislative program. In response, the caucus decided to meet again in closed session and reclaim its position as the center of party debate. The caucus was successful enough for one of its chairmen, Richard A. Gephardt of Missouri, to use this post to launch his 1988 presidential race.

The long-term fate of the caucus is uncertain. So far it appears strong only when the Republican party controls the White House and when debates are held in private. Because of its size, the caucus may not be the best forum for handling strategic problems or for making delicate party decisions. The caucus's Steering and Policy Committee may be the best arena for collective party leadership, and the Speaker remains the natural spokesperson for the party.

The Speaker

Throughout most of the twentieth century, parties in the House have been unwilling to invest power in their party leaders.[32] This reticence stems from early in the century when Speaker Joseph "Uncle Joe" Cannon, R-Ill., used the considerable authority of the speakership to dominate the House. An insurgency against Cannon in 1910 stripped the speakership of many of its major powers, including control over committee appointments, the Rules Committee, private and minor House business, the Special Calendar, and the party caucus. After Cannon's downfall and a short flirtation with party caucus government, the House turned to committee government and reliance on the seniority rule.

Efforts to revitalize the speakership began in the early 1970s, when the House majority party, the Democrats, needed strong leadership and a coherent strategy to thwart the efforts by the Republican president, Richard Nixon, to dismantle the Great Society. The move toward a stronger speakership took several years, with major reform efforts occurring in 1973 and 1975. These reforms activated the long-dormant Steering and Policy Committee, gave it the power of Committee on Committees (that is, the power to nominate committee members and committee chairs), made the Speaker its chair, and gave the Speaker the authority to select a number of its members. In addition, the Speaker was given the power to nominate the chair and Democratic members of the House Rules Committee, thus bringing that committee more clearly under the control of the Speaker and the party. These developments meant that, for the first time in decades, a Democratic Speaker had a major role in committee assignments, the election of committee chairs, and the choice of Democratic Rules members. Thus House Democrats seeking committee positions or leadership roles had far more reason to cooperate with the Speaker than in the past.[33]

Other reforms likewise strengthened the Speaker. First, increases in the financial and staff resources of the party whip office and in the number of whips appointed by the party leadership resulted in a stronger, more active whip system to assist the leadership in efforts to pass legislation.[34] Second, the Speaker regained some of the ground lost by Cannon concerning control over the referral of bills. Third, the creation of the new budget process provided mechanisms through which a skillful party leadership could control the budget and coordinate budget making by House committees.

The control of parliamentary procedures on the floor was one area in which the reforms of the 1970s did not seem to significantly redress the loss of ground that took place after Cannon's downfall. Recorded votes on amendments and electronic voting further reduced the Speaker's power as presiding officer. The Rules Committee has helped the Speaker gradually to overcome this problem of floor management. The sum of the changes constitutes a true resurgence of the speakership and a move back toward the power enjoyed by Cannon.

The Speakership: O'Neill to Wright to Foley

House Democrats adopted these various changes during Carl Albert's tenure, but it was Speaker Tip O'Neill, D-Mass., who first had access to them all. O'Neill's success in passing a controversial energy program during the early years of the Carter administration suggested to some that an era of strong party leadership had arrived. Their optimism, however, was premature. Subsequent defeats during the Carter years, and continuing struggles during the Reagan presidency, highlighted the limited resources of congressional leaders when faced with independent members during an era of united government or with a popular president of the opposite party during a period of divided government. Perhaps O'Neill's most distinctive contribution to the speakership was his success in becoming the first media celebrity in the history of the office and thereby bequeathing an office of historic visibility to his successor, Jim Wright of Texas.[35]

Wright's background was very different from O'Neill's. O'Neill, an Irish-American from Boston, had spent years on the Rules Committee; in the House he was concerned less with legislation than with "talking strategy with close friends over poker, golf, or dinner at a Washington restaurant." [36] Wright was a protégé of the most powerful Speaker of modern times, fellow Texan Sam Rayburn. Wright was a skilled legislator, having served most of his career on the Public Works Committee, and was a policy activist by temperament. As Speaker, he moved quickly to establish himself as a hands-on leader who would pursue an ambitious legislative agenda and act as "micromanager" of the legislative process. In doing so, he used the Steering and Policy Committee as a central policy committee, made aggressive use of the Rules Committee to restrict debate and to speed action on bills he considered top priority, and took a particularly powerful role in foreign policy, particularly on U.S. support for the Nicaraguan contras. During his speakership, in short, he transformed the office from consensus builder to agenda setter, from power broker to power wielder, and from congressional and national force into an international presence. Wright was able to assert the power of the speakership so strongly because of the fiscal crisis of the nation during the late 1980s and because, given the existence of divided government, the House Speaker was the most visible spokesperson for the Democratic party. In the end, however, Wright's aggressive and partisan style alienated both Republicans and many Democrats so that as the ethics grievance initiated by Newt Gingrich against Wright grew in severity Wright lacked the broad trust and friendship in the House that might have allowed him to weather the attack. In June 1989 Wright became the first Speaker in history to resign from office as a result of scandal.[37]

After Wright's resignation, the House chose as the new Speaker an individual with a more consensual and personable style, the Democratic majority leader, Thomas Foley.[38] Foley first won his House seat in the Johnson landslide of 1964 by defeating a twenty-two-year Republican incumbent in a wheat-growing district in the Inland Empire of Washington State. A lawyer by training and a liberal intellectual by temperament, Foley nevertheless solidified his electoral security in his conservative agricultural district by gaining appointment to the Agriculture Committee and remaining attentive to the agricultural needs of his district. In 1975 Foley became chair of the Agriculture Committee after only a decade in the House; in 1976 he was elected chair of the Democratic Caucus as well. In 1981 Speaker O'Neill named him majority whip because of his persuasive abilities with members and his effectiveness in building bipartisan cooperation on the Agriculture Committee. Democrats selected Foley as majority leader in 1986, when Wright succeeded O'Neill as Speaker.

Wright's resignation left Foley with the difficult task of solidifying his party's diminished prestige and rebuilding a sense of comity and cooperation in an institution that had become increasingly characterized by bitter partisan conflict and personal animosities.[39] Foley's task was made more difficult by divided party government and by the decision of House Republicans to take an aggressive approach to House politics. In March 1989 the growing aggressiveness of House Republicans was epitomized by their selection of their most partisan firebrand, Newt Gingrich, as the party's whip. In Gingrich and his Republican followers, Foley faced partisan opposition devoted to the removal of the Democratic party from congressional power through almost any means necessary. Those means included efforts to embarrass the Democrats through policy maneuvers and attempts to defeat them through continuing charges of corruption (charges that eventually came to be symbolized by the House banking scandal). Foley also faced considerable division within his own party. Some Democratic members, concerned with the immediate governance of the country, wanted to cooperate with Republicans to pass legislation that the president would sign; others, concerned with regaining the presidency in 1992, wanted to pass legislation that articulated the Democrats' policy agenda even at the risk of veto by the president.

Foley has attempted to lead his party and the House through mediation between the factions and the parties rather than through aggressive manipulation and arm-twisting.[40] He has been particularly respectful of the policymaking role of standing committees, perhaps because of his previous service as a committee chair. Thus at times he has allowed considerable leeway to such chairmen as Dan Rostenkowski, D-Ill., of Ways and Means, even in the face of calls for the Speaker to force more rapid and responsive committee action. Foley's conciliatory approach has led to visible policy defeats, including an embarrassing loss in his first major legislative effort—the move to defeat the president's 1989 proposal of a capital-gains tax cut—and the initial defeat in the 1990 budget battles. In response, many Democrats have called for the Speaker to show more aggressive policy leadership to offset the growing sense of organizational paralysis and disarray in the House.

Despite Foley's overt appearance of bipartisan forbearance, a deceptive degree of partisan effectiveness can be seen in his quiet and patient approach, particularly when held up against the difficulties he inherited from Speaker Wright. Thus the Democrats' willingness to work with President Bush in the budget summit of 1990 led the president to forgo his 1988 pledge of no new taxes, much to the president's regret and the Democrat's delight in the 1992 elections. And Foley's refusal to engage in a direct confrontation with Gingrich and Republican dissidents, but rather to manage and defuse their partisan thrusts in an incremental fashion, may have led House Republicans to become over-aggressive in their attack on the House as an institution. In the end, the Republican attack may have boomeranged on them. In the 1990 congressional elections, the vote margin for incumbent Republicans fell far more sharply than for incumbent Democrats. Likewise, the House banking scandal of 1992, generated by Republican dissidents, led to an anti-incumbency mood in the nation that was particularly potent in Republican middle-class districts and led thereby to the retirement or defeat of such Republican leaders as Vin Weber of Minnesota and Guy Vander Jagt of Michigan.

Although Foley has not had the dramatic effect of Jim Wright on policy, and although his tenure as Speaker has been a difficult one because of partisan and factional animosities set in motion during the Wright speakership, history may conclude that Foley was a wilier and more adept partisan politician than his contemporaries appreciated. Whether his Democratic colleagues, unhappy with the absence of glamorous leadership, will keep him as Speaker remains to be seen. Much depends on his ability to develop an effective relationship between the House and President Bill Clinton.

The Majority Leader and the Whip

The two other leadership positions within the majority party—and the Speaker's principal support team—are the majority leader and the whip. The majority leader is the party's point man on the floor of the House, ensuring that the party's daily legislative program flows smoothly while the Speaker presides over House deliberations. The majority leader also joins the Speaker in setting the legislative schedule and serving as party spokesperson. The majority whip is responsible for surveying party members on their policy positions and rounding up votes to pass party legislation.

The resignation of Wright as Speaker and Coehlo as whip in June 1989, and Foley's selection as Wright's replacement, set off a scramble for the majority leadership and whip positions.[41] The fight for majority leader was won by Richard Gephardt, chair of the House Democratic Caucus from 1984 to 1988 and a candidate for the 1988 Democratic presidential nomination. Gephardt was particularly attractive to members because he had "the kind of squeaky-clean image and well-scrutinized record" that Democrats felt they needed to repair the damage from the Wright and Coehlo affairs.[42]

The whip position was won by William H. Gray III, D-Pa., the sitting chair of the Democratic Caucus and former chair of the House Budget Committee (1984-1989). Upon his selection, Gray became the highest ranking African American in the congressional party hierarchy. In June 1991 he announced his retirement from the House to become president of the United Negro College Fund, and the Democratic Caucus replaced him with David E. Bonior, D-Mich., the party's chief deputy whip and a member of the Rules Committee. Although Bonior had an easygoing personality and was known as a skillful vote counter, he was a controversial choice: he added to the leadership team a third white male and nonsoutherner. To ensure greater heterogeneity within the leadership, Foley replaced Bonior as chief deputy whip with three chief deputy whips: a southern white male, Butler Derrick of South Carolina; a woman, Barbara B. Kennelly of Connecticut; and a southern black male, John Lewis of Georgia.[43]

As majority leader, Gephardt has drawn heavily on the media-oriented style that he developed in his 1988 race for the Democratic presidential nomination, and he has brought to the office some of the populist policy concerns of his presidential race. He has met extensively with the media and has emphasized a policy agenda focused particularly on tax cuts for the middle class and the protection of American jobs. Because of Foley's conciliatory and bipartisan style, Gephardt has had to assume the role of the leadership's "partisan point man" who articulates the party's position on key issues.[44]

As whip, Gray and then Bonior headed an elaborate organization that seeks to convey the views of the leadership to the members of the House, while determining members' views so that leaders can develop coalition strategies. The term "whip," first used in the British parliament, is derived from the fox-hunting term "whipper-in"—the person assigned to keep hunting dogs in a pack. During the past two decades the whip organization has grown enormously, more than doubling in size; by the early 1990s approximately a hundred members of the Democratic caucus served in the whip organization—as chief deputy whips or deputy whips serving the leaders in a close and strategic role, as assistant whips elected by regions to represent them to the leadership, and as at-large whips, who assist the leaders in general vote counts. Given his collegial and discursive style, Speaker Foley has relied heavily on meetings with the large whip organization to gauge policy sentiment in the party and to guide the party on a weekly basis.[45]

The Steering and Policy Committee

Another part of the Democratic leadership is the Steering and Policy Committee, a small "executive" committee composed of the Speaker's appointees and members selected by regional caucuses. Ideally, the committee would be a representative body that provides members with an opportunity for healthy debate and innovative direction on matters of public policy, gives guidance to committees and subcommittees, and spurs the party leadership to an articulate, persuasive policy role reflecting the dominant sentiment of the party. Since its reactivation in 1973, only occasionally has the committee shown that it can perform such functions. Under O'Neill, the primary role of the committee was to make nominations to the standing committees. Wright, who sought to use it more aggressively on policy matters, assigned his own staff to the committee. Foley has expanded by three the number of members of the committee appointed by the Speaker and has been known to use his power on the committee to deny choice committee assignments to members who crossed him on procedural votes on the House floor.[46]

If the leadership is to make the Steering and Policy Committee a more useful instrument and move the House closer to party government, it must clean up the jurisdictional nightmare of House committees and subcommittees. The current structure of committees and subcommittees invites jurisdictional disputes from those who see their influence threatened and from those who realize that such disputes can be used to delay and defeat legislation. Such disputes led House Democrats in the 97th Congress to include on the Steering and Policy Committee the chairs of the Budget, Appropriations, Ways and Means, and Rules committees. The presence of these chairs may foster better coordination, but jurisdictional disputes are not likely to end without reform of the committee system. Not until the problem of overlapping committee jurisdictions is thoroughly addressed and resolved will any majority party leadership and the Steering and Policy Committee, no matter how skilled and well organized, be able to provide the institution with clear policy direction.

Relations with the Loyal Opposition

The ability of the majority party to provide the House with effective leadership also depends on its relations with the minority party. In a highly diverse nation such as the United States, it is very difficult for the party consistently to maintain the high degree of voting cohesiveness needed to enact a legislative agenda without some cooperation from members of the loyal opposition. In addition, in a highly fragmented institution such as the House, the minority party will always have strategies that it can use to delay, obstruct, and sabotage the majority party. Finally, during periods of divided government, the power of the minority is particularly strong because it can override the majority party's control of the House by cohesive support of presidential vetoes. For this reason, and because of complications generated by the partisan struggle over Speaker Wright's ethics scandal, Speaker Foley sought over the past four years to establish a close working relationship with the Republican party in the House. In doing so, however, he faced a difficult task because of the increasingly aggressive stance of the House Republican party.

The Republican party has served as the House minority party continuously since 1955. Throughout most of this time, particularly as the conservative coalition declined in effectiveness during the 1960s and 1970s, the Republican party adopted a pragmatic method of legislating in which its members chose to work with the Democrats in drafting and passing legislation; they accepted modest influence on the House's legislative output as the alternative to an aggressive effort of obstructing the Democrats, building an alternative Republican agenda, and challenging the Democrats in a nationwide electoral contest for control of the House.[47] The pragmatic strategy seemed necessary because Democratic control of the House appeared so solid that a challenge to the House majority was likely to fail, leaving the Republicans with no influence whatsoever. The Reagan-Bush presidential victories in 1980, 1984, and 1988, however, convinced many Republicans that a well-organized assault on the Democratic majority might eventually succeed. In addition, many Republicans were becoming increasingly alienated by their continuing minority status and by the fact that, in cooperating with the Democrats, they were supporting an ever larger federal government and the persistence of social programs that seemed destined to solidify the Democrat's electoral success at the expense of the restrained fiscal policies envisioned by conservative Republicans. The "seething impatience" of the Republicans was reinforced by the tendency of the House Democrats to use their majority control to gain disproportionate control of such perks as congressional staff and to limit the Republican participation in amending processes in the House.[48]

In 1989 the House Republicans made a pivotal decision to adopt a more activist and aggressive approach when they elected Newt Gingrich as their party whip. The Republican minority leader, Robert H. Michel of Illinois, historically has adopted the pragmatic style of bipartisan cooperation, even in the face of Speaker Wright's partisanship, and had endorsed for party whip another pragmatist, Edward R. Madigan of Illinois.[49] Widely recognized as one of the Republican party's outstanding legislators, Madigan offered the party a traditional approach to the whip's job, emphasizing vote counts and coalition building, both among Republicans and with Democrats. By contrast, Gingrich had spent his previous ten years in the House harassing the Democratic leaders, plotting partisan strategy for Republican takeover of the House, and leading the ethics challenge to Speaker Wright. Gingrich had created the Conservative Opportunity Society, a small band of Republican activists who gained a national following by attacking Democratic leaders in "after hours" speeches on the House floor; these were televised nationally on C-SPAN. Gingrich's defeat of Madigan by a vote of 87-85 within the House Republican party conference was widely seen as a slap in the face of Republican "old bulls" such as Michel and as a decision by the Republicans to pursue a risky partisan strategy of attack and sabotage.

Since Gingrich's election as whip, much of the House Republican party has adopted an extraordinarily hostile approach to House Democrats, an approach that has produced tensions within the party and has some serious institutional consequences for the House.[50] The tensions within the party became most clearly evident in the fall of 1990, when minority leader Michel was almost alone among Republican House leaders in backing the initial 1990 budget agreements between President Bush and the congressional leadership. Tension was further highlighted in the winter of 1991, when Madigan left the House to join the Bush administration as secretary of agriculture. He acknowledged that his defeat by Gingrich and his feeling that his style of leadership was being rejected by fellow Republicans led to his departure. Finally, over Michel's initial objections and with Gingrich's blessing, a group of freshmen Republicans—called the Gang of Seven—initiated the aggressive inquiries into the management of the House bank that led to the "check bouncing" scandal of 1992 and increased the anti-incumbency mood that had surfaced in the 1990 elections in response to the government's 1990 fall budget crisis.

Whether or not the Democratic leadership will be able to work with the Republican minority in the future depends on their sensitivity to Republican grievances and on the willingness of Republicans to cooperate with the majority leadership. Certainly, some of the grievances of House Republicans could be addressed by the reform commission that the House voted to establish during the 102d Congress. Reforms could include a reduction in the use of multiple committee assignments and the abolition of proxy voting within congressional committees, which Republicans oppose because they believe such rules allow the Democrats undue dominance of committee policymaking; a reduction in committee staff, which Republicans believe gives the majority Democrats an undue administrative advantage over them; a more equitable distribution of office perks; and a more open process of floor debates and amendments. On the other hand, reforms will not satiate the desire of Republicans for control of the House. Much depends on whether House Republicans conclude that Gingrich's strategy of frontal attack on the Democrats and the House as an institution has proved to be effective over the past four years. If Gingrich is able to claim responsibility for the Republican gains in the 1992 election, he and his supporters will have greater leverage within the House Republican party and perhaps can solidify a hostile and confrontational strategy. If House Republicans conclude that Gingrich's strategy did little to improve the party's position in the House, and perhaps even was a major mistake that undermined their chances to make greater gains, the conciliatory and bipartisan styles that characterize both Minority Leader Michel and Speaker Foley could lead to closer partisan cooperation in the future.

The Future of Majority Party Leadership

During the years of divided government, the majority party leadership faced an increasingly difficult task. The country's growing fiscal crisis led to increased opportunity for a strong party leadership, in combination with the committee oligarchs, to shape congressional policymaking perhaps more directly and more thoroughly than at any other point in modern times. At the same time, the deepening fiscal crisis, combined with Speaker Wright's forced resignation and the House banking scandal, also served to tarnish the image of the House Democratic leaders and to undermine their support among members. During these twelve years, the House majority party experienced the most unstable period of central party leadership in the postwar era; it saw three Speakers, three majority leaders, and five majority whips. Turnover was attributed not just to normal retirement but also to the increasingly personalized conflict within the House. Should the nation's fiscal crisis continue, and should the public's unhappiness with Congress grow, additional turnover in House party leaders could occur.

With the Democrats maintaining majority control of the House, the critical issue for the House leaders will be to reestablish the sense that they can manage the business of the House in a responsible and ethical manner that addresses the nation's real policy needs. It is unlikely that the speakership and the majority party leadership can sustain many more years of scandal and policy drift analogous to the period from 1989 to 1992 without experiencing serious attacks on the power of the party leaders. Thus it is vital that the party leadership find ways in the 103d Congress and thereafter to refurbish the image of an effective and assertive leadership that serves the needs of the country and of the House membership. This refurbishment probably would come most rapidly if there were a significant movement toward a balanced federal budget and an improved domestic economy. Furthermore, additional attention might be given to reforms that would strengthen the speakership and the party leadership so that they would have the long-term clout necessary to building support among members and committees for the hard policy choices that the country must face in a period of declining resources, increasing demands for delivery of quality services, and adjustment to effective competition in the global economy.

Conclusion

Since the early 1970s the House of Representatives has been a remarkably fluid institution. Buoyed by an infusion of younger legislators dedicated to reform, the House overthrew a system of committee government that had dominated it for most of a century. In its place the members instituted a highly dispersed system of power in which subcommittees, assisted by the party leadership, were the emerging force. In the 1980s, however, in response to the nation's troubled fiscal and political environment, the role of subcommittees declined, and power became concentrated in a small number of committee oligarchs—particularly in those controlling the money committees—and in a more assertive party leadership. Because of this system of House governance, Jim Wright's speakership became the strongest policy speakership since Joseph Cannon's; yet in the aftermath of Wright's resignation, the House was left in a state of partisan conflict, policy gridlock, and institutional disarray. As the 102d Congress came to a close, the House had to face the public's disaffection with it as an institution and with individual incumbents that was unparalleled in modern times.

The pressing question for the House in the mid-1990s is whether it can reestablish a sense of orderly and legitimate decision making and address the nation's problems in a convincing fashion. If it can do these things, the public's preoccupation with scandal probably will recede and confidence in the institution and its members may return. If it fails, the House and its governing oligarchy will face serious problems in regaining public support and in maintaining a strong role in national policymaking.

The most serious threat to the stability of the House, and its greatest opportunity for institutional renewal, comes from the influx of new members into the 103d Congress. These members could insist on immediate institutional response to the nation's pressing policy problems, particularly the widespread unemployment of the early 1990s and the deficit spending underlying these economic difficulties. The new members could force the House to cut through the partisan conflicts and policy paralysis of the recent past and demonstrate assertive policy leadership. Alternatively, they could simply introduce new conflicts and confusion into the House and add to the sense of organizational disarray. Much depends on whether the new members and the country at large will interpret the 1992 election as providing Congress with a clear mandate for policy change and institutional action. At the very least, the anti-incumbency mood of the early 1990s should send a strong message that Congress must address the organizational and campaign finance issues that have helped generate policy paralysis and scandal. Although organizational reform is critical for the House over the long term, the most pressing issue is not reform but an effective response to the nation's policy problems, particularly its economic and fiscal dilemmas.

The fate of the House over the coming four years thus is tied to the ability of united party government to renew institutional cooperation between the legislative and executive branches and generate effective policy solutions to the nation's ills. With the election of a Democratic-president in Bill Clinton, and with the return of a Democratic Congress, the nation can discover whether these institutions, united by common party sentiments, can overcome our fragmented constitutional arrangements and address the severe economic and fiscal problems fostered by twelve years of divided party government. Most directly at issue in this endeavor are the leadership abilities of the new president and his capacity as a Washington outsider to work with Congress. But also at issue is whether Congress, particularly the House, can move beyond the organizational conflicts and disarray of recent years and establish a cohesive and cooperative approach to national policymaking. Given the recent legacy of organizational conflict within the House, and an influx of new and inexperienced members in the 103d Congress, this will be a daunting challenge.

Notes

1. The idea that incumbency in certain circumstances can be a negative cue is not a new one. For a discussion of the problems of incumbency, see Thomas E. Mann, *Unsafe at Any Margin: Interpreting Congressional Elections* (Washington, D.C.: American Enterprise Institute, 1978). For an assessment of conditions that could give rise to widespread revolt against incumbents, see Lawrence C. Dodd, "Congress, the Constitution, and the Crisis of Legitimation," in *Congress Reconsidered*, ed. Lawrence C. Dodd and Bruce I. Oppenheimer, 2d ed. (Washington, D.C.: CQ Press, 1981).
2. Martha Angle, "Voters May Not 'Clean the House,' but a Good Dusting Is Certain," *Congressional Quarterly Weekly Report*, Sept. 19, 1992, 2785. The largest House turnover in a single election since World War II occurred in 1948, when 118 new members were elected. The 1992 election brought 110 new members.
3. The data on House retirements and reelection defeats through 1990 is taken from Norman J. Ornstein, Thomas E. Mann, and Michael J. Malbin, *Vital Statistics on Congress, 1991-1992* (Washington, D.C.: Congressional Quarterly, 1992). Data for 1992 comes from *Congressional Quarterly Weekly Report*, Sept. 19, 1992, 2787.
4. Charles S. Bullock III, "House Careerists: Changing Patterns of Longevity and Attrition," *American Political Science Review* 66 (1972): 1295-1305. Bullock's operational definition of a House careerist is a member elected to ten terms or more.
5. Bruce I. Oppenheimer, James A. Stimson, and Richard W. Waterman, "Interpreting U.S. Congressional Elections: The Exposure Thesis," *Legislative Studies Quarterly* 11 (May 1986): 227-248.
6. Jon R. Bond, Cary Covington, and Richard Fleischer, "Explaining Challenger Quality in Congressional Elections," *Journal of Politics* 47 (1985): 511-529. For a discussion of challenger quality, see Peverill Squire, "Challengers in U.S. Senate Elections," *Legislative Studies Quarterly* 14 (November 1989): 531-547.
7. Indiana lost a seat in the 1982 reapportionment. The 7-4 Republican advantage in seats before the 1982 election eventually became an 8-2 Democratic advantage.
8. Bruce I. Oppenheimer, "Split Party Control of Congress, 1981-1986: Exploring Electoral and Apportionment Explanations," *American Journal of Political Science* 33 (August 1989): 653-669.
9. See, for example, Lawrence C. Dodd and Bruce I. Oppenheimer, "The House in Transition," in *Congress Reconsidered*, 3d ed., ed. Lawrence C. Dodd and Bruce I. Oppenheimer (Washington, D.C.: CQ Press, 1985), 37-38.
10. Ornstein, Mann, and Malbin, *Vital Statistics*, 201.
11. For the best analysis of the causes and consequences of the growing strength of political parties in the House, see David W. Rohde, *Parties and Leaders in the Postreform House* (Chicago: University of Chicago Press, 1991). The data on party unity scores that we present is adjusted to exclude the effect of absences.
12. John R. Cranford, "The New Class: More Diverse, Less Lawyerly, Younger," *Congressional Quarterly Weekly Report*, Nov. 7, 1992, 7-10.
13. Ibid.
14. See Herbert Asher, "The Learning of Legislative Norms," *American Political Science Review* 67 (1973): 499-513.
15. See Mark F. Ferber, "The Formation of the Democratic Study Group," in *Congressional Behavior*, ed. Nelson W. Polsby (New York: Random House, 1971), 249-267; and Arthur G. Stephens, Jr., Arthur H. Miller, and Thomas E. Mann, "Mobilization of Liberal Strength in the House, 1955-1970: The Democratic Study Group," *American Political Science Review* 68 (1974): 667-681. For a discussion of the reform efforts in the House and the initial role of the DSG, see Norman J. Ornstein and David W. Rohde, "Congressional Reform and Political Parties in the U.S. House of Representatives," in *Parties in an Anti-Party Age*, ed. Jeff Fishel (Bloomington: Indiana University Press, 1976).

16. For a more extensive discussion of the reform processes, see *Congress Reconsidered,* 1st ed., ed. Lawrence C. Dodd and Bruce I. Oppenheimer (New York: Praeger, 1977), 27-32. See also Ornstein and Rohde, "Congressional Reform and Political Parties"; and Leroy N. Rieselbach, *Congressional Reform in the Seventies* (Morristown, N.J.: General Learning Press, 1977).

17. For an excellent discussion of the Bolling committee, see Roger H. Davidson, "Two Avenues of Change: House and Senate Committee Reorganization," in *Congress Reconsidered,* 2d ed.; and Roger H. Davidson and Walter J. Oleszek, *Congress Against Itself* (Bloomington: Indiana University Press, 1977).

18. Janet Hook, "Congress OKs Step Toward Reform," *Congressional Quarterly Weekly Report,* Aug. 8, 1992, 2332.

19. *Congressional Ethics: History, Facts, and Controversy* (Washington, D.C.: Congressional Quarterly, 1992), 20-23.

20. See Janet Hook, "The Bank Buck Stops with Foley," *Congressional Quarterly Weekly Report,* March 14, 1992, 600.

21. For a summary of the bill's provisions, see Beth Donovan, "Campaign Finance Bill," *Congressional Quarterly Weekly Report,* June 6, 1992, 1651-1654.

22. See George R. Brown, *The Leadership of Congress* (Indianapolis: Bobbs-Merrill, 1922); Richard Bolling, *Power in the House* (New York: Capricorn, 1968); Richard F. Fenno, Jr., *Congressmen in Committees* (Boston: Little, Brown, 1973); and the essays by Ralph Huitt in *Congress: Two Decades of Analysis,* ed., Ralph K. Huitt and Robert L. Peabody (New York: Harper and Row, 1969).

23. On subcommittee government, see Lawrence C. Dodd and Richard L. Schott, *Congress and the Administrative State* (New York: Wiley, 1979); and Steven S. Smith and Christopher J. Deering, *Committees in Congress* (Washington, D.C.: CQ Press, 1984), 194-198.

24. David W. Rohde, "Committee Reform in the House of Representatives and the Subcommittee Bill of Rights," *The Annals* 411 (January 1974), 39-47; Norman J. Ornstein, "Causes and Consequences of Congressional Change: Subcommittee Reforms in the House of Representatives, 1970-1973," in *Congress in Change,* ed. Norman J. Ornstein (New York: Praeger, 1975), 88-114; and Lawrence C. Dodd and George C. Shipley, "Patterns of Committee Surveillance in the House of Representatives" (Paper presented at the annual meeting of the American Political Science Association, San Francisco, September 1975).

25. For case studies that demonstrate the legislative effect of committee change, see Norman J. Ornstein and David W. Rohde, "Shifting Forces, Changing Rules, and Political Outcomes: The Impact of Congressional Change on Four House Committees," in *New Perspectives on the House of Representatives,* ed. Robert L. Peabody and Nelson W. Polsby (Chicago: Rand McNally, 1977). For a discussion of the effect of committee change on legislative oversight, see Dodd and Schott, *Congress and the Administrative State.*

26. For a more extensive discussion, see Dodd and Oppenheimer, "House in Transition."

27. Alan Ehrenhalt, "Media, Power Shifts Dominate O'Neill's House," *Congressional Quarterly Weekly Report,* Sept. 13, 1986, 2136.

28. Andy Plattner, "Controlling the Floor: Rules Under Chairman Pepper Look Out for the Democrats,"*Congressional Quarterly Weekly Report,* Aug. 24, 1985, 672; and Janet Hook, "The Influential Committees: Money and Issues," Jan. 3, 1987, 22-23.

29. Quoted in Hook, "Influential Committees: Money and Issues," 23.

30. Pamela Fessler, "Read My Lips: No Conditions, Bush Tells Democrats," *Congressional Quarterly Weekly Report,* May 12, 1990, 1457; George Hager, "Defiant House Rebukes Leaders; New Round of Fights Begins," *Congressional Quarterly Weekly Report,* Oct. 6, 1990, 3183; George Hager, "One Outcome of Budget Package: Higher Deficits on the Way," *Congressional Quarterly Weekly Report,* Nov. 3, 1990, 3710.

31. For a discussion of different leadership strategies in the postreform era, see Barbara Sinclair, "Party Leadership and Policy Change," in *Congress and Policy Change,* ed. Gerald C. Wright, Leroy N. Rieselbach, and Lawrence C. Dodd (New York: Agathon Press, 1986).

32. See Joseph Cooper and David W. Brady, "Institutional Context and Leadership Style: The House from Cannon to Rayburn," *American Political Science Review* 75 (1981): 411-425.

33. On the Rules Committee in earlier eras, see James A. Robinson, *The House Rules Committee* (Indianapolis: Bobbs-Merrill, 1963); on the new Rules Committee, see Bruce I. Oppenheimer, "The Rules Committee: New Arm of Leadership in a Decentralized House," in *Congress Reconsidered,* 1st ed., 96-116.

34. On the whip system in an earlier era, see Randall B. Ripley, "The Party Whip Organizations in the U.S. House of Representatives," in *New Perspectives on the House of Representatives*; on the expanded whip system, see Lawrence C. Dodd, "The Expanding Roles of the House Democratic Whip System," *Congressional Studies* 6 (Winter 1979): 152-188; and Barbara Sinclair, *Majority Leadership in the U.S. House of Representatives* (Baltimore: Johns Hopkins University Press, 1983).

35. Ehrenhalt, "Media, Power Shifts Dominate O'Neill's House."

36. Alan Ehrenhalt, "Speaker's Job Transformed Under O'Neill," *Congressional Quarterly Weekly Report,* June 22, 1985, 1247.

37. See articles by Janet Hook in *Congressional Quarterly Weekly Report*: "House Leadership Elections: Wright Era Begins," Dec. 13, 1986, 3067, 3070; "Speaker Jim Wright Takes Charge in the House," July 11, 1987, 1487; "Jim Wright: Taking Big Risks to Amass Power," March 12, 1988, 623; "Passion, Defiance, Tears: Jim Wright Bows Out," June 3, 1989, 1289.

38. Janet Hook, "Foley: Rising to Top by Accident and Design," *Congressional Quarterly Weekly Report,* March 8, 1986, 551.

39. Janet Hook, "Budget Ordeal Poses Question Why Can't Congress Be Led?" *Congressional Quarterly Weekly Report,* Oct. 20, 1990, 3471-3473.

40. Chuck Alston, "The Speaker and the Chairmen: A Taoist Approach to Power," *Congressional Quarterly Weekly Report,* Nov. 2, 1991, 3177.

41. Janet Hook, "Gephardt, Gray Join Foley on Leadership Team," *Congressional Quarterly Weekly Report,* June 17, 1989, 1445.

42. Janet Hook, "Leadership Races Intensify; Foley Ascension Nears," *Congressional Quarterly Weekly Report,* June 3, 1989, 1296.

43. Janet Hook, "A Fast Start and Experience Gave Bonior Solid Votes," *Congressional Quarterly Weekly Report,* July 13, 1991, 1875-1876.

44. Janet Hook, "Rout of Democratic Party Leaders Reflects Fractured Party," *Congressional Quarterly Weekly Report,* Sept. 30, 1989, 2530.

45. Janet Hook, "Despite Whip's Political Role, Personal Ties Matter Most," *Congressional Quarterly Weekly Report,* July 6, 1991, 1818.

46. Chuck Alston, "Speaker and the Chairmen."

47. Phil Duncan, "House GOP: No More Mr. Nice Guy?" *Congressional Quarterly Weekly Report,* Feb. 9, 1991, 394.

48. Janet Hook, "Gingrich's Selection as Whip Reflects GOP Discontent," *Congressional Quarterly Weekly Report,* March 25, 1989, 625; and "Extensive Reform Proposals Cook on the Front Burner," *Congressional Quarterly Weekly Report,* June 6, 1992, 1579.

49. Janet Hook, "Battle for Whip Pits Partisans Against Party Pragmatists," *Congressional Quarterly Weekly Report,* March 18, 1989, 563; and "Gingrich's Selection as Whip Reflects GOP Discontent," *Congressional Quarterly Weekly Report,* March 25, 1989, 625.

50. Janet Hook, "Republican Contest Reflect Election Woes, Party Rift," *Congressional Quarterly Weekly Report,* Dec. 1, 1990, 3997; Phil Duncan, "House GOP: No More Mr. Nice Guy?"

3

Careerism in Congress: For Better or for Worse?

John R. Hibbing

The justices on the bench of the U.S. Supreme Court in 1892 had served an average of just over twelve years in that capacity. One hundred years later the sitting justices had logged only a few more years on the country's highest court—an average of just over fourteen years. In 1892 the president, Benjamin Harrison, had been on the job three years. In 1992 the president, George Bush, had been on the job three years. Those serving at the top of the judicial and executive branches in the United States in 1892 were about as experienced as they were in 1992.

The story is quite different for the legislative branch of the U.S. government. The members in the 1892 version of the House had on average fewer than five years of experience in that body. Fully 44 percent of the entire membership were in their first terms. Contrast these figures with the situation in the modern House. In 1992 the mean length of congressional experience possessed by the members was twelve years, and only 10 percent were in their initial House terms.[1] Length of careers in the executive and judicial branches has remained roughly constant over the past hundred years, but length of careers in Congress has increased by 150 percent.

In fact, career lengths in the twentieth-century Congress have occasionally reached monstrous proportions. Carl Hayden, D-Ariz., served fifty-seven years (fifteen in the House and forty-two in the Senate). Emanuel Celler, D-N.Y., and Carl Vinson, D-Ga., each spent five full decades just in the House. Jamie Whitten, D-Miss., with fifty-one years of service, recently broke their record for the longest continuous House service. This is a far cry from the situation one hundred years ago when those who stayed five years were a rarity.

By historical standards, the modern Congress is characterized by extremely long careers; on this there is little disagreement.[2] But when attention shifts and the question is whether the presence of extended-service legislators improves the governing process, agreement evaporates. We now have congressional careerism, but is that good news or bad news? Few attempts have been made to evaluate the consequences of careerism, even though it is one of the most important developments of modern American politics. As a result, where we should have meaningful and systematic evidence, we find only impassioned polemics based on unsubstantiated assertions.

For example, the current debate over whether to limit the number of terms that legislators can serve has been characterized by intense feelings but little evidence that would meet traditional canons of acceptability. Proponents of term limits wail about the low levels of turnover and the need for infusions of "fresh blood." Opponents of the reform contend that sufficient membership turnover still occurs and that legislative expertise is essential in our complex world.

In this essay, rather than merely documenting the existence of congressional careerism, I present evidence of its consequences. Specifically, I analyze the differences between junior and senior members of Congress. If there is little to differentiate new members from old, the effects of careerism could be rather modest. If, on the other hand, novice and experienced members behave in fundamentally different ways, the effects of careerism are likely to be substantial. What precisely comes with congressional experience? Only when we answer this question can we draw meaningful conclusions about careerism in general and term-limit proposals in particular.

Career Length and Membership Turnover

Before proceeding, however, it may be helpful to look at a few facts about the length of current and recent careers in Congress. All the talk of record-length careers and the need for term limits can be misleading. Originally, the most commonly mentioned service limit being proposed was twelve years in each house, but several states have now adopted twelve-year Senate limits and eight-year House limits. If a twelve-year limit had been in place in 1992, 163 representatives and 50 senators in the 102d Congress would not have been eligible to run for reelection (37 percent of the House and 50 percent of the Senate membership). All full committee chairs in both houses would have been removed (though only a fraction of the subcommittee chairs); so the immediate effect would have been substantial.

After this initial shock, however, the consequences in terms of membership turnover may be less than many imagine. As an illustration, consider the following data from the House of Representatives. In percentage terms, fewer new members entered the House in the 1980s than in any previous decade. On average, the five Congresses of that decade included about fifty new representatives (less than 12 percent every two years). This figure was down from about 16 percent in the 1960s, when incumbents still occasionally lost reelection bids, and the 1970s, when a surprising number of incumbents left voluntarily. Turnover increased substantially in 1992, when sixty-six members departed voluntarily and forty-three were defeated, thus at least partially confirming predictions concerning a huge retirement class and voter discontent with incumbents.[3]

A twelve-year limit on House service would guarantee a minimum of 100 percent turnover every twelve years, or somewhat more than 16 percent every two years. (Limits shorter than twelve years would, of course, stimulate slightly more rapid turnover.) Such a limit would constitute a small increase over turnover rates in the 1980s but would be about equal to turnover rates in the 1970s—and possibly less than those of the 1990s, if 1992 is any indication. Of course, the turnover under term limits could be more than the minimum if some members retired voluntarily or suffered electoral defeat before the expiration of their twelve-year leases. But in spite of a few well-publicized cases, early retirements are not all that common[4]—and junior members of late have been doing at least as well electorally as their senior colleagues.[5]

Furthermore, under term limits members and voters might begin to view the limit as a floor as well as a ceiling. It is likely that the number of early retirements and early defeats—already paltry—would drop to even lower levels. All told, term limits would increase membership turnover only modestly, perhaps by 1 or 2 percentage points over what they would have been without term limits.

So term limits would stimulate less additional turnover than most people realize. Moreover, if stimulating turnover is the main goal of reformers, other changes are probably preferable. Campaign finance reform, transferral of casework activities to a national ombudsman, and limitations on staff sizes and franking privileges immediately come to mind. What separates term limits from these other reform proposals is the members who would be turned over. Term limits specifically target senior members, whereas these other suggestions would result in turnover of all members.

Thus the real issue with term limitations, as well as with how we view lengthy congressional careers in general, is whether the senior members who would be summarily banished under term limits are contributing something to the legislative process that more junior members are not. This brings us to the key question of this chapter and, I would argue, of modern congressional research: What gains derive from legislative experience and from the general legislative professionalization or institutionalization of which extended careers are a part?

Congressional Service:
Life Cycle or Suspended Animation?

Thirty years ago, in his classic work *U.S. Senators and Their World*, Donald R. Matthews described the political life cycle that was thought to operate in Congress. This is how it worked. Electorally precarious new members attempted to gain supporters by aggressively pursuing casework and by reaching out directly to constituents. As the members survived repeated electoral challenges, becoming better known in Washington and more electorally secure at home, legislative responsibilities began to crowd out constituency service. After a very long time this behavior led to a weakening of electoral support and perhaps even to the defeat of legislators who were perceived to have contracted a case of Potomac Fever.[6]

Many subsequent works also detected substantial changes across the congressional career. Richard Fenno notes the shift from "expansionist" to "protectionist" tendencies as senior members gradually feel less need to "reach out for additional elements of support." Lawrence Dodd writes of an almost mystical legislative "mastery" that members acquire with the passage of the years. Similarly, Burdett Loomis, largely through his careful observation of the class of 1974 (a phrase used to refer to those members who entered the House of Representatives for the first time after the 1974 elections), believes that with experience members pick up the political skills they need to be quality legislators. Many observers believe there is a clear learning curve for members of Congress.[7]

Others, however, believe there is not. In fact, one of the recurring, if frequently implicit, themes of recent scholarship holds that congressional service is more static than cyclical. In stark contrast to the political life cycle view of congressional careers, the picture frequently painted now is that members come to Congress doing constituency service and leave Congress doing constituency service. They enter Congress as electoral neurotics, and they continue in this condition even if by most objective standards they appear safe. Furthermore, thanks to the death of the apprenticeship norm (the expectation that junior members will not play a vital role in the legislative process) and other changes, members are said to be free to participate meaningfully in the legislative process even when they first enter Congress.[8]

Generally, we are told, members rarely convert.[9] If change is to enter Congress, it must come by way of membership change because once members enter Congress they put their actions on cruise control. If all this is true, where is the learning curve? Where is the life cycle? Where are the benefits of legislative expertise?

Which of these two visions of congressional career contours is accurate? In the pages that follow, I address electoral careers, roll call careers, constituency activity, and legislative activity with an eye toward whether patterns in the modern Congress are cyclical or constant. First, we turn to electoral performance.

Electoral Careers

Congressional careers are now long because, the unusual events of 1992 notwithstanding, members have the desire and the ability to stay. The desire seemed to flicker momentarily in the 1970s, when the rate of voluntary retirement increased 77 percent. But we now know that this was an explainable aberration caused by demographics and reforms targeted against senior members already likely to retire.[10] In the 1980s voluntary retirement rates returned to the anemic levels of the 1960s. The ability of incumbents to secure reelection, on the other hand, had until 1992 remained an important part of the congressional scene for at least thirty years, as is attested to by the voluminous literature on the heightened advantage of incumbency.

The question before us now, however, is whether the cyclical pattern of electoral support that was presumed to be the engine for the political life cycle view of congressional service applies to the current scene. As it turns out, the "electoral career" of members of the House, even back in the 1950s, was never as cyclical as implied by the political life cycle literature. And we can state with even more certainty that by the 1980s virtually all traces of electoral cycles had vanished. Two factors account for the confusion on this point: first, a changing political climate across the decades and, second, the failure of scholars to appreci-

Figure 3-1 Electoral Performance of the House Class of 1970

Percentage of
vote

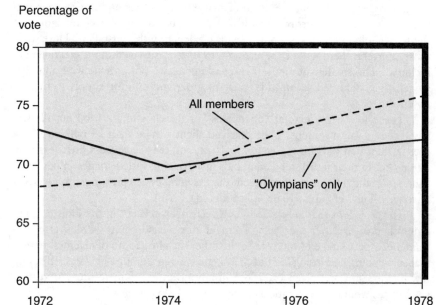

Source: Computed by the author.

Note: "Olympians" are the fourteen members who survived eight elections.

ate the importance of attrition, or what I am calling mortality effects.

To illustrate how mortality can affect conclusions, we consider the House class of 1970. Figure 3-1 shows the improvement in electoral performance experienced by this class over its first eight years of service. In 1972 the class of 1970 averaged 68.3 percent of the vote, and about the same two years later. But in 1976 the mean vote share rose above 73 percent before shooting up to 76 percent in 1978. These data would seem to provide excellent support for the notion that electoral performance improves with early experience, but there is more to the story.

The size of the class changes over time and mortality effects are registered. Although it began with forty-eight members, only about half (twenty-five) of the class remained in 1978. Now, if the half remaining were representative of the entire class, no harm would be done, but this is not the case. Mortality occurs because members lose or retire. Not surprisingly, those who lose tend to have been electorally more marginal than those who win. And it is also true that those who retire tend to be electorally more marginal than those who run for reelection.[11] Apparently, electoral uncertainty makes congressional service appear somewhat less attractive, a point made clear by the wave of retirements after the House banking scandal broke.

Thus the apparent improvement in electoral performance may really be attributable to the gradual removal of marginal members and not to an actual improvement on the part of any particular member or members. In Figure 3-1 the line labeled "Olympians only" lends credence to this suspicion. Here, only those fourteen members of the class of 1970 who survived eight elections are included. The smaller number of cases is a concern, but at least we know that any changes detected within this constant group are not due simply to mortality effects.

These fourteen electoral "olympians" of the class of 1970 do not register any electoral improvement. They received slightly more than 73 percent of the vote in their first bids for reelection in 1972, and they received a little less than 74 percent in their fourth reelection bids in 1978 with little variance in between. When mortality effects are controlled, the electoral cycles presumed to be a part of congressional life are actually quite muted.

To the extent that an electoral cycle has been present in the House, it has diminished in size over the years. To make this second point, we shift attention from mean percentage of the vote to the other major measure of electoral performance, winning and losing, and from a single class to a group of classes. (Because few members of any given class lose in any given election, results based on a single class would be so erratic as to obfuscate the message.)

In Figure 3-2, the percentage of incumbents successful in their bids for reelection is broken down by tenure, and the resultant patterns for two recent time periods are contrasted. What stands out immediately, of course, is the overall strong performance of incumbents, with well over 90 percent victorious. But beyond this widely known fact, the figure presents a slightly surprising message. In the 1966-1974 period, the chances of an incumbent losing a bid for reelection decrease with experience, from 16 percent in the first reelection bid to only 1 percent in the thirteenth. The line of best fit (the straight line that most closely approximates the actual data) has been added to the figure, and the linear slope is $+.65$, indicating that, on average, each additional term decreased the incumbent's chances of losing by nearly two-thirds of a percentage point.

In the 1976-1984 period, however, the results are quite different. In more recent years, long tenure has not improved the chances that incumbents will win reelection. First-termers won 94 percent of the time during this period, but congressional experience no longer seems to allow members to build on this high success rate. In fact, the slope of the line of best fit is negative (though it is small and statistically insignificant). The chances of a senior member losing in the modern Congress are every bit as great as the chances of a junior member losing.

What does this mean for visions of the electoral career? It means electoral performance across a typical congressional career is not very cyclical at all. Decades ago there was a modest cycle, with junior members performing more poorly in elections than senior members. But we now know that failure to appreciate mortality effects probably led to an overestimation of the variance between junior and senior members. Furthermore, the passage of the years has eroded whatever electoral cycle there was so that by the 1980s electoral performance

Figure 3-2 Chances of Incumbents Winning Reelection, 1966-1974 and 1976-1984

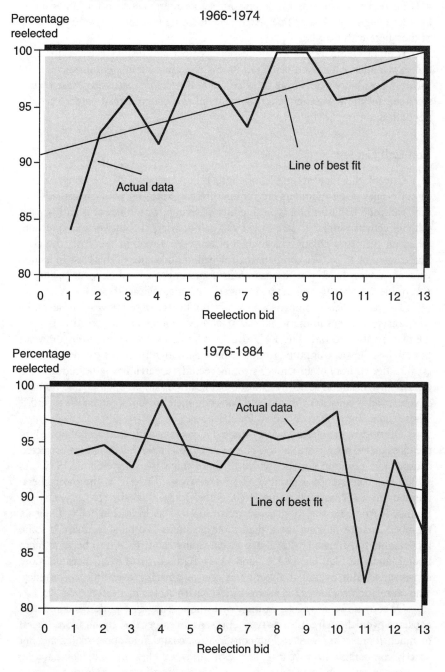

Source: Computed by the author.

over the course of a career in the House had become largely flat. In 1992 this trend continued, as questionable practices associated with the House bank probably created more electoral problems for senior members than for junior members (although it is notable that sixteen fast-learning first-termers were on the list of members with overdrafts).

If other elements of the congressional career still display cyclical qualities, the explanation cannot be electoral, unless of course members misperceive the threat, a possibility that cannot be ruled out.[12] But before discussing these points, we need to know whether other elements of the congressional career vary depending upon career stage.

Roll Call Careers

One of the highest profile of these other elements of the congressional career occurs when members are required to cast votes on policy matters. Does the "roll call" behavior of a typical legislator change with time, or is early-career roll call activity similar to late-career roll call activity? To answer this question, we again turn to a not untypical class of representatives, in this case, the class first elected in 1976. We compare the roll call performance of this class in its first year of service (1977) with that of its fourteenth year of service (1990) to determine whether the members changed their ideological stripes.

To make these comparisons, I rely on the representatives' conservative coalition scores, a summary indication of how liberal or conservative is each member's voting record. The 1977 scale was based on 156 votes during the year; the 1990 scale was computed from 54 votes. Although these scales are unable to capture the entirety of a member's voting record, research has indicated that the conservative coalition scale, like most other scales based on a reasonable number of votes, yields consistent results and does not misrepresent a member's record.[13] These scores have been corrected for absences.

Thirty-two members (twenty-three Democrats and nine Republicans) of the class of 1976 were still in the House in 1990. Table 3-1 compares corrected conservative coalition support scores of these thirty-two members in 1977 and 1990. The consistency is striking. Rep. Ted Weiss, D-N.Y., is the most liberal member in 1977 as well as in 1990. Reps. Jerry Huckaby, D-La., and Bob Stump, R-Ariz., are the most conservative in 1977 as well as in 1990. Only six members change ranking more than three positions. To be sure, there is some movement: Jim Leach, R-Iowa, and Arlan Stangeland, R-Minn., became more liberal, and Ike Skelton, D-Mo., and Doug Barnard, Jr., D-Ga., became more conservative. But overall the picture is one of amazing over-time consistency. The correlation coefficient of scores in 1977 with scores in 1990 is .95.

Of course, we must use caution with these data. The rankings could stay constant even though all thirty-two representatives became much more liberal or much more conservative. The conservative coalition support scores are not strictly comparable from year to year. Still, they are close to being comparable, and we can say with certainty that the relative roll call rankings of this particu-

Table 3-1   Roll Call Votes of the Class of 1976: Rankings from Most
                Liberal to Most Conservative, 1977 and 1990

	1977[a]		1990[b]	
Rank	Representative	Score	Representative	Score
1	Weiss, D-N.Y.	3	Weiss	0
2	Vento, D-Minn.	4	Bonior	6
3	Beilenson, D-Calif.	4	Vento	8
4	Bonior, D-Mich.	10	Markey	8
5	Markey, D-Mass.	11	Kildee	9
6	Kildee, D-Mich.	13	Beilenson	15
7	Pease, D-Ohio	17	Oakar	15
8	Oakar, D-Ohio	25	Panetta	17
9	Walgren, D-Pa.	25	Gephart	18
10	Gephart, D-Mo.	36	Pease	19
11	Dicks, D-Wash.	37	Walgren	34
12	Panetta, D-Calif.	38	Dicks	37
13	Murphy, D-Pa.	43	Rahall	37
14	Rahall, D-W.Va.	44	Glickman	38
15	Applegate, D-Ohio	46	Murphy	45
16	Volkmer, D-Mo.	47	Leach	52
17	Glickman, D-Kan.	50	Applegate	53
18	Pursell, R-Mich.	55	Pursell	78
19	Leach, R-Iowa	66	Volkmer	81
20	Skelton, D-Mo.	71	Walker	85
21	Flippo, D-Ala.	73	Flippo	87
22	Ireland, R-Fla.	77	Stangeland	89
23	Barnard, D-Ga.	82	Marlenee	90
24	Marlenee, R-Mont.	85	Jenkins	90
25	Jenkins, D-Ga.	86	Coleman	92
26	Coleman, R-Mo.	87	Ireland	93
27	Walker, R-Pa.	90	Watkins	93
28	Watkins, D-Okla.	93	Barnard	93
29	Stangeland, R-Minn.	95	Skelton	96
30	Edwards, R-Okla.	96	Edwards	96
31	Huckaby, D-La.	96	Stump	98
32	Stump, R-Ariz.	97	Huckaby	99

Source: Scores are conservative coalition support scores, corrected for absences.

Note: The correlation coefficient of scores in 1977 with scores in 1990 is .95.

[a] The 1977 scale was based on 156 votes.
[b] The 1990 scale was based on 54 votes.

lar class remained remarkably stable over a fairly lengthy time span. Less
certainty would obtain if our purposes required conclusions to pertain to actual
roll call behavior.

Perhaps more important, roll call behavior is now less flexible across a
typical House career than it was years ago. In Table 3-2, early roll call scales
are used to predict the same scales later in a career. Several R^2 values are

Table 3-2   The Ability of Roll Call Scales of First-Term House
Members to Predict Seventh-Term Roll Call Scales

		Party unity	Ideology[a]
Class	N	R^2	R^2
1946	26	.06	—
1948	28	.29	—
1950	25	.59	—
1952	31	.46	—
1954	19	.12	—
1956	9	.66	.79
1958	30	.39	.77
1960	19	.45	.85
1962	32	.82	.95
1964	30	.60	.93
1966	15	.75	.92
1968	19	.63	.92

Source: Computed by the author.

Note: The numbers reported are the R^2s generated when the member's roll call scale score in the seventh term is regressed on that same scale in the member's first term. (To be included, members of each class must have served at least seven terms.)

[a] Ideology is measured by conservative coalition scores, which were not computed and reported before 1956.

reported. R^2 is a commonly used measure of the ability of one variable or set of variables to predict or "account for" variation in another variable. In this case, the issue is the ability of early-career roll call behavior to predict late-career roll call behavior. The higher the value of the R^2, the higher the predictive ability of early roll call behavior. On all counts predictability has increased. Ideological odysseys, never common, are even rarer than before. For most members, how they vote the first year is now an incredibly accurate guide to how they will vote fifteen years hence.

Constituency-Service Careers

So far, we have seen that the votes cast for and by members of Congress now follow basically flat patterns. Is the same true for how members interact with constituents? Remember, a key element of the political life cycle was increasing attention to legislative matters and decreasing attention to constituent matters. Is there empirical confirmation of these expectations? First, we turn to constituency service.

Constituency service entails several separate concepts, all difficult to measure. Thus, like most of those working in this area, I must rely on two measures: the number of trips made by members to the home district and the number of staffers assigned to the home district. These measures are inadequate but helpful. Members who travel back to the district frequently and who assign a large proportion of their personal staffers to district offices are in some senses devoting scarce resources to constituent matters.

Unfortunately, common levels of activity in these areas have changed so significantly over the past few decades that these "period" changes must be neutralized before we can analyze life-cycle changes. Specifically, the proportion of staffers assigned to the district has increased tremendously, from an average of 14 percent of all personal staffers in the 86th Congress (1959-1961) to well over 40 percent in the 100th (1987-1989). Somewhat surprisingly, the number of trips home has been going in the opposite direction during the past ten to twelve years. Until the late 1970s trips home were on the rise, but in January 1978 congressional office allotments were changed so that the expenses members incurred in traveling home would reduce the amount of money available for other office-related matters.[14] Shortly after this change, trips home began decreasing by an average of about three or four per member per Congress.[15]

To control for these changes, we use an analysis that relies upon z-scores. Z-scores represent the relationship of a number to the mean of a set of numbers. For example, travel home is standardized in each Congress so that traveling home twenty-five times in 1980 means something quite different from traveling home twenty-five times in 1990, when many fewer trips, on average, were taken. The results presented in Figure 3-3 are really travel home relative to the rest of the members of the pertinent Congress. Similar procedures are necessary for determining the percentage of staffers assigned to the home district because this practice became much more common as the years went on.

When we conduct this standardization, changes attributable to life-cycle effects are easier to see. What is visible in Figure 3-3 is that, in relative terms, the number of trips members made home and the number of staffers assigned to the home district both decrease with tenure. Apparently, there is a little truth to the contention that senior members reduce their attention to constituents. But for several reasons such a conclusion must be drawn cautiously. First of all, the relative movement is slight and in the case of staffers almost nonexistent. At most, the change involves just a couple of tenths of one standard deviation and should not be overstated.

Moreover, although the data base is limited (going back only to 1970 for trips home and to 1960 for staff assignments), it appears that for more recent classes, as has been the case for all the other variables analyzed so far, life-cycle effects are much less pronounced (data not shown). In the modern Congress, senior members may do a little less doting on constituents than do their junior colleagues, but the differences between the two groups are modest and apparently are becoming more modest all the time.

Finally, when we analyze the actual (rather than relative) activity for individual members, it becomes apparent that constituency-oriented activities, in raw terms, generally increase with the age of the member of Congress. For example, Figure 3-4 presents information on the first eight terms of two representatives elected in 1970, Romano L. Mazzoli, D-Ky., and Ronald V. Dellums, D-Calif.

Figure 3-3   Standardized Contact of House Members with
                 Constituencies, by Tenure

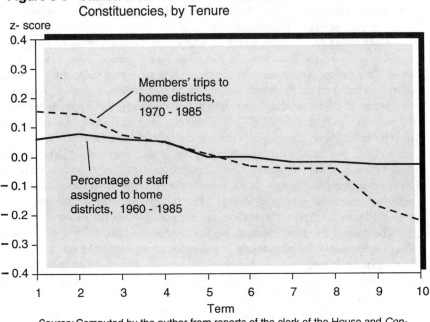

Source: Computed by the author from reports of the clerk of the House and *Congressional Staff Directory,* appropriate years.

These two representatives were selected for no other reason than that they entered Congress at this particular time, stayed awhile, and displayed patterns in constituency-service activities that are reasonably typical of their colleagues.

For the most part, the percentage of the personal staff assigned to home district offices by these two representatives increased over their first fifteen years in the House, from 40 percent (six of fifteen total staffers) to 58 percent (twelve of twenty-one) for Dellums and from 33 percent (three of nine) to 47 percent (seven of fifteen) for Mazzoli. The pattern for trips home is somewhat more complicated. Both Mazzoli and Dellums made the most trips home in the late 1970s, although predictably Dellums returned to California fewer times than Mazzoli returned to Kentucky. In the 1980s, however, both members cut back on their trips home. These drops, as mentioned earlier, parallel those of most members after reimbursement for travel was made to impinge upon the availability of other office necessities.

The bottom line? When the focus is on individual behavior, House members do not greatly reduce their constituency-oriented behavior as they age. The declining z-scores displayed in Figure 3-3 suggest that new members are relatively more active by a little, but the actual figures provide a slightly different slant. Even after a decade in the House, both Dellums and Mazzoli returned to their districts about twenty times a year and stationed approximately 50 percent of their staffers there. The actual change with their aging shows a slight increase,

Figure 3-4 The Constituency-Attention Careers of Romano Mazzoli and Ronald Dellums

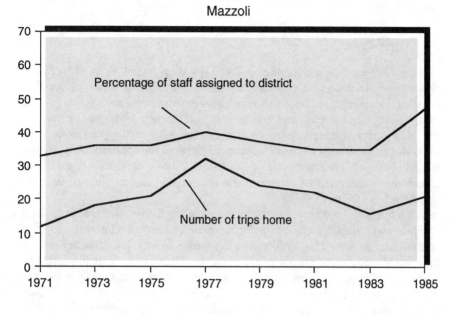

Mazzoli

Percentage of staff assigned to district

Number of trips home

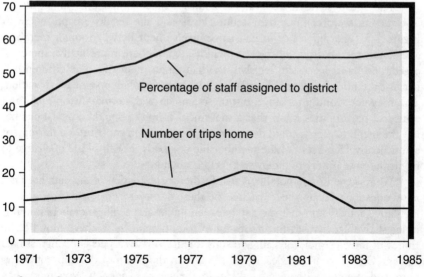

Dellums

Percentage of staff assigned to district

Number of trips home

Source: Computed by the author from reports of the clerk of the House and *Congressional Staff Directory,* appropriate years.

while the relative change shows a slight decline. On the whole, we must conclude that extended House stays bring little sizable change in the constituency-oriented activity of members.

Legislative Careers

So all these data are coming up flat. Typical careers in the modern House now show little change in electoral performance, roll call behavior, or constituency service. But what about members' involvement in legislation: introducing bills, offering amendments, and shepherding bills through the legislative process? Has this aspect of congressional careers also flattened in the postreform Congress? It certainly has if all the talk about the death of the apprenticeship norm is to be believed. According to this line of thought, junior members are no longer hamstrung by silly norms limiting their role in the process. But is there an empirical basis for this view?

To find out, I calculated three measures of legislative involvement for each member and standardized them in the same manner described in the section on constituency activity. The first measure, legislative activity, is a summary scale of bills introduced, amendments offered, and speeches made, equally weighted. The second, legislative specialization, is a measure of the percentage of the bills introduced by a member that are referred to a particular committee (rather than distributed across numerous committees). And the third, legislative efficiency, is a measure of the percentage of the bills introduced by a member that make it out of committee, with a special bonus given to members whose bills pass the scrutiny of the entire House.

The mean standardized values of these three components of legislative involvement were computed by tenure level, and the results are presented in Figure 3-5. The difference in legislative involvement between junior members and senior members is substantial. Senior members are more active, more focused, and more successful legislatively than junior members. The difference is not just a tenth of a standard deviation but more than half a standard deviation. This may not sound impressive, but those familiar with normal distributions and statistical probabilities know that a movement from .25 standard deviations below the mean to .25 standard deviations above the mean constitutes a movement across nearly 15 percent of the membership of a body. For this kind of change to be attributable purely to life-cycle effects is notable.

What is even more notable is that further manipulation of the data does not raise questions about the existence of these life-cycle effects in the area of legislative activity and that the gap between junior and senior members in terms of legislative activity has not narrowed in recent years, as we have found to be true with the electoral, roll call, and constituency-service aspects of congressional careers. On the contrary, despite all the talk of the death of the apprenticeship norm and of a newly democratized House, the gap has widened. Now more than ever, if we value legislators who are active, focused, and successful, we should value senior legislators.

Figure 3-5 Standardized Legislative Involvement of House Members, by Tenure, 1953 - 1985

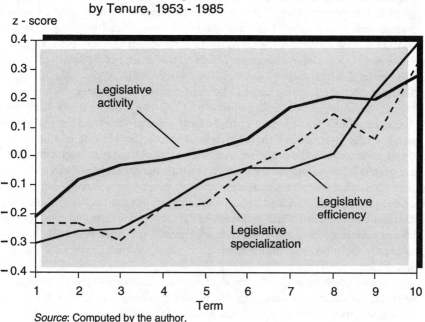

Source: Computed by the author.

Well, yes, it might be said, but senior members gobble up all the good party and committee positions, and this fact rather than legislative acumen explains their apparent superiority. This explanation fails at both the aggregate and the individual level. First, during the very years that positions in the House began to be distributed more equitably, senior members improved their relative performance. Second, it is possible to allow formal positions in the House to compete with pure length of service to see which is the most important and, more specifically, to determine whether the effects of extended legislative service operate directly on legislative performance or indirectly through the quality of the formal positions held.

When such a test is conducted at the individual level, the effect is direct. Senior members do have better positions, but this does not explain their superior performance on legislative matters.[16] This conclusion suggests that we could give every brand-new legislator a committee or subcommittee chair and the effects on their legislative performance would be minimal compared with the improvements that derive simply from their staying in the House for an extended period of time.

The Political Life Cycle Revisited

If we think back to our goal of determining whether modern congressional careers are static or cyclical, these findings may seem confusing: The electoral, roll call, and constituency-service components of the political life cycle in Congress have largely vanished, but actual work on legislation has become even more cyclical than it used to be. The confusion may be magnified by the expectation of conventional wisdom that legislative work is no longer the sole province of the old-timers. Upon closer inspection, however, this cluster of findings makes perfect sense. I would argue that legislative involvement is precisely where we should expect the learning curve to be most evident in Congress.

It would be surprising if members of Congress, who no doubt have been forced to solidify and to state publicly their political views before gaining entrance to the body, altered those views dramatically just because of a little additional information and experience. And we now know that members, before they are even officially sworn in, are presented with a battery of workshops on how to turn their offices into breathtakingly efficient constituency-service shops. Little on-the-job learning is needed here. Add to this the fact that the modern electoral environment is one in which candidate-centered elections with all their idiosyncrasies have replaced partisan-centered elections,[17] and there is not much reason to expect variation from junior to senior member on many aspects of congressional life.

Actual involvement in the legislative process is another story, however. No workshop is capable of providing the requisite information on this front. The legislative process is too intricate and subtle. The options are more varied than those present at roll call voting time. Coalitions and compromises, timing and jurisdiction, presentation and rules, all must be grasped—and these things simply take time. This is apparent in the results presented above.

The contrast between life-cycle effects on legislating but not on roll call voting illustrates a distinction nicely made by R. Douglas Arnold.[18] Arnold notes the difference between the decision environment on roll call matters and the decision environment facing what he calls coalition leaders. Although deciding how to vote on a roll call may be wrenching for a member, the options are framed very clearly: yea, nay, or take a walk. Contrast this situation with that confronting a coalition leader (often the bill sponsor), where the options are limited only by the member's imagination. Countless decisions are required on strategies, compromises, wording, external actors, timing, publicity, vote trading, the other house, and on and on.

As Arnold says, "On any given issue ordinary legislators face either a single dichotomous choice or a series of dichotomous choices ... [but] ... coalition leaders do not live in a dichotomous world. They do not choose among paired alternatives; they define those alternatives." [19] Is it any wonder that the growth of a legislator is more evident in activities related to coalition leading than in other aspects of congressional service?[20] And the so-called postreform Congress,[21] with its complex rules, omnibus bills, pay-as-you-go requirements, multiple actors, and divided government, if anything, places a greater premium on the skills and knowledge that Arnold has in mind. This may be part of the reason for Congress's growing dependence on senior members when it comes to legislative matters.

Term Limits

The political life cycle has been replaced by political stasis except when it comes to pure legislative involvement; and here, the distinction between junior and senior members is more pronounced than it has been in a long time. What does this finding mean for the way we view congressional careerism generally and proposals to limit terms specifically?

What would the exclusion of senior members do to the operation of Congress? It would not make members more vulnerable because junior members are no different from senior members on this score. It would probably not change the roll call tendencies of members because this tendency is set early anyway. And it would not do much to encourage members' attention to constituents. Most members and, particularly, their staffs are already working hard in this area, and only a slight diminution comes with age. But it would severely reduce the legislative potential of the membership. Senior members carry a disproportionate share of the legislative burden. Without them, legislative agendas would be less active, less focused, and less likely to become law than they are now.

Of course, some people believe the country's problems would be solved if our legislators were not as active and successful as they are. George Will, for one, complains about the mentality of Washington's entrenched incumbents; to wit, "Every good idea out there in America must become a slice of federal pork." [22] The implication that members would suddenly cease pursuing pork if they knew they would stay no longer than eight or twelve years is a bit puzzling. But it is true that if one opposes good ideas becoming law one should push for a system in which legislators are not competent, experienced, and knowledgeable enough to develop and pass a meaningful and coherent legislative agenda.

Many other wondrous consequences, we have been told, would flow from limiting congressional terms. In addition to Will's belief that limits would stop pork-barrel politics and restore government to its rightful role in American society, David Brady and Douglas Rivers as well as Gary Copeland and John David Rausch claim limits would resuscitate political parties. Jack Gargan thinks limits would reduce the "shady dealings" of legislators. And Mark Petracca sees limits as a way of replacing "permanent government with democratic government." At the same time, Petracca dismisses the potential problems with term limits by claiming that "there is no empirical evidence that professional politicians do a better job of governing than amateurs." [23]

In truth, the situation is just the reverse. As we have seen, there is solid evidence that more and better legislative work is undertaken by senior legislators than by junior legislators. But there is no evidence that junior members demur from playing the game of pork-barrel politics or that they are somehow immune from the fund-raising and other pressures attending senior members. [24] Nor is there any evidence that parties miraculously would flourish or that voters would feel empowered politically just because no one could spend more than eight years in the House or twelve years in the Senate. Indeed, a more likely possibility is that democracy would be weakened as novice legislators struggled to do battle with unelected but experienced staffers and bureaucrats.[25]

We know that in terms of legislative involvement congressional careerism has some beneficial consequences. There may also be some deleterious consequences. After all, increased legislative moxie obviously can be used for personal or overly parochial goals. Perhaps additional research will demonstrate that senior members are indeed more likely to be involved in fund-raising or other improprieties, but this is an empirical question and it, along with many other issues, should be pursued before we launch a full-scale attack on congressional careerism.

Legislative Professionalization

Although the current public debate has centered on term limits, the larger issue involves the pluses and minuses of a professionalized (or institutionalized) legislative body. Legislative professionalization is a phrase applied to the process by which legislatures develop large, independent infrastructures and unique rules, norms, and standard operating procedures in addition to stable memberships. Positions on term limits are often determined by deeper philosophical beliefs about the value of legislative professionalization. Put more simply, supporters and opponents of term limits usually have very different visions of what a legislature should be. Supporters believe it should be a mirror; opponents, a prism. Supporters want a legislature as good as the American people; opponents want a legislature that is better than the American people. Supporters hold the model representative to be Cincinnatus; opponents, Technocratus.

Who is right? If one pole of an imaginary spectrum is a legislature made up of issue specialists, highly informed but only tenuously connected to constituents, and the other pole is a legislature with a membership chosen by lot for short terms, a truly representative but unabashedly amateur body, should reform push our present Congress toward the former or the latter? This is a difficult question. Ambivalence on this important normative matter is perhaps most clearly seen in a recent proposal to push one house of Congress toward one pole and the remaining house toward the other.[26]

But putting aside for the moment what should be, there is no ambivalence about what is. Congress has for two hundred years been moving toward the first pole of this imaginary spectrum. Many writers have documented aspects of the institutionalization of Congress,[27] such as increasing complexity, increasing boundedness, and increasing devotion to standard operating procedures and institutional norms, emphasizing the origins and development of its committees, subcommittees, and support agencies; its banks, barbershops, and restaurants (perhaps to the subsequent regret of some members); and its norms, patterns of progression, and stable membership.

This kind of institutionalization is known to characterize virtually all entities as they struggle to survive and mature in an evolving, complex, and sometimes turbulent environment.[28] But the question that has not been addressed satisfactorily is whether a legislature can become institutionalized and still be responsive to the public mood—which after all is what a representative body is all about. Legislative institutionalization is not like the institutionalization of other bodies because the raison d'être of a legislature is not like that of other bodies. General Motors, IBM, and the U.S. presidency can institutionalize without a crisis of mission; the U.S. Congress cannot. After all, if the boundaries separating Congress from its environment have become hardened, if Congress has become frustratingly bureaucratized and complex, and if Congress's unique set of norms and rules has made it a world unto itself, where does this leave the people who are supposed to be represented by this creation? Can Congress be fully institutionalized and still be closely connected to constituents? Can institutionalization and representation reside in the same house?[29]

Perhaps the public is correct when it cries out, as it has been doing lately, that Congress is out of touch. The people need not have read political science journals to sense that the mechanized representation they are receiving is not what they want; to be baffled by the maze of subcommittees, perquisites, and staffers; and to conclude that, however many weddings the representative attends back in the district, there is somehow a distance between the people and the Congress. Two hundred years of congressional evolution away from the kind of representation many people apparently think they want is undoubtedly part of the reason for the recent dissatisfaction with Congress.

But we must determine whether the reforms serving as outlets for this dissatisfaction will in fact improve our governmental system. The evidence presented earlier in this essay helps in making this determination for term limits. We must also obtain and analyze parallel evidence for other aspects of professionalized legislatures. For example, legislative staffs have recently come in for heavy criticism. California in 1990 voted to cut by about one-half the large staffs of members of its state legislature. The larger and more diverse staffs of the U.S. Congress are even more vulnerable to attack than those of a state legislature.

Relative to the staffs of other national legislatures around the world, the U.S. Congress is nothing if not an outlier, having seven or eight times as many staffers as the next best staffed legislature in the world, the Canadian Parliament.[30] Voters are occasionally wondering whether these large entourages are really necessary. Party voting in Congress is higher now than it was fifteen years ago. When roll call votes deviate from the party line, the departure is often caused by a desire to support unadulterated local interests. Do we need nearly twelve thousand personal staffers and three thousand committee staffers to show members how to vote with their party or their district?

Questions have also been raised about congressional support agencies. Are they worth the taxpayers' money? Consider the following. In July 1991 the Office of Management and Budget (OMB) conceded that it had made a mistake. It had underestimated the deficit by $67 billion because it had based its calculations on certain taxes generating 20 percent of the base (the proper figure was 10 percent).[31] The Congressional Budget Office (CBO) employs well over two hundred people so that Congress does not have to rely on the executive branch's

OMB for budgetary data. A few weeks after OMB director Richard Darman issued his mea culpa, the CBO revised its estimates for the fiscal year 1992 deficit by, you guessed it, $67 billion. In this instance, CBO seems to have failed in the very thing it was set up to do: to provide Congress with accurate and unadulterated budgetary information.

In light of these events, an obvious question must be asked: Does the public derive much benefit from the massive infrastructure associated with the institutionalized Congress? Would calamitous events truly befall our government if Congress became a little less institutionalized, if staffs were cut and careers were shortened? The answer almost certainly is no. Those who oppose institutionalized legislatures and support ideas such as term limits have by no means cornered the market on hyperbole.

None of this is to say that Congress should ignore party lines, divest itself of all personal and committee staffers, sack the CBO, and pass legislation to limit terms.[32] The point is that the public, understandably, may see no accountability in an institution that is supposed to be built on that word. The public wants to know what return it is getting from its investment in a highly professionalized legislature. By not providing answers, we are only encouraging knee-jerk ideas such as term limits and drastic reductions of staff. By not delineating carefully the pros and cons of various features of congressional careerism and professionalized legislatures, we invite the muddled and overly emotional discussion of Congress now occurring.

Notes

1. The comparable numbers for the Senate at the beginning of the 102d Congress were mean length of service, 11.09 years, and percentage in their first congressional term, 4 percent (an unusually low figure).
2. See, for example, T. Richard Witmer, "The Aging of the House," *Political Science Quarterly* 79 (1964): 526-541; Nelson W. Polsby, "The Institutionalization of the U.S. House of Representatives," *American Political Science Review* 62 (1968): 144-168; H. Douglas Price, "The Congressional Career: Then and Now," in *Congressional Behavior*, ed. Nelson W. Polsby (New York: Random House, 1971); Charles S. Bullock III, "House Careerists: Changing Patterns of Longevity and Attrition," *American Political Science Review* 66 (1972): 1295-1300; and Morris P. Fiorina, David W. Rohde, and Peter Wissel, "Historical Change in House Turnover," in *Congress in Change*, ed. Norman J. Ornstein (New York: Praeger, 1975). The length of careers in recent Congresses looks much less unusual if the comparison is cross-national rather than longitudinal.
3. See Ronald D. Elving, "Congress Braces for Fallout from State Measures," *Congressional Quarterly Weekly Report*, Sept. 29, 1990, 3144-3146; and "Congressional Departures," *Congressional Quarterly Weekly Report*, May 2, 1992, 1139. In 1990 similar expectations of anti-incumbency voting turned out to be inaccurate, as virtually all incumbents won (only one lost in the Senate) and mean share of the vote for incumbents dropped only a little. For details, see Rhodes Cook, "Most House Members Survive," *Congressional Quarterly Weekly Report*, Nov. 10, 1990, 3798-3900.
4. For broader support of this point, see Daniel J. Reagan and Donald Davison, "Ambition and Retirement from the U.S. House of Representatives, 1957-1984" (Paper

presented at the annual meeting of the American Political Science Association, Washington, D.C., August-September 1991).

5. See, for example, John R. Hibbing, *Congressional Careers: Contours of Life in the U.S. House of Representatives* (Chapel Hill: University of North Carolina Press, 1991), chap. 2.

6. Donald R. Matthews, *U.S. Senators and Their World* (Chapel Hill: University of North Carolina Press, 1960), 241-242.

7. Richard F. Fenno, Jr., *Home Style: House Members in Their Districts* (Boston: Little, Brown, 1978), 173; Lawrence C. Dodd, "The Cycles of Legislative Change," in *Political Science: The Science of Politics,* ed. Herbert F. Weisberg (New York: Agathon Press, 1986); Burdett A. Loomis, "Political Skills and Proximate Goals: Career Development in the House of Representatives" (Paper presented at the annual meeting of the American Political Science Association, Washington, D.C., September 1988); and Burdett A. Loomis, *The New American Politician* (New York: Basic Books, 1988).

8. Morris P. Fiorina, *Congress: Keystone of the Washington Establishment* (New Haven: Yale University Press, 1977), 54-55; Gary C. Jacobson, *The Politics of Congressional Elections,* 2d ed. (Boston: Little, Brown, 1987); Herbert B. Asher, "The Changing Status of the Freshman Representative," in *Congress in Change.*

9. Glenn R. Parker, *Homeward Bound* (Pittsburgh: University of Pittsburgh Press, 1986), chap. 2.

10. Michael K. Moore and John R. Hibbing, "Is Serving in Congress Fun Again? Voluntary Retirements from the House Since the 1970s," *American Journal of Political Science* 36 (August 1992): 824-828.

11. Ibid.

12. Thomas E. Mann, *Unsafe at Any Margin: Interpreting Congressional Elections* (Washington, D.C.: American Enterprise Institute, 1978).

13. Keith T. Poole, "Dimensions of Interest Group Evaluation of the U.S. Senate, 1969-1978," *American Journal of Political Science* 25 (1981): 49-67.

14. Norman J. Ornstein, Thomas E. Mann, and Michael J. Malbin, *Vital Statistics on Congress, 1991-1992* (Washington, D.C.: Congressional Quarterly, 1992), 140.

15. With the number of trips home down and the number of staffers stationed in the home district up, it may seem at times as though we are moving toward a system of surrogate representation.

16. Hibbing, *Congressional Careers,* 163.

17. Gary C. Jacobson, *The Electoral Origins of Divided Government* (Boulder: Westview Press, 1990).

18. R. Douglas Arnold, *The Logic of Congressional Action* (New Haven: Yale University Press, 1990).

19. Ibid., 7.

20. Of course, constituency relations can also require artistry on the part of legislators. This theme receives its most thorough development in Fenno, *Home Style.*

21. Roger H. Davidson, ed., *The Postreform Congress* (New York: St. Martin's, 1992).

22. George Will, "Feds Can't Fund Every Good Deed," *Lincoln Star,* Oct. 7, 1991, 7.

23. David W. Brady and Douglas Rivers, "Term Limits Make Sense," *New York Times,* Oct. 5, 1991, 13; Gary W. Copeland and John David Rausch, Jr., "The End of Professionalism? The Dynamics of Term Limitations" (Paper presented at the annual meeting of the Southwestern Political Science Association, San Antonio, Texas, March 1991); Mark Petracca, "Term Limits Will Put an End to Permanent Government by Incumbents," *Public Affairs,* Report 31, Nov. 1990, 9. Jack Gargan ran a full-page paid political advertisement in several newspapers across the nation. See, for example, the *Denver Post,* July 15, 1990, 12G.

24. In 1988, for example, six House incumbents ran and lost; five were associated with some kind of scandal. The number of terms served by these five were, respectively,

one, two, two, two, and fourteen; so at least some junior members are open to questionable actions.

25. Nelson W. Polsby, "Limiting Terms Won't Curb Special Interests, Improve the Legislature, or Enhance Democracy," *Public Affairs*, Report 31, Nov. 1990, 9.

26. Robert Struble, Jr., and Z. W. Jahre, "Rotation in Office: Rapid but Restricted to the House," *PS: Political Science and Politics* 24 (1991): 34-37.

27. Samuel P. Huntington, "Congressional Responses to the Twentieth Century," in *Congress and America's Future,* ed. David Truman (Englewood Cliffs, N.J.: Prentice Hall, 1965); Polsby, "Institutionalization of the House."

28. S. N. Eisenstadt, "Institutionalization and Change," *American Sociological Review* 29 (1964): 235-247; Emile Durkheim, *The Division of Labor in Society* (Glencoe, Ill.: Free Press, 1947); and Max Weber, *The Theory of Social and Economic Organization* (Glencoe, Ill.: Free Press, 1947).

29. For discussion of this matter, see Kenneth A. Shepsle, "The Changing Textbook Congress," in *Can the Government Govern?* ed. John Chubb and Paul Peterson (Washington, D.C.: Brookings Institution, 1989).

30. Michael Malbin, *Unelected Representatives* (New York: Basic Books, 1980), 10.

31. George Hager, "Deficit Report Shows No Gain from Pain of Spending Rules," *Congressional Quarterly Weekly Report,* July 20, 1991, 1963-1964.

32. Defenders of staffs, presumably, will make their case much as I have done for experienced legislators: the benefits are to be found not in roll call voting but in formulating agendas and building coalitions.

Part II

◆◆◆

Elections and Constituencies

4

Voters, Candidates, and Issues in Congressional Elections

Robert S. Erikson and Gerald C. Wright

E lections for the U.S. House of Representatives fascinate observers of American politics almost as much as presidential elections do. Unlike Senate elections, which come at staggered six-year intervals, and gubernatorial elections, which have an irregular electoral cycle that varies from state to state, House elections provide a regular biennial measure of the national electoral pulse. Interest in House elections generally centers on the partisan balance of seats and the mood of the electorate that underlies this partisan verdict.

Another source of fascination with House elections is their large number. Every two years the composition of the new U.S. House is the result of 435 separate contests for 435 separate seats. In part, these 435 outcomes are determined by national electoral forces. But to a larger extent, they are determined by the candidates in these contests and the conduct of their individual campaigns.

In this essay, first we examine the national forces in House elections and their influence on the partisan divisions of the national vote and House seats. Next, we look at the role of candidates in individual House contests. Finally, we compare elections for the House with elections for the Senate.

The National Verdict in House Elections

The national result of House elections can be represented either as the partisan division of seats won or as the partisan division of the national vote. The partisan seat division receives the most attention because it reflects the parties' actual balance of congressional power. Naturally, the seat division is largely a function of how many votes the two parties receive nationwide. When one party gains or loses a certain percentage of the national vote, it expects on average to win or lose a particular share of the seats. The formula that translates votes to seats is called the swing ratio. For much of the post-World War II period, the swing ratio was about 2.0, meaning that for every percentage point a party gained in terms of votes, an additional 2 percent of the seats switched to its column.[1] (With a swing ratio of about 2.0, each party is about 1 percentage point short of victory in about 2 percent of the districts. When a party gains an additional 1 percent of the national vote, it captures the additional 2 percent of the seats it otherwise would have lost.)

Figure 4-1 shows the pattern of the two-party vote and the two-party seat division since 1952. Between 1952 and 1992 the seat division varied from about

Figure 4-1. House Seats and Vote, 1952-1992

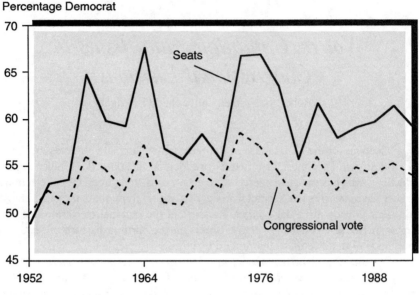

Percentage Democrat

Source: Compiled by the authors.

an even split between Republicans and Democrats to a Democratic edge of more than two-thirds of the seats. This major movement is a response to far smaller vote variations, from about 50 percent to about 58 percent Democratic.

Although Figure 4-1 shows the seats and votes generally moving in the same partisan direction, the swing ratio will vary from one election to the next. A definite downward trend is noticeable since the mid-1960s, with the swing ratio in some years dipping even below 1.0.[2] With the decline in the swing ratio, partisan change at the ballot box results in less movement in the partisan balance of power in Congress. There is an obvious underlying cause: a growing incumbency advantage. Increasingly, at least through the 1980s, incumbents have been able to insulate themselves from national partisan tides by manufacturing safe seats for themselves—winning by large margins in normal years and surviving with smaller but usually sufficient margins in years that are adverse for their party. This process frustrates either party when it senses the possibility of electoral gain. Since parties defeat few opposition incumbents when they gain votes, they must be satisfied with modest pickups of open seats (those with no incumbent running), which are unaffected by any incumbency advantage.

The Normal Vote

The Republican party has dominated contemporary presidential politics, for example, losing the White House only once between 1972 and 1988. Democrats, however, have dominated the House of Representatives for longer—holding a majority of seats continuously since 1952, with no letup in sight. The Democratic edge in congressional elections reflects the party's numerical lead within the electorate in terms of party identification. If most partisans were to vote for their party's candidate and the independent voters were to split about 50-50, the outcome of a national election would be about 54 percent Democratic and 46 percent Republican. Such an outcome, in which the election is decided on a party vote, is called the normal vote.[3] Observe in Figure 4-1 how the national House vote approximates the normal vote, with relatively small oscillations around the baseline of about 54 percent Democratic.

Election outcomes that depart from the normal vote stem from short-term defections by partisans and from temporary vote movement by independents. These temporary deviations from the normal vote are attributable to "short-term partisan forces" of the campaign. At a national level, short-term partisan forces intrude only lightly in House elections. But as we have seen, even small perturbations in the vote can have major consequences in terms of party seats.

Presidential Election Years

In presidential years the short-term forces of the presidential election and the short-term forces of the House election run in the same partisan direction: the party that wins more than its normal vote for president wins more than its normal vote in the congressional contests. Whether this happens because the House vote and the presidential vote are influenced by the same national issues or because people decide their congressional vote on the basis of their partisan choice for president is not clear. Whatever the cause, this phenomenon is called the coattail effect. Some House candidates seem to be carried into office by riding the coattails of their party's popular presidential candidate. Democratic coattails were at their strongest in 1964, when President Lyndon B. Johnson's landslide victory created an overwhelming 295-140 Democratic majority in the House of Representatives. Republican coattails were particularly strong in 1980, when Ronald Reagan won the presidency.

The size of the coattail effect is decidedly irregular. One statistical estimate for post-World War II elections puts it at $+0.31$ congressional votes nationally for every percentage point of the vote gained by the party at the presidential level.[4] Put another way, every added percentage of the vote gained by a presidential candidate also adds almost one-third of a percent of the vote to the presidential candidate's congressional running mates. Before World War II, presidential coattails appeared to be stronger than they are today; the national presidential vote and the national congressional vote marched more in lock step. One consequence of the weakening of the coattail effect is the increase in split-party control of government, with one party controlling the presidency and the other party controlling at least one house of Congress.

Midterm Years

One regular pattern of House elections is that the party that wins the presidency suffers a net loss of votes and seats in the following midterm election. Of the twenty-two midterms of the twentieth century, for example, in only one (1934) did the president's party gain seats. And in only one midterm (1926) did the president's party increase its share of the House vote. What accounts for this regularity?

Among political scientists, the conventional explanation for midterm loss has been the withdrawal of presidential coattails. The argument goes as follows: in presidential years the congressional vote for the president's party is inflated by presidential coattails. At the next midterm the congressional vote reverts toward the "normal vote" outcome. The result is a decline for the president's party.[5]

Although this argument is appealing, it is wrong. The vote at midterm is not predictably normal. Instead, at midterm the presidential party tends to get even less than its normal share of the vote. This means that each party does better at midterm when it is out of power at the presidential level. Moreover, the size of the midterm loss does not depend on the size of the presidential year victory, as the coattail argument would predict. Under all conditions, at midterm the congressional vote for the presidential party is about 4 or 5 percentage points lower than in presidential election years. Figure 4-2 illustrates this regularity for elections since 1946.[6]

It is as if the midterm electorate chooses to punish the president's party, no matter what the circumstances. Why would the electorate do this? According to one controversial theory, the electorate "punishes" the presidential party as an ideological hedge. Moderate voters, seeing themselves ideologically between the Democratic and Republican positions, have some incentive to balance the president's ideology with a congressional vote for the "out" party.[7] The process encourages divided government, with one party controlling the presidency and the other controlling Congress.

Electoral Change as a Search for Policy Direction

Every two years the national vote for Congress produces a change in the party composition of Congress. When the electorate collectively creates a change in the party composition of Congress, do voters have a specific policy purpose? Apart from the electorate's possible yearning for ideological balance between the president and Congress, what do congressional election results indicate about the electorate's policy preferences?

The popular view, often promoted by pundits at election time, is that partisan tides reflect the electorate's changing ideological mood—as if Democratic congressional gains signify growing liberal sentiment and Republican gains signify growing conservative sentiment. For example, the major Republican gains in 1980, at the time of Reagan's decisive presidential victory, were widely inter-

Figure 4-2 Democratic Congressional Vote by Election Year
and Presidential Outcome, 1944-1946 Through
1988-1990

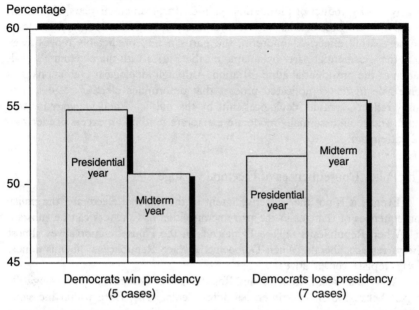

Percentage

Source: Compiled by the authors.

preted as a mandate for a new conservative agenda. Earlier, major Democratic gains at the time of Johnson's landslide 1964 election were interpreted at the time as a mandate for a new liberal agenda. Each instance was followed by major policy change—most notably Reagan's conservative tax cut and Johnson's liberal Great Society program. But in each instance, the electorate's desire for change was probably greatly exaggerated.

Reading turns in the electorate's ideological preference from the election returns can be hazardous. Public-opinion research shows little more than a trace of ideological movement over the short span between elections.[8] This trace can be important, however. Intriguingly, some recent statistical analysis suggests that the small shifts in the electorate's ideological mood actually do correlate with election returns.[9]

Still, even if election results respond to small changes in the public mood, other variables are more important as determinants of election results. In presidential elections, evaluations of the presidential candidates as potential national leaders loom large in the electorate's equation. These presidential evaluations involve the candidates' ideologies to some extent, with most voters preferring moderates to liberal or conservative ideologues. The evaluations also involve intangible considerations such as character and competence. The national economy presents one aspect of competence, as voters reward or punish the incumbent presidential party in proportion to the degree of economic prosperity it delivers.

In terms of national congressional elections, shifts in party fortunes are largely the byproduct of presidential politics. In presidential years, short-term forces from the presidential contest reverberate down to the congressional level as the coattail effect. At midterm, the partisan tide predictably moves away from the presidential party by an amount that varies with the electorate's evaluation of the presidential administration. Although ideological evaluations play some role in the complicated process that determines election results, they rarely reflect a simple ideological shift by the public. When ideology matters most, we see an essentially moderate electorate fend off an excess of ideological extremism.

The Policy Consequences of Electoral Change

Even if it is not the collective intent of the national electorate, the policy consequences of changes in the party composition of Congress can be substantial. When Republicans replace Democrats in the House, conservatives almost always replace liberals. When Democrats replace Republicans, liberals almost always replace conservatives.

As we shall see, Democrats and Republicans in Congress differ ideologically in part because their constituencies differ ideologically. Even within the same constituency, however, the two major-party candidates almost always diverge ideologically. This can be seen from several studies of the policy views of competing Democratic and Republican candidates. The most recent relevant data came from the 1982 election, when CBS News and the *New York Times* polled all congressional candidates on major issues. Candidates were asked their opinions on ten issues, which can be summed to make a ten-item scale of liberalism-conservatism. By this measure, the Republican was the more conservative candidate in 93 percent of the contests, the Democrat was the more conservative in 3 percent, and ties occurred in the remaining 4 percent.[10] A similar pattern was found for earlier studies of the 1966, 1974, and 1978 elections.[11] Thus a congressional voter usually has an easy way to cast a partisan ballot: to help elect the more conservative candidate, vote Republican; to help elect the more liberal candidate, vote Democratic.

The overall differences between the Republican and Democratic congressional parties can best be seen from a comparison of their ideological tendencies when voting on congressional roll calls. Conveniently, ideological interest groups provide frequencies with which members vote ideologically "correctly"—either conservative (as rated by the American Conservative Union, the ACU) or liberal (as rated by Americans for Democratic Action, the ADA). The indices of these two groups measure a common ideological dimension, with members who score high on ACU conservatism scoring low on ADA liberalism and vice versa. From these two indices, we created a composite index, which is simply the average of the percent liberal based on the two indices. On our index of "roll call ideology," 0 means a perfect conservative voting record and 100 means a perfect liberal record.

Figure 4-3 shows the ideological distributions for the two congressional parties for the 101st Congress, which served from 1989 to 1991. Republicans cluster at the conservative end; Democrats at the liberal end. This is no surprise. An important aspect of this graph, however, is that some members of Congress depart considerably from their party's norm. As we will see, these exceptions are important for the understanding of congressional representation.

District-Level Outcomes in House Elections

So far we have discussed congressional candidates almost solely in terms of their party affiliation, as if all Democrats were alike and all Republicans were alike. Similarly, we have discussed the electorate's choice as if it were solely between the national Democratic party and the national Republican party. In actuality, candidates within each party differ considerably. Candidates often take positions on issues that depart from their party's norm, perhaps out of electoral necessity. And whether by posturing on issues or by other actions, candidates do have considerable effect on district election outcomes. Local candidates can do more than watch helplessly while constituency partisanship and the national partisan trend determine whether they are elected or defeated. Although constituencies tend to vote according to their partisanship (the local normal vote) and the national partisan trend, constituencies also vote according to the capabilities they see in the candidates.

When voters cast their ballots in congressional elections, they have two sets of cues: the candidates' party affiliations plus whatever they have learned about the candidates. At first glance it would seem that voters generally possess insufficient information about the candidates to vote on anything more than a partisan basis. Consider some evidence from surveys: only about one-half of the voters can name their U.S. representative, and slightly fewer claim to have "read or heard" something about him or her. The content of this information is generally vague ("He is a good man." "She knows the job.") and rarely touches on policy issues or roll call votes. Only by the generous criterion of *recognition* of the representative's name does the electorate perform well. More than 90 percent claim to recognize their representative's name when supplied with it. Candidates for open seats are even less visible than incumbent candidates. And challengers trying to defeat incumbent representatives are the least visible of all. Typically, only about 20 percent of the voting electorate can recall the challenger's name or recall anything else about the challenger. Only about half will claim to recognize the challenger's name when supplied with it.[12]

Although voters generally are not well informed about their local House candidates, it does not follow that the candidates have little impact on election outcomes. Movements by relatively few voters in a constituency can create a major surge for or against a candidate. This movement, the "personal" vote, results from the constituency's reaction to the specific candidates, as opposed to

Figure 4-3 Distribution of House Roll Call Ideology, by Party, 1990

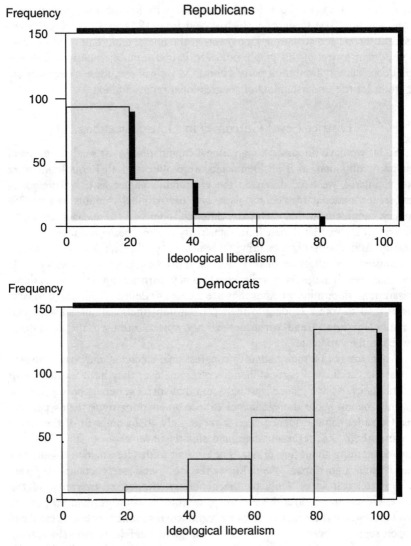

Source: Compiled by the authors.

Note: Ideological scores are based on ratings by the American Conservative Union and Americans for Democratic Action. Retirees are not included.

the "partisan" vote, which results from the constituency's partisanship. The personal vote is about as important as the partisan vote in deciding elections.

The Value of Incumbency

The first thing one notices about district-level House races is that when incumbents seek reelection they almost always win. In recent years incumbent candidates have enjoyed a phenomenal reelection rate of more than 95 percent. With such favorable chances, incumbents generally keep seeking reelection until presented with a compelling reason not to. The high retirement rate in 1992— about 20 percent—is the exception. In a typical election year only about 10 percent of sitting House members will actually retire. Those who do voluntarily leave often do so to run for another office. Some become lobbyists. Some quit because of illness or old age. And a few leave voluntarily in anticipation of the voters' wrath. Rarely do members leave because they prefer to abandon politics. They are essentially "career politicians."

Although several factors account for incumbents' electoral success, attention tends to focus on one specific reason: incumbents exploiting their "advantage of incumbency" over potential opponents. Incumbents can accrue an electoral advantage over potential challengers by using their many perquisites (perks) of office, such as free mailing privileges, generous travel allowances, and large staff largely devoted to serving constituents. Furthermore, incumbents hold an edge over potential opponents in their greater access to publicity and campaign cash. The result is that incumbents generate favorable images for themselves among their constituents, while their opponents must fight an uphill battle for even minimal visibility.

Exploiting this incumbency advantage is part of the reason that incumbents tend to be successful. But it is not the only one. Incumbents win for a variety of reasons besides an incumbency advantage or incumbency effect.

District partisanship. Most obviously, incumbents can win because they represent the majority party in their district. Every constituency has a particular partisan makeup or normal vote, to some degree tilting Democratic or Republican. When a constituency regularly gives a majority to one party, the incumbent does not need to do anything special to stay elected, other than to stay nominated. Few House districts are so safe for one party that they become electoral "locks," but most members represent districts that tilt in their party's favor. As we shall see, however, an interesting minority of candidates are able to win electoral favor despite representing their district's minority party.

Electoral selection. One simple but sometimes overlooked reason incumbents win is that incumbency status must be earned at the ballot box. Apart from district partisanship and partisan trends, elections are won on the basis of which party can field the stronger candidate. Strong candidates tend to win and by winning become incumbents. Upon winning, they survive until they falter or lose to even stronger candidates. Retirement of a successful incumbent starts the process again.

The process of electoral selection is independent of any incumbency advantage, but the two factors may reinforce each other. For instance, unusually strong candidates, with the help of a favorable partisan tide, can win in districts with adverse partisanship. Then, as the favorable partisan tide recedes, the strong candidates can stay elected by using the advantage of incumbency to enhance their personal appeal even further.

Weak challengers. A supplementary reason incumbents win easily is that strong candidates tend to draw weak challengers. Politicians who are electorally strong tend to run when their prospects of victory are strongest—for example with the occurrence of an open seat, the presence of a weak incumbent, or the anticipation of a favorable electoral tide. This we know from Gary Jacobson and Samuel Kernell's theory of strategic politicians.[13] When incumbents are strong candidates in their own right, they can scare off strong challengers even without using the leverage of incumbency. When they exploit the perquisites of incumbency, they scare off strong challengers further.

The incumbency advantage defined. Finally, we have the incumbency advantage itself. The incumbency advantage is the increment to the vote margin that a candidate gains by virtue of being the incumbent. Another way of stating this is that the incumbency advantage is the causal effect of incumbency on the vote.

The incumbency advantage over time. How large is the incumbency advantage? The best way to measure it is to observe the size of the "sophomore surge," the percentage of the vote that candidates gain from their first victory to their first reelection attempt. Averaged across elections and adjusted for the national partisan trend, the sophomore surge is a simple but accurate measure of the typical vote share gained from incumbency. During the 1970s and 1980s the sophomore surge averaged about 7 percentage points. That is, upon gaining incumbency status, incumbents tended to earn about 7 percentage points more than they otherwise would have earned.

The size of the incumbency advantage has increased over time. In the 1950s the sophomore surge—and therefore the incumbency advantage—averaged only about 2 percentage points. In the 1960s the incumbency advantage increased—rather suddenly, according to the evidence. By the 1970s the typical incumbency advantage reached its current value of about 7 percentage points.[14] As the incumbency advantage grew, so too did the incumbent success rate. As a byproduct, the swing ratio has declined—meaning less partisan turnover of seats.

The growth of the incumbency advantage corresponds in time with the declining importance of partisanship in congressional elections and the concomitant increase in the importance of candidates' personal characteristics. Beginning in the mid-1960s, the American electorate suddenly became less rigid in terms of party identification. The proportion of voters who called themselves independents rather than partisans rose dramatically. Among admitted partisans, the proportion who called themselves strong Democrats or strong Republicans noticeably declined. As partisanship declined as a determinant of vote choice, voters began to respond more to the personal attributes of the candidates than they had before. With elections being decided more on the basis of candidates than of partisanship, it became more important that candidates have strong vote appeal in their own right. Increasingly, congressional winners owed their success to their personal appeal. As incumbency status enhanced their visibility, congressional winners drew even more support from their constituency electorates.

Meanwhile, with their survival more dependent on their own behavior than on the fate of their party, incumbents began to invest in the kinds of constituency relations that pay off on election day. In the mid-1960s Congress changed the rules to bestow on its members several increases in their congressional perks. More so than previously, House members began to shower constituents with newsletters and other literature, travel home on weekends, and maintain large staffs not only in Washington but in their district offices. The process does not please all observers; some are particularly upset that House members can ensure their reelection at taxpayers' expense.

It may seem surprising that an incumbency advantage that averages only about 7 percentage points can work so strongly to ensure most incumbents of success. The explanation is that the incumbency advantage is not a simple 7 points across the board for all incumbents: some work harder than others to please their constituents. Members trying to stay elected in districts with adverse partisanship have the greatest incentive to dance for their constituents. Members from "safe" constituencies need not do anything exceptional to stay in office. Election results reflect this differential. Very safe members earn no incumbency advantage at all, while many of their more threatened brethren are able to garner far more votes than a candidate of the district minority party should.

Figure 4-4 offers an illustration from the 1990 election. This figure shows two scatterplots of the relationship between the district's 1988 presidential vote (as an indicator of district partisanship) and the vote for the U.S. House. The first scatterplot represents open seats (no incumbent running). The observations are reasonably close to the best-fitting regression line, which we call par. The diagonal line, par, represents the expected Democratic vote, given the district's partisanship (1988 presidential vote) and assuming an open seat. Note that most winners beat par, suggesting that the winner was the stronger candidate. (Most Democratic winners are above the par line, and most Republican winners are below it.)

The second scatterplot of Figure 4-4 represents the same scatterplot for seats in which the incumbent sought reelection in 1990. The par line from the first graph is reproduced in the second. Note that almost all incumbents perform better than par for their party. Those from very safe districts (almost all on the Democratic side), however, perform no better than par, and they do not need to do so to carry their safe districts. But candidates around the par level where the vote expectation is about 50-50 show a wide dispersal, with most incumbents far from par in their party's direction. Farthest from par are incumbents from districts where par favors the other party. This is because incumbents who come from the district's minority party need an exceptional vote appeal in order to stay elected, and generally, they are able to earn it.

A possible countertrend: Is there an anti-incumbent mood? Some popular accounts of recent elections insist that the electoral tide has turned against incum-

Figure 4-4 The Incumbency Advantage in the House, 1990

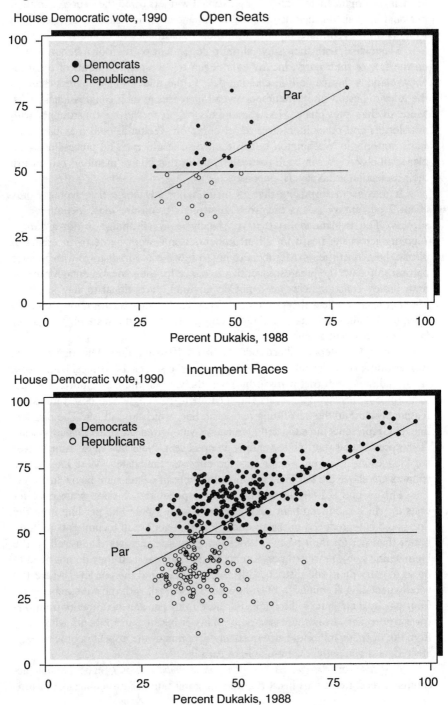

House Democratic vote, 1990   Open Seats

- ● Democrats
- ○ Republicans

Par

Percent Dukakis, 1988

Incumbent Races

House Democratic vote, 1990

- ● Democrats
- ○ Republicans

Par

Percent Dukakis, 1988

Source: Compiled by the authors.

bents and that the public is in the mood to vote incumbents out—whatever their party affiliation. As of the 1990 election, there has been little evidence of such activity. In 1990 veteran incumbents as a group did find a few percentage points shaved from their vote margins; these losses, however, were concentrated among those candidates with safe districts, and they could afford to waste some votes. In 1990 House members from marginal districts who needed the boost generally earned the usual incumbency advantage.[15] One reason incumbency has not turned from an advantage to a penalty is that both parties have been slow to run strong challengers where they might seem to have an opportunity to do so (see Chapter 5).

The incumbency advantage as an investment. Since incumbents almost always win, it might seem that incumbents can ignore their constituents' concerns. But that impression would be quite mistaken. A central source of the incumbency advantage is the careful tending to district interests. Incumbents like to stay elected, and they know that the way to do this is to provide constituents with what they want. Incumbents are well aware that their long-term electoral security depends on satisfying their constituencies. Even though House members know they are unlikely to lose the next election, they know that their chances are roughly one in three that they will *eventually* lose and be sent home by the voters. After all, roughly one in three got to Congress in the first place by defeating a sitting incumbent.[16]

If House members were to ignore their districts, we would see no incumbency advantage and rapid turnover. House members do not get their incumbency advantage automatically; they earn it by hard work. Part of this work is doing constituency service and bringing home "pork" in the form of government construction projects, local government contracts, and the like. But there is also a policy component to the incumbent's investment. One way House members earn their incumbency advantage is by representing their district's policy interests. Often, the district's policy interests can be expressed as an ideological preference. As we shall see in the next section, House members add to their vote margins by representing the ideological preferences of their constituents.

Candidates, Issues, and the Vote

In this section, we explore how House members hold on to their seats by offering their constituents ideological representation. As noted earlier, Republican candidates tend to be conservative and Democratic candidates liberal. The average constituent is caught in the middle, located between the two candidates on the ideological spectrum. When voters respond to ideology and issues, candidates can gain votes by moving away from their party's norm toward the center of the spectrum. In principle, each candidate would maximize his or her votes by moving in the direction of the opponent. If both candidates were to do so, they would meet in the center of the local ideological spectrum.[17]

In reality, candidates do not converge. The countervailing forces of their own liberal or conservative beliefs and those of their ideological supporters within their party work against such a tendency. Still, within each party the candidates do vary in their ideological positions. And the degree to which they moderate their stands by moving toward their opponents influences the vote.[18]

In terms of their personal ideological views, most House members are probably comfortable with the modal position of their congressional party—quite conservative for Republicans and quite liberal for Democrats. Those members who represent safe districts tend to reflect such views in their roll call voting. Their constituents allow this "ideological extremism" for two reasons. First, districts that are safe Republican or safe Democratic tend to be somewhat more ideologically extreme themselves. Second, and probably more important, safe districts tend to vote partisanly to an extent that overrides any considerations of ideological proximity. For instance, a safe Republican district may prefer a conservative Republican incumbent over a moderate Democratic challenger, whereas the verdict might be different in a district that is competitive in terms of partisanship.

Although representatives from safe districts have no strong incentive to engage in ideological moderation, this is not true for representatives of districts with marginal or adverse partisanship. The easiest way for a candidate from the minority party to win and hold a marginal or adverse district is to reflect the district's ideology. For a Republican to hold a competitive or Democratic district, for example, it pays to take a moderate or even liberal posture on issues. For a Democrat to hold a competitive or Republican district, it pays to take a moderate or even Republican posture.

We show the dynamic aspect of the relationship between incumbent ideology, district ideology, and the vote in a series of graphs and equations. Table 4-1 shows two regression equations (one for Democrats, one for Republicans) predicting the 1990 House vote from three independent variables. One predictor, included as an important control for district partisanship and ideology, is the district's 1988 presidential vote. A second is the net difference between the Democratic and Republican candidate in terms of (logged) campaign spending. This measure taps the important effect of money in politics.[19] The third variable is our chief variable of interest, the member's roll call ideology based on our composite scale of conservatism-liberalism. (We would also include a measure of the challenger's ideology, but none is available.)

Consistent with our theory, the table shows that member ideology is negatively related to the Democratic congressional vote in the district. The negative sign means that ideological liberalism on the part of the member predicts Republican voting (or, saying the same thing, conservatism predicts Democratic voting). To translate: for Republican incumbents, ideological moderation or even liberalism enhances the incumbent's vote margin; for Democratic incumbents, ideological moderation or even conservatism enhances the incumbent's vote margin. The statistical evidence is strong, with member ideology competing equally with the district presidential vote and the candidate's spending differential in terms of statistical benchmarks such as statistical significance, t-values, and the relative size of beta, or standardized regression, coefficients.

Table 4-1 Regressions of Democratic Vote on Incumbent Ideology, Candidate Spending, and District Presidential Vote, 1990

Independent variable	Regression coefficient	Standard error	t	Prob > t	Beta
Democrats (N=174)					
Roll call ideology[a]	−.11	.03	−3.39	0.00	−.23
Log (D−R spending)[b]	.51	.12	4.41	0.00	.24
Percent Dukakis[c]	.60	.05	11.57	0.00	.78
Constant	43.82	2.49	17.63	0.00	
Republicans (N=107)					
Roll call ideology[a]	−.22	.04	−5.04	0.00	−.54
Log (D−R spending)[b]	.34	.12	2.92	0.00	.25
Percent Dukakis[c]	.49	.12	4.21	0.00	.45
Constant	22.53	4.22	5.35	0.00	

Source: Compiled by the authors.

[a] Average liberalism on a 0-100 conservative-liberal scale based on American Conservative Union and Americans for Democratic Action roll call indices.

[b] Natural log of Democratic minus Republican spending difference (in thousands of dollars).

[c] Dukakis percentage of two-party vote in district, 1988 presidential election.

Figure 4-5 identifies the most ideologically deviant members in each party—Republicans who score more than 50 percent liberal and Democrats who score more than 50 percent conservative. We also identify each party's most extreme members—for Democrats, those with a greater than 97 percent liberal voting record, for Republicans, those with a 95 percent or more conservative voting record. As Figure 4-5 shows, each party's atypical members (liberal Republicans or conservative Democrats) generally get far more votes than par, which is represented by the diagonal line. Meanwhile, each party's extremists tend to do little better than the prediction from par—that is, little better than the typical candidate would do if the election were for an open seat.

Note also the kinds of districts that atypical members and extremists represent. The ideologically atypical tend to represent districts that are adverse for their party as measured by their 1988 presidential voting. But seemingly because of their ideological adjustments, they win by about an average amount for incumbents of their party. Meanwhile, the extremists show a tendency to represent districts that are relatively safe for their party, as measured by their 1988 presidential voting. Although, as mentioned, their personal vote margins are little better than par for their party in their district, they generally do not need safer margins because their districts are safe for their party to begin with.

Figure 4-6 presents a more complete picture of how the constituency affects the member's roll call voting. For each party's 1990 incumbents running for reelection, the figure shows the relationship between district presidential voting and the members' ideology score. Note how members from relatively one-party dis-

Figure 4-5 Ideology and the House Vote, 1990

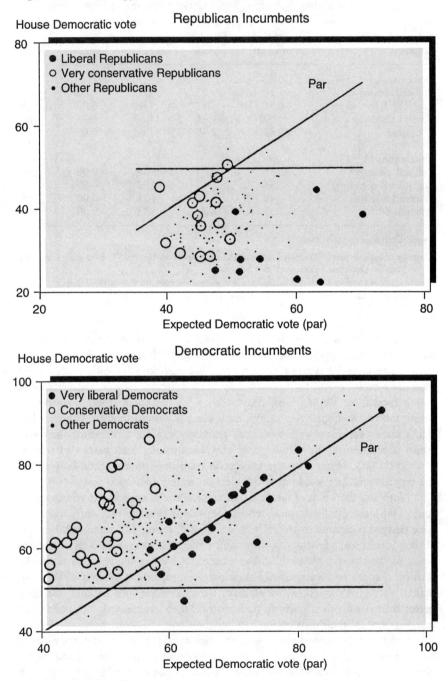

House Democratic vote — Republican Incumbents

- ● Liberal Republicans
- ○ Very conservative Republicans
- • Other Republicans

Par

Expected Democratic vote (par)

House Democratic vote — Democratic Incumbents

- ● Very liberal Democrats
- ○ Conservative Democrats
- • Other Democrats

Par

Expected Democratic vote (par)

Source: Compiled by the authors.

Note: Ideological scores are based on ratings by the American Conservative Union and Americans for Democratic Action.

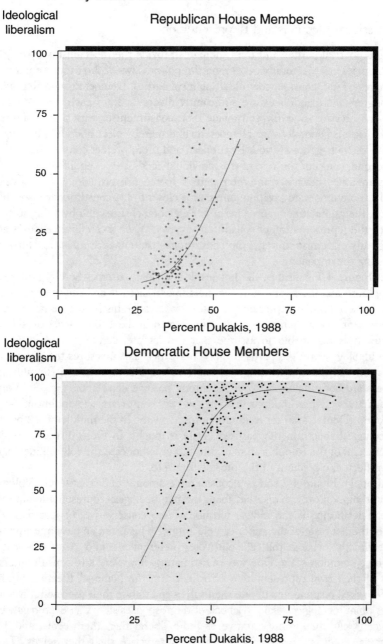

Figure 4-6   Republican and Democratic Roll Call Ideology (1989-1990) by 1988 District Presidential Vote

Ideological liberalism

Republican House Members

Percent Dukakis, 1988

Ideological liberalism

Democratic House Members

Percent Dukakis, 1988

Source: Compiled by the authors.

Note: Ideological scores are based on ratings by the American Conservative Union and Americans for Democratic Action; 0 = most conservative, 100 = most liberal.

tricts tend toward their party's ideological extremes, while members from relatively adverse districts veer ideologically in the direction of the opposition party.

Congressional Elections and Representation

The political parties and the candidates provide the mechanisms by which constituencies can electorally determine the policy views of their representatives in Congress. First, consider the role of political parties. Democratic and Republican congressional candidates are sufficiently divergent from each other on the liberal-conservative spectrum to provide their constituencies with a clear choice. Liberal districts generally vote Democratic and thereby elect liberals, while conservative districts generally vote Republican and thereby elect conservatives.

Second, consider the role of the individual candidates. Candidates for Congress sometimes deviate from their party's ideological orthodoxy. By moving toward a more moderate position, one that is closer to the constituency's prevailing view, the candidate enhances his or her electoral chances and by doing so can enhance the representation of constituency views. When a candidate chooses an ideologically extremist strategy, the constituency can enhance its representation by electing the opponent.

As Figure 4-7 indicates, the net result is a clear pattern whereby the most liberal House members represent the most liberal districts and the most conservative House members represent the most conservative districts. The horizontal axis represents constituency ideology, as reflected in the 1988 district presidential vote. It is reasonable to assume that district presidential voting in 1988 reflects ideology as well as partisanship. The vertical axis measures the representative's roll call liberalism using our usual index. Democratic and Republican members are both included. Note the strong positive correlation ($+.68$). Very pro-Bush and very pro-Dukakis districts get very conservative (Republican) and very liberal (Democratic) representation, respectively. In the middle of the partisan-ideological spectrum the partisan battle is fought. In these districts, either the Democrat or the Republican may win; but in either case the roll call ideology nicely reflects the gradient of the presidential vote.

Although Figure 4-7 shows a considerable amount of district-level ideological representation, we can also ask about the net ideological representation of the House. Specifically, is the House too liberal, too conservative, or just right in terms of the net taste of the American electorate? This is not an easy question to answer directly, because roll calls and voter preferences cannot readily be compared on a common scale. One way of estimating, however, is to consult voters' ratings of their own representatives. For instance, the National Election Study for 1990 asked respondents to rate themselves and to rate their representative on a seven-point ideological scale. A check of the responses shows an even balance: 14 percent saw their representative as more liberal than themselves, and 13 percent saw their representative as more conservative than themselves. The remaining 73 percent either declined to rate their representative or evaluated their representative's position to be the same as their own.

Figure 4-7 Roll Call Ideology (1989-1990) by 1988 District Presidential Vote

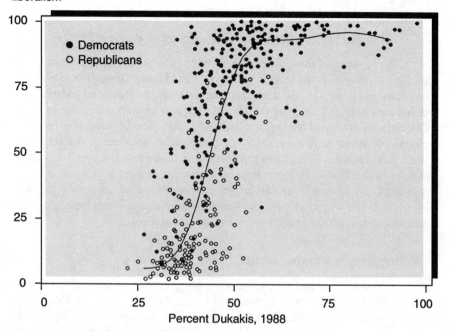

Ideological
liberalism

Democrats
Republicans

Percent Dukakis, 1988

Source: Compiled by the authors.

Note: Ideological scores are based on ratings by the American Conservative Union and Americans for Democratic Action; 0 = most conservative, 100 = most liberal.

But what if the American electorate were to desire electoral change from Congress? Ideological changes follow changes in the House's party composition, but, as we have seen, the forces behind these partisan changes do not involve any collective public desire for an ideological shift of direction.

Normally, the American electorate is rather static in its collective position on the ideological scale. But if the national electorate were to shift ideologically, could it get the House of Representatives to change with it? The likely answer is yes. The same forces that work at the constituency level to create representation would work at the national level to make the House responsive to a true ideological shift in the national mood. Because constituencies generally elect the candidate from the party most ideologically compatible with their views, an ideologically changed national electorate would elect a greater proportion of members from the more ideologically compatible party. Because local candidates tend to modify their ideological positions when the local constituency changes, candidates generally would tend to move in response to a national ideological drift. And because local candidates who are out of ideological step with their constituencies are the most likely to lose, candidates who are out of step with a national ideological movement would be more likely to lose. All these processes would ensure that an ideologically changed electorate would get an ideologically changed Congress.

House-Senate Differences in Electoral Representation

The Framers of the Constitution intended the Senate to be an elite chamber, isolated from the democratic demands of the House. Regardless of how well or poorly this intention has been realized, there are fundamental constitutional differences between the two chambers. The Seventeenth Amendment to the Constitution abolished the most remarkable difference by providing for direct election of senators. (Before 1918, state legislatures selected their state's senators.) Still, each state elects two senators rather than a number based on population, as in the House. Because senators have staggered six-year terms, they are free from the never-ending campaigns of representatives, who serve two-year terms. And, for the most part, the constituencies senators represent are larger and much more diverse than are those of representatives.

Election Results and the Senate

In terms of national election results, the party composition of the Senate reflects the same forces that determine the party composition of the House. The division between Democrats and Republicans in the Senate is influenced by presidential coattails in presidential years and the bounce to the out party at midterm. The Senate's partisan division responds more sluggishly to national trends, however, because only one-third of the senators are up for reelection in any election year.

As a general rule, Senate elections are more competitive than House elections. Senate races with no incumbent are almost always sharply contested by both parties. And an incumbent senator who seeks reelection has a considerably greater chance of defeat than does an incumbent House member who seeks reelection. Incumbent senators are reelected at about a 78 percent rate, compared with 92 percent for House incumbents. One reason for closer Senate races is that the statewide Senate constituencies rarely are dominated by one political party as the smaller House districts are. Another major factor is that Senate races attract strong challengers. A senator is far more likely than a House member to face a politically seasoned and well-financed election opponent. Finally, senators seem unable to obtain the strong incumbency advantage that House members enjoy, averaging no better than a few percentage points as their average sophomore surge. (Evidently senatorial challengers find it easier to generate visibility for their campaigns than do challengers to House incumbents.) Senators do perform well electorally, compared with nonincumbent candidates of their party, but this is because they had to be good candidates in the first place to survive electoral combat.

Although reelection to the Senate is more difficult than reelection to the

House, senators need to run only once every six years. The appropriate comparison of electoral security is a comparison of survival rates over the same period of time. Measured over six years, House members seeking reelection have a survival rate of approximately 78 percent—about the same as the re-election rate for senators.[20]

Thus the six-year term for senators almost exactly offsets the greater incumbency advantage of the House. Senators run less often but at more risk. The long-run survival rates for the two houses would appear to be roughly equal.

Representation: The House and Senate Compared

Is the Senate any less responsive to popular opinion than the House? Six-year terms would seem to provide senators with ample freedom from electoral concerns, except for the final run up to election. And when senators decide to be attentive to their electorates, their diverse constituencies make full representation difficult.

Like House members, senators are sensitive to constituency opinion, with each party's most conservative senators found in conservative states and most liberal members found in liberal states. In terms of partisan politics, the states are competitive enough that each party has a chance at a Senate seat. As a result, many states send both a Republican and a Democrat to the Senate, a pattern that baffles some observers. In a pattern similar to that of the House, senators from states in which the other party dominates often are ideologically atypical for their party.[21]

State Populations and the Senate

Although states vary considerably in population, each has two senators. California's twenty-five million people get the same number of senators as Alaska's one-half million. To some extent, this constitutionally designed "malapportionment" favors political conservatism. Indeed, state population correlates rather strongly $(+.34)$ with our measure of citizen liberalism, based on pooled CBS News/New York Times surveys.[22] Small, politically conservative states enjoy an extra margin of representation.

During the Reagan years, when the Republicans enjoyed a six-year Senate majority, the Senate was clearly the more conservative chamber. One is tempted to attribute this senatorial conservatism to the Senate's overrepresentation of small states. But the movement of national political tides may be strong enough to overcome any conservative bias. In past decades, the Senate was often thought to be more liberal than the more provincial House of Representatives.

The Six-Year Term

Because House members face election every two years, for them the election campaign, and hence the need to consider the electoral consequences of their behavior, is immediate. For senators, the six-year term can provide some leeway. Voters—so it sometimes seems—are electorally myopic, forgetting what senators do early in their terms and remembering only what they do close to the election.

Whether or not this view of the electorate is valid, there is a good deal of evidence that senatorial roll call voting responds to the six-year cycle.[23] In the year or two before they must run again, incumbents move away from their party's extreme. Democrats inch in a conservative direction and Republicans edge over to the left. The purpose in each instance is to appeal to moderate voters.

Issues and Senate Elections

Because senators moderate their ideological positions as reelection approaches, they presumably have good reason to do so: senators must believe that moderation enhances their chance of electoral success. Earlier we saw evidence that House members are more likely to be reelected with moderate ideological positions. Is the same true for senators?

Candidates' policy positions affect their reelection chances. For the Senate, candidates do better if they avoid their party's ideological extremes. Gerald Wright and Michael Berkman estimated the effect of candidates' issue positions by comparing different pairings of ideological positions while statistically controlling for the effects of several constituency characteristics and attitudes.[24] They estimated that whether a Senate candidate represents the party's moderate wing or more extremist wing creates a difference ranging from 5 to 8 percentage points. This effect is similar to that observed for House elections.

Conclusion

Along with presidential elections, congressional elections provide citizens with their main opportunity to influence the direction of national policy. When elections bring about significant changes in the party composition of Congress, we can be fairly confident of two things. One is that the new Congress will have a different ideological cast. Democratic and Republican candidates for House and Senate stand for quite different things. Therefore, electing more Democrats or more Republicans increases the likelihood of policy movement in the ideological direction of the advantaged party. Ironically, the second is that such changes stem less from the electorate's desire for new policy directions than from factors such as presidential coattails or the automatic slump the presidential party experiences at midterm.

Where we see the electorate's influence on policy direction is in the relationship between constituencies and their elected representatives. In terms of ideological direction, individual House and Senate members respond to their constituencies. In turn, ideological direction matters when constituencies decide which candidates they will elect and which they will not.

As individuals, voters know little about their representatives and only a bit more about their senators. House challengers are almost invisible, and only a portion of the electorate has even a modest amount of information about senatorial challengers. Nevertheless, this uninformed electorate manages to bring about very substantial levels of policy representation. The electorate is much more capable in the aggregate than as individual voters. It is as though all our individual ignorance and misinformed judgments cancel out, so that average perceptions and judgments are responsive to what the candidates say and do. The result is a more representative Congress than the electorate sometimes seems to deserve.

Notes

1. Gary C. Jacobson and Samuel Kernell, "Strategy and Choice in the 1982 Congressional Elections," *PS* 15 (Summer 1982): 426; John A. Ferejohn and Randall L. Calvert, "Presidential Coattails in Historical Perspective," *American Journal of Political Science* 28 (February 1984): 131.
2. Stephen Ansolabehere, David Brady, and Morris Fiorina, "The Marginals Never Vanished?" Research paper 970, Graduate School of Business, Stanford University, December 1987.
3. Philip E. Converse, "The Concept of the Normal Vote," in *Elections and the Political Order*, ed. Angus Campbell, Philip E. Converse, Warren E. Miller, and Donald E. Stokes (New York: Wiley, 1966), 9-39.
4. Ferejohn and Calvert, "Presidential Coattails."
5. Angus Campbell, "Surge and Decline: A Study of Electoral Change," in *Elections and the Political Order*, 40-62.
6. See also Robert S. Erikson, "The Puzzle of Midterm Loss," *Journal of Politics* 50 (November 1988): 1011-1029.
7. Alberto Alesina and Howard Rosenthal, "Partisan Cycles in Congressional Elections and the Macroeconomy," *American Political Science Review* 83 (June 1989): 373-398.
8. Robert S. Erikson, Norman R. Luttbeg, and Kent L. Tedin, *American Public Opinion: Its Origins, Content, and Impact*, 4th ed. (New York: Macmillan, 1991), chap. 3.
9. James S. Stimson, *Public Opinion in America: Moods, Cycles, and Swings* (Boulder: Westview Press, 1991).
10. Robert S. Erikson and Gerald C. Wright, "Voters, Candidates, and Issues in Congressional Elections," in *Congress Reconsidered*, 4th ed., ed. Lawrence C. Dodd and Bruce I. Oppenheimer (Washington, D.C.: CQ Press, 1989), 91-117.
11. John L. Sullivan and Robert E. O'Connor, "Electoral Choice and Popular Control of Public Policy: The Case of the 1966 House Elections," *American Political Science Review* 66 (December 1972): 1256-1268; Gerald C. Wright, "Elections and the Potential for Policy Change in Congress," in *Congress and Policy Change*, ed. Gerald C. Wright and Leroy Rieselbach (New York: Agathon Press, 1985), 94-119.
12. On voters' awareness of candidates, see Thomas E. Mann, *Unsafe at Any Margin: Interpreting Congressional Elections* (Washington, D.C.: American Enterprise Institute, 1978); Donald E. Stokes and Warren E. Miller, "Party Government and the Salience of Congress," *Public Opinion Quarterly* 26 (Winter 1962): 531-546; and Barbara Hinckley, *Congressional Elections* (Washington, D.C.: CQ Press, 1981), chap. 2.
13. Gary C. Jacobson and Samuel Kernell, *Strategic Choices in Congressional Elections*, 2d ed. (New Haven: Yale University Press, 1983).
14. Robert S. Erikson, "Estimating the Incumbency Advantage in Congressional Elections" (Paper presented at the annual meeting of the Political Methodology Society,

St. Louis, July 1990). For earlier estimates of the growth of the incumbency advantage, see Robert S. Erikson, "Malapportionment, Gerrymandering, and Party Fortunes in Congressional Elections," *American Political Science Review* 66 (December 1972): 1234-1245; David Mayhew, "Congressional Elections: The Case of the Vanishing Marginals," *Policy* 6 (Spring 1973): 295-318; Albert D. Cover and David R. Mayhew, "Congressional Dynamics and the Decline of Competitive Congressional Elections," in *Congress Reconsidered*, 2d ed., ed. Lawrence C. Dodd and Bruce I. Oppenheimer (Washington, D.C.: CQ Press, 1981), 62-82; and John A. Ferejohn, "On the Decline of Competition in Congressional Elections," *American Political Science Review* 71 (March 1977): 166-176.

15. On the lack of evidence of a strong anti-incumbent mood in 1990, see John Alford and John Hibbing, "The 1990 Congressional Election Results and the Fallacy That They Embodied an Anti-Incumbent Mood," *PS* 25 (June 1990): 217-219.

16. Robert S. Erikson, "Is There Such a Thing as a Safe Seat?" *Polity* 8 (Summer 1976): 613-632.

17. Anthony Downs, *An Economic Theory of Democracy* (New York: Harper and Row, 1957), chap. 8.

18. Robert S. Erikson, "The Electoral Impact of Congressional Roll Call Voting," *American Political Science Review* 65 (December 1971): 1018-1032; Gerald C. Wright, Jr., "Candidates' Policy Positions and Voting in U.S. House Elections," *Legislative Studies Quarterly* 3 (August 1978): 445-464; Robert S. Erikson and Gerald C. Wright, Jr., "Policy Representation of Constituency Interests," *Political Behavior* 1 (Summer 1980): 91-106.

19. Gary C. Jacobson, "The Effects of Campaign Spending in Congressional Elections," *American Political Science Review* 72 (June 1978): 469-491.

20. Amihai Glazer and Bernard Grofman, "Two Plus Two Plus Two Equals Six: Tenure of Office of Senators and Representatives, 1953-1983," *Legislative Studies Quarterly* 12 (November 1987): 555-563.

21. Robert S. Erikson, "Roll Calls, Reputations, and Representation in the U.S. Senate," *Legislative Studies Quarterly* 15 (November 1990): 623-642.

22. Gerald C. Wright, Robert S. Erikson, and John P. McIver, "Measuring State Partisanship and Ideology with Survey Data," *Journal of Politics* 47 (May 1985): 479-489. For more on population disparity and other explanations for House-Senate differences in ideology, see Bruce I. Oppenheimer, "Split-Party Control of Congress, 1981-86: Exploring Electoral and Apportionment Explanations," *American Journal of Political Science* 33 (August 1989): 653-669.

23. Richard F. Fenno, Jr., *The United States Senate: A Bicameral Perspective* (Washington, D.C.: American Enterprise Institute, 1982); Martin Thomas, "Electoral Proximity and Senatorial Roll Call Voting," *American Journal of Political Science* 29 (February 1984): 96-111.

24. Gerald C. Wright and Michael Berkman, "Candidates and Policy in United States Elections," *American Political Science Review* 80 (June 1986): 253-283.

5

The Misallocation of Resources in House Campaigns

Gary C. Jacobson

The 1990 congressional elections took place amid deep public discontent with national politics and politicians. Anger at Congress—simmering from the savings and loan debacle, a pay-raise fracas, and assorted scandals—was brought to a full boil by the squabbling over deficit-reduction legislation during October of the election year. Public approval of Congress approached its historic minimum, and vote for the average House incumbent dropped to its lowest level since 1974. Yet neither the public mood nor the vote swing against incumbents had much effect on the makeup of Congress. Only 15 of 406 House incumbents (9 Republicans and 6 Democrats) and but a single Senate incumbent (a Republican) met defeat in the general election.[1]

Why was neither party able to cash in on the public's anger? How did all but a handful of incumbents survive? The proximate answer is that turnover was modest because so many contests had been settled long before October 1990. They had been settled months earlier, when potential challengers made final decisions about whether to run for Congress, and during the summer, when campaign contributors and party officials were deciding where to invest their money, time, and effort. For these decisions yielded remarkably few challengers capable of exploiting the public's antigovernment mood.

Three elements create a formidable challenge: a good reason for voters to desert the incumbent, an acceptable alternative to the incumbent, and sufficient resources to acquaint voters with the first two. All three elements are necessary, none alone is sufficient, and all are interrelated. They are interrelated because potential candidates and contributors act strategically. Good candidates attract money, and the promise of money attracts good candidates. But both candidates and contributors also respond to the prospect of winning, which depends, in turn, on the availability of issues and arguments that might erode the incumbent's support. Without exploitable issues, even attractive, well-financed challengers can expect to make little headway. And more to the point for 1990, even incumbents who are vulnerable on the issues can count on reelection if they avoid challengers with the skill, appeal, and resources to exploit their vulnerability.[2]

By election day 1990 issues had emerged that offered considerable leverage against incumbents of both parties, but few incumbents faced challengers equipped to take advantage of them. Eighty-four House incumbents had no major party opponent at all, the most in any election since the 1950s (five senators were also unopposed in the general election). Those House incumbents who were opposed faced the least experienced set of challengers in any postwar election. Experience in elective office is a useful, albeit crude indicator of a challenger's quality.[3] Only 10 percent of the 1990 challengers had ever held any elective public office, a figure more than two standard deviations below the postwar mean of 21 percent. Predictably, little money flowed into the coffers of such an unpromising lot; they raised and spent less in real terms than any set of challengers since 1974.

More than a few postelection analyses argued that the 1990 election underlined the decisive power of incumbency because so few incumbents were defeated, even though the public's disdain for government was at a peak.[4] Considering the weakness of their opposition, however, the overall performance of House incumbents was unimpressive. Incumbents did much worse on election day than the quality and vigor of their opponents warranted.[5]

What accounts for the extraordinary weakness of both parties' challengers in the 1990 House elections? Part of the explanation surely lies in timing. The events that most angered voters took place late in the election year; national conditions earlier in the election cycle had been far less encouraging to challengers of either party. In addition, the prospect of redistricting after 1990 probably deterred some ambitious, career-minded candidates: Why endure the hard work, expense, and risk to one's political future by mounting a full-scale campaign to capture a district that may change drastically, or even disappear, before 1992? Wiser to wait a couple of years until the new boundaries are in place and the new districts, along with anticipated retirements, produce a bumper crop of open seats.[6]

But deeper currents are also at work. The dearth of vigorous challenges in 1990 continues a decade-long trend. The essential elements of a competitive House campaign—high-quality candidates, adequate campaign resources—have become narrowly concentrated in the most promising districts. A shrinking minority of districts get all the action; a growing majority are completely written off. The result is that opportunities of the kind that arose in 1990 are inevitably missed. This trend has continued despite the increasingly sophisticated information-gathering capacities of parties and other political organizations. Indeed, I shall argue that better information has led to a less productive allocation of campaign resources than ever. Moreover, this trend is but part of a broader decline in the efficiency with which campaign resources are distributed. My purposes in this essay are to examine the trends in campaign resource allocation, to try to account for them, and to show how they reduced both parties' ability to exploit unanticipated openings in 1990. The first step is to understand what distributive efficiency means in this context and why it is so difficult to achieve.

Allocating Campaign Resources: The Problem

Considered from a party's collective perspective, the chief electoral goal is to win as many seats as possible.[7] In the abstract, it makes little difference to the party which individual candidates win, only that the maximum number do. The party's individual candidates, on the other hand, care very much who wins. Although one can imagine a situation in which winning is of little value unless one is part of a majority (and thus a situation in which candidates would be willing to risk their own election to improve their party's chances), this is emphatically not true of congressional elections. The fruits of victory are by no means monopolized by the majority. The chief concern of candidates, then, lies in maximizing their own likelihood of winning. The party's collective interests are decidedly secondary.

This leaves the party and its candidates with conflicting preferences about the distribution of campaign resources. The party would, if it could, deploy personnel and campaign money in a way that promises to maximize the number of seats it wins. It would redirect resources from districts where it is strong to districts where it is weak up to the point at which the expected marginal gains (in seats won) among the latter are matched by the expected marginal losses among the former. The party's most promising prospective candidates, on the other hand, prefer to run when and where their chances of winning are highest, and its more affluent candidates resist giving up campaign funds if doing so would increase their risk of defeat. Losing candidates take little solace from a larger aggregate victory for their party.

The outcome of this conflict depends on who controls the resources. The greater the share controlled by the party, and the freer its officials are to pursue collective ends, the more efficiently it can allocate resources and the more seats it should therefore win. The more resources controlled by its stronger candidates, the less efficient the allocation and the fewer seats the party should win. In congressional elections, the main practical issues concern how candidates are recruited, how much campaign money is controlled by national party campaign committees, and how successfully these committees avoid domination by the party's incumbents. On every count, the parties face severe obstacles to efficiency.

Parties have little to say about the distribution of talented candidates. Congressional candidates are volunteers. Despite the considerable effort national party officials have made in recent years to discover and recruit promising candidates, party organizations have too little influence on politicians' career prospects to have much effect on their career choices.[8] Except in rare instances, parties do not make nominations; that authority is exercised by voters in primary elections, and it is not unusual for the candidate preferred by national party officials to lose. The persistent tradition of localism in American electoral politics precludes bringing in talented candidates from outside the district—a practice common in Great Britain. The parties thus have little control over the quality of candidates they field.

The parties also control only a small portion of campaign funds. Most campaign money is contributed by private individuals directly to the candidates. Political action committees (PACs) are the second largest source of campaign funds. In 1990 PACs supplied 23 percent of the money raised by Senate candidates and 42 percent of the money raised by House candidates who made it to the general election. Direct party contributions make up but a tiny share—on the order of 1 percent—of the money raised by congressional candidates. Parties may also spend money on behalf of candidates, however, and this coordinated spending, as it is called, may add up to a significant amount of money (the legal maximum was $50,280 in 1990 House races). Still, the total party contribution to congressional campaign finances is relatively small. In 1990 House and Senate candidates raised $428 million, of which $145 million came from PACs; national party committees contributed $4 million directly to candidates and spent about $26 million on their behalf.[9]

Most PACs (and many individual contributors) pursue objectives that readily lead them to ignore or subvert the collective electoral interests of the parties. For many business corporations, labor unions, and trade associations, the PAC is merely an aid to traditional lobbying for narrowly focused economic interests. Policy goals are specific and immediate: a tax break, regulatory relief, a higher price support, a loan guarantee. Money is given not so much to affect the outcome as to gain access and curry favor with whoever winds up in a position to serve or damage immediate economic interests. PACs of this kind contribute to sure winners who do not need the money, to members of both parties who sit on committees dealing with legislation they care about, and to newly elected members after the election. Even if a PAC is hostile to a member, it may be reluctant to give offense by supporting a challenger. This explains why PAC contributions as a whole so strongly favor congressional incumbents (illustrative data are presented in Figures 5-2 and 5-3 in the next section). Money spent on incumbents almost certain to win or on other candidates after they have won is, from the party's perspective, wasted.

Even campaign money controlled by party organizations may by wasted on secure incumbents if officeholders dominate the allocation process. The parties' House and Senate campaign committees are led by members chosen by party caucuses and thus must be at least somewhat responsive to the demands of their colleagues. In recent years these committees have managed to keep safe incumbents at bay and have been far more generous to challengers than have other donors. About 40 percent of their assistance still goes to officeholders, but most of it helps to shore up vulnerable members—a perfectly reasonable party strategy.[10] The parties' chief problem is that they control only a small portion of the money that flows through campaigns and so can contribute only a small increment of efficiency to its allocation.

These structural conditions may explain why campaign resources are distributed inefficiently, but they do not explain why the distribution has become increasingly skewed and, I believe, less productive over the past decade. The problem, from the parties' perspective, is twofold: more money going to incumbents and, among nonincumbents, an increasing concentration of resources in fewer and fewer districts. These are separable though related problems. The first has attracted the most attention, but the second may be equally detrimental to a party's ability to win seats from the opposition.

Overinvesting in Incumbents

The most widely noted inefficiency in the distribution of campaign resources is the overinvestment in campaigns of House incumbents.[11] Changes over time on both the demand and supply sides have only made things worse. Put simply, a large and growing portion of campaign money goes to sitting members with no electoral need for it. Much of it is not even spent on the campaign. In 1990, for example, after spending $163 million, House incumbents still had $77 million in unspent funds on hand at the end of December. The total spent by all challengers in 1990 was only $37 million, less than half the amount incumbents had left in their coffers.[12] For a party pursuing additional House seats, money unspent is money wasted.

Furthermore, the amount of money that incumbents spend on campaigns has become increasingly detached from objective electoral necessity. Incumbents have always spent reactively, in proportion to the quality and financing of their opposition. But their pattern of reaction has evolved in two important ways since accurate figures on campaign spending have become available, as the regression equations in Table 5-1 demonstrate. The equation treats the incumbent's spending as a function of the challenger's spending, the challenger's previous political experience, a trend term (to measure change over time), and interactions between the trend term and the other two variables. The coefficient on the trend term (1972=0, 1974=1, ... 1990=9), added to the intercept, shows that the average incumbent's spending more than quintupled over the period without regard to the challenger's spending or quality. In 1972 the average House incumbent would have spent about $70,000 (in 1990 dollars) against an inexperienced challenger who spent no money at all; by 1990 that figure had grown to $362,000. Second, the coefficients on the other variables show that the effects of the challenger's quality and spending have grown over the two decades; members respond more extravagantly to a challenge of a given strength than in the past. An incumbent would have spent, on average, an additional $.48 for every dollar spent by a challenger in 1972, $.71 in 1990; the incumbent would have spent an additional $30,000 if opposed by an experienced challenger in 1972, $87,000 in 1990.

As a consequence of these changes, the average amount (in constant dollars) spent by House incumbents nearly tripled between 1972 and 1990. Of even greater importance, though, is the fact that spending by the average challenger has remained comparatively flat. The stark contrast between the two trends is evident in Figure 5-1. Observe that the average House challenger's spending has fallen during the past decade; in 1990 it was 33 percent lower than in the peak year, 1982, leaving it only 12 percent higher than it had been in 1972. Because the marginal returns on campaign spending are much greater for challengers than for incumbents, a parallel increase in spending by both sides would have favored challengers.[13] This has not happened.[14] A vastly disproportionate share of the growing pot of campaign money has gone to incumbents and candidates for open seats. Notice that spending by candidates for open seats

Table 5-1   Reactive Spending by House Incumbents, 1972-1990

	Coefficient[a]	Standard error
Dependent variable		
Incumbent's spending		
Independent variables		
Intercept	69,927	8,149
Trend[b]	32,406	1,464
Challenger's spending	.479	.043
Challenger's spending X trend	.026	.007
Experienced challenger[c]	30,290	14,935
Experienced challenger X trend	6,258	3,059
R^2	.45	
Number of cases	3,228	

Note: Spending is expressed in 1990 dollars.

[a] All coefficients are significant at p<.05 or better.

[b] The trend is 1972=0, 1974=1,... 1990=9.

[c] Experienced challengers are those who have previously held elective public office.

increased as steeply as spending by incumbents; I will have more to say about this later.

Clearly, House incumbents' demand for campaign funds has boomed over the past decade. Developments on the supply side have also contributed to the increasing overinvestment in incumbents. As the financial role of PACs has grown, so has their bias in favor of officeholders. Since 1972 the share of House campaign contributions supplied by PACs has risen from 14 percent to more than 40 percent of the total, while the challengers' share of PAC dollars (in contested elections between incumbents and challengers) has fallen from nearly 30 percent to less than 10 percent. Figure 5-2 displays these trends graphically. The bias in the distribution of PAC funds has increased much more steeply than the bias in the distribution of total expenditures, as Figure 5-3 demonstrates. In 1972 the average incumbent outspent the average challengers 1.6:1; in 1990 the ratio was 3.9:1. In 1972 PACs favored incumbents over their challengers 2.6:1; by 1990 that ratio had grown to 10.1:1.

What accounts for these shifts in demand and supply? Growth on the demand side is at first glance something of a paradox, because the reelection rates of House incumbents have never been higher.[15] But the paradox dissolves when we recognize that members respond to subjective rather than to objective electoral risk, that risk is recurrent, and that uncertainty pervades electoral politics.[16]

Incumbents raise campaign money as much for insurance as for use in the campaign. The pursuit of a long-term career induces members to gird for the worst imaginable rather than the typical electoral threat. Uncertainty also breeds caution, and the grounds for uncertainty have widened in recent years. Party loyalty has diminished, leaving electorates less predictable, more volatile; a good

Figure 5-1   Campaign Spending by House Candidates, 1972-1990

Expenditures

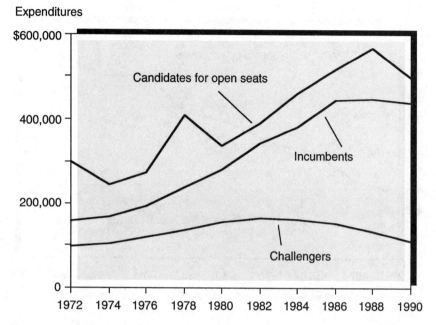

Source: Compiled by the author from Federal Election Commission data.

Note: Expenditures are expressed in 1990 dollars.

showing in one election has become a weaker guarantee of success in the next than it was in the past.[17] When a colleague's vote can drop more than 20 points from one election to the next—this has happened to at least one incumbent in every election for two decades—members take notice. The lesson was driven home again in 1990, when thirty-seven incumbents saw their vote decline by more than 10 percentage points from 1988 (another twelve incumbents went from running unopposed to winning less than 60 percent of the vote); most of them did not even face serious opposition.[18]

Other social and political developments have also spurred incumbents' demand for a reassuringly ample campaign account. Increasingly, politicians must take responsibility for tending their own careers because no one else can or will.[19] The electoral world in which they operate has become more difficult to understand or manage politically than ever before. Constituents are harder to find, harder to read, and harder to reach—and probably harder to please.

Modern American life does not nurture stable communities with dense social or political networks. The archetypal suburban couple with two careers, lengthy commutes, and a bewildering array of options for using whatever free time is left to them forms an elusive target for political messages. Increasingly, House candidates in competitive races feel compelled to use television, even

Figure 5-2 PAC Contributions to House Candidates, 1972-1990

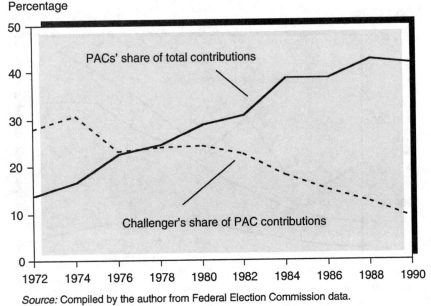

Source: Compiled by the author from Federal Election Commission data.

though it is expensive, often wasteful (you pay for the entire audience, although your constituents may constitute only a fraction of it), and cluttered with thousands of other messages competing for attention, for there is no other practical way to reach many voters. The principal alternative, direct mail, is also costly. Add to these expenses the price tag for consultants, accountants, lawyers, and everything else that goes into a full-dress House campaign, and it becomes obvious why such a campaign is so expensive. Moreover, the institutional flowering of party and political action committees has raised the stakes by greatly expanding the resources that could be mobilized against a member who has the misfortune to become a target.[20] Knowing this, incumbents raise far more money than they usually need as a hedge against the possibility, however remote, that they will find themselves facing a challenge that calls for an all-out response.

Contributors, PACs in particular, have been willing to fill the demand. We have already noted that many PACs distribute their funds to facilitate access to lawmakers and so naturally favor incumbents. But this does not explain why the share going to incumbents has increased so dramatically over the past decade. One possible explanation may be dismissed immediately: a change in the mix of PACs. Although the mix has indeed changed—corporate and nonconnected PACs (those without organizational sponsors) have expanded their activities faster than labor PACs[21]—a growing bias toward incumbents appears in all categories. Between 1978 and 1990 the incumbents' share of corporate PAC funds rose from 78 percent to 96 percent; of trade association funds, from 80 percent to 95 percent; and of nonconnnected PAC funds, from 37 percent to 83 percent.

Figure 5-3 House Incumbents' Advantage in Campaign Spending
and PAC Contributions, 1972-1990

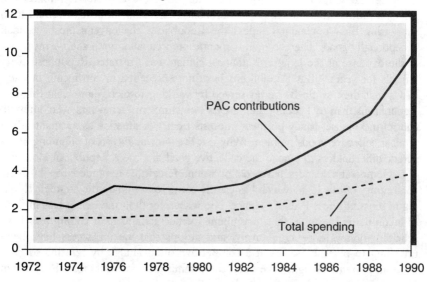

Ratio, incumbents to challengers

Source: Compiled by the author from Federal Election Commission data.

Note: The ratio is computed by dividing the amount for incumbents by the amount for challengers.

Labor PACs have also followed the trend (the incumbents' share has risen from 79 percent to 86 percent over these years), though in their case, unlike the others, the trend is more irregular and falls short of statistical significance. The growing bias of PACs toward incumbents reflects not a change in the mix of PACs but a change in their strategic behavior.

PACs may be arrayed along an implicit dimension according to their goals and the appropriate strategies for pursuing them. At one end are PACs that have narrowly defined economic interests, care only about access, and thus overwhelmingly favor prospective winners—mostly incumbents. At the other end are PACs with broad ideological agendas that seek to shape policy by maximizing the number of seats held by people in sympathy with their views. They support promising nonincumbent candidates (with "correct" views) and invest most of their money in close races, where campaign spending might actually influence the outcome. Such PACs support only those incumbents who are on their side and in electoral trouble. In this behavior, they resemble parties, though such PACs may, on occasion, subvert collective party interests when their objectives conflict with the party's simple goal of winning the seat.[22]

Most PACs care about both gaining access and electing sympathetic members and so pursue a strategy mix that puts them somewhere between these poles.

Their pattern of contributions varies according to their reading of political winds. They avoid offending incumbents who seem certain to win, but they are willing to switch to more congenial challengers whose prospects seem unusually promising. The best examples are the business-oriented PACs, who prefer Republicans in principle but continue to support incumbent Democrats (or at least refrain from supporting their opponents) unless the Republican challenger's prospects look exceptionally good. The common corporate preoccupation with short-term policy at the expense of the long-term political climate has frustrated Republican party officials for years.[23] But Republicans have not succeeded in convincing business PACs that they would be better served by working to elect more right-thinking Republicans than by keeping their access to incumbent Democrats, who, after all, control the House. Many business interests treat this situation as a variant of the familiar collective goods problem: Why risk the individual costs of offending Democratic officeholders to pursue the collective good of a more Republican House?

Democratic leaders have, on occasion, forcefully reminded the business community of this logic, which has clearly come to dominate the strategic thinking of most business PACs.[24] Hence, one reason for their increasing bias in favor of incumbents is simply that incumbent Democrats and their committees have solicited money more aggressively, and groups that vie for access have been unwilling to put themselves at a competitive disadvantage by refusing to give. More important, though, have been the diminishing prospects for a Republican House majority and for individual Republican challengers.

Business PACs were most generous to nonincumbent Republicans in 1980, joining the Republican tide that put Ronald Reagan in the White House, gave Republicans control of the Senate, and added thirty-three Republicans to the House, leaving them just twenty-six seats short of majority control. But prospects for a Republican House majority quickly faded when a deep recession cost the party twenty-six House seats in 1982, and it managed to add back only thirteen seats despite Reagan's landslide reelection in 1984. After 1984 no PAC could seriously doubt that Democrats would continue to run the House through at least the rest of the decade, and accommodation became the prudent strategy. Accommodation also made sense because the quality, and hence the prospects, of Republican House challengers declined throughout the decade. The proportion of Republican challengers with prior experience in elective office dropped from 19 percent in 1980 to less than 10 percent in 1988 and 1990.

The pattern of contributions from business PACs documented in Table 5-2 reflects these assessments. In the peak year for Republican challengers, 1980, corporate PACs gave 36 percent of their funds to incumbent Democrats and 20 percent to Republican challengers; by 1990 the equivalent figures were 49 percent and 3 percent. PACs in the Federal Election Commission's "Trade/ Membership/Health" category altered their distribution of funds similarly. Small wonder that Republican leaders, once the most zealous defenders of PACs, now propose to ban them outright.[25] They mistake effect for cause, however; their basic problem is not unfriendly PACs so much as a dearth of candidates with prospects sufficiently bright to justify a major investment of PAC dollars.

Table 5-2   PAC Contributions to Democratic Incumbents and Republican Challengers, 1978-1990 (in percentages)

Type of PAC	1978	1980	1982	1984	1986	1988	1990
Corporate							
Democratic incumbents	35	36	32	43	45	50	49
Republican challengers	16	20	9	11	3	3	3
Trade/Membership/Health							
Democratic incumbents	36	39	34	47	46	52	52
Republican challengers	14	17	8	7	3	2	2

Source: Norman J. Ornstein, Thomas E. Mann, and Michael J. Malbin, *Vital Statistics on Congress, 1989-1900* (Washington, D.C.: Congressional Quarterly, 1990), Table 3-18; "PAC Activity Falls in 1990 Elections," Federal Election Commission News Release, March 31, 1991, 3.

Narrowing the Range of Competition

The growing overinvestment in House incumbents is a familiar story, but another trend is at least as important in reducing the turnover in House seats during the 1980s. The essential elements of a serious effort to take a House seat from the other party—high-quality candidates, adequate campaign resources— are increasingly concentrated in the most promising districts. Both parties have moved toward a sharply bifurcated distribution of campaign effort, leaving fewer campaigns in the range where sudden tides can make a difference and surprises can happen. In part, this change takes the form of an increasingly disproportionate investment in open seats, but it appears as well in the increasingly skewed distribution of resources among challengers' campaigns. More and more districts are written off totally; only a small and diminishing minority of contests involve a high-quality challenger with the financial resources for a full-scale campaign.

Contests for Open Seats

Open House seats have always attracted a greater investment of campaign resources than seats held by an incumbent, for the obvious reason that a party's best chance for taking a seat from the opposition comes when it is no longer defended by an incumbent. During the past two decades the parties have taken 24.7 percent of the open seats held by the other party, compared with only 4.5 percent of seats defended by incumbents. In recent years, however, the financial gap between campaigns for open seats and those challenging incumbents has grown markedly. We have already noted the growing difference in average expenditures between challengers and candidates for open seats (recall Figure 5-1). The trend is similar, though not as pronounced, if we confine the comparison to open seats currently held by the other party, as Figure 5-4 indicates. In the four most recent elections, candidates for open seats held by the other party have spent an average of about $400,000, compared with less than $140,000

Figure 5-4   Campaign Spending by Nonincumbent House
Candidates, 1972-1990

Expenditures

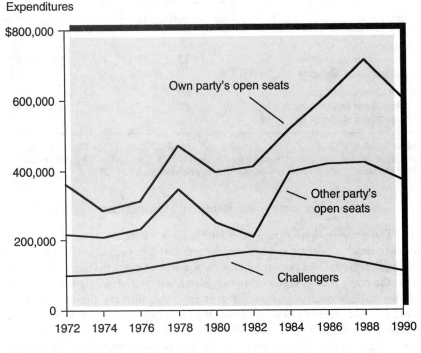

Source: Compiled by the author from Federal Election Commission data.

Note: Expenditures are expressed in 1990 dollars.

spent by the average challenger (the most money is spent by candidates for open
seats currently held by their party).

It is no accident that changes in the aggregate quality of candidates recapit-
ulate these trends. The percentage of experienced candidates representing both
the in party and the out party in contests for open House seats has grown
steadily, if irregularly, throughout the postwar period (see Figure 5-5). No trend
is evident in the aggregate quality of challengers for seats held by incumbents
until the early 1980s; but in each successive election from 1984 to 1990, the
number reached a new low. All three trends reached their furthest extent in
1990, when the proportion of experienced candidates for open seats reached
record highs (57 percent of out-party candidates, 80 percent of in-party candidates), while the proportion of experienced challengers fell to 10 percent.
Clearly, experienced candidates—who have a significantly greater likelihood of
winning in either context[26]—have been flocking to open seats while ducking
contests with incumbents. Because the relationship between campaign money
and candidate quality is reciprocal, it is not surprising that the trends in aggregate experience and campaign spending track one another so well. Both patterns

Figure 5-5 Experienced Nonincumbent House Candidates,
1946-1990

Percentage experienced

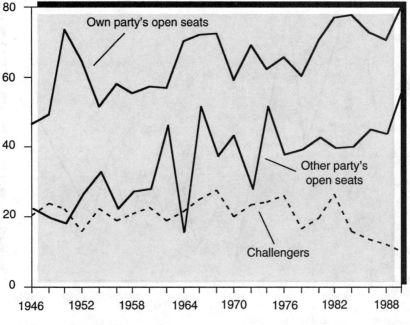

Source: Compiled by the author.

show that serious nonincumbent candidacies are increasingly confined to contests for open seats.

The Bifurcation of Challenges

Resources have also become concentrated in progressively fewer of the campaigns against incumbents. A growing number of incumbents face no major party opposition at all. Figure 5-6 displays the proportion of unopposed incumbents in postwar general elections. The dramatic drop in the early 1960s signaled the arrival of two-party competition in the South. After that, the percentage of unopposed incumbents drifted irregularly upward until the early 1980s, then took off steeply, reaching by the end of the decade levels not seen since the 1950s.

Among the challengers who have appeared, experience in elective office is increasingly rare (Figure 5-5), and a growing number of challengers have been so poorly funded that the incumbent was effectively unopposed. From 1982 through 1990 not a single challenger who spent less than $125,000 (in 1990 dollars) won. The proportion of challengers whose spending fell below this threshold increased steadily over the decade, from 56 percent in 1982 to 75

Figure 5-6 Unopposed House Incumbents, 1946-1990

Percentage unopposed

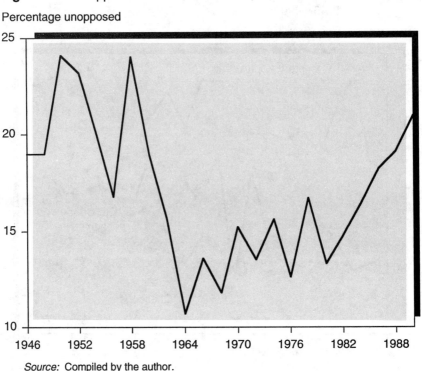

Source: Compiled by the author.

percent in 1990. At the same time, the proportion of challengers who spent at least $300,000—a conservative threshold for a serious challenge in the 1980s— declined from 18 percent in 1982 (and a peak of 21 percent in 1984) to 12 percent in 1990. If we include unopposed incumbents in the denominator, the proportion of incumbents who were financially or literally unopposed in general elections increased from 63 percent to 80 percent, and the proportion facing serious opposition declined from 15 percent (17 percent in 1984) to less than 10 percent, across the decade. The percentage of challengers spending in the middle range—between $125,000 and $300,000—also declined, from 27 percent to 13 percent (from 23 percent to 10 percent if uncontested seats are included in the denominator).

The distribution of campaign funds to challengers has grown more skewed over time. A standard measure of distributive inequality is the Gini index, which takes values between 0.0 (complete equality) and 1.0 (complete inequality: one gets everything, the rest, nothing).[27] The Gini index for challengers' campaign expenditures rose from .61 in 1972 (and a low of .59 in 1974) to .72 in 1990, when the top 10 percent of spenders accounted for more than half of all spending. The distribution of PAC contributions to challengers, always more skewed than total spending, has also become more unequal. The Gini index for PAC

Table 5-3   Spending by House Challengers, 1972-1990 (Tobit analysis)

	Coefficient[a]	Standard error
Dependent variable		
Challenger's spending		
Independent variables		
Intercept	−30,637	30,864
National swing[b]	7,686	1,109
Trend[c]	−33,265	5,016
Challenger's vote, t−1[d]	3,360	862
Challenger's vote, t−1 X trend	1,051	142
Experienced challenger[e]	34,263	17,829
Experienced challenger X trend	12,066	3,903
Sigma^2	3.6e10	9.9e8
log likelihood	−36,636	
Number of cases	2,949	

Note: Spending is expressed in 1990 dollars.

[a] All coefficients except the intercept are significant at p<.05 or better.

[b] The national swing is the change in the percentage of votes won by the challenger's party nationally from the previous election.

[c] The trend is 1972=0, 1974=1, ... 1990=9.

[d] The challenger's vote, t−1 is the challenger's percentage of the two-party vote in the same district in the previous election.

[e] Experienced challengers are those who have previously held elective public office.

contributions to challengers grew from .74 to .84 over the period. In 1990 more than 72 percent of total PAC contributions went to the top decile of recipients.[28]

The Tobit equation reported in Table 5-3 offers a multivariate depiction of what has occurred.[29] The equation estimates the challenger's total spending as a function of the national swing (a measure of national tides), a trend term, the marginality of the incumbent, the challenger's experience, and interactions between the trend term and these two latter variables. The positive and significant coefficients on the two interaction terms indicate that the effects on spending of a closer contest in the previous election or the presence of an experienced challenger have grown over time. For example, we can calculate from the coefficients that a challenger whose party's candidate won 35 percent of the vote in the previous election would have been predicted to spend about $87,000 in 1972 and $118,700 in 1990, an increase of 36 percent.[30] The same figures for a challenger whose party's candidate's previous vote was 45 percent would be $120,600 and $247,000, respectively, an increase of 105 percent. With a previous party vote of 25 percent, the challenger's expected spending would drop from $53,300 in 1972 to nothing at all in 1990. A challenger who had previously held elective office could expect to raise and spend an additional $34,300 in 1972, an additional $142,900 in 1990.

Increasingly, then, campaign money is concentrated in the most promising

Figure 5-7 Campaign Spending by Competitive and Uncompetitive
              Challengers, 1972 - 1990

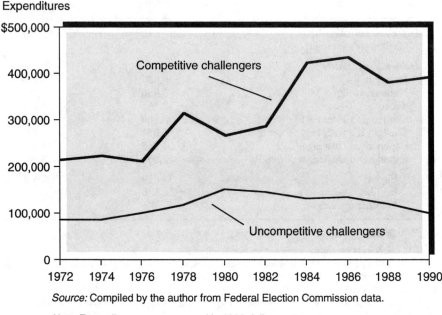

Source: Compiled by the author from Federal Election Commission data.

Note: Expenditures are expressed in 1990 dollars.

districts. Challengers among the shrinking fraction whose circumstances attract
generous contributions have continued to raise competitive sums; their spending
has grown at about the same rate as incumbent spending, while that of all other
challengers has stagnated, as Figure 5-7 indicates. It shows that money available
to challengers who have experience in elective office and who are running
against the most marginal incumbents (those who won with less than 60 percent
of the two-party vote in the previous election) has increased to the point that
such candidates typically spend about $400,000 on the campaign; that is, they
are as well funded as candidates for open seats held by the other party (all
figures are adjusted for inflation; 1990=1.00). Spending by the remaining challengers has declined steadily since 1980. And the proportion of challengers in
the first category has fallen sharply, from an average of 16 percent in 1972-1982,
to 10 percent in 1984-1988, and to an all-time low of 6 percent in 1990.

What accounts for these trends? In part, they reflect a straightforward expression of the same strategic thinking that has led to the overinvestment in
incumbents. The same logic that leads contributors to avoid antagonizing incumbents makes them skittish about supporting any challenger who has less than
exceptional prospects; thus, contributors invest only in the most promising challengers, otherwise putting the money not contributed to incumbents into contests for open seats, where there is no incumbent to risk offending. The pursuit
of access also justifies investment in only the most promising nonincumbents;

access to losers is worthless. Hence, as the access strategy has become prevalent, resources have been concentrated in progressively fewer contests.

The emphasis on access reinforces the view of many PAC managers that their performance is measured by how consistently they pick winners.[31] For groups seeking more than access—that are also hoping to improve the climate for their interests by electing a larger number of sympathetic members—this is a perverse standard, because it induces PAC officials to pad their records by playing it safe. With no penalty for missed opportunities—for withholding donations from losers who might have won had their campaigns found adequate financing—PAC officials have no incentive to risk investing in long-shot challengers. Risk taking among business PACs has also been discouraged by their experience with Republican challengers in the early 1980s, when the party oversold some of its candidates.[32] Interest groups that typically prefer Democrats have also found reason to play it safe. The Democratic majority already includes most of the seats to which the party could reasonably aspire, and it was not hard to justify a defensive posture—protecting incumbents—at a time when Republicans seemed to have a lock on the White House and were narrowing the gap in party identification.

The Decision to Run

Many of the same considerations that deter contributors from investing in challengers also deter ambitious, career-minded politicians from taking on incumbents. But other factors enter here as well. Imagine a simple schematic model of a potential candidate's decision calculus: Run when the value of winning, plus the value of running, minus the cost of running, discounted by the probability of winning is positive; otherwise, stay out. In recent years changes in all four variables in the model have probably worked against a potential candidate's decision to run.

Certainly, the personal cost of running has grown. The investment of time and energy (devoted as much to fund raising as to campaigning) required to run an all-out campaign is daunting. A serious House candidacy has become a full-time job—with plenty of overtime. Most nonincumbent candidates have to finance the campaign's start-up costs while forgoing income from their regular work for many months.[33] Candidates must also be prepared to sacrifice much of their privacy and family life. And the job, if won, comes with high fixed expenses (residences in both the Washington, D.C., area and the home district, for example) and a lower salary than most winners could earn with less effort in the private sector.

It is more difficult to discern changes in the benefits of running apart from the prospect of winning, because such payoffs tend to be psychological and hence are difficult to observe. But people are probably less inclined to view a congressional campaign as an opportunity to advertise their law practice or insurance or real estate business than they once did.

It is also conceivable that the value of holding a House seat has declined. Capitol Hill was not a happy place during the Reagan-Bush years. Divided gov-

ernment made legislating difficult; huge deficits stifled domestic initiatives; comity gave way to partisan guerrilla warfare; public scorn for the Washington
crowd was never higher. The list could go on. All of these things probably made
the job more frustrating, less attractive than ever. Moreover, with the federal
government in retreat, the states have taken on a large share of the important
political problems. It is not so surprising that career politicians hesitate to abandon what have come to be well-paid positions in fully professionalized state
legislatures to run for Congress.[34]

Whether or not the objective odds against knocking off an incumbent have
lengthened, subjective estimates of the likelihood of a successful challenge have
certainly declined. If potential candidates simply consider the frequency of successful challenges, the news is discouraging. Yet it is difficult to determine how
much the objective odds against winning have lengthened, because the frequency of formidable challenges has declined in parallel with the frequency of
successful challenges. Observe from the first column in Table 5-4 that the proportion of incumbents who lost fell sharply in the 1980s. But most of the change
is accounted for by a drop (of 55 percent) in defeats of incumbents who did not
face experienced challengers. The decline in the success rates of experienced
challengers is considerably more modest (24 percent), and the change across
decades does not achieve statistical significance. The success rate of experienced
challengers to marginal incumbents (those whose previous vote was below 60
percent) fell even less (15 percent). Again the decline falls far short of statistical
significance. Thus, the success rate for challengers with experience in office,
particularly those who oppose marginal incumbents, has fallen only modestly
(and the decline may be explained by the fact that the 1980s included only one
election with a strong partisan tide—1982—while the other decades included
two). But such challenges have certainly become less common; notice the shrinking number of cases over these decades in the two right-hand columns; in both
instances the decline is statistically significant (p<.001).

Finally, the most astute potential challengers would be deterred by the
growing disinclination of contributors to invest in their campaigns. They are fully
aware that, without at least several hundred thousand dollars to spend, their
prospects are bleak indeed. And when potentially formidable challengers are
deterred, so, naturally, are campaign contributors. The result of all these trends
is an increasingly polarized distribution of campaign effort. Convergent expectations of high-quality candidates and campaign contributors engender highly competitive campaigns in a small subset of highly promising districts; the same process writes off a growing number of districts entirely.

Missed Opportunities:
The Perils of Prediction

By the logic of this argument, the converging expectations of potential
candidates and contributors are, to a large degree, self-fulfilling. A cause judged
to be hopeless induces behavior that guarantees it will remain hopeless (viable

Table 5-4   House Incumbents Defeated in General Elections
(in percentages)

		Incumbents defeated		
Decade[a]	Total	No experienced challenger	Experienced challenger[b]	Experienced challenger, marginal seat[c]
1950s	6.2	3.8	15.8	19.9
	(1,963)	(1,570)	(393)	(277)
1960s	5.8	2.9	15.8	22.0
	(1,960)	(1,518)	(442)	(277)
1970s	5.7	3.6	13.6	17.6
	(1,902)	(1,483)	(413)	(227)
1980s	3.3	1.7	12.0	16.9
	(1,983)	(1,675)	(308)	(160)
F-statistic	6.7	4.7	1.0	0.8
Probability	<.001	<.001	.39	.50

Note: The number of cases from which the percentages were calculated are in parentheses.

[a] Decades are defined by reapportionment cycles; for example, the 1950s include 1952 through 1960, the 1980s include 1982 through 1990.

[b] Experienced challengers are those who have held elective office.

[c] Marginal seats are those won with less than 60 percent of the major party vote in the previous election.

challengers and contributors stay away). Belief that an incumbent is vulnerable leads to decisions that produce the kind of vigorous challenges that make for close contests which incumbents sometimes lose. The problem is that expectations are shaped by information that is far more unreliable than is commonly recognized. Indeed, the illusion of accurate information, based on polling and other research now carried out by potential candidates, party committees, and even some PACS, breeds overly cautious behavior and missed opportunities.

To understand why, consider an analogous dilemma from classical statistics. Statisticians recognize two types of errors that one can make when deciding whether to reject or accept a hypothesis: rejecting a true hypothesis (conventionally termed a type I error) and accepting a false hypothesis (a type II error).[35] The dilemma arises because the risks of type I and type II errors are inversely related; one can reduce the chances of making one type only by increasing the chances of making the other. Suppose the hypothesis is "this incumbent can be defeated by a vigorous challenge." The more careful potential candidates and contributors are to avoid type II errors—investing in a losing challenge—the more liable they are to type I errors—not investing in challenges that could succeed if enough resources were invested.

One might think that better intelligence should decrease both types of errors. But if the residue of uncertainty remains high, a decrease in errors does not necessarily follow. Some incumbents—those involved in scandals or those whose grip on the district is manifestly tenuous—are obvious targets, even without careful research. Other potentially vulnerable incumbents, on the other hand, may show little outward sign of weakness, and it may be exceedingly difficult to assess their vulnerability until voters know something about the alternative. Early in the campaign season, most incumbents will enjoy an enormous lead in polls against almost any potential challenger, if only because so few voters know anything about anyone but the incumbent. Discouraging research results for potential challengers may be taken far more seriously than their predictive accuracy warrants.

It is by no means always easy to determine which incumbents are ripe for plucking. In 1990, for example, only seven of the fifteen incumbents defeated in November, and only fourteen of the forty-three who received less than 45 percent of the vote, were identified as "vulnerable" or "potentially vulnerable" in Congressional Quarterly's July review of the campaigns.[36] Even projections published in October of the election year, when CQ puts out a special edition covering all the campaigns, regularly overlook emerging upsets. Of the ninety-six incumbents defeated in general elections from 1980 through 1990, eight had been classified by CQ in October as "safe," seventeen were listed as "incumbent favored," and twenty-six as "leaning to the incumbent." The rest had "no clear favorite" (forty-two) or leaned toward the challenger (three). Altogether, CQ thought the odds favored 53 percent of the losing incumbents but only 3 percent of the winning challengers (the rest were tossups). This is not because CQ does not know its business; on the contrary, CQ's ability to gather and evaluate information about House campaigns is unsurpassed. The point is that even the best informed observers overlook some vulnerable incumbents because a significant and irreducible measure of uncertainty surrounds House elections.

Outside events are an important source of this uncertainty. In the course of campaigns things happen, nationally and locally, that can alter the odds dramatically. Republican incumbents became increasingly vulnerable as unemployment continued to rise through the summer and into fall of 1982.[37] Prospects improved sharply for challengers of both parties in 1990, when, in late October, Congress handed them a potent issue by raising taxes and cutting benefits to consummate an unpopular deficit-reduction deal with the president.[38] Had the Iran-contra affair been exposed a month or two earlier rather then immediately after the 1986 election, Democratic challengers would certainly have enjoyed a windfall (Reagan's approval rating dropped twenty-four points in response to the scandal).[39] Politicians could—and did—anticipate that the economy would be in recession in the fall of 1982, though the depth of the recession was probably unexpected. But the deficit deal and Iran-contra were surprises.

Galvanizing local issues arise, and personal scandals and blunders occur unpredictably during the campaign. For example, in North Carolina in 1986, Democrat David Price's successful challenge was given an important boost when the incumbent's clumsy attempt to mobilize Christian fundamentalist supporters backfired.[40] In Rhode Island in 1988 Republican Ronald Machtley upset Democratic incumbent Fernand St Germain when the last-minute revelation of a Justice Department letter mentioning "substantial evidence of serious and sustained misconduct" on St Germain's part confirmed Machtley's central campaign theme.[41] The prospects of Rep. Pat Swindall, R-Ga., dropped sharply when it was revealed in mid-June of 1988 that he had accepted laundered drug money as a home loan; he was indicted in October and lost decisively in November.[42]

Unexpected events that favor challengers do not automatically endanger incumbents. Incumbents suffer real damage only when confronted by a challenger poised to take advantage of the windfall. If the challenger lacks the skill or resources to exploit an opening, the incumbent may lose votes but rarely the election. The eight challengers who defeated incumbents classified as "safe" in July 1990 spent an average of $348,000; five spent more than $300,000; only one spent less than $200,000 ($178,129). In the same election were fourteen challengers who won between 45.0 and 49.9 percent of the vote, gaining on average more than ten points over 1988, but who spent less than $200,000. This underfinanced group represents opportunities the parties missed. Even scandalous personal behavior may go unpunished in the absence of a plausible challenger. Robert Leggett, D-Calif., was reelected in 1976, even after he was exposed as a philanderer, forger, and alleged bribe taker. His challenger was an obscure retired state engineer who spent little money and believed that the election "was mostly up to God." [43]

The growing bifurcation of investment in campaigns to take seats from the other party, the increased incidence of type I errors that is the unavoidable byproduct of candidates' and contributors' growing obsession with avoiding type II errors, clearly reduce the potential for electoral change. The consequences are especially noticeable in the 1990 election, which juxtaposed exceptionally weak challengers with a strong, late-breaking swing against incumbents of both parties that reflected the public's disgust with budget politics. But the 1990 results are merely the inevitable result of a pattern that has been developing for a decade.

Prospects for Change

Neither party can be happy about wasting chances to pick up seats, but Republicans have special reason to be distressed. The status quo condemns them to permanent minority status in the House. Changes in PAC behavior have damaged Republican challengers more than Democratic challengers, because the Republicans' natural allies in the business PAC community have been far more reluctant to invest in challengers than have the Democrats' most loyal contributors, the labor PACs. The distribution of PAC funds is more skewed among Republican challengers (Gini index = .88 in 1990) than among Democratic challengers (Gini index = .78). Democratic House leaders have their own PACs, allowing them to use their fund-raising clout on behalf of Democratic challengers. More Republicans than Democrats were among the challengers who came close to victory in 1990 but were underfinanced and fell short.

The Republicans have enjoyed one major advantage for more than a decade—their party committees are much wealthier than those of the Democrats.

But their inability to derive any observable benefit from this advantage has led them in exactly the wrong direction. (Democratic committees have made the same mistake, but Democrats do not suffer from a continuation of the status quo.) Paul Herrnson notes with approval that

> over the course of the 1980s, the Hill committees greatly refined their ability to identify and participate in competitive races. In 1984, for example, each House campaign committee identified approximately one hundred "opportunity," or competitive races. Distinctions were made among these races, but party resources were not narrowly targeted.... Party resources were targeted more narrowly in ensuing election cycles.... In 1990, the DCCC [Democratic Congressional Campaign Committee] and the NRCC [National Republican Congressional Committee] each compiled a list of approximately forty "first-tier" races.[44]

Herrnson goes on to observe that "nevertheless, all four committees failed to allocate appropriate levels of resources in a few contests" in 1990 where their candidates' prospects proved better than expected.[45] Such mistakes inevitably increase with narrower targeting; a more productive strategy would target more contests, with the understanding that this would produce type II errors (money wasted on failed challengers) as the price of reducing type I errors (missed opportunities). The Democrats might justify narrow targeting by pointing to their limited resources; Republicans have no such excuse. The strategy adopted by the National Republican Congressional Committee in 1990—to "spend more money on fewer races and do so later in the election cycle"[46]—turned out to be exactly the wrong approach for taking advantage of opportunities that year.

The party committees presumably can learn from their strategic mistakes in 1990—if they recognize them as mistakes—but there are limits to what parties can do under the current laws to foster a more productive distribution of campaign funds. The maximum a party can put into a House campaign amounts to no more than 20 percent of what it takes, under most circumstances, to mount a full-scale challenge. Since parties can and do help direct PAC contributions, they might be able to improve somewhat the distribution of PAC funds as well. Considering the goals and strategies pursued by most PACs, however, parties are unlikely to achieve any major change in PAC behavior. Nor is there much prospect that parties can unilaterally improve the quality of their challengers. Despite more active national party recruiting in recent years, the quality of challengers has declined.

Some proposed changes in the laws governing campaign money could counteract the trends reviewed in this essay, though more by accident than by design. Various editorial writers, reform lobbies such as Common Cause, and their Democratic allies in Congress think campaign spending is out of hand and propose to limit it by law. The problem is not excessive campaign spending—competitive campaigns are unavoidably expensive—but underinvestment in potentially competitive districts. Limits on spending will help only if contributions that would have gone to surfeited incumbents are rechanneled into the campaigns of underfunded challengers. This rechanneling is by no means assured.

Spending limits are necessarily paired with some form of public subsidy, because the Supreme Court has deemed limits an infringement on free speech unless they are accepted "voluntarily" in return for public funds.[47] Indeed, much of the support in Congress for public funding stems from the desire to limit campaign spending. Any reasonable scheme of public subsidies—block grants, matching funds—would get more money into the hands of challengers and so would count as a distributional improvement; the down side is that unless the accompanying spending ceiling is set so high as to be almost pointless, challengers will have a harder time winning elections. Their average vote would increase, but their chances of winning would decline.[48] Spending limits, unless pegged at improbably high levels, are inherently detrimental to challengers, because most challengers need to spend a great deal of money to have any hope at all of overcoming the advantages incumbents enjoy before the first campaign dollar is spent.

PACs are another target of reformers. Proposals range from limiting the amount candidates may raise from PACs to banning them outright. Neither change is calculated to produce a distribution of campaign resources more productive of competition than the current system. Insofar as these changes would reduce funds available to challengers, they could make it even more difficult for challengers to win elections than it is now.

More promising are proposals to lift restrictions on the party committees. The parties have the greatest incentive to achieve a more productive distribution of resources (and party committees have, in fact, distributed their resources more efficiently than other contributors, though not as productively as they might). Furthermore, if PAC funds could be laundered (in a benign sense) through the parties, PACs that prefer a party's challengers but fear angering the other party's incumbents would have a solution to their strategic dilemma. The drawback is political: Republican committees raise much more money than their Democratic counterparts, and Democrats cannot be expected to vote themselves a major competitive disadvantage. In the long run, though, liberating the parties is the most promising solution to the problems examined in this essay.

Notes

1. Karlyn Keene and Everett Carl Ladd, "Public Opinion and Demographic Report," *American Enterprise* 2 (January-February 1991): 84; Gary C. Jacobson, "Divided Government, Strategic Politicians, and the 1990 Congressional Elections" (Paper presented at the annual meeting of the Midwest Political Science Association, Chicago, April 1990), 1.
2. Gary C. Jacobson and Samuel Kernell, *Strategy and Choice in Congressional Elections,* 2d ed. (New Haven: Yale University Press, 1983), 47-48; Gary C. Jacobson, *The Politics of Congressional Elections,* 3d ed. (New York: HarperCollins, 1992), 177.
3. Gary C. Jacobson, *The Electoral Origins of Divided Government* (Boulder: Westview Press, 1990), 50-57.
4. See, for example, Nancy Gibbs, "Keep the Bums In," *Time,* Nov. 19, 1990, 32-42.
5. Parameters from a model regressing the challenger's vote on the national swing, the previous vote in the district, campaign spending by the incumbent and challenger,

the quality of the challenger, and a trend term, estimated for 1972 through 1988 and applied to 1990, predict the average challenger to win 30.6 percent of the vote, much lower than the 35.5 percent the average challenger actually won. See Jacobson, "Divided Government," 4.

6. Ibid., 4-6.
7. The notion that rational politicians would pursue a "minimum winning coalition" does not apply; see Gary C. Jacobson, "Party Organization and Campaign Resources in 1982," *Political Science Quarterly* 100 (Winter 1985-1986): 604.
8. Paul S. Herrnson, "National Party Organizations and the Postreform Congress," in *The Postreform Congress,* ed. Roger H. Davidson (New York: St. Martin's, 1992), 55-57.
9. "1990 Congressional Election Spending Drops to Low Point," Federal Election Commission news release, Feb. 22, 1991, 7; Chuck Alston, "Those Who Needed It Least Often Got Campaign Help," *Congressional Quarterly Weekly Report,* Dec. 29, 1990, 4235.
10. Frank J. Sorauf, *Money in American Elections* (Glenview, Ill.: Scott, Foresman, 1988), 141-142.
11. See, for example, ibid., 155-161.
12. "1990 Congressional Election Spending Drops to Low Point," 7.
13. Gary C. Jacobson, *Money in Congressional Elections* (New Haven: Yale University Press, 1980), 136-157; Gary C. Jacobson, "The Effects of Campaign Spending in House Elections: New Evidence for Old Arguments," *American Journal of Political Science* 34 (May 1990): 334-362.
14. Alan I. Abramowitz, "Incumbency, Campaign Spending, and the Decline of Competition in U.S. House Elections," *Journal of Politics* 53 (February 1991): 48-49.
15. Jacobson, *Electoral Origins of Divided Government,* 38-39.
16. Richard F. Fenno, Jr., *Home Style: House Members in Their Districts* (Boston: Little, Brown, 1978), 13-18.
17. Jacobson, *Electoral Origins of Divided Government,* 15-23.
18. Most of these incumbents spent less than $100,000; no challenger spending less than $125,000 (in 1990 dollars) has won in more than a decade.
19. Alan Ehrenhalt, *The United States of Ambition: Politicians, Power, and the Pursuit of Office* (Washington, D.C.: Random House, 1991), 17-20.
20. Herrnson, "National Party Organizations and the Postreform Congress," 57-67.
21. Norman J. Ornstein, Thomas E. Mann, and Michael J. Malbin, *Vital Statistics on Congress, 1989-1990* (Washington, D.C.: Congressional Quarterly, 1990), 101.
22. In the 1984 Illinois Senate contest, for example, the National Conservative Political Action Committee supported a liberal Democrat against the moderate Republican incumbent on the ground that "the prospects are far less of Paul Simon, as a freshman Democrat, doing damage to the Western World than Chuck Percy as chairman of the Foreign Relations Committee." See Bill Peterson, "Strange Bedfellows in Illinois," *Washington Post National Weekly Edition,* June 11, 1984, 13.
23. Edward Handler and John R. Mulkern, *Business in Politics* (Lexington, Mass.: Lexington Books, 1982), 8-9.
24. Brooks Jackson, *Honest Graft: Big Money and the American Political Process* (New York: Knopf, 1988), chap. 4.
25. Chuck Alston and Glen Craney, "Bush Campaign-Reform Plan Takes Aim at Incumbents," *Congressional Quarterly Weekly Report,* July 1, 1989, 1648-1649.
26. Jacobson, *Electoral Origins of Divided Government,* 66.
27. Hayward Alker, Jr., *Mathematics and Politics* (New York: Macmillan, 1965), 36-42.
28. Regression analysis shows the upward linear trend of the Gini indices for both distributions to be statistically significant at $p < .01$.
29. G. S. Maddala, *Limited-Dependent and Qualitative Variables in Econometrics* (Cambridge: Cambridge University Press, 1983), 151-158. I perform Tobit rather than

regression analysis because it is the appropriate technique when the lower limit of values of the dependent variable is truncated at zero and many observations fall into this category; the coefficients may be interpreted the same way as regression coefficients.

30. These projections assume no swing to either party and an inexperienced challenger. The calculations are, for 1972, $35(3,360) - 30,673 = 86,927$, and for 1990, $35(9(1,051) + 3,360) - 9(33,265) - 30,637 = 118,643$. The other projections in this section are computed similarly.

31. Theodore J. Eismeier and Philip H. Pollock III, "An Organizational Analysis of Political Action Committees," *Political Behavior* 7 (1985): 196-197.

32. Jackson, *Honest Graft*, 77.

33. Clyde Wilcox, "'I Owe It All to Me: Candidate's Investments in Their Own Campaigns," *American Politics Quarterly* 16 (1988): 271-276.

34. Linda L. Fowler and Robert D. McClure, *Political Ambition: Who Decides to Run for Congress* (New Haven: Yale University Press, 1989), 99-100.

35. Statisticians actually state the problem in terms of the null hypothesis, but the analogy is clearer without this complication. See Thomas H. Wonnacott and Ronald J. Wonnacott, *Introductory Statistics*, 3d ed. (New York: Wiley, 1977), 255-256.

36. Dave Kaplan, "House Seats Ripe for Takeover Enliven Campaign Season," *Congressional Quarterly Weekly Report*, July 7, 1990, 2137-2139.

37. Jacobson, "Party Organization and Campaign Resources in 1982," 616.

38. Jacobson, "Divided Government," 6-9.

39. Harold W. Stanley and Richard G. Niemi, *Vital Statistics on American Politics*, 3d ed. (Washington, D.C.: CQ Press, 1992), 280.

40. Tom Watson, "A Year of Little Turmoil in House Elections," *Congressional Quarterly Weekly Report*, Nov. 8, 1986, 2843.

41. Peter Bragdon, "St Germain Out, but Incumbents Still Strong," *Congressional Quarterly Weekly Report*, Nov. 12, 1988, 3268.

42. Ibid.

43. David Johnston, "Leggett Likely to Win Despite Scandal," *Los Angeles Times*, Oct. 19, 1976, 3.

44. Herrnson, "National Party Organizations and the Postreform Congress," 58.

45. Ibid.

46. Chuck Alston, "Contest Raises Hard Questions About How NRCC Uses Funds," *Congressional Quarterly Weekly Report*, Dec. 1, 1990, 4001.

47. *Buckley v. Valeo*, 424 U.S. 1 (1976).

48. Abramowitz, "Incumbency, Campaign Spending, and the Decline of Competition," 52.

6

Personal and Partisan Advantage in U.S. Congressional Elections, 1846-1990

John R. Alford and David W. Brady

A great deal of the scholarly thinking about the contemporary House of Representatives holds that the need to be reelected is the dominant influence on its members. This need profoundly affects not only members' behavior but also the structure of the House and, more broadly, the nature of national politics and policy. Morris Fiorina argues that Congress funds and supports the Washington bureaucracy because the programs of various departments either serve the interests of constituents or are complex enough to require members' intervention in behalf of their constituents; both characteristics make members of Congress more needed and hence more reelectable.[1] David Mayhew points out that, in their attempt to ensure reelection, House members have structured the organization in a way that facilitates individual members' ability to (1) claim credit for service and projects in the district; (2) take positions on public issues that appeal to their constituents without having to bear consequences; and (3) advertise themselves to constituents so as to increase name recognition and thus electability.[2] The connecting thread in this argument is that House members' desire to be reelected causes them to structure the institution and its policy outputs in ways that do no harm to their reelection chances. And, in fact, incumbent representatives do get reelected at an impressively high rate—more than 95 percent in the 1980s—and their average margin of victory has increased substantially since 1965.[3]

This portrait of the House of Representatives is not without its critics. One point of view is that House members have always tried to serve their constituents; in the 1890s, for example, members from agricultural districts got themselves appointed to the Agriculture Committee and voted to increase the size of the Agriculture Department's budget. To counter this argument, we should point out that the research previously cited on the decline of competitiveness (that is, the success of incumbents) shows that incumbency as a dominant factor in House elections is a phenomenon of the mid-1960s and later.

If the incumbency phenomenon arose after 1965, the observation made by Fiorina and Mayhew about the House may well be correct; that is, Congress in the post-1965 period is more controlled than ever before by the ability of individual members to ensure their reelection. For the Mayhew-Fiorina interpretation to be plausible, at least two conditions must obtain: first, the incumbency factor must be a post-1965 phenomenon; and, second, individual members, not political parties, must exercise the greatest control over their electoral fate. We might call this second condition the decline-of-party condition. The weakening of political parties must be considered because the structure of the contemporary Congress and its policy outputs would be different if the United States had strong parties competing at the national level for majority status. The existence of strong parties implies that parties take definite stands on issues. One party, for example, might favor and implement budget constraints when elected, while the other would favor increased expenditures. Individual House members would be persuaded to act in the party's interest rather than their own. Under a stronger party system both the structure of the House and its policy outputs would be different.[4]

It seems clear that an important precondition for drawing reliable conclusions about the contemporary Congress entails determining when the incumbency factor arose as well as ascertaining the relative strength of partisan and individual electoral strength over time.

The Literature on Incumbency Advantage

The first study that specifically dealt with incumbency was Robert Erikson's 1971 article. After examining House elections from 1952 to 1960, Erikson concluded that, although incumbents had about a 2 percentage point advantage, most of the victory margin of incumbent candidates could be attributed to the strong party voting in their districts. In an update the following year, Erikson noted that his original findings might be time bound because in the 1966, 1968, and 1970 elections incumbency advantage had increased by about 3 percentage points.[5] David Mayhew, in his often cited 1974 article on the "vanishing marginals," argued that there had indeed been a sharp increase in incumbency advantage in the mid-1960s and this increase accounted for the decline in close (marginal) elections.

Since Erikson's discovery, a vast literature on incumbency advantage has appeared in the journals. Much of this literature has focused, inconclusively, on a search for the causes of the mid-1960s increase. The studies that focused on the degree of incumbency advantage have not changed the picture presented by Erikson and Mayhew, except to document the continuation of the trend into the 1980s. But because the focus has been almost exclusively on the post-World War II period, little is known about the long-term trend in incumbency advantage.

The only truly historical data on incumbency advantage in congressional elections are those provided in 1984 by James Garand and Donald Gross.[6] They present data on the competitiveness of House elections from 1824 to 1982; the trend over time in this data is quite interesting. They find, not unexpectedly, that incumbents always have had some advantage (the smallest advantage being about 3 percentage points in the late 1800s). This finding is in keeping with what one would have assumed, based on the general election literature; that is, many of the factors thought to contribute to incumbent success, such as name recognition, visibility, sources of campaign funding, campaign experience, district service, and voter inertia, are perennial characteristics of congressional elections.

The remainder of Garand and Gross's conclusions regarding the historical pattern of advantage are much less predictable and far more difficult to reconcile with the existing literature. Post-1965 levels of incumbency advantage are not uniquely high. Incumbency advantage was higher in the late 1920s than it was in the late 1970s. Even more surprising, the often cited increased advantage of the mid-1960s is, according to Garand and Gross, actually a decline from the general trend of increasing advantage that dates from 1894.

Reconciling these findings with the congressional election literature is a daunting task. Virtually all of the work of the past, both empirical and theoretical, concerning incumbency advantage is incompatible with Garand and Gross's observed mid-1960s decline. Even Garand and Gross are left with little to say about what might account for the trends they observed.

The difficulty of fitting the current literature to the historical trends provided by Garand and Gross may be the result of a problem fairly common in historical work, that of incommensurability—in other words, the comparison of two unlike sets of data. Garand and Gross have defined incumbency advantage as the margin by which incumbent winners outperform nonincumbent winners. It is not clear that this method translates in any direct fashion into what other studies of incumbency have measured, or even meant by, incumbency advantage. Thus Gross and Garand do not so much extend the current trend lines back into history as provide a largely novel series.[7] The task of placing the current incumbency data and literature in a historical perspective requires calculating measures of incumbency advantage for the pre-1946 period that are commensurable with the measures that are used in the existing literature to assess advantage, and the changes in that advantage, in the post-1946 era.

Data Collection

The scarcity of previous historical series in this area is no doubt due to the volume of data involved (there were more than ten thousand individual House elections in the post-World War II series alone), combined with the fact that the available machine-readable election returns do not include information on incumbency. Relying on published sources, we compiled data on House elections from 1846 to 1990; our data included the vote margins of the major-party candidates, specified whether an incumbent was running in the election, and, if so, gave the name of the party.[8]

The decisions we made concerning data coding bear mentioning. The vote results were coded as the percentage for the Democratic candidate, the percentage for the major opposition-party candidate (for the most part, this was the candidate of the Republican or Whig party, but occasionally it was the candidate of some other party—for example, the Populist party), and the percentage for the minor- or third-party candidates. Incumbency was coded in the same party categories as the vote. The election was coded as an open-seat election unless there was a previously elected member of the House running for reelection in the district that he or she had represented in the Congress immediately prior.

This fairly conservative definition of incumbency should yield a clear, stable picture of incumbency advantage regardless of its source.

Two major exclusions from the data set were necessary. The first election after a reapportionment of the House (1852, for example) was excluded from each decade because of the difficulty involved in assigning and interpreting incumbency status in areas where district lines have been shifted. Elections in which a candidate ran without major-party opposition, though included in the original data set, were excluded from the computed trends. Whether a measure is based on average vote or interelection vote shift, the inclusion of unopposed election results will bias any arithmetic measure of central tendency. This sort of exclusion is common to most of the incumbency studies.[9]

Incumbency in the House

The simplest measure of incumbency advantage is the mean share of the two-party vote earned by incumbents seeking reelection. Because the average share of the two-party vote for major-party candidates in open seats is always 50 percent (100 percent divided by 2), the average vote share for incumbents can be compared implicitly or explicitly to 50 percent. If we found that the mean vote for incumbents in a given election was not significantly higher than 50 percent, we would conclude that incumbents had no particular advantage over nonincumbents. Figure 6-1 presents the average incumbent share of the two-party vote, which is computed by election year from the major-party means. The mean share of the vote for Democratic incumbents and the mean share for Republican incumbents is computed separately; then the average of these two means is computed without regard to the number of observations on which each is based. This procedure yields a general measure of incumbent margin unbiased by the effects of a party tide in any given election.

The trend over time, presented graphically in Figure 6-1, is broadly consistent with the pattern reported by Garand and Gross. A general upward trend is evident throughout, with the series low coming in 1848 at 55.0 percent. The upward trend accelerates in the late 1800s, with temporary abrupt surges upward in 1904 and 1906 and in the 1920s. Indeed, the 1926 high point of 66.7 percent is not exceeded until 1986, when average incumbent vote rises above 68 percent. Unlike Garand and Gross, however, we do find a sharp upward trend after 1964, and the sustained high levels of advantage in the 1970s and 1980s are unprecedented in the series. Thus the post-1950 portion of our data, while at odds with the findings of Gross and Garand, is fully consistent with the remainder of the existing incumbency literature.

Incumbent Marginality

Another simple and widely used measure of incumbency advantage is the degree to which incumbent districts fall outside some arbitrary marginal range. The issue of marginality has been closely intertwined with the incumbency lit-

Figure 6-1   Average Incumbent Vote Share, House Elections
with Major-Party Opposition, 1846-1990

Percentage of vote

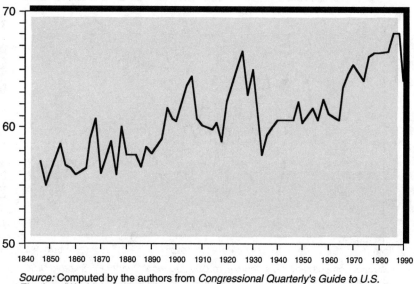

Source: Computed by the authors from *Congressional Quarterly's Guide to U.S.
Elections* (Washington, D.C.: Congressional Quarterly, 1985), and *Congressional
Quarterly Weekly Report,* various issues.

Note: No data are shown for the first election following the decennial census.

erature, beginning with Mayhew's investigation of the vanishing marginals.[10]
The figures for the proportion of districts in which the incumbent's share of
the two-party vote fell in the marginal (45-55 percent) range are presented in
Figure 6-2.

The pattern here is consistent with that of incumbent vote share (Figure
6-1). The declining marginality of incumbents is clearly not a new phenomenon.
Though somewhat erratic at times, the general trend has been one of declining
marginality since the 1848 high point of 60.6 percent of incumbent districts in
the marginal range. The low point is the 1988 election, when the proportion of
marginal incumbent districts drops to an extremely low 6.6 percent. Beyond the
overall trend, several other patterns are notable. The 1920s again are distinct, as
they were in Figure 6-1, for the degree of incumbent advantage: the 1926 low of
14 percent marginal was not reached again until 1968, when the proportion
marginal dropped to 11.7 percent, and as recently as 1980 the contemporary
proportion marginal has been higher (16 percent) than it was in 1926.

Looking only at the pattern since World War II, the numbers presented in
Figures 6-1 and 6-2 are entirely consistent with those in the current literature on
incumbency. Average incumbent vote share, which had been stable in the 60-62
percent range from the early 1940s through 1964, jumped upward sharply in

Figure 6-2 Percentage of Incumbents with Marginal Vote Shares,
             All House Elections with Major-Party Opposition, 1846-1990

Percentage of vote

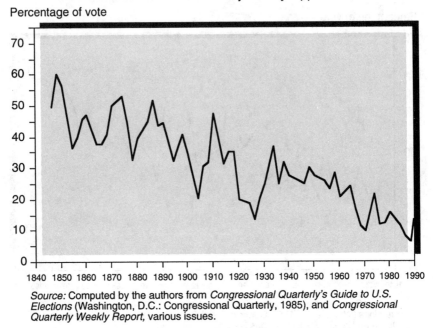

1840 1850 1860 1870 1880 1890 1900 1910 1920 1930 1940 1950 1960 1970 1980 1990

Source: Computed by the authors from *Congressional Quarterly's Guide to U.S. Elections* (Washington, D.C.: Congressional Quarterly, 1985), and *Congressional Quarterly Weekly Report,* various issues.

Note: Marginal vote share is defined as 45-55 percent of the two-party vote.

1966, and by 1976 was stabilizing in the 66-68 percent range, an increase of about 6 percentage points. Marginality, stable in the 25-30 percent range in the 1946-1964 period, dropped sharply in 1966, and by the late 1970s was in the low teens. Both patterns clearly contradict the Garand and Gross findings regarding the post-World War II period.[11]

Although the post-1950 data in Figure 6-1 fit well with the current literature, the earlier trends are more difficult to explain. Much of what is thought to explain the high contemporary levels of incumbency advantage, such as the role of television in campaigns, massive federal domestic spending, rapidly expanded use of the frank, new home styles, and constituency service, is of little use in explaining the broader pictures. The mid-1920s rise in advantage, for example, seems unlikely to be accounted for by any of these variables. Before we discredit any current explanations for their inability to explain similar past periods, however, we must look a bit more closely at the possibility that the similarity of the 1920s to the 1970s is more apparent than real.

The problem in comparing the 1920s with the 1970s is that the measures we have used so far do not sort out personal incumbency advantage from party advantage. A hypothetical example should make this point clear. Consider a midwestern congressional district in which the distribution of the vote is 58 percent Democratic and 42 percent Republican. The Democratic candidate wins elections with that exact vote share—58 percent. Imagine that a major automobile manufacturer buys up farmland in the district and builds a new factory employing thousands of union auto workers who are predominantly Democratic. Under these new conditions the average Democratic share of the vote reaches 65 percent. When we look at the average vote of incumbent House members, it will appear that the incumbent has increased his or her margin of victory when in fact it is the party that has increased its share of the vote.

Contrast this case with one in which a Democrat in a district similar to the one above wins a first election contest with 58 percent of the vote. Over the next three or four elections this representative works hard to be reelected—provides voters with services, claims credit for projects, advertises, and increases name recognition, thereby adding another 7 percentage points to his or her vote total. In terms of Figures 6-1 and 6-2, the 65 percent for the second incumbent will look just like the party-produced 65 percent in the first example. Yet a very important difference exists: in the second case there is a personal incumbency advantage that is not present in the first case. The Fiorina-Mayhew interpretation of the contemporary Congress rests on representatives having this kind of personal incumbency advantage rather than a purely partisan one, and the supposed effect of incumbency advantage on the institution of Congress derives specifically from the contradistinction between personal and party advantage. To discover whether a personal incumbency advantage exists, we must measure electoral results in a way that separates out the personal advantage factor.

Personal Incumbency Advantage

Early studies of incumbency advantage developed two parallel measures to isolate personal electoral advantage: sophomore surge and retirement slump. In each measure the personal advantage of incumbency is taken to be the difference between a party's vote share in an open-seat contest (one in which no incumbent is running) and the vote margin of an incumbent of that party in an immediately adjacent election. For example, a Republican incumbent runs for reelection in 1948, wins 58 percent of the vote, and retires before the 1950 election, creating an open seat. In the 1950 election a new Republican candidate wins with 56 percent of the vote; this member runs for reelection in 1952 and captures 59 percent of the vote. The 1948-1950 pair of elections produces a 1950 retirement slump estimate of -2 percentage points (the 1950 open-seat margin of 56 percent minus the 1948 preretirement margin of 58 percent). The 1950-1952 pair of elections produces a 1952 sophomore surge estimate of $+3$ percentage points (the 1952 first incumbent reelection margin of 59 percent minus the 1950 open-seat margin of 56 percent).

This approach to measuring incumbency advantage provides two benefits. By focusing on a single district and a set of adjacent elections, it controls for district characteristics. By determining the difference between an incumbent performance and an open-seat performance, the measurement removes from gross incumbency advantage that portion attributable to partisan advantage, as reflected by the party's performance in an open-seat contest. The remainder is the net personal advantage enjoyed by the incumbent, above and beyond that which comes from the partisan or party organizational strength of the district itself. It is this concept of personal incumbency advantage that most of the incumbency literature, and the related work in the congressional literature, implicitly turns on.

The data in Figure 6-3 depict sophomore surge and retirement slump in the House from 1846 to 1990.[12] In each case, the value for a given election year is derived by computing the mean slump or surge value separately for each party; then, as before, the average of these two means is computed without regard to the number of observations on which each is based. As noted above, this procedure removes the biasing effect of a party tide.

Any doubt as to the historically unique nature of incumbency advantage in the post-World War II era should be put to rest by the data in Figure 6-3. Before 1945 there is little to indicate any, even short-term, personal advantage to incumbency. Were there such an advantage, we would expect sophomore surge to be positive and retirement slump to be negative. Before 1945 such a configuration occurs in only eight of thirty elections (27 percent of the time, compared with an expected 25 percent of the time attributable purely to chance), while after 1945 it occurs in twelve of the fifteen elections. Moreover, slump and surge before 1945 are never both in the expected direction for any adjacent pair of elections.

If we use a modestly more rigorous test for the existence of personal incumbency advantage—that is, both slump and surge in the expected direction and both equaling or exceeding their respective standard errors (which is not a stringent test by usual statistical standards)—the pattern is even more distinct. This standard is not met even once until 1966, and in every election since that the magnitude of both slump and surge has been more than twice their standard errors. Personal incumbency advantage, the fluctuations of which figure so prominently in the congressional literature since 1971, scarcely predates that literature.

Ironically, this discovery brings the literature on incumbency advantage full circle. In his original 1971 article, Erikson presented the first quantitative assessment of incumbency advantage and concluded that the conventional wisdom of a considerable incumbent advantage was incorrect. The importance of this finding was quickly eclipsed by Erikson's own finding that incumbency had suddenly risen to levels that were, somewhat belatedly, in line with the conventional wisdom.[13] Our analysis suggests that Erikson's original conclusion was correct and remains significant. Moreover, even the modest levels of advantage that he found in the 1950s vanish when we move back just one decade. All of the numerous advantages that accompany incumbency yielded no electoral advantage to the incumbent until sometime after 1950.

An important implication of this historical pattern concerns what Nelson Polsby called the institutionalization of the House. Polsby's seminal work

Figure 6-3 Sophomore Surge and Retirement Slump, All House
Elections with Major-Party Opposition,1846-1990

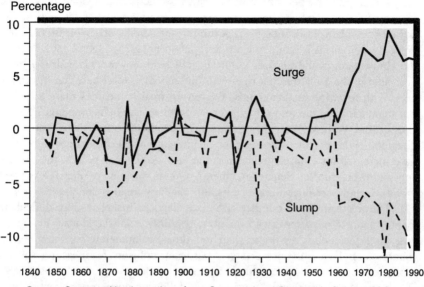

Percentage

Source: Computed by the authors from *Congressional Quarterly's Guide to U.S. Elections* (Washington, D.C.: Congressional Quarterly, 1985), and *Congressional Quarterly Weekly Report,* various issues.

Note: No data are shown for election years ending in 2 or 4.

showed that at about the turn of the century (1890-1910) the House of Representatives became a career for its members.[14] Specifically, the average length of service in the House increased, leadership positions became routinized—meaning that longer service was necessary before a member could advance—and housekeeping tasks, such as deciding contested elections, were done on a nonpartisan basis. In sum, the origins of the contemporary House are to be found in the House of the late nineteenth to early twentieth century. Although increases in the partisan advantage enjoyed by incumbents may have been associated with this shift, however, there is no indication that the hallmark of the modern House—substantial personal incumbency advantage—was in any way associated with these changes.

The data suggest that a second, much more contemporary, change in the House, perhaps along the lines of the Fiorina-Mayhew view of the modern Congress, must have taken place in the years just after World War II. Individual members seeking reelection may well have restructured the House's organization and policy to enhance their own electoral standing in their districts, rather than their party's standing. Although our work does not prove this theory, it does establish the initial condition necessary for the theory to be true.

Incumbency in the Senate

To this point we have discussed Congress, while presenting data only on the House of Representatives. We turn now to a consideration of the patterns in Senate incumbency advantage. In several 1980 studies of congressional elections, the consensus is that a greater electoral advantage to incumbency exists in the House than in the Senate.[15] Our concern here, however, is with the trend over time in the Senate rather than with differences in level between the chambers. With regard to Senate trends, Warren Kostroski concludes that "the postwar trend has been toward even greater safety for senatorial incumbents." Joseph Cooper and William West, using data that are more recent than Kostroski's, disagree: "Whereas the advantage of incumbents in elections does appear to have increased for House members in the late 1960's and 1970's, the reverse appears to be true for Senate members." Others, including Albert Cover and David Mayhew, are not willing to conclude that any trend is definite.[16]

The relatively small number of Senate elections makes it more difficult to identify short-term patterns with the same certainty as for the House. In a given year House elections are more than ten times as numerous as their Senate counterparts. This difference creates a particular difficulty for measures such as sophomore surge and retirement slump, which depend on a small subset of all elections (those immediately preceding and following open-seat elections). Any stable estimate of Senate patterns requires some aggregation of elections. We have chosen to aggregate by three-election triplets (see Figure 6-4). As we did with the House data, we computed each slump and surge separately by party and averaged them irrespective of the number of observations to remove the effects of party tides. Figure 6-4 begins with the election of 1920, since that was the first reelection opportunity for the class of 1914, the first to be directly elected.

The patterns over time for the Senate are quite similar to those for the House over the same period. If we use the same standard we applied earlier of both surge and slump in their respective expected directions, only two of seven election triplets before 1962 meet this standard, while all five of the triplets since 1962 exhibit the expected pattern. Again, as in the House, personal incumbency advantage in Senate elections is a post-1960 phenomenon. The magnitude of the advantage in the Senate, however, is much lower than that found in House elections, where slump and surge are typically 3 or 4 percentage points higher. Because senators generally have larger and more heterogeneous constituencies, in both population and geography, this lesser advantage is not unexpected. Much of the explanation offered earlier for rising personal advantage in the House depends on a fairly close relationship between individual members and their constituencies.

Origins of Incumbent Safety

Four reasons have been cited prominently in the literature for the rise of the personal incumbency factor in House elections: (1) congressional district lines

Figure 6-4 Sophomore Surge and Retirement Slump in the Senate
for Three-Election Triplets, 1920 - 1990

Percentage

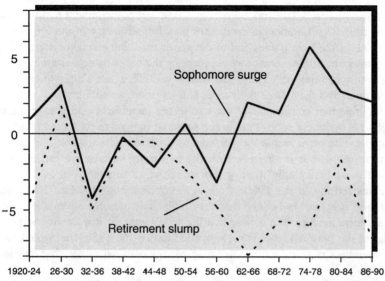

1920-24 26-30 32-36 38-42 44-48 50-54 56-60 62-66 68-72 74-78 80-84 86-90

Source: Computed by the authors from *Congressional Quarterly's Guide to U.S. Elections* (Washington, D.C.: Congressional Quarterly, 1985), and *Congressional Quarterly Weekly Report,* various issues.

have been drawn in the post-1960s period to favor incumbents; (2) incumbent members have increased resources (franking privileges, campaign funding advantages, and the like) to ensure reelection; (3) congressional challengers are weaker; and (4) changes in the electorate have weakened party identification.[17] Three of these explanations—redistricting, incumbent resources, and weaker challengers—are incumbent-related and essentially deal with the post-World War II period. The fourth explanation, changes in the electorate, postulates the decline of party identification in the electorate and dates the decline in competition to about the turn of the century.

Among the incumbent-related explanations, only redistricting seems to be clearly incorrect. The Senate patterns are similar to those for the House, and, of course, no redistricting takes place to affect the Senate. The evidence for the explanations centered on incumbent resources and weaker challengers is stronger yet inconclusive, and little has been done to explore their relevance for the Senate.[18] The interpretation based on decline of party identification may help to account for the present situation because we know that incumbent representatives get a disproportionate share of split-ticket votes, and the decline would explain the bicameral pattern of growth in advantage.[19] If the decline of party identification began in about 1900, however, it alone cannot account for the fact that the personal incumbency advantage began in the post-World War II period.

In short, there is no definitive answer to the question of what caused the rise in personal incumbency advantage.

Our own view is that during the 1950s and 1960s there emerged a new sort of congressional candidate and, inevitably, a new sort of incumbent member. For the first time large numbers of candidates took full advantage of the Progressive era reforms of the local parties and of the nomination and election system. They ran vigorous campaigns, sometimes supplanting the old party organization, sometimes simply ignoring it.[20] Their goal was to win office, not simply to carry the party banner, and they chose their races and ran them accordingly.

An important component of the rise in the incumbency advantage during the 1950s is members' motivation to run personal campaigns rather than partisan campaigns. The point is that the personal incumbency advantage so clearly visible in the mid-1960s is an artifact of who is retiring because we can measure personal incumbency only when a representative or senator retires. Thus the candidates retiring in the 1960s were in Congress during the late 1940s and 1950s, and it is hard to believe that they built their personal advantage during their last term in office. We believe that the 1950s hold the key to understanding the rise of the personal vote. What happened during the 1950s that would have given members of Congress an incentive to run personal rather than partisan campaigns?

The Eisenhower presidency is part of the answer, as is the rise of polling technology. When Dwight David Eisenhower took his second oath of office in 1956, he was the first president since Zachary Taylor in 1848 to face a Congress dominated by the other party. Moreover, public opinion polls had made it clear throughout the 1956 campaign that Eisenhower would be reelected by a comfortable margin. Democratic representatives thus knew that Eisenhower would be reelected and that campaigning against him and the Republican party would not ensure either their own or their party's reelection. Members seeking reelection had a strong incentive to run a different campaign, namely, a personal rather than a traditional partisan campaign. Eisenhower's victory in 1952 had followed the traditional pattern for successful presidential candidates in that he carried a Republican Congress to victory with him. The 1954 midterm elections replaced Republicans with a Democratically controlled Congress; more than a century of experience with such switches foretold a Democratic presidential victory in 1956. As polls made clear during 1955 and 1956, however, Eisenhower remained an extremely popular president. American voters were splitting their tickets in record numbers, and members of Congress knew that they were facing a new, less partisan electorate. In our view, members clearly had an incentive to respond to the less partisan electorate by selling themselves rather than their party.

Faced with a less partisan and thus more diverse set of potential reelection constituencies, representatives will alter their behavior to correspond to the new circumstances. The 1992 race for the sole congressional seat in Montana is a case in point. Throughout the 1980s Montana had two representatives: Pat Williams, a Democrat representing eastern Montana, a prounion, proenvironmental, university-dominated district, and Ron Marlenee, a Republican representing western Montana, a heavily agricultural and conservative district. As it became clear in the mid-1980s that Montana would have only one House seat after the 1990 census, both Williams and Marlenee began to change their behavior, knowing that simply courting their old constituencies would not suffice. From 1986 on, each spent more time in the other's district when he came home from Washington. Williams, whose symbol had been a map of Montana with the eastern part darkened under the heading "Pat Williams—Democrat," changed the symbol to a map of Montana under the heading "Pat Williams—Montana."

Marlenee began to support environmental legislation, in an effort to capture eastern voters, while Williams became more proagriculture, knowing he would need some agriculture votes in November. Representative Williams's switch away from his party identification clearly showed his understanding that the winning margin in Montana now is to be found among independent voters and split-ticket voters. The "new candidates" we alluded to earlier simply understood that with a dramatic rise in split-ticket voting their margin of victory would be found among split-ticket voters; thus they campaigned on personal factors—service, character, and policies that would appeal to these voters.

Is there any evidence for our thesis that the 1950s are the key to understanding the rise of the personal vote? One necessary condition for a rise in the personal vote is split-ticket voting. Research shows us that in House elections split-ticket voters split in the direction of the incumbent, and because more incumbents are Democrats, the House remains Democratic while Republicans win the presidency.[21] One measure of the importance of the 1956 election is that from 1900 through 1952 the percentage of congressional districts carried by House and presidential candidates of different parties was on average 15 percent, with 21 percent being the high point (1948). In 1956 a full 30 percent of all congressional districts were characterized by votes for House and presidential candidates of different parties. Moreover, after 1956 the average percentage of districts with split-party results is 34.5 percent.

The pattern of split-ticket voting in which voters choose Republican presidents and Democratic representatives also begins with Eisenhower. In 1952, 10 percent of all voters split tickets this way; in 1956 the number rose to 14 percent; it has averaged 15 percent over the following eight presidential elections. Incumbents of both parties thus realize that they cannot count on their party's presidential candidates to carry them to victory. Because neither their party identity nor their party's presidential candidate can do the job, incumbents have responded by doing the job themselves—by seeking the personal vote.

The earliest effect of this new blood in campaigns was felt in open seats, which these candidates made extremely competitive. Once in the incumbent ranks, the new members took steps to see that marginality would not stay with them long. What the new members faced in the old House must have seemed as outmoded to them as the system of local party bosses in the districts had seemed. Rigid adherence to seniority, limited staff, and autocratic committee chairmen meant that old-timers held most of the power and enjoyed most of the perquisites in the House. In his discussion of the status of freshmen representatives, Herbert Asher quotes a Republican member:

> The old political machinery, both in cities and rural areas, that used to provide Congress with new members is breaking down. Both political parties are under increasing pressure to reject so-called party hacks for candidates and put up the best possible men in these competitive two-party districts. Thus a new breed of man is being elected to Congress—bright, young, combative, and in a hurry. The seniority structure of the House of Representatives works against the man in a hurry, and there is growing restlessness.[22]

Beginning in the 1950s, with a variety of efforts aimed at procedural and structural reform, and continuing through to the 1973 Subcommittee Bill of Rights, the pattern of change in the postwar period has been one of distributing power within Congress more quickly and more broadly. Other changes, including increased personal staff, travel allowances, and use of the frank, assisted members in developing a personal district organization, further reducing their ties to the local party. Although the old days of patronage and graft were mostly gone, a new sort of federal largesse was available to distribute. The advent of the New Society programs in the 1960s accelerated the flow of federal dollars into the districts. The decentralization within Congress, combined with the growth of the federal domestic role, resulted in a situation that was highly conducive to the development of personal incumbency advantage.[23]

Personal incumbency advantage now rivals partisan advantage in its contribution to reelection margins, and the incumbent clearly has the upper hand in dealing with the local party. The local party no longer controls renomination or reelection, the value to the district of returning a member is high, the local benefits the member can claim credit for grow ever larger, and the opportunities for constituency service continue to expand.

Prospects for the 1990s

To this point we have focused on the past, examining the increase during the mid-1960s in incumbency advantage and placing that increase in historical context by looking back as far as the 1840s. We now turn to the current status of incumbency advantage and the prospects for the near future.

From its inception, the literature on incumbency has evidenced a common assumption of electoral advantage as a natural consequence of incumbency. The closest thing to dissent has been the work of a few authors, notably Melissa Collie and Gary Jacobson, arguing that the extent of the increase in advantage has been exaggerated.[24] Jacobson also has been an active advocate for the view that the future of incumbency advantage is by no means assured.[25] The notion that incumbency has seen its day gained considerable acceptance, particularly in the popular press, during the 1990 and 1992 congressional campaigns. Throughout the 1970s and 1980s the theme had been the near impossibility of dislodging a House incumbent, and observers expressed concern for the presumed lack of responsiveness in the electoral system. In 1990 the theme shifted to the anti-incumbent mood that was sweeping the country and the increasing insecurity of incumbents at all levels of government.[26] The most tangible expression of this anti-incumbent mood—mandated term limitations—developed a large and vocal following. The consensus was that the 1990s would not be a good decade for congressional incumbents.

The data for the 1990 election, as presented in each of the figures, provide us with the first evidence for what the decade of the 1990s might bring. Figure 6-1 certainly supports the view that 1990 represents a break from the general post-1965 pattern of increasing incumbent margins. The drop from the 1986 and 1988 level of just over 68 percent to the 1990 level of just over 64 percent is a sharp departure and reduces the vote share of incumbents to levels typical of the late 1960s and early 1970s. Vote share remains, however, well above the 60 percent level typical of the 1940-1965 period. Marginality (Figure 6-2) exhibits much the same pattern. The 1990 level of a 13 percent marginal, which is twice that of 1988, again looks like a move back to the levels common in the 1970s. Before we conclude that incumbents are in trouble, however, we must keep in mind that both incumbent vote share and marginality combine personal and partisan advantage. As we pointed out earlier, it is personal incumbent advantage—or perhaps for the 1990s personal incumbent *disadvantage*—that we want to isolate.

The data for sophomore surge and retirement slump in 1990 (Figure 6-3) present a much different picture. At more than 6 percentage points, sophomore surge is virtually unchanged from 1986 or 1988. Retirement slump, at 11 percentage points, is also in line with the levels of the 1980s and in fact is the second largest slump in the series. Put in more direct terms, new incumbents who first were elected to open seats in 1988 and first ran for reelection in 1990 ran on average more than 6 percentage points better in 1990, despite having to bear the hated label "incumbent." Districts in which local party leaders might have thought they were blessed by the retirement of an incumbent, so that they were free to run an outsider, found that on average the party suffered an 11-point decline. This is hardly evidence of the anti-incumbent voter mood so widely touted in the press. In fact, it does not even suggest the beginnings of a trend toward more moderate levels of incumbency advantage.

What do our data suggest for the remainder of the 1990s? Incumbents on average received less of the vote in 1990 than they did in the 1980s, but this decline was not attributable to any similar decline in personal advantage, as the much discussed anti-incumbent mood would suggest. Instead, incumbents lost ground from a weakening of the partisan base in their districts. Although it is always risky to generalize from a single observation, 1990 does tell us one thing: if this is what an anti-incumbent election looks like, incumbents have little to fear from their own district electorates. When the public mood turned against Congress in the 1970s, it was widely observed that voters hated Congress but loved their own member. Now it seems that voters hate incumbency but at least tolerate their incumbent.

Notes

1. Morris P. Fiorina, "The Case of the Vanishing Marginals: The Bureaucracy Did It," *American Political Science Review* 71 (1977): 171-181.
2. David R. Mayhew, *Congress: The Electoral Connection* (New Haven: Yale University Press, 1974).
3. See, for example, Robert S. Erikson, "A Reply to Tidmarch," *Polity* 4 (1972): 527-529; David R. Mayhew, "Congressional Elections: The Case of the Vanishing Marginals," *Polity* 6 (1974): 295-317; John A. Ferejohn, "On the Decline of Competition in Congressional Elections," *American Political Science Review* 71 (1977): 166-176; Albert D. Cover and David R. Mayhew, "Congressional Dynamics and the Decline of Competitive Congressional Elections," in *Congress Reconsidered*, 1st ed., ed. Lawrence C. Dodd and Bruce I. Oppenheimer (New York: Praeger, 1977); John R. Alford and John R. Hibbing, "Increased Incumbency Advantage in the House," *Journal of Politics* 43 (1981): 1042-1061; Melissa P. Collie, "Incumbency, Electoral Safety, and Turnover in the House of Representatives, 1952-1976," *American Political Science Review* 75 (1981): 119-131.
4. Joseph Cooper and David W. Brady, "Institutional Context and Leadership Style: The House from Cannon to Rayburn," *American Political Science Review* 75 (1981): 411-426.
5. Robert S. Erikson, "The Advantage of Incumbency in Congressional Elections," *Polity* 3 (1971): 395-405; Erikson, "Reply to Tidmarch"; Mayhew, "Congressional Elections."
6. James C. Garand and Donald A. Gross, "Change in the Vote Margins for Congressional Elections: A Specification of Historical Trends," *American Political Science Review* 78 (1984): 17-30.
7. See the discussion in Gary C. Jacobson, "The Marginals Never Vanished: Incumbency and Competition in Elections to the U.S. House of Representatives, 1952-1982," *American Journal of Political Science* 31 (1987): 126-141.
8. The election returns for 1852 to 1940 were compiled previously by Brady. The returns and incumbency data for 1946 to 1986 were compiled previously by Alford and John R. Hibbing. The election returns and incumbency data for the 1840s, as well as the incumbency data for 1854 to 1940, were compiled by Alford and Brady working together. The returns and incumbency data for 1988 and 1990 were compiled by Alford. In every case the source of the data was either *Congressional Quarterly's Guide to U.S. Elections* (Washington, D.C.: Congressional Quarterly, 1975, 1985) or the appropriate issues of *Congressional Quarterly Almanac* or *Congressional Quarterly Weekly Report*.
9. See, for example, Erikson, "Advantage of Incumbency"; and Cover and Mayhew, "Congressional Dynamics."
10. Mayhew, "Congressional Elections."
11. The differences between our findings and those of Gross and Garand are likely a function of the somewhat unusual measure of incumbent advantage they use. Incumbent winners' margins minus nonincumbent winners' margins is a troublesome and unstable way to assess advantage. Incumbent winners' margins obviously exclude incumbents who lose and thereby often misrepresent short-term shifts. As marginal winners drop into the losing range, for example, the margins of winning incumbents may actually rise as the weaker cases drop out. Nonincumbents are made up of two distinct classes: open-seat winners and challengers who defeat an incumbent. On average, we would expect the margins of the latter group to be significantly lower than those of the former group. Thus changes in the proportion of open seats will affect the average margin of incumbent winners, independent of any change in the performance of either group of candidates.
12. These measures are based on vote shifts between two elections. As such, the exclu-

sion of years following reapportionments, such as 1852, leads to the inability to compute surge and slump figures for the election immediately following. For this reason the slump and surge figures exclude both years such as 1852 and the following election of 1854, leaving us with the years ending in 6, 8, and 0 for each decade.

13. Erikson, "Advantage of Incumbency"; Erikson, "Reply to Tidmarch"; Robert S. Erikson, "Malapportionment, Gerrymandering, and Party Fortunes in Congressional Elections," *American Political Science Review* 66 (1972): 1234-1245.

14. Nelson W. Polsby, "The Institutionalization of the U.S. House of Representatives," *American Political Science Review* 62 (1968): 144-168.

15. See, for example, Alan I. Abramowitz, "A Comparison of Voting for U.S. Senator and Representative in 1978," *American Political Science Review* 73 (1980): 633-640; Hinckley, "American Voter"; Barbara Hinckley, "House Reelections and Senate Defeats: The Role of the Challenger," *British Journal of Political Science* 10 (1980): 441-460; Thomas E. Mann and Raymond E. Wolfinger, "Candidates and Parties in Congressional Elections," *American Political Science Review* 74 (1980): 617-632.

16. Warren Kostroski, "Party and Incumbency in Postwar Senate Elections," *American Political Science Review* 67 (1973): 1217-1218; Joseph Cooper and William West, "The Congressional Career in the 1970s," in *Congress Reconsidered*, 2d ed., ed. Lawrence C. Dodd and Bruce I. Oppenheimer (Washington, D.C.: CQ Press, 1981), 98; Cover and Mayhew, "Congressional Dynamics," 65.

17. For the redistricting argument, see Edward R. Tufte, "The Relationship Between Seats and Votes in Two-Party Systems," *American Political Science Review* 67 (1973): 540-554; for the resources argument, see Morris P. Fiorina, *Congress: Keystone of the Washington Establishment* (New Haven: Yale University Press, 1977); for the weaker challenger argument, see Mann and Wolfinger, "Candidates and Parties," or Barbara Hinckley, *Congressional Elections* (Washington, D.C.: CQ Press, 1981); for the change in the electorate argument, see Walter Dean Burnham, "The Changing Shape of the American Political Universe," *American Political Science Review* 59 (1975): 1-28, and Ferejohn, "On the Decline of Competition."

18. For a recent discussion, see John C. McAdams and John R. Johannes, "Congressmen, Perquisites, and Elections," *Journal of Politics* 50 (1988): 412-439.

19. Mann and Wolfinger, "Candidates and Parties."

20. See David R. Mayhew, *Placing Parties in American Politics* (Princeton: Princeton University Press, 1986), 329-332.

21. Mann and Wolfinger, "Candidates and Parties."

22. Herbert B. Asher, "The Changing Status of the Freshman Representative," in *Congress in Change*, ed. Norman J. Ornstein (New York: Praeger, 1975), 230-231.

23. Mayhew, *Congress: The Electoral Connection;* Fiorina, *Congress: Keystone of the Washington Establishment.*

24. Collie, "Incumbency, Electoral Safety, and Turnover"; Jacobson, "Marginals Never Vanished."

25. Gary C. Jacobson, "Divided Government, Strategic Politicians, and the 1990 Congressional Elections" (Paper presented at the annual meeting of the Midwest Political Science Association, Chicago, April 1991).

26. For a discussion of the anti-incumbent commentary surrounding the 1990 election, see John R. Alford and John R. Hibbing, "The 1990 Congressional Election Results and the Fallacy That They Embodied an Anti-Incumbent Mood," *PS: Political Science and Politics* 25 (1992): 217-219.

Part III

◆◆◆

Committee and Subcommittee Politics

7

Participation, Abdication, and Representation in Congressional Committees

Richard L. Hall

I n the aftermath of the 1992 congressional elections, it is natural to focus on the ways in which the Congress of the 1990s might be very different from those of the recent past. As the opening essay in this book points out, for instance, the dramatic turnover in membership may have significant implications for floor voting alignments, White House-Congress relations, congressional leadership, and the prospects for institutional reform. But if much may change, much will also stay the same. Among the features of congressional decision making that are likely to be unchanged is the decentralized means by which Congress makes most of its day-to-day policy decisions. Woodrow Wilson emphasized the importance of committees over a hundred years ago, and subsequent students of the institution have quoted him repeatedly ever since. Over the past two decades, in turn, numerous scholars have commented on the further devolution of legislative responsibility, citing the proliferation of work groups and at times lamenting the "fractured" nature of the institution.[1] Despite certain centralizing reforms in the budget process and enhancements in the role of party leaders, much of the legislative action in Congress occurs in congressional committees and subcommittees or, more accurately, through the network of formal and informal interactions that committee members and their staff control.

Like a large private firm, Congress stands to benefit in terms of better information and greater efficiency from an institutionalized division of labor, which the formal committee and subcommittee system is said to provide. As this essay attempts to show, however, committee jurisdictions and membership rolls provide at best only a rough indication of which legislators are likely to make the laws in specific policy domains. The division of labor in Congress, unlike that in a private firm, is not the product of some explicit institutional design intended to serve the collective purposes of the organization.[2] It bubbles up, as it were, from individual members' day-to-day choices about which matters warrant their scarce time, energy, and staff attention.

It is difficult to overestimate the importance of these decisions. Taken together, they determine which views and values matter on the particular issues that Congress takes up. With few exceptions, a sustained effort by a member and his or her staff is a necessary if not sufficient condition for significant influence on an issue before the member's chamber. This point is neglected in the substantial literature that views decision making as a process of building voting majorities, either in committee or on the floor. The act of voting is only one—and probably not the most important—form of participation in the legislative process. Except in cases where the lines of disagreement are very closely drawn, parliamentary suffrage gives a member relatively little influence over the several decisions that shape a piece of legislation. Authoring or negotiating a legislative vehicle, drafting particular amendments, developing procedural strategies, persuading colleagues to adopt one's point of view—all these activities weigh more heavily than voting in the decision-making calculus of most bills, especially in a legislature where committees, anterooms, and staff discussions are the principal forums for legislative deliberation. David Mayhew states the general principle: "In small working units, formal voting tends to recede in importance as a determinant of outcomes, and what individuals do with their time and energy rises in importance." [3]

This essay examines decision making in congressional committees, taking Mayhew's principle as its point of departure. Who makes the laws in congressional committees, and how do the patterns of legislative involvement affect the health of Congress as a representative assembly? [4]

Committee Assignments and the Accommodation of Interests

The analysis of committee decision making in Congress properly begins with the processes by which members seek and are selected for their committee assignments. Choices that members make about such assignments at the beginning of a session directly affect the patterns of participation and representation in the ensuing day-to-day decisions of their chamber. This is true for at least two reasons: one is related to the formal procedures governing participation at this stage; the second is related to the fact that, once assigned, the member's position provides informal opportunities and resources that subsidize his or her legislative involvement at the committee level.

The important legislative action in Congress—in contrast to most Western parliaments—tends to occur in and around the committees of jurisdiction.[5] The committee is the locus of most decisions regarding which matters within a given policy domain will move onto the chamber's legislative agenda. Once a decision to move forward has been made, in turn, the committee is where the original legislative vehicle normally gets formulated, the central issues are debated, and most of the substantive and technical amendments are reviewed and adopted. Although committee nonmembers normally are permitted to attend another committee's meetings, they enjoy no formal right to participate in these decisions: their presence cannot be counted toward establishing a quorum; they have no voting power; they cannot call up legislation, raise points of order, or offer amendments.

These constraints are considerably more important in the House than in the Senate, since there is no guarantee that a member will have full-blown opportunities to participate when a bill moves from committee to the House floor. Important floor action in the House normally is governed by the Rules Committee, which decides how much time will be allocated for floor debate, which members will control that time, and what sorts of amendments can be offered. Over the past two decades, in fact, the number of bills considered on the House floor under special rules that restrict the right of members to offer amendments has risen dramatically, especially for major pieces of legislation. Major health, tax, trade, environment, budget, and human services bills have come to the floor in recent years under rules that significantly limited the amending and speaking opportunities of the typical House member. Some members have complained that the restrictive rules frequently imposed by the House Rules Committee have been tantamount to "gag rules" that undermine the egalitarian principles that are supposed to govern the deliberative process in a majority-rule institution.[6]

In the Senate, floor consideration is far more open to committee nonmembers than it is in the House, rendering access to the committee stage less important. In addition, the potential of every senator to delay floor action (through holds, nongermane amendments, and filibusters) makes it more likely that a nonmember's views will be anticipated at the committee stage. Even so, committee members in the Senate as well as in the House possess distinct advantages. In particular, they gradually develop political and substantive expertise in their committee's policy domains; they are more likely to enjoy ongoing interactions with interested actors both on and off the committee; and they have greater access to committee and subcommittee staff. Taken together, these advantages are very important and go a long way toward explaining why committee members individually and committees collectively exert disproportionate influence over matters within their jurisdiction. As we will explore in greater depth in the next section, members face limitless demands on their time and attention, making it impossible to keep on top of all issues that are before their chamber at any given moment. On matters outside the jurisdiction of their own committees, members and their staff learn of legislative action from sources that are available to many outsiders: CQ's *Congressional Monitor*, the *Congressional Record*, the *Washington Post*, and various computerized information services. The legislative process on a particular matter can be well advanced before they learn of decisions already made, deals already cut, timetables already arranged. One former House staffer, now a legislative assistant for a Senate Democrat, observed: "In the Senate, you don't *have* to be on the right committee like we did in the House, but it helps. We've been wanting to do some things in the tax area. For instance, we've had all these farmers calling and writing, complaining about the diesel fuel tax.... I can't even get the Finance Committee staff to return my calls."

If a member is to play an effective role in a particular policy area, then, assignment to the committee of jurisdiction is more likely to place him or her close to the important legislative action and the community of relevant actors. For this reason, the business of seeking committee assignments normally involves strategic calculation and substantial effort. The process begins even before the formal start of a new Congress, as new members explore the range of committee vacancies and angle for particular slots. At the same time, sitting members take the opportunity to reassess their existing positions and weigh the benefits of adding another assignment or transferring to a new one.

Within certain important limits, which we shall note, the assignment process is largely self-selective.[7] As Kenneth Shepsle has observed, committee assignments are to members what stocks are to investors; they wish to acquire those that will maximize the value of their portfolio.[8] In this context, however, value is not economic profit but the advancement of the member's political goals or interests. Each member who seeks a change in portfolio calculates the value of particular assignments, discounts them according to the likelihood that they can be acquired, and then develops a rank order list to present to the party's committee on committees. After a sometimes protracted process of lobbying and bargaining, these committees allocate the available slots, sometimes renegotiating a committee's size, in such a way as to accommodate the interests of as many members as possible.

Of course, this abstract account renders the committee assignment process somewhat more systematic than it is. (When asked how he got a coveted seat on House Ways and Means in only his second term, Wyche Fowler, D-Ga., replied, "It beats the hell out of me.")[9] But it does convey the important point that committee assignments in Congress are largely interest-driven. What kinds of interests matter? One of the most common is serving one's constituents, which in turn enhances the member's ability to get reelected. Some committees are better suited to promote this goal than others, however. In a famous study of committees in the 1960s, for instance, Richard Fenno found that members of both chambers sought positions on the Interior and Post Office committees for "political help," to promote "district interests," or to obtain specific projects for their states.[10] More recent studies have emphasized the attractiveness of the committees dealing with agriculture, armed services, appropriations, and public works to members concerned with getting reelected.[11]

Like most of us, however, individual legislators are not single-minded seekers of any one particular goal.[12] In requesting their assignments, members hope to put themselves in a position to pursue interests other than reelection. Fenno identifies two additional goals that affect assignment behavior—making good public policy and acquiring influence within Congress—and suggests that "all congressmen probably hold all three goals" in different mixes.[13] Pursuit of the latter is something of a longer term strategy for most members, given that it requires assignment to highly coveted, "exclusive" committees such as Rules or Ways and Means, but pursuit of good public policy is a goal that is seldom very distant from the day-to-day calculations of members as they engage in their legislative work. Members can pursue their several purposes through one of two committee-centered strategies. One strategy is to diversify their portfolio by seeking positions on more than one committee, each of which is relevant to different interests. Many members do so, especially in the Senate, where each member normally receives more than one major assignment. For instance, when Paul Tsongas, D-Mass., began his Senate career in 1977, he requested a seat on Energy and Natural Resources, because of his state's concern over energy supplies, and Foreign Relations, because of a longstanding personal interest in Africa that dated back to his service in the Peace Corps.[14] In 1987 freshman senator Tom Daschle, D-S.D., sought assignment to Agriculture, whose jurisdiction was crucial to the economy of his state, and to Finance. One of his aides explained the latter choice:

> When Daschle came to the Senate, it was the first time in his political career that he didn't have to worry about reelection two years down the road. . . . [He] could go after a committee that he didn't feel he had to be on for political reasons. Finance gave him the chance to get involved in all the big issues he's interested in. Trade, tax, health—it's all right there.

A second, and perhaps more common, strategy is to seek assignment to a committee that has a jurisdiction suited to the pursuit of several purposes. In fact, most of the major committees in both chambers fit this description to some degree. Although the Finance Committee may place members close to some of the most important national issues, and although it may enhance a member's reputation for power within the Senate, it also provides members with opportunities to secure preferential tax and trade provisions for constituent groups. Health and consumer issues within the purview of House Energy and Commerce evoke members' deep-seated policy concerns, while fights over clean air, toxic waste cleanup, and Amtrak reauthorizations turn more on local and regional interests. For any particular member, in fact, assignment to even relatively narrow, "constituency" committees can simultaneously serve several goals. For instance, in 1991 freshman Calvin Dooley, D-Calif., actively sought and received assignment to House Agriculture. Dooley had been elected from a rural, agricultural, and economically depressed district in California's Central Valley that had much at stake in Agriculture Committee decisions on such issues as cotton and sugar price supports, pesticide regulations, and drought relief. But at the same time, he was an experienced farmer who came from a family that had farmed in the district for four generations, and he held an agribusiness degree from the University of California at Davis.[15] For less idiosyncratic reasons, likewise, relatively narrow committees such as House and Senate Agriculture can provide members with opportunities to pursue very different kinds of goals; although the Agriculture jurisdictions are dominated by issues of concern to rural districts with farm economies, they also include responsibility for federal food stamps, foreign hunger relief efforts, soil and wetlands conservation, groundwater pollution, and other nutrition and environmental issues that strike strong ideological chords.

In short, the committee assignment process is best understood as a set of institutional arrangements that channel member interests into positions of legislative advantage. But these arrangements are loose ones at best, and any notion of interest must be broad enough to encompass not only members' political self-interest but their personal policy concerns, prelegislative professional interests, and ideological commitments. At the same time, committee self-selection is not unconstrained. Rough limits on committee size, competition among members for scarce slots, and the requirement that the party ratios on most committees be roughly equal to the party ratio in the parent chamber—all of these considerations limit the extent to which members' interests map neatly onto their committee assignments.[16] Likewise, there are larger party and institutional interests that leaders charged with allocating scarce committee slots may introduce into the assignment process without necessarily violating their accommodationist principles. As Shepsle points out, for instance, there are strong reasons why the party committees on committees should try to accommodate members' reelection-motivated requests—the party as well as the individual member has a stake in ensuring against a strong electoral challenge.

But there is also a strong incentive for such actors to take into account the policy interests, expertise, or professional background of assignment seekers as well. In a recent and important book on legislative organization, Keith Krehbiel argues that the placement of individuals with prior expertise in committee issues is central to the committee assignment process. Committees composed of these "low-cost specialists" are, from the organization's point of view, "informationally efficient"; they enhance its capacity to develop policies that will have the real-world consequences that the chamber majority considers desirable.[17]

In sum, members' judgments about the desirability of particular committees involve "on-average, best-guess" evaluations of the relevance of their several interests to the various issues that might come before the committees in the coming two years. And even once those evaluations are made, members do not necessarily receive the assignments that they believe will best serve their short-term and long-term legislative objectives. For these reasons and more, participation in postassignment decision making is highly selective.

Activity and Abdication in Congressional Committees

Participation in committee activity in the Congresses of the 1940s and 1950s was far more structured than it is today. Both informal norms and institutional barriers dictated who would participate, more or less, on the various issues that the assembly considered. Members of a particular committee, for instance, were expected to concentrate on the thankless and the not-so-thankless matters assigned to them—to practice an ethic of hard work and specialization. Autocratic committee chairs controlled legislative activity through their substantial powers to set the legislative agenda, appoint subcommittee chairs, and make subcommittee assignments. Junior members, on the other hand, were admonished to be seen and not heard in the presence of their more experienced senior colleagues.[18]

In the postreform Congress, the limits to legislative involvement on any given issue lie less in the institution's norms or traditions than in the time and staff resources a member is able to commit. Such resources are decidedly scarce. "I feel like I'm spread thin all the time," one freshman House member noted. "There's never any time to read or think an issue through or anything like that." The pressures of the congressional workload extend to senior members as well. Elizabeth Drew quotes one representative who summarizes the almost universal frustrations of the job:

There are just too many votes, too many issues, too many meetings, too many attention-demanding situations. We're going to committee meetings, sub-committee meetings, caucuses—a caucus of the class with which you were elected here, the rural caucus, the steel caucus, you name it—and we're see-ing constituents and returning phone calls and trying to rush back and forth to the district, and then we're supposed to understand what we're voting on when we get to the House floor.[19]

Such observations have been systematically confirmed in a survey administered by the House Commission on Administrative Review. Analyzing data drawn from that survey, Thomas O'Donnell concluded that House members' "ability to concentrate time on any single activity is severely constrained by the abundance and complexity of the demands that confront them." [20]

If anything, the demands placed on the contemporary senator are even more severe.[21] Elected from larger and more heterogeneous areas, senators must represent a wider range of interests; they receive greater media and interest group attention; and given the relative size of the two chambers, individual senators face both greater obligations and greater opportunities for legislative involvement. These factors are reflected most clearly in their committee assign-ments. In 1988 the average number of committee and subcommittee positions for representatives was 6.6; for senators the average number was 11.1.[22] As one Senate staffer noted, the multiplicity of assignments produces scheduling con-flicts that are a major source of frustration—members' avarice in expanding their assignment portfolios at the beginning of a Congress can come back to haunt them during the everyday work of committee decision making:

[Scheduling conflicts] happen all the time, and it's a major pain. [The sena-tor's] almost always got more than one hearing going on at the same time. Or he'll need to be on the floor, and there'll be a committee markup. The staffer has to monitor the thing, leave the room, and get on the phone and track him down. [The senator] just has to make on-the-spot decisions about where to be and how much to do. It really gets crazy sometimes.

The problems of time management and scheduling at the committee level be-came so severe in the mid-1980s that the Senate, with self-conscious apprecia-tion of the irony involved, formed a select committee to study them. Named for Dan Quayle, the junior senator from Indiana who chaired it, the Quayle commit-tee received a litany of complaints that senators "have workloads which the hours of the day make it impossible to faithfully execute," are "burdened by a mass of obligations on [their] limited time," and face multiple "responsibilities [that] are often directly in conflict." [23] Testifying before the committee, Sen. Daniel Evans, R-Wash., summarized the prevailing view:

We would all agree that there is member inconsistency regarding participation, disappointment regarding performance due to conflicting committee assign-ments, frustration with committees scheduled at similar or the same times, ineffectiveness due to the oversized membership of some committees, and sometimes member disincentives to participate . . . at the maximum level.[24]

A clear illustration of such constraints is found in the truancy rates at com-

Table 7-1   Attendance and Voting in House Committees
(in percentages)

Committee	Absent	Voting by proxy or not voting
Education and Labor	30	45
Energy and Commerce	24	34
Agriculture	21	45

Source: Minutes and transcripts of committee markup sessions.

Note: Cell entries are averages across a saturation sample of bills marked up in each committee during one Congress: the 97th Congress (1981-1983) for Agriculture and Education and Labor; the 98th Congress (1983-1985) for Energy and Commerce.

mittee and subcommittee markups, which are often the most important meetings in the legislative process. Table 7-1 shows the incidence of nonattendance for a sample of approximately sixty bills in three House committees, where "attendance" is defined liberally by the committee clerk to mean whether a member appeared even momentarily during a particular markup. Given the relative importance of the markup stage, the figures shown in the column indicating absenteeism are striking. The average absenteeism for members of the House Education and Labor Committee, for instance, was 30 percent. In Energy and Commerce, thought to be one of the most powerful committees in the House, with jurisdiction over some of the most important legislation, one in four committee members failed to appear at any point during the typical markup. Nonattendance in committee, however, does not necessarily mean that a member does not vote, since most committees permit voting by proxy. In practice, though, proxy voting tends to augment the power of the active, not preserve the authority of the absent. Members often duck into a markup for a brief moment, leaving their proxy behind them with little knowledge of the way in which it will be used. The right-hand column of the table shows the considerable frequency with which members abdicate their voting rights during committee markups.

Patterns of truancy in Senate committees are similar. Several senators who testified before the Quayle committee noted the frequency with which committee or subcommittee chairs have trouble getting the 50 percent of the membership necessary to establish a quorum. At the commencement of its hearings, in fact, Chairman Quayle noted that "of the 12 members that are on this Select Committee, 9 of us have conflicts this morning with other committees and subcommittees in where we are supposed to be." An examination of the official record reveals that only three members of the select committee showed up for both days of its hearings, while five of the twelve did not appear even momentarily at either meeting.

Table 7-2 shows a more general picture of committee participation. The statistics summarize the number of members actively involved in ten bills that went through both House and Senate committees. The table reveals that, bill by

Table 7-2   Participation in Congressional Committees (in percentages)

Policy area/bill	Committee members active during prefloor consideration	
	House	Senate
Human resources		
Job Training Partnership Act of 1982	59	75
Older Americans Act Amendments of 1981	31	31
Head Start Reauthorization of 1981	28	19
Commerce		
Universal Telephone Service Preservation Act of 1984	64	41
Amtrak/Railroad Amendments of 1984	24	18
Textile Labeling Act of 1983	21	12
Agriculture		
Farm Credit Act of 1987	65	68
Wheat, Soybeans, and Feed Grains, 1981 Farm Bill	56	71
Conservation Title, 1985 Farm Bill	44	33
Cotton Title, 1981 Farm Bill	28	29

Source: Staff interviews, secondary accounts, and committee records from the House committees on Agriculture; Education and Labor; and Energy and Commerce and from the Senate committees on Agriculture, Nutrition, and Forestry; Commerce, Science, and Transportation; and Labor and Human Resources.

Note: Entries are the percentages of committee members who (1) offered at least one amendment during committee or subcommittee markup; (2) were major participants in markup debate; or (3) were cited in staff interviews, secondary accounts, or official records as having played a significant role behind the scenes.

bill, there is considerable variation in the breadth of participation across the eligible committee membership. We shall explore some of the factors that affect that variation in the next section. For now, two points are worth emphasizing. First, in only certain cases do we find a substantial proportion of a committee seriously involved in its deliberations. Charles Clapp, basing his conclusions on staff interviews in the early 1960s, estimated that "one-third to one-half of a committee's membership constitute the hard core that can be depended on in nearly every activity." [25] For the 1980s such estimates are clearly generous. In only half of the ten bills could even a third of the House or Senate committee be counted as full-fledged players in the decision-making process. Second, Table 7-2 confirms that the limits on participation are serious in both the Senate and the House. In almost every case, the proportion of Senate committee members participating is very close to the House proportion, suggesting that the greater time constraints and scheduling conflicts faced by the contemporary senator are at least partially offset by the greater staff support and range of legislative opportunities that the position confers.

In sum, it is an organizational fact of life that individual members of Congress act in some areas, abdicate in others. They cannot do everything; they must choose. In making these choices at the committee level, they resolve themselves into the working subsets, issue by issue, that normally drive the legislative action. As we shall see in the final section, these patterns have important implications for the nature and health of representation in a decentralized Congress.

Who Makes the Laws?
Decision Making in Committee

Who makes the laws that emerge from the committee rooms of Congress? A general answer to this question is not easy to formulate. Even on a single committee or subcommittee, the particular individuals who make up the active subset change from one bill to the next. Members themselves seldom have systematic strategies for allocating their time and staff among the various issues that come before their panels. In an attempt to explain why her boss got so involved in ꞏne bill before the House Subcommittee on Select Education, one staffer remarked, "One of [Subcommittee Chairman Austin] Murphy's staffers told me about the bill early on, and the congressman expressed an interest. So we just jumped in." Another staffer noted, "I don't know that we really [budget our time].... We just sort of react to things as they come up. [The representative] will say, 'This is something we need to go after,' and it's pointless to tell him that I've got sixteen other things going on. Some of them just fall by the wayside." Other staffers offer similar accounts. Asked how her boss sets his legislative priorities, an aide to one junior senator remarked:

> To [him] everything is a priority, which means that nothing is a priority. Last year he wrote a famous memo about what his priorities were going to be, where he wanted the staff to concentrate, and it basically included everything under the sun. Then he comes into the staff meetings and complains that he's not getting enough time to read and prepare.... Decisions about how we spend our time get made by default; it's not because we've got any kind of grand plan.

In short, members and their staff are constantly pulled between the lure of legislative opportunities and the limits on what they can do. In resolving this strain, moreover, they seldom have sufficient time, information, or foresight to consider the range of all viable activities, weigh their relative costs and benefits, and rank order them. Nonetheless, rough calculations do seem to emerge on an issue-by-issue basis as the office makes sometimes quick decisions about whether a particular issue is, as one staffer put it, "worth our time."

Participation and Interest

Several considerations influence those determinations. Perhaps the most important is some general perception that an issue affects the member's interests. That is, the same concerns that preoccupy the member in making committee assignment requests carry over to day-to-day decisions about committee involvement. The calculation of interest at this stage is simply more concrete and specific and hence has a more direct effect on committee outcomes. Serving one's constituents is a common theme in these calculations, even on committees that are not normally thought to be constituency oriented. Historically, Senate Labor and Human Resources and its House counterpart, Education and Labor, have been two of the most ideologically charged committees in Congress. Referring to his senator's activity on the Labor Committee, one staffer noted:

> There are certainly other committees that are better as far as our state is concerned. Appropriations would be better. But, then again, the education issues play well back home.... [The senator] was active in getting the elementary and secondary aid bill through last year, and it got us great press. He's probably given a dozen speeches on it back in the state.

Similarly, the legislative assistant to a senior member of House Education and Labor explained her boss's key role in reauthorizing the Older Americans Act: "Older Americans is so important to the district for demographic reasons. The district is the tenth most senior district in the country, the other nine being in Florida. It's a very stable community of immigrants, and [the Older Americans] programs affect them directly." More generally, though, members and their staffs cite a variety of interests that affect their participation in committee work. As in the committee assignment process, the member's personal policy views or chamber reputation are important determinants. Although he may later put it to good political use, Democratic representative John Dingell's Commerce Committee investigation of the Environmental Protection Agency cannot be wholly attributed to its direct electoral benefits; Dingell is virtually unbeatable in Southeastern Michigan, a circumstance that gives him substantial latitude to pursue his own agenda on Capitol Hill.[26] On Senate Foreign Relations, Republican Jesse Helms's vigorous opposition to economic sanctions against South Africa derived from his deep-seated conservatism, not from the issue's salience among his North Carolina constituency. In pushing the 1986 Tax Reform Act through House Ways and Means, Dan Rostenkowski, D-Ill., was concerned both with helping the average taxpayer and enhancing his reputation as an effective committee chairman.[27] Although members may seldom take the lead on issues that will do them direct political harm, concern with reelection is only one of several important interests that affect their committee participation. One senior Republican member explained his participation on the House Education and Labor Committee:

> First, you look at how it affects your district. What legislation would be beneficial to your constituents? Second, there's personal interests. I'm a former school superintendent, so I'm going to be involved in education matters. Even within education, I have some real pets. If you're talking about the training of administrators, that's something I'd be interested in. If you're talking about recruiting teachers, that's something I'd be interested in. If you're talking about school lunch or child nutrition, the same. Because that's something I feel strongly about.

In general, then, legislation that deals with broad issues or affects a wide range of states and districts is likely to evoke the various interests of a wide range of members. A quick review of the bills listed in Table 7-2 illustrates this point. In the human resources area, the Job Training Partnership Act of 1982 was probably the most important initiative during Reagan's first term, addressing major issues of national employment policy and affecting displaced workers in almost every state and district during a period of burgeoning unemployment. Similarly, the Farm Credit Act of 1987 followed on the heels of a deep depression in the agricultural economy, during which land values rapidly deflated and thousands of farmers nationwide were pushed into bankruptcy. For both of these bills, committee participation was broad, with more than half of the committee members in both House and Senate actively involved in the decision-making process. In contrast, several other bills listed in Table 7-2 involved a much narrower range of interests and generated much less participation. Although the federal Head Start program was originally designed to address basic issues of equal educational opportunity, the 1981 Head Start bill was a simple reauthorization of existing law, with only minor policy changes. For the most part, the 1983 Textile Labeling Act involved only a single regulatory issue and a single, regionally circumscribed industry. And the cotton title of the 1981 farm bill affected farmers in only a handful of states.

Legislative Resources

If participation in committees tends to be interest-driven, not all members are equally able to pursue their interests on more than a few bills with any efficacy. In both chambers, formal leaders enjoy a number of legislative advantages. In the first place, committee and subcommittee chairs and, to a lesser extent, ranking minority members enjoy certain procedural prerogatives not available to the average backbencher.[28] They have considerable control over the committee's agenda, the scheduling of meetings, and the progress of legislation. If committee action is likely to conflict with other business that the chair finds important or otherwise violates some strategic purpose, he or she is better able to adapt the nature and timing of committee events to suit his or her objectives.

House Energy and Commerce Committee Chair John Dingell provides something of an ongoing case study in how such prerogatives can be exploited to the leader's advantage. Consider, for instance, the Natural Gas Policy Act of 1984, a bill involving the deregulation of natural gas prices and hence the transfer of billions of dollars from one region to another and from consumers to natural gas corporations.[29] For almost a year during the 98th Congress, Dingell avoided bringing the bill to committee markup, fearing that proponents of deregulation had the votes to push through amendments that benefited the gas industry and hurt energy-consuming states, such as Dingell's Michigan. When Dingell finally convened a full committee markup, one member walked over to him and boasted, "John, we've got the votes." Dingell replied, "Yeah, but I've got the gavel." Dingell soon illustrated the difference. When markup began, he first allowed consideration on two amendments that would reveal the strength of his coalition. When he lost on both test votes, Dingell simply adjourned the markup, delaying consideration indefinitely.[30] He did not bring the bill up again until the following year, after he had managed to negotiate a substitute that was less favorable to industry. The committee then reported the substitute package over the vigorous objections of members from gas-producing states.[31]

Beyond their procedural prerogatives, committee leaders of both parties possess important resources that defray the costs of legislative involvement. Given their relative seniority and the repetitious nature of most committees' agendas, leaders are likely to have experience in the politics and substance of legislation that comes before their panel. Many have dealt with the same issues, heard the same arguments, and even questioned the same witnesses in previous sessions. If leaders start with superior expertise, in turn, they also possess greater resources to garner the political and technical information that is relevant to particular issues. Most important in such efforts is their greater access to and control over professional staff. In both chambers but especially in the Senate, the amount of staff time a member can allocate to an issue is a precondition for effective legislative involvement. One aide explained why his senator did so little to pursue his interests in the federal nutrition area during the 100th Congress:

> Well, it's not so much the political risks as it is the resources that we have to work with. Kennedy's been working on this for years. So has Panetta—his staffer is really sharp, really knowledgeable on the details. For my boss to take the lead on, say, something comprehensive in the hunger/nutrition area would take me years, given how little our office has to work with. . . . Notwithstanding the criticism of Hill resources, there is not a lot of staff around here.[32]

Finally, members with a formal institutional position occupy a central place in an information network that extends beyond the confines of the committee but plays a crucial role in the legislative process. Given their control over the committee's agenda, for instance, committee leaders and their staffs become the focal points for outsiders wishing to press their ideas, analysis, and demands upon the government. A case in point is the Federal Insecticide, Fungicide, and Rodenticide Act (FIFRA), a bill to regulate the agricultural use of potentially harmful chemicals. Although not likely to enthrall the average voter, FIFRA would have important implications for the environmental quality of lakes, rivers, and groundwater; for farmers and fruit growers who use chemicals in raising their crops; for agricultural workers whose health might be affected by exposure to such products; and for private companies that manufacture and market them. The act has been up for reconsideration in every Congress since 1980, generating countless studies and endless controversies among the various interest groups and policy specialists. An aide to the House subcommittee chairman, George Brown, D-Calif., described the drafting of one version of the bill:

> We spent weeks poring over all these reports and recommendations, and we finally put together a draft. But the environmentalists didn't like it, and there were fractures on the chemical industry's side—one side wanted some proposals relating to the release of health and safety data and the pesticide registration process. . . . So Brown said, "You guys sit down with my staff and go through this thing, point by point, and figure out where you want to be." That

was the beginning of four months of protracted negotiations with EPA, the industry, the environmentalists—sitting down, going back and forth, drafts and redrafts. Finally we got a negotiated settlement between the industry and the environmental groups and only then moved a bill, that comprehensive compromise, up to subcommittee markup.

If formal leaders, as a group, tend to be far more active in their committee and the policy community that surrounds it, there are important differences between the Senate and the House regarding the relative roles played by full and subcommittee leaders. Largely because of reforms passed in the early 1970s, House subcommittee leaders enjoy more advantages than do their counterparts in the Senate. Under the rubric "the Subcommittee Bill of Rights," the House Democratic Caucus limited the ability of full committee chairs to determine the number, composition, and chairmanships of the subcommittees; the authority of the committee chair to hold legislation at the full committee level was severely constrained; and each subcommittee chair was guaranteed a staff and budget.[33]

In the Senate the changes have been more modest. Most of the legislative markups are held at full committee, and Senate committee leaders retain greater control over the hiring, firing, and allocation of professional staff.[34] Even so, both subcommittee leaders and members exert disproportionate influence in the decision-making process of most Senate committees. In practice, subcommittee leaders normally enjoy at least some additional staff assistance. Equally important, subcommittee leaders and members tend to be more interested in matters that come before their panels. We have already seen how the committee assignment process serves to place on committees members who have general interests in the committee's jurisdiction. The subcommittee assignment process permits a more refined matching of specific interests to legislative jurisdiction, and the considerable flexibility in setting subcommittee sizes permits the committee to accommodate most members' requests. Although this matching process is far more precise in the House than in the Senate, subcommittee members in both chambers are more willing than their nonmember colleagues to expend their personal and staff time and forgo opportunities for legislative influence elsewhere. One aide to Sen. Bill Bradley, D-N.J., observed:

> Bradley's got certain interests. He's really got burning interests in trade, third world debt, and tax. He's on the trade subcommittee, he chairs the one on international debt, and all the tax stuff gets handled at full committee. He just doesn't get that involved in the rest of it. He doesn't have the time, or at least he doesn't think he has the time, to go into other things.

Another staffer commented on the important roles played by the chair and ranking minority member of the Senate Subcommittee on Health:

> There are really only a couple of senators who are really interested in Medicare—interested enough to understand it—and that's Mitchell and Durenberger. The others are intimidated and bored by it—intimidated because the discussion quickly progresses beyond their level of comprehension. It's such a technical program. I remember one day I was sitting alone in the anteroom

Table 7-3   Institutional Position and Participation in Committee
Decisions: A House-Senate Comparison (in percentages)

Institutional position	Committee members active during markup	
	House	Senate
Formal leaders		
Subcommittee	100	75
Full committee	80	70
Committee rank and file		
Subcommittee members	65	49
Subcommittee nonmembers	24	24
All		
Subcommittee members	72	58
Subcommittee nonmembers	29	32

Source: Staff interviews and committee records for the ten bills listed in Table 7-2.

Note: Entries are the percentages of members in the row category who (1) offered at least one amendment during committee or subcommittee markup; (2) were major participants in markup debate; or (3) were cited in staff interviews, secondary accounts, or official records as having played a significant role behind the scenes.

while Medicare hearings were going on. [One senator] walks out and says to me, "You know, my eyes just glaze over when they start talking Medicare this and Medicare that, Part A this and Part B that. I don't understand any of it." Not ten minutes later, another senator walked out and said to me, he was clearly being sarcastic, "That Medicare is really interesting stuff, isn't it?" It's not that senators don't care—at one level they have to care. But they're not really interested. Mitchell and Durenberger, maybe Bentsen, are the only ones who have any real influence.[35]

Although a sample of ten bills from three committees is too small to draw firm conclusions, Table 7-3 bears out several of the general tendencies described here. The first two rows show the significant roles played by full and subcommittee leaders: formal leaders were active in more than three-fourths of the observations. In the House, in fact, the subcommittee chair and the ranking minority member were major players in every case, despite the fact that these bills span three different committee and eight different subcommittee jurisdictions. House subcommittee members, in turn, were more than twice as likely to participate as were their full committee colleagues, reinforcing the general view that House decision making is highly decentralized. When one combines both the leader and rank-and-file categories, 72 percent of the reporting subcommittee members were active, compared with only 29 percent of the nonmembers. In the House, at least, the combination of institutional resources and member interests is markedly apparent in the behavioral patterns of committee decision making.

Table 7-4   Institutional Position and Amending Activity in Committee Markups: A House-Senate Comparison (in percentages)

	Successful amendments	
Institutional position	House	Senate
Formal Leaders		
Subcommittee	39	31
Full committee	5	15
Committee rank and file		
Subcommittee members	34	34
Subcommittee nonmembers	23	20
All		
Subcommittee members	72	65
Subcommittee nonmembers	28	35

Source: Committee records for the ten bills listed in Table 7-2.

Note: Entries are the percentages of all successful, substantive amendments offered during committee or subcommittee markup in the respective chambers for which members of the row category were responsible. Not included are amendments affected by subsequent substitutes or by successful second-degree amendments that the author of the first-degree amendment formally opposed.

Table 7-3 also illustrates important House-Senate differences in committee decision making. Specifically, the table confirms that subcommittees are more important in the House than in the Senate. For the ten bills studied, 100 percent of the House subcommittee leaders counted as principal actors, compared with 75 percent in the Senate. Likewise, 65 percent of the House subcommittee rank and file were active, compared with 49 percent in the Senate. In general, then, the behavioral differences between full and subcommittee members were smaller in the Senate. At the same time, however, Table 7-3 clearly shows that it would be incorrect to impute insignificance to Senate subcommittees; the House-Senate differences regarding subcommittees are matters of degree, not of kind. Although most Senate markups may take place at the full committee level, subcommittee members are much more likely to play important legislative roles there than are nonmembers, and a subcommittee leader is somewhat more likely to participate than is a full committee leader.

Table 7-4 provides additional evidence for each of the above propositions and better illustrates the effect of members' interests and resources on their legislative influence.[36] The table reports the extent to which members with and without some sort of institutional position are successful in amending the legislative vehicle during either full or subcommittee markup. In general, the patterns are strikingly similar to those of Table 7-3. Subcommittee leaders and members amend the legislative vehicle well beyond what their proportion of the total committee membership would suggest. Although House subcommittee members are normally outnumbered by nonmembers two to one, they are responsible for 72 percent of all successful amendments. The same pattern holds to a lesser extent in Senate committee decisions. For the committees studied here, sub-committee sizes averaged less than 40 percent of the committee membership, but subcommittee members were responsible for 65 percent of all successful amendments during markup action.

Table 7-4 likewise confirms the influential roles played by formal leaders in House and Senate committees. Again, the most important difference is in the relative roles played by subcommittee versus full committee leaders. We have already noted the crucial role played by subcommittee leaders in drafting legislation in the House. Table 7-4 shows that this domination of committee lawmaking continues into the markup stage. By themselves, the subcommittee chair and ranking minority member of the subcommittee with jurisdiction over a bill are responsible for almost 40 percent of all subsequent amendments to the bill; in contrast, full committee chairs account for only 5 percent. In the Senate, full committee and subcommittee leaders are more nearly equal in the extent to which they amend legislation that reaches the markup stage, but the number of amendments offered by the latter is still greater than those offered by the former by a 2-1 ratio.

In both chambers, the advantages of institutional resources, information, and member interest are clearly important in determining who makes the laws at the committee stage, but they cannot by themselves form the basis for a full-blown theory of legislative influence. Their effects are themselves contingent on political factors. Probably the most important of these are party, ideology, and the relative position of the administration. Other things being equal, the leader or backbencher who enjoys majority status will more easily shape committee legislation. The chairs far more than the ranking minority members dominate the drafting of the original vehicles, but even at the markup stage, members of the majority are more likely to attach additional amendments. For instance, of the several hundred successful amendments summarized in Table 7-4, approximately 68 percent in the House and 56 percent in the Senate were offered by majority party members, this despite the fact that majority party members already enjoy greater access to the behind-the-scenes negotiations that typically lead to the legislative vehicle that is ultimately subject to amendment. Similarly, the proximity of one's policy views to the current administration, the floor majority, or other important actors beyond the committee provides bargaining leverage that tends to affect the degree to which interest and institutional position translate into legislative effect.

Participation and Representation in a Decentralized Congress

Institutional critics have long reflected on the way in which the best democratic elections are undone in a legislative assembly that is itself oligarchic. Challenges to the uneven distribution of power within Congress have occurred periodically in this century with the occasional effect of changing the basic nature of the institution. In 1910 the House of Representatives revolted against the czarlike rule of Speaker Joseph "Boss" Cannon. In the 1950s and 1960s liberal activists berated the committee system, claiming that the power of southern conservative committee chairs prevented chamber majorities from working their will on major civil rights legislation, especially in the Senate. In the early 1970s the prerogatives of seniority and committee chairmanship were significantly curtailed in the House, such that institutional advantages were simultaneously shifted to the Speaker and to subcommittee chairs. More recently, institutional critics have advanced proposals to weaken further the power of committee chairs by giving the Speaker authority to appoint them, by restricting length of committee service of both chairs and members, and by curtailing committee staffs and budgets.[37] In the Senate, likewise, senatorial holds and other devices of minority obstructionism have come increasingly under attack. Such proposals, reformers hope, would not so much shift power in Congress from one set of oligarchs to another as invigorate party leaders who might serve as agents of their party's membership.

The ultimate success of reform notwithstanding, neither chamber is likely to exhibit soon any kind of rigid authority structure. But neither will the practice of decision making in Congress prove egalitarian, at least in the sense that a majority-rule voting model implies. As we have seen, legislative authority over a particular issue is often located in a small group of legislative players, but the size and composition of this group changes with each issue, and the distribution of influence is determined less by some formal bestowal of authority than by the distribution of members' interests and their ability to pay the time and information costs associated with effective involvement in the issue at hand. These are central tendencies of congressional decision making that are not likely to be affected much by procedural change.

The patterns of participation examined in this essay, then, have important implications for our evaluation of Congress. The focus of this final section will be on how they affect its representative character. The implications are not intuitively obvious. They become more clear when we first reflect on the traditional way in which the concept of representation has been defined and the principal way in which it has been studied.

Perhaps the most influential work on representation in Congress is an essay by Warren Miller and Donald Stokes entitled "Constituency Influence in Congress." [38] The principal purpose of their study was to employ available social scientific data to conduct a broad-based, empirical analysis of representation. Specifically, Miller and Stokes defined representation as the congruence between the roll call voting patterns of members and the general policy preferences of their constituents, a definition that squares well with ordinary language usage. Members who consistently vote in such a way as to contradict district opinion, for instance, are normally said to be "unresponsive," "out of touch," or "unrepresentative" of their districts. Periodic elections, in turn, serve to ensure that such relationships remain reasonably strong, that the westerner who votes against water projects and the Texan who supports domestic oil taxes are replaced by individuals more likely to represent their constituents.[39]

Implied in the Miller-Stokes formulation, then, is an important two-pronged premise: that representation is properly thought of as a relationship between a member and the member's constituency, one in which the former purposively reflects the views of the latter. To use language borrowed from Edmund Burke, the member is to act as a "delegate" of those who elected him or her. This view has received considerable play in the empirical research on representation[40] and has told us most of what we now know about the influence of constituents on members' postelection behavior. Although the results of that research appear somewhat mixed, the best work suggests that members do reflect constituent preferences when voting on the floor, especially when the issue is salient, the signal from the constituency is clear, and the consequences of the policy choice are easily traceable to the action of the representative.[41]

Whatever conclusions one draws from the study of legislative voting on the floor, however, a central theme of this essay has been that constituency considerations are common in member calculations during prefloor deliberations. Indeed, Mayhew has suggested that, in the extreme, committees can be viewed as platforms contrived for the purpose of expressing and advancing district interests.[42] And although I have suggested here that members have a diverse range of motivations, we have seen that constituency service is an especially important one. In selecting their committee and subcommittee assignments and in deciding how to allocate their time and energy in postassignment decision making, members regularly pursue opportunities to address concerns relevant to their district or state. This is especially true on committees widely characterized as parochial in outlook, such as House Agriculture. But it is also true on committees whose jurisdictions are less well known for their relevance to constituency interests, such as House Education and Labor or House Energy and Commerce.[43]

At the district-delegate level, then, the participation decisions of committee members provide reassurance that members are in fact responsive to their districts; representation, in this sense, is robust. Were the concept of representation properly focused only at the district-delegate level, the democratic critic could rest reassured that constituent interests are, in fact, represented in a decentralized Congress. But there is a second, perhaps more important level at which the study of representation must operate, a level at which the classic writings of John Stuart Mill on representative government are often pitched.[44] Mill suggests that the faithful representation of districts by individual members is not simply a democratic end in itself. Rather, it is something of a means to a larger institutional or collective end—the creation of an assembly that in the course of its collective deliberations gives expression to the views, values, and interests of a diverse citizenry. Such a perspective, then, emphasizes not so much the strength of the district-delegate connection but the representativeness of the collective deliberations.

Insofar as floor voting is concerned, there is little divergence in one's assessment of representation at these two levels. By constitutional requirement, each member has only one vote. Political prudence, in turn, requires that members miss few roll call votes, so that voting participation in both chambers averages more than 90 percent. But once one moves the analysis beyond an exclusive focus on floor voting, the first observation one must make is that participation is not universal. The second is that it is not equal. And the third is that there are good reasons to believe that, in certain conditions, the subset of members who do participate in the legislative deliberation will *not* be representative of the larger assembly.

The first two observations have been the focus of this essay to this point. At the committee stage, the stage at which most of the actual deliberation and decision making gets done, those two generalizations clearly hold. In the remainder of this section, I take up the third and identify two conditions that, when simultaneously met, lead one to worry that the selective participation of members within a committee will diminish the representativeness of the committee's deliberations.

The first condition is simply this: in deciding whether to become involved in an issue, constituency considerations are prominent. The second condition holds when the issue at hand involves policy choices in which the expected benefits are concentrated and the costs dispersed (or the expected costs concentrated and the benefits dispersed) such that the interests of different districts affected by the issue are mutually compatible. The more perfectly these two conditions are met, the *less* representative are the deliberations of the committee. There is, in short, a paradox central to our thinking about representation in an assembly charged with making collective choices about national policy. Responsiveness at one level may undermine representativeness at a second level.

Such conditions, of course, do not always hold, but they are common enough to distort the policy choices of Congress on many important matters in different policy domains. For instance, these conditions probably hold more often than not in the House and Senate committee deliberations over specific agricultural policies. To cite but one recent case, dairy assistance bills that emerged from both House and Senate agriculture committees in 1991 exhibited an unmistakable prodairy bias, this despite the opposition of the president, lobbying by a number of public interest groups, and severe budgetary pressures. With dairy subsidies and dairy farm income in decline during 1990-1991, both committees acted aggressively to shore up dairy farmers' income, advancing proposals that stood to impose (widely dispersed) costs on consumers of dairy products and, as an indirect consequence, threatened to cut by half a billion dollars the nutritional supplements to the widely dispersed beneficiaries of federal food stamps, school lunch programs, and the Women, Infants, and Children (WIC) feeding program.[45] Why did the committees act in this way? The makeup of the committees provides only a partial answer. Although there is a clear proagricultural bias on both committees, the overrepresentation of dairy state and district members is not dramatic. The prodairy bias among active *participants* within the committee was striking, however. The contribution of dairy production to the state economies of committee activists on the Dairy Assistance Act was three times greater than the average for committee nonmembers and 70 percent greater than the average for the already proagriculture committee members.[46] The pattern was even more striking in the House Agriculture Committee, with most of the principal players in the deliberation representing districts that ranked near the top in dairy production.[47]

The policymaking pattern exhibited in the recent dairy assistance deliberations is not unusual; indeed, the deliberations exhibit a pattern in dairy policymaking that has been evident for several decades. Neither are such patterns limited, within agriculture, to dairy policy, nor within the various domains of federal policy, to agricultural policy. Committee deliberations on farm credit, wheat and feed grains subsidies, peanut and sugar production controls—indeed, virtually every major nonnutrition agricultural program—exhibit patterns in which members from districts that have much to gain or lose dominate the action, with the remainder (often a nominal majority) of members (whose districts bear the mostly imperceptible costs) abdicating to their intensely interested colleagues.[48]

Outside agriculture, such behavioral patterns often appear in important areas that command significant federal resources. The clearest (if frequently overgeneralized) occasion involves decision making on Appropriations Committee provisions that provide for district- or state-specific projects—that is, classic pork-barrel spending programs. The magnitude of the difference between the benefits (to the local economy) and the costs (an imperceptible increase in tax burden or budget deficit) is huge for the districts in which the projects will be located. The same cannot be said for other districts. Although the benefits may be zero, the costs for them too are imperceptible; so the representatives of these districts have little incentive to devote scarce time and energy to opposing the efforts of their strongly motivated colleagues.[49] An important part of the explanation of why such nonmajoritarian measures get passed, then, is not so much logrolling, reciprocity, or deference as it is rational abdication by those members whose districts will not be significantly affected.[50]

The general principle at work here, however, is not limited to classic pork-barrel proposals—or proposals that involve identifiable projects earmarked for specific districts or states.[51] Other areas include certain kinds of urban aid, public works, transportation subsidies, merchant marine issues, tax policy, and even defense spending—an area in which one might most expect to see member participation driven by policy views about national security rather than by the desire to protect the stream of benefits to particular locales. During consideration of the fiscal 1993 defense authorization bill, for instance, Armed Services Committee members whose districts would be most hurt by impending defense cuts pushed through $1.2 billion in benefits in the form of economic adjustment assistance for affected communities, retraining for displaced defense industry workers, and loan guarantees to small defense companies attempting to diversify.[52] One staffer who participated in the negotiations likened them to the drafting of a disaster relief bill, noting that "anybody with defense-related layoffs showed up with a proposal, nobody else. There was no one there to say no."

Although important, these examples are not intended to characterize Congress and its members as single-minded seekers of district benefits. As I have already noted, not all issues that come before congressional committees are driven by state and district concerns. And members are not equally attentive to such concerns when they arise, even on committees known for a strong constituency orientation. The principal actors in Senate Agriculture's consideration of the 1988 Emergency Hunger Relief Act represented the states of Iowa, Kansas, Minnesota, and Vermont—hardly the states that benefit most from the Food Stamps program or other federal feeding efforts. The conservation titles of the 1985 and 1990 omnibus farm bills reflected the environmental and conservationist concerns of entrepreneurs on both the House and Senate Agriculture committees. One of the 1985 provisions imposed severe penalties on farmers who drained waterfowl habitat for crop production; another imposed unprecedented regulations on farmers who tilled highly erodible soil. And on other major committees—including those dealing with foreign affairs, the environment, human resources, housing, and health—issues frequently arise that evoke ideological or other deeply felt policy commitments. Any close observer of Congress can cite countless examples where the policy views and commitments of the major legislative actors were crucial to the shape of the ultimate legislation, and it is a rare case in which these factors are altogether absent.

Even where state and district concerns matter, many of the important legislative battles in Congress involve broad issues that are salient nationwide, and a wide range of competing interests come into play. On such issues, proposals may well be advanced that provide concentrated benefits, but those same proposals also imply concentrated or otherwise significant and perceptible costs. Under these conditions, there are strong constituency-based incentives for members with diverse preferences to be active on the issue. To cite but one example, the committee deliberations over reauthorization of the Clean Air Act (deliberations which spanned a decade culminating in the 1990 Clean Air Amendments) were rife with conflicts directly traceable to the effects that various clean air proposals would have on local, state, and regional interests—smog reduction in California, auto manufacturing in Michigan, oil producing in Texas, coal mining in West Virginia, acid rain in New York, and power plants in Indiana, to name but a few.[53] Similar patterns of participation appear for high-salience issues in other committees as well. For instance, recent committee deliberations over tax reform, higher education reauthorization, unemployment compensation, energy policy, and trade legislation exhibited fairly broad participation with a wide range of members' ideas and interests entering the decision-making calculus.

Still, the dairy assistance case illuminates a paradox that is central to any evaluation of Congress as a democratic institution. It reveals that under relatively common conditions constituency-minded behavior tends to undermine the representative character of the institution, not enhance it. Individual members, in allocating their legislative time and resources to constituency concerns, are in certain respects doing what we think representatives ought to do, what the electoral sanction—either through intimidation or natural selection—ensures that they do. They are, in short, meeting the standard of representation evident in the work of Miller and Stokes and a long line of analysis that has followed in their wake. Moreover, it is precisely where constituency benefits or costs are concentrated that the delegate-minded legislator sees the interests of the constituency most clearly and where the member's obligation as agent thus appears least ambiguous. But at the same time, it is precisely under these conditions that the interests and preferences of the participants are most likely to be unrepresentative of the larger set of legislators who hold the formal authority to act. Satisfied at one level, then, the democratic critic is frustrated at the other. A division of legislative labor that tends to exclude a wide range of views and values from the deliberative process, one in which large numbers of legislators effectively abdicate their legislative responsibilities to more directly affected, delegate-minded colleagues, raises serious problems for those who care about the representativeness of congressional deliberations.

Notes

All unattributed quotes come from interviews conducted by the author with members of Congress or congressional staff.

1. Although he overstates the extent to which committees are being replaced by informal work groups and task forces, Richard Cohen provides a good description of these trends. See *Washington at Work* (New York: Macmillan, 1992). For an earlier discussion of the fragmentation of the institution, see Roger H. Davidson, "Subcommittee Government: New Channels for Policymaking," in *The New Congress*, ed. Thomas E. Mann and Norman J. Ornstein (Washington, D.C.: American Enterprise Institute, 1981).
2. In fact, Michael Cohen, James March, and Johan Olsen and a long line of organizational theorists who have built on their work would contend that such a characterization does not apply all that well to firms or other organizations reputed to be hierarchical. See "A Garbage Can Model of Organizational Choice," *Administrative Science Quarterly* 17 (1972): 1-25.
3. David R. Mayhew, *Congress: The Electoral Connection* (New Haven: Yale University Press, 1974), 95. Mayhew here is echoing the more general observation made in Bauer, Pool, and Dexter's famous study of policymaking on foreign trade. The authors note that the member's principal problem is "not how to vote but what to do with his time, how to allocate his resources, and where to put his energy." See Raymond A. Bauer, Ithiel de Sola Pool, and Lewis A. Dexter, *American Business and Public Policy* (New York: Atherton Press, 1963), 405.
4. For more extensive treatments on these questions, see David E. Price, *Who Makes the Laws? Creativity and Power in Senate Committees* (Cambridge, Mass.: Schenkman, 1972); and Richard L. Hall, *Participation in Congress* (New Haven: Yale University Press, 1993). This essay is a revised version of the chapter on committee decision making that I wrote for the 4th edition of this reader. "Committee Decision Making in the Postreform Congress," in *Congress Reconsidered*, 4th ed., ed. Lawrence C. Dodd and Bruce I. Oppenheimer (Washington, D.C.: CQ Press, 1989).
5. In the British House of Commons, for instance, committees typically act on legislation only after it has been introduced by the executive minister and approved in general form by the Commons as a whole. Even so, the importance of congressional committees can be overstated and often is. Committees are part of what is normally a sequential legislative process, in which actors at other stages have formal authority to preempt or review what particular committees have done. Woodrow Wilson's claim that Congress is a body that regularly meets to ratify the work of its committees is

simply not true in the 1990s, if even it was true in the 1880s when he was writing (which it probably was not). In fact, it is increasingly common for committee bills to be amended on the chamber floor. Likewise, the congressional budget process has increased the importance of party leaders and the budget committees at the expense of the several authorizing committees. And there has been some tendency in recent years for certain highly partisan or politically delicate issues to be handled by task forces or ad hoc groups, especially in the Senate. None of these developments undermines the general point that committee activities are central to the legislative process, however.

6. On the changing uses and growing importance of special rules in the House, including alternative interpretations of their role in a majority-rule assembly, see Stanley Bach and Steven S. Smith, *Managing Uncertainty in the House of Representatives: Adaptation and Innovation in Special Rules* (Washington, D.C.: Brookings Institution, 1988). On Republicans' reaction to the growing use of restrictive rules, see Janet Hook, "GOP Chafes Under Restrictive House Rules," *Congressional Quarterly Weekly Report,* Oct. 10, 1987, 2449-2452.

7. See Kenneth A. Shepsle, *The Giant Jigsaw Puzzle: Democratic Committee Assignments in the Modern House* (Chicago: University of Chicago Press, 1978); Richard F. Fenno, Jr., *Congressmen in Committees* (Boston: Little, Brown, 1973), chap. 1; Richard L. Hall and Bernard Grofman, "The Committee Assignment Process and the Conditional Nature of Committee Bias," *American Political Science Review* 84 (December 1990): 1149-1166.

8. Shepsle, *Giant Jigsaw Puzzle,* chaps. 3-5.

9. Quoted in Richard E. Cohen, "The Mysterious Ways Congress Makes Committee Assignments," *National Journal,* Feb. 3, 1979, 183.

10. Fenno, *Congressmen in Committees,* 5-8, 139-140.

11. See especially Steven S. Smith and Christopher J. Deering, *Committees in Congress* (Washington, D.C.: CQ Press, 1984), 105-110.

12. Although he is often cited as having done so, Mayhew does not advance this position as a descriptively accurate empirical claim. See *Congress: The Electoral Connection,* esp. 13-17.

13. Fenno, *Congressmen in Committees,* 1.

14. Cohen, "Mysterious Ways," 184.

15. Phil Duncan, "Freshman Class Adds Some Spice to Congressional Blend," *Congressional Quarterly Weekly Report,* Jan. 12, 1991, 90-91.

16. Hall and Grofman, "Committee Assignment Process."

17. Keith Krehbiel, *Information and Legislative Organization* (Ann Arbor: University of Michigan Press, 1990).

18. Donald R. Matthews, *U.S. Senators and Their World* (Chapel Hill: University of North Carolina Press, 1960), 93-94; see also Charles L. Clapp, *The Congressman: His Work as He Sees It* (Garden City, N.Y.: Anchor, 1963).

19. Quoted in Thomas O'Donnell, "Managing Legislative Time," in *The House at Work,* ed. Joseph Cooper and G. Calvin Mackenzie (Austin: University of Texas Press, 1981), 128.

20. O'Donnell, "Managing Legislative Time," 138.

21. See Barbara Sinclair, *The Transformation of the U.S. Senate* (Baltimore: Johns Hopkins University Press, 1989).

22. Norman J. Ornstein, Thomas E. Mann, and Michael J. Malbin, *Vital Statistics on Congress, 1987-1988* (Washington, D.C.: Congressional Quarterly, 1987), 130.

23. U.S. Senate, *Hearing of the Temporary Select Committee to Study the Senate Committee System,* pts. 1 and 2, 98th Cong., 2d sess., July 31, 1984, and March 4, 1984.

24. Ibid., pt. 1, 41. In late 1987 the Senate was again holding hearings on many of the topics taken up before the Quayle committee. Freshman Democrats organized in 1988 to press the Senate leadership for reforms that would address the time con-

straints, scheduling conflicts, and general quality of life within the institution. Meanwhile, Senator Evans announced that he would retire at the end of the 1988 session, after only one term in office. See Martin Frazier, "Why Some Senators Feel Disenchanted, Burned Out," *Roll Call*, Dec. 20, 1987, 1, 19; Janet Hook, "Senators Look for Ways to Increase Efficiency," *Congressional Quarterly Weekly Report*, Dec. 5, 1987, 3001-3002.

25. Clapp, *The Congressman*.

26. Rochelle L. Stanfield, "Plotting Every Move," *National Journal*, March 26, 1988, 792-797.

27. Randall Strahan, "Committee Politics and Tax Reform" (Paper presented at the annual meeting of the American Political Science Association, Chicago, September 1987); Jeffrey H. Birnbaum and Alan S. Murray, *Showdown at Gucci Gulch: Lawmakers, Lobbyists, and the Unlikely Triumph of Tax Reform* (New York: Random House, 1987).

28. The advantages that a chair position confers are not what they were in the prereform Congress, however, and as I note above, they were under attack from reformers in the 102d and 103d Congresses. For the differences from the prereform period, see Smith and Deering, *Committees in Congress*, chap. 6.

29. See David Maraniss, "Power Play: Chairman's Gavel Crushes Gas Decontrol Vote," *Washington Post*, Nov. 20, 1983, A1.

30. Ibid.

31. For an excellent case study that reveals both the value and the limits of Dingell's procedural control over his committee's agenda, see Richard Cohen, *Washington at Work: Back Rooms and Clean Air* (New York: Macmillan, 1992).

32. The references are to Senate Labor and Human Resources Chair Edward M. Kennedy, D-Mass., whose committee has jurisdiction over school nutrition programs, and Rep. Leon E. Panetta, D-Calif., who chaired the House subcommittee with jurisdiction over food stamps and a number of other food assistance programs.

33. David W. Rohde, "Committee Reform in the House of Representatives and the Subcommittee Bill of Rights," *Annals of the American Academy of Political and Social Science* 411 (January 1974): 39-47.

34. See Smith and Deering's excellent discussion of House and Senate subcommittees in *Committees in Congress*, chap. 5.

35. The references are to the subcommittee chair, George J. Mitchell, D-Maine; subcommittee ranking minority member Dave Durenberger, R-Minn.; and full committee chair Lloyd Bentsen, D-Texas.

36. The problems of drawing strong inferences about influence from such data are several and important, however. See Richard L. Hall, "Measuring Legislative Influence," *Legislative Studies Quarterly* 17 (May 1992): 205-232. Still, better data and more systematic analysis confirm that subcommittee members and leaders are disproportionately powerful in committee decision making. See Richard L. Hall and C. Lawrence Evans, "The Power of Subcommittees," *Journal of Politics* 52 (May 1990): 335-355.

37. See Janet Hook, "Extensive Reform Proposals Cook on the Front Burner," *Congressional Quarterly Weekly Report*, June 6, 1992, 1579-1585.

38. Warren Miller and Donald Stokes, "Constituency Influence in Congress," *American Political Science Review* 57 (March 1963): 45-56.

39. Hannah Pitkin strongly emphasizes the importance of legitimate elections in her discussion of the theory and practice of representation, though she does not suggest that individual legislators be strictly responsive to district opinion in their legislative decisions. See *The Concept of Representation* (Berkeley: University of California Press, 1967), chap. 10.

40. For instance, see Donald J. McCrone and James H. Kuklinski, "The Delegate Theory of Representation," *American Journal of Political Science* 23 (1973): 278-300;

Christopher Achen, "Measuring Representation," *American Journal of Political Science* 22 (1978): 475-510; Morris P. Fiorina, *Representatives, Roll Calls, and Constituencies* (Lexington, Mass.: Heath, 1974). Richard Fenno's work on the subject pushes far beyond the delegate connection, though his focus remains at the member-constituency level. See *Home Style: House Members in Their Districts* (Boston: Little, Brown, 1978). More recent research by Jackson and King suggests that members represent constituents' preferences for public goods—policies that will not directly or materially benefit the constituents themselves—as well as their preferences for such things as water projects or energy tax breaks. See John E. Jackson and David C. King, "Public Goods, Private Interests, and Representation," *American Political Science Review* 83 (December 1989): 1143-1164.

41. The three best books on roll call voting all emphasize the importance of constituency: John Kingdon, *Congressmen's Voting Decisions*, 3d ed. (Ann Arbor: University of Michigan Press, 1989); Fiorina, *Representatives, Roll Calls, and Constituencies*; and John E. Jackson, *Constituencies and Leaders in Congress* (Cambridge: Harvard University Press, 1974). For a more recent work that takes up the conditions under which members will be most attentive to constituent preferences and upon which I build here, see R. Douglas Arnold, *The Logic of Congressional Action* (New Haven: Yale University Press, 1990). Still, a significant number of works do conclude that constituency effects are weak, but most such studies suffer from a common methodological problem that renders their conclusions suspect. For a summary of the literature challenging the constituency connection, see Robert A. Bernstein, *Elections, Representation, and Congressional Voting Behavior: The Myth of Constituency Control* (Englewood Cliffs, N.J.: Prentice Hall, 1989). For an analysis of the methodological problems that undercut that literature, see John E. Jackson and John W. Kingdon, "Ideology, Interest Group Ratings, and Roll Call Votes," *American Journal of Political Science* (1992), 805-823.

42. Mayhew, *Congress: The Electoral Connection*, 85-97.

43. See Hall, *Participation in Congress*.

44. See "Considerations on Representative Government," in *Three Essays* (Oxford: Oxford University Press, 1975), esp. chap. 5; John Chamberlin and Paul Courant, "Representative Deliberations and Representative Decisions: Proportional Representation and the Borda Rule," *American Political Science Review* 77 (1983) 718-733.

45. Alisa J. Rubin, "Attempts to Rewrite Farm Bill Stall in House Committee," *Congressional Quarterly Weekly Report*, July 13, 1991, 1894; Alisa J. Rubin, "Panel Raises Milk Subsidy, but Limits Production," *Congressional Quarterly Weekly Report*, July 20, 1991, 1977.

46. These estimates were calculated from data reported in Hall and Grofman, "Committee Assignment Process."

47. See Alissa J. Rubin, "Overhaul of Dairy Programs Propelled by Price Squeeze," *Congressional Quarterly Weekly Report*, July 6, 1991, 1822-1825. For a detailed description of the House subcommittee and full committee markups on the 1991 dairy legislation that reveals the dominant role played by dairy state representatives, see *Minutes of the Business Meetings and Hearings of the House Committee on Agriculture* (Washington, D.C.: U.S. Government Printing Office, 1991), 329-337, 558-570.

48. For an analysis of the bias evident in the behavioral patterns on a major farm credit bill, see Hall, "Committee Decision Making." For a more general discussion of selective participation in committee and its implications for representation in Congress, see Hall, *Participation in Congress*.

49. Although it is probably true that pork barrel is an overworked metaphor for characterizing all of congressional politics, it remains an important part of congressional spending decisions, even in a period of severe budgetary constraints on discretionary spending. For one recent example, see Mike Mills, "Home-State Projects Pave Way for Highway Bill Approval," *Congressional Quarterly Weekly Report*, July 20, 1991, 1976.

50. See Hall, *Participation in Congress,* chap. 7.
51. I should also add, however, that the principle at work in the mobilization of legislative agents can and often does extend beyond the case of geographically concentrated beneficiaries to groups or organizations that may be widely distributed across districts but whose intense interests within districts cause them to figure prominently in the member's perception of his or her constituency when thinking about a particular issue. Thus do the American Association of Retired Persons, the National Rifle Association, and various environmental groups exert considerable pressure on members from the grass roots. Other groups that may have no ability to claim representation of voters but have other election-relevant resources—most notably money—are likewise advantaged in mobilizing their supporters in Congress. On this point, see Richard L. Hall and Frank Wayman, "Buying Time: Moneyed Interests and the Mobilization of Bias in Congressional Committees," *American Political Science Review* 84 (September 1990): 797-820.
52. For background on these provisions, see Pamela Fessler and Pat Towell, "Senate, House Look for Ways to Cushion Spending Drop," *Congressional Quarterly Weekly Report,* May 23, 1992, 1460-1461.
53. See Cohen, *Washington at Work.*

8

Dan Rostenkowski:
A Study in Congressional Power

Randall Strahan

*Q: What do you like most about being chairman of
the Ways and Means Committee?*

A: (Grins) Having people think you're powerful.

—Dan Rostenkowski[1]

Rep. Dan Rostenkowski of Illinois seems to have acquired the adjective "powerful" as part of his title. It is not hard to understand why journalists who cover Capitol Hill often refer to him as "the powerful chairman of the House Ways and Means Committee." As chairman of the standing committee in the House of Representatives that has jurisdiction over federal tax and trade legislation as well as over two of the biggest federal spending programs (Social Security and Medicare), the Chicago Democrat presides over a panel with extraordinarily broad authority. Because of his committee leadership position, Rostenkowski was a prominent figure during the 1980s in the enactment of major reforms of the tax code, the welfare system, and the Social Security program. As long as he serves in the House, he will likely play an important role in any major policy changes that occur in the areas of tax, trade, welfare, and health policy.

Rostenkowski's approach to legislative politics invites use of the description "powerful." A product of the rough-and-tumble ethnic politics of one of America's last great urban political machines, Rostenkowski often appears out of step with the new age sensibilities and entrepreneurial, mass-media-oriented politics that are coming to define today's political class. He prefers and practices an older style of politics that emphasizes personal and tribal loyalty, deference to hierarchy, quiet negotiation, rewarding friends—and getting even with enemies. For example, in one incident that is well on the way to becoming part of the folklore of the modern House, Rostenkowski visited his wrath on Democrat Kent Hance of Texas. Hance, at the time a Ways and Means member, had cosponsored the 1981 Reagan administration tax-cut legislation that won out on the House floor over a bill written by Rostenkowski and Ways and Means Democrats. In response, during the House-Senate conference on the tax bill, the chairman pushed for deletion of provisions of personal importance to Hance, refused authorization for Hance to travel with a committee delegation to China, and even had the wheels removed from Hance's chair in the committee hearing room.[2]

Rostenkowski has actively attempted to assert control over the Ways and Means Committee and the legislation it develops. But it would be a mistake to dismiss him simply as a big-city arm-twister. During his tenure as Ways and Means chairman, he has built a reputation for taking public policy problems seriously and has recently been hailed "a master legislator" by the respected *Almanac of American Politics*.[3] Thus, when Dan Rostenkowski is described as powerful, it is not only because of his formal position but also because of his willingness to use power and his engagement in the important economic and social welfare issues over which his committee exercises jurisdiction.

Yet if power is viewed in light of the standard social science definition of A getting B to do something B otherwise would not have done, the closer one looks at Rostenkowski or other modern congressional leaders, the more elusive congressional power appears to be. Congressional leaders have limited rewards and punishments they can use to win compliance from their followers. They have almost no say in the decision to hire and fire legislators, a power that rests in the hands of members' local constituencies. As Charles O. Jones emphasized in his classic study of the limits of leadership in the House of Representatives, unresponsive or heavy-handed leaders who fail to maintain support of a "procedural majority" risk being stripped of their authority or voted out of leadership positions.[4] And in the case of House committee leaders, reforms enacted during the 1970s were designed expressly to limit the authority of committee chairmen over organizational and procedural matters and to make it easier for members of the majority party to remove committee leaders who fail to represent party members' views.[5]

As chairman of the House Ways and Means Committee, Dan Rostenkowski presents us with an interesting case in which to explore power and its limits in the House of Representatives. It will be helpful first to look at some historical background on the Ways and Means Committee and the leaders who preceded Rostenkowski as chairman. We will then survey the distinctive features of the institutional and political context within which Rostenkowski has worked since becoming Ways and Means chairman in 1981 and examine the leadership style Rostenkowski has developed as chairman. We will then consider two important cases, tax reform in 1985-1986 and capital-gains taxation in 1989, to illustrate Rostenkowski's use of power as Ways and Means chairman as well as the limits to that power. One goal of this essay is to convey how House members themselves view the exercise of power and leadership. To this end, the discussion will draw heavily upon interviews with Ways and Means members and staff.

The House Committee on Ways and Means

Dan Rostenkowski's importance as a political leader in the House stems in large part from the broad authority of the standing committee he chairs. The Committee on Ways and Means has existed as a standing committee in the House since 1795. During the nineteenth century, because of its jurisdiction over important economic policy issues, Ways and Means became closely linked to the political party leadership in the House. This connection was strengthened in 1911, when Ways and Means Democrats were assigned the power to make standing committee assignments for members of their party. With its members exercising this important organizational function and presiding over a jurisdiction that included, after the 1930s, Social Security and related social welfare programs as well as tax and trade policy, Ways and Means was considered one of the most important committees in the House. The committee probably reached the peak of its influence in the modern House during the years that Wilbur D. Mills, D-Ark., served as chairman (1958-1974).[6]

The Mills Era

During the years that Mills served as chairman, a relatively small Ways and Means Committee (twenty-five members) enjoyed considerable autonomy in framing economic and social welfare legislation for the House. The committee normally wrote legislation behind closed doors and brought its bills to the House floor under closed rules that prohibited amendments from noncommittee members. Another important feature of Ways and Means politics during this era was what John Manley termed "restrained partisanship."[7] Members of both parties generally took part in the deliberations through which legislation took form. Partisan conflict, when it occurred, was usually limited to votes in the final stages of committee decision making. In analyzing Ways and Means Committee politics during this period, Richard F. Fenno, Jr., found that most committee members agreed on two basic things: first, that they should try to protect the committee's prestige by writing legislation that would pass on the House floor; and second, that committee members should represent and defend their party's views in committee deliberations.[8]

Chairman Mills was an important influence on Ways and Means Committee politics because of the balance he struck between these two guiding premises. As Fenno described Mills's approach: "With the desire for floor success uppermost in mind, he does everything he can to facilitate and achieve a consensus on every bill." "His idea of consensus-building," Fenno added, "envisions not only Republican participation, but Republican votes at the decision stage. As a realist, he knows this is not always possible; and so, reluctantly, he also practices policy partisanship."[9]

For Mills, effective leadership meant protecting the committee's prestige in the House by making sure that Ways and Means bills were technically sound and capable of winning majority support on the House floor. Because subcommittees were abolished shortly after Mills became chairman, all of the committee's work occurred under his close direction. But according to those who observed the committee closely, the chairman's influence was based more on his mastery of issues and skill at discovering grounds for agreement among members of the committee and the House than on formal powers or the threat of sanctions.[10]

The Reform Era and the Ullman Chairmanship

The decade of the 1970s was a watershed period of institutional change and reform in the House of Representatives. The Ways and Means Committee was one of the principal targets of reform efforts. In part because of liberal Democrats' frustration with the cautious approach to new policy initiatives taken by the committee under Chairman Mills and in part because of demands for greater openness and participation by the large number of new members elected in the 1970s, the House enacted reforms that reduced the procedural autonomy of the committee and increased the influence of the majority party organization over the committee's operation.

As a result, by 1975 the context for exercising leadership on the Ways and Means Committee had changed dramatically. Committee chairs in the House were no longer assured of selection on the basis of seniority. Those who failed to be responsive to rank-and-file Democrats risked removal, under new rules that required election by a secret ballot of the Democratic Caucus. New rules were enacted to discourage committees from meeting in closed-door sessions. In addition, several reforms were targeted specifically at the Ways and Means Committee and at the centralized, consensus-oriented leadership exercised by Wilbur Mills. These reforms included transferral of the committee-assignment power from Ways and Means Democrats to a new Steering and Policy Committee chaired by the Speaker; changes in the closed-rule procedure to allow amendments to Ways and Means bills to be proposed by vote of the Democratic Caucus; a requirement that subcommittees be established; expansion of the committee's size from twenty-five members to thirty-seven members; and an increase in the majority-minority ratio on the committee from 3:2 to 2:1. Finally, budget reforms enacted in 1974 further reduced the autonomy of the Ways and Means Committee by creating new organizational units (the House and Senate Budget committees) and new procedures for coordinating money decisions.[11]

New patterns in appointments to the Ways and Means Committee also began to appear during the reform era. In some respects the selection process for new committee members showed continuity. State and regional representation continued to be important. Leaders in both parties remained active in the process, and most appointees had established records of party loyalty before winning a Ways and Means seat. But in a break with earlier practice, committee recruitment during the reform era was opened to junior members, including freshmen, and to members from highly competitive districts. In addition, changes began to appear in the goals legislators were seeking to advance through service on the Ways and Means Committee.[12]

During the Mills era most members who sought positions on Ways and Means did so primarily for reasons of prestige and influence.[13] In the aftermath of the reforms of the 1970s, which reduced the committee's power and autonomy and created broader legislative opportunities by expanding the committee and mandating use of subcommittees, this was no longer true. Interviews with members who have sought seats on Ways and Means since 1975 show that half or more cite policy interests as the reason for pursuing a seat on that commit-tee.[14] Thus, since the mid-1970s a broader range of views has been present about how the committee should operate, with more members seeking to ad-vance policy goals and fewer working primarily to protect the committee's pres-tige. The presence of more policy-oriented legislators, together with the reforms that reduced the committee's autonomy and increased the influence of the ma-jority party leadership and organization, made the context for exercising leader-ship on Ways and Means considerably more complex than it had been during most of the Mills era.

Mills resigned his chairmanship in late 1974 after a period of erratic per-sonal behavior. Al Ullman, D-Ore., who became chairman in 1975, brought a new perspective to the committee chair.[15] As he commented in a 1978 interview,

> I see my role as altogether different than chairmen used to see theirs. They were worried about image and not losing any bills and not bringing anything to the floor unless they had all the votes in their pocket. You can't operate that way any more. I see my role as one of leadership and trying to expand the thinking of Congress in new directions in order to meet the long term needs of the country.[16]

Rather than focusing his efforts as chairman on protecting the committee's pres-tige and record of floor success as Mills had, Ullman emphasized open debate and participation by committee members. He also demonstrated a willingness to take highly controversial bills to the House floor, risking (and sometimes incur-ring) defeat of the committee's recommendations or major amendments.

As one Democrat put it, "Mr. Ullman operated the committee in a collegial style. He didn't try to set a strong direction." When working on legislation, Ullman typically would endorse a position but then allow the committee to work its will without strong direction from the chair. He encouraged decentralization of authority on the committee by allowing broad discretion to subcommittee chairs in hiring staff. He rarely attempted to intervene or influence the develop-ment of legislation in Ways and Means subcommittees.

Some who served on the committee during the reform era enjoyed the legislative opportunities afforded by Ullman's permissive leadership style. But few described Al Ullman as a successful or effective chairman. Members of both parties were frustrated with his permissive approach to leadership and the volatile and unpredictable politics that resulted. The tone of many members' evaluations of the Ullman chairmanship is conveyed by one senior member's description of the period as a "time of wandering in the desert." Criticism of Ullman's leadership voiced by Ways and Means members suggests that at least some might have accepted stronger direction from the chair. Given his inclination toward a participatory, democratic approach to committee politics, however, Ullman showed little interest in reasserting leadership when the ex-traordinary passions of the 1970s reform era began to subside. When Ullman was defeated for reelection in 1980, his successor, Chicago Democrat Dan Rostenkowski, brought a very different view of politics and leadership to the Ways and Means chair.

Leadership and Power in the
Postreform Ways and Means Committee

Opportunities for, and limits on, the exercise of power by congressional leaders are defined primarily by three kinds of contextual factors. First are institutional factors. Institutional factors include constitutional forms and formal structures within the House as well as informal norms and practices that structure the expectations and behavior of members. Second are factors associated with electoral politics and the party system. The degree of unity or factionalism within the congressional parties and the configuration of partisan control of Congress and the White House are the most important factors of this kind.[17] Finally, at any given time the opportunities and constraints encountered by party and committee leaders in Congress are defined in part by the political forces arrayed around the issues on the congressional agenda or within the jurisdictions of specific committees.

Contextual Factors, 1981-1992

Institutional factors. As we have seen, during the 1970s the institutional context for leadership on the Ways and Means Committee had been restructured by reforms that reduced the procedural autonomy of the committee and increased the influence of the majority party organization and leadership. Under the institutional arrangements and budgeting procedures that have been in place during the years Rostenkowski has been chairman, the Ways and Means chairman has had to be attentive both to the concerns of the Democratic Caucus and to a succession of budgetary mechanisms that have constrained legislative options available to the committee.

In contrast to the Ways and Means chairman of the prereform years, the postreform chairman cannot give second priority to partisan objectives without risking removal by the Democratic Caucus. As David Rohde explains in his study of the "conditional party government" regime that has emerged from the 1970s reforms, "seeking and accepting positions of influence within the committee or party leadership meant accepting an implied contract: such leaders were obliged to support—or at least not to block—policy initiatives on which there was a party consensus."[18] Through budget procedures including reconciliation, the Gramm-Rudman-Hollings deficit-reduction act, and the 1990 budget agreement, House majorities have also defined constraints on the range of actions the chair and the committee may take—either by mandating specific actions (most often tax increases or cuts in entitlement programs) or by creating procedural obstacles to legislation that has an adverse budgetary effect.

The postreform institutional context also includes the patterns in committee recruitment noted earlier. Ways and Means members no longer share a consensus on protecting committee prestige. The current mix of members recruited to the committee builds into the committee's politics a tension between those who are primarily concerned with pursuing policy goals, especially partisan policy goals, and those who are concerned with protecting the prestige of the committee and drafting legislation that will become law.

Thus, the most prominent institutional factors affecting leadership on the postreform Ways and Means Committee include recruitment patterns that have produced a more heterogeneous committee membership and structural and procedural arrangements that require the committee to be more directly responsible to the majority party organization and to the preferences of House majorities on budgetary matters as expressed through reconciliation instructions and budgeting statutes. Like it or not, the Ways and Means chair today is not only responsible for leading a standing committee and overseeing a huge jurisdiction but is also an important part of the majority party organization and the congressional budget process.

Partisan and electoral factors. During Rostenkowski's chairmanship the distinctive features of the partisan context have been divided party government and, after a brief period in the early 1980s, the decline of the conservative coalition in the House, increased partisanship, and greater unity among House Democrats.[19] Although Republican presidents were elected and reelected in 1980, 1984, and 1988, the Democratic majority in the House since 1982 has been sufficiently large to allow—and at times to require—a partisan coalition-building strategy on Ways and Means. On issues on which House Democrats have been unified in opposition to Republican presidents, bipartisan cooperation between Democrats and Republicans on the Ways and Means Committee has been made very difficult if not effectively foreclosed. High-stakes partisan conflicts over tax and budget issues between House Democrats and a Republican White House also create opportunities for greater involvement by the majority leadership in developing legislation, further limiting the autonomy of the Ways and Means Committee and its chairman.

Jurisdiction and agenda factors. The Ways and Means agenda in the early 1980s centered on the tax- and budget-cutting initiatives of the new Reagan administration. Since that time the committee's agenda has been dominated by the large budget deficits that followed enactment of the president's program. With a jurisdiction encompassing both tax legislation and the biggest entitlement programs, the Ways and Means Committee and its chairman have been the focus of fiscal pressures to maintain (or raise) revenue and to restrain growth of entitlement spending. The committee has also been at the center of many highly partisan battles with Republican presidents Reagan and Bush over alternative approaches to economic policy and deficit reduction.

Dan Rostenkowski's Rise to Power

Daniel D. Rostenkowski's involvement in political life began well before his election to the House in 1958. His father, Joe Rostenkowski, had served as alderman and Democratic committeeman for Chicago's Thirty-second Ward. After abandoning a fledgling professional baseball career (as a pitching prospect in the Philadelphia Athletics organization) and attending Loyola University, Rostenkowski was elected to the Illinois state legislature in 1952 at the age of twenty-four. He served two terms in the state legislature. Rostenkowski then sought and won the support of Chicago mayor Richard J. Daley to run for the congressional seat that had come open in the Eighth District in 1958. With the blessing of Daley and the powerful Chicago Democratic organization, Rostenkowski began his House career when he was thirty.

Once in Congress, Rostenkowski maintained close ties to Mayor Daley and to local politics in Chicago, but he began also to seek out positions of influence within the House. Attracted by the political clout associated with the committee-assignment power then exercised by the Ways and Means Committee, Rostenkowski won a seat on the panel in 1964. Three years later he was elected chairman of the Democratic Caucus. In 1970 he won the sponsorship of Majority Leader Hale Boggs of Louisiana for appointment as majority whip, only to see the deal vetoed by Speaker Carl Albert of Oklahoma. After the 1980 election Rostenkowski had a second opportunity to join the top ranks of the majority leadership when an appointment as majority whip was offered by Speaker Thomas P. "Tip" O'Neill of Massachusetts. In something of a surprise move—for many had viewed Rostenkowski as a vote counter with little interest in or aptitude for substantive legislative work—he opted instead to fill the Ways and Means chair that was vacated by Al Ullman's defeat in the 1980 election.[20]

Steering the Cadillac Committee: Rostenkowski as Chairman

Rostenkowski's approach to leadership bears an unmistakable imprint from his political apprenticeship in the Chicago Democratic organization of the 1950s. As Leo Snowiss observed in a study of congressional recruitment written in the 1960s, members who came out of the Chicago machine tended to be nonideological types who were "well schooled in ... quiet bargaining, negotiation and compromise," who "value[d] party cohesion as a positive good in need of little or no justification," and who viewed politics "as a cooperative, organizational enterprise." They were also men who were accustomed to working within "a relatively hierarchic structure of authority." [21]

Rostenkowski has demonstrated impressive dexterity in adapting this older style of politics to a House dominated by independent, "new breed" legislators. One Democratic member who was elected at the height of the 1970s reform era described Rostenkowski's style of leadership:

> He talks about [Ways and Means] as the Cadillac of committees, and I say that you should refer to it as the Mercedes-Benz of committees. But he believes in these values of loyalty and stability, that there's a boss and the wise and compassionate boss checks it out with his minions before he leads them into battle. And he rewards and punishes. You know, these are all very Old Testament-type values. And they've worked very well.

Recalling Wilbur Mills's chairmanship, Rostenkowski's approach to leadership has focused on protecting and enhancing the power and reputation of the

Ways and Means Committee. "He wants his committee to look good, to pass legislation," stated one member. Said a second member,

> He constantly makes the argument that this is the elite committee in the House. [He says that] anybody who would want to serve on another committee ... doesn't know what he is talking about. He says this is the Cadillac committee.... He is very oriented toward reputation as such.

Ways and Means members and staff also describe Rostenkowski as a leader who seeks to maintain the committee's reputation as a body that writes "good law" and is capable of taking responsibility for difficult decisions, in addition to "winning" passage of committee bills on the House floor. Rostenkowski is quick to characterize the committee in these terms when asked about its role in the House:

> We're the best goddam committee in the House of Representatives. We work harder than anyone else. We take our jobs more seriously. We're the first ones to be criticized because we take the first bite of the apple. And sometimes there are a lot of worms in that apple.

A senior Republican commented that the chairman "feels a tremendous sense of responsibility" for the programs within the committee's jurisdiction. Although he participated actively in a tax-cut bidding war with the Reagan administration in 1981, Rostenkowski has been a consistent supporter of deficit-reduction efforts since that episode. On his role in fiscal matters, he says, "I'm not afraid of telling people that hogs get fat and pigs get butchered. I'm not afraid of telling people, it's your turn to pay."

Neither as a legislator nor as chairman has Rostenkowski been known to hold strong ideological views. Although he is instinctively loyal to the Democratic party as an institution, he is decidedly less enthusiastic than some House Democrats about using the federal government as an instrument of economic redistribution. When asked what "good law" means to Rostenkowski, a senior Ways and Means staffer explained:

> At the heart of it he is a fundamental—almost New Deal—Democrat who wants to make people's lives a little easier. He doesn't shy away from making people pay for it. He is not a sort of unreconstructed liberal.... The biggest portrait in his office, the one with the light over it, is FDR.

Others describe Rostenkowski as a pragmatist and as more business-oriented than most Democratic liberals.

Perhaps in part because of his more moderate views and in part because of his respect for hierarchy and preference for bargaining over public confrontation, Rostenkowski has been less partisan in dealing with Republican presidents than some in his party might like. "His basic philosophy is that if [legislation] is good for the country we get the benefit because we control the Congress—and there is no need to have this warfare," one Democrat explained. Said another, "There are times when it's wise to fight, to draw the lines, when you have both policy and politics on your side. I'm not always sure he grasps that."

As chairman, Rostenkowski has developed an assertive, yet highly personal leadership style. In contrast to Al Ullman, he has attempted to centralize authority on the committee and to oversee legislative activity in subcommittees as well as at the full committee level. Rostenkowski's approach to committee leadership has five main elements: he is actively involved in committee recruitment; he encourages group solidarity; he consults early, then negotiates to win firm commitments; he threatens dissidents and freezes out defectors; and he maintains centralized control over organizational resources.

Recruiting committee members. As Ways and Means chairman, Rostenkowski maintains a seat on the Steering and Policy Committee, the body that makes committee assignments for House Democrats. When asked if he takes an active interest in who is appointed to the Ways and Means Committee, Rostenkowski replies, "You bet your life I do." All the Democrats interviewed who joined the committee after 1981 mentioned that Rostenkowski was an important participant in the committee-recruitment process. It is difficult to know how influential he has actually been in determining appointments to the committee, but it is clear that for some Democrats his involvement has encouraged a sense of personal obligation to the chairman. "I wouldn't be on that committee if he had not wanted me there," volunteered one junior Democrat. Said another, "If you don't have his support, his active support, you can't get on that committee."

Rostenkowski has pushed to reestablish the prereform practice of restricting Ways and Means appointments to experienced members from relatively safe districts. As a senior committee Democrat who also served on the Steering and Policy Committee explained,

> Rostenkowski is a member of the old school. He doesn't want freshmen on the Ways and Means Committee. And he doesn't want anyone on that committee who is in trouble politically. It opens the door to too many compromise votes if you have a district that is 55 percent or so.

Discussing what he is looking for in new committee members, Rostenkowski commented:

> I want to see what kind of member he is or she is. I want to know if they can take a hard vote. . . . I've got to have people on that committee that are interested in the country, that will perform a leadership role and solicit other members to support the posture of the Ways and Means Committee, and that want to study and have some knowledge of what we have authority over. You can't make those kinds of judgments about people when they come here as freshmen.

In contrast to Democratic appointments during the Ullman years, no appointments of freshmen or members from marginal districts have been made to Ways and Means since 1980.[22]

Encouraging solidarity. Rostenkowski has tried to foster a sense of group identity and loyalty among Ways and Means members, particularly those on the Democratic side. "He has a different sense of loyalty and a different sense of comradeship about the committee than Mr. Ullman did," commented a Democrat who served under both chairmen. Rostenkowski's attempts to encourage group solidarity include informal dinners and gatherings with a circle of close allies on the committee; he also periodically convenes committee retreats in locations outside Washington.

Interviews with committee members suggest that Rostenkowski's involvement in recruitment and promotion of group solidarity have been important in rebuilding among junior members some of the concern for the committee's prestige and reputation that was characteristic of the prereform period. Note, for example, how one junior Democrat describes Rostenkowski's view of the committee:

> He likes a team player. That doesn't mean you have to march in lock step. But once you've tried your best to help whatever interest you might have or whatever issue you think is important—and you lose or you win—you don't embarrass the committee, you don't undermine the committee's work.

Consulting and negotiating firm commitments. When dealing with major legislative issues, Rostenkowski and his staff normally consult extensively with committee members before the chairman proposes a specific course of action. As one Democratic member observed:

> Rostenkowski is constantly calling caucuses. He is meeting with us all the time, catching us on the floor, calling us up. The way he keeps us in line is that he knows what his committee members want. By the time he is ready to make a decision, we've all played a role in it.

Rostenkowski's approach to building coalitions was described by a committee Democrat:

> When he's on a major piece of legislation he will have a series of conferences with the Democrats and let everyone speak their piece. He more or less sits back and listens and then goes to work on those he needs. . . . He works very closely with the ranking member on the Republican side . . . and another member or two on the Republican side if he needs to. Then he knows where he's going. He will forge a bill. He gets solid commitments, even if he has to trade a bit. . . . Then he'll pass that bill out of committee because he will know that he has a majority of votes.

"We know what areas an individual member is interested in," Rostenkowski explains. "You sit and talk with these fellas, and if you listen, they'll tell you everything that's on their minds." "And what I've done," he continued, "I'd ask certain people, what do you want to see in the bill? And after I'd seen that I'd got about nine or ten fellas that want the same thing, I'd do them all a favor and I'd put it in the bill."

Rostenkowski's approach to building coalitions in the full committee has been first to solidify a base of support among committee Democrats and then, if possible, to negotiate to attract Republican support. As was the case with Chairman Wilbur Mills, Rostenkowski's emphasis on protecting the committee's power and "winning" on the House floor encourages him to build bipartisan coalitions when political conditions allow. Rostenkowski makes clear his preference for reporting legislation with bipartisan support: "I think the members of my committee want to show some progress. And I know as a basic number if I can't get better than half the Republicans and my Democrats, then I have a hard time passing a bill on the floor of the House of Representatives."

The highly partisan nature of many of the issues within the committee's jurisdiction, together with Rostenkowski's ingrained partisan instincts and his responsibility to the Democratic Caucus, however, limit the possibilities for reviving the restrained partisanship that prevailed on the prereform committee. Committee Republicans emphasized that Rostenkowski's interest in including minority members in committee decisions fades quickly on issues where partisan confrontation occurs. "In the preliminary steps of almost every issue," a Republican member noted, "he makes an extra effort to be bipartisan and let everybody be a player. However, when push comes to shove . . . he has a natural reaction to become extraordinarily partisan." Commented a second Republican, "When he works with me on a trade bill I see a whole hell of a lot of him, he relies on me, and the stuff I do works. When we work on a bill where we [Democrats and Republicans] fall apart, it isn't fair to say it's an icy relationship, but the relationship dries up." Some Republicans have expressed frustration over limited legislative opportunities that have been present for the minority when major legislation is crafted primarily through negotiations between the chairman and committee Democrats. "The thing that adds some civility to it all," noted a senior Republican, "is that if the issue is such that it is going to be treated in a partisan manner, that's communicated. You're not surprised by it one way or the other."

Threatening dissidents and freezing out defectors. Rostenkowski's approach to leadership combines consultation and negotiation with the overt threat of sanctions against those who defect from the agreements that have been negotiated. Especially among Democrats, one member commented, "once that consensus is developed, he expects you to pull together for whatever is decided." In describing his own approach to negotiating with committee members, Rostenkowski once remarked, "If you're against me, I might as well screw you up real good." [23]

One Democrat emphasized Rostenkowski's willingness to punish uncooperative members when explaining how the chairman had asserted control over the operation of the committee:

> Every member of the committee knows that they're going to have at some point a parochial matter that's going to be before the jurisdiction of the Ways and Means Committee. They know that Rostenkowski and his staff may undermine the attempt to get it on the agenda. I think it is the threat that you are going to be frozen out when things are important to you that gives him a great deal of that power.

Having witnessed or heard about cases in which the chairman has frozen out or retaliated against those who fail to support committee bills (such as the chairman's treatment of Kent Hance), committee members now accept this treatment as part of the normal operation of the committee. According to one committee Republican, the prospect of retaliation from the chairman was a significant element in his decision to support the tax-reform package developed by the committee in 1985. Realizing that a "no" vote might result in retaliation from the chairman at the conference committee stage, he explained, "There comes a certain point where you've won enough that if you abandon the bill itself, then all those issues you had in there are probably going to get stricken."

Given the limited autonomy of committee leaders in the postreform House, it would be a mistake to place too much emphasis on the use of punishment in explaining Rostenkowski's effectiveness as a leader.[24] Sanctions can be effective only if used sparingly and in a manner generally consistent with the legislative goals desired by the Democratic majority on the committee and in the House. To use them otherwise would be to risk undermining the procedural majority in the Democratic Caucus to whom the chairman is now directly responsible.

As one Ways and Means Democrat commented about Rostenkowski:

> He knows how to wield power. With power you can hurt members. I've never been on the receiving end of it, but I do know of cases where he has not allowed bills to come up. But no chairman, especially the chairman of the Ways and Means Committee, can maintain the kind of support he has by being a negative leader. His leadership is mainly by the force of his personality and communication.

Another member emphasized that Rostenkowski operates with a "strict code of fairness." "Danny has generally always treated the committee members fairly," a committee Republican observed. "He's tough. If he's against you, he's against you, and he'll beat the hell out of you. But he'll tell you up front he's going to do it."

Controlling organizational resources. When he became chairman in 1981, Rostenkowski ended his predecessor's practice of allowing subcommittee chairs to hire subcommittee staff. Instead, subcommittee chairs are allowed to make only one professional appointment and one clerical appointment, as mandated by House rules. The remainder of the majority staff are hired by and are responsible to the full committee chairman. "The chairman provides an element of control by controlling the staff on the subcommittees," one senior Democrat commented. "All the staff view Rostenkowski as the boss, not the subcommittee chairman."

In part because of this more centralized staffing arrangement, Ways and Means subcommittees are less independent under Rostenkowski than they were during the late 1970s. According to one subcommittee chairman, "His is the flagship, and we all have little frigates. But there's no doubt that his is the ship of the line. He allows us to go out and do things, but he keeps control." Subcommittee chairmen are expected to obtain the chairman's approval for holding subcommittee hearings and markups. Rostenkowski prefers to defer to subcommittee chairmen, but he monitors legislation being drafted at the subcommittee level through his staff. A subcommittee chairman explained, "Unless the staff is saying that what we are doing is harebrained, as long as we are politically responsible, he gives us tremendous latitude." Staffers indicated that both political and budgetary concerns have at various times attracted the chairman's intervention in subcommittee deliberations. Concerning Rostenkowski's attitude toward bills being written in subcommittee, a senior committee staffer observed: "He is very much like [former chairman Wilbur] Mills, in that, if you're going to legislate, let's legislate something that's going to become law." [25]

Congressional Power and Its Limits

During his years as chairman of Ways and Means, Rostenkowski has been involved in developing important legislation in the areas of taxation, Social Security, welfare reform, and health care. But he has enjoyed varying success in maintaining control of the "Cadillac committee" and the legislation it reports. A brief discussion of Rostenkowski's role in two important legislative battles—tax reform in 1985-1986 and capital-gains taxation in 1989—will help to illustrate the conditions under which his approach to leadership works best and those under which even the "powerful" chairman of the Ways and Means Committee encounters the limits of congressional power.

Tax Reform, 1985-1986

In May 1985 President Reagan submitted to Congress a comprehensive tax-reform proposal. Tax reform, as it became defined in 1985, involved restricting or eliminating tax preferences enjoyed primarily by corporations and wealthy individuals in order to lower income tax rates and remove millions of low-income taxpayers from the tax rolls. Because tax reform advanced a number of diffuse, general interests (economic growth, greater equity, increased compliance with the tax code) and poorly organized interests (low- and middle-income taxpayers) at the expense of many well-organized beneficiaries of existing tax preferences, few observers in 1985 thought tax reform would become law. But tax reform did become law in 1986, and Dan Rostenkowski made an important contribution to its passage by skillfully maneuvering the bill through a reluctant Ways and Means Committee.[26]

Ways and Means members of both parties agreed that Rostenkowski's active leadership was critical to the committee's approval of tax-reform legislation in 1985. Said one Democrat, "He really brought the Democrats along on this. There was no real interest—well maybe from [Don J.] Pease [D-Ohio] and [Byron L.] Dorgan [D-N.D.] and one or two others—but most of us did not want to do tax reform." A committee Republican commented, "I don't know of anybody else who could have gotten a consensus—or created a consensus—on a bill given the obstacles in its way at the beginning. There was no political consensus out among the rank-and-file for a bill." The chairman's leadership techniques, together with appeals directed at prestige, policy, and partisan and electoral concerns of committee members, all came into play in Rostenkowski's successful coalition-building effort on tax reform.

In the early stages of committee deliberations, Rostenkowski appealed for support mainly on the ground that the Reagan administration tax-reform proposal had created an unusual opportunity to advance good public policy. Rostenkowski described his approach:

I said we're going to take six or seven million people that are poor off the rolls. We're going to do more for the lower end of the tax structure, and corporate America is going to wind up paying more in taxes. Those are the arguments I kind of shamed my colleagues into accepting.

To galvanize support for tax reform, Rostenkowski organized a committee retreat at Airlie House in the Virginia countryside. He met privately with Ways and Means members and delivered an emotional appeal for making the tax code more fair. He emphasized that the committee's prestige would be riding on its ability to produce a credible tax-reform bill. A committee Republican recalled the chairman's appeals:

> Airlie House was important in terms of bringing the committee together and really did help to develop a sense of history. [Rostenkowski] ... said this was an historic moment, a great opportunity for the committee to recapture some of the glory it had lost because we had lost fights on the floor in the years before.

Once the committee agreed to take up the task of writing a tax-reform bill, Rostenkowski shifted his strategy and began negotiating changes in the bill to accommodate local or group interests of concern to committee members. He made concessions in exchange for commitments to support the overall reform package. In one important instance, Rostenkowski agreed to maintain the full deductibility of state and local taxes at the request of a group of committee members from northeastern states. "He said, 'OK, I'm gonna give in to this but now you have to support it [the committee bill],' " one member of the group recalled. Concerning other revisions Rostenkowski allowed in the bill, another Democrat said, "In some of the major areas we have been left to write the legislation, but we have almost signed on in blood."

In the later stages of the committee markup, Rostenkowski made it clear that committee members who voted against him would stand to lose out in writing the transition rules for the bill (special exceptions to new tax provisions that may be used to confer tax breaks on particular individuals, industries, or localities). One member described the chairman's response to an unwanted amendment that threatened to derail the bill:

> He just looked at all of us sitting there and said, "I just want to tell you that if this thing passes, any accommodations I have made to any member of the committee for this are null and void." He just said that. Two or three people changed their votes.

Throughout the markup Rostenkowski reminded committee members, especially Democrats, that they would be blamed if the committee failed to report a strong reform package. When the markup appeared to be faltering in October 1985, rough treatment by the press reinforced the chairman's contention that unfavorable electoral consequences might follow a failure to act on tax reform. In the end the tax-reform bill was reported out of the Ways and Means Committee in November 1985. After an even more radical reform package passed the Senate, the bill was signed into law in October 1986.

Dan Rostenkowski's leadership on the tax-reform issue was as impressive a display of congressional power as one is likely to find in the postreform House. Persuasion, negotiation, threats, personal loyalties, control over the committee's agenda, and effective staff work were all skillfully employed to build a majority on a committee whose members were at first mostly indifferent—and some even hostile—to the idea of tax reform. Tax reform presented the chairman with an unusual opportunity to enhance the prestige of the Ways and Means Committee, to advance a partisan objective of House Democrats, and to write some "good legislation," all in one bold stroke. But as important as Rostenkowski's personal commitment and political skill were to the outcome, the political context cannot be overlooked if the reasons for Rostenkowski's success in bringing the Ways and Means Committee around on this issue are to be fully understood.

Although proposed by a Republican president, tax reform became a legislative priority of House Democrats for two reasons: it had potential appeal to voters, and there were concerns that Ronald Reagan would bring his considerable communications skills to bear in blaming Democrats if reform efforts died in the Democratically controlled House. In addition, an unusually broad consensus had developed among policy experts and across the ideological spectrum that tax reform was a good idea—that it was in the public interest. This view was reflected in press coverage of the issue, leaving representatives who opposed tax reform at risk of being portrayed within the Washington community and before their constituents as captives of "special interests"—as legislators who cared more about the favored few who benefited from tax loopholes than the majority who would stand to get lower tax rates. Thus, the politics of the issue as it developed in 1985 created incentives to support reform for those concerned with prestige in Washington, partisan considerations, and reelection, as well as for those who may have been motivated by the fact that virtually all the experts were in agreement that tax reform was good public policy. Rostenkowski's masterful use of the power of the chairmanship consisted in his intuitive grasp of the full range of committee members' motivations and his skill in appealing to all of those motivations in building a legislative coalition.

Capital-Gains Taxation, 1989

"Tax Vote Overhauls Rostenkowski's Image," announced a front-page *Washington Post* article in December 1985.[27] After his difficulties in maintaining control of two major tax bills during the early 1980s, Rostenkowski's successful effort on tax reform seemed to establish his reputation as a leader who could combine power and purpose. By 1989, however, the chairman's sense of direction and ability to control the Ways and Means Committee seemed less clear. As the *New York Times* had it in November 1989, "Mr. Rostenkowski, perhaps the most powerful chairman of the most powerful committee in Congress, has been stumbling."[28] What changed between 1985 and 1989 was not the institutional context or Rostenkowski's power as chairman but the politics of the issues on the committee's agenda and the opportunities they offered for Rostenkowski to advance the goals he values as chairman.

One issue on which the committee seemed to veer out of control in 1989 was capital-gains taxation. Through the reconciliation procedure of the congressional budget process, the House had instructed the Ways and Means Committee to report tax legislation in 1989 that would raise $5.3 billion in new revenues over two years. Finding little support for a major tax increase and facing a threat from President Bush to veto any new taxes, Rostenkowski allowed publicly in June 1989 that a cut in tax rates on gains from sales of capital assets might be part of the tax bill the committee would write to satisfy the reconciliation instructions. From the chairman's perspective a capital-gains cut was attractive because it would produce a substantial short-term revenue gain—revenues that would go a long way toward reaching the $5.3 billion mandated by the budget process. Rostenkowski was also looking for revenues to fund several tax preferences and credits that committee Democrats wanted to incorporate into the bill for housing, education, child care, and other purposes. Because a capital-gains cut had been the centerpiece of George Bush's 1988 presidential campaign, Rostenkowski saw the provision as a revenue raiser and as a way to attract bipartisan support and avoid a presidential veto.

What Rostenkowski failed to anticipate was the intensity of his fellow Democrats' opposition to a capital-gains cut. At a committee caucus held after his public statements about a capital-gains tax cut, a majority of committee Democrats vehemently opposed the idea. Delivering what Rostenkowski later described as a verbal hazing, members of the committee majority "complained that capital gains was a tax break for the rich that Democrats had no business promoting." [29] Respecting the wishes of the committee caucus, Rostenkowski backtracked on the issue and announced his opposition to a capital-gains cut. But in the meantime, six Ways and Means Democrats (the "gang of six") led by Ed Jenkins of Georgia had already agreed to vote together in support of a capital-gains cut. With all the committee Republicans supporting the reduction, the votes of the "gang of six" would produce a one-vote majority on the committee.

The result was a rancorous intraparty debate and an embarrassing situation for a chairman who takes pride in maintaining control of his committee. Faced with the prospect of losing to the coalition led by Jenkins and Ways and Means ranking Republican Bill Archer of Texas, Rostenkowski delayed a final committee vote on the issue for weeks while trying unsuccessfully to develop a compromise capital-gains provision acceptable to Ways and Means Democrats and the House majority leadership. Ultimately, neither he nor the Democratic leadership was able to stop passage of an amendment in committee and on the House floor that incorporated the Jenkins-Archer capital-gains cut in the House version of reconciliation legislation in 1989.

Speculation was heard at the time that Rostenkowski personally favored a capital-gains cut and thus did not push as hard as he might have to stop the Jenkins-Archer provision.[30] Committee Democrats and staffers who were interviewed generally rejected this interpretation. According to one member of the "gang of six," the dissident Democrats agreed among themselves that "they would stay with the issue regardless of the consequences, regardless of the pressure." Discussing the chairman's position, the same Democrat said, "He opposed it once a majority of the committee caucus opposed." A second committee Democrat also discounted the view that Rostenkowski was pulling punches: "He doesn't like to lose on the committee. Believe me, if he *could* have stopped it, he *would* have stopped it." A majority staffer explained that

> by the time it surfaced it was a done deal. They had the votes and they were unshakable.... They had made commitments to each other.... Jenkins hit the hole and was through it and was running for a touchdown before we knew it.

The issue of capital-gains taxation illustrates the complex contextual forces that define opportunities and limits for the exercise of power by the chairman of the postreform Ways and Means Committee. Explaining why he had entertained the possibility of a capital-gains cut in June 1989, Rostenkowski said, "I'm looking for a way to get to $5.3 billion, and not disappoint the Democrats, and not give President Bush the opportunity to veto the bill." [31] By virtue of his position, Rostenkowski is responsible for seeing that the committee meets its responsibilities under the budget process and for representing the concerns of his fellow Democrats on the committee and in the House.

Preferring to negotiate a legislative solution that could become law, Rostenkowski needed to raise $5.3 billion in new revenues in 1989. The chairman's attempt to craft a bipartisan solution involving a capital-gains cut was rejected by a Democratic committee caucus that chided him for failing to represent partisan goals. When the chairman recognized that he had to change direction, he was faced with a large dissident faction on the committee that could not be reined in. That a determined and skillful leader like Rostenkowski could not get his way in either case demonstrates the limits of power in the contemporary House.

Conclusion: Leadership and Power in the House of Representatives

If these limits on the exercise of power are present in the Ways and Means Committee and in the House, is it accurate to describe Dan Rostenkowski—or any other House leader—as powerful? In addressing this question, we should keep two points in mind. First, power is partly a matter of interpretation; conclusions about congressional power depend in part on how congressional politics are viewed. Second, congressional power, especially in the modern House, consists primarily of legislators' taking advantage of opportunities presented by the interplay between partisan politics, changing political issues, and the institutional forms that allocate authority within the institution. For even the most skillful congressional leader, opportunities to exercise power wax and wane as political conditions change.

For scholars who have viewed Congress mainly from a sociological perspective, the power of leaders may have been obscured somewhat by a tendency to view leadership as a "group process" or as a "role" that functions to advance the goals of the collectivity (party, committee, and so forth). In this view of legislative politics, leadership is almost entirely "followmanship": effective leaders exert influence rather than power.[32] Effective leaders in the modern Congress usually do have to appeal to followers' goals or opinions through persuasion or means other than threats of punishment; but it does not necessarily follow that leadership is best understood as followmanship. Leaders continue to have opportunities to direct what happens in Congress. Recent work drawing on more individualistic purposive theoretical frameworks may help provide a more complete understanding of congressional leadership by emphasizing that leaders can exert power over legislative outcomes through skillful use of procedural prerogatives and asymmetries in information created by institutional arrangements.[33] To this newer perspective should be added the observation that in some cases the power of leaders may extend beyond outcomes on particular bills to restructuring of the institutional forms within which legislative politics and leadership take place.[34]

Dan Rostenkowski presents an interesting study in congressional power because he is unusually attuned to seeking out and acting on opportunities for exercising power. In the aftermath of the unsettled politics of the 1970s reform era, he has reasserted an active leadership style and established a centralized organizational structure on the Ways and Means Committee. Rostenkowski's approach to crafting legislation sometimes alienates those of his colleagues who prefer a more ideological politics as well as those outside Congress who think politics should be more about deliberation and less about deals. But he has proved that an "Old Testament" style of committee leadership can work surprisingly well in the postreform House. (The unusually large turnover that will occur in the House and in the Ways and Means Committee in the 103d Congress will provide yet another test of the chairman's political dexterity.) Finally, although he has made his missteps as chairman, Dan Rostenkowski has developed into a leader with a strong sense that power brings with it responsibility for governing. (Whether he may also have seriously abused some of the prerogatives that came with power is uncertain as this volume goes to press.)

But is he as powerful as people think? Perhaps appreciating the elusive quality of power in the postreform Congress, Rostenkowski responds, "I don't know. I really don't."

Notes

The author gratefully acknowledges helpful comments from Charles O. Jones and Richard F. Fenno, Jr., and research support from the Dirksen Congressional Center.

All unattributed quotations are from interviews conducted by the author with current and former members and staff of the House Ways and Means Committee. Between 1985 and 1992 thirty-one members and eight committee staffers were interviewed. With the exception of Chairman Dan Rostenkowski, who was interviewed on three occasions

(March 8 and 9, 1989, and Feb. 4, 1992), all those interviewed were promised ano-
nymity.

1. Rep. Dan Rostenkowski, interview with author, Feb. 4, 1992.
2. See Pamela Fessler, "Rostenkowski Seeks More Influential Role," *Congressional Quarterly Weekly Report*, Jan. 29, 1983, 195; Jeffrey H. Birnbaum and Alan S. Murray, *Showdown at Gucci Gulch* (New York: Random House, 1987), 105; Barber B. Conable, Jr., *Congress and the Income Tax* (Norman: University of Oklahoma Press, 1989), 67.
3. Michael Barone and Grant Ujifusa, *The Almanac of American Politics, 1992* (Washington, D.C.: National Journal, 1991), 363.
4. Charles O. Jones, "Joseph G. Cannon and Howard W. Smith: An Essay on the Limits of Leadership in the House of Representatives," *Journal of Politics* 30 (August 1968): 617-646.
5. See Steven S. Smith and Christopher J. Deering, *Committees in Congress*, 2d ed. (Washington, D.C.: CQ Press, 1990), chap. 2.
6. The most comprehensive treatment of the history of the committee is Donald R. Kennon and Rebecca M. Rogers, *The Committee on Ways and Means: A Bicentennial History, 1789-1989*, H. Doc. 100-244 (Washington, D.C.: U.S. Government Printing Office, 1989).
7. John F. Manley, *The Politics of Finance: The House Committee on Ways and Means* (Boston: Little, Brown, 1970). On the politics of the committee during the Mills era, see also Richard F. Fenno, Jr., *Congressmen in Committees* (Boston: Little, Brown, 1973).
8. Fenno, *Congressmen in Committees*, 55-57.
9. Ibid., 115, 117
10. Manley, *Politics of Finance*, chap. 4.
11. For more detailed treatment of reforms affecting the Ways and Means Committee, see Catherine E. Rudder, "Committee Reform and the Revenue Process," in *Congress Reconsidered*, ed. Lawrence C. Dodd and Bruce I. Oppenheimer (New York: Praeger, 1977); and Randall Strahan, *New Ways and Means: Reform and Change in a Congressional Committee* (Chapel Hill: University of North Carolina Press, 1990), chaps. 2, 3.
12. Strahan, *New Ways and Means*, 60-78.
13. Manley, *Politics of Finance*, 56.
14. Strahan, *New Ways and Means*, 75-78; Smith and Deering, *Committees in Congress*, 87, 91-93.
15. For a more detailed discussion of the Ullman chairmanship than the brief account that follows, see Strahan, *New Ways and Means*, chap. 5.
16. Richard E. Cohen, "Al Ullman—the Complex, Contradictory Chairman of Ways and Means," *National Journal*, March 4, 1978, 347.
17. On the influence of party unity and factionalism on leadership, see Joseph Cooper and David W. Brady, "Institutional Context and Leadership Style: The House from Cannon to Rayburn," *American Political Science Review* 75 (June 1981): 411-425; and David W. Rohde and Kenneth A. Shepsle, "Leaders and Followers in the House of Representatives: Reflections on Woodrow Wilson's Congressional Government," *Congress and the Presidency* 14 (Autumn 1987): 111-133.
18. David W. Rohde, *Parties and Leaders in the Postreform House* (Chicago: University of Chicago Press, 1991), 161.
19. A careful analysis of the partisan context in the House during the 1980s may be found in ibid. For evidence of increased cohesion among Ways and Means Democrats on tax votes during the 1980s, see Strahan, *New Ways and Means*, 160-161.
20. On Rostenkowski's background and political career before becoming Ways and Means chairman, see Irwin B. Arieff, "New Role for Rostenkowski Gets Him into

the Thick of House Power-Playing," *Congressional Quarterly Weekly Report*, May 16, 1981, 863-866; Michael Barone, "The Tax Writers," *Washington Post*, Dec. 10, 1985, A21; Birnbaum and Murray, *Showdown at Gucci Gulch*, 103-106; Iris Krasnow, "Power Drive," *Chicago*, November 1991, 119-123, 140, 144-149; and Thomas P. O'Neill, Jr., with William Novak, *Man of the House* (New York: Random House, 1987), 211-220.

21. Leo M. Snowiss, "Congressional Recruitment and Representation," *American Political Science Review* 60 (September 1966): 630; 629.

22. Strahan, *New Ways and Means*, 69, 73.

23. Elizabeth Wehr, "Rostenkowski: A Firm Grip on Ways and Means," *Congressional Quarterly Weekly Report*, July 6, 1985, 1318.

24. It would also be a mistake to overlook the fact that the judicious use of sanctions can be an effective tool for legislative leadership, even in the postreform House. For a game theoretic explanation of the logic of using sanctions to foster cooperation (something Rostenkowski no doubt learned about from tribal elders in Chicago), see Randall L. Calvert, "Reputation and Legislative Leadership," *Public Choice* 55 (September 1987): 81-119.

25. For more detailed treatments of subcommittee politics on the Ways and Means Committee, see Randall Strahan and R. Kent Weaver, "Subcommittee Government and the House Ways and Means Committee" (Paper presented at the annual meeting of the Southern Political Science Association, Memphis, Tenn., Nov. 2-4, 1989); and Linda Kowalcky, "The House Committee on Ways and Means: Maintenance and Evolution in the Post-Reform House of Representatives" (Ph.D. diss., Johns Hopkins University, 1991), chap. 4.

26. The following account is based on Strahan, *New Ways and Means*, chap. 7. On the politics of tax reform during 1985-1986, see also Birnbaum and Murray, *Showdown at Gucci Gulch;* Timothy J. Conlan, Margaret T. Wrightson, and David R. Beam, *Taxing Choices: The Politics of Tax Reform* (Washington, D.C.: CQ Press, 1989); and Cathie J. Martin, *Shifting the Burden: The Struggle Over Growth and Corporate Taxation* (Chicago: University of Chicago Press, 1991), chap. 7.

27. Dale Russakoff, "Tax Vote Overhauls Rostenkowski's Image," *Washington Post*, Dec. 19, 1985, A1, A10.

28. Susan F. Rasky, "For the Chairman of a Powerful Committee, the House Is No Longer a Home," *New York Times*, Nov. 11, 1989, 12Y.

29. Jeffrey H. Birnbaum, "Rostenkowski, Buttered by Bush and Battered by Democrats, Erred Badly on Capital Gains," *Wall Street Journal*, Sept. 19, 1989, A32. See also Jeffrey H. Birnbaum, "Rostenkowski Won't Cut Tax on Gains in His Plan for Revenue-Raising Bill," *Wall Street Journal*, July 18, 1989, A2.

30. Elizabeth Wehr, "Bush May Be the Big Winner as Panel Completes Work," *Congressional Quarterly Weekly Report*, July 15, 1989, 1752; Ronald D. Elving, "Democrats Pursue Consensus on Capital Gains Cut," *Congressional Quarterly Weekly Report*, Sept. 9, 1989, 2299-2302.

31. Jeffrey H. Birnbaum, "Rostenkowski Won't Seek Cut in Gains Tax," *Wall Street Journal*, June 29, 1989, A3.

32. See, for example, John F. Manley, "Wilbur D. Mills: A Study in Congressional Influence," *American Political Science Review* 63 (June 1969): 442-464.

33. See C. Lawrence Evans, *Leadership in Committee* (Ann Arbor: University of Michigan Press, 1991), chap. 6.

34. One House leader who stands out for having exercised congressional power in this fashion is Republican Thomas B. Reed of Maine. See Randall Strahan, "Reed and Rostenkowski: Congressional Leadership in Institutional Time," in *The Atomistic Congress*, ed. Allen D. Hertzke and Ronald M. Peters (Armonk, N.Y.: M. E. Sharpe, 1992).

9

Multiple Referral and the Transformation of House Decision Making

Garry Young and Joseph Cooper

One of the most important, but least analyzed, of the reforms in the House of Representatives in the mid-1970s is the change in the rules that permitted a bill to be referred to more than one committee. Certainly, other changes—including the creation of the budget reconciliation process, the increased influence of subcommittees, and the heightened influence of party caucuses over committee chairs—have had a tremendous effect on the operation of and distribution of power in the postreform House.[1] Nonetheless, no other reform rivals multiple referral in the range of its effects across all the stages of legislative decision making.[2]

Common perceptions of the legislative process are still dominated by images of what may be called the textbook Congress—a way of depicting the House, offered in textbooks and certain other works, that quickly caught on and gained wide acceptance.[3] The textbook view was caricature as well as portrait, but its cardinal error was to assume that House operations are timeless and impervious to change.

The defining characteristics of the textbook Congress were tied to a particular House, the House that emerged in the late 1930s with the rise of the conservative coalition and persisted until the reforms of the Watergate era were completed in the mid-1970s. Some features of this portrait, to be sure, do capture historical aspects of House procedure. For example, in this period, as in preceding periods, bills were singly and exclusively referred to the standing committees with predominant jurisdiction, and the means available to the chamber to alter a referral or discharge a bill were very difficult to employ and were rarely used. Still, the images of the textbook Congress embraced far more than procedure and were far from timeless. The textbook view rested on and reflected the distinctive manner in which the mid-twentieth-century House combined traditional procedures with distinctly contemporary patterns of partisan division and House organization to create an oligarchic pattern of committee power. Thus the portrait of the textbook Congress highlights the ability of standing committees and their chairs to dominate decision making in the House in their policy areas.

The procedures and processes of multiple referral represent significant departures from textbook norms, both with respect to the referral and reporting of bills and with respect to the dimensions of committee power. Multiple referral is thus part and parcel of a new House, a House that is very different from that of Speakers Sam Rayburn, John McCormack, and Carl Albert. In this House a substantial portion of the most important business is multiply referred, and this practice has significantly altered patterns of legislative decision making and distributions of power among key units and actors.

In this essay we describe and assess the effect of multiple referral on decision making and performance in the modern House. After briefly explaining the major procedural aspects of multiple referral, discussing its origins, and outlining patterns of usage, we proceed to a detailed discussion of the legislative process when bills are multiply referred. This analysis is organized in terms of decision-making stages, and at each stage practice as presented in the textbook view is contrasted with practice under multiple referral.[4]

The Advent and Development of Multiple Referrals

Under House rules, jurisdiction over proposed legislation is generally confined to standing committees. This is true whether bills are singly or multiply referred. Single referrals are by definition uniform; multiple referrals are more complex.

Types of Multiple Referrals

There are three types of multiple referral: joint, sequential, and split. In a joint referral a bill or resolution is referred concurrently to two or more committees. For example, during the 100th Congress (1987-1989), the Homeless Assistance Act (HR 558) was jointly referred to the Energy and Commerce Committee and to the Banking, Finance, and Urban Affairs Committee.

A sequentially referred bill initially is referred to only one committee. Unlike singly referred bills, however, it is not placed on a floor calendar after the committee has reported the bill. Rather, the bill is referred to one or more additional committees.[5] An example of a sequential referral is the banking reform bill (HR 6) considered during the 102d Congress (1991-1993). The bill was referred initially to Banking, Finance, and Urban Affairs. After Banking had reported the bill, it was referred sequentially to the Energy and Commerce, Agriculture, Judiciary, and Ways and Means committees.

Finally, under a split referral, specific provisions of a bill are divided up and sent concurrently to two or more committees. Some of the sections can and do overlap among committees. For example, during the 99th Congress (1985-1987), the Superfund reauthorization bill (HR 2817) was referred to three committees: Ways and Means, Energy and Commerce, and Public Works and Transportation. Energy and Commerce received all or part of Titles I, II, and III. Public Works received all or part of Titles I and II, and Ways and Means received Title IV.

In general, committees may consider only the provisions of a bill that fall under their jurisdiction, as stated by House rules and precedent. Because jurisdictions tend to overlap substantially, this means in practice that for most multiply referred bills, several committees deliberate on the same provisions. In the case of many sequential referrals, the Speaker specifically limits the provisions secondary committees can consider.

Additionally, the Speaker has the authority to impose time limits on committees. When a time limit is imposed, the committee must report the bill within the set period or face automatic discharge of the bill. Typically, in a sequential referral time limits are placed on the secondary committees, though no bar exists to impose time limits on the initial committee as well. The Speaker may also place time limits on any of the committees in a joint or split referral. Although Speakers have not made extensive use of this power formally, their ability to threaten to impose a time limit provides them with an effective means of countering obstruction.

The Creation of Multiple Referrals

The factors that led to the collapse of the textbook Congress are complex and are explained elsewhere.[6] Multiple referral was adopted in 1974 in the midst of a series of reform movements within the House. The defining goal of the unit established to reform the committee system—led by Richard Bolling, D-Mo.—was to redesign committee jurisdictions radically in order to reduce overlap. Recognizing that totally exclusive jurisdictions would be impossible to define, multiple referral was introduced as a supplement to jurisdictional reform. Still, the expectation was that multiple referral would not be used often or would not prove to be particularly important to the institution.

As it turned out, the Bolling reforms lost to a considerably less ambitious reform package that made only minor alterations to committee jurisdictions. Multiple referral, however, was adopted with very little opposition.[7] With old jurisdictional alignments—and thus substantial overlaps—intact, the use of multiple referral had the potential to alter the very nature of the legislative process and the distribution of power in the House. This potential has been realized over time as members have become more and more familiar with the mechanism and understand the rich variety of new opportunities for influencing outcomes that it provides.[8]

Frequency and Importance of Use

Statistics on the use of multiple referral are presented in Table 9-1. These data indicate that the percentage of multiply referred bills introduced, considered, and passed has grown impressively since the 94th Congress (1975-1977).[9] More important, the fact that singly referred bills continue to outnumber multiply referred bills in all these categories should not be misinterpreted. Major legislation, as indicated by the fact that the number of bills considered under a special rule averages only about 100 per Congress, accounts for only a small percentage of the total business.[10] Typically, multiply referred bills are complex and controversial, not minor or routine. As a consequence, whereas multiply referred bills constitute only 15 to 20 percent of the total number of bills introduced and reported, they

Table 9-1 Bills and Resolutions Multiply and Singly Referred, 94th-101st House of Representatives

Action	94th Congress	95th Congress	96th Congress	97th Congress	98th Congress	99th Congress	100th Congress	101st Congress
Referred as a percentage of total measures								
Single	94.0	89.7	88.3	90.4	88.4	86.0	82.5	81.8
Multiple	6.0	10.3	11.7	9.6	11.6	14.0	17.5	18.2
(N)	(20,532)	(19,633)	(11,801)	(10,306)	(9,316)	(8,883)	(7,322)	(7,716)
Reported as a percentage of total measures [a]								
Singly referred	97.5	94.6	88.6	86.8	86.2	83.7	83.0	84.3
Multiply referred	2.5	5.4	11.4	13.2	13.8	16.3	17.0	15.7
(N)	(1,495)	(1,490)	(1,286)	(805)	(983)	(839)	(929)	(840)
Passed as a percentage of total measures								
Singly referred	98.5	96.6	94.9	94.2	93.0	94.2	88.7	91.0
Multiply referred	1.5	3.4	5.1	5.8	7.0	5.8	11.3	8.9
(N)	(1,624)	(1,615)	(1,478)	(1,058)	(1,375)	(1,368)	(1,278)	(1,420)
Reported as a percentage of referred								
Singly referred	8.0	8.8	12.2	8.2	11.3	10.5	12.8	11.2
Multiply referred	3.3	4.4	11.8	11.7	14.0	12.6	12.4	9.4
All referrals	7.7	8.4	12.2	8.6	11.6	10.8	12.7	10.9
Passed as a percentage of referred								
Singly referred	8.8	9.8	15.1	11.7	17.1	19.2	18.8	20.5
Multiply referred	2.2	3.0	6.0	6.7	9.9	7.3	11.3	9.1
All referrals	8.4	9.1	14.0	11.3	16.3	17.5	17.5	18.4

Sources: 94th-99th Congresses: Roger Davidson, Walter Oleszek, and Thomas Kephart, "One Bill, Many Committees: Multiple Referrals in the U.S. House of Representatives," *Legislative Studies Quarterly* 13 (February 1988): 3-28; 100th-101st Congresses: Compiled by the authors.

[a] Data are reports filed. For multiple referrals, any measure in which at least one committee reported is included.

constitute a substantial proportion of the most important business deliberated on each session. For example, in the three most recent Congresses (1987-1993), multiply referred legislation has concerned such issues as budget reconciliation, trade, aid for the homeless, clean air, health care reform, welfare reform, creation of a national energy strategy, and reform of the banking system.

Most multiple referrals are joint referrals. Although sequential referrals occur less often than joint referrals, fifty to sixty multiple referrals per Congress are sequentially referred. In addition, they constitute a considerable proportion of the multiple referrals that are reported from committee. The actual number of sequential referrals may be deflated because of strategic considerations among committees. Split referrals occur only occasionally. Bills that cross multiple jurisdictional boundaries strongly resist division into a set of parts that can be comprehensively distributed to a group of committees with overlapping jurisdictions. Because split referrals occur so infrequently, we do not discuss them further in this chapter. Finally, most multiple referrals involve just two committees, although cases involving more than two committees are not uncommon. Indeed, the total number has been as high as fifteen.[11]

Introduction and Referral of Bills in the Modern House

As suggested earlier, the modern House is very different from the textbook House. Because of a variety of structural reforms as well as changes in party coalitions and issues, this is true even when major legislation is singly referred. When bills are multiply referred, however, the model loses much of its correspondence to actual practice. Because multiple referral now plays a critical role in important areas of legislative business, a new model of the legislative process is required.

Although scholars have focused intensively on what happens in the legislative process after referral to committee, little attention has been paid to the politics of bill introduction and referral. This is largely because bill referral under a single referral system tended to be simple and automatic, with little recourse for those who were unhappy with the referral. Nevertheless, at least one observer claims that bill referral is much like an iceberg: it is very important but largely below the surface of congressional politics.[12] The actions taken at this stage of the process determine to a great extent the ultimate success or failure of legislation; this is especially true for multiple referrals.

The Textbook Congress

Under the textbook Congress the stage before committee deliberation on a bill was mechanical. Introduced legislation was referred to the committee of predominant jurisdiction, as determined by House rules and precedent. Exclusive committee jurisdiction coupled with single referral limited the preintroduction strategy of a bill's proponents and limited the Speaker's discretion over the referral and scheduling of the bill. The committee that received a bill generally enjoyed tremendous influence over its fate. Modification of the original referral was difficult and rarely achieved; discharge of a bill from obstructive committees tended to be very rare.

In limited cases the writer of legislation could craft a bill in a way that would get it referred to a friendlier committee. The classic case is the 1963 civil rights bill, which was strategically written so that it could be referred to the Judiciary Committee.[13] Nevertheless, such opportunities tended to be highly constrained, and committees protected their jurisdictional claims later in the process to prevent egregious jurisdictional poaching.

Upon introduction of a bill, the Speaker (in practice, the House parliamentarian, an agent of the Speaker) referred the legislation to the relevant committee. Opportunities for discretion occurred only in cases where jurisdiction was extremely ambiguous, for example, when new issues emerged that were not governed by established precedents.[14]

Multiple Referral

The creation and use of multiple referral has changed the whole process of introducing legislation, making it more varied and strategically complex in several ways. From the outset a committee faces the implications of sharing responsibility for legislation with other committees. Consequently, committees can opt for one of two strategies: cooptation or cooperation. Cooptation entails an attempt by a committee to bypass completely or to limit severely the effect of other committees in the process. A cooperative strategy, on the other hand, entails cooperative interaction between relevant committees from the beginning.

Examples of cooptive strategies can best be seen in the drafting of legislation. When committee members draft a bill, they must now consider the possibility of the bill's referral to a number of committees. Which committee receives a particular bill depends on what particular areas of jurisdiction are included in it. Consequently, the way a bill is drafted, in regard to the areas of jurisdiction covered, affects whether or not a bill is multiply referred as well as the conditions of referral.

Proponents must carefully consider whether the bill should be drafted broadly, thus crossing a number of committee jurisdictions and increasing the chances that the bill will be multiply referred, or whether it should be drafted narrowly, thus ensuring a single referral. Which choice to make depends on how the trade-offs are assessed. If a broad bill increases the chances that committees hostile to the bill will gain some control over it, proponents may draft a narrower bill despite their preference for a broader one. An example is the Homeless Assistance Act (HR 558), passed during the 100th Congress. Proponents of the legislation wanted to include a provision for homeless veterans. Adding such a provision to the bill, however, would have resulted in the bill's referral to Veterans Affairs and possibly to Armed Services, two potentially hostile committees. Instead, they wrote a narrower bill to confine it to two friendly committees: Energy and Commerce and Banking, Finance, and Urban Affairs.[15]

Narrow drafting of legislation can also give proponents an important procedural advantage on legislation certain to be opposed by another committee farther along in the process. An example is the Uniform Product Safety Act (HR 1115), also of the 100th Congress. An Energy and Commerce Committee member designed the bill to look like product safety legislation. The intent, however, was to reform product liability laws by placing a limit on the awards plaintiffs could gain in tort suits. The result was a sequential referral, with Energy and Commerce gaining the initial referral. This cooptive strategy enabled the bill's proponents to move the legislation farther along in the process because the committee with jurisdiction over product liability, the Judiciary Committee, strongly opposed the reform.[16]

In other cases proponents write bills more broadly than necessary, or preferred, to circumvent a hostile committee. If the narrow bill would go singly to the hostile committee and subsequently would be squashed, writing a broad bill and obtaining a multiple referral may allow the supportive committees a chance to report a bill and get the Speaker's support in forcing the hostile committee to report it. A good example is the ethics reform package offered in 1977 by the Obey commission, headed by David Obey, D-Wis. The bill was written broadly both to achieve the objectives of the commission and to subject several hostile committees to overwhelming leadership and caucus pressure.[17]

Cooptive strategies clearly increase conflict among committees in the House. At times, the use of multiple referral has exacerbated disputes over jurisdiction and led to the demise of legislation that otherwise would have been passed into law. Use of the mechanism, however, also has led to impressive cooperative ventures by committees in behalf of important legislation. Proponents of a bill—in many, if not most, cases—realize that coalition building must begin considerably earlier in the process than was necessary in the textbook Congress. In recognition of this fact, committees interested in passing legislation now engage in a number of cooperative interactions at the prereferral stage.

This interaction generally takes one of two forms. One form involves committee members, staff members, and sometimes the Speaker mutually writing a bill before it is introduced. An example of this form is the health care legislation considered during the 102d Congress.[18] The second form involves the construction of prereferral bargains. These bargains usually include an agreement on the type of referral to be sought (subject to the acquiescence of the Speaker), and they often include agreements about such issues as which committee will have jurisdiction over particular segments of the bill.[19]

These two kinds of interaction serve several purposes. First, they can reduce uncertainty about a bill's viability. If members can work out their major differences early, or at least agree on a mechanism to resolve their differences, the committees may be more willing to expend valuable time and energy on the bill. Second, such agreements can prevent substantive and jurisdictional conflict. Finally, as Roger Davidson and Walter Oleszek note, such agreements can make the Speaker's task easier in developing the referral.[20]

Once drafted and introduced, a bill goes to the next step: referral to a committee or group of committees—another stage of the process that has generated little research.[21] Within broad parameters set by the rules, the Speaker may opt to refer the legislation singly or multiply.

In many cases, though not all, it is known at the outset that a bill initially referred to one committee will be sequentially referred to one or more additional committees. Other sequential referrals occur because the initial committee of reference amended the bill to include topics in the jurisdiction of another committee. Consequently, the referral process is now open-ended, not fixed. Indeed, it is probable that a number of bills that would have been sequentially referred are not because the initial committee of reference chooses not to report.

Together, the multiple referral option and existing ambiguities in jurisdiction have expanded the Speaker's ability to use referral authority to help or impede proposed legislation. For example, during the 99th Congress Speaker Thomas P. "Tip" O'Neill, Jr., D-Mass., referred a Republican-sponsored bill jointly to four committees, while sending a virtually identical bill, sponsored by a Democrat, singly to a sympathetic committee.[22] Depending on the preferences of the Speaker, adding committees to a joint referral reduces the chances that a bill will proceed to the floor.[23] Likewise, strategic imposition of a sequential referral may effectively kill a bill, because of added delay, or may force an outcome more in line with the Speaker's wishes.

In addition, the Speaker has the power to impose time limits. Here, the modern House makes a dramatic departure from the textbook House because committees charged with a time limitation cannot obstruct the bill in question. In practice, the Speaker rarely imposes a time limit on the initial committee in a sequential referral but usually imposes such limits on the secondary committees. For joint referrals, the Speaker has the authority to impose a time limit on all the committees of reference. Alternatively, the Speaker may designate one committee as a primary committee with unlimited time, while the secondary committees are required to release the legislation within some period after the primary committee has reported. Except in cases of legislation of great importance, the use of time limits for joint referrals is infrequent. Still, the Speaker can use the threat of a time limit to advance important legislation.

The availability and flexibility of the time limits has expanded the Speaker's choices considerably. By imposing a time limit, the Speaker can prevent a committee or group of committees from obstructing a bill; by declining to impose one, the Speaker can impede a bill. Furthermore, by structuring time limits strategically, the Speaker can heighten or limit the impact of particular committees. Short time limits make it difficult for a committee to influence complex legislation, and long ones may effectively kill a bill's chances of passage.

Understandably, committees prefer and will lobby the Speaker for the least restrictive time limitations possible. In the 102d Congress, for example, Energy and Commerce chair John Dingell, D-Mich., wrote to Speaker Thomas Foley, D-Wash., requesting unlimited time to consider the banking reform bill (HR 6), which would be referred sequentially to Dingell's committee. Foley ultimately gave Energy and Commerce a time limit of two months, a common length for sequential referrals.[24]

Finally, the Speaker can direct deliberation by specifying what parts of the legislation can be considered by various committees. In general, committees are restricted to consideration of portions of legislation that fall within the committee's jurisdiction. Referral of an entire bill to a committee makes policing jurisdictional boundaries very difficult, however, and conflict occurs quite frequently.

In some cases the Speaker formally limits committees to particular provisions of a bill. Although split referrals are infrequent, in many cases of sequential referrals the Speaker will formally designate which parts of the bill the secondary committees may consider or limit the secondary committees to those parts of the legislation amended by the initial committee.

Committee Deliberation in the Modern House

The bulk of the House's work continues to be carried out at the committee stage. In this stage committee members and staff determine much of the final content of a bill. Under the textbook Congress a single committee of reference dominated consideration of—and thus the important substantive details of—legislation. Under multiple referral, however, this exclusive control, including the power to obstruct legislation, is greatly mitigated.

The Textbook Congress

During the textbook Congress, once a committee received a bill, that committee—and that committee alone—controlled the bill. Although committee success on the floor required sensitivity to majority sentiment in the chamber, interaction with other committees at this stage in the process was not necessary.

Most bills referred to committee received little consideration and failed to go farther in the process. The decision to consider a particular bill generally was made by the committee chair, who enjoyed significant autonomy over committee agendas. Decisions to report legislation depended on the support of a majority of the committee as influenced by the committee chair and the particular interest groups that enjoyed an influential relationship with the committee.

Multiple Referral

Under multiple referral, committees no longer enjoy exclusive control of a bill. Once in possession of a bill, a committee must pay close attention to other committees. Decisions on a bill's progress and content depend on the combined preferences of the multiple committees involved as well as the preferences of the Speaker.

With joint referrals, if the legislation has basic support, one of the committees will begin the process of consideration by referring the bill to a subcommittee. The subcommittee then holds hearings and decides whether to report the bill, amended or not, to the full committee. Other committees in the reference will delay their consideration until it is clear that a lead or primary committee wishes to act. On bills of great importance and complexity—the omnibus trade bill in the 100th Congress, for example—several committees will work on the bill at the same time.

Committees holding joint referrals often communicate during the course of their deliberations. Such communication can save duplication of effort—through the sharing of information—and foster the reconciliation of differences. What does not appear to have occurred, contrary to some prior expectations, is an increase in the number of jointly held committee hearings. Committees continue to protect their autonomy, including monopoly control over hearings.

Once a bill is reported by one of the committees, attention shifts to the other committees. Each committee in the reference is authorized to amend only the portions of the bill that fall within its jurisdiction. As noted earlier, however, some jurisdictional poaching does occur, particularly when the Speaker has not specifically assigned bill sections. In many cases jurisdictional conflict can hamper a bill's progress far more than substantive differences between or among committees. Even if a bill is reported by one of the committees of reference, it must still clear the other committees before it can go to the floor. As noted, the Speaker's power to impose time limits may significantly affect the fate of a bill. For this and other reasons, the Speaker's support is critical if a single committee wants to take a joint referral to the floor.

The committee deliberation stage for sequential referrals works quite differently. Only one committee receives a bill; then, upon that committee's report, further committees receive the bill. This changes the strategic context, especially for the original committee of reference. To limit the number of additional committees receiving discretion over a bill, the initial committee may avoid amending the bill in a way that would affect other committees. For example, in the 100th Congress, the Merchant Marines Committee voted down an amendment to the Arctic National Wildlife Refuge bill to prevent it from being sequentially referred.[25] Alternatively, the original committee of reference may choose not to report a bill because it fears the changes a subsequent committee will adopt; or it may first settle its differences with the secondary committee. These committees must weigh their policy desires against the possibility of opening up a bill to a hostile committee.

When the initial committee reports the bill, the Speaker has the option of sequentially referring the bill to more committees. In practice, chairs of interested committees ask the Speaker for the referral, and the Speaker has full discretion over whether to make the referral and the time limit to be placed on each committee. Once a subsequent committee has received a bill, that committee must report it, with whatever amendments the committee desires, within the deadline (extensions are occasionally granted by the Speaker).

Floor Action in the Modern House

The next stage in the legislative process, after committee deliberation and reporting, is the floor stage. Processes at this stage are structured by procedures for bringing bills to the floor and for considering bills once on the floor. Over the past century the House has evolved a complex set of arrangements for handling business at the floor stage, and these procedures play a critical role in the passage of any bill. Nonetheless, these procedures like all others of the House, are subject to change; differences in procedure and practice from one era to another can significantly alter the nature of the legislative process. Here again, the introduction of multiple referral, combined with other political and organizational changes, has made the floor stage in the modern House quite different from that in the textbook Congress.

The Textbook Congress

In the textbook Congress individual committees maintained a high degree of autonomy and control over legislation after a bill left committee. Although a bill could reach the floor through several methods, a single committee determined the content of the bill. No negotiation or reconciliation with other substantive committees was necessary.

For important public legislation the typical method of bringing a bill onto the floor was through the granting of a special order or rule by the Rules Committee. A rule or special order, which must be passed in the form of a resolution by the House, specifies the conditions under which a bill will be considered on the floor. Generally, a rule determines when the bill will be brought up for consideration, the amount of time allowed for general debate, and the number and the type of amendments that will be permitted. By far the most common type of rule granted in the textbook Congress was the open rule. An open rule permits the proposal of any amendment germane to the bill in question. Occasionally, closed rules, which bar amendments, were used. The major alternative method for bringing public legislation to the floor was suspension of the rules. This procedure, however, was used very infrequently.[26]

During this period the Rules Committee was the major hindrance to committee power. It operated independently of the House leadership and was exceedingly difficult to bypass. When it wished to block access to the floor, the Rules Committee was a formidable obstacle. Still, the Rules Committee exercised its leverage with caution and sought to block only a restricted number of bills each Congress.

Once their bills were on the floor, committees generally succeeded in working their wills. If suspension occurred, the major obstacle was the requirement of a two-thirds majority. But committees limited suspensions to uncontroversial bills, and they were rarely defeated. Nor did reliance on open rules impair committee power. The chair and ranking minority member controlled general debate time, and members of the committee of reference usually dominated such debate. In addition, the chair had superior rights with respect to recognition and thus usually could aid the bill by immediately offering counteramendments to hostile floor amendments.[27] Equally important, norms of deference and reciprocity were strong. Noncommittee members respected and relied upon the expertise of committee members and expected the same consideration to be given to the committees on which they sat.[28] In sum, committees generally succeeded in getting their proposals passed with few changes.

Multiple Referral

The two hallmarks of the textbook Congress at the floor stage no longer exist. Most members of the Rules Committee are now appointed by the Speaker and are responsive to both the Speaker and the majority party caucus. In addition, committees have lost much of their autonomy and control at the floor stage. Obviously, reliance on multiple referral in important areas of business is not the only factor responsible for these changes. Nonetheless, in important areas of policy it has contributed significantly to altering the process of decision making on the floor.

In determining the context in which a bill is brought to the floor, multiple referral introduces a new and important step. Before a bill can move to the floor, differences between the various committee proposals must be resolved either by compromising or by permitting competing amendments on the floor. As discussed earlier, committees may communicate and work out compromises before reporting their respective versions of a bill. Inevitably, some differences between the respective committee reports will remain. The typical method for resolving these differences is for the chairs and staff of the respective committees to get together and bargain. For example, during the 99th Congress two committees, Energy and Commerce and Public Works and Transportation, held split reference over the main section of the Superfund reauthorization bill (HR 2817). After each committee had made its report, the chairs of the two committees engaged in a long series of negotiations that ultimately resulted in a compromise package that went to the floor.[29]

In some cases, especially those involving party programs, the leadership or the Rules Committee will act as brokers and sometimes arbitrators. Speaker Jim Wright, D-Texas, for example, is reported to have made individual decisions on conflicting committee versions of the omnibus trade bill (HR 3), passed in the 100th Congress. The Rules Committee can force committees to compromise by threatening either to refuse to grant a rule (thus blocking the bill from moving forward) or to grant a rule that would pit varying committee versions against each other on the floor.

As a result of this process, a very different version of a committee bill from the one reported may go to the floor. Negotiations between committees generally involve only a few members, typically the full committee chairs, and sometimes relevant subcommittee chairs. Consequently, rank-and-file committee members may be unhappy with the final results. Although chairs presumably are sensitive to the wishes of ordinary committee members, opportunities for discretion are clearly bountiful and have led to conflict. The most notorious example is the banking reform legislation (HR 6) in the 102d Congress. The Banking, Finance, and Urban Affairs Committee reported a bill that would have radically reduced and redirected banking regulations. The Energy and Commerce Committee, fearing that the reform would damage the securities and insurance industries, offered a version of the bill that, if anything, increased regulation on banks. The chairs of Banking and Energy and Commerce—Henry Gonzalez, D-Texas, and Dingell, respectively—got together and worked out a compromise version of the bill. The compromise incensed many members of Banking because it essentially accepted the most important provisions of the Energy and Commerce version. Ultimately, the bill was defeated on the floor, with most Banking members voting against it.[30]

In most cases the Rules Committee prefers that the substantive committees work out their differences on their own and resists sending highly conflicting committee versions of a bill to the floor. Such compromises extricate the Rules Committee from disputes over jurisdiction and legislative substance. In general, the committee provides rules favorable to the compromises. At a minimum, the rules will allow the compromise version to be the bill that goes to the floor (as opposed to its becoming an amendment to the floor proposal). In many cases the rule granted hinders floor amendments to the compromise language. In the banking reform case, not only did the Rules Committee send the bill to the floor with the Dingell-Gonzalez compromise, but it also prevented the Banking Committee version from being offered as an amendment.[31]

As the last example suggests, the floor stage under multiple referral differs from that in the textbook Congress both because of the impact of the mechanism and because of the manner in which the mechanism combines with new aspects of practice and procedure. Two such features are especially influential in structuring decision making at the floor stage in the modern House: the growth of restrictive rules and the expanded use of suspension.

Restrictive rules confine amending activity far more than open rules do but less than closed rules. These rules can fairly be regarded as an invention of the modern House. Such rules, once rare, are now quite common. Moreover, only in recent decades have they been perfected in terms of their complexity and power. In large part, current practice stems from the fact that committees in the modern House are far more vulnerable to being challenged, and challenged successfully, than were committees in the textbook era. Restrictive rules are especially useful with multiple referral. They greatly facilitate committee compromises by removing uncertainty over whether the bargains made can be protected on the floor. At the same time, they provide committees and party leaders with flexibility in forging committee agreements and structuring floor voting to win majority support. Committee leaders can agree to leave selected, highly controversial issues to a floor vote without fear that the bulk of the package will be dismantled. Similarly, party leaders can provide the minority with opportunities to challenge selected, but important, aspects of a bill without fear of being victimized by minority voting strategies. Multiple referral thus powerfully reinforces the inclination to use restrictive rules. It is no accident that multiply referred bills tend to receive more restrictive rules than do singly referred bills.

Multiple referral affects floor decision making under a rule in several other important ways. First, debate after a rule is passed is necessarily more complex. All the committees involved, including the majorities and minorities, share the time allotted. Second, in cases in which committees are presenting compromise legislation or are engaged in settling differences on the floor, they must coordinate floor amending activity. Finally, the degree to which the committees involved present a united front can critically affect outcomes. In cases in which committees have compromised most of the issues, the bill has the advantage of multiple committee support. In cases in which committees are allowed to come to the floor despite great differences, the bill operates under the great disadvantage of multiple committee conflict. An excellent example is the banking reform bill of the 102d Congress, discussed earlier. The two main committees— Banking and Energy and Commerce—went to the floor in complete disagreement over the bill. A number of House members voted against the bill simply because contradicting arguments were presented.[32]

A second distinctive feature of floor procedure in the modern House that has combined with multiple referral to alter patterns of floor decision making is an expanded reliance on suspension of the rules. Indeed, in recent decades the number of bills brought to the floor under suspension substantially exceeds those brought to the floor under all types of rules.[33]

In large part, the increasing use of suspension parallels the increasing time pressure in the House. Suspension provides a quick and easy method of bringing bills to the floor if they are not controversial and enjoy bipartisan committee support. Accordingly, the modern House has increased the number of days on which suspension may be used and has allowed votes on suspensions to be grouped rather than requiring them to follow debate on particular bills.[34] Here again, however, suspension provides an especially useful mechanism for bringing multiply referred bills to the floor. The growth in the use of suspension thus is related to the growth in the use of multiple referral. In the 98th Congress (1983-1985), for example, 59 percent of the multiply referred bills that reached the floor did so through suspension.[35]

Suspension facilitates the movement of multiply referred bills to the floor in several ways. First, suspension allows new language in a bill to be brought to the floor without formal review by other units of the chamber (such as committees of reference or the Rules Committee). The parties involved in a committee negotiation can write out the compromise language and allow one of the committees to offer it on the floor right away as part of a motion to suspend the rules. Second, as with restrictive rules, suspension prevents reneging on the compromises since no amendments to the legislation are allowed. Finally, suspension provides a way around the problem of getting all the committees involved in a joint or split referral to report the legislation. In some multiple referrals, one committee might have little interest in considering the bill but maintain no opposition to its being passed. Also, it is common for one of the committees of reference to amend a bill to remove the provisions of the legislation that affect the jurisdictions of the other committees of reference. In both types of cases, suspension is a convenient way to bypass the onerous task of having all committees report a bill.

In sum, on many important bills the floor stage of the legislative process in the modern House is only barely recognizable to those familiar with the textbook Congress. Multiple referral has been both a cause and a component of the new patterns of decision making that have emerged.

Resolving Chamber Differences in the Modern House

For a piece of legislation to become law it must pass both the House and the Senate in identical form and then either be signed by the president or be passed by the House and Senate over a presidential veto. Yet the two chambers often produce substantially different bills. Several methods exist for resolving conflict between the House and Senate. One chamber can simply adopt the other chamber's version outright, or the two chambers can send amendment proposals back and forth until agreement is reached. In many cases, however, and especially when conflict concerns important and controversial legislation, the two chambers create a conference committee, which is composed of members of both bodies, to resolve their differences.

The Textbook Congress

Formally, the power to appoint House conferees is a prerogative of the Speaker. During the textbook Congress, however, the Speaker generally relied on the chair and ranking minority members of the committee of reference to make the actual choices. With rare exceptions the House delegation was made up entirely of members from the committee of reference. Typically, the senior member of the House delegation, usually the committee chair, chaired the delegation. The conference committee appointed one of the two delegation chairs to be conference chair. The conference chair controlled the agenda and subsequently exercised great influence over outcomes.[36]

Because conference meetings could be closed, the two sides could bargain over the legislation privately. Before the committee could reach agreement, a majority of each delegation had to concur. The agreement was written up as a conference report and was presented to each chamber. In the House floor action on the committee report occurred under restrictive conditions. Essentially, the chamber could vote in favor of the compromise version, vote against it, or order the conference to reconvene. On occasion, particular sections of the bill could be considered in the same fashion, piece by piece.[37]

Allowing the House delegation to be dominated by the committee of reference ensured that members who were generally supportive of the bill and knowledgeable about its contents would deal with the Senate. The House conferees worked to protect those parts of the legislation of special concern to the committee members. In some cases amendments added on the House floor against the committee's will could be deleted from the conference version of the bill. Such an exercise of committee power was necessarily limited by the preferences of the Senate and its delegation as well as by the willingness of the House to support the modified bill.[38] Nonetheless, in general the conference stage in the textbook Congress served as a final facet of committee power. Committee members dominated conferences and protected committee interests and influence.

Multiple Referral

Conference committee procedures and processes mirror much of the conflict and cooperation of multiple committee referrals seen earlier in the legislative process. During the textbook Congress members from a single committee comprised the House delegation to conference. In contrast, under multiple referral members from all the committees involved serve on the conference committee. The result is greater complexity and conflict at the conference stage.

The Speaker appoints the delegation members for multiply referred legislation. Although the advice of senior committee members is often accepted, the Speaker is now far more likely to use discretion independent of the committees when making these appointments.[39] Equally important, because of multiple committee representation, House conferees are likely to be far more disparate in their interests and views.

Generally, the apportionment of each committee's representation on the conference depends on the extent to which the legislation bears on the committee's jurisdiction. Furthermore, the Speaker often specifies which members of the delegation can work on which parts of the bill. For example, to work on the Superfund bill discussed earlier, Speaker O'Neill appointed forty-six members: eleven members from Energy and Commerce, eleven from Ways and Means, ten from Public Works and Transportation, ten from Merchant Marines and Fisheries, five from Judiciary, and two from Armed Services. (Three were appointed from more than one committee.) Additionally, O'Neill designated which sections of the bill each committee's representatives could consider.

As Lawrence Longley and Walter Oleszek have noted, when conference committees are composed of members from multiple committees, the mechanics are different from conferences composed of members from a single committee.[40] First, some of the conferences can be quite large. An extreme example is the omnibus trade bill of the 100th Congress. The House sent 155 members to conference, and the Senate sent 44, nearly 40 percent of the membership of Congress. Second, a multiple committee delegation complicates the choice of a delegation chair and, accordingly, the conference chair. Finally, because of the size of the conference, the complexity of much of the legislation, and the restriction of particular members to particular sections of a bill, many multiple committee conferences break down into subconferences, which consider their respective sections and report back to the full conference committee.[41]

The designation of members and their duties for multiply referred legislation can be a difficult task for the Speaker. The designation of the delegation chair and the responsibilities for each committee's representatives can result in severe jurisdictional infighting among the committees, occasionally leading to the demise of coalitions that had held up on the floor. At the same time, these decision-making needs also serve to expand the Speaker's discretion and influence.

In conference, the basic task of the respective delegations remains one of resolving the differences between the two chambers' versions of the bill. But there are several important differences for bills that are multiply referred. First, subconferences add another step to the legislative process and increase the rigidity of the bargaining process because individual subconferences do not have the luxury of bargaining across the range of issues contained in the bill.

Second, multiple committee delegations are not as cohesive as single committee delegations. Typically, members from the same committee are accustomed to working closely with each other; they often share procedural norms that differ from committee to committee. Indeed, intercommittee conflict within the delegation can be severe. Furthermore, chairs still enjoy some influence over their own committee members, but such influence rarely transcends committees.[42]

Third, the ability of any one committee to remove unwanted amendments added at the House floor stage is greatly reduced. Such attempts must get by the members of the other committees. The presence of mixed committee delegations also increases the chances that one of the groups will complain and seek the Speaker's intervention as arbitrator.

An example is the Superfund bill of the 99th Congress, discussed earlier. Deliberation over the main nontax provision of the bill went to members from the Energy and Commerce and Public Works and Transportation committees. Dingell from Energy and Commerce chaired the delegation. At the committee stage the two committees clashed bitterly over provisions in the bill, with Public Works generally supporting the more liberal provisions. The final House version more closely resembled the Public Works version, while the Senate passed a version closer to the original Energy and Commerce version. In conference, a coalition led by Dingell attempted to produce a much more conservative bill, even to the point of refusing to accept Senate acquiescence to the more liberal House language. In response to Dingell's actions, Public Works chair James Howard, D-N.J., and several others walked out of the conference meeting and immediately appealed to Speaker O'Neill, arguing that a majority of the House delegation was not forthrightly supporting the House position. Eventually, Dingell and company backed down, and the conference reached agreement on a compromise bill that was roughly in the middle of the original House and Senate bills.[43]

Finally, as the previous example suggests, the Speaker's role and influence at the conference stage has increased. The Speaker can be called in as arbitrator to protect the original House intent and to resolve conflicts among different committee contingents so that a common House position vis-à-vis the Senate can be forged. An example here is Speaker Wright's role in the reconciliation bill during the 100th Congress.[44]

Once a conference has come to a decision, the conference report is considered on the House floor. This process has not been radically altered by reliance on multiple referral, except in the case of the complexities introduced with respect to debate. Whereas conference reports are privileged and can be brought to the floor without a rule, rules are frequently secured in order to allocate and organize general debate time among the various committees.[45]

The Effects of Multiple Referral

The primary effect of multiple referral has been to alter the entire context of strategic decision making in important areas of policymaking. At every stage of the legislative process, multiple referral has created a variety of new options and has played a significant role in altering sources of leverage or advantage for committees, committee leaders, and party leaders. Increased complexity and altered patterns of advantage among major units and actors have increased the degree of contingency and uncertainty in the legislative process and have made the political skills of House leaders even more influential than they were.

Committee Roles

On balance, multiple referral has had more negative than positive consequences for committee power. The bedrock of the power of committees in the textbook Congress was their ability under the rules of the House to monopolize the consideration and reporting of all bills within their jurisdictions. These procedural advantages combined with patterns of political division to place committees in a position in which their negative power to block the bills they opposed was exceedingly difficult to challenge and their positive power to pass the bills they favored was substantial. Although multiple referral was not the only, or even the prime, reason for the demise of oligarchic committee power, the process has contributed to that result. Under multiple referral, the power of committees to block legislation they oppose or to pass bills they favor is far more restricted. Not only are committees subject to the Speaker's time limits, but they must interact and compromise with other committees to move a bill to the floor and pass it.

Nonetheless, it would be a mistake to exaggerate the negative consequences multiple referral entails for committees or to ignore its benefits. Speakers have been hesitant to impose or threaten time limits in cases in which the various committees involved are deeply divided. The imposition of time limits accordingly has been sporadic rather than routine, except for secondary committees in a sequential referral. Similarly, the Rules Committee is reluctant to move legislation to the floor when the various committees of reference cannot agree on the basic features of a bill. If Rules, nonetheless, on occasion allows important bills to come to the floor, it will usually insist that the committees agree to restrict conflict on the floor to a few salient issues. House committees thus retain substantial amounts of negative power over bills, even when they are multiply referred.

As for benefits, the choice between single and multiple referral systems hinges on the trade-off between monopoly power over a set of policy concerns and shared power over those concerns.[46] In a complex world of highly overlapping policy issues, formally defined systems of jurisdiction that assume single referral and exclusive control may well not provide committees with the scope they need to attain their policy goals. To abandon rigid systems of allocating bills for flexible ones is thus not at all necessarily adverse to the interest of the committees. Of course, the benefits involved will vary in terms of the nature of a particular committee's position in the existing jurisdictional system. Committees with relatively broad and ambiguous jurisdictions, such as Energy and Commerce, will experience substantial net increases in influence through the expanded opportunities to share in the business of other committees. In contrast, committees with relatively narrow and precise jurisdictions, such as Agriculture, may suffer net losses when other committees with overlapping jurisdictions are allowed to share in business that previously was theirs exclusively. Overall, House committees must have gained more than they have lost. Otherwise, it is difficult to explain why House members allowed the mechanism to be perfected and its use to be expanded rather than voting to restrict or destroy it.

Similarly, multiple referral benefits committees by institutionalizing a process of cross-fertilization between or among committees and by providing earlier and broader opportunities for negotiating and bargaining.[47] For a variety of reasons, both of these elements contribute to assembling a majority coalition on the floor. Different committees bring different perspectives and forms of expertise to a problem. In addition, a wider set of interested members can be involved before differences and positions become rigid either substantively or politically.[48] Finally, multiple referral, operating through either restrictive rules or suspension, engenders trust by guaranteeing that the bargains reached will be protected on the floor.

All this is not to deny that multiple referral limits the ability of a committee to bring a bill to the floor when it wants or in the form it wants. Nor is it to deny that the changes in strategic advantage that multiple referral involves at the committee stage significantly affect policy results. For example, in the case of the Superfund legislation, proenvironment interests were forced into a disadvantageous compromise in the 96th Congress (1979-1981), when the nontax provisions were singly referred to the Interstate and Foreign Commerce Committee (now Energy and Commerce). In contrast, during the 99th Congress, when such provisions were jointly referred to Energy and Commerce and Public Works and Transportation, environmentalists secured legislation far more in line with their policy views.[49] Even so, the modern Congress is not the textbook Congress. Given the greater complexity of substantive issues and voting coalitions, it should not simply be assumed that a committee whose policy desires are frustrated by the processes of multiple referral could obtain them if bills had been singly referred. It is equally arguable that, more often than not under current circumstances, committees that do not engage in early and extensive attempts at accommodation on important bills with other interested committees will fail on the floor.

Leadership Power

On balance, multiple referral has contributed to the power of committee leaders and party leaders. In the context of the other limits placed on the power of chairs, multiple referral has done far more to stabilize and reinforce their power than to undercut it. First, greater access to legislative business gives aggressive chairs the opportunity to affect policy agendas and ultimately policy substance. Conversely, the vulnerability of all committees to poaching by other committees requires chairs to assume the mantle of guardian of the committee's collective interests. Both roles enhance the power of committee chairs, particularly on chairs of committees with broad jurisdictions. Thus, despite the contemporary image of weak committee chairs, it is difficult to imagine more powerful committee chairs than John Dingell of Energy and Commerce and Dan Rostenkowski, D-Ill., of Ways and Means.

Second, the role that chairs play in reconciling committee differences provides them with substantial opportunities for discretion over policy outcomes and leverage over committee members. The compromises that a chair makes with other committees, after his or her committee has reported, are not subject to approval by the committee. Such discretion, to be sure, is not absolute. As our previous example of the defeat of the Dingell-Gonzalez compromise on banking reform legislation teaches, the chair must be sensitive to the preferences of committee members. But chairs at every stage of the process have opportunities to advance their policy preferences while bargaining on behalf of the committee. Furthermore, chairs can help or punish committee members through judicious use of the bargaining power conferred on them by multiple referral in negotiating with other committees. They can, for example, at any of several stages of the process either ensure that a member's pet provisions or project will stay in the bill or allow them to be struck.

The effect of multiple referral on party leaders is clear and needs little qualification. Multiple referral, both alone and in combination with other recent changes, has substantially enhanced the Speaker's leverage in the legislative process. As demonstrated in this essay, because of the advantages multiple referral provides, the Speaker has increased ability to influence outcomes at every stage of the process. It is nonetheless true that the Speaker's enhanced leverage is something of a two-edged sword. The Speaker can be drawn into bitter committee or party battles which result in outright defeats or Pyrrhic victories that permanently alienate broad groups of members. The inevitable consequences of such outcomes are losses of trust and prestige. Although overly aggressive uses of the sources of leverage multiple referral provides may lead to loss of influence, there is no substitute for strong and active day-to-day involvement by the Speaker when complex and controversial bills of prime importance are at issue.

Consider the omnibus trade bill of the 100th Congress. This legislation was very complex and controversial, but it was high on the list of the Democratic party's political agenda. The bill was jointly referred to six committees, all of which wanted as much freedom as possible to produce whatever version of the legislation they preferred. In this case Speaker Wright imposed a very short time period. In so doing he put all the committees involved on notice that failure to produce a bill within the specified period would result in a discharge and loss of influence over the legislation. Once all the committees had reported, the daunting task of reconciling the version into a coherent and uniform bill had to be faced. Here again, there was plenty of opportunity for delay as each of the six committees attempted to extract as many concessions as possible from the other committees. By stepping in and aggressively brokering the bargaining, Wright effectively moved the legislation to the floor.[50]

If the Speaker fails to use such influence aggressively, a legislative logjam can result and the institution may be unable to pass legislation of importance. This failure to use his influence has been the accusation made against the current Speaker, Thomas Foley. Generally, Foley has given committees tremendous latitude on legislation and has not involved himself in resolving conflicts among committees. An example is the highway bill of the 102d Congress. Foley's failure to resolve conflict between the Public Works and Ways and Means committees over the legislation contributed to its long delay and caused bitter criticism, directed against Foley, from House Democrats.[51] Ironically, then, passivity when important bills are multiply referred can be as detrimental to the prestige and power of a Speaker as highly aggressive behavior.

House Performance

One question remains to be addressed: Does multiple referral contribute to or impede the House's ability to fulfill its lawmaking responsibilities under the Constitution? There is no simple answer to this question, and no broad consensus exists among students of Congress. Multiple referral has made the legislative process more participatory by allowing committee leaders and members to exercise influence in a wider variety of policy areas. Thus it can be argued that multiple referral involves more negative than positive consequences for effective lawmaking because on balance it has weakened committee power and multiplied veto points.[52] It should be remembered, however, that oligarchic committee power in the textbook Congress obstructed the legislative process in a number of important areas of legislation and that issues and coalitions are now far more complex than they were.

In an age of complexity, no linear relationship exists between committee power and institutional performance. Rather, both program effectiveness (given the need to coordinate a wide variety of substantive concerns and forms of expertise) and political effectiveness (given the need to assemble a wide variety of interests into a winning coalition) may well be better served by mechanisms, such as multiple referral, that reduce committee power, broaden participation, and expand the power of party leaders. Indeed, we might well ask whether the House in recent years could have succeeded in passing comprehensive trade, health, budget reconciliation, and energy bills if the multiple referral mechanism had not been available. Critics nonetheless reply that multiple referral places an excessive burden on the party leadership and encourages disruptive forms of aggrandizement on the part of committee leaders. Their preferred solution is thus to redraw existing committee jurisdictions in a thorough and comprehensive manner and to abandon or restrict multiple referral.[53]

While admitting that the effects of multiple referral are mixed both in terms of distribution of power and successful performance, we have a positive view. Whatever problems the mechanism has, we see no substitute for it. It follows that the legislative process should be seen as one that is more contingent on the interplay between a variety of strategic choices and more dependent on the political skills of legislative leaders than has been true in the past. For multiple referral to work, leaders must be bold and committed enough to take risks to advance their policy desires but wise and resourceful enough to choose substantive compromises and political strategies that will succeed. That is no mean demand to place on legislative leaders. It reflects an age in which political and substantive complexity have grown so great that the institutional arrangements created to handle it deroutinize decision making rather than regularize it. In this respect, experience in Congress is similar to experience in other sectors of American politics and society generally. As we approach the twenty-first century, uncertainty has become the haunting presence in politics, as it is in most of contemporary life.

Notes

1. Some examples include Thomas E. Mann and Norman J. Ornstein, eds., *The New Congress* (Washington, D.C.: American Enterprise Institute, 1981); Aaron Wildavsky, *The New Politics of the Budgetary Process* (Glenview, Ill.: Scott, Foresman, 1988); David W. Rohde, *Parties and Leaders in the Postreform House* (Chicago: University of Chicago Press, 1991); and Roger H. Davidson, ed., *The Postreform Congress* (New York: St. Martin's, 1992).

2. Works that focus exclusively on multiple referral in the House include Roger H. Davidson, Walter J. Oleszek, and Thomas Kephart, "One Bill, Many Committees: Multiple Referrals in the U.S. House of Representatives," *Legislative Studies Quarterly* 13 (February 1988): 3-28; Melissa P. Collie and Joseph Cooper, "Multiple Referral and the 'New' Committee System in the House of Representatives," in *Congress Reconsidered*, 4th ed., ed. Lawrence C. Dodd and Bruce I. Oppenheimer (Washington, D.C.: CQ Press, 1989); Roger H. Davidson and Walter J. Oleszek, "From Monopoly to Interaction: Changing Patterns in Committee Management of Legislation in the House" (Paper presented at the annual meeting of the Midwest Political Science Association, Chicago, 1987); Kathleen Bawn, "Ex Post Vetoes After Multiple Referral: Institutional Power in the Post-Reform House" (Unpublished manuscript, University of California, Los Angeles, 1992); and David Austen-Smith, "Interested Experts and Policy Advice: Multiple Referrals Under Open Rule," *Games and Economic Behavior* (forthcoming).

3. Kenneth A. Shepsle, "The Changing Textbook Congress," in *Can the Government Govern?* ed. John Chubb and Paul Peterson (Washington, D.C.: Brookings Institution, 1989).

4. Although multiple referral has been available in the Senate for most of this century, it was not formally included in the Senate rules until 1977. Multiple referral is used with considerably less frequency in the Senate than in the House, however. See

Roger H. Davidson, "Multiple Referral in the Senate," *Legislative Studies Quarterly* 3 (August 1989): 375-392. Despite the Senate's infrequent use of multiple referral, the use of multiple referral by the House can affect the business of the Senate. One example of this occurred in the 102d Congress. In the House, a bill to create a national energy strategy was multiply referred. One of the committees of reference—Ways and Means—added some uncontroversial tax provisions to the bill. The change caused problems in conference because the Senate committee with jurisdiction over taxes—the Finance Committee—had not received the original bill. The Senate was forced to refer the bill to Finance so that it could review the tax provisions. This led to new, and controversial, additions to the bill by Finance that threatened the bill's passage. See Thomas Lippman, "Powerful Legislation That Is Running Out of Gas Fast," *Washington Post National Weekly Edition,* July 13-19, 1992, 34.

5. Sequential referrals also occasionally occur in tandem with joint or split referrals. In the 100th Congress, for example, this combination occurred seven times.

6. Steven S. Smith, *Call to Order* (Washington, D.C.: Brookings Institution, 1989); Shepsle, "Changing Textbook Congress."

7. Roger H. Davidson and Walter J. Oleszek, *Congress Against Itself* (Bloomington: Indiana University Press, 1977).

8. Davidson, Oleszek, and Kephart, "One Bill, Many Committees"; Collie and Cooper, "Multiple Referral."

9. The overall number of referrals has been decreasing over time. In the 94th Congress 20,532 measures were referred to committees, while in the 101st the numbers had dropped to 7,716. The absolute frequency of multiple referrals had been declining as well, but this trend has reversed in the 100th and 101st Congresses.

10. Stanley Bach and Steven S. Smith, *Managing Uncertainty in the House of Representatives* (Washington, D.C.: Brookings Institution, 1988), 21.

11. Davidson, Oleszek, and Kephart, "One Bill, Many Committees."

12. Charles Tiefer, *Congressional Practice and Procedure* (New York: Greenwood, 1989), 110.

13. Lewis Froman, *The Congressional Process: Strategies, Rules, and Procedures* (Boston: Little, Brown, 1967), 36-37.

14. Tiefer, *Congressional Practice and Procedure.*

15. *Congressional Record,* May 5, 1987, H1001.

16. Rochelle Stanfield, "Plotting Every Move," *National Journal,* March 26, 1988, 797.

17. Allan Katz, "The Politics of Congressional Ethics," in *The House at Work,* ed. Joseph Cooper and G. Calvin Mackenzie (Austin: University of Texas Press, 1981), 111-115.

18. Richard Cohen, "Faulting Foley," *National Journal,* Aug. 10, 1991, 1969.

19. Davidson and Oleszek, "From Monopoly to Interaction"; Tiefer, *Congressional Practice and Procedure.*

20. Davidson and Oleszek, "From Monopoly to Interaction."

21. One exception is Joseph Cooper and Cheryl Young, "Bill Introduction in the Nineteenth Century: A Study of Institutional Change," *Legislative Studies Quarterly* 14 (February 1989): 67-106.

22. Davidson and Oleszek, "From Monopoly to Interaction," 28.

23. Garry Young, "Legislative Decision Making Under Multiple Referral" (Ph.D. diss., Rice University, 1993).

24. John Cranford, "Walls Around Banking System May Face Congress Chisel," *Congressional Quarterly Weekly Report,* June 15, 1991, 1564.

25. Joseph A. Davis, "ANWR Bill Clears One Hurdle but Real Test Is Yet to Come," *Congressional Quarterly Weekly Report,* May 7, 1988, 1206.

26. Samuel Cooper, "Gateway to the Floor: Suspension of the Rules in the House of Representatives" (Honors thesis, Harvard University, 1990); Bach and Smith, *Managing Uncertainty.*

27. Barry R. Weingast, "Floor Behavior in the U.S. Congress: Committee Power Under

the Open Rule," *American Political Science Review* 83(September 1989): 795-815.

28. Steven S. Smith and Christopher J. Deering, *Committees in Congress*, 2d ed. (Washington, D.C.: CQ Press, 1990).

29. Joseph Davis, "Compromise Reached Between Committees," *Congressional Quarterly Weekly Report*, Dec. 7, 1985, 2552.

30. John Cranford, "Deal Smooths Overhaul's Path to Floor, but not to Passage," *Congressional Quarterly Weekly Report*, Oct. 26, 1991, 3114-3115. Why did Gonzalez renege against his own committee? Part of the explanation is that he strongly disliked the reform package. Perhaps more important, he expressed concern about Energy and Commerce's encroachment upon Banking's jurisdiction. He agreed to the compromise in return for Dingell's promise that the jurisdiction belonged to Banking.

31. John Cranford, "Banking Overhaul Losing Ground to Complexity, Controversy," *Congressional Quarterly Weekly Report*, Nov. 2, 1991, 3182-3185.

32. Pamela Fessler, "Halloween on the House Floor," *Congressional Quarterly Weekly Report*, Nov. 2, 1991, 3184.

33. Sam Cooper, *Gateway to the Floor*, 41-42.

34. Ibid., 43-46.

35. Davidson, Oleszek, and Kephart, "One Bill, Many Committees," 18.

36. Walter J. Oleszek, *Congressional Procedures and the Policy Process*, 3d ed. (Washington, D.C.: CQ Press, 1988), 249; Lawrence Longley and Walter J. Oleszek, *Bicameral Politics* (New Haven: Yale University Press, 1989), 260.

37. Oleszek, *Congressional Procedures*.

38. For discussions of committee power derived from conference committee participation, see Kenneth A. Shepsle, Barry R. Weingast, and Keith Krehbiel, "Why Are Committees Powerful?" *American Political Science Review* 81 (September 1987): 929-945; and Steven S. Smith, "An Essay on Sequence, Position, Goals, and Committee Power," *Legislative Studies Quarterly* 2 (May 1988): 151-176.

39. Davidson and Oleszek, "From Monopoly to Management," 141.

40. Longley and Oleszek, *Bicameral Politics*.

41. Subconferences are not exclusive to multiply referred bills.

42. Given that the Senate uses multiple referral far less frequently than does the House and, accordingly, has fewer mixed committee delegations than does the House, multiple referral may have an effect on who wins in conference. Presumably, this effect is in the Senate's favor.

43. "Dissension Splits House 'Superfund' Conferees," *Congressional Quarterly Weekly Report*, May 3, 1986, 1002. For an alternative discussion of multiple referral and conferences see Bawn, "Ex Post Vetoes After Multiple Referral."

44. Janet Hook, "Budget Deal Enacted at Last, Congress Adjourns," *Congressional Quarterly Weekly Report*, Dec. 26, 1987, 3183-3184.

45. Longley and Oleszek, *Bicameral Politics*.

46. Davidson and Oleszek, "From Monopoly to Interaction."

47. Ibid.

48. Collie and Cooper, "Multiple Referral."

49. The Superfund examples are derived from various articles in *Congressional Quarterly Weekly Report* and *National Journal* as well as the *Congressional Record* from the 96th and 100th Congresses.

50. The trade bill example is derived from various articles in *Congressional Quarterly Weekly Report* and *National Journal* from the 100th Congress.

51. Cohen, "Faulting Foley."

52. Burton Sheppard, *Rethinking Congressional Reform* (Cambridge, Mass.: Schenkman, 1985).

53. Ibid.

Part IV

✦✦✦

Congressional Leadership and Party Politics

10

House Majority Party Leadership in an Era of Divided Control

Barbara Sinclair

The 1992 elections end twelve continuous years during which control of the House of Representatives and the presidency was divided between Democrats and Republicans. For twenty of the twenty-four years from 1969 through 1992, Democratic House majorities faced a Republican in the White House. That experience strongly influenced the way the House majority party leadership functions. In the 1980s a highly active, broadly involved, and yet inclusive House Democratic party leadership emerged. In this essay I argue that the emergence of a strong majority leadership was a response to divided control and to other major alterations in the political and institutional environment.

To understand why and how divided control and other contextual factors have shaped the party leadership, we need to grasp the essential character of legislative party leadership. Elected by their fellow partisans in the chamber, legislative party leaders are best understood as agents of those members who charge them with advancing members' goals, particularly but not exclusively in ways that require collective action. Specifically, members expect their leaders to facilitate the enactment of legislation, the core task of a legislature and one that requires collective action. Thus, House Democrats expect their leaders to perform the coordination and coalition-building tasks necessary to pass legislation that furthers members' reelection and policy goals. In the modern House, however, collective action is not the only route toward attaining such goals. The modern House offers members a variety of ways to further their goals through individual entrepreneurial activities. House Democrats also expect their leaders to facilitate where possible—and certainly not to hinder unduly—individual goal-advancing activity. Since members expect both the passage of legislation and considerable autonomy of action and freedom from coercion, party leadership is always a balancing act.

What members consider the optimal balance will vary over time as a function of the costs and benefits of assertive versus permissive central leadership. Those costs and benefits, in turn, are a function of the political and institutional context. For example, as I shall argue, divided control makes enacting legislation satisfactory to majority party members very difficult, especially when, as was the case in the 1980s, the president's and the House majority party's policy preferences are far apart. Consequently, divided control increases the benefits of an assertive, active leadership that can boost the party's chances of success.

This essay begins with an overview of the characteristics that distinguish the contemporary majority party leadership and then briefly discusses its evolution. To understand the way the leadership functions now, the focus of the remainder of the essay, it is necessary to understand the elements that shaped it.

Majority Party Leadership: A Contemporary Profile

Majority party leaders in the contemporary House are more active, more frequently involved in all stages of the legislative process, and more engaged in a broader range of legislative and political activities than were their predecessors of the 1950s, 1960s, and 1970s. A comparison of leadership activity in selected Congresses over the past two decades shows the magnitude of the change.[1]

To make rigorous comparisons across time possible, we must define the congressional agenda. I have used Congressional Quarterly's list of major legislation, augmented by those measures on which key votes occurred (again according to Congressional Quarterly). Together, these sources produce a list of legislation considered major by close contemporary observers.

Leadership involvement in the legislative process may take a variety of forms: the leadership may involve itself in shaping legislation, in structuring floor choices through procedure, in mobilizing votes, or in managing other aspects of legislative strategy. To make comparisons over time possible, I constructed summary measures based upon these modes of activity but did not attempt to make fine distinctions among them. The first measure, intended to distinguish some involvement from no involvement, is based upon answers to the following three questions: (1) Was the bill part of the leadership's agenda? (2) Did the Speaker or the majority leader advocate passage during floor debate? (3) Did Congressional Quarterly's account report the leadership as being involved? If any one of the answers is "yes," I considered the leadership to have been involved.

A second, more refined measure distinguishes major involvement from minor involvement on the basis of the modes of involvement reported by Congressional Quarterly. Four modes are distinguished: (a) the leadership uses its control over scheduling, over the Rules Committee, or over other procedures to advantage the legislation; (b) the leadership is involved in a floor vote mobilization effort; (c) the leadership is centrally involved in some other aspect of legislative strategy, or (d) the leadership participates in shaping the content of the legislation by talking or negotiating with or among the committee(s) or with the Senate or the president. I define major involvement as the leadership's engagement in (d), shaping legislation, or in any two of the other activities outlined here (that is, 1, 2, a, b, c).

The majority party leadership's level of activity has increased dramatically during the past two decades (see Table 10-1). In the 91st Congress (1969-1971), the first Congress of the Nixon presidency, the House majority party leadership was involved in less than half (46 percent) of the items on the congressional agenda; on only 28 percent the items was leadership involvement

Table 10-1 Increase in Leadership Involvement on the Congressional Agenda (percentage of agenda items)

Congress	Leadership involvement	
	Some	Major
91st (1969-1971)	46	28
94th (1975-1977)	60	40
97th (1981-1983)	67	38
100th (1987-1989)	83	60
101st (1989-1991)	68	54

Source: Compiled by the author.

major. During the Congresses of the 1980s and early 1990s, by contrast, the rate of leadership involvement varied between 67 and 83 percent; and during the 100th and 101st Congresses (1987-1991) leadership involvement was major on well over half the agenda items. Because of the way the variable was defined, the growing frequency of major involvement signifies an increase in the scope of leadership activity. In the 91st Congress, party leadership involvement occurred primarily at the floor stage; party leaders attempted to help pass legislation written by autonomous committees when those committees needed help. Contemporary leaders are more frequently involved earlier in the process, working to ensure that legislation reaches the floor in a timely fashion and in a form broadly acceptable to their membership.

A distinct and important form of early involvement is agenda setting, a set of activities aimed at focusing attention on and attempting to build pressure toward action on a problem, issue, or policy proposal. Because the president is considered the premier governmental agenda setter in the American political system, agenda setting by the House party leadership must be assessed relative to presidential agenda setting. Presidents use standard forums for agenda setting, the State of the Union address being the most important.[2] The majority party leaders also have available forums that routinely receive considerable press coverage; they favor these channels for agenda-setting activities. The president's agenda is here defined as items mentioned in the State of the Union address or its equivalent and in special messages of some prominence.[3] Agenda setting by the majority party leadership, if it occurs, will become manifest in the Speaker's address, delivered when the Speaker is elected to that office at the beginning of a Congress; in the party's reply to the president's State of the Union address; in the leadership's reply to special presidential speeches; or in statements at major news conferences.

Presidents tend to dominate the congressional agenda during their first Congress. (Bush was an exception.) In contrast, during the last Congress of an eight-year administration, the president is only one of several players. The Democratic party leadership's role in agenda setting also shows a cyclical pattern; the leadership tends to be most active late in a presidency when the opposition party president is least active. A distinct trend toward greater leadership activity is evident, however. (See Table 10-2.) In the 91st Congress, Nixon's first, agenda setting by the Democratic House leadership was minimal. During Reagan's first Congress, the 97th, the leadership was significantly more active, despite the conservative tide. The first Bush Congress, the 101st, again saw an increase in leadership agenda-setting activity. Leadership activity also increased—and more dramatically—from the last Congress of the Nixon-Ford presidency, the 94th, to the last Reagan Congress, the 100th. In the 100th Congress, the Democratic leadership was a more prominent agenda setter than was the president.

The leadership's increased involvement in agenda setting, like its greater activity in other stages of the legislative process, is a response to its members' needs and expectations. When control is divided, House Democrats usually will be dissatisfied with the president's agenda. Given the president's advantages in the struggle to define the agenda, members have come to expect their leaders to aid them in getting their preferred issues onto the agenda.

In the 1980s House Democrats came to expect their leaders to act as their spokesmen in other ways as well. In the early 1980s Reagan's media skills, in combination with the political climate, allowed the president to dominate political discourse and to propagate a highly negative image of the Democratic party. Unable as individuals to counter this threat to their policy, power, and reelection goals, Democrats expected their leaders to take on the task. Unlike rank-and-file House members, the party leaders have considerable access to the national media.

It is now always the top party leaders who appear on television to give the party's response to the president's State of the Union address. Hardly a weekend goes by without at least one of the Democratic top echelon appearing on the prestigious Sunday interview shows. And these are only the most visible manifestations of the leadership's performance of the party spokesman role.

The contemporary House Democratic leadership is also characterized by its highly inclusive style. Although stronger in the sense of being more consequential in the legislative process, the party leadership has not become more hierarchical, more closed, or more directive. To the contrary, beginning in the 1970s Democratic House leaders developed strategies for including more of their members in leadership efforts. As we shall see, such an approach was necessary to enable the leaders to satisfy their members' desires for legislative results and for opportunities to participate broadly in the legislative process. To be sure, members' expectations of their leaders changed during the 1980s; House Democrats came to expect more activist and aggressive leadership, an expectation that continues in the 1990s. Members, however, still expected their leaders to facilitate when possible and not to hinder the rank and file's pursuit of their goals through individualistic strategies. The ideal point on the spectrum—from permissive, passive leadership to aggressive, activist leadership—has shifted, but successful leadership is still a balancing act.

Table 10-2 The Leadership's Expanded Agenda-Setting Role
(percentage of agenda items)

Congress	Agenda setter			
	President	Leadership	Other	N
91st (1969-1971)	48	2	34	50
94th (1975-1977)	23	17	35	48
97th (1981-1983)	44	9	16	45
100th (1987-1989)	23	33	23	40
101st (1989-1991)	18	12	n.a.	50

Source: Compiled by the author.

The Contextual Determinants of Activist Leadership

Before we examine in more detail the way contemporary party leadership functions, it will be useful to look briefly at the elements that have shaped House members' expectations and the leadership's response. Divided control is an important element, but by no means is it the only one. The House reforms of the 1970s increased uncertainty in the legislative process. As the powers of committee chairmen declined, the opportunities and resources for rank-and-file members to participate in the legislative process increased. Floor amendments proliferated, and committees became less able to pass their legislation on the floor without change. By the end of the 1970s many Democrats had become concerned about the unexpected policy consequences of the reforms. The wide-open, participatory process that the reforms established, however, became much more legislatively problematical within the context of the political environment of the 1980s. With the election of Ronald Reagan in 1980, House Democrats faced a conservative, confrontational president who threatened their goals. Backed by a Republican Senate and widely perceived as having a policy mandate, Reagan was a formidable opponent. Even after the perception of a mandate had faded, Democrats had difficulty in passing legislation they favored. Republicans controlled the Senate until 1987, and since the early 1980s large and growing budget deficits have severely constrained legislative activity.[4]

The reformers of the 1970s had given their party leaders new powers and resources that, aggressively used, could significantly increase the probability of legislative success. In the immediate postreform period, Democrats had been unwilling to allow their leaders to employ those new resources expansively. Now, faced with a much more difficult legislative context, members were not only willing to allow but increasingly came to demand that their leadership use those powers and resources aggressively to help pass legislation that would advance Democrats' policy and reelection goals.

By making satisfactory legislation so difficult to pass, the political context raised the potential benefits of strong leadership. An increase in the ideological homogeneity of the Democratic membership lowered the potential costs. The change in southern politics set off by the civil rights movement and the Voting Rights Act of 1965 had, by the early 1980s, resulted in a less conservative southern Democratic contingent in the House. In addition, expensive new social programs were ruled out by the federal deficit. This constraint upon policy proposals seriously considered also contributed to the Democrats' increasing voting cohesion, which becomes particularly evident after 1982.

In the late 1980s and early 1990s the voting cohesion of the Democrats reached levels unprecedented in the post-World War II era. During the period from 1951 through 1970, the average party unity score for House Democrats was 78 percent; this figure fell to 74 percent during the period from 1971 through 1982. The scores began rising after the 1982 election, and they averaged 86 percent during the period from 1983 through 1991. During these same years the proportion of roll calls on which a majority of Democrats voted against a majority of Republicans also increased, averaging 55 percent compared with 37 percent during the 1971-1982 period. As policy differences among Democrats declined, so did fears that the exercise of strong leadership would pose a threat to the policy or reelection goals of individual members.[5]

A look at the changing structure of conflict on the congressional agenda of major legislation, as defined earlier, shows the Democrats' increased voting cohesion and the extent to which their policy preferences and those of the president conflicted in the 1980s and early 1990s. During the 91st Congress only 18 percent of the agenda pitted two-thirds or more of House Democrats against Nixon; splits among Democrats and the ideological ambiguity of some of Nixon's policy positions contributed to this low level of clear-cut partisan conflict. The frequency of such conflict increased to 42 percent in the 94th Congress, rose to 47 percent in the 97th Congress, and reached a high of 61 percent during Reagan's last Congress. During Bush's first Congress the figure was a little lower (53 percent) but still higher than during the ideologically charged 97th Congress (1981-1983). House Democrats and the president continued to be at odds on policy. And, given that the president is a formidable opponent, House Democrats continued to need leadership assistance.

Democratic Leadership in the 1990s: Organization, Activities, Strategies

As the needs and expectations of members evolved in response to changes in the political and institutional context—and as the leadership attempted to meet their expectations—party organization, leadership activities, and leadership strategies also changed. The challenge the leadership faced in the 1980s and continues to face in the 1990s is to provide members with those things that require collective action—satisfactory legislation, preeminently, but also a favorable party image. The leadership must do these things, however, without infringing excessively on the members' capacity to pursue their goals through individual means. Members want legislative results, but they also want to participate fully in the legislative process; they want to enact legislation that furthers their policy goals, but they do not want to have to cast votes that pose a reelection risk. Ideally, leadership strategies should simultaneously provide protection, opportunities for participation, and legislative success.

Organizing to Communicate and Mobilize

The House Speaker, the majority leader, and the majority whip have traditionally constituted the core of the majority party leadership. As demands on the leaders have increased, the core group has expanded. By the late 1980s the chief deputy whip and the chairman and vice chairman of the Democratic Caucus were clearly members of the inner circle. At least on the periphery of the inner circle are the three chief deputy whips who replaced the single chief deputy whip, David E. Bonior of Michigan, when he succeeded William H. Gray III of Pennsylvania as whip in 1991.

The core leadership group—Speaker Thomas S. Foley of Washington; Majority Leader Richard A. Gephardt of Missouri; Majority Whip Bonior; Chief Deputy Whips Butler Derrick of South Carolina, Barbara B. Kennelly of Connecticut, and John Lewis of Georgia; Caucus Chair Steny H. Hoyer of Maryland; and Caucus Vice Chair Vic Fazio of California—is relatively large and also diverse. Diversity gives the leadership ties to all segments of the membership and is important to coalition-building success. As the leadership has become more central to the legislative process, members' desires for representation in the leadership have intensified. (When Speaker Foley split the single chief deputy whip position into three, he appointed a southerner, a woman, and an African American in response to those groups' importunings.)

The combination of the leadership's need for assistance and the membership's desire for inclusion within the leadership circle has led to a massive expansion of the Democratic whip system. Consisting of the majority whip, a deputy whip, and approximately eighteen regionally elected zone whips in the early 1970s, the whip system has grown to more than a hundred members. In 1992 it consisted of the whip, three chief deputy whips, fifteen deputy whips, three task force chairmen, sixty-six at-large whips, and eighteen zone whips. Except for the majority whip, who like the Speaker and the majority leader is elected by the full Democratic Caucus, and the zone whips, who are elected by regional groups of members, the whips are appointed by the top leaders.

The whip system performs two important and related functions: it serves as a central conduit for information between members and leaders, and it plays an important role in mobilizing votes. Information about the preferences—and the moods, activities, and plans—of the membership is critical for the inner circle to exercise effective legislative leadership. The whip system provides the leaders with information in two distinct ways.

First, upon the leaders' instructions, the whips conduct a formal poll to ascertain members' voting intentions on upcoming legislation. The results of whip polls are an important guide to legislative strategy, as we shall see. A poll may indicate that a vote should be postponed until a few more members can be brought around or even that substantive changes must be made in a bill if it is to pass. Conversely, a poll may show a solid majority in favor of the legislation and so indicate that no more resources need be put into the effort.

Second, the weekly whip meetings are another important source of information for the leaders. At those generally well attended meetings, leaders hear the opinions, reactions, and gripes of a cross section of their membership. Discussion tends to be wide ranging and frank. A major benefit of being a whip is that the meetings give members the opportunity to convey their views directly to the leadership.

The whip system is centrally involved in mobilizing the votes required to pass legislation important to the party. The whip polls provide the leadership with information essential for strategy planning. In addition, efforts to persuade the rank and file are generally orchestrated through the whip system. A special whip task force, which includes a subset of the large whip system membership, oversees the effort to pass each major bill; we shall elaborate on this process later.

The whip system serves the needs of both leaders and members. For the leadership, its seemingly inflated size is actually beneficial, ensuring that the whip meetings reflect the diversity of member sentiment and providing a large pool from which to draw workers for vote-mobilization efforts. For members, regular access to the leaders became increasingly attractive as the leadership became more active; being a whip provides access without committing a member to working for the party position across the board.

Members and leaders have another forum for communicating with one another. The Democratic Caucus, the organization of all House Democrats, meets monthly and at the request of fifty members. The caucus can be used by groups of members or by the leadership. When important and controversial legislation is nearing floor consideration, party and committee leaders may hold a caucus meeting to inform their membership of the substance and the politics of the bill and to gauge their members' reactions. Groups of members may request a special meeting to discuss an issue or problem, often hoping thereby to send a message to committee or party leaders about the direction and intensity of member sentiment. The caucus can instruct committees or party leaders, though it seldom does so. Intense member sentiment, however, exerts pressure on leaders—committee as well as party—because all are dependent upon the membership for their positions.

Orchestrating Floor Strategies

About 11:00 a.m. on May 26, 1988, Republicans, without warning, offered an amendment to the intelligence authorization bill to lift restrictions on CIA aid to the contras. Believing passage of the amendment would scuttle the talks between the Nicaraguan government and the contras, which were scheduled to begin the next day, the Democratic leadership went into its "fire drill." The deputy whips were told to work the doors; a computer list of members absent for the last roll call was printed, and those who supported the leadership were located and asked to vote; a whip call alerting all Democrats that an important vote was imminent was sent over the automatic phone system.

The members of the task force on Nicaragua were called to the floor. The task force's mission was to inform and persuade. Each member of the task force was assigned some of the fifty-one Democrats with no hard-and-fast position whose votes would make the difference. Meanwhile, the task force chair asked the most active Republican opponent of contra aid to make sure the small band of like-minded Republicans were on board. The chair also persuaded an influential moderate Democrat to lobby other moderates.

As the vote approached, the leadership still lacked reliable information on sixteen members. Because votes on contra aid generally had been close, the task force was assigned to "baby-sit" these sixteen. Each task force member sat with an assignee, making sure that person was informed about the substantive and political effects of the vote. When the vote came at about 1:30 p.m., the Republican amendment was defeated, 214-190.

The House floor is the traditional domain of the party leaders. Facilitating the passage of legislation at the floor stage is a task the leadership has long been expected to perform. As floor passage became more problematic, the frequency of leadership involvement increased and new strategies were developed. To be sure, only a small proportion of the more than nine hundred bills passed by the House each Congress engages the leaders' attention.[6] Most of the bills are neither controversial nor highly consequential. The party leadership is increasingly likely to take an active part in getting major legislation passed, however.

Legislation important to a substantial part of the Democratic membership or to the party or to the institution as a whole will elicit leadership involvement, particularly if difficulty is expected. Thus in the 100th Congress the leadership worked actively on farm credit legislation because Democrats from farm states hard-hit by the agricultural recession needed this legislation for reelection. For ideologically committed liberals and for members with large numbers of minority constituents, civil rights legislation to overturn restrictive Supreme Court decisions has been a major legislative goal. These members have expected and received their leadership's help in this endeavor. In 1991 the extension of unemployment benefits for workers who had exhausted their regular benefits was particularly important to Democrats from districts hurt by the recession; it was also important to the party's image. Going into an election year, all Democrats would benefit if the party appeared both compassionate and capable. Much the same was true of the huge transportation bill enacted in late 1991; many individual members benefited, and so did the party as a whole. In contrast, the 1991 banking bill that provided the Federal Deposit Insurance Corporation with a $30 billion line of credit to close failed banks was "must-pass" but no-benefit legislation. If Congress had not enacted the legislation, dire financial consequences would have resulted. George Bush would have delighted in pointing out who was responsible, and the public image of Congress and its majority party would have suffered. Yet voting $30 billion for failed banks in a time of recession and tight federal spending was unpalatable to members as individuals. The Democratic leadership had no choice but to get involved in all these legislative battles. The farm credit, unemployment benefits, and transportation bills offered opportunities to advance the policy and reelection goals of their members. The leadership's task with the banking bill was to protect their members collectively by persuading a sufficient number to cast individually risky votes.

The extent of leadership involvement depends upon how important the bill at issue is deemed to be, how much trouble is anticipated, and what the expected difficulties are. Leadership activity can vary from last-minute persuasion when a bill runs into unexpected trouble on the floor, as in the case of the contra aid amendment, to full-fledged orchestration of the process from bill introduction to enactment.

The contemporary leadership will monitor the progress of major legislation from its inception, even if its involvement will be focused primarily on the floor stage. Staffers assigned to keeping tabs on committee activities regularly give the leaders updates on the status of important bills and alert them to developing problems. Sometimes incipient trouble can be averted by a well-timed word with committee members.

At some point the party and the committee leadership will discuss floor scheduling. If the party leaders consider a bill central to the party's agenda, they will often hold a discussion at the beginning of the Congress and set a target date. The Speaker may assign the bill one of the coveted low numbers that symbolically convey priority; thus, in the 102d Congress the civil rights bill was designated HR 1, and family and medical leave legislation, HR 2, indicating the central places of these bills on the party's agenda.

The aim in scheduling major legislation is to bring the bill to the floor when its chances of success are greatest and its effect on the party's image most favorable. The majority party's near total control over the floor schedule is an important leadership tool. The leadership can wait until it has the votes for passage or, conversely, it can schedule legislation quickly before the opposition has time to mobilize. Of course, deadlines and public pressure from the president can constrain the leadership's use of its scheduling powers.

Committee and party leaders discuss the political and substantive aspects of the bill likely to affect its floor fate. As the target date for floor consideration draws near, they decide which floor roll calls are likely to be the difficult ones. Will the critical vote or votes be on approving the rule, on one or several amendments (and, if so, which ones), or on final passage? Accurate prediction is essential because so much of strategy depends upon it.

The special rule that specifies the conditions under which a bill is considered on the floor can often determine which votes will be the critical ones. If the rule allows no amendments, the key vote is likely to be on the rule itself. If the rule allows only a few specific amendments, determining which are likely to be the key votes will be fairly easy. If any germane amendment is allowed, however, the bill's proponents may well face much more uncertainty.[7]

The decision about the special rule is obviously one of the most important strategic decisions. The Rules Committee makes that decision, but, because the committee's Democratic members are chosen by the Speaker, the committee's decisions are heavily influenced by what the leadership wants. If the Speaker makes his wishes known, the committee almost always complies.

Usually, the whip system swings into action only after at least a preliminary decision on the rule has been made. A whip's aide drafts the questions to be asked in the whip poll, and the questions are conveyed by fax to the zone whips. Each zone whip (or more frequently an aide) calls the Democrats in the whip's regional zone, ascertains their answers to the questions, and reports the results back to the majority whip's office.

The leadership will have set up a special task force to work on the legislation, usually by inviting all whips, committee Democrats who support the legislation, and, sometimes, other particularly interested Democrats. The task force members work from the vote count of the zone whips. Every Democrat not listed as voting "yes" on the critical votes is assigned to a task force member and is contacted again. The initial count is often done staff to staff; now contact is member to member. The task force members must not only ascertain the voting intentions of their assignees, but they must also persuade them to support the party position. If the first task force member is unsuccessful in persuading an uncommitted Democrat, another member may try. The process of refining the count and of persuading the uncommitted continues until floor success is assured. Often during the persuasion process the task force will work with friendly interest groups. Only if, at the very end, a few more votes are needed do the top leaders personally become involved in persuasion.

At some point the leadership may conclude that the legislation as drafted by the committee cannot be enacted. Changes must be made if the bill is to pass at all or if it is to pass with a majority large enough to pressure the president to sign or to compromise. (Leadership involvement in shaping substitute legislation is discussed in the next section.) Sometimes, what is needed to engineer passage is not a significant change in the substance of the legislation but an opportunity for members to cast a protective vote. The leadership can ensure that members get that chance. Thus, for example, in 1989 Sen. Jesse Helms, R-N.C., and other right-wing Republicans mounted a campaign against the National Endowment for the Arts (NEA) for purportedly supporting pornographic art. The budget and the artistic freedom of the NEA were endangered. The appropriations bill that included NEA funding could not have been passed without change. Casting a favorable vote would have left many members vulnerable to charges of supporting federal funding of pornographic art. The party leadership cooperated with the committee leadership to arrange for a vote that would cut the budget by $45,000, the amount of the two controversial grants. Having protected themselves by supporting this cut, most Democrats voted for the legislation, which passed without real damage to the NEA.

Most of the work to mobilize votes is done before the legislation reaches the floor. On major legislation, when one or more key roll calls are expected to be close or when unexpected trouble arises, the task force will continue active work throughout the period of floor consideration. Task force members will work the doors, signaling the party position to Democrats as they stream into the chamber to vote. The task force will make sure that members committed to the party position show up to cast their votes. If the party position is short of votes as the clock runs down, task force members will push their colleagues to change their votes and will have the top leaders lean on waverers.

Whip task forces provide the assistance a party leadership subject to enormous demands on its time and resources badly needs. When several important and problematic bills must be brought to the floor in quick succession, only the task force device makes active leadership involvement on each bill possible. During the 100th and 101st Congresses task forces operated in approximately seventy instances per Congress. Clearly, that level of leadership involvement would not have been possible if the core leadership had had to rely only upon its own numbers. Task forces also allow the top leaders to hoard their resources by making it possible for them to limit their personal persuasion.

Task forces contribute to legislative success. In addition, they enable many Democrats to participate meaningfully in the legislative process and in leadership efforts, thus helping the leadership to fulfill this facet of members' expectations. The whip task force system is a central element of a strategy of inclusion developed by Democratic party leaders to aid them in reconciling these two potentially conflicting expectations: legislative results and broad participation. Task forces provide Democrats with the opportunity to become significantly involved on legislation they care about, even if they are junior members or not members of the originating committee. And many representatives take advantage of the opportunity; in the 100th Congress, for example, about 60 percent of House Democrats served on one or more task forces.

Control of the Rules Committee provides the basis for another important leadership strategy. Carefully crafted rules can reduce uncertainty and structure the choices members face on the floor. In 1989 the party leadership brought a combined congressional ethics and pay-raise package to the floor. This was done under a closed rule to prevent amendments that might pick apart the carefully balanced bipartisan deal. In 1990 the proposed constitutional amendment outlawing flag burning, which the leadership wanted to defeat, was also considered under a closed rule. As with the combined ethics and pay-raise bill, Democrats did not want to have to go on record on a series of difficult, no-win votes. The leadership also wanted to head off any changes that would make the constitutional amendment more palatable. More frequently, however, rules allow a limited number of amendments, usually including a Republican substitute for the Democratic-supported committee bill. Republicans, thus, are given an opportunity to vote on their preferred version, which under the Reagan and Bush administrations often reflected the president's preferences; they—and other opponents—are not given the chance to unravel the compromises worked out at the prefloor stage by offering a multitude of amendments. The rule under which the civil rights bill was considered in 1991, for example, allowed votes on the Republican-administration substitute, on a liberal substitute, and on a committee amendment. Republicans were denied a motion to recommit with instructions (which provides another way of amending the bill) because that would have, as a Rules staffer explained, "given them two bites at the apple."

In the mid-1970s the Speaker was given the power to nominate Rules Committee Democrats, subject only to ratification by the Democratic Caucus, and the committee became an arm of the leadership. But members' desires and expectations limited the leadership's use of rules for strategic purposes. Democrats then wanted to be free to offer any germane amendments on the floor. Nowhere is the change in members' expectations more evident. Democrats now expect their leaders to use restrictive rules on most major legislation. In the 95th Congress (1977-1979), only 15 percent of all rules granted for initial consideration of legislation were restrictive; by the 101st Congress well over half (55 percent) were.[8] When only the congressional agenda of major items, as defined earlier, is considered, the change is even greater. In the early and mid-1970s most major legislation was brought to the floor under a simple open rule; in the 91st Congress (1969-1971) and the 94th Congress (1975-1977), about 80 percent of major agenda items were. By the 101st Congress this figure had shrunk to about 20 percent. Bills on which the leadership is involved in a major way are even more likely to be considered under closed or complex and usually restrictive rules; during the 101st Congress, 92 percent were.

Every rule requires majority approval on the House floor. Since Republicans increasingly vote against most restrictive rules, approval depends upon a large proportion of Democrats voting in favor. The big increase in the use of such rules, thus, signifies that most Democrats approve of the leadership's aggressive use of this strategy. It also suggests that leaders use the strategy skillfully. The leadership frequently employs carefully crafted and often restrictive rules to enable its members to vote their policy preferences without paying too big a reelection price. Closed rules, for example, may provide members with "cover" by making the crucial vote a procedural one. Unpopular but necessary measures may be bundled with more popular provisions and voted on as a package under a restrictive rule. Thus members could justify a vote for a congressional pay raise by the inclusion of a stringent ethics code in the package. When a group of Democrats really needs to offer an amendment for policy or reelection reasons, they are given the opportunity to do so. On the civil rights bill, for example, the Black Caucus and a group of women members were given the chance to offer a liberal substitute for a more moderate version drafted to have broad appeal.

The Democrats' willingness to approve restrictive rules routinely also suggests that they are, by and large, reasonably satisfied with the bills that come to the floor. Vote-mobilization task forces and carefully crafted rules can increase a bill's probability of floor success but only within the limits set by the substance of the legislation.

Shaping Legislation

When the leadership decided civil rights legislation would be a top priority in 1991, the Speaker asked Whip William H. Gray to oversee the effort. Congress had failed to override a bill Bush had vetoed in 1990; furthermore, by vocally and repeatedly labeling the legislation a quota bill, Bush had made supporting it electorally risky for some members. Under those circumstances, merely passing the bill would not be sufficient. "Given the kinds of numbers we needed to come out looking good, ... we had no margin for error, because it meant we needed incredible Democratic cohesion; we needed almost all the Democrats, 95 percent or something," a senior leadership staffer explained. "And the only way that we were going to do that was to put together some pretty appealing compromises." Working with committee Democrats, with members— particularly southerners—concerned about supporting legislation that could be labeled a quota bill, and with interest groups on both sides of the issue, Gray worked out a compromise that was substituted for the original committee version on the floor. On final passage 250 Democrats voted for the bill, and only 15 voted against.

The contemporary majority leadership, as this example shows, does not confine its activity to the floor; meeting member expectations of legislative results requires that leaders take an active interest in all stages of the legislative process. They often involve themselves early and sometimes take a hand in shaping legislation.

Committees can expect considerably less deference now than they could in the prereform era; consequently, the form in which they bring legislation to the floor is even more important than it used to be.[9] When a committee is incapable of putting together a bill satisfactory to the bulk of the Democratic membership and one that can command a majority of the House, the party leaders often step in if the legislation is important to the party. In 1989, for example, the liberal Education and Labor Committee approved a generous minimum wage bill. Although an early whip poll indicated that, with work, the bill might squeak through the House, many Democrats would have been forced to take a difficult vote on a bill that would never be enacted in its original form. The Democrats could not possibly muster a two-thirds vote to override an inevitable veto. Under the leadership's auspices a compromise version of the legislation was worked out and offered as a substitute amendment on the floor. It passed easily.

On both minimum wage legislation and the civil rights bill, the party leadership's involvement extended far beyond matters of procedure and floor strategy into matters of legislative substance. Democratic committee leaders and committee contingents allow the party leaders to involve themselves in this way because they want to pass their legislation and, to do so, they need the leadership's help.

In addition, committee leaders are responsive to a leadership they perceive as representing the sentiments of the Democratic membership because committee chairmen are dependent upon Democratic Caucus approval. Party leaders can and do lean on committee leaders to report out legislation that the Democratic membership wants. In 1991, for example, some pressure was required to persuade the chairman of the Ways and Means Committee to report out legislation extending unemployment benefits. To give his members a major accomplishment to take home, Speaker Foley was determined that by the end of 1991 transportation legislation would be enacted. To that end, he kept the pressure on House conferees. "He is on our back continuously," the committee chairman said.[10] Differences between the House and the Senate were resolved, and both chambers gave final approval to the bill before Thanksgiving.

Recent Speakers have differed somewhat in how quick they are to intervene in committee and lean on committee chairmen. Speaker Jim Wright used the leverage his position gave him expansively. Tom Foley, as a former committee chairman, defers more to chairmen and tends to wait longer before intervening. These are, however, marginal differences. House Democrats expect their leaders to produce legislative results. When doing so requires pressuring a committee and its chairman, they expect their leaders to do so.

Since the mid-1970s, when the multiple referral of legislation to all committees with a jurisdictional claim was instituted, the party leadership has been drawn much more deeply into the prefloor legislative process. A substantial proportion of most major legislation is referred to more than one House committee and so requires the approval of each committee.[11] In 1989-1991, for example, 32 percent of the congressional agenda of major bills, as defined earlier, was referred to multiple committees. When a bill is referred to many committees, leadership coordination is often necessary to bring it to the floor in passable shape and in timely fashion. Even when only two committees are involved, committee leaders are not always able to negotiate a solution to their differences. Often brokering and pressure by the leadership are required to get the committees to reach an agreement. The trade bill in the 100th Congress and the Americans with Disabilities Act (ADA) in the 101st Congress are examples of legislation that, because of the sheer number of committees involved, required leadership coordination. The trade bill was referred to eleven committees, ADA to four.

The handling of ADA is indicative of Speaker Foley's style. He frequently designates a member to take the lead on each major bill. Steny Hoyer, chairman of the Democratic Caucus, was the "designated hitter" on ADA; Hoyer monitored the numerous subcommittee and full committee meetings on the legislation, encouraged action, and negotiated agreements on substantive matters in conflict.[12]

When the politics surrounding a bill are particularly complex and delicate, the leadership may supersede the committees as the key actor. In 1989 the congressional ethics and pay-raise bill was crafted by a special task force appointed by the leadership. During the 100th Congress the leadership put together several contra aid bills. The campaign finance bill passed by the House in 1991 was drafted by another special task force designated by the leadership.

By fostering budget summitry, the political and policymaking environment of the 1980s and early 1990s has further drawn the party leadership into the prefloor legislative process. Divided control of government and the constraint of big budget deficits have made legislative stalemate an ever-present threat. The president and the congressional majority were deeply divided on basic questions of priorities during the 1980s and early 1990s. Yet despite their lack of agreement and the inability, after 1982, of either the president or the congressional Democrats to impose their preferences on the other, legislation making budgetary decisions must be passed. By the late 1980s basic decisions on spending and taxes were frequently made in interbranch budget summits. The magnitude of the issues and the partisan stakes involved dictated that top party leaders speak and act for their membership in negotiations with the administration.[13] To be sure, most members dislike summitry as a decision-making procedure because it cuts them out of the process. But when it becomes unavoidable, Democrats prefer having their elected leaders make those decisions rather than any other small group of members.

Conveying the Message

On November 26, 1991, as Congress was frantically finishing its legislative business for the year, President Bush unexpectedly endorsed a tax cut proposal that conservative House Republicans were pushing. "I want to see the package passed and I want to see it done fast," he told the press.[14] The statement was a surprise. Most officials in the administration had opposed any immediate tax cut, and the House Republican package was hastily crafted legislation that had not been subjected to scrutiny. In fact, the president's endorsement appeared to represent not true support but an attempt to solve several political problems. Democrats had been criticizing the president for his lack of an economic recovery program. Their concerted attack was receiving media attention and was probably contributing to Bush's falling popularity in the polls. Only hours away from planned adjournment, Congress appeared to be in little danger of passing that bill or any other tax cut. By endorsing the conservative Republicans' package, Bush would put Democrats on the defensive and satisfy House Republicans who, of course, wanted their president's support.

The Democratic leadership responded quickly. "It was unbelievably irresponsible for the President to suggest that he would like us to vote today on a proposal that wasn't even a legislative proposal until last night and has been cost-estimated at $23 billion," Speaker Foley told the press. "It is totally irresponsible."[15] In an unusual speech on the House floor, the Speaker called for "an end to the gamesmanship." He challenged Bush to phone him and ask for Congress to return in December if Bush really wanted a tax bill.[16]

At a caucus of House Democrats late in the evening of November 26, the leadership outlined its strategy. The House would not formally adjourn when it finished its business; then the leadership easily could recall members should Bush decide to bash Congress for not passing a tax cut. In December the Ways and Means Committee would hold hearings to highlight the troubled economy, expose problems with the conservative Republican plan, and begin to build support for a Democratic alternative.

The media found this high-stakes confrontation riveting and devoted extensive coverage to the leadership's adept response to the president's political ploy. The consensus was that the Democrats had called Bush's bluff and come out well ahead. The interest created by this imbroglio probably increased media coverage of the December Ways and Means hearings. Carefully orchestrated to showcase the difference between Democratic proposals for middle-class tax relief and Republican plans to cut the capital-gains tax, which would benefit the rich, the hearings clearly put the Democrats on the offensive and the president on the defensive.

With Congress out of town, the president had expected to monopolize the spotlight, using that media attention to repair some of the damage done to his popularity by the bad economy and the Democrats' effective exploitation of the issue. He had hoped, in fact, to turn the tables on his political opponents, blaming the country's economic woes on congressional Democrats. In this instance, the House Democratic leaders, by their adept response to the threat, not only protected the party's image and their members but transformed the issue into an opportunity to promote the party's image and its policies.

Democratic members of the House now expect their party leaders to act as their spokesmen in this fashion. During the long period of divided control, Democrats had come to understand that the president's great access to the media gave him an enormous advantage in political and policy struggles and that they as individuals could never compete with the president in the realm of public opinion. The skill with which Ronald Reagan used the president's access to the media to further his policy and political agenda and to denigrate Democrats made congressional Democrats realize they needed their own spokesmen to counter the president.

The party leadership has developed a variety of mechanisms to enhance its effectiveness as spokesman. All the leaders employ one or more staffers whose primary charge is press relations. Every day that the House is in session, the Speaker holds a fifteen-minute press conference. When the Speaker leaves to convene the House, the other top leaders and senior leadership staff stay behind to answer more questions. The leaders hold occasional press luncheons with selected reporters. They appear frequently on the Sunday interview shows and periodically on the morning network news programs and on the "MacNeil-Lehrer Newshour."

When the House is in session, a group of activist, media-savvy Democrats meet daily with the majority leader to agree upon a message for the day and to plan press-related efforts. Usually, the message is derived from the major legislation of the day. It attempts to link that legislation to broader themes that reflect favorably on the Democratic party. For example, family and medical leave legislation, one of the party's priorities in the 102d Congress, was defined as both a family issue and a fairness issue.

Although members want their leaders to act as spokesmen, they do not thereby take a vow of silence. Getting everyone "to sing from the same hymn book" is a perpetual problem. When the party is split, media coordination cannot solve the problem, but when there is considerable agreement, it can help.

The leadership uses a variety of forums to convey its message. Press conferences, sometimes including participants with special media appeal, may be held. When the family and medical leave bill was on the floor, several people faced with the agonizing choice between caring for a severely ill child and working at a job needed for family support were featured at press conferences. A coordinated series of one-minute speeches on the House floor at the beginning of business is a favorite technique, one used throughout the week the family leave bill was under consideration. Although C-SPAN televises House floor activities, the major aim of these activities is to get coverage in newspapers and on network television, a goal amply realized during the campaign for family leave legislation. All three evening network news programs had segments about the issue and the legislation.

Highlighting some issue through a dramatic event designed to get media coverage can be an effective component of legislative strategy. In 1988 the Democratic party leadership attempted to enact legislation requiring companies to notify workers sixty days before they closed a plant. The leadership carefully orchestrated a day-long series of events featuring workers thrown out of work without any notice. These events received extensive media coverage. Strong public support for the notification requirement eventually persuaded Reagan, who had adamantly opposed the provision, to let the legislation become law without his signature. By making the issue highly visible, Democrats had made an election-year veto too politically expensive for the president. In late October 1991 Democrats staged an all-night House debate on the suffering of the nation's jobless. Carried live on C-SPAN, the debate kept the pressure on President Bush to agree to an extension of unemployment benefits. The vigil was part of a campaign that contributed to Bush's ultimate acceptance of legislation he had formerly opposed.

The president's standing as head of state and his greater access to the media are enormous advantages in getting the administration's interpretation, especially of complex and abstruse matters, accepted by the public over that of congressional opponents. The congressional leadership cannot compete with the president on an equal footing; their efforts, however, have modestly narrowed the gap. When external developments work in favor of the Democratic position—as they did on plant closing and the extension of unemployment insurance—the leadership is now more capable of amplifying the effect of positive developments through its media efforts than it ever was before.

Leaders, Followers, and Policy: An Assessment

Today, House Democrats display, according to the usual voting measures, substantial ideological homogeneity. Their party leaders possess a considerable capacity to provide legislative leadership—to deliver the coordination and coalition-building services necessary for legislative success and even to act as party spokesmen with some effectiveness.

Why, then, have the 1980s and early 1990s witnessed so much dissatisfaction with Congress in particular and with government in general? If conditions analysts have long considered necessary for effective policymaking were being met, why was almost everyone unhappy with policy results?

Divided control is a large part of the answer. The U.S. system of government requires that the president and Congress work together if much is to be accomplished. Sufficient strength for one branch to impose its will on the other is rare. When control is divided, an ideologically homogeneous, reasonably strongly led majority party in Congress actually increases the chances of stalemate. Certainly stalemate results when, as has been the case in recent years, the parties strongly disagree on what is good public policy. In these circumstances, the president is less able to break off enough majority party members to pass his proposals; yet, because he possesses the veto, he can usually thwart majority party efforts at significant policy innovation.[17]

With control now united, a period of productive policymaking can be expected. The changes that have occurred in the Democratic party in the House make Bill Clinton's admittedly formidable task of bringing about major policy change easier. The Democratic leadership, always an ally of a Democratic president, brings impressive tools to the task; Speaker Foley and the rest of the leadership group can give Clinton considerable help in putting together and holding together majorities at the various stages of the legislative process. The Democratic House membership came out of the 1992 elections united in its conviction that its collective fate rested upon producing effective policy responses to the economic problems the country faces.

Still, the Democrats' high level of voting cohesiveness and the majority leadership's central role in the policy process have developed, in good part, in response to adversity. Can the Democrats maintain that state of affairs in a less threatening environment?

Two related temptations confront Democrats and pose a danger to the party's legislative performance. Members on the left of the party's spectrum may see the election of a Democratic president as an opportunity to place scores of expensive new social programs on the agenda. A massive expansion of the agenda would likely create dissension and reduce cohesion. Members from all parts of the spectrum may reassess the costs and benefits of the leadership's structuring of choices. In a seemingly more favorable political climate, many Democrats may be attracted to the freelance policy entrepreneurship prevalent in the 1970s; thus they may be less willing to acquiesce in restrictive rules than they were under divided control.

If Democrats succumb to these temptations, the policy costs will be high. The reforms of the 1970s changed the legislative process in such a way that significant, sustained legislative accomplishment requires active involvement and direction by the party leadership. The success of any Democratic administration depends upon active congressional leadership, and such leadership depends upon the expectations and desires of the party's congressional members. If Democrats are able to resist these temptations, however, a period of real policy achievement is likely.

Notes

This essay is based, in part, upon participant observation in the House Speaker's office in 1987-1988 and upon interviews with House members, staff, and informed observers over a number of years. I am grateful to Jim Wright, D-Texas, and his staff for giving me the opportunity to see how the speakership operated from the inside. I also thank all those who gave up some of their precious time to talk with me. All unattributed quotations are from interviews conducted by the author. Grants from the Academic Senate Research Committee of the University of California, Riverside, and from the Dirksen Center greatly helped the research.

1. A more detailed presentation and analysis of these data can be found in Barbara Sinclair, "The Emergence of Strong Leadership in the 1980s House of Representatives," *Journal of Politics* 54 (August 1992): 657-684. For an analysis of leadership in the 1950s and 1960s, see Randall Ripley, *Party Leaders in the House of Representatives* (Washington, D.C.: Brookings Institution, 1967).
2. See Paul Light, *The President's Agenda* (Baltimore: Johns Hopkins University Press, 1982); and Mark A. Peterson, *Legislating Together: The White House and Capitol Hill from Eisenhower to Reagan* (Cambridge: Harvard University Press, 1990).
3. Routine administration requests for reauthorization of legislation without major change do not qualify the items for presidential agenda status. In Congressional Quarterly's account, there are cases in which some other identifiable individual or group—most frequently one or a group of liberal entrepreneurs or a group such as labor—is the primary agenda setter. These are classified into a looser category, labeled "other." Not all items are classified. Fairly frequently, an item attains congressional agenda status through routine processes—the need for reauthorization, the appropriations process, and so forth.
4. Barbara Sinclair, "Strong Party Leadership in a Weak Party Era—The Evolution of Party Leadership in the Modern House," in *The Atomistic Congress,* ed. Allen D. Hertzke and Ronald M. Peters (Armonk, N.Y.: M. E. Sharpe, 1992); and Barbara Sinclair, *Majority Party Leadership in the U.S. House* (Baltimore: Johns Hopkins University Press, 1983).
5. *Congressional Quarterly Weekly Report,* various dates; and David W. Rohde, *Parties and Leaders in the Postreform House* (Chicago: University of Chicago Press, 1991).
6. Norman J. Ornstein, Thomas E. Mann, and Michael J. Malbin, *Vital Statistics on Congress, 1991-1992* (Washington, D.C.: Congressional Quarterly, 1992), 151.
7. For a fuller discussion of rules, see Stanley Bach and Steven S. Smith, *Managing Uncertainty in the House of Representatives* (Washington, D.C.: Brookings Institution, 1988). For more on the relationship between the Speaker and the Rules Committee, see Bruce I. Oppenheimer, "The Changing Relationship Between House Leadership and the Committee on Rules," in *Understanding Congressional Leadership,* ed. Frank H. Mackaman (Washington, D.C.: CQ Press, 1981); and Sinclair, *Majority Party Leadership in the U.S. House.* For a more general analysis of the enterprise of structuring choices and its effect on outcomes, see R. Douglas Arnold, *The Logic of Congressional Action* (New Haven: Yale University Press, 1990).
8. Don Wolfensberger, "Open vs. Restrictive Rules, 95th-101st Congresses" (Manuscript prepared by the Minority Counsel, Subcommittee on the Legislative Process, Committee on Rules, 1991).
9. Steven S. Smith, *Call To Order: Floor Politics in the House and Senate* (Washington, D.C.: Brookings Institution, 1989).
10. Quoted in Chuck Alston, "The Speaker and the Chairmen: A Taoist Approach to Power," *Congressional Quarterly Weekly Report,* Nov. 2, 1991, 3178.
11. See Melissa P. Collie and Joseph Cooper, "Multiple Referral and the 'New' Committee System in the House of Representatives," in *Congress Reconsidered,* 4th ed., ed.

Lawrence C. Dodd and Bruce I. Oppenheimer (Washington, D.C.: CQ Press, 1989).

12. See Barbara Sinclair, "House Majority Party Leadership in an Era of Legislative Constraint," in *The Postreform Congress,* ed. Roger H. Davidson (New York: St. Martin's, 1992), 103-105.

13. For a discussion of budget summit politics in 1990, see ibid., 105-110.

14. Quoted in Chuck Alston, "First Session Winds Down after Tax-Cut Dither," *Congressional Quarterly Weekly Report,* Nov. 30, 1991, 3506.

15. Quoted in William J. Eaton and Douglas Jehl, "Democrats Plan Vote on Tax Cut," *Los Angeles Times,* Nov. 27, 1991, A1, A12.

16. Alston, "First Session Winds Down," 3507-3508.

17. Barbara Sinclair, "Governing Unheroically (and Sometimes Unappetizingly): Bush and the 101st Congress," in *The Bush Presidency: First Appraisals,* ed. Colin Campbell and Bert Rockman (Chatham, N.J.: Chatham House, 1991).

11

Forces of Change in Senate
Party Leadership and Organization

Steven S. Smith

I n the 1880s political scientist and future president Woodrow Wilson wrote
that in the Senate

> no one is the senator. No one may speak for his party as well as for himself; no
> one exercises the special trust of acknowledged leadership. The Senate is
> merely a body of individual critics, representing most of the not very diversified
> types of society substantially homogeneous; and the weight of every criticism
> uttered in its chamber depends upon the weight of its critic who utters it,
> deriving little if any attention to its specific gravity from connection with the
> designs of a purposeful party organization.[1]

In the 1970s Wilson's immoderate depiction of the Senate was cited by another
insightful scholar, Charles O. Jones, as fitting the modern Senate as well. Jones
insists that "strong substance-oriented policy leadership by party leaders is neither possible nor desirable in the United States Senate." The best that can be
expected of Senate leaders, Jones argues, is that they will sometimes exploit
their "traditional procedural functions in such a way that it has considerable
impact on the substance of legislation."[2] The limits on leadership in any democratic institution, as well as the Senate's unique rules and enduring individualism, appear to severely constrain the ability of party leaders to shape policy
choices.[3]

Nevertheless, the Senate's current party leaders, Democrat George Mitchell of Maine and Republican Robert Dole of Kansas, are among the most powerful Washingtonians. To be sure, Mitchell and Dole do not dictate policy choices
to their party colleagues; nor do they consistently assume a leading role in shaping legislation. But the Mitchell-Dole pair are notable for their assertiveness and
involvement in substantive policy questions. They even have been contrasted to
the "weaker" House leaders, Speaker Thomas Foley of Washington and Minority Leader Robert Michel of Illinois.

The concern of this essay is how party leaders and their organizations have
adapted to the great changes that have occurred in the Senate since the 1950s. I
shall argue that leaders now are more immersed in substantive policy matters.
They more frequently appoint party task forces on important legislation outside
the system of standing committees and more aggressively manage the policy
agenda of their party and chamber. The parties meet more frequently to discuss
substantive and political matters, perform more political and service functions,
and for most senators are a more central feature of the communications network.

And yet the Senate's procedures and individualism limit the ability of its central party leaders to move far beyond their duties as floor and party managers to take the lead on substantive policy matters.

Historical Origins

Modern leadership posts were created in the early twentieth century, well after Wilson offered his testimony on Senate politics.[4] Soon after the publication of Wilson's book, the party caucus chairmen gradually began to assume responsibility of representing the parties on the floor. By World War I, when Wilson was president of the United States, caucus chairmen were also floor leaders, running the Senate's business. But not until 1920 for the Democrats and 1925 for the Republicans did the Senate parties formally use the modern title of leader.

Since the 1920s the formal positions of majority leader and minority leader have been institutionalized in party rules and recognized in the formal precedents of the Senate. The terms "floor leader" and "majority leader" (or "minority leader") are now used interchangeably in the Senate. Until 1945 the floor leader of each party also served as the party's conference chairman. In that year Republicans implemented rules providing for a separate party conference chairman. Democrats continued to make their floor leader the conference chairman. The prominence of the floor leaders is reflected in the front-and-center location of their desks on the Senate floor. Table 11-1 lists the floor leaders since the mid-1950s.[5]

The formal powers of floor leaders under the Senate's standing rules are important but limited. Jointly, the majority leader and minority leader may increase a committee's size temporarily to preserve a majority of seats for the majority party, they may waive rules providing that committees not meet while the Senate is in session and that committee reports be available for three days before floor action, and they may refer legislation to two or more committees. The use of these powers increases efficiency in the Senate, but the powers are granted to the joint leadership to ensure that partisan advantage is not gained by their use. As a result, they seldom play a role in shaping outcomes on important policy matters.

More important than the Senate's standing rules are Senate precedents. Senate precedents, which date back at least to the 1930s, require that the presiding officer recognize the majority leader, minority leader, majority bill manager, and minority bill manager, in that order, before other senators.[6] The majority leader's preferential recognition bestows the ability to set the Senate's agenda and to avoid the recognition of senators whose motions might upset the leader's plans. This privilege, along with resources granted to the floor leaders by their parties, are the foundations of Senate leaders' influence.

Forces Shaping Leaders' Strategies

Explaining the strategies of Senate leaders has proved to be a difficult task for congressional scholars. It is now conventional to note that Senate leaders lack

Table 11-1 Senate Party Leaders Since the Mid-1950s

Party leader	Position
Democratic	
Lyndon B. Johnson, Texas	Minority leader, 1953-1955 Majority leader, 1955-1961
Mike Mansfield, Mont.	Majority leader, 1961-1977
Robert C. Byrd, W.Va.	Majority leader, 1977-1981 Minority leader, 1981-1987 Majority leader, 1987-1989
George Mitchell, Maine	Majority leader, 1989-present
Republican	
Robert A. Taft, Ohio	Majority leader, 1953
William Knowland, Calif.	Majority leader, 1953-1955 Minority leader, 1955-1959
Everett M. Dirksen, Ill.	Minority leader, 1959-1969
Hugh Scott, Pa.	Minority leader, 1969-1977
Howard H. Baker, Tenn.	Minority leader, 1977-1981 Majority leader, 1981-1985
Robert Dole, Kan.	Majority leader, 1985-1987 Minority leader, 1987-present

strong formal powers; so their influence turns on personal factors—their personalities, talents, and interests—as well as on their colleagues' idiosyncrasies. Nevertheless, several sets of conditions shape the behavior of leaders in predictable ways. These include the expectations of colleagues, various aspects of the Senate's political environment, and the cohesiveness, polarization, and strength of the Senate parties.

Expectations of Party Colleagues

Former Senate parliamentarian Floyd Riddick wrote that "the position of the floor leader is not that of an army general over a multitude of soldiers. Unlike army officers, the floor leaders must maintain continued support. They are subject to periodic re-election by the same persons they have been leading." [7] That is, Senate floor leaders are, first and foremost, *party* leaders. Indeed, they are appropriately viewed as agents of their party colleagues. Their success and failure is largely dependent on the cooperation of those party colleagues. Consequently, leaders' goals and strategies are shaped by the demands and expectations of their party colleagues, whose own behavior is driven by three major goals. [8]

First, senators seek reelection, at least in most cases. They demand a Senate schedule that frees them to pursue reelection activities. Senators also seek direct campaign assistance from party leaders. Leaders attend receptions in Washington, travel to colleagues' home states as attractions to fund-raisers and other events, and offer endorsements and testimonials. And leaders influence the use of the party campaign committees' resources and often contribute small sums themselves. The campaign committees provide members with assistance in campaign planning, media strategy, fund raising, and research.

Leaders also are expected to help create and maintain a favorable party reputation.[9] All senators carry a party label, a brand name, which has a reputation or an image with the general public. Evidence for the effects of party reputation on senators' reelection prospects is abundant.[10] Thus senators have a good reason to demand that party leaders work to build and sustain a favorable party reputation.

Second, most senators have policy commitments originating in either personal beliefs or political circumstances. By its nature the pursuit of policy commitments is a collective enterprise—legislation must find a place on the Senate agenda, majorities must be mobilized to support legislation, and so on. Because leaders shape the agenda and have resources that are useful in coalition-building efforts, they regularly are subject to demands from colleagues for assistance and favorable consideration. And for members of the majority party, particularly, judicious construction of the Senate agenda—avoiding certain issues, timing the consideration of other issues wisely—may contribute to building or maintaining a favorable party reputation.

Third, senators often are interested in personal power, sometimes for its own sake and sometimes as a means to an end—gaining reelection, passing legislation. Whatever the purpose, senators in the majority party are advantaged by their committee and subcommittee chairmanships, control of staff, parliamentary privileges, and sheer party size. Of course, majority party status turns on the party's aggregate electoral success; so senators concern themselves with those national conditions that affect their party's reputation and influence aggregate election outcomes.[11] Thus senators, out of concern for their personal power, have reason to insist that their leaders work for a favorable party reputation and facilitate the campaign activities of their party colleagues.

The demands placed on party leaders can be generalized as four expectations. Leaders are expected to (1) serve the personal political needs of party colleagues, (2) help the party gain or maintain majority party status, (3) work for a favorable party reputation, and (4) pursue the collective policy objectives of the party. The most immediate and fundamental expectation is the first one, serving the personal political needs of party colleagues.

The character of senators' political needs has changed dramatically in recent decades.[12] A swelling interest group community, new forms of mass communication, and greater ease in transcontinental travel have produced an expanding political universe for senators. Senators are in a better position to develop national constituencies and build nationwide coalitions in behalf of legislative causes. At the same time, running for reelection has become more expensive and time consuming as senators have become less dependent on state party organizations. And more constituents are soliciting senators' assistance on personal problems and demanding senators' attention to their policy problems. Even the number of constituents visiting senators' Capitol Hill offices and expecting to see them has skyrocketed.

More staff, larger office budgets, more paid trips home, and more committee and subcommittee assignments have given senators the wherewithal to manage many of the new demands and opportunities. Senators take on more issues, more frequently pursue legislation unrelated to the jurisdictions of their assigned committees, and offer more floor amendments to committee bills. While they have become more active legislatively, senators also have taken more trips home. Between the 1950s and late 1970s the number of days senators spent in their states increased from an average of fewer than 20 to more than 160 per two-year Congress, while Senate sessions became somewhat longer.[13]

Self-reliant, individualistic, outward-looking, and active senators create problems for leaders. Senators demand scheduling favors and party support in order to take advantage of new opportunities and carry the burdens of campaigns. Attendance on the floor is a severe problem—the Senate often comes to a halt to wait for someone to make it to the floor. With more senators seeking to participate and protect their privileges, negotiations on legislative substance and procedure are more complicated and protracted. Obstructionism is a routine tactic as senators exploit their parliamentary prerogatives in response to pressure from organized groups and vocal constituencies. Uncertainty about the schedule and outcomes is the normal state of affairs.

External Political Context:
Public Opinion and the President

The one-way trend in Senate individualism since the 1950s stands in sharp contrast to the ebb and flow found in major features of the Senate's political environment. One such feature is public opinion. Public opinion influences the nature of the demands senators place on their leaders, as well as senators' receptivity to leaders' initiatives. The degree to which public opinion favors one party over the other probably shapes the intensity of demands on leaders—bad times tend to generate demands for more effective leadership. The degree of consensus about public policy in each party's electoral constituency probably influences the consistency of its members' political needs and so affects the ability of the leader to satisfy colleagues.

Characterizing the multiple dimensions of public opinion over several decades is beyond the scope of this essay, but two indicators of public opinion are worth noting. The first concerns the homogeneity of political views within party constituencies, which is likely to affect senators' willingness to cooperate with party colleagues and leaders on policy matters and influence the degree to which senators of the same party have similar definitions of a favorable party reputation.

The relative homogeneity of Senate party constituencies is visible in the pattern of presidential voting across the states. A second indicator of public opinion is the reputation of the parties in the general public, which, I have noted, has a measurable influence on Senate election outcomes.[14] Table 11-2 lists the variance in presidential voting across Senate constituencies, as well as the party favored by the general public on Gallup Poll questions concerning the party most able to keep the country prosperous and out of war.

Democratic leaders have experienced a constituency diversity ranging from a moderate level under Lyndon Johnson of Texas and Mike Mansfield of Montana to a high level under Mansfield in the late 1960s and early 1970s, and then back to moderate-to-low levels under Mansfield, Robert Byrd of West Virginia, and Mitchell. Only for Mansfield in the late 1960s and early 1970s did constituency diversity take a strongly disadvantageous turn, and it has improved somewhat in recent years for Byrd and Mitchell. Republican leader Everett Dirksen of Illinois experienced only a modest increase in constituency diversity in the late 1970s.

The sharpest negative changes in party evaluations occurred for Johnson (on war and peace during the Korean conflict), Mansfield (on prosperity and war and peace in the late 1960s), and Byrd (on prosperity late in the Carter administration). Abrupt negative shifts in the party reputation on prosperity were borne by Dirksen in 1958, Hugh Scott of Pennsylvania in 1970-1971, and, to a lesser extent, Baker in 1982. Dirksen had to weather 1964 on issues of war and peace, thanks, no doubt, to Barry Goldwater's candidacy. In the past decade or so, conditions generally have favored the Republicans, creating pressure on Democratic leaders to improve their party's standing with the public.

Beyond public opinion, Senate leaders must deal with the views, strategies, and popularity of the president. Table 11-2 indicates when Senate leaders have served with a president of the same party. Because modern presidents are expected to promote substantial legislative programs, devise their parties' legislative strategies, and work to enhance their parties' reputations and electoral prospects, much of the leadership burden rests with the president rather than the Senate leader when the two are of the same party. Influencing the president on behalf of colleagues then becomes a central part of the Senate leader's job. And the strategies of opposition leaders often respond to, and influence, those of the president. The recent Democratic leaders, Byrd and Mitchell, have been constrained in their ability to attack incumbent Republican presidents by the weakness of the Democrats' reputation with the general public.

Party Cohesiveness, Polarization, and Strength Within the Senate

The ability of Senate leaders to move beyond service functions to more political, partisan, and policy-oriented functions depends on the degree of consensus within their parties and the presence of a partisan stimulus, a stimulus that usually comes from polarized differences between the parties and from serving with a president of the other party.[15] Assertive, policy-oriented leaders often face resistance from senators whose personal needs are being shortchanged or whose power as committee leaders is threatened by leadership involvement. Such resistance is particularly difficult to overcome when the party is internally divided on what constitutes a favorable party reputation or a desirable direction for party policy initiatives. But when the parties are internally cohesive, and particularly when the two parties hold opposing points of view, conditions favor assertive party leadership. Leaders' success in such endeavors turns on the strength of their party. All three factors—party cohesiveness, polarization, and strength—vary considerably over time.

Party cohesiveness and polarization vary from issue to issue as well as from Congress to Congress.[16] Figure 11-1 indicates the values for measures of intraparty cohesiveness and interparty similarity for roll call voting on the most important votes—those identified by Congressional Quarterly as key votes. Intraparty cohesiveness and interparty differences declined between the 1950s and late 1960s, remained relatively low in the 1970s, and have increased since then. Democratic leader Mansfield and Republican leaders Dirksen and Scott led the parties during the period of low cohesiveness and polarization, while Democrats Byrd and Mitchell and Republican Dole led the parties during the period of enhanced, though far from perfect, intraparty cohesiveness in the late 1980s and early 1990s. These changing conditions influence the degree to which the leader can turn to the party organization as a basis for building winning coalitions.

Of course, when it comes to legislative outcomes, nothing matters as much to Senate party leaders as having the votes. The sheer size of the Senate parties matters, as does the cohesiveness of the parties. In fact, it is possible to conceive of party strength as a product of size and cohesiveness. Leaders must work the hardest to achieve policy objectives when party strength is low. When party strength is high, policy victories are easy to obtain, assertive leaders may not be needed, and tolerance for domineering leaders may be low. Figure 11-2 illustrates party strength since the early 1950s.

Until after the 1958 elections the Senate parties were of roughly equal strength, a circumstance that greatly limited the ability of Majority Leader Johnson to gain policy victories for his party. The 1958 elections marked the beginning of nearly a decade in which Johnson and his successor, Mike Mansfield, could count on a majority from their own party on the average vote. Neither party has been so advantaged since the 1968 election. Thus, although party cohesiveness and polarization ebb and flow, creating variation in the conditions associated with strong leadership, only for a brief period in the past forty years has a Senate party been so strong that it could win most votes without help from the other party.

Senate Leaders' Responsibilities

In response to changing political forces, leaders have adjusted their strategies in performing their basic responsibilities. The long-term trend toward

Table 11-2 Elements of Senate Leaders' Political Environment Since the Mid-1950s

Year	Majority leader[a]	Minority leader[a]	Constituency homogeneity[b]		Favored party on two issues[c]		President's party
			Democratic states	Republican states	Prosperity	Peace/War	
1955	Johnson	Knowland			Neither	Republicans	Republican
1956	Johnson	Knowland	6.7%	4.4%	Neither	Republicans	Republican
1957	Johnson	Knowland			Neither	Republicans	Republican
1958	Johnson	Knowland			Democrats	Republicans	Republican
1959	Johnson	Dirksen			Democrats	Republicans	Republican
1960	Johnson	Dirksen	5.4	5.1	Democrats	Republicans	Republican
1961	Mansfield	Dirksen			Democrats	Neither	Democrat
1962	Mansfield	Dirksen			Democrats	Neither	Democrat
1963	Mansfield	Dirksen			Democrats	Democrats	Democrat
1964	Mansfield	Dirksen	12.4	7.6	Democrats	Democrats	Democrat
1965	Mansfield	Dirksen			Democrats	Democrats	Democrat
1966	Mansfield	Dirksen			Democrats	Neither	Democrat
1967	Mansfield	Dirksen			n.a.	n.a.	Democrat
1968	Mansfield	Dirksen	11.8	8.3	Neither	Republicans	Democrat
1969	Mansfield	Dirksen/ Scott			n.a.	n.a.	Republican
1970	Mansfield	Scott			Democrats	Republicans	Republican
1971	Mansfield	Scott			Democrats	Neither	Republican
1972	Mansfield	Scott	7.4	6.0	Neither	Republicans	Republican
1973	Mansfield	Scott			n.a.	n.a.	Republican
1974	Mansfield	Scott			Democrats	Democrats	Republican
1975	Mansfield	Scott			n.a.	n.a.	Republican
1976	Mansfield	Scott	6.3	6.0	Democrats	Neither	Republican

Year	Leader 1	Leader 2					
1977	Byrd	*Baker*			n.a.	n.a.	Democrat
1978	Byrd	*Baker*			Democrats	Democrats	Democrat
1979	Byrd	*Baker*			n.a.	n.a.	Democrat
1980	Byrd	*Baker*	7.2	8.2	Neither	Democrats	Democrat
1981	*Baker*	Byrd			Republicans	Democrats	Republican
1982	*Baker*	Byrd			Democrats	n.a.	Republican
1983	*Baker*	Byrd			Democrats	Democrats	Republican
1984	*Baker*	Byrd	4.6	6.5	Republicans	Democrats	Republican
1985	*Dole*	Byrd			Republicans	Democrats	Republican
1986	*Dole*	Byrd			Republicans	Republicans	Republican
1987	Byrd	*Dole*			Neither	Democrats	Republican
1988	Byrd	*Dole*	5.0	6.3	Republicans	Neither	Republican
1989	Mitchell	*Dole*			n.a.	n.a.	Republican
1990	Mitchell	*Dole*			Republicans	Neither	Republican
1991	Mitchell	*Dole*			Republicans	Republicans	Republican

Sources: Homogeneity data are compiled by the author from various editions of *Almanac of American Politics (National Journal)*, *Congressional Quarterly Almanac*, and *Congressional Quarterly Weekly Report*; favored party columns are compiled from *Gallup Reports, 1935-1968*, and various editions of *Gallup Poll Monthly* and *Gallup Report*.

[a] Names of Republican leaders are in italics.

[b] Each entry is the standard deviation in the Democratic presidential vote across the states with a senator from this party. The two columns are not mutually exclusive sets of states because states may be represented by a senator from each party.

[c] A party is the favored party when at least 5 percent more Gallup Poll respondents choose one party over the other on the questions concerning the party most able to create prosperity and maintain peace, averaged over the polls taken in any one year. Years in which data are not available because Gallup did not ask the questions are listed as "n.a."

Figure 11-1 Senate Partisanship on Key Votes, 1953-1989

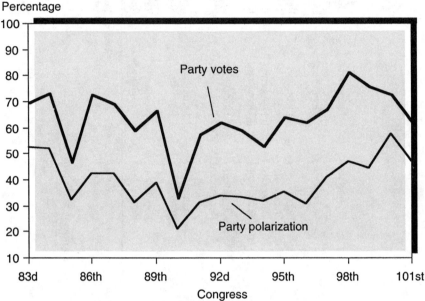

Percentage

Congress

Source: Congressional Quarterly Almanac, appropriate years.

Note: The vertical axis for party votes is the percentage of key votes that are party votes (Democratic majority opposes a Republican majority); the vertical axis for party polarization is the Rice Index of Party Unlikeness (mean absolute value of the difference between the percentage of Democrats voting yea and the percentage of Republicans voting yea).

greater individualism and uncertainty in the flow of business have led Senate leaders to expand party service functions, share leadership duties with more senators, and employ their procedural and organizational resources more creatively. The ebb and flow of public opinion and party control of the presidency and the Senate have produced shifts in leaders' approaches to nearly all of their responsibilities. And greater partisanship in the past two decades has generated more interest in the party organizations, as well as a more partisan, assertive approach to relations with the president and policy leadership.

Managing the Flow of Senate Business

The majority party leader's first, most visible, and most time-consuming responsibility is managing the flow of legislation, particularly on the Senate floor. Yet the Senate's rules handicap the majority leader's efforts to perform this indispensable function. Because the Senate lacks a general germaneness rule for amendments, senators can circumvent or ignore committees by offering a bill in the form of an amendment to nearly any measure that is taken up on the floor. There also is no general limit on debate; senators can filibuster legislation,

Figure 11-2 Party Strength in the Senate, 1953-1990

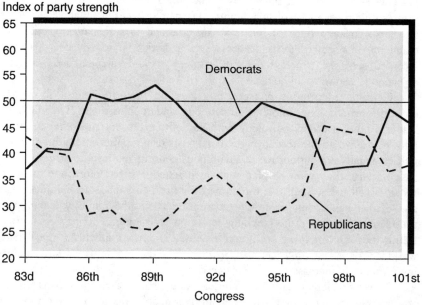

Index of party strength

Congress

Source: Roll call votes are from the Inter-University Consortium for Political and Social Research.

Note: Party strength is the product of (a) party size in percent and (b) party cohesiveness as the mean proportion of party members voting with the party majority on all roll call votes.

amendments, and any debatable motion. Under the current rule, cloture may be invoked—debate may be cut off—only if at least three-fifths of all senators, or sixty senators, agree to do so. If cloture is invoked, subsequent amendments must be germane. The process requires advance notice of a cloture vote and up to thirty hours of debate after cloture is approved. The rule makes it possible for a sizable minority to block action or to extract concessions by filibustering or threatening to do so.

Thus scheduling legislation for floor consideration entails much more than a regular survey of standing committees to anticipate what is coming next to the floor. Leaders must anticipate amendments and obstructionism from all quarters, particularly from minority party members. They must adjust to the timing of presidential nominations and treaties. And they must deal with their colleagues' demands for personal scheduling considerations.

All recent majority leaders have sought predictability in the flow of business by exploiting their right of first recognition, crafting unanimous consent agreements, and taking advantage of the minimal deference given to them on scheduling matters. With unanimous consent, the leader may set aside the standing rules of the Senate and impose restrictions on debate or amendments or set specific times for votes. But the necessity of gaining unanimous consent places substantial power to obstruct in the hands of individual senators. Naturally, senators insist on advance notice of unanimous consent requests that might affect their interests. To keep track of senators' concerns and to anticipate objections to unanimous consent requests, leaders of both parties for several decades have recorded senators' expressed concerns in a "marked calendar." A senator's objection is known as a "hold."

Gaining unanimous consent engages the majority leader in nearly ceaseless negotiations, cajolery, adjustment, and readjustment. The minority leader always is consulted, along with committee leaders and other senators known to have an interest in particular pieces of legislation. Senators of both parties usually are supportive of unanimous consent requests to structure debate because they want to plan their own schedules, but often one or more senators will use a hold or a threatened filibuster to gain a tactical advantage and extract concessions from the committee chair, the majority leader, the president, or someone else seeking action on legislation. This process is frustrating, but it has become both more essential and more difficult as the Senate workload, floor amendments, obstructionism, holds, and demands for scheduling favors have increased in recent decades.

These developments led Senate leaders to change their floor management strategies in several ways. First, the monthly schedule was altered. In campaigning for their election to the post, all of the past four majority leaders promised to alter the Senate's schedule to enhance the efficiency and predictability of floor sessions. Republican leader Baker promised, and largely succeeded in providing, more advance notice, fewer roll call votes, and fewer weekend and late-night sessions. Dole eventually pressed the Senate into four-day work weeks, Tuesday through Friday, an increase over the Tuesday through Thursday routine that the Senate had adopted for the purpose of floor voting. And Byrd even called votes on Fridays just to keep his colleagues from leaving early for home. In 1988 Byrd adopted the most important innovation—giving senators every fourth week off and insisting on five-day work weeks for the other three weeks. This arrangement has worked well for many senators, and Mitchell has chosen to maintain it.

Nevertheless, keeping to a schedule remains nearly impossible. Even attendance is a problem. In 1991 Majority Leader Mitchell opened a floor session with a common plea:

> I strongly encourage Senators who have amendments to be here when we return to the bill shortly after noon so that we do not have another day in which we spend all of the afternoon hours waiting for Senators to come to offer amendments, and then find we are here late into the evening with Senators complaining about being here late in the evening. That is a decision that is made by Senators themselves. If no one will come to offer an amendment during the daylight hours, inevitably we are in here very late at night considering amendments.[17]

Roll call votes are still held open longer than the fifteen minutes provided by the rule, to give senators more time to make it to the chamber floor from their offices, from committee rooms, and often from locations off Capitol Hill. In 1987 Byrd explained the pressure put on the majority leader: "I have Members on my side who do not make it here by the time the 15 minutes are up and I try to check on them. I hear they are on the subway, they have left the office and they will be here, should be coming in the door any moment. So we wait." [18]

Moreover, quorum calls are still used to give leaders and bill managers time to get sponsors to the floor to offer their amendments, make speeches, or consult on unanimous consent agreements. The resulting delays continue to undermine the most carefully designed schedules.

Second, leaders sought to reduce obstructionism and delay by changing the cloture rule. In 1975 Mansfield supported a successful effort to change the 1959 rule requiring a vote of two-thirds of senators present and voting to invoke cloture to the current three-fifths of all duly elected senators. The rule did not prevent obstructionist tactics in the form of dozens of procedural motions after cloture was invoked; so in 1979 the Senate agreed to Byrd's proposal to include all floor activity in the hundred-hour limit for postcloture debate. At Dole's insistence that provision was tightened to thirty hours in 1986.

The ability to invoke cloture was improved only marginally by the changes. Mansfield, faced with numerous filibusters in the late 1960s and early 1970s, followed his whip's advice and began to "track" legislation so that a filibustered measure would not block the consideration of all legislation. Subsequent leaders have followed this practice, even though it may occasionally encourage filibusters by reducing the friction generated by blocking action on a measure. Although leaders have pursued various halfway measures to make it easier to curb debate and amendments, they have not yet succeeded in getting new rules adopted. Mitchell endorsed the general thrust of such efforts in his 1988 campaign for majority leader, but he has not crusaded in their behalf.

Third, with ever increasing scheduling pressures and no major change in the cloture rule, leaders developed a deeper repertoire of tactics for using unanimous consent agreements. Majority Leader Johnson is reputed to have transformed agreements into a genuine tool of the leadership during the 1950s. Generally, Johnson's unanimous consent requests were fairly simple; they included provisions to limit debate on the measure and amendments and to bar nongermane amendments.

Since the 1950s unanimous consent agreements have become more common and complex as leaders have adjusted to new circumstances. Leaders since Mansfield have vigorously pursued agreement to structure and often limit debate and amendments in order to streamline floor consideration of complex or controversial bills and to make the floor schedule more predictable. For example, agreements have more frequently provided amendment-specific limits on debate and second-degree amendments, and they have frequently set specific times for roll call votes on measures, amendments, or motions. To improve his ability to respond to unpredictable developments on the floor, the majority leader now frequently asks consent for authority to schedule certain actions after consulting with the minority leader.

Fourth, leaders attempted to reduce obstructionism by establishing a new understanding about holds. By the early 1970s holds were a firmly established means for senators to block action on a bill. Most of the time, majority leaders refrained from calling up a measure on which a hold had been placed until the hold was removed. Minority leaders usually objected to the majority leaders' unanimous consent requests to take up a bill when a hold was placed on the bill by a party member. This process required that most measures be cleared in both parties before they are considered on the floor. Although holds usually were not observed on "must-pass" bills, such as appropriations bills, they had become more of a problem for Senate leaders as incentives increased for senators to fully exploit their prerogatives on behalf of outside interests. Holds also became a more effective tool of obstructionism as the Senate's schedule was swamped with legislation.

In the 1980s Republican leaders Baker and Dole announced on separate occasions that they would consider holds to be nothing more than requests for advance notice. They reported that senators would have to come to the floor themselves to register objections to unanimous consent requests or to filibuster. But not much changed for Senate Republicans. The convenience of having leaders represent them and voice their objections on the floor may have been too great for the practice to be set aside.

Backed by a group of junior Democrats who had formulated a variety of reform proposals in 1988, Democratic leader Mitchell, upon taking office, distributed a statement to his Democratic colleagues that "reaffirmed the traditional definition" of a hold as an opportunity for notice—a right to be notified—and not a mechanism for delaying Senate action.[19] In his view, Democrats took his admonition seriously, and he has had little problem with Democratic holds. Republican holds are another matter. Dole continues to object to the Democratic leader's requests to call up measures on behalf of his Republican colleagues. In fact, in the 102d Congress there appears to be an increase in Republican objections, which has led Mitchell more frequently to seek cloture on the motion to proceed.

Mitchell has made two other contributions to floor management. First, he seems to have defused the procedural arms race that had developed between Byrd and Dole. The relationship between Byrd and Dole was civil but lacked trust—a result, perhaps, of both partisanship and personal rivalry. Mitchell has lived up to a promise not to surprise Minority Leader Dole, and they consult each other on Senate business with a sense of common purpose. Mitchell reports, "I've tried very hard to be cooperative with Senator Dole, to the extent it's possible. . . . We both recognize that we do not always agree on the Senate's agenda. But we recognize that we have a responsibility for the functioning of the Senate." [20] Mitchell's approach appears to have generated far more support for cloture votes from Dole than Byrd managed to acquire.

Second, Mitchell reverted to the style of Johnson and Mansfield in sharing floor oversight duties with party colleagues. Byrd preferred to oversee floor activity personally as much as possible, but Mitchell has sought a more collegial leadership and freed himself for activities off the floor and away from the Capitol. Several senators regularly assist Mitchell in monitoring floor debate—Wendell Ford of Kentucky, his whip; Tom Daschle of South Dakota, his Policy Committee co-chair; and Wyche Fowler, Jr., of Georgia, the first occupant of a position Mitchell created, assistant majority leader. And Mitchell, somewhat like Dole, frequently creates negotiating teams to work out differences among Democrats and with Republicans in order to gain unanimous consent on how to proceed with important legislation. These developments reflect Mitchell's deliberate strategy to include party colleagues in floor management and instill a greater appreciation of his predicament as floor leader.

Thus intensified individualism and partisanship have complicated the leader's job of managing the flow of business. Gradually, and in fits and starts, leaders have moved away from confining and antiquated scheduling practices, such as reliance on a party committee, and moved toward more flexible approaches that give a greater voice to rank-and-file party members and allow leaders to adjust more creatively to rapidly changing circumstances on the floor.

Managing the Party Organization

The floor leader and secondary party leaders share responsibility for party organization and staff. Nevertheless, the policymaking and political roles of party organizations depend directly on the use the floor leaders choose to make of them. In recent years, however, senators' demands and partisan concerns have led both parties to strengthen the services and, to a lesser extent, the policymaking role of their conferences and party committees.

Created in 1947, the Policy Committees were designed to produce legislative proposals for the parties and coordinate the work of their standing committee contingents. Generally, the Policy Committees have not performed such functions.[21] At first, the majority party's committee played a minor role in scheduling legislation for the floor. Johnson presented his schedule to the Democratic Policy Committee—which was stacked with senior members—biweekly, and his plans were routinely approved most of the time. On occasion, the committee's meetings were a convenient place to float ideas and work out differences within the party. And Johnson used the Policy Committee as a place to house a small staff that he controlled. Calendar Committees (later called Legislative Review Committees), operating under the auspices of both Policy Committees, more carefully reviewed legislation to clear it for floor consideration, but even these had fallen into disuse by the mid-1960s.

Under Republican Dirksen in the late 1950s and 1960s, and under Democrat Mansfield in the 1960s, the Policy Committees became somewhat more important as forums for discussion, vehicles for issuing policy statements, and sounding boards for leaders seeking colleagues' views. The scheduling function died as the leaders assumed full responsibility. Dirksen and his Policy Committee chairman, Bourke Hickenlooper of Iowa, organized weekly luncheon discussions for the full conference, a practice adopted by all of his successors. Dirksen did not like his Policy Committee to limit his own flexibility, so he did not use the committee to establish formal policy positions.

For the majority party Democrats, the demise of the Policy Committee's scheduling role in the early 1960s seemed to be related to electing an assertive Democratic president and allowing the president's legislation a right-of-way to the floor.[22] Mansfield expanded the size of the committee, appointed more junior members, made the committee more representative of the conference, and called more meetings for the purpose of discussing policy questions. After Republican Richard Nixon took over the White House, Mansfield used the committee aggressively. The hope was to develop policy positions that would improve the party's image and generate greater party cohesiveness within the Senate.[23]

After assuming the top spot in 1977, Byrd discontinued meetings of the Democratic Policy Committee, perhaps at first because Senate Democrats were following the lead of the new Democratic president, Jimmy Carter. Byrd preferred to meet with the chairs of the standing committees and to use the Policy Committee only as a place to house staff experts responsible to him.

After the 1980 elections, in which Republicans won control of the Senate and the White House, Republican leader Baker made the Republican Policy Committee a council of standing committee chairs. Although some of the reformers of the 1940s had hoped that the majority party's Policy Committee would serve as a sort of executive committee for the Senate, Baker did not use the committee to devise policy or set the Senate schedule. Rather, the committee was a convenient place to bring chairs together and prod them to keep legislation moving. Senior committee leaders, along with secondary party leaders, still make up the Republican Policy Committee.

The role of the Democratic Policy Committee took a turn after the election of Mitchell as Democratic leader.[24] Pushed by junior Democrats seeking a more active party organization and more influence over party strategy, Mitchell reactivated the Policy Committee and appointed a co-chair, Tom Daschle, who had initiated junior Democrats' reform proposals in 1988. Supervision of the staff is split between Mitchell and Daschle, with Mitchell controlling the foreign policy, public relations, and floor staff and Daschle controlling the domestic policy and service staffs. The committee, which meets weekly to discuss approaches to policy problems, has sponsored retreats and policy-specific seminars for Democrats and has been the source of annual Democratic legislative agendas.

Over the past two decades, the most obvious development in party offices is the tremendous expansion of services to senators and their offices. This expansion reflects a response of secondary leaders, particularly the Republican Policy Committee and conference chairs and now the Democratic Policy Committee co-chair, to the increasing needs of individual senators and their staffs for timely information and expertise that are more efficiently provided collectively. Republicans led the way, beginning in the 1970s, by expanding services provided by the staffs of the Policy Committees, conferences, and leadership offices (see Table 11-3). Services now include a variety of publications on the Senate schedule, legislation, policy problems, and political matters;[25] electronic mail commu-

Table 11-3 Senate Leadership and Party Staffs, 1959-1991

Year	Democrats		Republicans			
	Floor leader	Policy Committee	Floor leader	Policy Committee	Conference	Conference secretary
1959	3	13	2	17		
1961	2	6	4	16		
1963	2	7	3	10		
1965	3	8	3	11		
1967	1	5	3	11		
1969	1	6	2	12		
1971	2	8	3	25[a]		
1973	1	8	4	23[a]		
1975	1	8	4	29[a]		
1977	2	13	5	15	14	
1979	3	20	4	14	13	
1981	3	22	15	15	14	
1983	3	37	14	20	19	
1985	4	32	16	16	20	3
1987	4	35	20	12	19	2
1989	5	33	16	10	18	3
1991	6	36	22	19	15	2

Source: Charles B. Brown, ed., *Congressional Staff Directory* (Mount Vernon, Va.: Congressional Staff Directory), various years.

Note: Empty cells indicate no separate staffs in those years.

[a] Policy Committee and conference staff combined.

nications; clearinghouses for job applicants; in-house cable television to provide senators' offices with up-to-the-minute information on floor developments; analyses of floor voting records; assistance in the production of newsletters and graphics material; and facilities and staff assistance for the production of radio and television messages and programs. The parties now maintain satellite uplink equipment, so senators can make live appearances on local stations or at meetings away from Washington.

Party whips and their staffs also have gained a more important role. The whips—or the assistant majority and minority leaders, as they are formally designated—traditionally have little role beyond assisting the leader in overseeing floor activity. Their deputy whips are junior members who have shared the burden of monitoring the floor. Only occasionally have whip polls of the party membership been conducted; this function is often left to bill managers. The core duties of House whips—keeping track of members' locations before important votes, soliciting their attendance, and even counting votes—are handled in the Senate by party staff members, the party secretaries, on a day-to-day basis. The role Senate whips play has turned on the needs of the floor leaders. Some whips have performed virtually no floor or leadership duties, while Byrd, serving under Mansfield, actually assumed most of Mansfield's floor generalship duties. Byrd, on the other hand, conducted no whip polls because Mansfield never requested them. And Byrd's whip, Alan Cranston of California, conducted polls infrequently and at his own discretion.

Since the 1950s the duties and services of the whip and assistant whips have expanded somewhat.[26] Assistant whip positions were created in the late 1960s; additional assistant whips have been added to help floor leaders monitor floor activity and look out for party interests. Their jobs have increased in importance as complicated unanimous consent agreements, obstructionist tactics, and unexpected amendments have become common. Both parties' whip offices have added weekly publications, "whip notices," to announce the expected floor schedule, and scheduling notices were made accessible by computer in the 1980s. Perhaps most important, whips have become more truly assistant leaders—substituting for the floor leader, meeting frequently with the floor leader and assistant whips on policy and political matters, and representing the party. Although the duties of Senate whips are still not as firmly established as those of their House counterparts, the whips are clearly a central part of a more collegial leadership than they were in the 1950s.

Finally, both parties have turned increasingly to task forces to coordinate party strategy on some important pieces of legislation. Byrd made use of a task force on tax policy in 1980. According to a keen observer of Congress, "His willingness to create the task force shows his belief that Senate leaders need to play a greater role in helping their party set policy." [27] Byrd followed that experiment with nine task forces in 1981, an effort designed to provide the Democrats with a coherent response to the Reagan administration and to generate a sense of party purpose after the devastating loss of majority party status.[28]

More recently, both Democrat Mitchell and Republican Dole have appointed task forces on a variety of issues.[29] These task forces are a flexible way to handle issues that involve two or more standing committees; sometimes they help the leader find solutions to problems that divide party members; they give senators without a relevant committee assignment an avenue of participation; they provide the party leader with a somewhat more direct connection to the development of a party proposal than would be possible if issues were left to standing committee members; and they more clearly identify the proposal as a party proposal.

Serving as Intermediary with the President

One of the Senate leaders' special responsibilities is to serve as intermediaries between Capitol Hill and the White House. Senators of the president's party, who generally support the president's program, expect their leader to serve as the president's point man, at least at first. Weakening support within the president's party, or personal differences between a leader and a president on policy or political matters, often produces a shift in the relationship. The leader of the opposition party, if in the majority, feels responsible for giving the president's policy proposals, treaties, and nominations timely consideration. This expectation is particularly strong in the Senate because that body shares in the president's treaty-making and appointment power.

The specific nature of the relationship between presidents and leaders is a function of choices made by each participant, but the initiative in this relationship generally rests with the president. As Majority Leader Mitchell put it recently, "The terms and pace of the relationship are dictated by the president." [30] Leaders do not decline presidential requests for consultation, but presidents have spurned Hill leaders, even of their own party, from time to time. Since the 1950s the relationship between presidents and Senate leaders appears to have become less personal, more formal, more partisan, and restricted to necessary business.

Eisenhower's relationship with congressional leaders is a useful baseline because it is often touted as the model of bipartisan cooperation. With respect to leaders of his own party, Eisenhower held weekly breakfast meetings with his party's top two or three leaders from each chamber, and sometimes others, while Congress was in session.[31] Frank discussion often took place at these meetings, but the quality of the discussion seemed to decline over the years.[32] His working relationship with the Republican leader of the mid-1950s, William Knowland of California, was not strong. Knowland's whip and successor, Everett Dirksen, was Eisenhower's most important lieutenant. Dirksen toed the line on foreign policy requests from Eisenhower, unlike Knowland, and frequently had private breakfasts with the president.[33]

In 1954 Eisenhower began to hold formal and informal meetings with Democratic leaders, including nineteen formal bipartisan leadership meetings in the 1954-1960 period. The bipartisan meetings were devoted almost exclusively to foreign and defense policy matters and were not conducive to personal consultation and candid exchange. The meetings usually included a large number of committee leaders and took place over lunch. The usual format was a briefing, normally by Cabinet officers, followed by legislators' comments and questions.

More important, Eisenhower cultivated the goodwill of Johnson and the Democratic House Speaker, Sam Rayburn of Texas, in evening get-togethers over cocktails, perhaps as often as once a month.[34] These sessions were sometimes supplemented with meetings that included foreign policy committee leaders, particularly Sen. Walter George of Georgia and William Fulbright of Arkansas. Genuine consultation occurred at many of these meetings. At times, the interparty, interbranch relationship appeared to be a truly cooperative, consultative one. Beginning in 1957 a series of foreign developments occasioned objections to Eisenhower's policies from Johnson and even from the more deferential Rayburn.[35] By late 1958, with the impending election promising to yield Democratic gains in Congress, the relationship between Eisenhower and the Democratic leaders had lost much of its warmth and the number of personal meetings declined. Eisenhower appeared to become more assertive and partisan during the next two years, when he called only one formal bipartisan leadership meeting. The Eisenhower administration ended with a more partisan pattern of rhetoric and consultation.

All presidents since the 1950s have scheduled weekly meetings, usually breakfast meetings, with leaders of their own party while Congress is in session. These weekly meetings generally have concerned legislation currently before Congress and so have tended to emphasize domestic policy. These meetings are a well-established norm, the violation of which would risk the wrath of congressional leaders whose support is vital to the success of the president's legislative program. The nature of the weekly meetings has varied, as has the frequency of special meetings and phone conversations with party leaders. Sporadic meetings with opposition leaders, usually jointly with leaders of their own party, also are common features of presidents' schedules in recent decades. But as with Eisenhower, Johnson, and Rayburn, the relationship between presidents and Hill leaders often has turned on more private and informal relations. It is in this area that the decline of bipartisan consultation is most notable.

Democratic presidents Kennedy and Johnson worked well with Mansfield and Dirksen. John F. Kennedy invited the Republican Dirksen for a private meeting about once a month.[36] But Johnson's relationship with Dirksen was extraordinary. Congressional reporter and Dirksen biographer Neil MacNeil explains:

> The very frequency with which Johnson and Dirksen conferred let Dirksen speak with confidence on how the President stood on almost any public question and encouraged the view that they worked out their differences in private. Where President Kennedy invited Dirksen to the White House perhaps once a month and telephoned him only a little more frequently, President Johnson was constantly talking to Dirksen, to the extent that he seemed to depend on Dirksen for advice. Johnson asked Dirksen to the White House two or three times a week in normal times and even more frequently at times of travail. His telephone calls to Dirksen were numberless, sometimes as many as ten in a single day.[37]

Dirksen, much to the chagrin of many fellow Republicans, particularly House Republican leader Gerald Ford of Michigan, supported Johnson's Vietnam War policies and was seldom critical. He generally intimated that he had the inside track to Johnson's thoughts and refused to bow to Republican pressure to be more partisan in foreign affairs.

President Richard Nixon maintained cool relations with congressional leaders. He began in the usual pattern by conducting weekly meetings with his party's leaders, but little consultation appears to have taken place at these sessions.[38] Senate Republican leader Hugh Scott, Dirksen's successor, was listed among Senate Republican liberals that Nixon "reviled," even though Scott appeared to have become a loyal party soldier when he joined the leadership.[39] Instead, Nixon preferred to work with other senators who were ideological or personal friends.[40] And Nixon increasingly relied on his enlarged congressional liaison staff to communicate with Hill leaders.

Proportionately, Nixon held about as many bipartisan leadership meetings as Kennedy and Johnson did. During his first term he even attempted to establish a more meaningful, private relationship with Mansfield, inviting Mansfield to breakfast once a month, and sometimes more frequently, for discussions about foreign affairs.[41] The arrangement did not last.[42] Nixon's meetings with Hill leaders often amounted to no more than briefings following his international trips. Nixon held few meetings with Mansfield or the collective bipartisan leadership during the last half of his administration.

After ascending to the presidency, Gerald Ford reestablished relations with his party's elected congressional leaders as his primary conduit to the Hill and kept his commitment to hold weekly meetings with them.[43] He, too, held many bipartisan leadership meetings, most of which were devoted to foreign policy.[44] Democratic leaders were pleased with the turnaround in their relations with Republican presidents, although Ford—unlike his four predecessors—did not have special private rendezvous with any opposition leader, and he very seldom consulted Democrats on domestic policy. Moreover, Ford shared Nixon's views about the obstructionism of Congress in international affairs and avoided consulting congressional leaders before making most of his military decisions.[45]

President Carter's problems with his own party's congressional leaders are now notorious.[46] At first, troubles stemmed from a lack of consultation on major legislative proposals, distrust of established insiders on Capitol Hill, inattentiveness to—and sometimes disdain for—the courtesies usually extended to members of Congress, and the absence of White House support for congressional leaders' efforts to enact Carter's legislation. Relations improved considerably during Carter's term in office. Senator Byrd came to develop an effective working relationship with Carter, particularly on foreign policy matters, and the two men consulted privately on substance and process from time to time.[47] Carter's relations with his party's leaders remained businesslike.

Carter developed a fruitful relationship with Republican leader Baker. Concerning the Panama Canal treaties, Carter recorded in his diary that Baker "wants to work closer with me, as did his father-in-law, Senator Dirksen, with Presidents." [48] But the Carter-Baker relationship never approached the strength of the Johnson-Eisenhower, Dirksen-Kennedy, or Dirksen-Johnson relationships. Baker was not often invited to the White House for private consultations, and he opposed Carter on some important foreign policy matters.

President Reagan maintained the established pattern of regular sessions with his party's Hill leaders and continued the practice of occasional meetings with opposition leaders. But his meetings with Democrats often were scripted by his aides and seldom involved any meaningful consultation or exchange of views. Even Republican leader Dole seemed to lack patience with Reagan's aloofness and frequently went his own way in the absence of a clear program from the White House.

President Bush's administration fits the long-term trend toward greater personal distance and partisanship in the relationship between presidents and leaders. Republican leader Dole, a rival of Bush's for the presidency, managed to overcome his competition with Bush to work hard in behalf of most of the Bush program.[49] Dole sometimes struck out on his own, particularly on foreign policy issues, and he sometimes refused to pursue Bush proposals that appeared to be doomed in the Senate. Dole did not appear to have a close, personal relationship with Bush.

Predictably, Bush was even more distant from Mitchell. Upon Bush's election to the presidency and Mitchell's election as majority leader in late 1988, there was reason to believe that these two pragmatic, low-key leaders might develop an effective working relationship. Mitchell promised to work in a nonpartisan manner on foreign policy questions and hoped that Bush would consult with him in that area. That did not happened. Mitchell occasionally received a phone call from Bush soliciting information or advice, but there were no personal meetings and little important consultation between the two men.[50]

In summary, it appears that since the Nixon administration, presidential relations with opposition leaders have been generally circumscribed and formal. The private bonds that Eisenhower, Kennedy, and Johnson shared with at least some opposition leaders were not present in subsequent administrations. Relative dependence on formal meetings increased, and the frequency of meaningful consultation, including consultation on foreign affairs, was much lower after the Johnson administration. Formal meetings are not conducive to the exchange of off-the-record views. The format may well encourage Hill leaders to present partisan views. Intensifying partisanship, as well as the expansion of the White House staff, which buffers presidents from Capitol Hill, may have contributed to the distance between presidents and legislative leaders.

Serving as Party Spokesman

All leaders since the 1950s have made interaction with the press an important part of their leadership activities. As partisanship has increased in the past two decades, and as television has become the dominant means of political communication, effectiveness as a party spokesman has become a more central component of members' expectations for floor leaders. The change is most noticeable among Senate Democrats, whose leaders between 1961 and 1988, Mansfield and Byrd, were perceived as weak and sometimes indifferent party spokesmen. Minority party status in the 1981-1986 period, a long period without a Democratic president, and the high media profile of House Speakers Thomas P. O'Neill of Massachusetts and James Wright of Texas appeared to sensitize Senate Democrats to their party's inability to communicate an effective message.

In the Senate of the mid-1950s, Democratic leader Johnson actively courted the press—applying heavy doses of the "Johnson treatment" in private interviews. He followed Rayburn's lead by instituting briefings before the beginning of each day's session and called frequent press conferences in his office as well. Republican Knowland sometimes was openly hostile to the press and had little time for regular press conferences. But Dirksen began his own weekly press conferences upon assuming the floor leadership in 1959 and proved to be President Eisenhower's chief defender against the charges of Democratic critics. He became a television celebrity during the 1960s. Subsequent Senate leaders have held daily briefings, although they have varied in their use of press conferences.

In the 1950s leaders' relations with the press and media appeared to serve personal as much as party purposes. Robert Peabody's 1976 examination of leadership contests, *Leadership in Congress*, makes plain that service as a party spokesman was seldom a major consideration in leadership selection in the 1950s, 1960s, and early 1970s.[51] Service to colleagues, mastery of the mechanics of the legislative game, and position among party factions were given greater weight. Perhaps because of their weak institutional position and lack of national media coverage, only House Republicans made media skills much of an issue in leadership contests. In general, party leaders took a back seat to committee chairs as opinion leaders on matters of policy. In fact, studies on party leadership of the 1960s did not catalog service as party spokesman or anything similar among the major functions or techniques of leaders.[52]

Expectations have changed. Leaders now are expected to be effective party spokesmen.[53] The increasing importance of television as a medium of political communication, presidents' domination of television news, and the growing number of news programs seem to have increased the demand for good television presence in leaders. Since the mid-1960s opposition congressional leaders have sought and have been granted time on the television networks to respond to presidential addresses.[54]

By the early 1980s the spokesman's role had become so prominent as to warrant listing it among leaders' primary responsibilities.[55] On the Republican side, Baker has been compared favorably with Scott. Both Baker and Dole have larger press and speech-writing staffs than did their predecessors. On the Democratic side, the quality of media representation became a critical issue in 1986, when Byrd was challenged for reelection as Democratic leader by J. Bennett Johnston of Louisiana. Byrd's effectiveness as a spokesman was a major issue and led him to hire a media consultant after defeating Johnston.[56] In 1988 the majority leadership contest seemed to turn in part on the perception that Mitchell would be a better spokesman for his party than his competitors, Johnston and Hawaii's Daniel K. Inouye.[57] Sen. Joseph R. Biden, Jr., of Delaware noted that "the Democrats have realized the need, in the presence of the Republican administration, to have a person who can not only make the Senate function well, but who can be a party spokesman." [58] Mitchell has encouraged the efforts of his Policy Committee co-chair, Tom Daschle, to develop party messages and organize floor speeches by Democratic senators on pressing issues.[59]

What leaders want most from the press and the electronic media is favorable coverage of themselves and their party. Regrettably, it is difficult to measure how favorable the coverage is. But the volume of coverage is measurable, thanks to indexes of newspapers and television news broadcasts. The volume of coverage reflects leaders' efforts and newsworthiness, as well as the judgments of reporters, editors, and directors about what is newsworthy. It yields a picture of the attention gained or granted to leaders and of the policy content of the coverage.

Figures 11-3 and 11-4 indicate the great variation in newspaper mentions and television appearances among leaders. Interpreting the pattern for the *New York Times* is complicated by the fact that the paper cut back on the number of stories about Congress in the late 1970s.[60] The relative standing of congressional leaders is plain, however. From the 1950s through the mid-1970s Senate leaders were far more visible in the *Times* and in television news than were House leaders. The Speaker of the House has gained prominence since the 1970s, and Speakers O'Neill and Wright were about as visible as the two Senate leaders.

Also notable is the prominence of the Senate minority leader. The Senate minority leader, whether of the president's party or not, regularly receives about as much attention in print and on television as the majority leader. The contrast to the prominence of the House minority leader could not be more stark. There is little doubt that the power of the Senate minority and the Senate's prestige give the Senate's minority leader a big advantage over his House counterpart in attracting media attention.

Most striking among recent Senate leaders is Byrd's relatively low visibility in the 1980s. He virtually disappeared from television in the early 1980s, just as Senate Democrats, as the minority party and out party, seemed most to need an effective spokesman. Speaker O'Neill, still leading a Democratic majority in the House, overshadowed Byrd as the media voice for the Democrats. Mitchell, Byrd's successor, has been mentioned only slightly more frequently in the *Times* than Byrd, but, perhaps far more important, Mitchell has nearly doubled Byrd's number of annual appearances on the network news programs. Mitchell's visibility on television puts the Democratic leader back in the range of the previous two Republican leaders and the House Speaker.

Serving as a Policy Leader

Genuine party leadership—formulating policy proposals and assuming primary responsibility for soliciting support of them—is one function that Charles Jones argued was beyond the reach of Senate party leaders. Indeed, the conventional and historically accurate characterization of Senate party leaders is that they are managers, facilitators, mediators, brokers, and middlemen in the legislative game.[61] In 1977, in fact, one keen observer emphasized that the Senate party leadership's

> prime function now is to process the work of the Senate, but with so many Members potentially active it no longer can assure that the work will get done. As a more open body, the Senate is more likely to flounder. It is difficult to chart the course of debate in advance because no one can be certain which amendments will be offered. Moreover, once floor consideration is underway, it may be difficult to arrange an expeditious conclusion because so many Senators are involved.
>
> In response to this dilemma, leaders have become more and more absorbed in procedural aspects of Senate work and this trend has led them further away from substantive concerns.[62]

In the mid-1970s leaders appeared to be mere managers and mediators.

Figure 11-3 Mean Number of Stories Mentioning Party Leaders in the *New York Times*, 1956 -1991

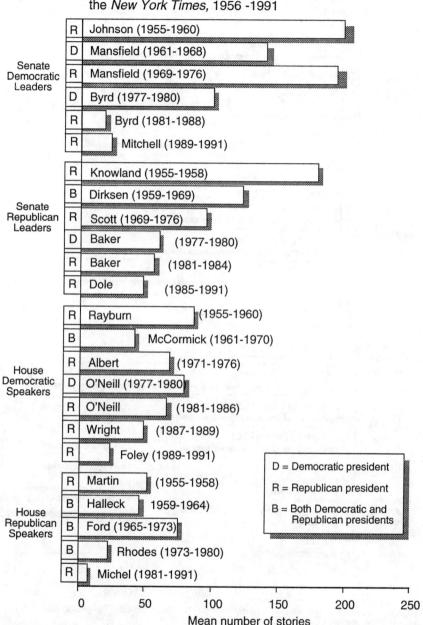

Source: *New York Times* and *New York Times Index*, 1956-1990.

Note: Only stories concerning issues of public policy are included; personal stories without obvious policy content and those concerning campaigns or other political events are excluded. The number reported is the annual mean number of stories for the years indicated

Figure 11-4 Mean Number of Stories Mentioning Party Leaders on Network Television Evening News Programs, 1968 - 1990

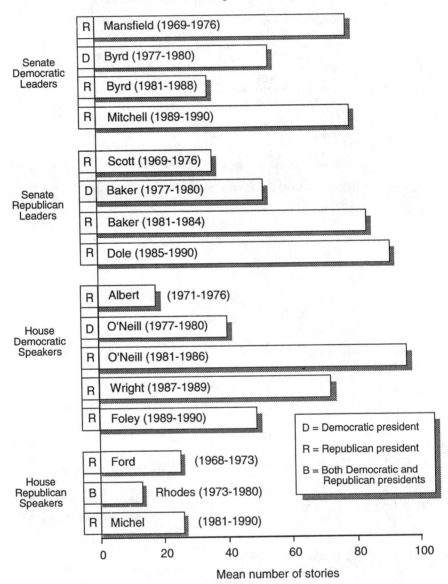

Source: *Television News Index and Abstracts* (Nashville: Vanderbilt Television News Archives, appropriate years).

Note: Only stories covering issues of public policy are included; personal stories without obvious policy content and those concerning campaigns or other political events are excluded. The number reported is the annual mean number of stories for the years indicated.

Of course, all modern Senate leaders have occasionally taken a leading role on a few issues, usually those of longstanding personal interest or importance to their home states. Most notably, Johnson took a keen interest in space policy and defense preparedness, Knowland led the charge against Communist China, Mansfield made Asian policy a specialty and led the fight to reduce American troop commitments in Europe, Scott pursued legal issues and some foreign policy questions, Byrd led the Senate on energy issues, Dole championed agriculture issues, and Mitchell pursued environmental legislation. Each of these efforts represented interests that the leaders had pursued in committee posts before they assumed floor leadership.

Moreover, foreign policy has been a central interest of all modern Senate leaders, even those who showed little interest in the subject before their election as floor leaders. Several factors seem to be at work here: the Senate's special role in ratifying treaties, the expectation that leaders comment on international events, leaders' formal and informal functions as conduits to the Senate for information from the executive branch, and the opportunity to attend various ceremonial and quasi-diplomatic functions. Recently, Dole and Mitchell, two senators who sat on neither the Armed Services nor the Foreign Relations Committee, have been vocal critics of American foreign policy on several issues. Mitchell has been especially critical of the administration's policies toward the former Soviet Union and the Communist Chinese government.

Some change toward policy-oriented leadership has occurred since the mid-1970s. Demands for assertive leaders, facilitated by more intraparty cohesiveness and interparty differences, have led recent leaders to be more policy-oriented. Both Baker and Mitchell prepared more legislative agendas than did their predecessors. These have been substantially more detailed than the short lists that Johnson and Mansfield prepared. And the agendas clearly reflect party priorities, in contrast to the more personal lists of their immediate predecessors.

The change is greater for the Democrats than for the Republicans. "My intention from the start was to place more emphasis on substance," Mitchell explained. "The party must stand for something. . . . I made it clear that I intended to use the position to advance my positions." [63] The Democrats' task forces, rejuvenated Policy Committee, and policy agendas represent a sample of Mitchell's intensive efforts to generate interest in party activities and promote party cohesiveness behind legislative proposals at an early stage. Mitchell cannot dictate policy directions to his party, of course, but he has pushed hard to generate party policy proposals and promote them.

Leaders of both parties have acquired resources that allow them to become more involved in the substance of policymaking. Democratic leaders, by virtue of their chairmanship of the Policy Committee, have used the Policy Committee to house much of their "leadership" staff, while Republican leaders have had to borrow from the Policy Committee staffs or place staff directly in the leadership office. Refer back to Table 11-3, which shows the expansion in the size of the Democratic Policy Committee staff since the 1970s and of the Republican leaders' office staffs in the 1980s.

In sharp contrast to Mansfield, who regularly failed to spend a large part of his budget allotment, Byrd began to add staff upon his election as majority leader in late 1976. By the time he left the majority leader's post, he had quadrupled the staff by adding policy specialists as well as media consultants, political advisers, and speech writers. When Mitchell took over in 1989, he shared control of the policy staff with Senator Daschle, the new co-chairman of the Policy Committee. On the Republican side, Baker greatly expanded the leadership staff upon becoming majority leader in 1981, and Dole has expanded the staff further in recent years.

Even with their expanded resources, Mitchell and Dole assert themselves on the substance of policy very selectively. Only issues of exceptional importance and controversy require their close attention. The increasing demands of their other responsibilities, including representation of their home states, make it impossible for Senate leaders to devote the necessary time to bill management and policy leadership on a regular basis. Besides, there often is little reason for them to run the show. Committee leaders, with the aid of large committee staffs, usually are pursuing policies and strategies that are fully compatible with leaders' own views and approaches. As a result, party leaders Mitchell and Dole exercise some care and diplomacy in choosing issues to take on as their own.

Conclusion

In the past two decades the party apparatus of the Senate has become substantially more elaborate. This is most evident in the provision of services to meet the needs of individual senators and their staffs. It also is evident in the increasing, though still sporadic, ventures of party leaders, task forces, and committees in crafting legislation and strategy on behalf of their parties. This mix reflects the dual patterns of unrestrained individualism and intensified partisanship experienced by the Senate since the early 1970s.

Top Senate leaders remain caught in the vise of competing expectations. Demands for efficiency and predictability in floor activity conflict with demands for personal services and considerations. Even when the parties are internally cohesive, conflicts between the interests of individual senators and of the party collectively are ever present. Demands for effective party spokesmen and clearly identified party positions conflict with the committee leaders and rank-and-file senators seeking media attention for themselves and their pet causes.

In some institutional settings, leaders can overcome these tensions by force of their formal powers. In the Senate, there are few powers to exercise forcefully and usually unacceptable costs for doing so. Limited policy leadership from top party leaders is the typical result. But limited policy leadership should not be equated with ineffective policy leadership. Recent leaders have bolstered their capacity to pursue a more central role in policymaking. They have shown that effective policy leadership can come from party leaders who are selective in choosing the place and time for asserting themselves.

Notes

1. Woodrow Wilson, *Congressional Government: A Study in American Politics* (1885; reprint, Baltimore: Johns Hopkins University Press, 1981), 147.
2. Charles O. Jones, "Senate Party Leadership in Public Policy," in *Policymaking Role of Leadership in the Senate,* a compilation of papers prepared for the Commission on the Operation of the Senate, 94th Cong., 2d sess. (Washington, D.C.: U.S. Government Printing Office, 1976), 20, 19-20.
3. See Ralph K. Huitt, "Democratic Party Leadership in the U.S. Senate," in *Working Within the System* (Berkeley, Calif.: Institute of Governmental Studies Press, 1990), 73-93.
4. Floyd M. Riddick, *Majority and Minority Party Leaders of the Senate: History and Development of the Offices of Floor Leaders,* S. Doc. 92-42, 92d Cong., 1st sess. (Washington, D.C.: U.S. Government Printing Office, 1971).
5. Several other party positions have been created in this century. For the Republicans, the several leadership posts—conference secretary, whip, Policy Committee chair, Committee on Committees chair, and National Republican Senatorial Committee chair—are held by different senators. In contrast, the Democrats, whose steering committee handles committee assignments, until very recently reserved their Policy Committee and Steering Committee chairmanships for their floor leader. In late 1988 newly elected majority leader Mitchell appointed another senator to chair the Steering Committee and named a co-chair for the Policy Committee. He also created a new post, assistant floor leader, but he continues to chair his party's conference.
6. Riddick, *Majority and Minority Party Leaders of the Senate,* 11.
7. Ibid., 13.
8. See also Robert L. Peabody, "Senate Party Leadership: From the 1950s to the 1980s," in *Understanding Congressional Leadership,* ed. Frank H. Mackaman (Washington, D.C.: CQ Press, 1981), 86.
9. Gary W. Cox and Mathew D. McCubbins make this argument for the House of Representatives. See their *Legislative Leviathan: Party Government in the House* (Berkeley: University of California Press, forthcoming), chap. 6. Richard F. Fenno, Jr., notes how important party reputation was for Senate Republicans, and particularly for Republican leader Howard Baker, in the early 1980s. See *The Emergence of a Senate Leader: Pete Domenici and the Reagan Budget* (Washington, D.C.: CQ Press, 1991), 67, 95, 101, 113.
10. For example, Senate incumbents' reelection chances are affected by the public's assessment of the parties' ability to solve the country's most important problem and to promote prosperity. Similarly, a senator's own reelection chances are related to how his or her party colleagues fare, even after the senator's previous electoral history is taken into account. The supporting evidence is reported in Steven S. Smith, *Leading the Senate* (Washington, D.C.: Brookings Institution, forthcoming), chap. 1.
11. For a review of existing models, see Michael S. Lewis-Beck and Tom W. Rice, *Forecasting Elections* (Washington, D.C.: CQ Press, 1992). It turns out that a Senate party's seat gains or losses are predicted well by a statistical model that incorporates four factors: (1) change in national real disposable income six months before the election, (2) whether the election is a presidential midterm election, (3) the number of seats up for reelection, (4) and party reputation, as measured by the Gallup Poll questions on the party most likely to provide prosperity and peace.
12. See Barbara Sinclair, *The Transformation of the U.S. Senate* (Baltimore: Johns Hopkins University Press, 1989).
13. Glenn R. Parker, *Characteristics of Congress* (Englewood Cliffs, N.J.: Prentice Hall, 1989), 30; Norman J. Ornstein, Thomas E. Mann, and Michael J. Malbin, *Vital Statistics on Congress, 1989-1990* (Washington, D.C.: Congressional Quarterly, 1990), 156.

14. Presidential popularity is also sometimes noted as an aspect of public opinion influencing party strategies in Congress. See Jon R. Bond and Richard Fleisher, *The President in the Legislative Arena* (Chicago: University of Chicago Press, 1990), chap. 7.

15. David Brady, Richard Brody, and David Epstein, "Heterogeneous Parties and Political Organization: The U.S. Senate, 1880-1920," *Legislative Studies Quarterly* 14 (May 1989): 205-223.

16. Leaders, of course, have something to do with the level of party cohesiveness and polarization observed in roll call voting. In the 1950s Lyndon Johnson worked harder than other leaders to keep issues dividing Democrats off the Senate floor, keeping the expressed level of party cohesiveness artificially high. Nevertheless, the level of partisanship in recent years is fairly represented in Figure 11-1 as being relatively high. Thus, leaders Mitchell and Dole, more than most of their predecessors, have been in a good position to assert themselves on matters of policy.

17. *Congressional Record,* Nov. 14, 1992, S16661.

18. Ibid., Aug. 7, 1987, S11603.

19. Sen. George Mitchell, interview with author, Washington, D.C., March 28, 1992. See also Richard E. Cohen, "Campaigning in the Club," *National Journal,* March 9, 1988, 948-951.

20. Richard E. Cohen, "Teaming Up in a Chamberful of Egos," *National Journal,* June 23, 1990, 1553.

21. Hugh A. Bone, *Party Committees and National Politics* (Seattle: University of Washington Press, 1958).

22. Harry McPherson, *A Political Education* (Boston: Little, Brown, 1972), 183-185.

23. On the early 1970s, see John G. Stewart, "Central Policy Organs in Congress," in *Congress Against the President,* ed. Harvey C. Mansfield, Sr. (New York: Praeger, 1975), 20-33.

24. See Donald C. Baumer, "Senate Democratic Leadership in the 101st Congress" (Paper presented at the annual meeting of the American Political Science Association, San Francisco, Sept. 2, 1990).

25. For a summary of party publications in 1991, see Samuel C. Patterson and Thomas H. Little, "The Organizational Life of the Congressional Parties" (Paper presented at the annual meeting of the Midwest Political Science Association, Chicago, April 1992), Table 2. See also Baumer, "Senate Democratic Leadership in the 101st Congress."

26. Walter J. Oleszek, *Majority and Minority Whips of the Senate,* 98th Cong., 2d sess., S. Doc. 89-45 (Washington, D.C.: U.S. Government Printing Office, 1985). Also see Robert L. Peabody, *Leadership in Congress* (Boston: Little, Brown, 1976), 331-332; and David T. Canon, "The Institutionalization of Leadership in the U.S. Congress," *Legislative Studies Quarterly* 14 (August 1989): 418-419.

27. Richard E. Cohen, *Congressional Leadership: Seeking a New Role* (Beverly Hills, Calif.: Sage, 1980), 69.

28. Richard E. Cohen, "Minority Status Seems to Have Enhanced Byrd's Position Among Fellow Democrats," *National Journal,* May 7, 1983, 958-960.

29. For example, see Richard E. Cohen, "Making His Mark," *National Journal,* May 20, 1989, 1232; Richard E. Cohen, "Crumbling Committees," *National Journal,* Aug. 4, 1990, 1876; and Spencer Rich, "Senate GOP Task Force Unveils Plan to Expand Coverage for Health Care," *Washington Post,* Nov. 8, 1991.

30. Interview with author, March 28, 1992.

31. See *President Eisenhower's Meetings with Legislative Leaders, 1953-1961* (Frederick, Md.: University Publications of America, 1986), taken from a file at the Eisenhower Library. Also see James MacGregor Burns, *The Deadlock of Democracy: Four-Party Politics in America* (Englewood Cliffs, N.J.: Prentice Hall, 1963), 255.

32. Stephen E. Ambrose, *Eisenhower: The President* (New York: Simon and Schuster,

1984), 549.

33. See ibid.; Burns, *Deadlock of Democracy;* Robert J. Donovan, *Eisenhower: The Inside Story* (New York: Harper, 1956); and Neil MacNeil, *Dirksen: Portrait of a Public Man* (Cleveland: World, 1966).

34. Rowland Evans and Robert Novak, *Lyndon B. Johnson: The Exercise of Power* (Cleveland: World, 1966), 168-169.

35. Alfred Steinberg, *Sam Rayburn: A Biography* (New York: Hawthorn, 1975), 318-321.

36. MacNeil, *Dirksen,* 281.

37. Ibid.

38. John Erlichman reports that the Republican leaders "rarely were given a chance to say anything" at the weekly breakfast sessions. See his *Witness to Power* (New York: Simon and Schuster, 1982), 204.

39. Rowland Evans and Robert Novak, *Nixon in the White House: The Frustration of Power* (New York: Random House, 1971), 108; and Nicol C. Rae, *The Decline and Fall of the Liberal Republicans from 1952 to the Present* (New York: Oxford University Press, 1989), 106.

40. Charles O. Jones, "Presidential Negotiation with Congress," in *Both Ends of the Avenue: The Presidency, the Executive Branch, and Congress in the 1980s,* ed. Anthony King (Washington, D.C.: American Enterprise Institute, 1983), 117; Peabody, "Senate Party Leadership," 95.

41. Ross K. Baker, "Mike Mansfield and the Birth of the Modern Senate" (Paper presented at the Everett McKinley Dirksen Center symposium on Senate leadership, Washington, D.C., May 17, 1990), 45. Mansfield claims that he encouraged Nixon to pursue his China initiatives at these meetings.

42. Evans and Novak, *Nixon,* 106-107.

43. Gerald R. Ford, *A Time to Heal* (New York: Harper, 1979), 140.

44. Walter Kravitz, "Relations Between the Senate and the House of Representatives: The Party Leadership," in *Policymaking Role of Leadership in the Senate,* 129.

45. In the case of the *Mayaguez* incident, Ford briefed congressional leaders after issuing orders for the use of force to free the captured Marines. See Ford, *Time to Heal,* 280-281, 283.

46. Charles O. Jones, "Congress and the Presidency," in *The New Congress,* ed. Thomas E. Mann and Norman J. Ornstein (Washington, D.C.: American Enterprise Institute, 1981), 240; Peabody, "Senate Party Leadership," 94-95.

47. Several instances are noted in Jimmy Carter, *Keeping Faith: Memoirs of a President* (New York: Bantam, 1982).

48. Ibid., 224.

49. See Richard E. Cohen, "Still a Chill Between GOP's Top Two," *National Journal,* Nov. 11, 1989, 2775.

50. Mitchell, interview with author, March 28, 1992.

51. Robert L. Peabody, *Leadership in Congress.*

52. Randall B. Ripley, *Party Leaders in the House of Representatives* (Washington, D.C.: Brookings Institution, 1967), chaps. 3, 5; Randall B. Ripley, *Majority Party Leadership in Congress* (Boston: Little, Brown, 1969), 44-45; Randall B. Ripley, *Power in the Senate* (New York: St. Martin's, 1969), 24.

53. On leadership and the media, see Cokie Roberts, "Leadership and the Media in the 101st Congress," in *Leading Congress: New Styles, New Strategies,* ed. John J. Kornacki (Washington, D.C.: Congressional Quarterly, 1990), 85-96.

54. Joe S. Foote, *Television Access and Political Power: The Networks, the Presidency, and the "Loyal Opposition"* (New York: Praeger, 1990), 33-34.

55. Roger H. Davidson, "Senate Leaders: Janitors for an Untidy Chamber?" in *Congress Reconsidered,* 3d ed., ed. Lawrence C. Dodd and Bruce I. Oppenheimer (Washington, D.C.: CQ Press, 1985), 236. Stephen Hess notes that top party leaders always have been among the most visible senators and continue to be so. See Stephen Hess, *The*

Ultimate Insiders: U.S. Senators and the National Media (Washington, D.C.: Brookings Institution, 1986).

56. See Roberts, "Leadership and the Media," 95.
57. Richard E. Cohen, "A Consensus Builder to Lead the Senate," *National Journal*, Dec. 3, 1988, 3079.
58. Jennifer Spevacek, "Mitchell Wins Leadership Post," *Washington Times*, Nov. 30, 1988, A8.
59. For example, see *Congressional Record*, Jan. 23, 1992, S208-14.
60. Center for Responsive Politics, *Dateline: Capitol Hill* (Washington, D.C.: Center for Responsive Politics, 1990), 61-62.
61. David B. Truman, *The Congressional Party: A Case Study* (New York: Wiley, 1959), 104-106. With respect to leaders as ideological middlemen, see Aage R. Clausen and Clyde Wilcox, "Policy Partisanship in Legislative Leadership Recruitment and Behavior," *Legislative Studies Quarterly* 12 (May 1987): 243-263.
62. Allen Schick, "Complex Policymaking in the United States Senate," in *Policymaking Role of Leadership in the Senate*.
63. Mitchell, interview with author, March 28, 1992.

12

The Republican Parties in Congress: Bicameral Differences

John B. Bader and Charles O. Jones

On election night, November 4, 1980, it became apparent that a major event was occurring. For the first time in this century an incumbent Democratic president was going down to defeat. Jimmy Carter was losing—and losing big—to Ronald Reagan. Just before 6:00 p.m., western time, President Carter interrupted Reagan's shower to concede.[1] Once that stunning concession had been comprehended, analysts turned to another political development that promised to be of equal importance. As the evening wore on, it looked as if the Republicans had an excellent chance of winning control of the Senate. Many Senate races were close—eleven races were settled by 3 percentage points or fewer. In the end, Republicans won nine of the eleven contests, and party control shifted to the Republican party for the first time since 1954.

The reaction of incumbent Republican senators to these results fully matched the excitement of analysts. Only one of their number had been in the Senate when the Republicans were last a majority, and that member—Strom Thurmond of South Carolina—had then been a Democrat. The prospect of taking charge—of becoming committee chairmen, of increasing committee staff, of managing the legislative schedule—made Republican senators giddy. It would be their Senate.

Meanwhile, on the House side, the Republicans had a net gain of 33 seats—their largest in any presidential election since 1920. Although the gain left them 26 votes shy of a majority (matching the post-1958 high of 192 seats achieved in 1968 and 1972), they saw possibilities for cross-partisan majorities on issues in which southern Democrats could be persuaded to join them. Still, that alliance was less dependable than having a Republican majority. Therefore House Republicans looked forward to the party realignment that was predicted by some of those reading the 1980 election returns.

The 1982 elections, however, reduced House Republican numbers once again; the party had a net loss of 25 seats. Whatever complex shifts were occurring among the voters to produce the extraordinary split government of the 1980s, these shifts did not mark a comprehensive partisan change sufficient to produce major changes in the House of Representatives. And so after a taste of cross-party management, House Republicans assumed the unrewarding minority party functions of supporting presidential bargains with Democrats, awaiting the legislative initiative of Senate Republicans, and opposing the growing policy aggressiveness of the majority House Democrats.

This partisan and institutional division of the early 1980s offers a thematic backdrop to this essay on congressional Republicans. It illustrates that there are two Republican parties on Capitol Hill: the House Republican party and the Senate Republican party. They differ from one another and they differ in the way they relate to the White House. The principal purpose of this essay is to identify those differences and to discuss their importance for the national policy process.

Differences Between House and Senate Republicans

Much of the press and scholarly attention to Congress is directed toward the Democratic party for the very good reason that the Democratic party has dominated that institution since 1945. Even Republican presidents have courted votes among House and Senate Democrats to build majorities for their programs. There is, however, much to be learned about contemporary congressional politics by studying House and Senate Republicans. Among the lessons are the concerns associated with an emerging system of divided government and the roles played by the legislative parties in each chamber.

The following are some of the important differences between the House and Senate Republican parties in the post-World War II period:

- House Republicans have been in the minority since 1955—thirty-eight, soon to be forty, consecutive years. Senate Republicans managed majorities for six years during that period.[2]
- The average number of House Republicans declined during the most recent twenty-four-year period (1969-1993) over the previous twenty-four-year period (1945-1969), whereas the average number of Senate Republicans increased (see Table 12-1).
- A higher proportion of House Republicans retire than do Senate Republicans.
- House Republicans tend to have their highest incumbent return rates when they have the lowest number of total members. In recent elections, however, Senate Republicans have had high return rates and a large base, thus capturing the Senate or remaining competitive.
- The proportion of House Republican freshmen has decreased slightly; the proportion of Senate Republicans has increased slightly.
- In roll call voting, House Republicans are consistently less supportive of the president than are Senate Republicans.

The Democrats too have changed during this time—with significant effects for congressional Republicans. In large part because of increased homogeneity and cohesion, House Democrats have come to be aggressive in countering Republican presidents. Democrats essentially are playing the role of an opposition party. Party unity among House Democrats has increased impressively, with presidential support declining markedly. And Democrats have taken firm control of House procedures, often to the exasperation of House Republicans.[3] Senate

Table 12-1   Republican Composition of the House and Senate, 1945-1993

	House Republicans		Senate Republicans	
	Average no. per Congress	Average % per Congress	Average no. per Congress	Average % per Congress
1945-1993	181	41.5%	43	43.4%
1945-1969	189	43.3	41	42.0
1969-1993	172	39.6	45	44.8

Source: Calculated from data in Norman J. Ornstein, Thomas E. Mann, and Michael J. Malbin, *Vital Statistics on Congress, 1989-1990* (Washington, D.C.: Congressional Quarterly, 1990), 38-39.

Democrats have had to be more cautious than formerly for several reasons. The Democrats have been in the minority themselves, the Republicans have shown strength even while they were in the minority, and Senate traditions encourage a collegial atmosphere. Steven Smith talks about a "revolution" in the House; he refers to an "evolution" in the Senate.[4]

House Republicans: A Supportive Opposition

The setting is the cavernous and ornate hearing room of the House Committee on Ways and Means. On February, 12, 1992, all members are in attendance as the committee takes up various tax proposals intended to stimulate the economy. President Bush had offered his plan in the State of the Union message, proposing both short-term and long-term solutions. He urged passage of the short-term proposals by March 20. The committee's ranking Republican, William Archer of Texas, introduced the smaller, quick-fix package, but the Democrats rejected it. The Democratic floor leader, Richard Gephardt of Missouri, introduced the whole Bush package—including the longer term proposals that the president judged could wait:

> By sending the "Gephardt-Bush" measure to the full House, the Democrats on the Ways and Means Committee hoped to kill it and embarrass Republicans at the same time. That is because it would require a vote on all of President Bush's tax proposals at once. It includes measures he or House Republicans would rather forget about . . . or at least put off.[5]

Committee Republicans were apoplectic. "We're not going to play," ranking member Archer shouted. Democrat Thomas J. Downey of New York responded, "If you want to walk out on George Bush, we'll give you the chance." [6]

Such are the frustrations of the participating minority. The most that House Republicans can hope for is the occasional cross-partisan majority, more often than not led by someone other than their own leaders. Typically, they are caught in the middle or left out altogether. The White House expects them to support the president's initiatives or the compromises he works out with House Democrats. They are also expected to sustain vetoes, even when they may have voted originally for the bill the president rejected. For House Republicans, seeking an identity in these circumstances cannot be easy. And an identity crisis lasting several decades surely takes its toll. We can see their frustration by examining three areas: leadership changes in the House, the electoral connections between House Republicans and the president, and policy options for Republicans within the House.

Leadership Changes in the House

House Republicans have had vigorous leadership contests, often following disappointing election results. In 1959, after a net loss of 47 seats, Charles A. Halleck of Indiana defeated the longtime Republican floor leader, Joseph W. Martin of Massachusetts. In 1963 Gerald R. Ford of Michigan defeated the incumbent conference chairman, Charles B. Hoeven of Iowa. Two years later House Republicans suffered a net loss of 38 seats, reducing their numbers to 140, their lowest total since 1938. Halleck was challenged by Ford and lost 73-67. In a careful study of this change, Robert L. Peabody quotes one member as saying, "We need to look for constructive alternatives, not just . . . vote 'no.'" Another member remarked, "I'm tired of always painting ourselves into a corner." [7]

House Republicans have not ousted a leader since 1965, though spirited contests occur frequently. Table 12-2 profiles House Republican leaders during the period of the new split-party politics in Washington. Leadership changes during this period were due to incumbents leaving office, either to retire or to accept another position. All involved contests except the accession of John J. Rhodes of Arizona.

In recent years many House Republicans have exerted pressure on leaders to play a more aggressive role in policymaking. The Conservative Opportunity Society (COS) has been particularly vocal in this regard. The COS began engaging in tactics bound to irritate Democrats and cause conflict among Republicans as well. COS members used special orders (speeches following the day's regular business) to attack Democrats. They used delaying tactics on the House floor, pressed for investigations of wrongdoing, supported reform, and offered a far-reaching set of policy positions. The putative leader of the COS, Newt Gingrich of Georgia, argues that playing along with the Democrats will not work. According to Gingrich, the system under which Republicans live their political lives must be changed. For example, responding to the House banking scandal, Gingrich pressed for full disclosure of those who had overdrawn their accounts in the House bank (even though he too had overdrafts):

> This is about systemic, institutional corruption, not personality. To ask the Democratic leadership to clean things up would be like asking the old Soviet bureaucracy under Brezhnev to reform itself. It ain't going to happen.[8]

Gingrich won election as the minority whip in 1989. Until then leaders

Table 12-2   House Republican Leaders, 1969-1993

	Tenure	Initial selection	Previous position	Reason left
Floor leaders				
Gerald R. Ford, Mich.	1965-1973	Elected, 73-65	Conference chairman	Became vice president
John J. Rhodes, Ariz.	1973-1981	Elected, no opponent	Policy committee chairman	Did not seek reelection
Robert H. Michel, Ill.	1981-	Elected, 103-87	Whip	—
Whips				
Les Arends, Ill.	1943-1975	Elected	None	Retired
Robert H. Michel, Ill.	1975-1981	Elected, 78-38-22 (two opponents)	Campaign committee chairman	Elected leader
Trent Lott, Miss.	1981-1989	Elected, 96-90	Research committee chairman	Ran for Senate
Newt Gingrich, Ga.	1989-	Elected, 87-85	None	—

Source: Compiled from information in various issues of *Congressional Quarterly Weekly Report.*

were "regular" Republicans who promised more vigorous, but not revolutionary, leadership. Gingrich's narrow win was of a different order, however. Janet Hook described it this way:

> Gingrich's promotion from backbench bomb thrower to minority whip was an expression of seething impatience among House Republicans with their seemingly permanent minority status.
> Against this backdrop, the election was the political equivalent of a Hail Mary pass in football.[9]

Gingrich has not always been a team player, either with the minority leader or with the president. It remains to be seen what the precise effects of selecting a maverick whip will be. Most assuredly, however, House Republicans will continue to chafe under the yoke of conflicting expectations and naturally will look to their leaders for changes that they often are in no position to effect.

Electoral Connections Between House Republicans and the President

How might House Republicans be expected to view the White House after an election? They were, of course, always in the minority during the period

Table 12-3   Republican Results in House, Senate, and Presidential
                  Elections, 1968-1990

Year	Presidential candidate	Percentage of vote		House GOP		Senate GOP	
		Popular	Electoral College	No.	%	No.	%
1968	Nixon	43	56	+4	+2	+6	+17
1970				−12	−6	+2	+5
1972	Nixon	61	97	+12	+7	−2	−5
1974				−43	−22	−5	−12
1976	Ford	48	45	−1	−.7	+1	+3
1978				+11	+8	+3	+8
1980	Reagan	51	91	+33	+21	+12	+29
1982				−26	−14	+1	+2
1984	Reagan	59	98	+14	+8	−1	−2
1986				−5	−3	−8	−15
1988	Bush	54	79	−2	−1	0	0
1990				−8	−5	−1	−2

Sources: Calculated from data in Norman J. Ornstein, Thomas E. Mann, and Michael J. Malbin, *Vital Statistics on Congress, 1989-1990* (Washington, D.C.: Congressional Quarterly, 1990), 37-39; and Harold W. Stanley and Richard G. Niemi, *Vital Statistics on American Politics* (Washington, D.C.: CQ Press, 1988), 82-83.

Note: The number of gains and losses is based on changes from the beginning of the previous Congress.

1969-1993. The variation in their status was in their proximity to majority status and, therefore, in their capacity to fashion a meaningful cross-partisan majority on certain issues. Table 12-3 outlines the comparative election results for House, Senate, and presidential candidates in the years 1968-1990. (The comparative Senate results will be discussed in the next section.)

During these years Republican electoral results were the most volatile under Nixon. His 1968 victory was extremely narrow, and the House Republican gain in that year was small, too. Still, taking into account the party's sizable net gain in 1966, the Republicans came within 26 seats of a majority, their closest bid since the 1956 election. The modest losses in 1970 were recouped in 1972, when President Nixon enjoyed one of the greatest victories in history. In popular votes he ran ahead of more than half of the winning House Republicans in their districts, doubtless an impressive result. Yet this remarkable win did not produce a majority for House Republicans, and the president's resignation and subsequent pardon contributed to a disastrous result at the polls for House Republicans in 1974.

Surely the high point for House Republicans in recent decades occurred in the 97th Congress (1981-1983), when Ronald Reagan's huge victory was complemented by a substantial increase in his party's House seats. Here was the first total victory for the party—White House, House, and Senate—since 1952. Yet it still left House Republicans with the hope, not the reality, of majority status. That hope was dashed in 1982. Although Reagan won a smashing reelection in

1984, House Republicans failed to match their earlier numbers. Disappointment continued under the Bush administration. The president's substantial win in 1988 was not accompanied by an increase in the number of House Republicans. He ran behind most of the winners in their districts.

There is little evidence to suggest strong electoral ties between House Republicans and their president. Yet Republican representatives know they will be called on to support his program, even when many judge that program to be inimical to their personal or constituency interests. Meanwhile, House Democrats have successfully capitalized on the continuity of their majority status to fashion impressive legislative tools with which to manage the House of Representatives as though the Republicans were not there.

Policy Options for House Republicans

David R. Mayhew has identified 267 major acts passed in the post-World War II period; 142 of them were passed in the years 1969-1992, the period focused on in this essay. We sampled one-fourth of these acts (36) to identify the policy options available to House and Senate Republicans. (Table 12-5, found later in this chapter, lists the acts included.) Our review shows that House Republicans are significantly more constrained than are Senate Republicans. Unquestionably, the difference is due in part to the organization and traditions of the two legislative bodies: individual senators have more prerogatives, regardless of party, than individual representatives. Representatives' options are constrained for three collateral reasons:

- Most of the work in the House is done in committees and subcommittees. Even when Republicans wield influence, their work tends to be subsumed within that of the Democratic leadership.
- Floor debate and the amending process are often tightly managed through leadership control of the Committee on Rules. Therefore, short of divisiveness among House Democrats, Republicans can seldom expect to have much influence on the floor.
- A Republican president must, perforce, work with House Democrats in building majorities for his program. Therefore much of the compromising will be in the direction of the Democrats—sometimes to such an extent that Republicans will oppose their own president.

In his study of the postreform House, David W. Rohde describes the weakened policy position of the House Republicans:

> Since the reforms and the increase in Democratic homogeneity . . . things have become quite different. Both within committees and on the floor, Republicans' ability to have an impact has declined. Increasing Democratic unity has reduced the Democrats' need to seek Republican support. Unless the majority is divided, in most instances it can do as it pleases. As Henry Waxman (D-Cal.) succinctly put it, "If we have a united Democratic position, Republicans are irrelevant." [10]

Former Speaker Tip O'Neill, D-Mass., is reported to have said, "Republicans are just going to have to get it through their heads that they are not going to write legislation." [11]

A brief review of a sample of major legislation, from 1969 through 1992, shows that Republicans resisted O'Neill's advice but lived frustrating lives as lawmakers. They tried hard to support the president, many times with disappointing results. On occasion during the first Nixon administration, House Republicans worked with Democrats at the committee stage to shape a bill ultimately acceptable to the president. Their efforts were subsumed within the Democratic bill, but they had the satisfaction of having contributed to the legislation. On other occasions, when committee Democrats either defeated or ignored the president's proposal, House Republicans sometimes introduced the proposal on the floor as a substitute for the Democratic bill. If they were successful (as they were with the Equal Employment Opportunity Act of 1972), victory lasted only until the conference committee met.

With the approach of the 1972 election, House Democrats sought substantial increases in Social Security benefits over those proposed by the president, certain that he would not veto the changes. House Republicans essentially stepped aside from a bidding process over which they had little or no influence. After their devastating defeat in 1974, House Republicans were limited to supporting bargains between President Gerald Ford and House Democrats or having to sustain Ford's vetoes. (This will be discussed later in this essay.)

Twice during the Nixon administration the Republicans joined forces with the Democrats to support Congress as an institution. The first case was the War Powers Resolution of 1973. Although both houses of Congress passed this legislation with substantial Republican support, President Nixon vetoed the measure as constituting a threat to presidential prerogatives. Nearly one-half of the House Republicans voted to override the veto. The second case was the Budget and Impoundment Control Act of 1974. Designed to provide Congress with an independent capability to analyze the budget, the act was passed overwhelmingly in both houses and signed by the president (an act he later regretted). [12]

House Republicans had more flexibility under Carter than under Nixon, primarily as a consequence of a divided Democratic party. [13] Thus, for example, Republicans worked with Democrats in fashioning substitute legislation (as with the Clean Air Act Amendments of 1977), they successfully delayed legislation (as with rules concerning the creation of the Department of Education), and they supported certain initiatives (as with a modified synthetic fuels program). William Connelly shows a substantial increase in the number of policy statements issued by the House Republican Policy Committee during the Carter administration. [14] Freed of having to answer for the administration, House Republicans were in a position to take initiatives, fully aware that few would come to fruition.

Clearly, House Republicans were the most active in the early months of the Reagan administration. With the support of the so-called boll weevils—a group of southern Democrats—they virtually managed the House on budgetary and tax policy. Even then, however, they were in no position to take the kind of leadership displayed by Sen. Bob Dole, R-Kan., then chairman of the Senate Finance Committee, in regard to the Tax Equity and Responsibility Act of 1982. Rather, they were left to cry "shame" when Rep. Dan Rostenkowski, D-Ill., decided not to push for a House tax plan, thus raising the constitutional issue of the Senate initiating a tax proposal.

After their serious losses in 1982 and on into the Bush administration, House Republicans were never again in a position to lead the House. They often mounted serious opposition to the compromises between the president and House Democrats or to Democratic efforts to go it alone on legislation. Occasionally, they introduced their own substitute proposals (as they did with catastrophic health insurance and welfare reform). With the anticrime package, they simply outmaneuvered Democrats on the floor. Overall, however, they fought rearguard actions—working within committees to have influence, seeking to delay the inevitable, displaying their own proposals on the floor before these proposals went down to sure defeat, and supplying the votes to sustain vetoes. It has not been satisfying work. Not surprisingly, when House Republicans were asked to endorse a budget agreement worked out between congressional Democrats and President Bush in early October 1990, many of them rebelled, joining an equally disgruntled group of liberal Democrats and voting no.

In the era of divided government the relationship between House Republicans and the president is tenuous at best. A complete experience for a legislator-representative must include constituency service and lawmaking. Staff increases and other perquisites now provide House Republicans with very nearly the same resources for serving the congressional district that House Democrats enjoy. What they lack is the reward of seeing a major piece of legislation through to final passage. House Republicans, are, for the most part, spectators. They have choice seats, to be sure, and sometimes they are called in as substitutes when a pickup team is needed. A few, like Bill Gradison of Ohio, are even permitted to participate on a regular basis. But circumstances have prevented them from serving as complete legislators.

At one point on January 30, 1890, when Speaker Thomas B. Reed, R-Maine, was single-handedly defeating the dilatory tactics of Democrats, the Democrats demanded to know, "What becomes of the rights of the minority?" Reed responded, "The right of the minority is to draw its salaries and its function is to make a quorum." [15] It is fair to say that the House Republicans, like all members of Congress, have more duties today than ever before, but they may feel no more effective as lawmakers than did the Democrats of Reed's time.

Senate Republicans: Legislative Partners

House Republicans are frequently trapped into awkward political positions, such as when Ways and Means Democrats forced them to vote against their president in February 1992. Senate Republicans rarely face such helplessness. For them, negotiations over the 1991 civil rights bill may be more typical and illustrative. Those negotiations highlight some critical differences between the two chambers of Congress: Republican senators enjoy extensive and constructive policy input, they play a wide variety of roles in the process, and they are accorded respect by the president.

After President Bush vetoed a civil rights bill in 1990, moderate Republicans led by John Danforth of Missouri worked with liberal Democrats, such as Edward Kennedy of Massachusetts, to draft an acceptably bipartisan bill. Some Republicans, such as Danforth and his floor leader, Bob Dole, feared that recent battles over racial issues were ruining their party's efforts to broaden their appeal to minorities.

Although Danforth played a crucial role as policy leader and bipartisan cosponsor, Dole intervened in the eleventh hour to facilitate a compromise. Dole managed to postpone final consideration of the bill while he pressed senators and the president to come to agreement. He asked that C. Boyden Gray, White House counsel, join a meeting of Republican senators on October 23, 1991, in Dole's office on Capitol Hill. Hours passed. By midafternoon, Gray concluded, "This is going to go." [16] Danforth spent much of the day shuttling between Gray and Kennedy. Kennedy and two aides came to Dole's office. Huddling in a hallway with Danforth, Kennedy agreed to a Dole proposal concerning damage limits for businesses. Inside Dole's office, Gray had been joined by White House chief of staff John Sununu. After they had reviewed Kennedy's concession, Sununu called the president at 10:00 p.m. "We have a deal," he said simply.[17]

As the civil rights bill illustrates, Republicans in the Senate have considerable political and policy leverage. Even as minority leader, Dole could affect scheduling to allow room for compromise. Filling a variety of policy roles, Dole, Danforth, and other Republicans made important contributions to a major piece of legislation. They worked with liberal Democrats, such as Kennedy, who found themselves coming to Republican offices to make the final deal. Likewise, the White House showed significant deference to Republican senators by coming to the Hill and accepting their proposals. This leverage and a secure sense of identity can be seen as we examine leadership changes in the Senate, the electoral independence of Republicans from the president, and the variable roles Republicans play in the Senate's policy process.

Changes in the Senate

Although the selection of House leaders seems to turn on electoral loss and internal frustration, Senate leaders come to their positions for more personal, individualized reasons. Senate contests for party positions tend to be vigorous but lacking an ideological or strategic mandate. This may be because the atmosphere of a party caucus in the Senate is more intimate than a party caucus in the House, but it also reflects the fluid nature of policy positions in the Senate (see Table 12-4).

In 1969 the Republican Senate leadership went through considerable change. The venerable Everett M. Dirksen of Illinois, minority leader for ten years, wanted his friend and fellow conservative Roman Hruska of Nebraska to

Table 12-4   Senate Republican Leaders, 1969-1993

Leaders	Tenure	Initial selection	Previous position	Reason left
Floor leaders				
Everett M. Dirksen, Ill.	1959-1969	Elected, 20-14	Whip	Died
Hugh D. Scott, Jr., Pa.	1969-1977	Elected, 24-19	Whip	Retired
Howard H. Baker, Jr., Tenn.	1977-1985	Elected, 19-18	None	Retired
Robert J. Dole, Kan.	1985-	Elected, 28-25	Finance Committee chair	—
Whips				
Hugh D. Scott, Jr., Pa.	1969	Elected, 23-20	Campaign Committee vice chair	Elected leader
Robert P. Griffin, Mich.	1969-1977	Elected, 23-20	None	a
Ted Stevens, Alaska	1977-1985	Elected unanimously	None	b
Alan K. Simpson, Wyo.	1985-	Elected, 31-22	Veterans Affairs Committee chair	—

Source: Compiled from information in various issues of *Congressional Quarterly Weekly Report* and *Congressional Quarterly Almanac.*

[a] Griffin sought to be floor leader and was defeated by Baker; he did not seek reelection.

[b] Stevens sought to be floor leader and was defeated by Dole; he did not seek reelection.

become the party whip. But Hugh Scott of Pennsylvania upset Hruska 23-20. When Dirksen died in September of that year, Scott was well positioned to run for floor leader. Hruska challenged Scott, but this time Hruska bowed out of the race to support Howard Baker of Tennessee. Baker, Dirksen's son-in-law, had been in the Senate only a few years. His lack of seniority proved his undoing, and he was defeated 24-19. As Robert Peabody writes, "In the final analysis, seniority proved more decisive than ideology." [18]

Senate Republican leadership turned over again in 1977. Again, the results were surprising and the causes largely personal, not ideological or policy-related. Robert Griffin of Michigan, the minority whip, seemed poised to assume the floor leadership post. Howard Baker, however, quietly gathered a bare majority and upset a stunned Griffin by a single vote. Griffin probably should not have acted so surprised, for Baker clearly was an ambitious man. Twice considered as a vice presidential candidate and twice as a candidate for floor leader, Baker made sure he would not be left out again.

When Baker announced his retirement in 1984, sixteen Republicans scrambled to take his place. The party clearly showed that it lacked a stable ladder of succession as once again the sitting whip—this time Ted Stevens of Alaska—lost. The new leader, Bob Dole, promised to be a strong negotiator and party spokesman. Dole and, to some extent, Alan K. Simpson of Wyoming, elected party whip, came from the center of the party, whose members had become increasingly conservative. Both were known for their pragmatic willingness to compromise. They had come to lead their party principally for personal reasons.

Since 1969 changes in the Senate Republican leadership—fluid and personal—have reflected the nature of the Senate as well as the secure position held by Republicans in that body. In contrast to House Republicans, Senate Republicans have felt no need to punish their leadership for party misfortunes or to choose leaders whose selection made strategic or ideological statements. Rather, they have rewarded members who have personally sought their respect, loyalty, and support.

Electoral Independence of
Senate Republicans from the President

By constitutional design, Senate and presidential elections are only partially connected. One-third of the Senate is up for reelection every two years. The exact proportion of each party will vary depending on its share of seats in that one-third. Thus, for example, in 1992 Republicans held fifteen of the Senate seats up for reelection—almost exactly one-third of their total of forty-three seats. In 1980, however, only ten Senate seats were held by Republicans—slightly less than one-fourth of their membership.

House and Senate election results are often different either in direction or in volume of change (refer back to Table 12-3). On just two occasions did the results appear to be similar and substantial in terms of projecting a congruous message. In 1974 both House and Senate Republicans experienced significant net losses, with many of the losers no doubt believing that President Nixon had caused their defeat. In 1980 the opposite occurred. Many of the Republican winners could be expected to thank Ronald Reagan (whether or not coattails could be demonstrated to have worked for them).

Placing the Senate results alongside those of the president and the House confirms the separateness we know is there. But it reinforces the character of recent American national politics. Republican senators, like their counterparts in the House, live their political lives independently of the president. Their challenge in participating in policymaking is, therefore, defined primarily by the nature of their status within the Senate. And that status has improved since 1968.

Variable Policy Roles for Senate Republicans

Unlike their partisan brethren in the House, Senate Republicans have experienced the power and satisfaction of being the majority party. Republicans had dreamed of gaining such status since they lost it in 1955. They would return to such dreaming immediately after the 1986 election. The post-1969 period, then, includes the minority eras (1969-1981 and 1987 to the present) and the majority era (1981-1987).

If partisan status is so critical, we should expect a clear bifurcation of policy roles. Members of the majority would be "responsible," crafting and passing legislative solutions to pressing national problems, while minority members would dissent, obstruct, and complain. In the minority, Republicans would master the filibuster—a delay tactic in which members hold the floor—and the "killer amendments" that would destroy support for an entire bill. Suddenly—if partisan status is so important—on a clear, cold day in January 1981, Republicans would have dropped such tactics and become responsible majority members. Just as suddenly, almost magically, they would have returned to their roles as dissenters in 1987.

But Washington is no magic kingdom, and the Senate cannot be described so easily. In fact, Republicans in the Senate have played a surprisingly wide variety of legislative and political roles. In a survey of the histories of thirty-six major pieces of legislation passed since 1969, we have identified eight broad Republican roles: policy leader, bipartisan cosponsor, contributor by amendment, collective cooperator, dissenter by amendment, obstructor/critic, filibusterer, and wallflower (see Table 12-5).

These variable roles generally transcend partisan alignments and status. They overlap temporally and even over a single piece of legislation. During consideration of the 1973 War Powers Resolution, for example, Jacob Javits of New York was a critical policy leader, credited as the author of the Senate version. Meanwhile, fellow Republicans Barry Goldwater of Arizona, Roman Hruska of Nebraska, Peter Dominick of Colorado, and John Tower of Texas played the role of obstructor/critic. Likewise, it often does not matter very much who is president or who are floor leaders. As Table 12-5 illustrates, these roles are scattered fairly evenly over the five presidencies and three floor leadership changes since 1969. Instead, policy and ideological differences seem to have more importance in determining which role a particular senator will play in the legislative process than do presidential relations or party leadership.

Table 12-5 reveals something perhaps more surprising than the variety of roles played by Republican senators. The distribution of roles over the thirty-six bills examined suggests that Republicans play a far more active and constructive role in the legislative process than their usual minority status would seem to indicate. The list of legislation under "policy leader" and "bipartisan cosponsor" is especially striking both for the numbers of bills and for their importance. These include legislation that greatly altered the powers and capacities of Congress, such as War Powers and Budget and Impoundment Control, as well as landmark policy changes affecting the environment, Social Security, international trade, taxation, civil rights, and welfare. One might expect policy leadership by Republicans when they were in the majority, but the list under cosponsorship shows that at least three critical bills during that period were introduced with Democratic partners. They were the 1983 Social Secu-

Table 12-5 Policy Roles Played by Republican Senators in Selected Pieces of Major Legislation, 1969–1991

Year	Legislation	Policy leader	Bipartisan cosponsor	Contributor by amendment	Collective cooperator	Dissenter by amendment	Obstructor/ critic	Filibusterer	Wallflower
1969	Coal Mine Safety Act					X			
1969	Environmental Policy Act								X
1969	Social Security increases								X
1969	Tax Reform Act			X					
1970	OSHA	X		X					
1970	Organized crime control		X		X				
1970	Postal Reorganization Act	X	X	X		X			
1972	Equal Employment Opportunity Act	X	X						
1972	Social Security increase (COLAs)								X
1972	Supplemental Security Income approved	X							
1972	State/local fiscal assistance								
1973	Employment and Training Act		X						
1973	War Powers Resolution	X	X				X		
1974	Budget and Impoundment Control Act	X		X	X	X	X		
1975	Energy Policy and Conservation		X		X	X			
1975	Securities Act Amendments					X			
1975	Toxic substances control	X							
1977	*Clean Air Act Amendments*							X	
1978	*Airline deregulation*					X	X		
1978	*Comprehensive energy package*						X		
1979	*Creation of Education Dept.*				X				
1980	*Depository Institutions and Monetary Control Act*			X					
1980	*Synthetic fuels program*	X					X		
1981	**Economic Recovery Tax Act**	X		X					
1982	**Tax Equity and Responsibility Act**	X							X

Legislation								
1983 **Social Security Amendments**	X	X						
1984 **Anticrime package**	X	X						X
1985 **Gramm-Rudman-Hollings**	X	X					X	
1986 Immigration reform	X		X					
1986 **Tax Reform Act**	X		X		X			
1988 Catastrophic health insurance	X							X
1988 Family Support Act (welfare reform)	X							
1988 Omnibus foreign trade measure	X	X						
1990 Clean Air Act	X					X		
1990 Deficit reduction package	X							X
1991 Civil Rights Act	X							X
Totals	18	9	8	5	8	9	1	4

Source: The list of legislation is drawn from David R. Mayhew, *Divided We Govern: Party Control, Lawmaking, and Investigations, 1946-1990* (New Haven: Yale University Press, 1991), 52-73; policy roles are drawn from descriptions in various editions of *Congressional Quarterly Almanac.*

Note: Legislation passed when Republicans were in the minority during a Republican administration is in regular type; legislation passed when Republicans were in the minority during a Democratic administration is in italic; legislation passed when Republicans were in the majority is in bold.

rity amendments, the 1984 anticrime package, and the 1985 Gramm-Rudman-Hollings amendment.

Other participatory roles include those of contributor by amendments and collective cooperator, in which both parties agree with near unanimity. This cooperation spans partisan and presidential arrangements, such as the Securities Act Amendments of 1975 (Republicans were in the minority with a Republican president), the establishment of the Department of Education in 1979 (Republicans were in the minority with a Democrat in the White House), and the anticrime package of 1984 (Republicans were in the majority under Reagan, a Republican). In the role of contributor by amendment, Republicans have a long history both in the minority and the majority of contributing to the development of legislation. A Javits amendment to the Occupational Safety and Health Act (OSHA) to establish a presidentially appointed review board proved critical to gaining passage and avoiding a Nixon veto. After long negotiations with the White House, John Heinz of Pennsylvania successfully added a provision to the 1988 catastrophic health bill to cover medical prescriptions.

Ultimately, this propensity of Republican senators to participate no matter the political circumstance may be attributed to their primary role as legislators. As members of Congress, they have a great deal invested in a productive legislative process. As politicians who gain respect, satisfaction, and power by contributing, they often feel the need to participate, not obstruct. Furthermore, they worry that consistent obstructionism would shut them out of the process altogether, a situation that often characterizes House Republicans. Thad Cochran of Mississippi points out that "Republicans are sensitive to their minority status and don't want to be completely shut out." He continues, "We're groping for ways to ensure we have .ole in the legislative process. We're not going to be content to be spectators." [19] When minority leader Dole was considering retirement in late 1991, he worried that shrinking numbers would make life in the minority discouraging. "I want to make certain that if it's going to be a minority, we're going to be a viable minority and have some influence on policy." [20] Minority members may remain in Congress year after year, despite their status, to stay near the center of events, but they do worry about being dismissed as unimportant.

Overused obstructive tactics can help to marginalize the minority even further. Abuse of the filibuster worries many of its more active practitioners, such as Paul Laxalt of Nevada. "We just don't filibuster for the hell of it around here." [21] On many occasions, perhaps most occasions, Senate Republicans seek and usually find ways to have substantive input—to play active, contributing roles—in the policy and legislative processes.

Nevertheless, Republicans also play a variety of dissenting and noncontributing roles. These roles fall along something of a continuum from dissenting participation to almost complete abstention: dissenter by amendment, obstructor/critic, filibusterer, and wallflower. As previously noted, these dissenting roles may be played by some while others in the party fulfill policy leadership and participatory roles. This complex and often contradictory matrix of role playing reveals a legislative party composed of numerous ideological factions and strong individuals.

When dissenting by amendment, Republican senators vigorously attempt to affect the policy direction set by a piece of legislation, often out of concern for their constituencies. In 1969 John Sherman Cooper of Kentucky, representing a state with significant mining interests, attempted to soften and redirect the coal mine safety bill. Democrat Don Riegle and Republican Robert Griffin, both representing Michigan, showed obvious concern for the automobile industry by fighting, if unsuccessfully, for lower auto emission standards in the 1977 Clean Air Act Amendments.

Of the many roles played by Republicans in the Senate, the most widely recognized are those that are the most aggressively resistant: obstructor/critic and filibusterer. Most often, these roles are played by conservative members. Jesse Helms of North Carolina may be the most notorious of these conservative dissenters, often pushing an agenda at odds with leaders of his own party. Majority Leader Howard Baker, full of confidence from legislative successes and high levels of party unity, was nevertheless unable to deal with the "Helms factor." Helms had tried to attach an antibusing rider to the 1975 energy and conservation bill. Riders, amendments to nonrelated bills, are a favorite obstructive tactic of conservative Republicans when in the minority. If adopted, they often serve as "killer amendments" by undermining support for the entire bill. In 1981 Mark Hatfield of Oregon, chairman of the Appropriations Committee, claimed he had Helms's promise to refrain from proposing riders because Republicans were then in the majority. Helms apparently could not help himself. In that same year he forced several divisive votes on busing and abortion that Baker wanted to avoid.

Helms does not seem to care that his amendments are frequently defeated. School prayer has never been legalized, although he has pushed for it with amendments to such legislation as the creation of the Department of Education in 1979. While Republicans were in the majority, Helms continued his strong, if doomed, policy positions against several Reagan appointees and in favor of food stamp cuts. Nevertheless, he seems comfortable in the role of obstructor/critic. He has even institutionalized this position by building a network of like-minded think tanks, political action committees, direct-mail organizations, and lobbying groups.[22]

The filibuster may represent the ultimate tool of dissension. Unique to the Senate, filibusters are talkathons designed to delay, to frustrate, and often to derail legislation. A minority of one can gain enormous leverage over a majority of ninety-nine. Orrin Hatch of Utah argues that the tactic has a corrective effect. "The filibuster rule is the only way the majority of the people, who are represented by a minority in the Senate, can be heard." [23] Whether or not Hatch is right, James Madison and his fellow authors of the Constitution were clearly concerned about the rights of the minority; the filibuster strongly supports that concern. Curiously, of the thirty-six pieces of legislation studied, the only successful example of this tactic is Utah senator Jake Garn's filibuster of the Clean Air Act Amendments in 1976. This paucity of examples may reflect the concern

Republicans have of being shut out if they overuse dissenting devices. More likely, Republicans usually decide that their policy and ideological concerns can be more constructively advanced if they play participatory roles, roles demanding viable policy input. Except for the wallflower role—in which Republicans seem to have disappeared temporarily from the process—any other role would be more constructive, involved, and participatory than the role of filibusterer.

Our role typology for Senate Republicans intentionally has two conspicuous gaps—the roles of follower and of presidential proxy. The modern Senate has been a particularly difficult body to lead, given its individualistic, nonhierarchical structure and the absence of institutional mechanisms for demanding or even encouraging party loyalty.[24] Although most studies have focused on Democratic floor leadership, our survey of important legislation supports a similar conclusion for Republican leaders. Floor leaders gave active, substantive attention to very few of the bills listed in Table 12-5, though leaders always play a critical scheduling role. As noted, Dole played both facilitative and scheduling roles for the Civil Rights Act of 1991. The 1990 Budget Agreement is an important exception to more typical and lower substantive input by leaders. There, both Majority Leader George J. Mitchell of Maine and Minority Leader Dole were heavily involved in negotiating and developing an initial budget proposal. The defeat of the proposal in the House left the leaders as much bewildered as defeated.

Instead, formal leadership of Senate Republicans has been limited in influence to periods of intense partisanship or of clear policy mandates. Republicans have been forced to be opportunists, exploiting circumstances when they seem favorable. Howard Baker's experience as majority leader from 1981 to 1985 serves as a good example of Republicans being at the mercy of the elements. Nevertheless, because of the leadership's control over scheduling, we cannot characterize leaders as being completely marginalized even in the most adverse circumstances.

Baker became majority leader when the Senate switched to Republican control after the 1980 election. During 1981, the Republicans' first year in the majority, Baker enjoyed the giddy unity of a party finally granted institutional power with an apparent policy mandate shared with President Reagan. Baker stood at the helm of a party with sixteen freshmen. The last time Republicans had so many freshmen, after the 1946 election, they also gained the majority. Except for the run-ins with Helms discussed earlier, Baker had strong support from his fellow Republicans, who at first were willing to give the president's agenda priority.

But the praise Baker received began to fade after 1981 as challenges came from all quarters. At first grateful for Baker's easy-going tolerance, members could no longer resist abusing their privileges. Absenteeism rose, committee chairs became impatient and sought to push their own agendas, and ideological factions began to emerge. Conservatives pressed for attention. to their social policy concerns and several of them, particularly Laxalt and James McClure of Idaho, emerged as possible rivals to Baker's own leadership position. Simultaneously, moderates formed a caucus of sorts and felt free to vote as a bloc against their party, giving Democrats a working majority on several issues. Baker quickly learned that large numbers may produce majority status, but maintaining discipline and unity becomes difficult.

A second role missing from our typology is that of presidential proxy. To fulfill this role, Senate Republicans would seek to advance and secure passage of the president's legislative and policy agenda. Given that Republicans have lived in the White House for all but four years since 1969, such a role for Senate Republicans would seem natural. Turning again to 'Table 12-5, we see that Republicans in the Senate do play the proxy role with some regularity. Baker introduced the Nixon administration version of the 1972 state and local fiscal assistance bill. The 1984 anticrime package was strongly pushed by Reagan; these crime bills were cosponsored by Republicans Laxalt and Thurmond with Democrats Joseph Biden of Delaware and Edward Kennedy. Even when in the minority, Senate Republicans generally have a strong personal and policy affinity with a Republican president. As previously noted, Senate Republicans more consistently support the president than do House Republicans. Perhaps presidents return the favor by giving Senate Republicans greater substantive policy input. House Republicans rarely experience an affinity with the president, perhaps because they are so far from gaining a majority of seats. Senate Republicans have held an average of 44.8 percent of seats since 1969, while House Republicans have held less than 40 percent. This greater competitive advantage has made a difference in the attention and respect Republican senators receive from the president and from the Democrats.

This is not to say that Senate Republicans are there to do the president's bidding. The policy process in the two houses of Congress has a life and dynamic independent of the president. Issues and legislation may be discussed and reintroduced for years, as presidents come and go, before blossoming with enough support to reach enactment. The president is but one actor, albeit a powerful one, in an ongoing process. Many of the thirty-six pieces of legislation examined were developed with pointed disregard of the president and his concerns. And, in fact, Republicans played critical policy leadership roles in two pieces of legislation—the War Powers Resolution of 1973 and the Budget and Impoundment Control Act of 1974—that directly limited presidential power, while a Republican, Richard Nixon, held the office. Senate Republicans filled equally critical roles in the Tax Reform Act of 1986 and the Family Support Act of 1988 (welfare reform). Reagan may have provided legislators with critical ideological cues as to the general shape he wished these bills to have, but Republicans were more than willing and capable of handling the legislative details and negotiations on their own.

Republicans in the Senate have benefited from the freedom and power afforded by majority status. Even in the minority, however, they continue to have the resources, the access, and the desire to choose among constructive lawmaking activities. Specific roles may not be dictated by partisan status, but the reality or proximity of becoming the majority party lends the Republican party greater legitimacy and authority in the Senate than it does in the House. When we couple this vantage with the individualistic traditions and prestige of the Senate, we begin to understand why Senate Republicans have greater discretion to play various policy roles than do their House colleagues. They have a choice, a freedom they exercise in a wide variety of political and policy circumstances. Members of the House have not been so lucky.

Veto Politics

No discussion of congressional Republicans would be complete without mentioning their role in sustaining presidential vetoes. For a president facing congressional majorities, the veto is an important tool for two important reasons. First, it permits him to thwart the policy initiatives of those majorities. Second, it enables him to have a greater effect on legislation by threatening the veto in advance of passage.

Vital to these uses of the veto is the president's capacity to maintain sufficient unity within his own party that his action will not be overridden. All that is required to sustain a veto is one-third of the members plus one. But there are times when that number is not easily attained. Furthermore, sustaining vetoes is basically unsatisfying work. Legislators are put in the position of supporting a negative proposition, not to mention that they must bear the criticism of having thwarted a majority. The process can become downright tiresome when the majority Democrats pass legislation they know will be vetoed, thereby forcing Republicans to sustain the president's action—all done in order to develop a campaign issue to use against the president and his congressional party.

Table 12-6 summarizes the vetoes by Republican presidents since 1969. (Pocket vetoes are not included.) The record shows the power of the weapon. Nixon, Reagan, and Bush had only 15 of 100 vetoes overridden (15 percent). Ford's case clearly reflects his weakened position as an unelected president and his party's weakened state. (The Republicans had less than one-third of the House seats and only slightly more than one-third of the Senate seats.) Just over one-fourth of Ford's vetoes were overridden. Perhaps more remarkable, however, is that 9 of his vetoes—nearly one-fourth—were sustained in the House (3 of these were initially overridden in the Senate).

Bush's record is remarkable. He exercised the veto power with considerable skill and had only one of his vetoes overridden. In all but the one case, he succeeded in having the veto sustained even when that outcome was not predicted from the original vote in each body. Consequently, Bush's record enhanced his influence through the mere threat of a veto. Rep. Vic Fazio, D-Calif., made this observation: "We have fallen into the trap of thinking that if we don't have a two-thirds vote we should do nothing." On the other hand, some Democrats concluded that they might just as well send bills to the president to define differences on issues. Sen. John Kerry, D-Mass., had this to say about the president's use of the veto: "If he intends to veto everything, we ought to put out things that demonstrate the differences between him and us. You're going to see more of that." [25]

Table 12-6 Congressional Action on Vetoes by Republican Presidents, 1969-1992

President	Number of vetoes[a]	Sustained		Overridden			No effort
		House	Senate	House	Senate	Both	
Nixon (1969-1972)	13	3	4	1	0	4	2
Nixon (1973-1974)	11	5	4	0	2	1	1
Ford (1974-1976)	42	9	6	4	3	11	16
Reagan (1981-1984)	18	2	1	0	0	4	11
Reagan (1985-1988)	21	2	2	1	0	5	12
Bush (1989-1992)	37[b]	11	10	5	2	1	14
Totals	142	32	27	11	7	26	57

Source: Calculated from various editions of *Congressional Quarterly Almanac.*

[a] The number shows regular vetoes, not pocket vetoes.

[b] The tax bill that Bush vetoed shortly after the 102d Congress adjourned was not considered a pocket veto; it is included in this figure but is not included in the column labeled "no effort."

No doubt veto politics will continue to be featured in divided government. The veto is a potent weapon in the partisan battle between the White House and Congress. And it places a significant burden on the Republicans—particularly those in the House who, as we have shown, have fewer policy options as individual members and therefore do not welcome the essentially negative posture of confirming a "no."

Conclusion

A spate of books and articles recently have drawn attention to divided government. Most of these works focus on why this condition persists, how it works, and how it might be changed. Study of the various components of this new politics is to be recommended. As we have shown in this essay, the Republican party operates under different conditions and performs different functions in the House and the Senate. House Republicans live in a frustrating political and policy world. They have ample resources to serve their constituencies and therefore are reelected at respectable rates. But they play minimal roles in lawmaking, while being called on to defend Republican presidents, support legislative bargains reached between presidents and congressional Democrats, and sustain presidential vetoes. Many look longingly to the Senate where they observe former colleagues enjoying a more rewarding political life than the one they have.

Senate Republicans have been in a competitive position much of the time since 1969, and they have had the chance to serve in the majority during three Congresses. Thus the naturally greater opportunities for individual influence in the smaller chamber are enhanced by the experience of having been in charge. A review of major legislation shows the impressive variety of policy roles that Republican senators can play even when in the minority.

A permanent congressional minority can be rejuvenated only through a turnover of members. Yet experience is required for a minority to play a meaningful role in the lawmaking process. Congressional Republicans may be able to win only if they have a coherent policy message, as the Conservative Opportunity Society argues. But it is difficult to promote such a message without an occasional legislative success. It is said that House Republicans can win a majority only if they get better candidates.[26] Yet recruiting able candidates for an unrewarding career is difficult. Having realized a breakthrough in the Senate, Republicans perhaps can hope that the House will continue to serve as a good training and recruiting base for the Senate. As for the House, Republicans may have to depend on redistricting and an anti-incumbent mood in the electorate to produce the long hoped for majority.

Notes

1. By the president's own account in Ronald Reagan, *An American Life* (New York: Simon and Schuster, 1990), 221-222.
2. Both chambers smashed previous records. House Democrats earlier served in the minority for sixteen years (1895-1911), as did House Republicans (1931-1947). Senate Democrats twice served in the minority for eighteen years (1861-1879 and 1895-1913).
3. See David W. Rohde, *Parties and Leaders in the Postreform House* (Chicago: University of Chicago Press, 1991), chap. 3; and Steven S. Smith, *Call to Order: Floor Politics in the House and Senate* (Washington, D.C.: Brookings Institution, 1989).
4. Smith, *Call to Order,* 86.
5. Adam Clymer, "To Republicans' Ire, Bush's Tax Package Advances in House," *New York Times,* Feb. 13, 1992, A1.
6. Quoted in ibid, D8.
7. Robert L. Peabody, *Leadership in Congress* (Boston: Little, Brown, 1976), 105.
8. Quoted in Clifford Krauss, "Gingrich Takes No Prisoners as Attacks Sink House Bank," *New York Times,* March 17, 1992, C23.
9. Janet Hook, "Gingrich Selection as Whip Reflects GOP Discontent," *Congressional Quarterly Weekly Report,* March 25, 1989, 625.
10. Rohde, *Parties and Leaders in the Postreform House,* 128.
11. Quoted in ibid., 128. Former minority leader John J. Rhodes of Arizona reported this statement by O'Neill. Rhodes also quoted O'Neill as saying, "The people gave us the mandate and we're not going to give it up." John J. Rhodes, *The Futile System* (Garden City, N.Y.: EPM Publications, 1976), 33.
12. Nixon especially regretted this act as it related to impoundment controls. See Richard M. Nixon, *In the Arena: A Memoir of Victory, Defeat, and Renewal* (New York: Simon and Schuster, 1990), 206.
13. Rohde confirms this point in *Parties and Leaders in the Postreform House,* chap. 5.
14. William Connelly, Jr., "The House Republican Policy Committee: Then and Now" (Paper presented at the annual meeting of the American Political Science Association, Washington, D.C., September 1989), 18. Actually, the increase began in 1975 with the substantial loss of Republican seats in 1974.
15. Quoted in Hubert Bruce Fuller, *The Speakers of the House* (Boston: Little, Brown, 1909), 231.
16. Quoted in David Lauter, "Rush of Events Broke Rights Bill Impasse," *Los Angeles Times,* Oct. 26, 1991, A1.
17. Quoted in ibid. and with description by Lauter.

18. Peabody, *Leadership in Congress*, 433.
19. Quoted in Janet Hook, "Senate GOP Flexes Muscles of the Minority," *Congressional Quarterly Weekly Report*, May 23, 1987, 1061.
20. Quoted in Ronald Elving, "As Hope for Senate Control Fades, GOP Still Looks for Gains," *Congressional Quarterly Weekly Report*, Nov. 9, 1991, 3306.
21. Quoted in "Dusting Off the Filibuster," *Congressional Quarterly Weekly Report*, Aug. 5, 1978, 2023.
22. Irwin Arieff, Nadine Cohodas, and Richard Whittle, "Sen. Helms Builds a Machine of Interlinked Organizations to Shape Both Politics, Policy," *Congressional Quarterly Weekly Report*, March 6, 1982, 499.
23. Quoted in "Dusting Off the Filibuster."
24. See Ralph K. Huitt, "Democratic Party Leadership in the Senate," *American Political Science Review* 55 (June 1961): 331-344; Roger H. Davidson, "The Senate: If Everybody Leads, Who Follows?" in *Congress Reconsidered*, 4th ed., ed. Lawrence C. Dodd and Bruce I. Oppenheimer (Washington, D.C.: CQ Press, 1989), 275-305; Samuel C. Patterson, "Party Leadership in the U. S. Senate," *Legislative Studies Quarterly* 14 (August 1989): 393-414.
25. Both quotes in Janet Hook, "President's Mastery of Veto Perplexes Hill Democrats," *Congressional Quarterly Weekly Report*, July 27, 1991, 2041, 2045.
26. Gary C. Jacobson, *The Electoral Origins of Divided Government* (Boulder: Westview Press, 1990), 102.

13

Deliberation: An Untimed Value in a Timed Game

George E. Connor and Bruce I. Oppenheimer

In 1924, as the House began consideration of HR 6820, the naval appropriation bill, Rep. Burton French, R-Idaho, asked and received unanimous consent "that the time be equally divided between the gentleman from South Carolina and myself, without agreement as to time." [1] *The subsequent debate consumed twenty and one-half hours, of which nine and one-half hours were spent in general debate and the remainder on amendments. Similarly, debate on the appropriation for the War Department (HR 7877) took twenty-one hours, of which general debate comprised seven hours. Combined, these bills funded military operations for the fiscal year. In 1979 the corresponding bill, the Department of Defense appropriation (HR 5359), required only seven hours, just two of them for general debate. Despite the fact that HR 5359 was a more complex and expensive appropriation than those passed sixty-five years earlier, deliberation on the House floor lasted about one-sixth as long.*

Most complex organizations face the problem of how to deal with conflicting goals. Congress is no exception. In an effort to perform a range of functions and to preserve democratic values, Congress must address goals that at times compete with each other. A few examples will clearly illustrate the dilemma: (1) House members (and senators to a lesser extent) are expected to represent and voice the views of local constituencies in the national arena, but they are also expected to develop policies in the national interest; (2) Congress is expected to resolve conflicts, and in doing so it should foster majority rule yet protect the rights of minorities; (3) Congress is expected to respond flexibly to the needs of the country and its citizens yet ensure that its decisions are made wisely and only after careful deliberation.

These goals do not necessarily conflict, but the potential for conflict is evident. And a consideration of more of the goals and expectations of Congress—to make laws, be representative, work efficiently, be deliberative, act wisely, be responsive, oversee the executive branch, avoid meddling—sensitizes one to the potential for contradiction of purpose.

Through much of its history Congress has had one crucial resource that has made dealing with conflicting goals possible. That resource is time. Congress could deal with its workload in the available time. Several factors affect the use of time in Congress. First, many policy problems in the past did not seem urgent. It has been suggested that American society was normally tolerant of stalemate when decisions could not be reached. Thus Congress was not often placed in the position of having to rush to uncover a legislative solution. Second, the range, number, and complexity of issues with which Congress and the national government were expected to deal were more limited. Clearly, the role of the national government in the economy, health care, education, environmental concerns, energy, and civil rights (not to mention a range of new defense and foreign policy concerns) has primarily developed in the post-World War II era. And making good legislative policy decisions on many of these issues requires expertise.

Until the 1960s Congress normally could complete its work with four to five months remaining in the calendar year. Without pressures of time and workload, the potential for conflict in underlying values and expectations was reduced. Congress could get through its legislative program and thus appear relatively responsive and efficient; yet there was time available to listen to one more speech or give careful consideration to one more amendment. There was time to deal with the parochial concerns of members from diverse constituencies through private bills and public works programs, thus allowing more national attention to be given to important issues of broad concern. This does not mean that there was no conflict of values or that the public viewed Congress as unflawed. What it does mean is that the ample time available gave the institution the leeway to cope with competing expectations.

By the early 1970s this leeway had disappeared. Since then, Congress has normally operated from January through December. Many bills do not pass because there is not sufficient time to get them through the process, not because a majority of representatives or a majority of senators oppose their passage. The legislative game, which had been for all practical purposes an untimed game, has become a timed game. And some democratic values have been sacrificed in an effort to meet others.

Midway through the second session of the 96th Congress, Robert G. Byrd, D-W.Va., then Senate majority leader, discussed the workload and time problems of the Senate in explaining why he was pushing for cloture on a piece of legislation:

> Only 60 working days remain for Senate floor activity, excluding Saturdays— and, of necessity, there undoubtedly will be some Saturdays on which the Senate will have to be in session. . . . On Tuesday, when the vote occurs on cloture, only 57 working days will be remaining after that day. . . .
>
> So, with only that limited time remaining and with 50 authorization bills dealing with expiring authorization . . . yet to be taken up, the first concurrent budget resolution yet having to be resolved, at least one supplemental appropriation bill, 13 general appropriation bills, and a number of other measures, it is obvious that the Senate cannot delay action on any of these measures and expect to get its work done prior to October.[2]

Byrd's prediction proved accurate. After recessing for the election, the Senate returned in mid-November and did not finish its work until December 16.

In this essay we examine how the changing workload of Congress and corresponding time constraints have affected one democratic value that resides at the heart of legislatures: deliberation.

Why Is Deliberation Valuable?

Although deliberation is not specified in the classic triumvirate of popular sovereignty, majority rule, and political equality, it has always been a crucial component of democratic theory. Furthermore, "the idea of government by deliberative process had been central to the American political tradition since the early 1600s." [3] We find it useful to divide the concept of deliberation into two components: interinstitutional deliberation and intrainstitutional deliberation.

Interinstitutional deliberation can be seen very clearly in the constitutional design of checks and balances, separation of powers, and bicameralism. These three features were "recognized as a means of making legislative action more deliberate." [4] Defined in terms of slow, purposeful action, interinstitutional deliberation can be regarded as one of the "fundamental and enduring values ... of a constitutional democratic state." [5] This form of deliberation is familiar to most students of American politics. But there is a second, less familiar type of deliberation that is more important to the deliberative functioning of legislatures like the U.S. House of Representatives and the U.S. Senate: intrainstitutional deliberation.

Intrainstitutional deliberation can be defined as rational discussion tempered by reasoned debate. It has been argued that internal processes "that depend on compromise and concurrence" complement "substantive principles of natural rights, consent, and limited and balanced power." [6] Steven Smith distinguishes between debate, "a verbal contest between people of opposing views," and deliberation, "reasoning together about the nature of a problem and solutions to it." [7] For purposes of this analysis, and because it is difficult to tell when deliberation leaves off and debate begins, we prefer to subsume both of Smith's categories under the heading of intrainstitutional deliberation. Although both forms of deliberation have consequences for democratic government, intrainstitutional deliberation is of primary interest to us in this essay. This is because intrainstitutional deliberation serves three important functions in democratic theory—inclusiveness, avoidance of error, and legitimacy.

In Book VII of the *Politics*, Aristotle maintained that for matters of "public interest" a deliberative body was essential. He advocated an inclusive body because "the results of deliberation are better when all deliberate together." [8] Elaborating on Aristotle's doctrine, John Stuart Mill asserted that

> the only way in which a human being can make some approach to knowing the whole of a subject, is by hearing what can be said about it by all persons of every variety of opinion, and studying all modes in which it can be looked at by every character of mind.[9]

For the Founders the issue of inclusiveness was raised with respect to the size of the legislative districts. Although seeking to avoid the " 'confusion and intemperance of the multitude,'" Madison argued that "the House should be large enough to ensure 'free consultation and discussion.'"[10] Inclusion, in turn, fosters the two other purposes of deliberation.

Because of its inclusive character, deliberation serves as a means of avoiding error. Mill contends that deliberation assists the government in its duty "to form the truest opinions [it] can. . . . There is the greatest difference between presuming an opinion to be true, because, with every opportunity for contesting it, it has not been refuted, and assuming its truth for the purpose of not permitting its refutation."[11] For Alexander Hamilton, "the oftener a measure is brought under examination, the greater the diversity in the situation of those who are to examine it, the less must be the danger of those errors which flow from want of due deliberation."[12]

With respect to the length of House terms, the Federalists recognized that "making deliberation possible cannot itself make members of Congress deliberate." By advocating two-year terms, the Federalists asserted that "for the whole process to work, members must look forward and deliberate with each other—an impossibility if every moment is spent looking over the shoulder at the home constituency."[13] Intrainstitutional deliberation, then, affords the legislature with a democratically conceived process for arriving at the "truest opinions."

By distinguishing between majority rule as an outcome and majority rule as a process, Elaine Spitz illuminates the linkage between deliberation and its third function, legitimacy. Why don't minority members "take their ball and go home"? Spitz suggests:

> The intrinsic goodness of the majority decision rule depends on the bonds within the group using it, and on an operational procedure that encourages the participation of all, excludes no one arbitrarily, and provides for a mutual exchange of views.

According to Spitz, the function of discussion is

> to facilitate the articulation of interests; to encourage understanding of diverse positions; to permit estimates of the intensity of preferences and the likelihood of resistance; to prod everyone toward an accommodation with opponents; and finally, to promote a temporary, viable, peaceful agreement.[14]

"The ultimate result of the discussion process," Spitz argues in the words of Ernest Barker, "is opinion based on modifications or adjustments that attempt to do justice to all points of view, and an opinion thereby entitled to ask the greatest concession of acceptance or toleration by all."[15] Intrainstitutional deliberation serves a legitimizing function because it provides a vehicle for conflict to be diffused, for consensus to develop, and for legislative decisions to be accepted broadly.

Deliberation in Operation

It is one thing to expound on a democratic value in theory and quite another to put it into operation and keep it working. Joseph Cooper in *The Origins of the*

Standing Committees and the Development of the Modern House describes and analyzes how tension between theory and practice grew. In the First Congress, the primacy of deliberation was clearly accepted. It was the practice that "subjects ought to be referred to a Committee of the Whole so that their principles could be determined." Permission even to introduce legislation was given "only after the subject had been discussed and determined by the whole House, preferably in a Committee of the Whole if the subject was at all important." [16]

Practical considerations required adjustments in this routine. As the House membership grew and the number of measures before it increased, concern developed with the increased tendency of the House to rely on the executive. By the Fourth Congress adherence to Committee of the Whole discussion as a prerequisite for lawmaking activity had begun to slip, and "the stringency and hold of traditional notions declined as the years passed."

> Members simply ceased to believe that rational deliberation and majority rule were dependent on a free or unstructured process of interchange among roughly equal members, that differential distributions of influence stemming from structural or institutional arrangements were evil.[17]

Of course, deliberation did not disappear. But as the nineteenth century progressed, the combined effect of an increasing workload and a growing membership brought additional restrictions—growing dependence on standing committees and limitations on floor debate. Other functional needs of the institution placed constraints on the norm of deliberation. These constraints, however, ought to be viewed within the broader context. There were no serious time problems, and deliberation could survive, even if it no longer flourished on the House floor.

The 1900s and the Progressive Critique

As part of their efforts to reform governmental processes, the Progressives and reform-minded political scientists critiqued the internal operations of the House of Representatives. Woodrow Wilson was clearly the most prominent of these. His book *Congressional Government* is noteworthy for its attack on the committee system and the consequent shifting of "the theatre of debate upon legislation from the floor of Congress to the privacy of the committee-rooms." Although Wilson was critical of deliberation in "small sections," he focused on the amount of time spent processing legislation:

> Time would fail it [Congress] to discuss all the bills brought in, for they every session number thousands; and it is to be doubted whether, even if time allowed, the ordinary processes of debate and amendment would suffice to sift the chaff from the wheat in the bushels of bills every week piled upon the clerk's desk.

Wilson concluded that "it is impossible for Congress to do wisely what it does so hurriedly." [18]

Echoing Wilson's theme of "disintegration," Rep. William Cockran, D-

N.Y., noted that "the House had fallen to the level of the electoral college," where "members vote in silence," and instead of deliberation and debate, "imaginary contributions are inserted into the Record." [19] Developing this critique of the quality of legislative decisions, political scientist Lindsay Rogers contended in a 1920 article in the *American Political Science Review:* "Judged by the legislative grist, Congress spends an astonishing proportion of its time on picayune matters, to say nothing of the private legislation, which is, by all odds, the chief interest of many members." Rogers in a subsequent article summarized the Progressive critique with reference to the 68th Congress, noting the tension between the ideal of deliberation and the functional realities of the modern House. "There was raised in an acute form a question which is difficult in any legislative assembly: how to square the necessity for certainty and a time table in legislative business with due notice to members and freedom of discussion." [20]

Our research indicates that although Rogers and others were correct in noting the rise of special orders, the increased usage of suspension of the rules, and the general decline of deliberation in the House, they erred by analyzing deliberation as a discrete rather than a continuous variable. As we shall see by today's standards, the House of the 1920s, and even the House of the 1950s, operated in an atmosphere normally unconstrained by time and workload pressure. This historical perspective is essential if we are to develop an accurate portrayal of the role played by deliberation in legislative processes.

House Floor Deliberation in Three Congresses

Writing in 1919, Rogers set forth a challenge that fits nicely with our concern about time and deliberation. He observed:

> In connection with this question of legislative procedure an investigation of how Congress spends its time would be very interesting. It is well enough to point out the delays on various measures, but what is done in the meanwhile? An investigator studying the *Congressional Record* with this purpose in view would have an exceedingly tedious and enervating task, but the results would be very valuable.[21]

Like Rogers, we ask how Congress spends its time and to what extent deliberation has been sacrificed to the explosion of the congressional workload. And what have the consequences been? To investigate these questions, we examined in detail the floor activities of the House of Representatives in three Congresses using information gathered from the *Congressional Record*. We selected the 68th (1923-1925), the 84th (1955-1957), and the 96th (1979-1981) Congresses. Although the selection is somewhat arbitrary, these Congresses have certain similarities. They were free of major upheavals (such as wars or depressions). They came in the second half of presidential terms—of Coolidge, Eisenhower, and Carter, respectively. They occurred at relatively evenly spaced intervals, and they all postdate the Budget and Accounting Act of 1921, which established the modern appropriations process. Finally, it can be argued that they all demonstrated some unity of government control. Coolidge and Carter

Table 13-1 Use of Time in Three Congresses

Congress/ Session	Opening date	Closing date	Days meeting	Hours meeting	Mean hours per day	No. of bills
68th Cong., 1st sess.	12-6-23	6-7-24	139	794	5:43	52
68th Cong., 2d sess.	12-3-24	3-4-25	69	369	5:21	41
Total 68th Cong.			208	1,163	5:35	93
84th Cong., 1st sess.	1-22-55	9-2-55	91	454	4:59	76
84th Cong., 2d sess.	1-18-56	7-27-56	101	451	4:28	91
Total 84th Cong.			192	905	4:43	167
96th Cong., 1st sess.	1-15-79	12-20-79	155	956	6:10	122
96th Cong., 2d sess.	1-22-80	12-16-80	146	907	6:13	89
Total 96th Cong.			301	1,863	6:11	211

Source: Compiled by the authors from the *Congressional Record,* appropriate years.

operated with their parties in control of the Congress, and Eisenhower had a functional majority with the conservative coalition, although the Democrats were the majority party during the 84th Congress.

Our purpose in examining House floor activity in these three Congresses is to understand better the House's reaction to changes in workload and time pressures and the implication of those changes for the ability of the House to engage in deliberation. To begin, it is useful to compare some general indicators of workload and use of time in the three Houses. The data in Table 13-1 are revealing. In terms of session length, the 96th Congress is very different from the two earlier ones. Both of its sessions ran nearly the entire year. Neither of the sessions in either the 68th or 84th Congresses lasted much more than seven months. Three of the four sessions could have been extended; only the lame duck 68th Congress, second session, had to make way for a new Congress. In fact, at the end of the first session of the 68th Congress, a few House members urged that the body not adjourn.[22]

The difference in session lengths is reflected in the number of days the House met as well. The 96th House met on about 50 percent more days than the 68th and 84th did (excluded from these totals are pro forma meetings, those that last less than forty minutes). The contrast is even clearer when one examines the number of hours the Houses met. The 1,863 hours of House meetings in the 96th Congress are more than double the total of the 84th and 60 percent greater than that of the 68th. Equally surprising is that the House in the 68th Congress actually was in session for more hours than the House in the 84th. In addition, the daily meetings during the 96th Congress were the longest of the three. On average, daily meetings exceeded six hours in both sessions.

Two other facets regarding time matters are worth noting. First, except for Christmas breaks, the 68th House met nearly every day other than Sundays for regular legislative business. There were no recesses for trips home to the district. Second, the House floor in the 96th Congress took more than a month before it considered "regular legislation," while the 68th and 84th had regular legislation on the floor almost immediately.[23] This change reflects the growing dependence of the floor on committees—and, by the 96th Congress, on subcommittees—for legislative work.

The last column in Table 13-1 is a single indicator of workload, the number of pieces of legislation considered under regular legislative procedures. It demonstrates an increase across the three Congresses and suggests a significant growth in workload. Clearly, the indicator does not include all legislation nor does it indicate anything about the complexity of the legislation under consideration.

These data suggest that there has been a marked increase in the workload of the House of Representatives. As late as the 1950s the increase could be handled without corresponding increases in the length of sessions. But by the 96th Congress, the House was operating year round in an effort to complete its work.

Shortening General Debate

One area of adjustment to compensate for the growing workload of the House floor has been in the time allowed for general debate. General debate occurs before a bill is considered for amendment. For regular legislation such time is provided by rule, unanimous consent, or otherwise specified. Table 13-2 presents data on the distribution and mean of general debate time for three Congresses. In the 68th Congress on average a bill was allowed slightly more than 3 hours of general debate. General debate time had dropped to under 2 hours by the 84th Congress and to 1.59 hours by the 96th. Actually, the change has been greater than these figures reveal. Nearly all the bills in the 96th Congress that were given 6 hours or more of general debate were ones on which the House was bound under existing law to provide lengthy general debate. These included legislation related to the Budget and Impoundment Control Act and to the Trade Act. But the time allotted was not completely used. For example, in considering the Trade Act Amendments of 1979 (HR 4537), the House was required by the Trade Act of 1974 to provide 20 hours of general debate. In fact, the House consumed only 4 hours and 25 minutes. If we remove these exceptional cases in calculating the mean for general debate in the 96th Congress, the time drops to about 1.5 hours. Generally, the House in the 96th Congress allowed for more than a single hour of general debate only for bills that had been referred to more than one committee—each committee had to be allowed time in general debate.

This general debate indicator is the best representation of Steven Smith's conceptualization of deliberation. It has clearly been one of the areas of floor activity that has been sacrificed as the House has attempted to cope with the demands of work and the constraints of time.

Because of problems in determining the amount of time consumed by voting on amendments in the three Congresses, we shall not attempt to com-

Table 13-2   Hours Allotted for General Debate in Three Congresses

No. of hours	Number of bills		
	68th Congress	84th Congress	96th Congress
1.0 or fewer	21	83	141
1.5	2	2	7
2.0	36	47	31
2.5	2	2	0
3.0	9	12	7
4.0-5.0	10	14	3
6.0-10.0	8	7	4
More than 10	4	0	1
Avg. per bill	3.13 hours	1.88 hours	1.59 hours

Source: Compiled by the authors from the *Congressional Record,* appropriate years.

pare the time used in this part of bill consideration. The comparison of appropriation bills with which this essay began suggests that change has occurred. Moreover, we can find few instances of House members in either the 68th or the 84th Congress expressing frustration with the use of time or with extended amending periods. The same cannot be said about the 96th Congress. For example, after nearly four and one-half hours of debate on HR 3930, the Defense Production Act Amendments, Speaker Thomas P. O'Neill, Jr., D-Mass., interrupted the proceedings to complain: "It is my understanding from the members of the committee that when this bill came out of committee, 39 to 1, that it would be through the House in a couple of hours. It is necessary that we complete this bill." [24]

Increased Use of Suspension of the Rules

Another way the House has responded to workload and time problems has been to use suspension of the rules for floor consideration of legislation. Under suspension of the rules, floor debate is limited to forty minutes on a piece of legislation. Although the procedure requires a two-thirds vote for passage of an item, it significantly limits the amount of floor time that will be consumed. The procedure was available in all three Congresses. The frequency with which suspension of the rules was used changed modestly between the 68th and 84th Congresses, from 47 bills to 69 bills. In the 96th Congress, however, the House considered 397 pieces of legislation under suspension of the rules. This indicates, first, how much the workload of the House has grown; second, how precious floor time has become; and, third, how willing the House has become to sacrifice deliberation in the face of time and workload pressures.

Decrease in Private Bills

One auxiliary change in House floor activity that reflects an effort to cope with the growing workload problem has been the decline in the private calendar. Private bills, those introduced by House members to address the problems of particular parties, were once an important part of congressional activity. (In legislatures outside the United States private bills remain an important responsibility for the members.) Private bills normally dealt with subjects such as individual immigration problems, exceptions from specialized tariff duties, and resolution of civil claims. It was one way House members could demonstrate attentiveness to their constituents.

In the 68th Congress the House passed 378 private bills, and in the 84th Congress it passed 1,105. But despite the attention that House members are credited with giving to constituent problems in recent years, the House passed only 125 private bills in the 96th Congress. There simply is no longer any time available for the House as an institution to devote to these matters. Although the decline in private bills does not reflect on deliberation, it does offer additional evidence of changes in time constraints. Floor time is in short supply. There is little time for general debate, even on major issues. Relatively uncontroversial bills are taken up under suspension of the rules. And private bills are an endangered legislative species.

Can Deliberation Occur
If No One Is There to Listen?

Both the House as an institution and its individual members have been affected by the growth in the workload. In addition to increased floor activities, members are faced with more committee and subcommittee meetings to attend, larger office staffs to manage, an increased number of trips home to the district, a growing interest group community seeking access, a flood of information to read and digest, more constituents in Washington, and an escalating need to raise campaign funds, among other things.

Realizing the impossibility of being several places at the same time, House members have chosen to spend less time on the House floor. Our evidence of this change comes from an examination of division votes. Unlike roll call votes, for which bells ring in the House side of the Capitol and in the office buildings so that members have time to get to the floor and cast their votes, division votes come without warning and offer no grace period. Members are simply asked to stand and be counted on each side of the issue under consideration. Accordingly, division votes are a good measure of how many members are present on the House floor during debate.

In Table 13-3 are the data for division vote participation in the three Congresses. We had expected to find a steady decline in floor attendance from the 68th to the 84th to the 96th Congress because we thought that floor attendance would drop as workload increased. The fact that more members voted on divi-

Table 13-3 Attendance for Division Votes in Three Congresses

Congress/ Session	No. of division votes	Mean no. of members voting
68th Cong., 1st sess.	435	130
68th Cong., 2d sess.	202	116
84th Cong., 1st sess.	106	165
84th Cong., 2d sess.	93	150
96th Cong., 1st sess.	225	72
96th Cong., 2d sess.	113	68

Source: Compiled by the authors from *Congressional Record,* appropriate years.

sions in the 84th Congress than in the 68th leads us to offer two possible explanations. First, in the concentrated sessions of the 68th Congress—without recesses and with Friday, Saturday, and Monday meetings—and with the slowness of cross-country transportation, House members absent from Washington for one reason or another were bound to miss votes. By the 84th Congress, sessions were not as concentrated, and a member could leave Washington, D.C., on Thursday evening and return by Tuesday morning without missing many votes. Second, there is every indication that the legislative workload of the 84th Congress was heavier than that of the 68th. But there is little evidence that the workload exceeded the time available to the House as an institution. Sessions ran only about seven months. Suspension of the rules was used infrequently. And there was plenty of time to deal with a large private calendar. Daily floor sessions averaged fewer than five hours. For the most part, the congressional game was still an untimed one. In that environment House members, too, had less hectic schedules and more time to spend on the House floor.

What is more striking in Table 13-3 is the drop in House floor attendance by the 96th Congress. For division votes, on average, only about one in six House members were present. True, by the late 1970s members could watch the proceedings on television in their offices—yet there is no indication that televising the House has affected floor attendance.

The drop in floor attendance has two implications, aside from demonstrating the effect of competing activities for the attention of House members. Both deal with deliberation. First, if floor debate occurs when few members are on the floor to listen to it or engage in it, can deliberation and the functions it fosters—inclusiveness, error avoidance, and legitimacy—be well served? Of course, deliberation may occur elsewhere, in a committee or subcommittee, for example. In those arenas, however, discussion involves a limited number of not always representative participants. Members active on committees are, in fact, the ones most likely to be on the floor as well. Second, low floor attendance suggests that members may not place a high value on deliberation. Many of the important decisions may already have been made elsewhere, and when recorded votes are called, members have plenty of time to get to the floor. Clearly, they choose to spend their time meeting other demands.

Deliberation: A Qualitative Glance

In the opening of this essay we contrasted the defense appropriations of the first sessions of the 68th and 96th Congresses. It is worthwhile to return to these appropriation bills to consider some of the qualitative aspects of deliberation. Until this point, our analysis has focused on quantitative measures, such as floor attendance. But attendance figures offer only a glimpse of deliberation and do not address the issue of participation. We have chosen to return to the naval and war appropriations of the 68th Congress (HR 6820 and HR 7877) and the defense appropriation of the 96th Congress (HR 5359) to illustrate the quality of deliberation: How broad is floor participation, and what impact does it have? By examining the number of members speaking during general debate, the number introducing amendments, and the success of amending efforts, we find some useful comparisons.

In 1924, during general debate over the naval and war appropriations, 103 members addressed their colleagues on the floor. By comparison, only 13 members spoke during general debate on the defense appropriation in 1979. Similarly, 32 members offered amendments to the navy and war bills, while only 7 introduced amendments to the defense bill. Finally, a total of fifty-five amend· ments were offered on the 1924 appropriation, of which thirty passed and twenty-five failed. During 1979 only eight amendments, all minor ones, were considered, and three of these failed. (It should also be noted that roll call votes on three of these amendments took up a substantial amount of the time. By contrast, none of the 1924 amendment votes were roll calls.)

For our middle Congress, 35 speakers participated during general debate of the first-session defense appropriation (HR 6042), and 10 members offered a total of eleven amendments. Of these amendments, six passed and none was considered by roll call. Although amending activity was only slightly higher than that in the 96th Congress, it appears that floor attendance was fairly high. An average of 225 members voted on the three divisions. On the single division vote on HR 5359 in 1979, only 33 members voted.

Not only were more people listening, but more people were participating in discussion and debate. Although these data are suggestive rather than definitive, this case comparison supports our earlier quantitative findings on the decline of deliberation.

Is Deliberation Conducted Elsewhere?

Although it is apparent that floor deliberation has declined, it is possible that deliberation simply occurs elsewhere. The most likely candidates in our search for deliberation are committees and subcommittees. Indeed, during the Progressive era, Lindsay Rogers and Woodrow Wilson criticized the committee system for its usurpation of legislative authority. Three aspects of committee and subcommittee operation—membership self-selection, primary activities, and member attendance—indicate that deliberative functions suffer at those levels as well.

Richard Hall argues that in order to be fully effective in a particular policy area, most members require "assignment to the committee of jurisdiction ... close to the important legislative action and the community of relevant actors." By identifying the principle of self-selection, Hall demonstrates that these particularized subsets of the legislative whole fall short of our deliberative criteria (Chapter 7). Significantly, they fall short of meeting the inclusiveness function of deliberation.

Second, even if one concludes that "the evidence for what have been called 'preference outliers,' 'high-demand committees,' 'self-selection tendencies,' and ultimately 'committee' power is inconclusive," it is not at all certain that deliberation is a valued part of committee activity.[25] One scholar of committees contends that "congressional committees have shifted their attention away from processing legislation toward such matters as oversight, executive messages and reports, and the exchange and dissemination of information." [26]

Finally, the time constraints that are so prominent for the House as a whole are prominent in the committee room as well. Data on attendance and participation during bill markups vary but generally are unimpressive, even when a generous measure of attendance is used. Hall concludes that "the truancy rates at committee and subcommittee markups, which are often the most important meetings in the legislative process," are one indicator of constraints affecting committees (Chapter 7).

At one time it may have been accurate to claim that the locus of deliberation simply had moved from the House floor to the committee room. If that was the case, deliberation has declined in committee rooms as well.

The Consequences of Declining Deliberation

The picture we have painted of House floor activity since the 1970s is far different from that of the 1920s or 1950s. The House has become a year-round operation. The daily floor meetings are longer. More legislation is handled, and that legislation is more complex. Less time is available for general debate. Legislation is considered more quickly. Because of the conflicting time demands, members give House floor debate low priority. Even if congressional critics like Wilson and Rogers were correct in their day, recent Congresses make the ones they studied appear heavily involved in deliberation.

We have suggested here that a prime reason for this decline in deliberation has been the growing legislative workload and the resulting time constraints under which Congress operates. In a timed game the expectations and goals of Congress, as a democratic legislative body, have been placed in conflict. The need to process a growing legislative workload, to be responsive to an impatient public, and to compete with the other institutions for national policy influence has resulted in a sacrifice of deliberation. Put simply, in the context of late twentieth century American democracy, the values of responsiveness, expertise, and efficiency have displaced deliberation as they have come into conflict. Increasingly, the House floor is a processor of bills rather than an arena of deliberation.

It is often assumed that deliberation occurs elsewhere. But, as we have seen from studies of committee and subcommittee participation, there is strong reason to question that assumption. Moreover, the deliberation that does occur at those levels, because those venues include only unrepresentative samples of House members, is functionally inferior.

On occasion, members do engage in some semblance of deliberation on the House floor. The debate on the resolution authorizing the president to commit troops to military action in the Persian Gulf is a recent example. It is no accident that that debate received high praise in the media and from the public. Furthermore, the event illustrated the functional values of deliberation. In that case inclusiveness, avoidance of error, and legitimacy were major concerns. Significantly, in the end those opposing the resolution accepted the outcome and were supportive of its implementation.

Is there reason to think that something of importance has been lost because of this decline in deliberation? We think the answer to that question is yes. First, deliberation, like representation, is a democratic value for which legislatures are particularly well suited. When Richard Fenno wrote about the superiority of Congress to the other institutions of national government in its capacity as a representative institution and the need to strengthen that strength, he might almost as well have been discussing deliberation.[27] In part, the two are linked. By fostering inclusiveness and legitimacy, Congress's representativeness makes it well suited for deliberation. Unlike representation, deliberation has been allowed to decline. At a time when public discontent with political institutions is high, Congress might be well served by revitalizing its capacity for deliberation.

Second, among the complaints most frequently voiced by representatives and senators, especially those leaving Congress voluntarily in 1992, is a frustration with the deadlock and a feeling of being left out in the development of policy.[28] Because the function of inclusion is one of Congress's strengths, deliberation could act as an important component in easing the frustration of members.

Third, an increase in deliberation might well relieve some of the inefficiencies of the legislative process. Certainly, more attention to deliberation will require floor time. But by developing consensus and giving the minority its say, the "losers" may be more willing to accept the outcome and may be less likely to engage in direct and indirect obstruction.

Finally, deliberation is one of the values that separates representative democratic governments from administrative states. Even if the procedural steps in lawmaking remain intact, the continued decline of deliberation is a threat to democratic government.

Of course, it is one thing to be critical of the decline of deliberation and quite another to suggest how the trend can be reversed. Such an undertaking may be appropriate for more detailed discussion elsewhere. An observation drawn from this research suggests one avenue where deliberation might be fostered. In the 96th Congress, and to some degree in subsequent Congresses, there was one point at which time was available on the House floor. That point occurred at the beginning of the Congress, when committees and subcommittees had not yet advanced much legislation to the floor. (In recent years Democratic House leaders have used some of this time to push through already well defined items on the party program.) It would be entirely feasible during the first month or so of a Congress to schedule time for major floor debates on key issues that the House hopes to address during that Congress. The purpose of these debates would be to discuss given issues without the confines of a committee product, to listen to alternative perspectives, to develop consensus where possible, and to focus the work of the committee or committees to which the subject matter is to be referred.

Thus, hypothetically, the House might debate the health care issue. After a period of careful deliberation, during which a full range of approaches could be put forth and discussed, it might decide to pursue a policy providing for universal public coverage, or it might pursue one of universal private coverage with subsidization of insurance premiums or some other broadly defined approach. The appropriate committees would then be charged to produce legislation establishing a health care system within that defined approach. This approach to deliberation would not be a return to the process as it worked in the early nineteenth century, when the Committee of the Whole set forth general principles and then referred the matter to a committee to work out the details. Clearly, the complexity of many current issues means that committees would still have a major role, and the deliberating procedure probably could be reserved for only a few major issues in each Congress. This change would, however, be in sympathy with that earlier time. Because the decisions made during these debates would be important in setting the agenda, members would be likely to give them high priority, and the debates would stimulate significant public attention. Such an experiment in deliberation might be just the catalyst Congress needs to revitalize this democratic value.

Notes

1. *Congressional Record*, 68th Cong., 1st sess., 4254.
2. *Congressional Record*, 96th Cong., 2d sess., 13454.
3. Donald Lutz, *Popular Consent and Popular Control* (Baton Rouge: Louisiana State University Press, 1980), 199.
4. Herman Belz, "Constitutionalism in the American Founding," in *The Framing and Ratification of the Constitution*, ed. Leonard W. Levy and Dennis J. Mahoney (New York: Macmillan, 1987), 340.
5. Joseph Cooper, "Organization and Innovation in the House of Representatives," in *The House at Work*, ed. Joseph Cooper and G. Calvin Mackenzie (Austin: University of Texas Press, 1981), 327.

6. Belz, "Constitutionalism," 340.
7. Steven S. Smith, *Call to Order: Floor Politics in the House and Senate* (Washington, D.C.: Brookings Institution, 1989), 238-239.
8. Aristotle, *Politics,* trans. Ernest Barker (London: Oxford University Press, 1980), 301, 192.
9. John Stuart Mill, *On Liberty* (New York: Norton, 1975), 21.
10. Michael J. Malbin, "Congress During the Convention and Ratification," in *The Framing and Ratification of the Constitution,* 193.
11. Mill, *On Liberty,* 21.
12. Alexander Hamilton, James Madison, and John Jay, *The Federalist Papers* (Middletown, Conn.: Wesleyan University Press, 1961), 495.
13. Malbin, "Congress During the Convention and Ratification," 195, 196.
14. Elaine Spitz, *Majority Rule* (Chatham, N.J.: Chatham House, 1984), 153, 205-206.
15. Ibid., 150.
16. Joseph Cooper, *The Origins of the Standing Committees and the Development of the Modern House,* Rice University Monographs in Political Science, vol. 56, no. 3 (Houston: Rice University, 1970), 10, 17.
17. Ibid., 13, 58.
18. Woodrow Wilson, *Congressional Government* (Baltimore: Johns Hopkins University Press, 1981), 70, 62, 68.
19. Quoted in Lindsay Rogers, ed., "American Government and Politics," *American Political Science Review* 16 (1922): 50.
20. Lindsay Rogers, ed., "American Government and Politics," *American Political Science Review* 14 (1920): 661; Lindsay Rogers, ed., "Record of Political Events," *Political Science Quarterly* 40 (Supplement 1925): 70.
21. Lindsay Rogers, ed., "American Government and Politics," *American Political Science Review* 13 (1919): 263.
22. In the 68th Congress, 1st sess., the Adjournment Resolution, H. Con. Res. 27, was adopted 221-157.
23. We define regular legislation as bills or resolutions that were considered under a rule, with unanimous consent as to debate time, or under the regular rules of the House (which allow one hour of debate per side). Regular legislation does not include conference reports, bills considered under suspension of the rules, or the debate over the adoption of the rules.
24. *Congressional Record,* 96th Cong., 1st sess., 16677.
25. Keith Krehbiel, "Are Congressional Committees Composed of Preference Outliers?" *American Political Science Review* 84 (1990): 150.
26. Roger H. Davidson, "The New Centralization on Capitol Hill," *Review of Politics* (1988): 355.
27. Richard F. Fenno, Jr., "Strengthening a Congressional Strength," in *Congress Reconsidered,* ed. Lawrence C. Dodd and Bruce I. Oppenheimer (New York: Praeger, 1977), 261-268.
28. For example, see "Lent's Retirement Leaves Hole on House Energy Panel," *Congressional Quarterly Weekly Report,* June 27, 1992, 1857.

Part V

...

Congress, the Executive, and Public Policy

14

Congress and Foreign Policy: The Misperceptions

Eileen Burgin

A lexis de Tocqueville wrote that "in the control of society's foreign affairs democratic governments do appear decidedly inferior to others." [1] The "inferior" qualities causing Tocqueville unease are most acute in Congress, the most democratic branch of the U.S. government. Tocqueville's concerns undoubtedly strike a responsive chord in many Americans today: criticizing Congress's actions has become nothing less than a national pastime. Indeed, Congress often appears as a gadfly, if not the sole culprit, hindering our foreign relations; few commentators defend Congress's activities or even hint at a silver lining. [2]

Observers highlight a full spectrum of problems with congressional participation. At the extremes, Jim Lindsay classifies critics as "irreconcilables" and "skeptics." [3] Irreconcilables argue that Congress overreacted to an "imperial presidency"; now an "imperial Congress" "fetters" an "imperiled presidency." [4] Those who contend that the president has become Congress's "servant" maintain, in part, that 535 secretaries of state "micromanage" our foreign policy. [5] At the opposite end of the critics' spectrum are skeptics, who believe that although Congress may bark it does not bite. Harold Koh argues, for instance, that "Congress has *persistently* acquiesced in what the President has done." [6] Commentators' complaints also cover other aspects of congressional foreign policy activity that fall between the spectrum's extremes of an imperial or impotent Congress. Congressional involvement may be problematic because of institutional inadequacies (for example, inefficiency), inconstancy, ignorance, or perhaps most important members' reelection orientations. [7] Critics may stress, for example, that an inconstant, ignorant, or parochially minded Congress encourages, or even dictates, policies that are "inexcusable from the standpoint of genuine concern for national security." [8]

Certainly, criticizing Congress in the foreign policy field is easy as well as amusing, for colorful anecdotes and intuitively appealing stories of misguided acts are not lacking. But is the situation as bad as critics contend? The central argument here, simply stated, is that while many of the often contradictory criticisms have some merit, Congress does have a significant role to play in the foreign policy arena and may even contribute effectively to forming U.S. foreign policy. Congress is neither imperial nor impotent; Congress is not so institutionally inadequate, inconstant, or ignorant to warrant grave concern; and although institutional players themselves may be electorally obsessed, members' parochial interests do not automatically translate to congressional contamination of foreign policy making. Thus I advocate that we strive not to exaggerate vices and overlook virtues. We also must remember that Congress is not the only branch of government that makes flawed decisions or is "remote from . . . perfect wisdom and perfect virtue" [9]—just consider the Reagan administration's actions in the Iran-contra scandal.[10]

In this essay, I first examine the constitutional framework in the foreign policy arena and, more specifically, Congress's constitutional powers. Next, I explore how Congress exercises its constitutional prerogatives; understanding how Congress asserts itself is crucial for evaluating its actions. Then I describe the various types of criticisms of congressional foreign policy involvement. Finally, I evaluate critics' concerns and offer a more balanced assessment.[11]

The Constitutional Framework

Something of the wonder that suffuses a child upon learning that a mighty oak sprang from a tiny acorn fills one who peers behind the tapestry of conventional learning and beholds how meager are the sources of presidential claims to monopolistic control of foreign relations.

—Raoul Berger [12]

Presidential claims to monopolistic power in foreign affairs *are* inaccurate.[13] Our constitutional system of "separated institutions sharing powers" did not intend to create an omnipotent executive.[14] Rather, the Framers designed two active and combative branches, with many overlapping foreign policy roles. In so doing, the Founders sought to safeguard against the arbitrary exercise of authority. As James Madison wrote, "Ambition must be made to counteract ambition." [15] Indeed, thwarting ambition was so important that the Framers chose that goal over efficiency in conflicts between the two. Justice Brandeis observed, "the doctrine of the separation of powers was adopted . . . not to promote efficiency but to preclude the exercise of arbitrary power." [16]

In terms of specific constitutional grants of authority, the president has fewer prerogatives related to foreign policy than does Congress. The president is "Commander in Chief of the Army and Navy"; the president has the power with the Senate's "Advice and Consent" both to "make Treaties" and to "appoint Ambassadors"; and the president receives "Ambassadors and other public Ministers." In addition, some of the president's general authority is relevant: the president is vested with the "executive Power"; takes an oath to "preserve, protect, and defend the Constitution"; and "shall take Care that the Laws be faithfully executed."

The specific issues within Congress's constitutional purview, in contrast to those within the president's purview, are vast.[17] Congress is foremost the lawmaking branch. And it may "make all Laws which shall be necessary and proper for carrying into Execution" its enumerated powers, about half of which pertain to foreign affairs. Congress's constitutional prerogatives in five substantive policy areas related to foreign policy stand out. First, Congress has substantial power over the purse. This power derives from the authority to determine how funds should be spent (that is, "No Money shall be drawn from the Treasury, but in Consequence of Appropriations made by Law"), along with the power to raise revenue (that is, "To Lay and collect Taxes, Duties, Imposts, and Excises, to pay the Debts and provide for the common Defence and general Welfare"). Madison regarded the power of the purse as "the most complete and effectual weapon with which any constitution can arm the immediate representatives of the people." [18] Second, in Article 1, Section 8, Congress's national security or war powers are enumerated: Congress is given the power to "declare War," to "raise and Support Armies," to "provide and maintain a Navy," to "make Rules for the Government and Regulation" of the armed forces, to "provide for calling forth the Militia," and finally to "provide for organizing, arming, and disciplining the Militia." In discussing Congress's war powers, Michael Glennon goes so far as to say that the president's powers "are paltry in comparison with, and are subordinate to, [the] grants to Congress." [19] Even such a consistent advocate for a strong executive as Alexander Hamilton stressed that the president was less threatening than the British king, for Congress, not the president, has power that "extends to the *declaring* of war and to the *raising* and *regulating* of fleets and armies." [20] Third, Congress has the power to "regulate Commerce with foreign Nations." This ensures congressional prerogatives over foreign trade apart from the taxing powers. The last two substantive policy areas in which Congress is granted power in foreign affairs fall under the Senate's purview: the Senate is given the power of "Advice and Consent" on both treaties and ambassadorial appointments.

A listing of specific constitutional grants of authority pertaining to foreign policy, such as the above, should not be misleading; ambiguities, areas of concurrent power, and omissions exist. Important foreign policy prerogatives lie in what Justice Jackson coined a "zone of twilight." [21] (For instance, consider questions regarding which branch deploys military forces and regulates covert action as well as the role of executive agreements and executive privilege.) With such uncertainty surrounding two vigorous and ambitious branches, therefore, it is not surprising that the Constitution created, as Edward Corwin stated, "an invitation to struggle for the privilege of directing American foreign policy." [22] In the consequent "tug for more of the foreign policy blanket," various influences beyond constitutional powers often have been significant; historical precedents, presidents broadly construing their constitutional authority, crises confronting the nation, and Supreme Court decisions have all affected the struggle between the branches.[23]

Congress's Powers in Practice

Given Congress's ample—albeit sometimes ambiguous and shared—constitutional powers, we may consider how Congress asserts itself in the foreign

policy field. The classic congressional method for exercising foreign policy prerogatives is legislation. Binding legislative tools—including bills, joint resolutions, and obviously amendments to these measures—only succeed in a technical
sense (that is, by becoming law) when a majority of a quorum in both houses
agree, assuming that two-thirds majorities are not necessary to override a presidential veto. (Treaties require a two-thirds majority in the Senate, and nominations require a simple Senate majority.) Yet Congress does not limit itself to a
purely legislative strategy in the foreign policy arena, as most observers would
lead us to believe; Congress supplements its legislative authority with informal or
nonlegislative mechanisms (for instance, consultations, public appeals through
the press, and hearings). Congress employs its two means of influence independently and symbiotically. Legislative and nonlegislative vehicles often are inex-
tricably intertwined: the tools are employed in tandem; legislation mandates the
use of informal mechanisms; and nonlegislative tools serve as the precursor to
formal legislation. Members wield both kinds of instruments regarding all substantive foreign policy areas in which Congress exercises constitutional authority.

Legislative Tools

Binding legislation is the traditional congressional mechanism for trying to
influence foreign policy and exercise constitutional prerogatives. Many binding
foreign policy measures are issue specific and reactive in nature. Rather than
attempting to make broad procedural and structural changes in the foreign policy
making environment that may not affect the particular subject engendering congressional interest and concern, issue-specific legislation directly addresses a current foreign policy problem.

Issue-specific measures include bills and joint resolutions that fulfill constitutional prerogatives in a straightforward manner. Senate approval of nominations and treaties, trade policy (especially that aimed at specific countries), and
authorization and appropriations measures all may offer examples of such legislation. In 1986, for instance, Congress imposed trade sanctions against South
Africa (overriding Reagan's veto).[24] Using its power of the purse, Congress also
approves legislation that determines how money contained in foreign aid bills
will be spent by earmarking most of the available funds.[25] Congress responds to
special executive requests for funds as well, as it did when it passed the $8.4
billion quota increase to the International Monetary Fund in 1983.[26] And Congress may even take the lead: in the mid-1980s Congress pushed emergency
relief bills to aid African drought victims.[27]

Some issue-specific legislation contains critical restrictive provisions. These
provisions typically involve Congress exercising negative powers to prohibit certain actions or to decrease the room for executive interpretation. The so-called
Boland amendments, and more generally U.S. policy during the Reagan years
regarding aid for the Nicaraguan contras, provide illustrations of restrictive legislation: the Boland amendment attached to the continuing resolution for fiscal
1983 forbade the use of funds "for the purpose of overthrowing the government

of Nicaragua"; for 1984, Congress limited the funds available for U.S. intelligence activities supporting military or paramilitary activities in Nicaragua; and for 1985, Congress barred any spending for the contra rebels before February 28 and made other funds available thereafter if Congress approved assistance by joint resolution.[28] Thus through the power of the purse Congress attempted to restrict the purposes for which contra aid funds could be used as well as the quantity of funds. Another case in point concerns U.S. policy toward El Salvador in the early 1980s—from 1981 through 1984 Congress passed restrictive legislation making military aid to El Salvador conditional on specific requirements.[29]

Issue-specific legislation also may be directive in nature. In directive legislation Congress generally gives the president what he wants, yet adds hurdles, mandating that the executive undertake certain activities. The most common requirement concerns issue-specific executive reports; the Congressional Research Service (CRS) recently identified close to seven hundred foreign policy reporting requirements.[30] Reports enable Congress to achieve a number of objectives. Through reporting requirements, Congress may monitor the executive branch, without tying its hands. Congress requires reports as well, to force the executive to acknowledge certain facts. Thus Congress passed an amendment to the fiscal 1991 foreign aid appropriations bill obligating George Bush to report on any military cooperation since 1986 between the U.S.-aided noncommunist resistance in Cambodia and the Khmer Rouge, cooperation considered to be "common knowledge" outside administration circles.[31] Reports are also intended to enable Congress to remain part of the process, at least nominally. In authorizing the use of force against Iraq in January 1991, for instance, Congress directed the president, before using force, to report to Congress his determination that "all appropriate diplomatic and other peaceful means" to obtain Iraqi compliance with United Nations (U.N.) resolutions had not been and would not be successful.[32]

In addition to issue-specific legislation, Congress passes prospective-procedural legislation. Prospective-procedural legislation seeks to influence foreign policy making in a non-case-specific manner, hence moving beyond the triggering event. Unlike issue-specific bills and joint resolutions, prospective-procedural legislation attempts to improve the functioning of the foreign policy system in the future by altering the policy process or broad procedural and structural mechanisms. Ultimately, prospective-procedural legislation may establish a framework for Congress to assert its institutional prerogatives; it often creates a convenient, policy-neutral foil for criticizing future executive actions as well.

The classic prospective-procedural measure is the War Powers Resolution, passed over Nixon's veto in 1973. This law, which sought to design a formula for congressional-executive codetermination in the area of troop involvement abroad, included three principal procedures: (1) presidential consultation with Congress "in every possible instance . . . before introducing United States Armed Forces into hostilities or into situations where imminent involvement in hostilities is clearly indicated by the circumstances"; (2) executive reports to Congress within forty-eight hours when armed forces are sent into one of several situations without a declaration of war—the reporting requirements under Section 4(a)(1) trigger a sixty-day clock for presidential withdrawal of troops; and (3) congressional action regarding military ventures, including how Congress may extend, sustain, or terminate the use of force.[33] The War Powers Resolution contains three provisions common to many prospective-procedural measures, namely, consultations, reports, and a legislative veto.

Prospective-procedural legislation sometimes includes provisions delegating authority to the executive branch. Yet in delegating authority to the executive, Congress strives to ensure congressional influence. Take the Omnibus Trade and Competitiveness Act of 1988. A CRS report explained that although the law delegates power "it provides a greater, participatory role for the Congress" in such ways as the following: it requires "increased consultation"; it requires "an annual statement" from the U.S. trade representative; it gives Congress "leverage" to ensure adequate executive branch consultations "during trade negotiations"; it "provides for congressional withdrawal of fast-track procedures"; and it significantly changes the trade remedy provisions, "primarily by limiting the discretion of the President and making action by the executive branch more likely." [34] Further examples of prospective-procedural legislation, discussed below, include the Intelligence Oversight Act of 1980, the Goldwater-Nichols Reorganization Act of 1986, the Arms Export Control Act of 1976, and the 1977 act creating the State Department's Bureau of Human Rights and Humanitarian Affairs.

Nonlegislative Tools

In studies on Congress and foreign policy, nonlegislative tools—or more precisely, non-legally binding tools—receive little attention.[35] Yet we cannot evaluate critics' concerns without understanding the less traditional ways in which Congress exercises power. All non-legally binding instruments can influence policy—and influence it without the widespread consensus needed for passing, and overriding presidential vetoes on, bills and joint resolutions. Most informal mechanisms influence policy in several ways. First, nonlegislative vehicles may provide members with a forum to sway public, congressional, executive, or even a foreign government's opinion. If successful in swaying opinion, members utilizing these tools may affect agendas, decision making, and critical actions in the legislative and executive branches as well as abroad. Second, non-legally binding tools may allow legislators similarly to influence policy, by offering them the opportunity to inform or educate—whether it be constituents, the American public, members of Congress, or people and officials in other nations. Third, through nonlegislative instruments members may send out signals about possible future legislative and nonlegislative moves, hence achieving desired results by generating anticipated reactions in the executive branch and in foreign governments. Because other actors may base their behavior and decisions on expectations of what Congress will do, these signals may prompt responses obviating the need for further congressional action.[36] In addition to influencing policy, all nonlegislative mechanisms may enable members to pursue personal political objectives, such as winning reelection, maintaining or gaining power in Congress, and seeking higher elected office.

A host of factors help define what legislative and nonlegislative tools Congress will employ. The nature of a congressional response may depend upon the specifics of an issue, for instance, content, surrounding controversy, timing, and duration.[37] A short-lived foreign policy problem occurring during a lengthy congressional recess (such as the 1989 Panama invasion, for example) will tend to stimulate less legislative activity than a long-lived issue occurring during a legislative session; simple logistics compel members to rely upon nonlegislative tools.[38] A broad array of factors within Congress, ranging from institutional and structural considerations to more personal ones, also affect congressional action. More specifically, the committee (or committees) with jurisdiction over an issue, the role of the majority party leadership, and the personality and power of the individual leaders on a subject may influence the kind of action taken.[39] The use of legislative and nonlegislative instruments may reflect the impact of divided government as well.[40]

While various considerations do affect the nature of a congressional response, it should be remembered that legislative and nonlegislative mechanisms usually become part of one process of Congress asserting its power in foreign policy. Take the efforts to impose sanctions against South Africa. The groundwork for legislation had been laid for several years through the use of many non-legally binding instruments. Then in 1985, to preempt legislative action, Reagan issued an executive order—Congress was on the verge of passing a measure aimed at dismantling apartheid. Culminating action taken over several years, Congress in 1986 passed sanctions legislation.[41]

To illustrate further how non-legally binding tools may influence policy, I now briefly review nine specific indirect mechanisms. The following discussion also highlights the number and variety of ways in which Congress may influence foreign policy and, consequently, the flaws implicit in limiting an analysis to legally binding legislative tools.

Nonbinding legislation. Although called "legislation," simple and concurrent resolutions lack the binding, mandatory effect of bills and joint resolutions and do not require presidential action. In fact, nonbinding legislation resembles nonlegislative tools in intended and actual impact. When Congress approved a nonbinding resolution expressing opposition to the 1984 mining of the Nicaraguan harbors, for instance, the action did not force Reagan to change his policies, but it did publicly demonstrate his lack of support and the possibility of binding legislative retribution.[42] Nonbinding legislation may also be directed at other countries: the passage of resolutions in 1989 condemning specific rights violations in Bulgaria, Czechoslovakia, and Romania enabled Congress to communicate with and pressure nations over which Congress had little leverage since they already were barred from trade benefits.[43]

Informal advice. Informal advice covers everything from suggestions made by members during perfunctory White House telephone calls to inform them of impending action to exchanges that may occur because of member observance of treaty negotiations and foreign elections. The Senate's Arms Control Group, which visited Geneva several times a year from 1983 through 1989, for instance, talked with U.S. and Soviet negotiators, hoping to increase the likelihood that congressional concerns would be weighed before a treaty's presentation to the Senate. Sen. Richard G. Lugar, R-Ind., when chair of the Foreign Relations Committee, also offered informal advice to Reagan officials after he headed an American observer team to the 1986 Philippine elections.[44]

Consultation. Consultation with the executive branch presents a more formal means of influence than does informal advice. Often consultation occurs in response to legislative requirements, such as those in the 1988 Omnibus Trade and Competitiveness Act. Because theoretically consultation furnishes members with a meaningful chance to share their views and influence policy (perhaps by blocking proposals before they become a fait accompli), Congress tries to mandate increased consultation in a range of policy areas.

Direct dealings with foreign governments. Members' direct dealings with foreign governments come in two forms. First, members regularly meet with foreign personnel stationed in Washington embassies, with other dignitaries visiting Washington, and with officials abroad when members travel. For instance, Saudi ambassador Prince Bandar Bin Sultan met with legislators in January 1991 and discussed the possibility of a huge U.S. arms deal.[45] Second, occasionally members engage in personal or private diplomacy. Most such diplomatic efforts follow an executive's invitation, as with former Speaker Jim Wright's 1987 involvement in peace process negotiations with top foreign leaders concerning the contras. This activity ensued from the administration's earlier invitation to Wright to participate in the peace process (although Reagan officials later criticized Wright for undermining the executive's position).[46] Not all personal or private diplomacy has an executive link; truly independent "lone ranger diplomacy," however, is the more uncommon form of personal diplomacy.[47]

Public appeals through the press. Activities such as press conferences, interviews, op-ed pieces, and less formal "photo opportunities" are all regularly used means of influence. For instance, in January 1981 Sen. Gary Hart, D-Colo., sought to begin moving the policy agenda toward military reform and thus published a piece in the *Wall Street Journal* in which he called for change.[48] In contrast, Rep. Walter Fauntroy, D-D.C., chose a "photo opportunity" in his protest of and endeavor to alter U.S. policy toward South African apartheid—he held a sit-in at the South African ambassador's office in 1984.[49] A prominent group of protesters following Fauntroy's lead gathered outside the embassy and were photographed being taken away by police.[50]

Hearings. A wide range of subcommittees and committees hold hearings on foreign policy issues; most committees have some jurisdiction over these matters.[51] In addition to the objectives common to all nonlegislative vehicles, hearings also provide Congress with a vehicle to conduct oversight. Consider the hearings held by several committees in December 1990 concerning what appeared to be an impending war in the Persian Gulf. At the time of the hearings, President Bush had already altered the nature of the U.S. mission from defensive to offensive by nearly doubling the troops in Saudi Arabia—without congressional approval while Congress was in recess—and had received the U.N. Security Council authorization to use "all necessary means" to force Iraqi compliance with U.N. resolutions. Given Congress's exclusion from these actions, the hearings furnished members with an avenue to become more active players: the committees attempted to influence policy and conduct oversight, and many committee members sought personal benefits from participation.[52] The 1991 hearings on Robert Gates's nomination to direct the Central Intelligence Agency (CIA), and the 1987 Iran-contra hearings, although substantively different kinds of hearings, offered members similar opportunities.[53]

Floor statements. Speeches on the House and Senate floor occasionally go beyond simple "position taking" aimed at constituents.[54] A case in point is the three-day speech in 1987 by Sen. Sam Nunn, D-Ga., chair of the Armed Services Committee, about the Reagan administration's reinterpretation of the Anti-Ballistic Missile (ABM) Treaty. When Reagan officials attempted to justify forging ahead with "star wars" technology, in part by reinterpreting the ABM Treaty, Nunn took to the floor, critically and exhaustively analyzing the reinterpretation. Nunn's decision to use floor statements as part of his strategy to influence events underscores this nonlegislative vehicle's potential.[55]

Letters. Members also write letters to the executive, although this tool is less publicized than most other nonlegislative tools. Substantively, much correspondence resembles the letter 111 members sent to Reagan concerning contra aid in March 1987. The letter writers, many of whom were so-called swing votes, hoped "to exert pressure on the administration in exchange for their support, and they sought to impose conditions involving changes in the contra forces, the goals of the aid policy, or both." [56]

Lawsuits against the president. Perhaps the least typical nonlegislative measure is members pursuing judicial avenues. Legal victories, though, are rare. The Supreme Court usually refuses to deal with claims, rebuffing members primarily on the basis of the political question doctrine, which is a device federal courts use to insulate themselves from what are deemed to be essentially political disputes. When the Court does rule on the merits of a case, it tends to favor the president.[57]

The Negative Ledger Entries

Having examined Congress's constitutional powers and Congress's exercise of its prerogatives, we now shall look at observers' criticisms in greater detail. In this section I review critics' diverse concerns about Congress's actions. After considering somewhat contradictory arguments by commentators at the spectrum's extremes—an "imperial" or an "impotent" Congress?—I address other criticisms of congressional foreign policy involvement.

An "Imperial" Congress?

Critics who see an "imperial" Congress "fettering" an "imperiled presidency" complain about the legislative and nonlegislative devices used to exert influence. Legislative and nonlegislative vehicles allow Congress to "micromanage" the executive, observers contend, by taking over the detailed administration of foreign policy and curtailing the president's flexibility. For instance, earmarking in foreign aid gives Congress the opportunity to make specific decisions that constrain the executive's ability to spend appropriated funds as necessary. And restrictive measures such as the Boland amendment present similar problems; repeating a common refrain, Douglas Jeffrey argues that "the congressional majority foreordained something like the Iran-Contra 'scandal' by attempting to hog-tie the president with the Boland Amendment." [58] Congress also allegedly micromanages when it holds a president "hostage" through restrictive legislation that limits or withholds funds. Observers maintain that reporting requirements in directive and prospective-procedural legislation offer further evidence of congressional meddling. Bush complained, for example, that the Pentagon alone spent $50 million and 500 "man-years" in fiscal 1989 writing reports to satisfy Congress.[59] Critics contend that nonlegislative mechanisms as well are notorious for hampering and undermining the executive: hearings increasingly and capriciously interfere with administration officials' time through requested testimony and pry into executive matters; informal advice and consultations may circumscribe executive freedom of action; and private diplomacy undercuts the president in his dealings and negotiations with foreign governments. Beyond micromanaging, commentators argue that an "imperial" Congress also oversteps its constitutional prerogatives. The War Powers Resolution is these critics' favorite illustration of an unconstitutional law hamstringing the presidency.[60]

An "Impotent" Congress?

Observers at the opposite end of the critics' spectrum see an "impotent" Congress. An "impotent" Congress almost always loses to the president in foreign policy making because it complies with or acquiesces in what the president wants or has done, even if clearly contrary to Congress's stated will.[61] Three related points are particularly relevant to this argument.

First, critics stress that laws are not self-executing, and administrations often exploit weaknesses.[62] Commentators say the War Powers Resolution is a case in point: the executive branch typically construes consultation obligations narrowly, holding informational briefings in which it presents a fait accompli and fails to solicit legislators' counsel, rather than seeking members' "advice and opinions" when "a decision is pending"; and the executive circumvents the law's sixty-day clock by submitting reports "consistent with" the act instead of pursuant to section 4(a)(1), as Congress intended.[63] Critics also highlight Congress's attempt to influence military aid to El Salvador in the early 1980s as an example of executive noncompliance. Kenneth Sharpe writes, "The administration . . . provided false and misleading information in order to certify that the conditions required for aid existed, despite overwhelming evidence to the contrary."[64] And when Congress used the power of the purse to limit military appropriations to El Salvador, Sharpe explains that Reagan violated the laws' intent and circumvented Congress by increasing military assistance through the president's special defense drawdown authority and the authority to reprogram budgetary allocations.[65] Thus critics argue that even appropriations cutoffs do not ensure good executive behavior. (And since Congress frequently attaches cutoffs to continuing appropriations measures to deter vetoes, the provisions are subject to yearly reconsideration.[66]) Complaints about executive branch noncompliance with the Intelligence Oversight Act of 1980 also abound. The CIA's failure to inform Congress adequately about the agency's own role in the 1984 mining of the Nicaraguan harbors, for instance, prompted this protest from Rep. Norman Y. Mineta, D-Calif.: "We've dug, probed, cajoled, kicked and harassed to get facts from the CIA, but Casey wouldn't tell you that your coat was on fire unless you asked him."[67]

Second, and related to the first point, these commentators contend that the legislative cry has more resonance than substance—the hallmark of binding legislation is ambiguities, loopholes, and giveaways to the executive. The Intelligence Oversight Act, according to critics, illustrates the common problems. An "impotent" Congress passed loosely written legislation that codified executive practice, rather than clearly revamping the intelligence oversight system and establishing ironclad requirements on such matters as prior notification.[68] Instead of a blanket requirement on prior notification of all intelligence activities, for instance, Congress allowed the executive to act without prior notice in some cases as long as appropriate committees were informed "in a timely manner." Another ambiguity or loophole, critics complain, concerns covert operations affecting "vital" U.S. interests—in such cases only the "Gang of Eight" congressional leaders must be notified.[69]

Third, and again intertwined with the previous points, critics maintain that presidential evasion of statutes typically prompts weak congressional responses.[70] Congress usually suffers from collective-action troubles, these commentators argue, unable to defeat, let alone override, the executive; a critical mass is rarely willing to reign in any president—and especially a popular president—on foreign policy issues. Observers contend that concerns about being blamed for policy failures make members powerless. Even when a president openly flouts a law's spirit—such as the War Powers Resolution, the Intelligence Oversight Act, or the military aid restrictions to El Salvador—Congress has been unable to muster the requisite will to demand faithful execution of the law.

An "Institutionally Inadequate" Congress?

Still other commentators stress the significance of institutional inadequacies in evaluating Congress's foreign policy participation; these inadequacies make it difficult, if not impossible, for Congress to be an effective foreign policy player. Several institutional inadequacies stand out. Most important, critics argue that Congress is an inefficient body that cannot act quickly. The glacial pace of the legislative process is legendary, these commentators maintain. Procedural mechanisms available to senators on the floor, for instance, may stymie Congress's ability to respond promptly to a problem. Gregg Easterbrook in the *Atlantic Monthly* criticized Congress for what he saw as a fiasco in the congressional response to the African famine crisis in 1984: the House passed a simple $60 million emergency aid package to assist drought victims, but, because the Senate attached thirty-six nongermane amendments to it and the House-Senate differences then needed to be resolved, the measure was not enacted into law until four months later.[71] The proliferation of filibusters and the threat of filibusters also is indicative of the system's inefficiencies, observers contend. Critics note that structural factors often make it difficult for Congress to exercise power with dispatch. The internal organization of Congress is "collegial and sequential," whereas the executive is "hierarchical and centralized." [72] And according to a bipartisan panel of the National Academy of Public Administration (NAPA), the "increasing [committee] redundancy and jurisdictional overlap," and the consequent rise in joint and sequential referrals of bills, has slowed the legislative process "to the point of near paralysis on major issues." [73] Commentators stress the similar impact of the decentralized nature of Congress, the breakdown of the seniority system, and the increase in staff people; when all members think they can be "players," movement is gradual.

Critics concerned about institutional inadequacies detect other weaknesses. Commentators underscore the deficient instruments Congress uses to influence policy. Excessive reliance on blunt legislative instruments, they argue, eliminates the flexibility a president needs on complex foreign policy issues and may reveal U.S. strategy and policy to other governments.[74] Along these lines, another institutional inadequacy plaguing Congress is the lack of secrecy. This problem takes two forms. Some observers complain that Congress acts publicly; in other words, Congress is institutionally ill-suited to participate in the foreign policy arena where subtle nuance is paramount.[75] The more typical grievance about the lack of secrecy, though, is that members leak classified information. During the Iran-contra hearings, Oliver North even justified lying to Congress because he said Congress could not be trusted with sensitive intelligence material.[76]

An "Inconstant" Congress?

Critics who lament Congress's inconstancy believe that Congress is an unreliable policymaking body because it does not have long-term policy vision; Congress lacks the steadfastness in a course that Tocqueville identified as an indispensable quality to foreign relations.[77] This problem appears especially acute with legislative vehicles. Critics contend that shifts on policy questions—sometimes due to Congress's responsiveness to public opinion swings—result in foreign policy instabilities and program management inefficiencies. The twists and turns on contra aid policy in the 1980s, according to the minority report from the Iran-contra investigation, exemplify "vacillating congressional policy" and "constantly changing laws." [78] In 1985, fewer than two months after reaffirming its yearlong opposition to contra aid, Congress reversed itself and allowed the legal flow of assistance to resume; about six months after resuming contra aid, Congress rejected a $100 million aid package the Reagan administration had requested; and fewer than six months later, Congress approved the president's $100 million aid package.[79] Similarly, on defense policy Barry Blechman states that Congress is "sacrificing overall consistency and coherence of national policy for narrow interests and short-term objectives." [80] In addition to causing instability, this "inconstant" Congress harms U.S. policy because it leads to inefficiencies in program management. When Congress changes its mind in the middle of multiyear defense projects, for instance, Blechman explains that there have been "start-up costs and inefficiencies as programs [began], just as there [will be] termination costs and inefficiencies on the way down." [81] Hence, frequent shifts in course are costly and counterproductive.

An "Ignorant" Congress?

The lack of expertise, according to another criticism, may be Congress's fatal flaw in the foreign policy realm. Foreign policy issues are often complex matters requiring an appreciation of what Richard Nixon called the "interrelationship of international events." [82] Yet, commentators argue, members do not have such an appreciation of foreign affairs. Most people enter Congress with little experience in foreign policy. And while in Congress, members do not obtain the knowledge necessary to make informed decisions on these complicated issues.[83] Not only do time constraints curtail legislators' ability to master foreign policy issues, but Congress also lacks the executive's foreign policy and national security apparatus. Thus critics maintain that nonlegislative and legislative tools just enable members to intrude upon executive actions beyond their ken.

A "Reelection-Oriented" Congress?

Other observers advocate the "self-interest axiom," namely, that members are "single-minded seekers of reelection." [84] Critics detect several disturbing results of the reelection orientation on congressional foreign policy involvement. First, critics suggest that because members focus only on their own political futures, not on substantive policy problems, Congress cannot be an effective and judicious foreign policy participant and will contaminate U.S. policy. The subtle prevalence of this kind of criticism is noteworthy. In January 1991, before U.S. hostilities commenced in the Persian Gulf, for instance, a *Newsweek* article on congressional redistricting stated, "Forget . . . the Persian Gulf: the secret obsession of all 435 members of the U.S. House of Representatives is reapportionment and redistricting." [85] The implicit assumption is that members are so anxious about reelection that it is difficult for them to make "wise" foreign policy decisions. Second, and related to the first concern, commentators contend that reelection-oriented members inappropriately consider and evaluate complex foreign policy issues through narrow, parochial lenses; in other words, reelection-oriented members may serve as "delegates" rather than as "trustees," losing sight of broad policy issues in responding to constituents' detailed concerns. For instance, on defense procurement issues, pork-barrel politics rather than the common good may govern spending decisions; on trade issues, politically profitable tinkering with statutes that weigh only local interests may create "a regulatory patchwork—an expanding fabric of rules, with new layers stitched to older ones";[86] on treaties, senators may undercut diplomats and harm U.S. policy by using constituent mail, not actual treaty packages, to assess proposals; and on issues involving the interests of powerful political action committees (PACs), the availability of money for constantly campaigning members may determine votes and policies rather than the "national interest." Third, a reelection-oriented Congress, critics maintain, impedes U.S. foreign policy making, for it leads to an uncreative, stagnant Congress unable to pass innovative legislation; innovation signifies risks, risks suggest responsibility, responsibility may imply blame, and blame may be registered at the polls. Consequently, members may focus excessively upon "safe" foreign policy issues, exploiting them for publicity at home.[87]

A More Balanced Assessment

Before we evaluate critics' concerns by assessing what Congress does, several points merit underscoring. We must not consider commentators' complaints about Congress according to whether we agree or disagree with what Congress tries to accomplish. If we allow our values and policy preferences to intrude on these judgments, our assessments will be ever changing and essentially meaningless. An accurate evaluation cannot be based on criticisms serving as smoke screens for dissatisfaction with a Democratic Congress's interaction with a Republican administration. In addition, we must remember that although different elements in American society may favor different foreign policy decisions and outcomes, there is no single position that necessarily serves the "national interest." Such judgments are inevitably subjective and should be divorced from an analysis of this kind. Similarly, responsiveness to public opinion is not tantamount to a policy hindering the national interest, as some observers imply. Another caveat relates to the Constitution. In many cases the Founders envisioned, and the constitutional framework created, the very structures, procedures, and processes about which critics complain; therefore, commentators essentially are expressing dissatisfaction with the constitutional system itself. Yet rather than considering the rationale for the framework or honestly addressing the objections to the Constitution, critics usually simply insinuate that Congress has erred. Finally, while in this section I offer another side to the critics' complaints; the critics are correct that problems exist—many of their concerns are valid. Nonetheless, the conclusions drawn about Congress's ability to participate effectively in foreign policy making tend to be much less valid than some of the specific criticisms about Congress's actions.

An Influential, but Not Dictatorial, Congress

Congress is neither "imperial" nor "impotent." Despite Congress's vast constitutional grants of authority in foreign affairs, the presidency currently is the more powerful branch in the foreign policy arena, enjoying substantial "informal and extraconstitutional techniques for the management of foreign affairs." [88] Thus Congress does not control foreign policy making. Yet that does not make Congress "impotent." Congress is a foreign policy player, influencing policy directly and indirectly. As a discussion of Congress's use of legislative and nonlegislative instruments will illustrate, fixations with Congress's alleged powerlessness and imperialism obscure more than they illuminate.

Contrary to what certain critics suggest, legislative tools sometimes achieve intended results. Cases of Congress influencing policy, checking the president, or imposing wishes on the executive through issue-specific, reactive measures, as described previously, are not lacking. Congress forced South African sanctions on a displeased Reagan administration in 1986, overriding the president's veto to do so. And Congress pushed legislation to aid African drought victims in the mid-1980s. Although in both cases press coverage helped to stimulate a public and relatively unified outcry, hence facilitating Congress's actions, that does not diminish the laws' significance. [89]

Congress also may accomplish its objectives through issue-specific, reactive legislation containing restrictive provisions. In 1984 Congress passed legislation restricting economic assistance to El Salvador, withholding 30 percent of such aid until the Salvadoran government held a trial regarding the killings of four American churchwomen. Congress's use of the purse strings produced a response—a trial was held within months. [90] More generally, restrictive "congressional action on human rights [targeting Latin American countries] did affect [Reagan's] conduct," according to David Forsythe. "Security or economic assistance was blocked, limited, or delayed." [91] Congress has achieved its goals with restrictive provisions in the defense area as well. In 1983 Congress held Reagan's budget request on the MX missile "hostage" and succeeded in eliciting "concessions from the administration on related issues"; and in 1985 Congress "barred the air force from deploying more than fifty MX missiles in fixed silos," one-half of Reagan's request. [92]

Directive legislation, too, may furnish an effective tool. A 1988 CRS study found that Congress may accomplish its objectives through reporting requirements by raising a subject's priority within an agency. [93] Human rights reports did just that, and the 1992 NAPA investigation thus discovered "almost universal agreement" that human rights reports have had a "significant" effect. [94] These reports may keep Congress better informed, making the executive more accountable and less likely to disregard a congressional majority. [95] The reporting requirements in the fiscal 1991 foreign aid appropriations bill regarding the use of U.S. aid in Cambodia similarly furnished Congress with what it wanted—Bush officials were unable to deny that cooperation existed between the U.S.-aided noncommunist resistance and the Khmer Rouge, and this admission served as the foundation for restrictive measures regarding aid.[96]

Congress also may achieve its goals through prospective-procedural laws. The NAPA study concluded that "had Congress not carved out a larger formal role for itself in foreign military sales decisions [through the 1974 Nelson-Bingham amendment, modified in the Arms Export Control Act], the United States would have sold more arms abroad than it had during the 1970s and through the mid-1980s. Moreover, larger numbers and more sophisticated weapons would have been sold to Middle Eastern countries that have historically been enemies of Israel." [97] The NAPA study stressed the Goldwater-Nichols Act accomplishments as well: it "made Congress a stronger and more active player in defense organization and process issues," even "without the [executive's] full support and cooperation." [98]

In addition to achieving intended results, binding legislation influences policy and presidential actions in unanticipated, yet significant, ways. Thus, even if a president circumvents a law or ignores its spirit and intent, the measure is not necessarily useless. The War Powers Resolution is a case in point. Although widely regarded as a failure—because of presidential violations and congressional inability to demand compliance—the law has provided members with a framework for asserting prerogatives and a convenient foil for criticizing executive military actions.[99] Moreover, the simple existence of the War Powers Resolution has affected presidential decisions about whether, how, and for how long to commit troops.[100] Similarly, "general" human rights legislation, though often failing to achieve a stated objective as planned, may achieve an objective in a different way from that intended or it may accomplish another goal. Forsythe explains:

> Though one can seriously question the *direct* importance of a law like Section 502B of the Foreign Assistance Act pertaining to security aid and human rights, especially during the Reagan administration, that legislation may have indirect importance through country-specific legislation. The general legislation becomes a talking point in congressional proceedings. The law legitimizes congressional concern. It socializes persons into thinking about the linkage between human rights and security assistance, and thus it may contribute indirectly to U.S. action on human rights.[101]

Beyond accomplishing its objectives by enacting legislation into law, Congress also often achieves desired results by threatening legislative actions, particularly when Congress exhibits the consensus and will to pass a measure. When Congress was on the verge of passing (and subsequently overriding Reagan's expected veto of) a 1985 South African sanctions bill, for instance, Reagan sought to preempt congressional action by issuing an executive order. The executive order addressed many of Congress's concerns. Congress hence succeeded in influencing policy without passing the bill, forcing Reagan to alter his approach of "constructive engagement." [102] And from the president's vantage point, he forestalled congressional action, at least temporarily. Thus, when assessing Congress's legislative influence, one must look past the scorecard of legislation enacted into law.

Congress's means of influence are not limited to legislative vehicles—those enacted into law and simply threatened—as some critics imply. Congress also affects foreign policy through nonlegislative tools. Nonlegislative tools offer members opportunities to influence agendas, decision making, and actions by swaying opinions, informing and educating, and generating anticipated reactions. Several examples illustrate the potential effect of nonlegislative tools. When Bush failed to offer a far-reaching new defense strategy in response to the end of the Cold War, members in early 1990 began employing a variety of nonlegislative devices. In floor statements, public appeals through the press, and committee hearings, "legislators excoriated Bush's 'business as usual' FY 91 [budget] request, and highlighted the need for a quick and dramatic revision of U.S. military strategy." [103] Congress's "evident willingness" to act spurred Bush; he subsequently offered a revised proposal "sufficiently consistent with the congressional demands for change." [104] Congressional nonlegislative activism similarly influenced Reagan's policy toward the Philippines in 1985-1986. Informal advice, direct dealings with foreign governments, public appeals through the press, and floor statements are only a few of the nonlegislative tools members employed in that case.[105] Senator Lugar's public protests of Ferdinand Marcos's efforts to steal the election finally swayed an obstinate Reagan, who had been reluctant to concede that the Philippine election was not a situation of fraud "on both sides." [106] Nonlegislative devices, applied relentlessly and extraordinarily effectively, have even prompted a unilateral Pentagon decision to kill a weapon already in production. In 1985 the Pentagon terminated the DIVAD program (conceived in the mid-1970s to furnish antiaircraft protection for army tank divisions against the Soviets) following intense nonlegislative activism—former defense secretary Caspar Weinberger announced the cancellation after former representative Denny Smith, R-Ore., threatened to publicize the real results of DIVAD's operational tests.[107] Legislators' direct dealings with foreign governments also sometimes have dramatic results: after a January 1991 meeting with members, for instance, Saudi ambassador Prince Bandar Bin Sultan apparently suggested postponing the huge U.S. arms deal to Saudi Arabia because of concern about significant congressional opposition.[108]

In evaluating Congress's influence, critics also must recognize that the legislature's effectiveness varies by issue. Consequently, it is misleading to stress Congress's impotence based only on its actions in crisis situations. Congress often appears unable to wield any weapon—let alone its most potent weapon, the power of the purse—when faced with a fait accompli such as an undeclared war, for Congress then would be responsible for stranding soldiers in the field. Furthermore, presidential power is at its greatest under such crisis conditions.[109] Yet on "strategic" policy (for example, specifying "goals and tactics") and "structural" policy (for example, "procuring, deploying, and organizing military personnel and material"), Jim Lindsay and Randall Ripley argue that Congress's influence increases.[110] Especially when a "policy vacuum" exists, Congress is more apt to be able to assert itself successfully.[111]

The preceding discussion has illustrated that Congress is a player in the foreign policy arena and can influence policy. Sometimes legislation achieves intended results; sometimes legislation succeeds in unexpected ways; sometimes the threat of legislation generates desired actions; and sometimes nonlegislative mechanisms accomplish members' goals. Despite successes, though, critics who see an impotent Congress correctly raise a few problems, albeit they greatly overstate the extent and consequences of these problems. In particular, binding legislation is not flawless. Presidents do ignore the letter and intent of laws, and Congress may fail to confront presidents with such violations. Moreover, in order to garner adequate support for passing legislation and because of poor drafting, laws may have loopholes and ambiguities (even if giveaways are not the norm). Limits on Congress's effectiveness thus exist; nonetheless, we have seen that Congress can be an effective foreign policy participant and should not be considered impotent.

The fact that Congress is not impotent, however, does not validate claims of an imperial Congress. Four points deserve further attention in this regard. First, critics significantly exaggerate the degree to which Congress engages in micromanagement. Critics typically fail to offer evidence documenting that this activity is as extensive as they suggest, instead extrapolating from a few specific examples to imply that the cases exemplify Congress's work. Yet although Congress at times uses the purse strings to assert itself, and although members have undertaken actions of "lone ranger diplomacy," for instance, it is misleading to draw sweeping conclusions from isolated occurrences. Indeed, the president has substantial flexibility on most issues, especially on those relating to crisis situations. Similarly, complaints of Congress increasing demands on the executive through nonlegislative means are overblown—the number of hearings and requested testimonies on defense activities, for example, has been relatively stable.[112] Critics also exaggerate the burden of reporting requirements. It is unlikely that $50 million in reporting expenses strained a $300 billion Pentagon budget, for instance, as Bush suggested.[113]

Second, the criticism of an imperial Congress is often disingenuous. The argument may serve as a smoke screen for critics unhappy with the constitutional structure because it allows a Democratic Congress to oppose or check a Republican president and hinder the "national interest." In other words, the "imperial" grievance may stem both from policy disagreements with a Democratic Congress and a concomitant belief that a Republican president knows best. As Lindsay explains, "Many of the same [critics] who today denounce the 'imperial Congress' applauded when conservatives on Capitol Hill obstructed Jimmy Carter's diplomatic initiatives." [114] If protests were sincere, moreover, executive branch officials complaining about micromanagement through reporting requirements, for instance, would make significant and numerous suggestions to abolish reports when so asked. Yet Congress alone has worked to abolish unnecessary reports.[115] (Also suggestive of the hypocrisy here is the occurrence of presidential requests for Congress to require some reports. Facing the possibility of an aid cutoff to Jordan because of Jordan's support for Iraq in the 1991 Persian Gulf war, Bush sought a provision allowing $27 million in military assistance to Jordan if he reported that it had both terminated Iraqi aid and backed the Middle East peace efforts.[116]) The executive reaction to cases of congressional "intrusion" further illustrates the criticism's hollowness. Despite administration cries that Congress undermines the president and curtails his flexibility, the executive may in fact desire congressional action. The White House may appreciate being able to blame Congress for having done what it wanted to do but felt that it could not.[117] Similarly, "good cop" presidents may find congressional power over the purse handy, warning foreign governments of severe "bad cop" retribution if certain conditions are not fulfilled.[118]

Third, an imperial Congress is an unrealistic possibility under our constitutional framework. Just to form a consensus among a majority of both bodies is often so difficult that it is unlikely that Congress could pass measures forcing the president to be Congress's "servant." And even if a majority in both houses defy a president, mustering the requisite two-thirds to override a veto is improbable—Congress has only overridden one foreign policy veto since the War Powers Resolution in 1973. Congress could not even block Reagan's controversial 1981 sale of advanced-technology AWACS (airborne warning and control system) radar planes to Saudi Arabia, for instance, when a simple majority for a concurrent resolution of disapproval would have sufficed. As Blechman writes, "With Ronald Reagan at the height of his popularity, members could not successfully stand up against him, even with the Democratic party and the Israeli lobby behind them." [119]

Fourth, when congressional micromanagement occurs, it sometimes happens in reaction to executive actions that invite a response—that is, a refusal to discharge the constitutional obligation to "take care that the laws be faithfully executed." And as Louis Fisher states, if an administration chooses "to sabotage statutory programs and . . . implement White House policy instead of public law, the light for congressional intervention turns green." [120] Thus rather than an insidious Congress waiting to pounce on an unsuspecting executive, a reactive Congress simply may be responding to executive misdeeds.

A Deliberative Congress
(Not Necessarily Inefficient or Indiscreet)

Institutional inadequacies do indeed exist. In selected instances Congress may move too slowly, members may manipulate procedural devices and delay action on urgent measures, and individual legislators may leak classified information. These flaws, however, do not render Congress unable to contribute effectively to foreign policy making.

Congress is, and was designed to be, a deliberative body. As discussed earlier in the section on the constitutional framework, the Founders did not intend Congress to be the paragon of efficiency—they preferred to preclude the arbitrary exercise of power. Nonetheless, although Congress is a deliberative body not designed for fast action, and although it does move more slowly than may be desirable in some cases, it also can, in the words of Rep. Lee Hamilton, D-Ind., "act quickly upon occasion." [121] When speed is paramount, Congress can enact and follow expedited procedures.[122] In considering whether to authorize the use of force in the Persian Gulf in January 1991, for instance, Congress responded promptly to Bush's request for congressional action. Bush asked, in a letter of January 8, for a resolution stating support for the "use of all necessary means to implement" the U.N. resolution. The House and Senate each then considered two separate resolutions, and Congress finished action on January 12, four days after Bush's request and three days before the January 15 U.N. deadline.[123] Congress's speed here—regardless of how one feels about its final vote—is noteworthy. Along these lines, procedural delays in the Senate by nongermane amendments and filibusters often can be managed. When controversial nongermane amendments bogged down the African famine relief bill in March 1984, for instance, African drought victims did not have to wait four months for U.S. aid (until House-Senate disagreements were resolved), as critic Easterbrook suggested. Instead, Congress ensured that food aid would not be "held hostage" by irrelevant funding disputes; it immediately attached emergency food aid to an urgent low-income energy supplemental aid bill, which was enacted into law within weeks.[124] And in the House, too, majority party leaders manipulate rules and procedures to thwart others' efforts to delay or kill measures they favor. Just observe how the leadership and former Banking Committee chairman Fernand St Germain, D-R.I., moved the unpopular $8.4 billion International Monetary Fund quota increase through the House in 1983; they attached the bill to a popular housing measure and brought the package to the floor in such a way that it could not be debated for more than one hour or amended.[125]

Sometimes, though, Congress is simply inefficient. In certain cases this inefficiency can be problematic; at other times it can be beneficial. In other words, an efficient Congress is not tantamount to a wise Congress. "Deliberation often prevents error." [126] Open debate in formulating legislation may help ensure that policies reflect public attitudes and have the public support needed to sustain them over the long term. And on major, controversial issues, prolonged congressional deliberation not surprisingly mirrors the public debate. Even widespread committee participation, as part of the deliberative process, may not be patently harmful; broad involvement may counter the often narrow executive decision making and the possibility that policies will fall prey to distortions of "groupthink." Furthermore, there are few instances in which speed is as critical as commentators would have us believe. Even in crisis situations, a decision rarely needs to be made so quickly that Congress cannot participate.

Congress also is not a sieve, leaking whatever comes its way. In fact, the executive branch leaks significantly more information than does Congress.[127] Near the beginning of his first term as vice president, Bush considered leaks to be the Reagan administration's "biggest failure." [128] "Everything from classified intelligence reports to accounts of a spat between Secretary of State

Alexander Haig and Defense Secretary Caspar Weinberger [had] found its way into the press." [129] And the question of the two leaks that North raised in the Iran-contra hearings to support his contention that Congress could not be trusted came from the executive branch, not from Congress; North himself had leaked one of the stories.[130]

A Flexible Congress Grappling with Some Long-Term Issues

Congress can be shortsighted. Yet contrary to conventional wisdom, it is not always shortsighted. Indeed, Congress at times strives for both consistency and a long-term approach to problems. Through issue-specific legislation Congress may confront the underlying causes of crises. In the mid-1980s, for instance, congressional legislation addressed not only the immediate African famine emergency but also the long-term problems associated with the emergency.[131] In addition, with prospective-procedural measures Congress may attempt to construct a broad framework in a specific policy area that will ensure constancy of approach over an extended period of time. For example, the 1980 Intelligence Oversight Act requires prior congressional notification of covert operations. All executive agencies dealing with intelligence must report to the House and Senate intelligence committees unless the president determines that an operation affects vital U.S. interests. In that case, prior notification is limited to eight specified congressional leaders.[132] And the 1988 Omnibus Trade and Competitiveness Act requires, among other things, increased consultation with Congress (even during trade negotiations) and annual reports from the U.S. trade representative on policy objectives and actions taken to achieve the objectives.[133] In the human rights area, Congress created the Bureau of Human Rights and Humanitarian Affairs in the State Department in 1977; the bureau now compiles annual reports on the human rights situation in every U.N. member state. Congress succeeded here in institutionalizing human rights in the State Department's bureaucratic structure, with a human rights officer working on the annual reports in every bureau and overseas post.[134]

Obviously, though, Congress is at times inconstant and myopic. But this inconstancy is not necessarily problematic, as it may allow for flexibility.[135] Congressional policy shifts often simply reflect eroding public support for unwavering policy approaches. And it is not axiomatic that such responsiveness to public opinion, even if it yields inconstant policies, hurts the "national interest" as critics assume. The ability to mirror public ambivalence, as discussed below, is one of Congress's attributes; a president may be less apt to appreciate prevailing attitudes and less able to respond.[136]

Congress is not the only branch that struggles with inconstancy and a proclivity for shortsightedness. Presidents, too, are guilty of myopia and making policy changes. According to Maynard Glitman, chief negotiator for the Intermediate-Range Nuclear Forces (INF) Treaty and former ambassador to Belgium, "presidents may be more prone to short-sightedness than Congress, whose members have almost guaranteed life tenures." [137] Incoming presidents, on the other hand, "often approach issues in the context of a four-year term," that is, to "make a mark" they must act quickly. [138] Consider Reagan's inconstancy and shortsightedness on the matter of terrorism. At the very time that Reagan was advocating a policy of not dealing with terrorists or their sponsors, he covertly did just that in the Iran-contra affair, secretly trading arms for hostages. [139] Albeit the relative level of inconstancy and myopia between Congress and the president cannot easily be gauged, it is important to appreciate that this is not exclusively Congress's problem—it is unfair to level criticisms only against Congress that similarly apply to the executive.

A Congress with Foreign Policy Expertise

The majority of members are not foreign policy specialists. Members may enter Congress with little knowledge of foreign policy issues, and while there they may not become well schooled in these matters. Nonetheless, ignorance is not a serious defect in the foreign policy realm; Congress as an institution has, and utilizes, foreign policy expertise.

The congressional leaders on foreign policy issues who influence the legislative agenda, the parameters of debates, the votes of rank-and-file members, and the policy outcomes tend to be members with much more expertise than the average member and with more expertise than critics concede. With larger and more highly qualified staffs and with the increase in foreign travel, these members have become better informed. And because of long service in Congress, members in fact may "possess a degree of expertise and kind of institutional memory rarely found in the upper echelon of Executive Departments." [140] Representative Hamilton, for instance, a leader in the foreign policy field, was elected to the House in 1965; he has seen six presidents in the White House and eight secretaries in the State Department. Senior congressional aides also typically remain on the job much longer than secretaries and assistant secretaries. Hamilton's "foreign policy alter ego," Michael Van Dusen, has been on the representative's staff since 1971. [141] And because other members rely on the expertise of knowledgeable members and staff, such as Hamilton and Van Dusen, Glitman found in his experience that "it is not necessary for everybody to be an expert." [142] During Senate consideration of the INF Treaty, for instance, Glitman stressed that senators looked to Chairman Nunn of the Armed Services Committee, who is known for his and his staff's specialized knowledge.

The criticism of an "ignorant" Congress often rests on the assumption that only presidential actions, based on broad knowledge of complex issues, promote the national interest. But this assumption is problematic. As Samuel Huntington explained, "The more important a policy issue is, the less important becomes detailed technical information and the more relevant becomes broad judgments on goals and values, i.e., political judgments, where presumably the congressman's competence is greatest." [143] In other words, members may not always need a sophisticated appreciation of the "interrelationship of international events," as Nixon suggested.

A Reelection-Oriented Congress—
No Cause for Alarm

Most members are reelection oriented. Since a legislator's survival in office hinges on adequate district support, a member will try to respond to perceived constituent—and particularly supportive constituent—pressures.[144] Yet the consequences of the reelection orientation are not as negative as critics believe. Although in some foreign policy cases a reelection obsession and a consequent fear of retribution at the polls may prompt individual members to undertake questionable actions and to be uncreative and risk-averse, by and large Congress is not critically harmed by this phenomenon.

Commentators exaggerate the ramifications of members' reelection orientation. Congress, even a reelection-oriented Congress, may not pander to special constituent interests as consistently as critics contend—consider Congress's independence from the pro-Israel lobby in the fall of 1991, when this powerful lobby was actively supporting the proposed $10 billion loan guarantees to Israel.[145] Key legislators backed Bush's request that Congress delay action on the loan guarantees until early 1992 because of concerns that granting the loan guarantees at that time "could jeopardize plans for an Arab-Israeli peace conference." [146] PAC money as well tends not to govern congressional vote outcomes. Although it may affect a few particular members' votes, more generally it buys access.[147] The effects of parochialism on specific issues also may be overblown, for critics sometimes ignore the multidimensional aspects of policy questions. Kenneth Mayer writes, "To suggest that Congress would find it easy to cancel the MX if the system produced no economic benefits ignores the tremendous uncertainty surrounding the debate over the future of U.S. strategic nuclear forces." [148]

Critics similarly overstate the consequences of the electoral orientation on individual members' involvement and thus on the actions of Congress as a whole. Responsiveness to constituents is primarily symbolic in nature; constituents affect whether members participate much more than how extensively they participate.[149] Members' perceptions of supporters' preferences generally do not lead members to engage in forms of involvement likely to affect the outcome of a debate; instead, their perceptions prompt activities that simply may help electorally. Hence, the impact of responsiveness to constituents is minimal in terms of actual policy formation. Congressional foreign policy leaders and activists are driven not by constituents but by personal policy interests, committee and leadership position, and the desire for influence.[150]

Commentators also assume that members allow parochial concerns to sidetrack national objectives, essentially because the public does not encourage actions consonant with the national interest. Yet judgments about the national interest are inevitably subjective; hence, it is not axiomatic that constituents promote policies contrary to the good of the nation. Furthermore, as Rep. Patsy T.

Mink, D-Hawaii, wrote after time in Congress and the State Department, "It is folly to believe . . . that good foreign policy necessarily stands above the pressures of . . . constituent interests. Politics is the art of reconciling and educating, not of avoiding, those interests." [151] A foreign policy, to be pursued effectively over an extended period of time, typically requires a foundation of legitimacy, and it may gain that legitimacy through public backing. Representative Hamilton explained that "congressional support is a primary expression of the people's approval. The President is not likely to gain the support of the American people if he cannot gain [Congress's] support." [152]

Finally, it is noteworthy that the Framers recognized that self-interest would be a significant motive and sought strong constituent links. According to Madison, "Duty, gratitude, interest, ambition itself, are the cords by which [representatives] will be bound to fidelity and sympathy with the great mass of the people." [153] Consequently, the standard for judging the use of legislative and nonlegislative vehicles should not be purity of motives—purity of motives is not a precondition for a tool to be helpful or for Congress to contribute to foreign policy making.

Summary

Congress is, and will remain, a participant in the foreign policy making process. And contrary to what critics contend, that prospect is a positive feature of our system of government. Considering how Congress exercises its constitutional prerogatives, we have seen that the criticisms of congressional participation in foreign policy making are often overblown and misguided; effective congressional participation in foreign affairs is not an oxymoron for the reasons critics have identified. Congress is neither imperial nor impotent; Congress is not so institutionally inadequate, inconstant, or ignorant to render it incapable of contributing to foreign policy making; and members' interests in reelection do not disqualify Congress from playing a productive role. Although it is convenient and intuitively appealing to use Congress as a receptacle for blame, little here suggests that such an orientation is correct. In fact, Congress often contributes effectively to foreign policy making, offering such strengths as greater deliberation of policies, discretion, flexibility, expertise, and representation of public sentiment. Perhaps it is time to appreciate some of Congress's virtues rather than simply harping on its vices.

Notes

For their comments on this essay or other assistance with this project, I thank Vaughn Altemus, Christopher Bumstead, Morris Fiorina, James Lindsay, Bruce Oppenheimer, Mark Peterson, Tom Rice, Robert Taylor, and most especially George Young.

1. Alexis de Tocqueville, *Democracy in America,* ed. J. P. Mayer, trans. George Lawrence (Garden City, N.Y.: Doubleday, 1969), 228.
2. For two recent works in the area of defense policy that offer a more positive per-

spective than this, see James M. Lindsay, *Congress and Nuclear Weapons* (Baltimore: Johns Hopkins University Press, 1991); and Kenneth R. Mayer, *The Political Economy of Defense Contracting* (New Haven: Yale University Press, 1991).

3. James M. Lindsay, "Congress and Diplomacy," in *Congress Resurgent: Foreign and Defense Policy on Capitol Hill,* ed. Randall B. Ripley and James M. Lindsay (Ann Arbor: University of Michigan Press, forthcoming).

4. L. Gordon Crovitz and Jeremy A. Rabkin, eds., *The Fettered Presidency* (Washington, D.C.: American Enterprise Institute, 1989); Gordon S. Jones and John A. Marini, eds., *The Imperial Congress* (New York: Heritage Foundation, 1988); and quote of former president Gerald R. Ford in Marvin Stone, "Presidency: Imperial or Imperiled?" *U.S. News and World Report,* Jan. 15, 1979, 88.

5. See Herman A. Mellor, "Congressional Micromanagement: National Defense," in *Imperial Congress,* 107-129; and commentary by Richard N. Perle, in *Fettered Presidency,* 103-104.

6. Harold Hongju Koh, "Why the President (Almost) Always Wins in Foreign Affairs: Lessons of the Iran-Contra Affair," *Yale Law Journal* 97 (June 1988): 1297. Emphasis added.

7. For instance, see Les Aspin, "Congress Versus the Defense Department," in *The Tethered Presidency,* ed. Thomas M. Franck (New York: New York University Press, 1981), 245-263; I. M. Destler, "Executive-Congressional Conflict in Foreign Policy: Explaining It, Coping with It," in *Congress Reconsidered,* 3d ed., ed. Lawrence C. Dodd and Bruce I. Oppenheimer (Washington, D.C.: CQ Press, 1985), 343-363; and J. William Fulbright, "The Legislator as Educator," *Foreign Affairs* 57 (Spring 1979): 719-732.

8. Higgs used the phrase in reference to a "selfish, parochial, and wasteful" Congress. See Robert Higgs, "Hard Coals Make Bad Law: Congressional Parochialism Versus National Defense," *Cato Journal* 8 (Spring-Summer 1988): 80.

9. *The Federalist Papers,* No. 6 (New York: New American Library, 1961), 59.

10. Even former representative Dick Cheney, a staunch supporter of the "fettered presidency" school of thought, admonished John Poindexter in the Iran-contra hearings: "The reason for not misleading the Congress is a practical one. It is stupid." House Select Committee to Investigate Covert Arms Transactions with Iran and Senate Select Committee on Secret Military Assistance to Iran and the Nicaraguan Opposition, *Joint Hearings on the Iran-Contra Investigation,* 100th Cong., 1st sess., 1987, 246.

11. Throughout the essay I refer mainly to recent issues, that is, those from the 1980s and early 1990s. Three factors encourage this concentration. First, as Mann states, the "pace of congressional involvement [in foreign policy making] actually accelerated during the presidency of Ronald Reagan." See Thomas E. Mann, "Making Foreign Policy: President and Congress," in *A Question of Balance: The President, the Congress, and Foreign Policy,* ed. Thomas E. Mann (Washington, D.C.: Brookings Institution, 1990), 1. For a different view, see Ralph G. Carter, "Congressional Foreign Policy Behavior: Persistent Patterns of the Postwar Period," *Presidential Studies Quarterly* 16 (Spring 1986): 329-359. Second, scholars have already lavished much attention on congressional assertiveness in the immediate post-Vietnam period. For example, see Thomas M. Franck and Edward Weisband, *Foreign Policy by Congress* (New York: Oxford University Press, 1979); James L. Sundquist, *The Decline and Resurgence of Congress* (Washington, D.C.: Brookings Institution, 1981); Charles W. Whalen, Jr., *The House and Foreign Affairs: The Irony of Congressional Reform* (Chapel Hill: University of North Carolina Press, 1982). And, third, reader familiarity with recent issues is likely to be greater.

12. Raoul Berger, *Executive Privilege: A Constitutional Myth* (Cambridge: Harvard University Press, 1973), 131.

13. Note that the term "foreign affairs" is not used in the Constitution itself.

14. Richard E. Neustadt, *Presidential Power: The Politics of Leadership with Reflections on Johnson and Nixon* (New York: Wiley, 1976), 101.
15. *Federalist Papers*, No. 51, 322.
16. *Myers v. United States*, 272 U.S. 52 (1926), 293.
17. See, for instance, Cecil V. Crabb, Jr., and Pat M. Holt, *Invitation to Struggle: Congress, the President, and Foreign Policy*, 4th ed. (Washington, D.C.: CQ Press, 1992), 39-55; Mann, "Making Foreign Policy," 4-7. An argument has emerged recently, however, that presidents have inherent constitutional powers, making them dominant in conducting foreign policy. See Committees Investigating the Iran-Contra Affair, *Minority Report of the Congressional Committees Investigating the Iran-Contra Affair*, 100th Cong., 1st sess., 1987, H. Rept. 100-433, S. Rept. 100-216, pt. 2, chap. 2.
18. *Federalist Papers*, No. 58, 359.
19. Michael J. Glennon, *Constitutional Diplomacy* (Princeton: Princeton University Press, 1990), 72.
20. *Federalist Papers*, No. 69, 418. Emphasis in original.
    This is not to imply, however, that there are not differing interpretations of the war power. See David Gray Adler, "The Constitution and Presidential Warmaking: The Enduring Debate," *Political Science Quarterly* 103 (Spring 1988): 1-36; J. Terry Emerson, "The War Powers Resolution Tested: The President's Independent Defense Power," *Notre Dame Lawyer* 51 (1975): 187-216; and Abraham D. Sofaer, *War, Foreign Affairs, and Constitutional Power: The Origins* (Cambridge, Mass.: Ballinger, 1976).
21. *Youngstown Sheet and Tube Company v. Sawyer*, 343 U.S. 579 (1952), 637.
22. Edward S. Corwin, *The President: Office and Powers, 1787-1957*, 4th rev. ed. (New York: New York University Press, 1957), 171.
23. The phrase is Louis Henkin's in "Foreign Affairs and the Constitution," *Foreign Affairs* 66 (Winter 1987-1988): 285.
24. House Committee on Foreign Affairs (hereafter HCFA), *Congress and Foreign Policy, 1985-1986*, 1987, Committee Print, 24-36.
25. Bruce W. Jentleson, "American Diplomacy: Around the World and Along Pennsylvania Avenue," in *Question of Balance*, 172-174.
26. HCFA, *Congress and Foreign Policy, 1983*, 1984, Committee Print, 110-133.
27. HCFA, *Congress and Foreign Policy, 1985-1986*, 142-157.
28. See Cynthia J. Aronson, *Crossroads: Congress, the Reagan Administration, and Central America* (New York: Pantheon, 1989).
29. Kenneth Sharpe, "The Post-Vietnam Formula Under Siege: The Imperial Presidency and Central America," *Political Science Quarterly* 102 (Winter 1987-1988): 556-559.
30. Pamela Fessler, "Complaints Are Stacking Up as Hill Piles on Reports," *Congressional Quarterly Weekly Report*, Sept. 7, 1991, 2562.
31. Ibid., 2564.
32. PL 102-1.
33. See PL 93-148. Reprinted in HCFA, Subcommittee on Arms Control, International Security and Science, *The War Powers Resolution: Relevant Documents, Correspondence, and Reports*, 100th Cong., 2d sess., May 1988, Committee Print, 1.
34. HCFA, *Congress and Foreign Policy, 1988*, 1989, Committee Print, 94-95.
35. For some exceptions, see Thomas M. Franck and Clifford A. Bob, "The Return of Humpty-Dumpty: Foreign Relations Law After the Chadha Case," *American Journal of International Law* 79 (October 1985): 912-960; Susan Webb Hammond, "Congress in Foreign Policy," in *The President, The Congress, and Foreign Policy*, ed. Edmund S. Muskie, Kenneth Rush, and Kenneth W. Thompson (Lanham, Md.: University Press of America, 1986), 67-91; James M. Lindsay, "Congress and Foreign Policy: Why the Hill Matters," *Political Science Quarterly* (forthcoming); and

James M. McCormick, "Decisionmaking in the Foreign Affairs and Foreign Relations Committees," in *Congress Resurgent.*

36. Lindsay, "Congress and Foreign Policy," 9, describes the phenomenon of anticipated reactions well: "Just as chess players consider their opponent's possible moves and plan several steps ahead, Congress and the executive branch anticipate one another's behavior and modify their own behavior accordingly." Admittedly, though, the effect of anticipated reactions cannot be evaluated perfectly. Peterson writes, "the processes are so complex, the participants are so varied and numerous, and executive decisions about legislative issues are often not discrete events." Mark A. Peterson, *Legislating Together* (Cambridge: Harvard University Press, 1990), 46.

37. For a discussion of the effect of issue-related factors on the influences affecting a representative's participation in foreign policy issues, see Eileen Burgin, "Representatives' Participation in the House: The Impact of Issue-Related Factors on Foreign Policy Involvement" (Paper presented at the annual meeting of the American Political Science Association, Washington, D.C., Aug. 29-Sept. 1, 1991).

38. For background on the timing and duration of the Panama incursion, see Eileen Burgin, "Congress, the War Powers Resolution, and the Invasion of Panama," *Polity* (forthcoming).

39. See McCormick, "Decisionmaking in the Foreign Affairs and Foreign Relations Committees"; and Barbara Sinclair, "Congressional Party Leaders in the Foreign and Defense Policy Arena," in *Congress Resurgent.*

40. Yet little empirical evidence exists documenting the consequences of split-party control of the two branches on the nature of legislative behavior in the foreign policy arena. See Morris P. Fiorina, *Divided Government* (New York: Macmillan, 1992); and David R. Mayhew, *Divided We Govern* (New Haven: Yale University Press, 1991). Moving beyond the effect of divided government on kinds of actions undertaken to consider results, we do have the basis for clear observations. Fiorina states that "there may be some small degree of increased conflict over presidential appointments when different parties control the presidency and the Senate, and the president may be marginally less successful" *(Divided Government,* 99). It certainly appears likely, considering the partisan Senate vote, for instance, that a Republican Senate would have confirmed Bush's first nominee for secretary of defense, John Tower. See Pat Towell, "Senate Spurns Bush's Choice in a Partisan Tug of War," *Congressional Quarterly Weekly Report,* March 11, 1989, 530-534.

41. HCFA, *Congress and Foreign Policy, 1985-1986,* 16-36.

42. Martin Tolchin, "House Vote Opposes Mining of Nicaraguan Ports," *New York Times,* April 13, 1984, sec. A.

43. HCFA, *Congress and Foreign Policy, 1989,* 1990, Committee Print, 28.

44. Raymond Bonner, *Waltzing with a Dictator: The Marcoses and the Making of American Policy* (New York: Times Books, 1987), 410-440.

45. Rochelle Stanfield, "Weighing Arms Sales for Saudis," *National Journal,* Jan. 12, 1991, 79.

46. HCFA, *Congress and Foreign Policy, 1987,* 1989, Committee Print, 70-84.

47. Lindsay, "Congress and Diplomacy."

48. Daniel Wirls, "Congress and the Politics of Military Reform," *Armed Forces and Society* 17 (Summer 1991): 489-490.

49. See the following articles from the *Washington Post:* Kenneth Bredemeier and Michel Marriott, "Fauntroy Arrested in Embassy," Nov. 22, 1984, sec. A; Philip Smith, "Fauntroy Released in Sit-In Case," Nov. 23, 1984, sec. B; and Courtland Milloy, "Blacks Form 'Free South Africa Movement,'" Nov. 24, 1984, sec. C.

50. For instance, from the *Washington Post,* see Saundra Saperstein and Michel Marriott, "Protest Grows at Embassy," Nov. 28, 1984, sec. A; Karlyn Barker and Michel Mariott, "1960s Tactic Revived for Embassy Sit-Ins," Nov. 29, 1984, sec. A; Karlyn Barker and Chris Spolar, "Tutu Hails Embassy Protestors," Dec. 3, 1984, sec. B;

Allister Sparks, "South Africa Notes Washington Protests," Dec. 8, 1984, sec. A; Karlyn Barker, "Rosa Parks, New Groups Join Protest," Dec. 11, 1984, sec. A; John Ward Anderson, "Clergy, Boxer Protest at Embassy," Dec. 14, 1984, sec. A.

51. For a listing of House and Senate committees with some foreign policy jurisdiction, see Hammond, "Congress in Foreign Policy," 77.

52. For a brief discussion of the hearings held by the Senate Armed Services and Foreign Relations committees and the House Foreign Affairs Committee, see Crabb and Holt, *Invitation to Struggle,* 155-157.

53. For two conflicting views of the Iran-contra hearings, see William S. Cohen and George J. Mitchell, *Men of Zeal,* rev. ed. (New York: Penguin, 1989); and Harold Hongju Koh, *The National Security Constitution: Sharing Power After the Iran-Contra Affair* (New Haven: Yale University Press, 1990), chap. 1. On the Gates nomination, see Senate Select Committee on Intelligence, *Nomination of Robert M. Gates to be Director of Central Intelligence,* 102d Cong., 1st sess., 1991, Exec. Rept. 102-19.

54. The phrase is Mayhew's. See David R. Mayhew, *Congress: The Electoral Connection* (New Haven: Yale University Press, 1974), 61-73.

55. In the *Congressional Record,* 100th Cong., 1st sess., see the following: March 11, 1987, S2967-S2986; March 12, 1987, S3090-S3095; and March 13, 1987, S3171-S3173.

56. HCFA, *Congress and Foreign Policy, 1987,* 67.

57. See Thomas M. Franck, "Courts and Foreign Policy," *Foreign Policy* 83 (Summer 1991): 66-86; and Koh, *National Security Constitution,* chap. 6.

58. Douglas A. Jeffrey, "Executive Authority Under the Separation of Powers," in *Imperial Congress,* 62.

59. Fessler, "Complaints Are Stacking Up," 2562.

60. For instance, see Caspar W. Weinberger, "Dangerous Constraints on the President's War Powers," in *Fettered Presidency,* 95-101. And for a more sweeping challenge to the constitutionality of congressional foreign policy actions, see John Felton, "Bush Throws Down the Gauntlet on Provisions He Opposes," *Congressional Quarterly Weekly Report,* Feb. 24, 1990, 603-604.

61. Koh, *National Security Constitution,* 117.

62. For instance, see Sharpe, "Post-Vietnam Formula Under Siege," 556-559.

63. These arguments are reviewed in Burgin, "Congress, the War Powers Resolution, and the Invasion of Panama."

64. Sharpe, "Post-Vietnam Formula Under Siege," 556.

65. Ibid., 556-559.

66. Koh, *National Security Constitution,* 129.

67. Martin Tolchin, "Congress: Of C.I.A. Games, and Disputed Rules," *New York Times,* May 14, 1984, sec. A.

68. Koh, *National Security Constitution,* 58-59.

69. For a review of the act's provisions, see Congressional Research Service, "Covert Actions: Congressional Oversight," IB87208, Oct. 14, 1988.

70. For instance, see Koh, *National Security Constitution,* 131-133.

71. Gregg Easterbrook, "What's Wrong with Congress?" *Atlantic Monthly,* December 1983, 57-84.

72. Glennon, *Constitutional Diplomacy,* 28.

73. Panel of the National Academy of Public Administration (hereafter NAPA), *Beyond Distrust: Building Bridges Between Congress and the Executive* (Washington, D.C.: National Academy of Public Administration, 1992), 109-110.

74. For instance, see Franck and Weisband's discussion of two congressional actions: (1) the decision to allow bombing in Cambodia only until August 15, 1973 (or for forty-five more days); and (2) the cutoff of military aid to Turkey in 1974, with the cutoff's implementation suspended for almost two months, theoretically to allow for executive diplomatic flexibility. *Foreign Policy by Congress,* 17-23, 35-45.

75. The Bush administration voiced such complaints about congressional handling of China's most-favored-nation status. See Eduardo Lachica, "Senate Imposes Curbs on China's Trade Status," *Wall Street Journal,* Feb. 26, 1992, sec. A.
76. See Cohen and Mitchell, *Men of Zeal,* 183.
77. Tocqueville, *Democracy in America,* 229.
78. Committees Investigating the Iran-Contra Affair, *Minority Report,* 438, 511.
79. On the shifts described here, see Philip Brenner and William M. LeoGrande, "Congress and Nicaragua: The Limits of Alternative Policy Making," in *Divided Democracy: Cooperation and Conflict Between the President and Congress,* ed. James A. Thurber (Washington, D.C.: CQ Press, 1991), 222-233.
80. Barry M. Blechman, *The Politics of National Security: Congress and U.S. Defense Policy* (New York: Oxford University Press, 1990), 21.
81. Ibid., 56-57.
82. Report to the Congress, Feb. 18, *1970, Public Papers of the Presidents of the United States: Richard Nixon,* 1970, 179.
83. For instance, a Bush White House official explained why any House measure on most-favored-nation status for China would be unacceptable: "It is just too hard to educate that many members." David S. Cloud, "White House Looks to Senate to Maintain China Status," *Congressional Quarterly Weekly Report,* June 1, 1991, 1434.
84. The argument, in its initial and general form (that is, not relating to foreign policy) appears in Morris P. Fiorina, *Congress: Keystone of the Washington Establishment,* 2d ed. (New Haven: Yale University Press, 1989); and Mayhew, *Congress: The Electoral Connection.*
85. Tom Morganthau, "A Not So Simple Game," *Newsweek,* Jan. 14, 1991, 20.
86. Pietro S. Nivola, "Trade Policy: Refereeing the Playing Field," in *Question of Balance,* 239.
87. Fulbright, "Legislator as Educator," 719-732.
88. Crabb and Holt, *Invitation to Struggle,* 19-23.
89. See HCFA, "Congress and Foreign Policy, 1985-1986," 24-26, 142-157.
90. Certainly, though, the quality of the proceedings may be questionable. David P. Forsythe, *Human Rights and U.S. Foreign Policy: Congress Reconsidered* (Gainesville: University of Florida Press, 1988), 140.
91. Ibid., 157.
92. See, respectively, Blechman, *Politics of National Security,* 90-91; Lindsay, *Congress and Nuclear Weapons,* 146.
93. Fessler, "Complaints Are Stacking Up," 2565.
94. NAPA, *Beyond Distrust,* 47.
95. Forsythe, *Human Rights and U.S. Foreign Policy,* 140.
96. Fessler, "Complaints Are Stacking Up," 2564.
97. NAPA, *Beyond Distrust,* 60.
98. Ibid., 45-46.
99. Burgin, "Congress, the War Powers Resolution, and the Invasion of Panama."
100. See, for instance, testimony of Rep. Dante Fascell, D-Fla., in Senate Committee on Foreign Relations, Special Subcommittee on War Powers, *The War Power After 200 Years: Congress and the President at a Constitutional Impasse,* 100th Cong., 2d sess., July, August, and September 1988, 942-943; HCFA, *The War Powers Resolution: A Special Study of the Committee on Foreign Affairs,* 97th Cong., 2d sess., April 1982, Committee Print, 278-280; and Christopher Madison, "Despite His Complaints, Reagan Going Along with Spirit of the War Powers Law," *National Journal,* May 19, 1984, 989-993.
101. Forsythe, *Human Rights and U.S. Foreign Policy,* 156-157.
102. HCFA, "Congress and Foreign Policy, 1985-1986," 22-23.
103. Paul Stockton, "Congress and Defense Policymaking for the Post-Cold War Era," in *Congress Resurgent.*

104. Ibid.
105. See Bonner, *Waltzing with a Dictator*, chaps. 16, 17; and Gregory F. Treverton, "Intelligence: Welcome to the American Government," in *Question of Balance*, 97-99.
106. Bonner, *Waltzing with a Dictator*, 422.
107. Hedrick Smith, *The Power Game: How Washington Works* (New York: Random House, 1988), 168-173.
108. Rochelle Stanfield, "Weighing Arms Sales for Saudis," *National Journal*, Jan. 12, 1991, 79.
109. James M. Lindsay and Randall B. Ripley, "How Does Congress Matter in Foreign and Defense Policy Making?" in *Congress Resurgent*.
110. Ibid.
111. Stockton, "Congress and Defense Policymaking for the Post-Cold War Era."
112. General Accounting Office, *Legislative Oversight: Congressional Requests for Information on Defense Activities*, Report to Chair of the Armed Services Committee (Washington, D.C.: U.S. Government Printing Office, 1986).
113. Fessler, "Complaints Are Stacking Up," 2562.
114. Lindsay, "Congress and Diplomacy."
115. Fessler, "Complaints Are Stacking Up," 2566.
116. Ibid., 2565.
117. Blechman, *Politics of National Security*, 132-133.
118. Recall Bush's response to congressional threats about allies' paltry contributions at the beginning of the Persian Gulf crisis. Crabb and Holt, *Invitation to Struggle*, 280.
119. Blechman, *Politics of National Security*, 125.
120. Louis Fisher, "Micromanagement by Congress: Reality and Mythology," in *Fettered Presidency*, 155.
121. Lee H. Hamilton, "Congress and the Presidency in American Foreign Policy," *Presidential Studies Quarterly* 18 (Summer 1988): 509.
122. Franck and Bob, "Return of Humpty-Dumpty," 943-944; and ibid.
123. Carroll J. Doherty, "Bush Is Given Authorization to Use Force Against Iraq," *Congressional Quarterly Weekly Report*, Jan. 12, 1991, 65-71.
124. *Congressional Quarterly Almanac, 1984* (Washington, D.C.: Congressional Quarterly, 1985), 429-439.
125. HCFA, "Congress and U.S. Foreign Policy, 1983," 110-133.
126. Hamilton, "Congress and the Presidency in American Foreign Policy," 509.
127. Ibid.
128. "Reagan Runs Up Against the Real Washington," *U.S. News and World Report*, May 25, 1981, 43.
129. Ibid.
130. Cohen and Mitchell, *Men of Zeal*, 184-186.
131. HCFA, "Congress and Foreign Policy, 1985-1986," 147.
132. James M. McCormick and Steven S. Smith, "The Iran Arms Sale and the Intelligence Oversight Act of 1980," *PS: Political Science and Politics* 20 (Winter 1987): 29-37.
133. HCFA, "Congress and Foreign Policy, 1988," 94-95.
134. Crabb and Holt, *Invitation to Struggle*, 253-255; Forsythe, *Human Rights and U.S. Foreign Policy*, 119-128.
135. Stockton, "Congress and Defense Policymaking for the Post-Cold War Era."
136. Ibid., for a discussion of presidential problems in responding to such shifts.
137. Glitman entered the Foreign Service in 1956. (Maynard Glitman, interview with author, University of Vermont, Burlington, March 5, 1992.)
138. Ibid.
139. Cohen and Mitchell, *Men of Zeal*; and Walter Pincus, "President Was Told Arms Were Key to Iran's Help," *Washington Post*, Nov. 14, 1986, sec. A.

140. Francis O. Wilcox, "Cooperation vs. Confrontation: Congress and Foreign Policy Since Vietnam," *Atlantic Community Quarterly* 22 (Fall 1984): 277.
141. Christopher Madison, "Hamilton's Foreign Policy Alter Ego," *National Journal*, Dec. 22, 1990, 3097.
142. Glitman, interview with author.
143. Samuel P. Huntington, *The Common Defense: Strategic Programs in National Politics* (New York: Columbia University Press, 1961), 130-131.
144. See Eileen Burgin, "Influence of Constituents," in *Congress Resurgent.*
145. Christopher Madison, "Considering Gates, Competently," *National Journal*, Oct. 19, 1991, 2573; and Christopher Madison, "A Not-So-Sure Thing," *National Journal*, Sept. 14, 1991, 2200-2203.
146. Madison, "Not-So-Sure Thing," 2200. Bush subsequently altered his stance; on Aug. 11, 1992, Bush and Israeli prime minister Yitzhak Rabin announced a U.S.-Israeli agreement on loan guarantees.
147. For instance, see Mayer, *Political Economy of Defense Contracting.* And for a different perspective on this issue, see Richard L. Hall and Frank W. Wayman, "Buying Time: Moneyed Interests and the Mobilization of Bias in Congressional Committees," in *American Political Science Review* 84 (September 1990): 797-820.
148. Mayer, *Political Economy of Defense Contracting,* 219.
149. Burgin, "Influence of Constituents."
150. Eileen Burgin, "Representatives' Decisions on Participation in Foreign Policy Issues," *Legislative Studies Quarterly* 16 (November 1991): 521-546.
151. Patsy T. Mink, "Institutional Perspective: Misunderstandings, Myths, and Misperceptions: How Congress and the State Department See Each Other," in *Tethered Presidency,* 74.
152. Hamilton, "Congress and the Presidency in American Foreign Policy," 509.
153. *Federalist Papers,* No. 57, 353.

15

Can Congress Govern?

Catherine E. Rudder

I t is ironic that Americans hold their national governing institutions, especially "the people's branch," in such low regard at a time when emerging democracies are striving to emulate those very institutions. U.S. citizens' contempt for Congress can be traced to four sources of varying degrees of seriousness and treatability. These include scandals in Congress, the poor performance of the economy, the policy performance of Congress and the president, and the public's lack of understanding of what Congress does.

The Public's Disenchantment with Congress

The most notable but least important source of contempt is scandal, a concept whose definition varies with time and place. In the contemporary Congress scandals range from poor ethical judgment of members to doubtful institutional practices. For example, in 1986 five senators allegedly gave preferential treatment to major campaign contributor and subsequent felon Charles H. Keating, Jr. One of the five, as chair of the Banking, Housing, and Urban Affairs Committee, was especially well situated to intimidate federal regulators overseeing Keating's activities. Another senator, Brock Adams, D-Wash., was accused of sexual improprieties and declined to run for reelection in 1992. Yet another, David Durenberger, R-Minn., claimed questionable reimbursements and is reported to be under criminal investigation. The all-male Senate Judiciary Committee put on a salacious, unseemly spectacle in the 1991 Supreme Court confirmation hearings of Clarence Thomas and in the process gave the impression of institutional degradation.

Other recent scandals have included a poorly managed and perhaps pilfering House post office; a House restaurant that tolerated deadbeats; a House "bank" (more properly, a cooperative holding station for members' deposits) that allowed overdrafts without penalty; a congressional pay raise passed on the sly; exemptions for members from employment and workplace rules such as civil rights and safety laws; and a variety of longstanding perquisites for representatives and senators—such as free prescription medicine, cheap haircuts, and reserved parking spaces at Washington, D.C., airports—that were once generally accepted privileges of office.

These practices have come to be seen by the public as symptomatic of a Congress that has lost touch with those whom it represents. With reelection rates as high as 98 percent in the House, members have become, many have thought, removed from their electorates. Even if this analysis were correct, it does not get to the heart of the matter. (If anything, members of Congress are too responsive to their constituents' short-term, immediate interests—if not to their sensitivities—to legislate wisely, and those reelection rates support such a contention.)

Many of these problems, once they are defined as problems and exposed, are in effect self-correcting. The House bank has been closed. The House post office and other functions will be professionally run (and indictments have been handed down in the case of the post office). A record number of well-funded women ran competitive races for the Senate and House in 1992, with the result that 11 percent of the members of the House in the 103d Congress will be women—up from 7 percent (twenty-nine) in the 102d Congress—and that women's numbers in the Senate will rise from three to six.[1] The number of House incumbents defeated in primaries (nineteen) reached a post-World War II high in 1992, as did the number of voluntary retirements from the House. Almost one-quarter of the members of the 103d Congress will be new members. Perquisites are under review and are being curtailed. Term limits are not required to create turnover in Congress. A free, energetic press; competitive elections; and a mildly attentive public are.

A second reason for the public's disenchantment with Congress stems from the poor performance of the economy. Although in a technical sense the current recession has not been as severe as the one in 1982 (after which the United States experienced enormous economic prosperity), the recent downturn has been more protracted and has affected more white-collar workers. Moreover, the prosperity of the 1980s was not evenly shared: household incomes of the most wealthy one-fifth of the population soared, while those of the bottom one-fifth fell. Middle-class incomes—despite more workers per household—stayed about even.[2] If the economy were to improve, so would assessments of Congress.

A third reason stems from the policy performance of Congress and the president. Even when the government is divided by party, with a Republican in the White House and a Democratic majority in the House and Senate, the fortunes of the two branches are tied by whether they are producing public policy—although the public holds the president more accountable for program success than it does Congress.[3] From the congressional perspective, if the president does not set priorities and push for them effectively, and if he systematically vetoes legislation that Congress manages to conjure up on its own, he undermines Congress's reputation and its ability to govern.

Finally, even without scandals and with a booming economy and legislative accomplishment, Congress as an institution would probably be held in low esteem by the American public. Citizens, although they may like their own representative, do not appreciate what Congress does or understand the enormity of the tasks before it. This ignorance of both theory and process does not obviate the concern that the modern Congress may not be up to the task of governing: hence, the popularity of dubious constitutional amendments to tinker with the structure. This lack of public understanding may, however, reflect poorly on the civic education of Americans, the quality of congressional press coverage and attention to it, and the willingness of elected officials to perform their educative functions.

In sum, the cause of low public regard most amenable to treatment but least important to the ability of Congress to govern is scandal. It is, in fact, self-correcting under our system of government. Least controllable is the economy. In between are policy performance and public understanding. It is to these last two matters that this essay is addressed.

The Issues Confronting Congress

Although the end of the Cold War requires a paradigmatic shift in foreign policy thinking, the most pressing issues that national lawmakers face are difficult domestic problems. These include the short-run and long-term need to strengthen the economy, to make an effective transition to a peacetime economy, and to reduce unemployment without triggering inflation or raising interest rates significantly. This difficult task is made more difficult by the quadrupling of the national debt since 1980, created by yearly deficits that absorb about 15 percent of annual federal spending. Thus the staggering size of the federal deficit not only constrains government's ability to use fiscal stimuli without causing other economic damage but it also uses up money that could be applied to employment and investment programs.

To the degree that yearly deficits (if not the overall, cumulated debt) are to be reduced, programs will have to be cut, not expanded, and taxes will have to be raised—a prescription opposite to what is needed if short-run economic problems are to be addressed. To the degree that a high-wage economy is to be created, spending for education, training, research, development, and infrastructure will have to be increased, not decreased as a deficit-reduction program would require. To the extent that the government is to have a role in resolving social problems such as crime, drugs, homelessness, deteriorating cities, and rising epidemics (including tuberculosis and AIDS), more, not less spending is needed.

These choices are not easy ones, nor is the proper course obvious. Furthermore, the nation has not reached a consensus as to which route to take. Similarly unpleasant trade-offs await the country in the areas of health care, energy consumption, and environmental protection. If not intractable, the problems confronting national lawmakers are daunting. Citizens have reason to believe that national governing institutions are not up to the task. This pessimism stems from a suspicion that modern problems are not amenable to democratic solutions, at least as American institutions have been designed and developed.

Paralyzing Forces

Under the American system of shared powers, creating and maintaining majorities has always been difficult. For a variety of reasons, the challenge seems to have grown in modern times.

Divided government. In the post-World War II period, divided government has become as much the norm as unified party control. The inherent conflict between institutions—between the executive branch and Congress and from 1981 to 1987 between the House and the Senate—is exacerbated by the overlapping cleavage of party. If Congress and the president have reasons to disagree, Democrats and Republicans certainly do. To sharpen party distinctions in the mind of the public and thus to try to create electoral advantage, parties have an incentive not to come to agreement on legislative matters unless there is some overriding reason for them to do so. According to this line of reasoning, governing is made that much more difficult by the increasingly common phenomenon of divided government.

This argument is vulnerable on two grounds, that of empirical evidence comparing policy performance under periods of divided and party government and that of research demonstrating the decline in importance of party in the electorate. In an already classic work, *Divided We Govern,* David R. Mayhew examines major legislation from 1946 through 1990 and finds that divided government makes little or no difference in the amount of important legislation enacted.[4]

Thus divided government does not necessarily produce more deadlock than unified government does. The Tax Reduction Act and the Omnibus Budget Reconciliation Act of 1981, the Social Security Amendments of 1983, the budget acts of 1982 and 1984, the Tax Reform Act of 1986, the Clean Air Act of 1990, and the Budget Enforcement Act of 1990 were all enacted under divided government.

Party division between institutions does, however, present a serious strategic choice, the outcome of which can lead to low legislative productivity. Party leaders can decide it is to their electoral advantage not to cooperate and to try to make the other party seem the villain. The president can decide not to present a realistic budget or not to set much of an agenda. He can decide not to compromise or not to bargain. He can veto major legislation. Like the Republican minority in Congress, the Democratic majority, for its part, must decide whether it is an opposition party or part of the governing coalition.[5]

Part of the complaint about divided government, however, is that it encourages dishonesty and destructive collusion, not just deadlock. To gain partisan advantage, the president may present a budget based on overoptimistic economic estimates in order to reduce the apparent need for painful tax increases or spending cuts. The more Congress is honest in its economic estimates, the more pain it will have to inflict on the American public. Not wanting to suffer the blame for tax increases or spending cuts that the president refuses to propose, Congress has an incentive to go along with the president's faulty estimates.[6]

A similar pattern can be seen in the proceedings leading to the Tax Reduction Act of 1981. These discussions degenerated into a bidding war and caused huge losses to the federal Treasury, much greater than President Reagan had originally proposed and greater than most disinterested observers felt could be justified—all to garner credit for being the most friendly to specific interests and to the American taxpayer. Other examples of collusion include the savings and loan deregulation of 1982 (and the subsequent underwriting of that industry by the government) and the unwillingness or inability of the Republican president or the Democratic majority in Congress to curtail leveraged buyouts by altering tax incentives. Billions of federal dollars are being spent to guarantee the savings of Americans after the reckless behavior of savings and loan institutions, and tens of thousands of jobs are lost as companies are dismantled after buyouts. Yet neither party can be held responsible for either outcome. Because both parties are culpable, citizens have no party to vote for in protest of policies that many voters consider ill-conceived.[7]

This kind of party cooperation contributes to the low esteem in which Congress is held and to the anti-incumbency mood of the electorate. Thus Mayhew's analysis does not answer the less frequently articulated, but nevertheless serious, complaint about divided government—that it contributes to unaccountability and irresponsibility. His work does show that even when different parties control different branches of the government, important legislation can be enacted, not all of which, it should be added, is irresponsible.

Campaigns and elections. Evidence pointing to legislative performance under divided government is not the only reason to question the sufficiency of the deadlock thesis. To blame party conflict for the inability of Congress to act perhaps misses a major, but probably overstated, political development of our time—namely, the decline of party in the electorate and the emergence of the independent politician barely more than nominally connected to his or her party. This development complicates the task of governing and is contrary to the idea that the two parties are phalanxes locked in deadly combat.

The litany is familiar: Parties do not control who their nominees are; party organization at the local level has all but vanished; candidates create and maintain their own electoral organizations; many candidates shun their party label, raise their own money, get elected on their own, and owe little loyalty to their party. For their part, electorates are less strongly attached to parties than ever. They split their tickets and base their voting decisions more on candidates and candidate image than on party preference.[8] An attenuated connection to party means greater reliance on thirty-second advertisements and on episodic and noncontextual news reports.[9] The public becomes more volatile, less predictable, less reliable, and more susceptible to hit-and-run, negative attack campaign strategies.

If one were to extrapolate from these facts exclusively, the question whether Congress can govern must be answered in the negative. Members of such a Congress would not necessarily have anything in common and would have no apparent reason to work together. Members would act atomistically. There would be nothing to bring them together. The fortunes of Congress and the president, even if they were of the same party, would be disconnected.

Under such a system, it should be added, deadlock would be likely, absent other sources of coercion, but such inaction would be born of anarchy, not of divided party government. Furthermore, in such circumstances members not given to political suicide would have little inclination to cast public votes for painful policies that might be in the best long-run interests of the country.

Fortunately, the two parties bring about some cohesion. Difficult votes are cast. Still, candidate-centered campaigns and elections do weaken the ability of each party to create ongoing governing coalitions,[10] especially ones that can deal with problems involving unpleasant choices.

Congressional reforms. The decentralizing effects of the congressional reforms of the 1970s, like the effects of the rise of the independent candidate, have perhaps been overstated, but they have in fact made governing more difficult. Ordinary members are more important than their counterparts were two decades ago. Committee chairs are less independent, they must pay more attention to the committee members of their party, and they must share their power with sub-committee chairs. This erosion of centralized power can, however, strengthen American democracy by giving voice to diverse constituencies and by reining in the exercise of arbitrary, dictatorial chairs. For Congress to govern, there must be a way of bringing these voices together rather than silencing them, as was the tendency before the reforms.

Thus, although creating majorities for legislation has never been easy, it is much more complicated now than previously. It is also worth noting that many of the elements that assisted action in the past are the same today. For Congress to retain its legitimacy, however, reforms were necessary, and, as will be apparent, several of the reforms provide Congress with the basis from which to govern accountably and responsibly.

Interest groups. If divided government, independent politicians, and decentralizing congressional reforms are not sufficient impediments to policy performance by Congress, the sway that interest groups hold over Congress may be. Through their political action committees these organizations provide members with a large share of the campaign funds needed to wage expensive media campaigns. Such groups can often command voters' support, and they can threaten to generate election opposition. Because they control resources that members need, they gain access and members' attention.

Given the broad range and number of groups, one could reasonably argue that they represent the legitimate organization of interests in a free society. The problem such groups pose, however, is that many exist to protect the status quo—making such changes as health care reform or budget cuts very difficult propositions—and they are barriers to legislators' addressing virtually "constituentless" issues (such as deficit reduction, the poverty of 20 percent of the country's children, and other concerns representing "a diffuse, ill-organized interest") as opposed to "particularistic, well-organized, putatively very powerful interests."[11]

In short, the very issues facing Congress today, offering difficult choices and possibly painful results for some or all segments of the population, are those on which entrenched interest groups are most likely to obstruct action. Like the other barriers, however, this one is not impossible to scale, nor is it wholly negative.

How members spend their time. Not only has much of the American public given up on Congress, but so have many sitting members. A record number of representatives declined to run for reelection in 1992, many expressing frustration with the system in which they found themselves. The complaints varied and were not new. Still, the inability of Congress to deliberate and legislate is a common concern. An important source of that inability is the amount of time members must spend, year-round, raising money for their next reelection campaign. The system of campaign finance distorts the legislative product here if nowhere else.

Countervailing Forces

Although the constitutional structure makes enacting legislation difficult in any circumstances, modern developments—from the increasing frequency of divided government to the effects of some of the congressional reforms—heighten the challenge. The nature of the issues and the lack of consensus among the public, appropriately reflected in Congress, are complicating factors as well. Nevertheless, divided government does not necessarily lead to deadlock, nor is divided government always the case. Moreover, forces that paralyze action or lead to irresponsible collusion can be and sometimes are countervailed.

Presidential leadership. In study after study, legislative performance has been found to be dependent on the willingness of the president to set an agenda, to work for that agenda, to compromise, and to stay engaged in the process.[12] Congress must be willing to engage in negotiation as well.

It is true that a forceful congressional leader, such as former Speaker Jim Wright, D-Texas, can set out and effectively pursue his own agenda,[13] and Congress sometimes initiates action, as it did with the 1982 and 1984 budget acts. The president, however, can provide a sustained focus, can command the attention of the mass media, can reasonably claim to represent the nation, and can explain to the public the need for particular legislation in a way that Congress cannot.

Congressional parties and leaders. Far from describing the atomistic Congress of each member looking out for himself, David Rohde has documented the increasing degree to which roll call votes in the House, and to a lesser extent in the Senate, are divided along party lines.[14] Congressional reforms and changes in the party within the electorate account for this cohesion.

Specifically, although politicians may run candidate-centered campaigns, they are still attached to a party. Thanks to the Voting Rights Act and the party realignment that has taken place in the South, Democrats are more similar in their constituencies and policy preferences than they were when southern Democrats were apt to vote with Republicans. By the 1980s the party caucuses had become more homogeneous. This wider difference between the congressional parties and greater similarity within them has resulted in "conditional party government"—that is, a somewhat stable, continuous governing coalition.[15] The congressional parties can act as parties and by implication can be held accountable for what they do.

Congressional reforms have contributed to party coherence as well. It is true that the rank and file gained influence after changes in rules were instituted in the 1970s and that consequently party leaders must pay close attention to the needs and preferences of their members. The reforms, however, also strengthened the powers of leaders and the majority party. For example, the establishment of the Democratic Steering and Policy Committee—half elected and half controlled by the leadership—has the power to make Democratic committee assignments and to recommend actions concerning scheduling of legislation, legislative priorities, and party policy. Other reforms gave the Speaker the power to appoint the chair and Democratic members of the Rules Committee, with the concurrence of the caucus; to refer bills to multiple committees; and to set deadlines for committee action on legislation. An expansion of the whip system increased the likelihood that Democrats would vote together. The reforms strengthened not only the leadership but also the Democratic Caucus and caucuses within committees. As Rohde explains, the reforms help to "foster collective control." [16]

Speakers have varied in the extent to which they have used their powers to provide their congressional party with forceful leadership. Even Speaker Wright, who perhaps has most effectively exploited those powers to push a legislative agenda, saw his role as no more than "a hunting license to persuade." [17] The reforms require extensive consultation on the part of successful party leaders with their members. Leadership tools, however, must be used if they are to result in congressional policy performance. Taken together, the reforms provide Congress with a basis on which to govern—namely, through the majority party guided by forceful, consultative leadership.

Trumping interest groups. With the exercise of presidential leadership and the new coherence of the majority party in Congress, interest groups need not stymie the legislative process. On those occasions in which there is only a diffuse public interest on one side and well-defined interest groups lined up on the other, Martha Derthick and Paul Quirk and Randall Strahan have demonstrated that organized opposition can be overcome with the right combination of factors; among them are the development of consensus of elite opinion on an issue and the exercise of leadership by officials.[18] Alternatively, as Richard Cohen makes clear in his case study of the Clean Air Act, interest groups can be brought directly into the process and decent legislation can emerge.[19]

Public understanding. Despite the success of the Clean Air Act, the public was excluded from the process, though, ironically, its interests were represented. This neglect stemmed from the fact that many of the negotiations were held behind closed doors, that the press hardly covered the legislation as it was being developed, and that members and the president did not bother to perform the educative function that is fundamental to informed consent.[20]

Many observers have noted that difficult compromises may be best hammered out in private, but before the bargains are made and once they are set, citizens must be engaged in knowing what the choices were and they must be told why a particular agreement was accepted. If the public is not brought in on such decisions and does not know when Congress and the president have effectively worked together, it should come as no surprise that citizens assess Congress and the president on what the media report: scandal, conflict, and stalemate.

When President Bush did not bother to explain to the public why he broke his pledge in 1990 not to raise taxes, he undermined his own political support and increased many voters' cynicism about the political system. A possibly admirable decision to compromise and develop a new budget enforcement mechanism was derided rather than appreciated. Further complicating the task of governing was the general unwillingness of the president and Congress to explicate the implications of issue choices and help the public to understand long-term, general interests. Although the pledge of "no new taxes" may have been effective campaign rhetoric, it made responsible governing considerably harder.

Conclusion

The issues facing the contemporary Congress are formidable and the task of legislating is made more difficult when the government is divided, politicians are independent of party and party leaders, voters are volatile in their loyalties, interest groups are powerful, and huge amounts of money are needed for reelection campaigns. Congress can govern, however, and most particularly it can govern when the president leads in a strategic and engaged manner. In fact, the stage is set for conditional party government, as Rohde calls it, by congressional reforms and by electoral forces that provide coherence without muffling the voices in the rank and file.

Reducing the power of Congress under the justification that the issues are too difficult and congressional conflict too rancorous for the legislative branch to govern sells democracy short. Such a justification is intellectually lazy and reduces the power of people to have a say in their government.

The low esteem in which Congress is held by the public and by some legislators speaks less to the question of whether Congress can govern than it does to the failure of Congress, the press, and educators to explain what Congress does, what citizens can expect and demand of it, and what voters can do to hold members accountable for their actions.

Notes

1. For a brief time three women served in the 102d Congress. Jocelyn Birch Burdick, D-N.D., was appointed to succeed her husband Quentin N. Burdick, who died Sept. 8, 1992.
2. Patricia Ruggles and Charles F. Stone, "Income Distribution Over the Business Cycle: Were the 1980s Different?" (Washington, D.C., Urban Institute, 1991, Research Paper).
3. Jon R. Bond and Richard Fleisher, *The President in the Legislative Arena* (Chicago: University of Chicago Press, 1990).
4. David R. Mayhew, *Divided We Govern: Party Control, Lawmaking, and Investigations, 1946-1990* (New Haven: Yale University Press, 1991).

5. Janet Hook, "Budget Ordeal Poses Question: Why Can't Congress Be Led?" *Congressional Quarterly Weekly Report,* Oct. 20, 1990, 3473.
6. Louis Fisher, "Elimination of Budget Resolutions" (Congressional Research Service, Washington, D.C., 1992, Mimeographed).
7. Donald L. Bartlett and James B. Steele, *America: What Went Wrong?* (Kansas City: Andrews and McMeel, 1992).
8. Martin P. Wattenberg, *The Decline of American Political Parties, 1952-1988* (Cambridge: Harvard University Press, 1990); and Wattenberg, *The Rise of Candidate-Centered Politics: Presidential Elections of the 1980s* (Cambridge: Harvard University Press, 1991).
9. Shanto Iyengar, *Is Anyone Responsible? How Television Frames Political Issues* (Chicago: University of Chicago Press, 1991).
10. Anthony King, "The American Polity in the Late 1970s: Building Coalitions in the Sand," in *The New American Political System,* ed. Anthony King (Washington, D.C.: American Enterprise Institute, 1978), 371-395.
11. Martha Derthick and Paul J. Quirk. *The Politics of Deregulation* (Washington, D.C.: Brookings Institution, 1985), 237.
12. Mark A. Peterson, *Legislating Together: The White House and Capitol Hill from Eisenhower to Reagan* (Cambridge: Harvard University Press, 1990); Bond and Fleisher, *President in the Legislative Arena;* David W. Rohde, *Parties and Leaders in the Postreform House* (Chicago: University of Chicago Press, 1991); Richard E. Cohen, *Washington at Work: Back Rooms and Clean Air* (New York: Macmillan, 1992).
13. Barbara Sinclair, "The Changing Role of Party and Party Leadership in the U.S. House" (Paper presented at the annual meeting of the American Political Science Association, Atlanta, September 1989); Rohde, *Parties and Leaders in the Postreform House.*
14. Rohde, *Parties and Leaders in the Postreform House.*
15. Ibid., 116.
16. Ibid., 28.
17. Hook, "Budget Ordeal Poses Question," 3472.
18. Derthick and Quirk, *Politics of Deregulation;* Randall Strahan, *New Ways and Means: Reform and Change in a Congressional Committee* (Chapel Hill: University of North Carolina Press, 1990).
19. Cohen, *Washington at Work: Back Rooms and Clean Air.*
20. Ibid.

16

The 1990 Budget Enforcement Act: The Decline of Congressional Accountability

James A. Thurber and Samantha L. Durst

Throughout American history tumultuous battles have raged between the executive branch and Congress over the power of the purse. Recent battles dominating the national political agenda have been fought over which branch of government should be held accountable for federal spending and taxing priorities and over the continued growth of the deficit and debt. These conflicts have led to major changes in the way the congressional budget process works. The latest changes are incorporated into the Budget Enforcement Act of 1990 (BEA).[1] In this essay we evaluate how this act affects the way Congress makes budget decisions. We also assess the effect these reforms have on presidential and congressional budgetary power and on the complexity, openness, and timeliness of the budget process. In conclusion, we suggest that the Budget Enforcement Act has several implications for Congress's capacity to make difficult budgetary decisions.

The Congressional Budget Process

The congressional budget process is only one part of the financial system that governs federal revenues and outlays. The president is responsible for proposing a federal budget to Congress. To formulate the budget, the president relies on his staff and advisers, the Office of Management and Budget (OMB), the Council of Economic Advisers, the Treasury Department, and the government agencies that administer federal programs. The budget accounts for past expenditures, gives the president's recommendations, and estimates receipts and outlays for the coming fiscal year. It includes the current services budget and makes technical assumptions about how the economy will perform during the new fiscal year.

After the president has submitted the budget to Congress (each year on the first Monday after January 3), the congressional budget process formally begins. The 1990 Budget Enforcement Act allows the president to delay the submission of his budget proposal until the first Monday in February, but it stipulates that "this increased flexibility be used very rarely to meet only the most pressing exigencies."[2] Congress legislates the actual level of federal receipts and outlays. Although the president submits his budget first, Congress has no obligation to accept it. Congress is free to alter the president's budget in any way it wishes or to pass its own budget.

Taxes and other revenue-raising measures are specified by legislation that follows the normal legislative process. Major committee responsibilities for revenue policy lie with the Budget committees in both chambers of Congress, the Ways and Means Committee in the House, and the Finance Committee in the Senate. All revenue legislation must originate in the House, although in recent years this procedure has been sidestepped.

Legislative authorizations and appropriations designating how much money can be spent and how it will be spent must be passed by Congress and signed by the president before they can take effect. Authorizing legislation establishes the federal agencies that will administer federal programs or allows existing agencies to continue. Authorizing legislation is typically enacted for a limited time, after which Congress must pass new authorizing legislation. Each legislative committee must develop authorizing legislation for every federal program over which it has jurisdiction. Sometimes authorizing legislation even stipulates the maximum amount of federal funds that can be appropriated for a given federal program.

Appropriations legislation grants federal agencies budgetary authority, which allows them to incur debts. Budgetary authority, like authorizations, can be granted for varying periods of time. Under the current budget process, most agencies must be given budgetary authority each year. Appropriations legislation falls within the jurisdiction of the House and Senate Appropriations committees, but, like revenue legislation, it is usually first considered by the House. Once the House has passed appropriations legislation, it is sent to the Senate for consideration. If the Senate passes legislation that differs from the House version, a conference committee resolves the differences, just as with other forms of legislation. Once the differences are resolved, and both houses of Congress have passed the same legislation, the bill is sent to the president for his signature. The president can either sign the legislation or veto it. (See Figure 16-1.) All this activity is supposed to be accomplished before October 1, the beginning of the government's fiscal year. In recent years, however, that goal has been difficult, if not impossible to reach. In addition, the federal budget deficit and debt have continued to grow.

To combat rising deficits and improve accountability, Congress has reformed the budget process. In the past twenty years the congressional budget process has undergone four major reforms: the Congressional Budget and Impoundment Control Act of 1974; the Balanced Budget and Emergency Deficit Control Act of 1985 and 1987, known as Gramm-Rudman-Hollings I and II; and the Budget Enforcement Act of 1990.[3] Supporters of these acts suggested that their passage would promote discipline in congressional budgeting, reduce deficits, and make the process more timely and effective. In the years since these reforms were adopted, however, concern about the budget process has increased.

The 1974 Budget Process Reforms

The most important change in the way Congress collects and spends money in the past fifty years was the 1974 Congressional Budget and Impoundment

Figure 16-1 Budget Appropriations Process

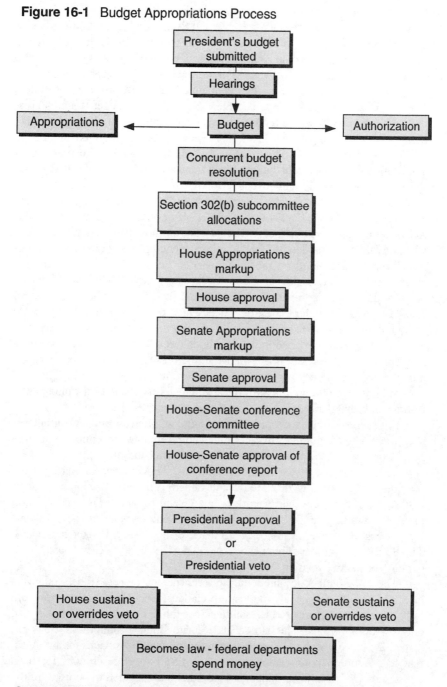

Source: Adapted from James A. Thurber, "Budget Continuity and Change: An Assessment of the Congressional Budget Process," in *Studies of Modern American Politics,* ed. D.K. Adams (Manchester, England: Manchester University Press, 1987), 81.

Control Act, also referred to as the Congressional Budget Act.[4] The Congressional Budget Act created standing House and Senate Budget committees, which are responsible for setting overall tax rates and spending levels. It also required that Congress annually would establish levels of expenditures and revenues with prescribed procedures for arriving at those spending and income totals. The procedures included three important elements. First, the Congressional Budget Act established a timetable to set deadlines for action on budget-related legislation. This timetable was intended to ensure completion of the budget plan before the beginning of each fiscal year. Second, the act required the annual adoption of concurrent budget resolutions (which do not require presidential approval). Initial concurrent budget resolutions set targets for total budget authority, budget outlays, and revenues for the upcoming fiscal year. The two chambers then adopt a "binding" concurrent resolution with ceilings on budget authority and outlays and a floor on revenues. After enactment of the conference report to the concurrent budget resolution, the Appropriations committees adopt what are called the Section 302(a) committee spending allocations. The committee allocations are based on the recommended Section 302(b) subcommittee allocations contained in the concurrent budget resolution. They determine how much of the upcoming fiscal year "pie" each of the thirteen subcommittees can spend for programs under their jurisdiction. Third, the Congressional Budget Act instituted a reconciliation process to conform revenue, spending, and deficit legislation to the levels specified in the final budget resolution.[5] The budget resolution largely can be seen as an alternative to the president's budget, containing a mix of Congress's policy preferences and the president's preferences. The concurrent budget resolution sets forth the spending levels, theoretically binding the Appropriations and authorization committees to these levels.

Under the reconciliation process the House and Senate Budget committees may direct other committees to determine and recommend revenue or spending actions deemed necessary to conform authorizations and appropriations to the determinations made in the budget resolutions. The Budget committees have the option of mandating that House and Senate committees report legislation that will meet budget authority, outlays, and revenue targets.[6] The reconciliation process allows the Budget committees to direct one or more of the legislative committees to change existing laws to achieve the desired budget reductions. The Budget committees submit the recommended changes to each house "without any substantive revision."

The 1974 budget act intended the reconciliation process to be a relatively brief and simple exercise. By most interpretations, reconciliation measures were to be in the second concurrent resolution (not the first) and were to be applied only to appropriations. The House and Senate Budget committees, however, turned the process around. They included reconciliation directions for authorization and Appropriations committees in the first budget resolutions for fiscal 1981. Although clearly the budget act intended reconciliation to be used for the second—binding—resolution, the strategy of placing ceilings on the first resolution worked. The Budget committees were successful in invoking the reconciliation process (that is, specifying the level of program reductions each committee should make to achieve the spending ceiling) for fiscal 1981. They required several congressional committees to reduce spending by about $6.2 billion, and they asked the tax-writing committees to recommend revenue increases of $4.2 billion. The fiscal 1981 reconciliation bill established an important precedent. Furthermore, for fiscal years 1981-1985 it resulted in savings of more than $50 billion in outlays (not budget authority) and $29 billion in additional revenues for the same period.

The reforms established by the 1974 Congressional Budget and Impoundment Control Act focused attention on the budgetary effectiveness of Congress. The legislation's ability to enable Congress to control the size of the budget and the deficit remains questionable, however. Since the act was implemented, the deficit has continued to grow and the budget process has been completed by October 1 in only two years. And because many of Congress's favorite programs risk having their funding limited, one effect of the act has been to increase the complexity involved in formulating a budget and the difficulty of gaining congressional support for the final budget.

Gramm-Rudman-Hollings

Increasingly concerned with its inability to control the budget process and curtail large deficits, Congress enacted the Balanced Budget and Emergency Deficit Control Act of 1985 (amended in 1987). This act is commonly known as Gramm-Rudman-Hollings (or GRH) I and II, after Sens. Phil Gramm, R-Texas, Warren B. Rudman, R-N.H., and Ernest F. Hollings, D-S.C. By the early 1980s projected budget deficits were in the $200 billion range, far more than had ever been experienced before.[7] In July 1990 the Office of Management and Budget estimated the fiscal 1990 deficit to be $218.5 billion (the final figure was $220 billion) and the fiscal 1991 deficit to be $231.4 billion ($167.4 billion more than the GRH target). Changing economic conditions and estimates of increased expenditures related to the savings and loan crisis continued throughout 1990, and by October 1990 the fiscal 1991 deficit estimate had risen to nearly $300 billion.[8]

The GRH legislation revised established budgetary deadlines for each of the major aspects of the congressional budget process.[9] Its goal was to bring discipline to congressional budgeting, to make the process efficient, and to focus attention on deficit reduction. The central enforcement mechanism of GRH is a series of automatic spending cuts that occur if the federal budget does not meet or does not fall within $10 billion of the deficit targets. These automatic spending cuts are referred to as sequestration.[10] Sequestration requires federal spending to be cut automatically if Congress and the president do not enact laws to reduce the deficit to the maximum deficit amount allowed for a given year. The deficit targets for fiscal years 1986-1996 are listed in Table 16-1. If the proposed federal budget does not meet the annual deficit targets established under Gramm-Rudman-Hollings, the president must make across-the-board spending

Table 16-1   Federal Deficit Reduction Targets, 1986-1996
(in billions of dollars)

Fiscal year	1985 GRH targets	1987 GRH targets	1990 BEA targets	CBO deficit projections	Actual deficits
1986	172	—	—	—	221
1987	144	—	—	—	150
1988	108	144	—	—	155
1989	72	136	—	—	152
1990	36	100	—	—	195
1991	0	64	327	331	269
1992	—	28	317	425	290
1993	—	0	236	331	—
1994	—	—	102	268	—
1995	—	—	83	244	—
1996	—	—	—	254	—

Source: Congressional Budget Office (CBO) estimates of the deficit are from *An Analysis of the President's Budgetary Proposals for Fiscal Year 1991* (Washington, D.C.: Congressional Budget Office, March 1990), 8; *The Economic and Budget Outlook: An Update* (Washington, D.C.: Congressional Budget Office, July 1990), x, xiii; and House Budget Committee staff, Dec. 15, 1992.

Note: Budget figures include Social Security, which is an off-budget expense but is counted for the purposes of the Gramm-Rudman-Hollings targets. For comparability with the targets, the projections exclude the Postal Service, which is also off budget.

cuts evenly divided between domestic and defense programs until those targets are met. Most entitlement programs (approximately 43 percent of the budget) and interest payments (approximately 14 percent of the budget), however, are partially or totally exempt from the potential cuts.

The 1985 GRH legislation gave the General Accounting Office (GAO) the responsibility for triggering sequestration. In 1986, however, the Supreme Court declared that part of the legislation to be unconstitutional because it gave the GAO, a legislative support agency, executive functions.[11] The Supreme Court's decision would have prevented the implementation of GRH, but Congress responded by passing the Balanced Budget and Emergency Deficit Control Reaffirmation Act of 1987 (GRH II). GRH II altered the original deficit-reduction plan by directing the Office of Management and Budget, an executive agency, to issue the report that would trigger sequestration if deficit-reduction targets were not met. The new legislation also revised the original deficit-reduction targets in accordance with more realistic economic assumptions.

Gramm-Rudman-Hollings I and II promised long-term progress toward lower deficits and a balanced budget, but these goals were elusive and overly optimistic. For example, as Table 16-1 shows, since the GRH legislation was enacted in 1985 and revised in 1987 the deficit never has been as low as the law requires.

Under GRH, presidential and congressional attention to each budget year was increased, but neither branch considered long-term budgetary goals. Since

1980 more than half of all roll call votes in Congress have been on budget-related bills, with a high of 56 percent in the House and 71 percent in the Senate.[12] Although GRH II revised the original deficit targets, the new targets were well out of reach as early as 1990, when Congress considered the fiscal 1991 budget.

GRH sequestration was supposed to threaten the interests of all participants in the congressional budget process enough to make them want to avoid it. The threat of sequestration, however, did not always have the intended effect. Comparing the projected effects of sequestration on their favored programs with the potential effects of cuts from regular legislation, policymakers simply decided that their interests were best served by delaying the passage of authorization and appropriation bills until after sequestration had occurred.[13]

Two other factors contributed to the failure of GRH. First, and most important, legislators could avoid sequestration by using overly optimistic economic and technical assumptions as substitutes for actual policy changes—a common practice in recent years. In the past, presidents underestimated federal outlays, largely because they tended to overestimate performance of the economy (and thus revenues) and to underestimate the current services outlays.[14] In fiscal 1987, for example, the administration's estimates for current services outlays were $27 billion below the Congressional Budget Office's "current policy" outlay estimates.[15] The difference in estimates was due almost entirely to divergent economic or technical assumptions. Interest accounted for 64 percent of the difference between estimates of the current services outlays by the administration and Congress; lower OMB estimates of inflation accounted for almost all of the remaining difference. Second, enforcement of the deficit targets was not effective after the final budget "snapshot." Before the BEA was passed in 1990, Congress evaluated the budget only once a year to ascertain whether it was meeting the GRH deficit-reduction targets. The result was a snapshot of the budgetary situation. After the snapshot was taken, indicating that the deficit target had been met, Congress could adopt legislation that would raise the deficit in the current year and in following years as well.[16] The budget reforms of the 1970s and 1980s, in spite of their goals, did not curb federal spending, reduce the deficit, force Congress to complete budgeting on time, reorder national spending priorities, allow Congress to control fiscal policy, or eliminate the need for continuing resolutions. Clearly, something needed to be done to counteract these loopholes. In 1990 Congress again reformed the budget process.

The 1990 Budget Process Reforms

The Budget Enforcement Act of 1990 makes significant programmatic and procedural restrictions in the way federal budgets will be evaluated in the 1990s. This bipartisan agreement is designed to bring more control over spending. At the same time, it is intended to ease potential conflicts over the budget, allow more efficient negotiated compromises to difficult economic and political questions, solve the problems of increasing deficits, and provide political cover for unpopular election-year decisions.[17]

The new budget rules further centralize power within Congress and force Congress to make "zero-sum" choices; that is, legislators must trade visible reductions in one program for visible increases in another or cut taxes for some interests in exchange for tax increases for others. The BEA includes substantive changes in budgetary procedures to bring more top-down control over the budget process and reduce the deficit. In December 1990 the Congressional Budget Office estimated that the tax hikes, spending cuts, and procedural changes of the BEA summit agreement would reduce the cumulative deficit by about $496 billion for the 1991-1995 period.[18] The most visible change is the elimination of fixed deficit targets as established in GRH I and II. Other innovations—such as categorical sequesters, pay-as-you-go (PAYGO) provisions on taxes and spending, and an enhanced role for the Office of Management and Budget—also affect the budgetary powers of Congress and the president.

The BEA comprises six major provisions: (1) new sequestration rules, (2) spending ceilings and "fire walls," (3) pay-as-you-go reforms, (4) multiyear budgeting, (5) changes in the way technical and economic assumptions are made, and (6) revisions in program accounting during the budget process.[19]

Sequestration rules. The Budget Enforcement Act changes the process of sequestration if deficit limits are not met. Sequestration had been the hallmark of the GRH legislation. The 1990 law requires a specified amount of savings for each of the five years covered by a multiyear budget plan. Through fiscal 1993 sequestration is linked not to the total federal budget but to limits, or "ceilings," for discretionary spending in three categories of government programs: defense, domestic, and international programs.[20] (Discretionary spending is spending for programs that must be appropriated each year.) BEA eliminates the $10 billion cushion between the actual deficit and the deficit target for fiscal 1991-1993 that was the norm under GRH. Through fiscal 1993, if the deficit exceeds the targets for any reason other than changes in policy (that is, an expansion in benefits or tax cuts), there is no requirement for a general or categorical sequestration; instead, the deficit targets will simply be readjusted. After fiscal 1993 the GRH sequestration process will go back into effect, with a $15 billion cushion and fixed deficit targets. Although the president can adjust the deficit targets for economic and technical reasons in fiscal 1994 and 1995, this option is not required.[21]

Spending ceilings. Perhaps the most significant aspect of the BEA reforms are the spending ceilings it establishes. The ceiling of each discretionary spending category is enforced by an end-of-session sequestration applied across the board to all programs within the category or categories that exceed their spending limits. (For example, if the ceiling for discretionary spending in the international category is exceeded, the end-of-session sequester would apply to all programs within the international category.) This process is referred to as categorical sequestration. Categorical sequestration will be triggered only if the spending limits of any or all of the categories are exceeded because of changes in legislation (for example, an extension of the benefits of a program or of the number of people eligible to receive benefits or tax cuts). If the spending limits are exceeded because of changes in economic conditions (or because the number of eligible recipients increases, as is the case with many domestic programs), sequestration will not be triggered. If more funds are appropriated for discretionary spending than are allowed under the discretionary limits, automatic sequestrations will be imposed, but they will be imposed only on the accounts in the category in which the breach has occurred. The fire walls do no allow the transfer of funds between the three spending categories for fiscal years 1991-1993. Those wanting more domestic spending may not "raid" funds from the "peace dividend" in the defense category.

In fiscal years 1994-1995 the system will return to fixed deficit targets enforced by the same sequestration rules used before the 1990 act, unless OMB fully exercises its option to adjust the 1994 and 1995 deficit targets in light of more up-to-date economic and technical estimates. A single ceiling will be in effect for all discretionary spending in fiscal years 1994-1995.

The law also provides for a "look-back" at each legislative session to ensure that legislation does not cause the spending limits to be exceeded. In the past, Congress evaluated the budget only once a year to ascertain whether it was meeting the GRH deficit targets. After that evaluation, it was relatively free to add new expenditures to the budget, often increasing the level of the deficit. Look-back legislation enacted by BEA requires that any amount added to the current year's deficit by policy changes made after the final budget snapshot will also be added to the following year's deficit-reduction target. Although this eliminates incentives for deficit increases after the final budget snapshot and for schemes that reduce one year's budget deficit by shifting spending into the next fiscal year, it also reduces the flexibility of fiscal policy in cases of emergencies or changing national or international situations. The law, however, provides for exemptions to spending ceilings for "emergency needs." For example, the expenditures for the Persian Gulf war in 1990-1991 were designated an emergency need and were not counted against the defense spending ceiling.

Pay-as-you-go reforms. All tax and direct spending legislation must be "deficit neutral" in each year through fiscal 1995. This major reform is called a pay-as-you-go procedure. PAYGO will cut nonexempt entitlement spending automatically to make up for any increase in the deficit because of the passage of legislation that increases entitlement benefits or extends benefits to more people or that would lead to revenue reductions.[22] This change makes the budget process a zero-sum game. Pay-as-you-go reforms are based on the notion that any increase in outlays above the previous year's base level must be paid for by offsetting outlay reductions or tax increases. Although each bill need not be deficit neutral, the net result of all bills must be deficit neutral.

BEA supporters argue that any kind of pay-as-you-go approach is an improvement over the procedures of the 1980s, when a Republican president and a Democratic House allowed the explosion in defense spending and entitlement programs that were paid for with borrowed money. Pay-as-you-go reforms are not necessarily intended to reduce the deficit. Their purpose is to limit growth in existing budgets and deficits by requiring that new expenditures be linked to cuts in expenditures for existing programs or to tax increases.[23] With pay-as-you-go reforms, the ceiling for each year's new budget will be set as if every program had been frozen at the previous year's amount. If members of Congress propose higher expenditures for existing programs or expenditures for new programs, they will also have to propose tax increases or cuts in existing programs to produce the revenues required to fund their new or more expensive programs. Under the BEA, increases in direct spending (or reductions in revenues) must be paid for by offsetting spending reductions (or revenue increases) within each category. If the increase or decrease is not offset, a special reconciliation process will eliminate any net revenue loss and a sequester will eliminate any deficit increase. According to Robert D. Reischauer, CBO director in the Bush administration, "This pay-as-you-go requirement . . . proved to be an effective poison pill that . . . killed a number of legislative efforts to cut taxes and expand entitlements." [24]

Like the limits on categorical spending, pay-as-you-go provisions can be exempted if there is an emergency need. The 1990 budget agreement, however, also requires that all new revenues go to reduce the deficit. If the economy grows faster than expected and revenues exceed projections, the increased revenues will not be available to pay for increased spending.

Multiyear budgeting. BEA's multiyear budget plan is intended to reduce the federal deficit by $492 billion over the five-year period from 1991 through 1995, through revenue increases roughly equal to $137.2 billion and outlay reductions roughly equal to $281.4 billion. The remainder of the deficit reduction will come, principally, from savings in debt servicing. These debt-service savings and the estimated reduction in the deficit will be achieved through the other provisions of the 1990 budget law .

Changes in economic and technical assumptions. The 1990 budget law provides for OMB to make additional adjustments in the deficit targets, based on changes in economic and technical assumptions, before the fiscal 1992 and 1993 budget cycles. OMB can also adjust the targets in fiscal 1994 and 1995.[25] In addition, under BEA the economic and technical assumptions made by OMB (which are used in estimating the president's budget proposal each January) will be "locked in" for the purposes of the sequestration projection to be made later in the year. This provision gives OMB and the president new power in the budget process. Congress will no longer be aiming at "moving targets" as the president alters his estimating assumptions during the year.

Revisions in program accounting. Furthermore, as part of the 1990 budget agreement several programs that are part of the budget (such as the savings and loan cleanup and the military operations in the Persian Gulf) are not counted against the spending limits of their categories. Moreover, Social Security receipts and disbursements are taken completely off budget. None of these transactions will be considered in estimating the deficit or in calculating for sequestration.[26] In both the House and the Senate the Social Security trust fund will be protected by "fire wall" points of order against legislation that would reduce trust fund balances.[27] An immediate consequence of this action was to increase the deficit to an unprecedented $269 billion for fiscal 1991.[28]

House and Senate points of order against "budget busting" provisions are an important enforcement mechanism in BEA. Under the 1990 act, legislation is subject to a point of order for breaching either the budget-year spending levels or the sum of the five-year levels set in a budget resolution. (The five-year enforcement mechanisms apply to all budget resolutions through the 1995 resolution, after which the act's enforcement powers end.) To prevent temporary savings through shifts in the timing of spending (such as military pay delays), BEA specifies that budget resolutions in each year through fiscal 1995 will be for five years, with five-year discretionary spending allocations, revenue floors, and reconciliation instructions.

The multiyear pact led the House and Senate to create different procedures for the appropriators. House appropriations will be allowed to proceed on May 15, even in the absence of a budget resolution. The House Appropriations Committee must use the statutory caps for domestic, defense, and international discretionary spending allocations and proceed on the basis of those spending decisions. Senate committees other than the Appropriations Committee will be allowed to proceed in the absence of a new budget resolution if their bills conform to the out-year allocations in the most recent budget resolution. This procedure establishes more spending control by Appropriations committees over other committees, and it allows the House and the Senate to move spending bills even if the budget resolution is late.

Effects of the 1990 Budget Reforms

What are the consequences of the BEA reforms? We can evaluate the possible effects in terms of the degree of centralization of the process (that is, the extent of top-down versus bottom-up budget making), the budgetary powers of the president versus those of Congress, the amount of openness in the decision-making process, the extent of complexity in decision-making rules, and the effect of the BEA revisions on the timeliness of the process.[29]

Collectively, in the next decade these changes will significantly affect the way Congress budgets. The BEA sets spending caps for five years for both budget authority and outlays in discretionary appropriations. Spending ceilings and floors imposed upon discretionary spending in the three appropriations categories in fiscal 1991-1993 are followed by a single ceiling on total discretionary spending in fiscal 1994-1995. Discretionary spending, severely limited in the past decade, is projected to be about 35 percent of the total budget, or $540 billion, for fiscal 1993. Appropriations bills that breach any of the three appropriations categories would trigger sequestration in programs within the breached category. The BEA provides that the caps can be adjusted for several reasons: among them are changes in inflation rates, revision of budgetary concepts and definitions, reestimates of credit and debt forgiveness costs as specified by the

Table 16-2 Possible Effects of the 1990 Budget Enforcement Act Reforms

Reform	Presidential/ executive branch power	Congressional power	Budget complexity	Openness of the process	Budget timeliness
Costing and assumptions	Increase	Decrease	Less complex	More open	More time-consuming
Fire walls and categorical sequesters	Increase	Decrease	More complex	More open	More time-consuming
PAYGO	Increase	Decrease	More complex	More open	More time-consuming
Five-year budget	Increase	Decrease	More complex	More open	Less time-consuming

Source: The format and evaluation criteria for this table are adapted and reformulated from James A. Thurber and Samantha L. Durst, "Delay, Deadlock, and Deficits: Evaluating Congressional Budget Reform," in *Federal Budget and Financial Management Reform*, ed. Thomas D. Lynch (Westport, Conn.: Greenwood Press, 1991), 76.

IRS and the International Monetary Fund, and appropriations for emergency needs. In addition, a cushion for estimating discretionary spending targets is included. (In early 1992 budget leaders were still discussing the definition of what constitutes an emergency—a major loophole in the budget agreement.) The discretionary caps on spending and the so-called fire walls between spending categories establish more controls and fewer degrees of freedom for members and committees, especially for the appropriators, because they do not allow funds from one category to be used to offset spending that breaks the cap in another category. For example, for at least the first three years of the agreement, shifts in allowable discretionary spending from the defense category to the domestic category will not be allowed.

Generally, because the 1990 law establishes a zero-sum budget, its provisions establish more budget control, expand the power of the Appropriations committees, and narrow the scope of influence other committees have enjoyed. At the same time, by publicly revealing the trade-offs that formerly were allowed in discretionary and entitlement program spending, the congressional budget process is made more accessible and accountable to the public, to interest groups, and to the administration. A zero-sum game, with controls on the number of behind-the-scenes tricks that can be played, makes the budget process more accountable to everyone. Although an open, more accountable zero-sum budget process may have the potential for more conflict than the old method did, the reforms are intended to create a more congenial budget process. The 1990 budget agreement ensures that the president and Congress will not fight over the size of the deficit, but they will continue to battle over domestic discretionary and entitlement spending priorities in a controlled, zero-sum environment.

The 1990 BEA shifted the "score keeping" function from the Congressional Budget Office to an executive office agency, the Office of Management and Budget. (Score keeping is the process of accounting for the cost of authorizations and appropriations bills and determining whether they are consistent with the budget resolution.) This shift of responsibility was a major gain for the president, greatly enhancing his power, and a loss for congressional committees and party leadership. The shift makes the budget process less complex, more open, yet more time-consuming than it was before the reform because of potential conflicts over cost estimates (see Table 16-2). The House Democratic Caucus, however, revised the budget agreement in late 1990 by requiring the Congressional Budget Office and the Joint Committee on Taxation to assume the role of scorekeeper for spending and tax actions. President Bush immediately objected: "This rule would change the new pay-as-you-go enforcement mechanism by overturning a specifically negotiated and agreed scoring provision. More important, if the proposed rule is adopted, the House of Representatives will have begun the 102d Congress by undercutting the credibility of the entire budget agreement." [30] Despite the president's harsh words, the revision held and retained the important power of score keeping within the legislative branch. The 1990 budget agreement also required that all new revenues go to reduce the deficit, further limiting the budgetary power of members and committees.

The 1990 BEA changes clearly show that when budget outcomes are perceived to be unacceptable, and when the causes of the outcomes cannot be easily influenced, legislators exert pressure to reform the budget process to create new outcomes.[31] Although the coalition of BEA supporters had a wide variety of policy goals, they supported change for two main reasons. They feared the projected massive negative impact of a fiscal 1991 GRH sequestration to reduce the budget deficit (an estimated 20 percent across-the-board cut), and they perceived the underlying causes of the deficit to be complex and uncontrollable in the short term. The changes have led to ever increasing centralization, top-down control, and a better grasp of the scope of budget problems by the budget makers and those affected by their work. The 1990 reforms further changed the process in response to Congress's and the president's goals of gaining control over budget outcomes and ultimately over the deficit. Those goals may continue to be elusive, however.

Presidential Versus Congressional Budgetary Power

"A balance of power between the executive and the legislature, so one actor can catch the other at bad practice," Irene Rubin argues, "is probably more sound over the long run than the weakening of one and the continual strengthening of the other." [32] Most of the 1990 reforms increased the budget power of the president relative to that of Congress. The reforms, however, have affected congressional and executive branch power in different ways. In the first half of the 1990s the battle between the president and Congress will not be about how much money should be spent, as it has been in the past. Theoretically, that issue was settled in the five-year budget pact. Instead, the conflict between the president and Congress will be about how that money should be spent. The reforms that impose new deficit targets, set the Social Security surplus off budget, and establish PAYGO do not directly affect the president's power in the budget process. But the reforms do increase the president's resources to negotiate budget policies and priorities with Congress. Furthermore, the BEA sets limits on total spending, something that President Bush, Republican members of Congress, and conservative Democrats wanted. Those structural and policy changes have indirectly increased the president's power.

Before the BEA reforms, Congress had significant flexibility in budget decision making, despite the self-imposed limits made by the Congressional Budget Act and the two GRH acts. The new deficit targets, Social Security trust fund surpluses being taken off budget, pay-as-you-go provisions, and categorical sequestration all decrease Congress's ability to appropriate the level of funding it might wish. The five-year budget agreement made new tax increases more public and more painful, thus limiting new spending by Congress. Through fiscal 1992 the pay-as-you-go proposals especially limit the prospects for new programs, and thus the power of the authorizations committees, because they require funding for new programs to be taken from existing programs or from new taxes. The separate spending limits set for military, domestic, and international programs mean that

Congress cannot use military savings to finance domestic programs. Instead, domestic programs must compete with one another for funding. This zero-sum game gave more budget power to a president and conservative members who wanted to limit domestic spending. It took power away from members who would like to allocate money for new programs and expand old ones.

Notably, the 1990 budget agreement has mixed consequences for the distribution of power within Congress. The pay-as-you-go, zero-sum reforms have a centralizing effect: the reforms discourage individual members from initiating their own "budget proposals" because cuts and revenue enhancements will have to be instituted in other programs in order to save individual proposals. On the other hand, enforcing categorical sequestration more strictly, initiating PAYGO provisions, and taking the Social Security trust fund surplus off budget raise the public's understanding of spending priorities and the specter of heavy lobbying. These changes intensify the pressure on members and committees to protect their favorite programs and make cuts in other programs. Such controls also centralize more of Congress's budget decision making around the leadership and the Budget committees, institutions with the power to negotiate trade-offs in the zero-sum game.

Although the rigid constraints set by the 1990 budget agreement may have further reduced the autonomy of the Appropriations committees, most budget participants argue that the Appropriations committees were the big winners in the 1990 pact. The new budget process rules diminish the role of the House and Senate Budget committees, by giving more freedom to the appropriations panels. One budget expert summarized this shift: "Since the pot of money the Appropriations Committees will have to work with has already been decided, they needn't wait for a spending outline from the budget committees before divvying it up." [33] Appropriators will be more able to determine the legislative details within the BEA constraints than through the old reconciliation process and sequestration under GRH. A budget summit observer concluded, "As chairman of the Senate Appropriations Committee, a panel whose control of spending has been enhanced by the current budget pact, Robert C. Byrd [D-W.Va.] is again squarely at the center of power." [34]

Appropriators have more control over backdoor spending by the authorizers in reconciliation bills. The budget process reforms also encourage appropriators to favor "pain-deferral budgeting," or slow-spending programs over fast-spending programs, to limit the projected spending for the next year. An example of pain-deferral budgeting is the failure of Congress (and the Bush administration) to terminate any of the major programs whose budgetary requirements are likely to escalate sharply in future years, such as the space station and the superconducting super collider. "The camel's nose is being allowed under the tent; next year the camel's shoulders will want in, and then his hump," according to Reischauer.[35] The reforms give the Appropriations committees more control over their own policy preferences, but they still allow delay of hard budget decisions. The big losers are the authorizing committees, which have significantly reduced freedom under the new zero-sum controls.

Openness, Complexity, and Timeliness

The BEA reforms have made the congressional budget process more open to the public. The discretionary spending limits and PAYGO controls over entitlement spending for the five-year budget agreement are well known to all the players. The new rules reduce freedom for the congressional actors while revealing the budget decisions to interest groups and the administration. According to Rubin, "closing the budget process is often considered one way to help control increases in expenditures; opening it is usually a way of increasing expenditures." [36] The BEA attempts to do the opposite: it opens the process and places more controls on expenditures, thus putting tough spending and taxing decisions in full public view. As a consequence of these changes, constituents, lobbyists, and the administration will continue to turn to the appropriators for discretionary spending decisions and to the revenue committees for entitlement and tax decisions. At the same time they will be watching the Budget committees with special care.

The five-year budget agreement simplifies the process only if members abide by the agreement. According to Leon E. Panetta, D-Calif., chairman of the House Budget Committee, members are not likely to do so.[37] Hence, when it comes to timeliness, the innovations may work at cross-purposes. Theoretically, a five-year budget agreement should make it easier for Congress to pass budget resolutions on time.

Several reforms of the Budget Enforcement Act increase the complexity and thus the potential delay in Capitol Hill budget making. Steps in the process have multiplied, as have the decision-making rules. Typically, the more complex the process, the more time-consuming it is. Categorical sequestration and PAYGO provisions will slow the process by increasing the number of confrontations within Congress and between Congress and the president. Additionally, confrontations increase complexity and delay in the process as more cuts (or more tax increases) are made to meet the spending caps. Already difficult budget decisions may have been made more difficult because of the changes in the process, but doing something about limiting spending or increasing revenues depends upon the political will of the members and pressure from their constituents. Furthermore, the budget categories are frustratingly complicated and inconsistent. The twenty-one functional categories in the budget resolutions do not neatly fit the thirteen separate appropriations bills nor the three categories of spending in the 1990 BEA. There is no one-to-one relationship between line items and functional categories of the budget. So the House and Senate Appropriations committees must translate the functional allocations from the Budget committees into appropriations allocations and report the result. It is then necessary to compare those results to the ceilings and guidelines set out in BEA to determine whether sequestration is required, thus increasing the complexity and delay in the budget process.

Conclusions

Although major cuts from defense spending are part of the agreement, specific policy outcomes are not likely to change dramatically as a result of the BEA. The constraints of previous budget decisions, especially the huge deficits and mandatory entitlement spending for social welfare programs, will continue. Congress is attempting to be more honest about budget deficits by showing the "real" numbers for each of the next five years rather than playing budgetary tricks, but it will be impossible to say who is to blame for the increasing deficits under the 1990 "remote control" budget process rules. All the budget actors will play "no fault" blame avoidance to help ensure their reelection, just as they did during the past decade. The BEA has further diffused the target of responsibility for the deficit. One budget observer remarked, "The new budget agreement has acted as a kind of fiscal neutron bomb, leaving the deficit standing but for the time being eliminating the fighting over it." [38]

Who will take the blame for the deficit? Not the Budget and appropriations committees, not the tax-writing committees, the party leadership, or the president. Budgetary politics will continue to be center stage in Congress, but the responsibility for macrobudget decisions will be diffuse. The temptation of members to try to "game" the new budget system continues to threaten the revised process. This behavior is not surprising, considering that the BEA has not been popular. The key votes for the budget agreement in the fall of 1990 were very close. The changes in the budgeting process were accepted by members from a desire to get home to campaign for reelection as much as from any real conviction that the agreement represented desirable policy.[39]

Budget and party leaders will continue to build coalitions to formulate the budget and to negotiate with the president about spending priorities. The major effect of the 1990 agreement is a tighter zero-sum budget game with more control and with top-down, centralized budgeting by the congressional party leadership. The trade-offs between program reductions and increases are more visible at the aggregate level, as are tax reductions and increases, but the responsibility for them is more diffuse. The BEA's emphasis is on spending and taxing, not on deficits. The budget battles will be struggles over spending priorities within zero-sum limits defined by the 1990 reforms. The reforms imply larger roles for budget and party leaders. Ultimately, conflict over further centralization of the budget power is inevitable, but the intent of the reforms is to create a more harmonious budget process that will not focus solely on deficits.

Naomi Caiden has suggested that "budgeting implies the capability to make deliberate choices for both aggregates and parts, as well as to achieve some balance between what is bought and what is paid for," but the BEA seems to limit Congress's ability to do just that.[40] We suggest that the BEA is actually another move toward "no thought" budgeting, reflecting a breakdown in the government's will to budget. Under the 1990 budget agreement, Congress has abdicated its role as guardian of the purse and has lost some of its ability to make policy in favor of a more congenial budget process. For example, by taking Social

Security off budget, Congress will move toward having less control over the Social Security Administration and its use of Social Security trust funds. This decision could be used as a precedent to set other trust funds off budget. The surpluses in other major trust funds in 1993 will be approximately $62 billion, according to CBO estimates. Spending restraints on these funds will be loosened at the same time that the trust fund program areas could still be receiving general-fund support and competing with general-fund programs lacking the protection of trust fund status. Moreover, the ability of OMB to modify the deficit targets and of Congress to exempt some of its costliest programs from the categorical spending limits may make the deficit targets impossible to miss and as a result make them useless in the struggle against higher deficits.

The features that make the Budget Enforcement Act attractive insulate Congress from accountability and make it difficult to assign responsibility for the growth of the federal budget or the size of the deficit. Because the BEA provides no regular review procedure of its provisions, its effectiveness in achieving budgetary and policy goals cannot be evaluated easily. In fact, the budget agreement's structure limits Congress's ability to pursue new or changing budgetary or policy goals (by favoring existing programs over new programs and prohibiting savings in one category from being applied toward programs in other categories). The budget's complexity makes the process accessible only to the experts. Putting the budgetary process on automatic makes it unnecessary for even the experts to examine the process. We agree with Caiden's argument that the post-BEA budget process is overly complex and obscures spending decisions:

> The automatic readjustment of targets and "no fault" budgeting make some mockery of the idea of deficit reduction, as does the exemption of very large expenditure items, such as Operation Desert Shield and the savings and loan bailout. The entrusting of critical calculations on scoring and assumptions to OMB rather than an independent body may also diminish trust in budgetary honesty. If . . . BEA promises further abdication of power, and thus responsibility, honesty in budgeting may continue to be a scarce quality.[41]

While budgetary problems continue to grow, Congress and the president blame the process and make themselves less accountable. Instead of forcing itself to pass a budget in a timely, fiscally responsible manner, Congress continues to change the rules of the budget game. Instead of facing the tough spending and taxing choices necessary to make the budget meet the GRH deficit-reduction targets, Congress and the White House agreed to new targets and a new process in the 1990 BEA.

Just as there were objections to GRH because it could be used as a crutch, enabling Congress and the president to avoid difficult decisions needed to remedy budgetary problems, there are objections to the 1990 BEA. It encourages both branches of government to make short-term decisions that complicate the long-term problems associated with the federal budget process and to emphasize process reform rather than long-term policy solutions. Already there are signs that members of Congress and the president are dissatisfied with the five-year budget agreement and the new budget process. Some have even suggested that it may be time to replace the BEA agreement with a new one.[42] President Bush in an interview on December 23, 1991, suggested breaking the 1990 budget agreement: "There are ways to live within the caps and then juggle around inside, but that would take new legislation." [43] In his 1992 State of the Union message, however, President Bush promised not to allow any changes to the BEA. President Clinton will face a movement to reform the process further when the debt limit hits $4.145 trillion early in his administration.

Senate Budget Committee chairman Jim Sasser, D-Tenn., suggested that further reform is unnecessary. "The problem is not the process. . . . The problem is that revenues do not match outlays." [44] In other words, the problem is the problem. Increasingly, however, the response on Capitol Hill is the problem is the process. House Budget Committee chairman Panetta revealed this in his review of the BEA. "We knew there was trouble on the horizon. To some extent the budget agreement was designed to slow down the catastrophe." [45] (Early in 1992 Chairman Panetta put before the House a budget with increased domestic spending and no "fire walls," and it lost.)

No budget process is policy neutral. Policy outcomes and budget process reforms cannot be separated politically, as the 1990 budget negotiations demonstrated. The BEA controls have a conservative bias; they are intended to control spending. Like earlier reforms, they centralize budget power, reinforce top-down budget control, open up the process, and encourage more discipline in congressional spending and taxing. The budget process continues to require presidential and party leadership if Congress is to do its work.

Budget process reform does not work by itself; it must have the support of the actors. Members of Congress create the budget process reforms and try to abide by them. If the policy outcomes do not comply with the preferences of the members, however, they may change the process again. The budget process rules are important, but in the battle over the budget the preferences of the major budget actors are much more important in determining the policy outcomes. Presidents and members of Congress must demonstrate that they have the leadership and political will necessary to eliminate the budget deficit and to formulate a budget responsibly and intelligently for the benefit of their constituencies and of the country as a whole. The Budget Enforcement Act may be just another means by which Congress and the president temporarily avoid budget deadlock by delaying the time in which they must come to grips with the deficit. The major effect of the 1990 reforms may have been to eliminate the struggle over the budget process by moving "away from deficit control and toward no-fault budgeting, where process compromises have been made to ameliorate divisions among budget participants in the White House and Congress who wanted dramatically different policies." [46] In fact, the 1990 BEA may have moved Congress and the president beyond no-fault budgeting to "no thought" or "remote control" budgeting. In general, the BEA reflects a breakdown in the government's capacity to make hard budget decisions and to reduce the deficit.[47]

The BEA faces a highly uncertain future and will probably be changed before fiscal 1995. Several pressures on the process will lead to these changes.

First, the categorical discretionary caps of the BEA will disappear in fiscal 1994, creating pressure to redistribute spending. Those fearing that defense and international spending will be cut severely will want to negotiate a new agreement. Second, Congress and the president will be tempted to adopt policies to stimulate the economy and provide tax relief and spending increases in the post-1995 period, pushing the deficit higher; those who want to control the deficit will push for an extension of BEA discipline. Third, the debt ceiling ($4.145 trillion), the legal limit placed on the gross borrowing of the federal government, will be reached by early 1993. At that point Congress must raise the ceiling to prevent the government from grinding to a halt, thus leading to another round of political conflict and procedural reforms designed to reduce the deficit.

Further changes in budget making will come, if at all, from the American electorate when citizens make demands for deficit reduction. If voters wanted a balanced budget, Congress would pass a balanced budget without new procedures. (In mid-1992 the House and Senate failed to pass a balanced-budget amendment.) At present American voters and interest groups seem to want to go to heaven without dying: they support spending for desired programs, but they resist increased taxes—thus mandating deficit financing. Notably, a poll taken by the *New York Times* before the 1990 budget agreement indicated that Americans overwhelmingly expected their federal taxes to go up to reduce the budget deficit, and they were willing to accept some new taxes.[48] (And indeed taxes did go up in the 1990 budget pact.) In the past the American electorate has failed to make this kind of commitment; in the Clinton era this may change.

Process reforms cannot compensate for the lack of political will. Neither the American electorate nor its elected officials in the White House and on Capitol Hill have displayed the political will necessary to make revenues match outlays. It may be that the 110 new members of the House in the 103d Congress and President Clinton will change this pattern. It is too soon to tell.

Notes

This chapter is based in part upon interviews with House and Senate members, staff, and informed observers. We are grateful for the time they gave and for their observations about the congressional budget process. We especially thank Nicholas A. Master, senior staff member, House Budget Committee, for sharing his knowledge.

1. The Budget Enforcement Act of 1990, PL 101-508, U.S. Code Congressional and Administrative News (St. Paul, Minn.: West Publishing, 1990), 104 Stat., 1388-573 (hereafter U.S.C.C.A.N.). See, generally, Louis Fisher, "Federal Budget Doldrums: The Vacuum in Presidential Leadership," *Public Administration Review* 50 (November-December 1990): 693-700, which suggests that the federal budget process is in crisis due to a lack of presidential leadership and accountability.
2. Budget Enforcement Act of 1990, U.S.C.C.A.N., 104 Stat., 1388-608, 1388-609.
3. For a discussion of these reforms, see James A. Thurber, "The Impact of Budget Reform on Presidential and Congressional Governance," in *Divided Democracy: Cooperation and Conflict Between the President and Congress,* ed. James A. Thurber (Washington, D.C.: CQ Press, 1991), 145-170; James A. Thurber, "Budget Continuity and

Change: An Assessment of the Congressional Budget Process," in *Studies in US Politics*, ed. D. K. Adams (Manchester, England: Manchester University Press, 1989), 78-118; Harry Havens, "Gramm-Rudman-Hollings: Origins and Implementation," *Public Budgeting and Finance* 6 (Autumn 1986): 4-24; Lance T. LeLoup, Barbara Luck Graham, and Stacy Barwick, "Deficit Politics and Constitutional Government: The Impact of Gramm-Rudman-Hollings," *Public Budgeting and Finance* 7 (Spring 1987): 83-103; and Raphael Thelwell, "Gramm-Rudman-Hollings Four Years Later: A Dangerous Illusion," *Public Administration Review* 50 (March-April 1990): 190-197.

4. One of the important reforms instituted by the 1974 Budget Act was the creation of the Congressional Budget Office (CBO). This agency serves as Congress's principal source of information and analysis on the budget and on spending and revenue legislation. The CBO's specific mandate is to assist the House and Senate Budget committees and the spending and revenue committees. Secondarily, it responds to requests for information from other committees and from individual members of Congress. Before the CBO was created, Congress had to rely upon the president's budget estimates and economic forecasts and upon the Joint Economic Committee's annual analysis of the economy and fiscal policy.

5. Thurber, "Budget Continuity and Change," 80.

6. See Allen Schick, *Reconciliation and the Congressional Budget Process* (Washington, D.C.: American Enterprise Institute, 1981); Dale Tate, "Reconciliation Breeds Tumult as Committees Tackle Cuts: Revolutionary Budget Tool," *Congressional Quarterly Weekly Report*, May 23, 1981), 887-891.

7. Another measure of budget deficit problems is the imbalance of outlays and receipts as a percentage of the gross national product (GNP). As a percentage of GNP, the deficit is decreasing. For example, in 1983 outlays were 24.3 percent of GNP and receipts were 18.1 percent; in 1986 outlays were 23.7 percent to 18.4 percent revenues; and in 1989 outlays were 22.2 percent to 19.2 percent revenues. See U.S. Congress, Congressional Budget Office, *The Economic and Budget Outlook: Fiscal Years 1991-1995* (January 1990), Appendix E, table E-2, 123.

8. James Edwin Kee and Scott V. Nystrom, "The 1990 Budget Package: Redefining the Debate," *Public Budgeting and Finance* 10 (Spring 1991): 4.

9. These deadlines significantly altered previous budget process deadlines. Notably, the new deadlines have been delayed or modified informally each year since GRH I and GRH II were passed.

10. See Rudolph G. Penner and Alan J. Abramson, *Broken Purse Strings: Congressional Budgeting 1974-1988* (Washington, D.C.: Urban Institute Press, 1988), 97.

11. *Bowsher v. Synar*, 478 U.S. 714 (1986).

12. Thurber, "Impact of Budget Reform," 148.

13. U.S. Congress, House Budget Committee, *The Fiscal Year 1991 Budget*, 101st Congress, 2d sess., Feb. 2, 1990, Committee Print.

14. Current services outlays are the costs associated with maintaining existing government services and programs. See Thurber, "Impact of Budget Reform," 159-160.

15. U.S. Congress, Congressional Budget Office, memorandum, 1986.

16. See U.S. Congress, Senate Committee on Governmental Affairs, "Proposed Budget Reforms: A Critical Analysis," in *Proposed Budget Reform: A Critical Analysis*, 100th Congress, 2d sess., prepared by Allen Schick (Washington, D.C.: Congressional Research Service and the Library of Congress, April 1988), 52.

17. John E. Yang and Steven Mufson, "Package Termed Best Circumstances Permit," *Washington Post*, Oct. 29, 1990, A4.

18. U.S. Congress, Congressional Budget Office, *The 1990 Budget Agreement: An Interim Assessment*, December 1990.

19. Detailed explanations of the Omnibus Budget Reconciliation Act of 1990 (OBRA) and Title XIII of that act, the Budget Enforcement Act of 1990, can be found in

Richard Doyle and Jerry McCaffery, "The Budget Enforcement Act of 1990: The Path to No Fault Budgeting," *Public Budgeting and Finance* 10 (Spring 1991): 25-40; and U.S. Congress, Congressional Budget Office, *1990 Budget Agreement: An Interim Assessment.*

20. Budget Enforcement Act of 1990, Sec. 13101, U.S.C.C.A.N., 104 Stat., 1388-574. See also Kee and Nystrom, "1990 Budget Package," 8.

21. Doyle and McCaffery, "Budget Enforcement Act of 1990," 34.

22. Budget Enforcement Act of 1990, Sec. 13204, U.S.C.C.A.N., 104 Stat., 1388-616.

23. U.S. Congress, Congressional Budget Office, "Pay-as-You-Go Budgeting," staff memorandum, March 1990.

24. Robert D. Reischauer, speech presented to the National Tax Association, 84th annual conference on taxation, Williamsburg, Va., Nov. 11, 1991.

25. John E. Yang, "Gramm-Rudman-Hollings Redux," *Washington Post,* Oct. 30, 1990, A19.

26. Budget Enforcement Act of 1990, Sec. 13301, U.S.C.C.A.N., 104 Stat., 1388-573.

27. Budget Enforcement Act of 1990, Sec. 13302 and 13303, U.S.C.C.A.N., 104 Stat., 1388-623. The "fire wall" points of order provisions provided for in the 1990 budget act differ between the House and the Senate. In the House the provision "creates a 'fire wall' point of order (as free-standing legislation) to prohibit the consideration of legislation that would change the actuarial balance of the Social Security trust funds. In the case of legislation decreasing Social Security revenues, the prohibition would not apply if the legislation also included an equivalent increase in Medicare taxes for the period covered by the legislation." The Senate "also creates a fire wall to protect Social Security financing but does so by expanding certain budget enforcement provisions of the Congressional Budget Act of 1974. The Senate amendment expands the prohibition in Section 310(g) of the Budget Act to specifically protect Social Security financing, prohibits the consideration of a reported budget resolution calling for a reduction in Social Security surpluses, and included Social Security in the enforcement procedures under Sections 302 and 311 of the Budget Act. The Senate amendment also requires the Secretary of Health and Human Services to provide an actuarial analysis of any legislation affecting Social Security, and generally prohibits the consideration of legislation lacking such an analysis." Conference Committee Report, Final Draft, 101st Cong., 2d sess. (1990), Sec. 6, "Treatment of Social Security," 10.

28. As a result of the 1977 and 1983 Social Security amendments, there is a growing annual Social Security trust fund surplus, which is financed through payroll taxes. The surplus will be about $68 billion in 1990 and about $103 billion in 1993.

29. See Thurber, "Budget Continuity and Change," and James A. Thurber and Samantha L. Durst, "Delay, Deadlock, and Deficits: Evaluating Congressional Budget Reform," in *Federal Budget and Financial Management Reform,* ed. Thomas D. Lynch (Westport, Conn.: Greenwood Press, 1991).

30. President George Bush, press release, Dec. 21, 1990.

31. Irene S. Rubin, *The Politics of Public Budgeting: Getting and Spending, Borrowing and Balancing* (Chatham, N.J.: Chatham House, 1990), 63.

32. Ibid., 234.

33. John E. Yang, "Budget Battle Set to Begin on New Terrain," *Washington Post,* Feb. 3, 1991, A12.

34. Lawrence J. Haas, "Byrd's Big Stick," *National Journal,* Feb. 9, 1991, 316.

35. Reischauer, speech to National Tax Association, Nov. 11, 1991.

36. Rubin, *Politics of Public Budgeting,* 66.

37. Rep. Leon E. Panetta, interview with authors, Washington, D.C., Feb. 26, 1991.

38. Yang, "Budget Battle Set to Begin on New Terrain," A12.

39. The House passed the conference report on the omnibus reconciliation bill on October 27, 1990, by a 228-200 vote; the Senate passed it by a 54-45 vote.

40. Naomi Caiden, "Do Politicians Listen to Experts? The Budget Enforcement Act of 1990 and the Capacity to Budget," *Public Budgeting and Finance* 10 (Spring 1991): 46.
41. Ibid., 45.
42. Eric Pianin, "Panetta's Deficit Solution: Cut Military by 40%, Pare 8 Cabinet Depts.," *Washington Post,* Oct. 8, 1991.
43. Quoted in Ann Devroy, "Bush Considers New Defense Cuts," *Washington Post,* Jan. 3, 1992, A1.
44. Quoted in Yang, "Budget Battle Set to Begin on New Terrain," A12.
45. Quoted in ibid.
46. Doyle and McCaffery, "Budget Enforcement Act of 1990," 38.
47. For a complete discussion of the government's budgeting capability, see Allen Schick, *The Capacity to Budget* (Washington, D.C.: Urban Institute, 1990).
48. Michael Oreskes, "Grudging Public Thinks Tax Rise Must Come," *New York Times,* May 27, 1990, A1.

Part VI

✦✦✦

Congress and Political Change

17

Can Inattentive Citizens Control Their Elected Representatives?

R. Douglas Arnold

How much are ordinary citizens—people who pay only occasional attention to politics and public affairs—able to control the behavior of their elected representatives? In principle, it might seem relatively straightforward for citizens to control legislators. If legislators wish to be reelected and if citizens reward and punish them for their actions in office, one should expect legislators to do whatever citizens desire. In practice, the issue of control is more problematic. How can citizens control legislators when most citizens pay scant attention to public affairs? Why should legislators worry about citizens' preferences when they know most citizens are not really watching them? How, in fact, can even the most conscientious legislators follow their constituents' preferences when so many of those preferences are unformed, unclear, and unstable?

Popular beliefs about citizens' control appear to follow the more pessimistic line. Many believe that legislators give greater weight to special interests and to their personal interests than to constituents' interests. In a national survey in 1990, only 20 percent of those interviewed agreed that "most members of Congress are more interested in serving the people they represent than in serving special interest groups," whereas 71 percent believed that members are more concerned with special interest groups. Similarly, only 31 percent agreed that "most members of Congress are more interested in serving the people they represent than in serving themselves," whereas 58 percent believed that members are more concerned with serving themselves.[1] This is hardly a ringing endorsement of democratic control.

Scholars' beliefs about the extent of citizens' control are more complicated, but the general theme is still pessimistic. In their classic article "Constituency Influence in Congress," Warren Miller and Donald Stokes found some evidence that local constituencies controlled the actions of their representatives, but their influence seemed restricted to the domain of civil rights and did not embrace the equally important domains of social welfare and foreign policy.[2] A more recent book by Robert Bernstein, subtitled "The Myth of Constituency Control," finds even less supportive evidence and declares that "elections do not serve as a mechanism through which citizens control their government."[3] Although some scholars have found greater evidence of democratic control than these findings suggest, it is fair to say that the scholarly literature supports more than it refutes the notion that ordinary citizens have little control over their elected representatives.

This essay explores the mechanisms by which citizens can control elected representatives. My quarrel with previous research on the subject is that most scholars have focused on a single mechanism for control. Failing to find evidence that citizens use that method, they conclude that citizens lack any meaningful control. The mistake is to assume that a single mechanism is necessary for effective control. Although I am prepared to believe that a single mechanism is a sufficient condition for citizens to control their representatives, I am not convinced that such a mechanism must also be a necessary condition for control. As long as there are other ways in which citizens could control legislators, scholars are in no position to conclude that examination of a single method says anything definitive about either the existence or the extent of democratic control of government.

The first section of this essay explores the assumptions that other scholars have made when they study constituency influence and reviews briefly the evidence that either supports or refutes their hypotheses about citizens' control. The second section questions why these assumptions are thought to be necessary for effective control. I discuss what we mean by control, how social scientists have studied control relationships in other settings, and how those lessons apply to questions about constituency control of Congress. The third section sets forth an alternative mechanism by which citizens can control legislators and discusses its plausibility in the American setting. The final section returns to the original question and assesses what is known about the extent of citizens' control.

Legislators as Instructed Delegates: The Standard Control Model

The standard control model presumes that citizens are active controllers. Citizens are conceived to be much like automobile drivers. They know where they want to go, they can select the best routes (policies) to get there, and they are capable of steering their vehicles (legislators) to reach their chosen destinations. The proper test for how well motorists control their vehicles is their success in navigating unfamiliar routes, bypassing various obstacles, and arriving at their destinations in time for their appointments. The proper test for how well citizens control legislators is their success in getting legislators to support and enact their most preferred policies.

The most basic assumption of the standard model is that citizens have both outcome preferences and policy preferences. Outcome preferences are attitudes about the desirability of specific ends, such as safe communities, clean air, protection from foreign attack, and the maintenance of a sound economy. Policy preferences are attitudes about the proper means toward those ends. Examples are preferences about instituting a seven-day waiting period before handguns can be purchased, requiring mechanical scrubbers on coal-powered plants, increasing the number of aircraft carriers in the Navy, or cutting federal expenditures across the board to bring the budget into balance.

The second assumption is that on the important issues of the day citizens evaluate legislative candidates by focusing on both their positions and their actions. For challengers, the focus is on the policies they promise to support and those they promise to oppose. For incumbents, the focus is on both their promises and their past actions. Citizens are presumed to be especially attentive to legislators' roll call votes. The logic of the model is that citizens reward and punish legislators based on how compatible legislators' roll call positions are with citizens' own policy preferences.

The third assumption is that legislators are strongly interested in being reelected to Congress. Most legislators are career-minded politicians who seek to retain their current positions—at least until a more promising political position becomes available. With citizens choosing among candidates by focusing on their positions and their actions in office, it follows that legislators will work diligently to reflect their constituents' current policy preferences. It also follows that challengers will work to position themselves even more closely to citizens' current policy preferences.

These three assumptions are all that is required for citizens to control legislators in office. Legislators act as instructed delegates, working to discern their constituents' policy preferences and doing their best to follow the majority's preferences. When individual legislators fail to act as good delegates, either by intentionally following the preferences of a minority or by failing to discern the majority's preferences, citizens replace them with those who promise to be better delegates.

The standard control model is far from perfect in allowing citizens to control governmental decisions. First, it works only for items that are placed on the governmental agenda and for which roll call votes are required. Citizens can hardly punish their individual legislators for failing to support a given policy when their legislators were never given the opportunity to vote. Second, it fails to consider the strategic aspects of voting and the ability of clever leaders to structure the order in which legislators vote on amendments so that majorities win on each successive vote but nevertheless attain a less-preferred policy. Third, it works only for citizens who vote. Given that voter turnout in congressional elections has been less than 50 percent for each national election since 1972, citizens' control under the standard model is, at best, control by a majority of the minority.

Despite these and other defects, the standard control model allows for an impressive amount of influence. If the assumptions were all true, legislators would feel tightly controlled by their constituents' policy preferences, and legislators' actions would be largely congruent with citizens' preferences. The questions that remain are empirical ones. Do citizens have both policy preferences and outcome preferences? Do citizens evaluate legislative candidates by focusing on both their positions and their actions? Do legislators actually respond to constituents' policy preferences?

There can be little doubt that citizens have preferences about a wide range of outcomes. On some issues they have practically identical outcome preferences. Most citizens prefer a strong defense, a sound national economy, safe communities, and a cure for cancer to the alternatives of invasion, depression, crime, and early death. On other issues citizens have conflicting outcome preferences. Some people prefer quiet lakes; others enjoy fast boats. Some enjoy pornography in the privacy of their homes; others are offended by its very existence. Citizens may also have conflicting preferences about the necessary trade-offs among competing ends. Some people seek a clean environment but are unwilling to pay much to achieve it; others favor redesigning everything from the automobile to beverage containers in the pursuit of the cleanest environment possible.

Citizens are far less likely to have preferences about the scores of policy alternatives that are designed to achieve a particular end. The existence of policy preferences depends in part on citizens' awareness of the alternatives and in part on the simplicity of the various remedies. If one asks most citizens their attitudes toward coal scrubbers, tradable emissions rights, or effluent taxes, the answers will contain more noise than information. Few people have genuine preferences about the principal alternatives for reducing emissions from utility plants because they are only dimly aware of the alternatives. If one asks citizens their attitudes toward more general policies, such as increasing (or decreasing) spending on defense, education, or the environment, one is far more likely to elicit genuine information about their preferences. Visible problems that seem to have simple remedies also generate policy preferences easily. Most citizens have strong, though conflicting, policy preferences about proposals such as a constitutional amendment to outlaw flag burning, a bill to ban the possession of handguns, or a proposal to require the use of seat belts.

The assumption in the standard control model that citizens have both outcome preferences and policy preferences is only partially met. Although citizens easily past the test for outcome preferences, most citizens do not have policy preferences for the hundreds of policy alternatives that Congress considers each year. This limitation necessarily restricts the range of issues for which citizens can control elected legislators, given that preexisting policy preferences are essential to the instructed-delegate model. Control is still possible, however, for the many alternatives for which citizens do have genuine policy preferences.

The assumption that citizens evaluate legislative candidates by focusing on candidates' positions on the important issues of the day is more difficult to assess. Although it is relatively easy to identify citizens' preferences about the various candidates, it is far from easy to determine the causes of those preferences. Citizens themselves may not know why they prefer candidate A to candidate B any more than they know why they prefer corn flakes to bran flakes, Harrison Ford to Kevin Costner, or country music to jazz.

At least some of the findings from past studies raise doubts about the notion that citizens rely heavily on candidates' policy positions when they decide how to vote in legislative elections. First, citizens do not appear to have extensive information about candidates' policy positions. Although 46 percent of a 1988 sample of voters were able to express general agreement or disagreement with their representative's votes in Congress, only 16 percent were able to express agreement or disagreement with their member's vote on a specific bill.[4] Second, policy and ideology are not the most frequently mentioned reasons for liking or disliking legislative candidates. In the same 1988 survey, voters were far more likely to mention candidates' personal qualities, experience in office, and attention to constituency matters as justifications for their preferences than they were to mention candidates' specific policy positions or general ideological stances.[5]

When citizens do have information about candidates' general voting records or specific policy positions, however, that information does affect their evaluations of the candidates. Citizens who agree with their representative's vote on a specific bill tend to support the incumbent, whereas those who disagree are more likely to support the challenger. The same is true for citizens who express general agreement with the incumbent's votes or who believe the incumbent would handle the most important issue of the day better than the challenger.[6] The extent of agreement or disagreement also affects the probability of their voting for the challenger. Voters who see themselves in fundamental disagreement with their representative tend to support the challenger, whereas those who see more modest ideological differences are more likely to stick with the incumbent.[7]

The problem with the second assumption, then, is one of information more than of behavior. When citizens have good information about the candidates' policy positions, it appears that the information affects their voting decisions. The problem is that too few citizens know where the candidates stand on the issues or what their representatives have done in office for the standard control model to operate effectively.

The third assumption—that legislators actually respond to constituents' policy preferences when they make decisions in office—is the most difficult to assess. The difficulty is not in identifying legislators' policy decisions, for members of both House and Senate vote publicly on several hundred policy alternatives each year, but rather in estimating citizens' policy preferences within each legislative district. Although there is nothing inherently difficult about conducting opinion surveys in all districts (or in a sample of districts), surveys are enormously expensive. Administering a survey in a single state or congressional district is not noticeably cheaper than doing so throughout the entire nation.

The expense of district-level surveys has encouraged scholars to try other approaches. Warren Miller and Donald Stokes first attempted to use a single national sample to estimate constituency opinion in House districts, but their district samples were too small and too biased to allow reliable estimates.[8] The more common approach is to use indicators of each district's economic interests as surrogates for constituents' opinions about a proposed policy. For example, Robert Bernstein and William Anthony used each state's share of contracts for the antiballistic missile system as a measure of statewide opinion toward the proposed system.[9] Other scholars have been less explicit in equating economic interests with constituents' preferences, but they imply that economic indicators are adequate surrogates for constituency opinion.[10] In fact, this approach tells one very little about constituents' true opinions. Given that most citizens do not have preferences about most policies, it is very odd to assume that they have preferences about each proposal and that their policy preferences are a simple function of their supposed economic interests.[11] The only reliable way to estimate constituents' policy preferences is with survey research in which legislative districts are the primary sampling units.

The best research employing survey evidence from congressional districts demonstrates that legislators do respond to constituency opinion when voters have strong policy preferences. Larry Bartels, who used the 1980 National Election Study survey of 108 congressional districts to estimate citizens' preferences about defense spending, showed that constituency opinion had powerful effects on representatives when they were voting on the level of defense appropriations.[12] In 1981 constituency opinion accounted for most of the legislative support for a 9 percent increase in real defense spending. Bartels also estimated the effect that each district's stake in the Pentagon budget had on legislators' decisions. Although he discovered that representatives responded to their districts' economic interests, these responses were quite distinguishable from their responses to constituency opinion. At least in this case, economic indicators were not acceptable surrogates for evidence about constituents' actual policy preferences.

The various empirical studies, then, provide each of the three assumptions in the standard control model with some support. These findings make it difficult to accept the most pessimistic conclusion that legislators' actions are completely beyond the control of their constituents. It is equally difficult, however, to accept the view that legislators act as well-instructed delegates, working to carry out their constituents' detailed instructions about policy. The main problem with this view is that most citizens do not have preferences about most policy alternatives. A secondary problem is that most voters do not have much information about legislators' policy positions or about their performance in office.

My reading of the evidence suggests that citizens can and do control some of the actions of their representatives in office. They do so when they have strong preferences about policy and good information about legislators' actions in office. The extent of citizens' control, however, falls far short of the normative ideal embodied in the standard control model.

The Nature of Political Control

The standard control model is not the only way in which citizens can control their elected representatives. Although this statement may seem obvious to many readers, it has not been obvious to most scholars working on the subject. For example, after reviewing the evidence for and against the standard control model, Bernstein concludes: "Constituencies do not control the policies adopted by their representatives; they have some influence over what those policies are, but members are by and large free to adopt what they think best." [13] This statement would be true only if there were no alternative mechanisms for controlling legislators' actions.

Establishing the existence of control relationships is no easy task. Social scientists have long debated how to observe and measure power, influence, control, and all the other variations on the same theme.[14] A control relationship is easiest to observe when one person issues a direct order and another obeys. No one can doubt that a kindergarten teacher is in control when a single word quiets an entire class. What makes this case so easy to evaluate is that the controller's preferences are crystal clear and the students' responses are directly opposite to their habitual behavior. Most control relationships are far more subtle than this, however, and require careful detective work to unravel.

One of the most common mistakes is to confuse the frequency with which one person monitors another person's behavior with the extent of control. Careful monitoring and tight control are very different things, and frequent monitoring may not be necessary for tight control. Scholars once concluded that Congress had little influence over the bureaucracy because legislators devoted so little time to monitoring what the agencies were doing. It was the signal contribution of Mathew McCubbins and Thomas Schwartz to show that Congress had other mechanisms for learning about bureaucratic compliance—ones that were more efficient and more effective than legislators themselves gathering information.[15] McCubbins and Schwartz argued that Congress relied on individual citizens and organized interest groups to monitor bureaucratic decision making. When legislators heard complaints, they assumed there was a problem; when they heard nothing, they assumed all was well. Millions of citizens can monitor bureaucratic compliance far more effectively than can a few hundred legislators holding hearings and conducting field investigations.

A second mistake is to assume that in order to influence another person's choices the person in control must have well-established preferences about all the alternatives under consideration. Well-established preferences make the scholar's job easier, but they are not necessary for control itself. Consider the relationships between generals and fighter pilots in two air forces. In country A, the generals specify what a pilot should do in every imaginable situation, threatening serious punishment for pilots who deviate from detailed flight plans. In country B, the generals give pilots latitude to react to new and changing circumstances, reserving punishment only for those who cannot defend the reasonableness of their actions in a subsequent review. In which air force do the generals have the greater control? If the question is control over every flight maneuver, clearly country A's generals are the more powerful. If the question is control over the outcomes that generals actually prefer—high kill ratios in combat—country B's generals may well be the more influential. Detailed policy preferences are not necessary for effective control so long as the controllers have clear outcome preferences.

A third mistake is to confuse the frequency of punishment with the extent of control. Many proponents of term limits for legislators have fallen into this trap, arguing that legislators operate beyond the control of constituents—the evidence being that so few legislators are ever defeated at the polls. The problem with this argument is that the contrary hypothesis is observationally equivalent. A setting in which legislators responded perfectly to constituency opinion would produce no defeats at the polls just as certainly as one in which legislators operated independently of constituency opinion. Punishment is evidence of imperfect control; no punishment is consistent with both perfect control and perfect independence.

A fourth mistake is to fail to appreciate the changed nature of control relationships when two actors play (or expect to play) a repeated series of games together. When a rental company loans a car for even a single day, it demands that a customer sign a legal document specifying what the customer can and cannot do with the car. The company details its expectations about every possible eventuality because it presumes a customer has no interest in a continuing relationship and therefore no interest in pleasing the company. When a mother loans her son the car for an evening, no elaborate agreements are necessary. Most children treat their parents' cars with greater care than any rental car because they hope to borrow the car on subsequent occasions and because they know that getting caught doing something stupid (no matter whether it had been directly prohibited) might eliminate future borrowing rights.

Those who believe that the standard control model is the only way for citizens to control their elected legislators have committed each of these errors. They assume that citizens need to have preferences about all the alternatives under consideration in order to influence legislators' choices among those alternatives. They assume that citizens need to monitor carefully legislators' actions in office in order for legislators to have an incentive to serve citizens' interests. They accept as evidence of citizens' inability to control legislators the fact that voters rarely remove legislators from office. They fail to appreciate how legislators' aspirations for long political careers give them incentives to avoid actions that might displease voters. These errors do not diminish the empirical research that shows the inadequacy of the standard control model for explaining legislative activity. They do, however, undermine the argument that the standard control model is a necessary condition for citizens to control elected legislators.

Before we can develop an alternative model about how citizens can control their elected legislators, it is important to define carefully the concept of control. In common usage, control means "to exercise restraining or directing influence" over something or somebody "in order to keep within bounds or on a course." [16] Drivers who control their automobiles and parents who control their children keep their cars' and their children's actions within accepted bounds. By extension, citizens who control their legislators keep legislators' behavior within the bounds of what citizens want legislators to do.

The concept of control is closely related to the concept of influence—a term for which social scientists have a precise definition. Jack Nagel defines influence as "a causal relation between the preferences of an actor regarding an outcome and the outcome itself." [17] In this essay, I consider citizens influential (or in control) to the extent that legislators' decisions reflect in some way citizens' preferences about policy issues. Establishing what citizens prefer is, thus, essential to measuring citizens' influence over legislators' behavior. In fact, the principal difference between the standard control model and the alternative control model offered in this essay is the way in which citizens' preferences are conceived.

Legislators as Controlled Agents: The Alternative Model

The alternative control model presumes that citizens are somewhat more passive than the citizens of the standard control model. Citizens are regarded more like tax auditors, who notice when things are seriously out of line, than like drill sergeants, who direct troops to march left and right in precise formations. Passivity, however, should not be confused with a lack of influence. Auditing can be an efficient and effective means of controlling legislators' behavior.

The alternative control model rests on four basic assumptions, one of them identical to an assumption in the standard control model, two of them modifications of the original assumptions, and one completely new. The identical assumption is that legislators are strongly interested in reelection. This simple motivational assumption is basic to any model of representation in which legislators respond to citizens' preferences. In settings where legislators are not strongly interested in reelection, legislators lack the basic incentive to discover and follow citizens' wishes.[18]

The second assumption in the alternative control model is that citizens have outcome preferences and can easily acquire policy preferences after the legislature acts, even though they may not have had policy preferences in advance of legislative action. This is a modification of the assumption in the standard control model in which citizens are presumed to have both outcome and policy preferences in advance of legislative action. The modified assumption is considerably more realistic than its predecessor. It allows citizens to develop policy preferences as a response to debates among policy experts and politicians rather than in advance of such debates. Citizens may acquire policy preferences as a direct consequence of legislative debate or when they first notice a change in governmental policy or in the middle of a subsequent electoral campaign, when a challenger questions the wisdom of an incumbent's actions in office.

The third assumption is that citizens are capable of evaluating incumbent legislators by focusing on their policy positions and their actions in office. This is a modification of the assumption in the standard control model in which citizens actually evaluate legislative candidates according to their positions and actions. The revised assumption simply states that citizens are capable of such evaluations once they become aware of what their representatives have done in office.

The new assumption is that the system contains activists who have incentives to monitor what legislators are doing in office and to inform citizens when legislators fail in their duties. Challengers to incumbent legislators have perhaps the strongest incentives for monitoring legislators' behavior and mobilizing voters. Few challengers fail to sift through incumbents' voting records in search of issues that can be used against incumbent legislators. In addition, groups that bear major costs under a particular governmental policy may help publicize what incumbent legislators have done to contribute to their plight. Whereas challengers seek to replace incumbents, these groups may seek to persuade incumbents to avoid electoral repercussions by altering their positions and working for the groups' benefit.

These four assumptions recognize a division of labor between citizens and professional politicians. Legislators, challengers, and activists do most of the real work. Citizens act more like spectators who register their approval or disapproval at the end of a performance. This division of labor reflects the incentives that drive each type of actor.

In the political world described by these four assumptions, legislators have strong incentives to anticipate citizens' future preferences. Even when citizens seem unaware of an issue or indifferent toward it, legislators do not assume that they are free to vote as they please. Instead, legislators consider the possibility that someone might work to inform their constituents about their policy positions before the next election and that their constituents might not be pleased by their positions and might be inspired to oppose their reelection. To forestall such a reaction, legislators choose their policy positions very carefully. Although it is true that most issues do not present legislators with life or death choices in which a single wrong decision can lead to electoral defeat, legislators create acceptable voting records one issue at a time. They vote carefully on every issue because that is the safest way to guarantee that their voting records cannot be used against them in future elections.

Challengers have equally strong incentives to uncover potentially unpopular positions that incumbents have taken on past roll call votes. Most challengers begin their campaigns with serious disadvantages. Ordinarily, incumbents are better known than challengers, and most incumbents have spent their years in office showering their districts with newsletters, baby books, press releases, services, and an unending stream of favorable publicity. Challengers need to find ways to generate negative publicity about incumbents and favorable publicity about themselves. Scandal aside, challengers have discovered that unpopular roll call votes provide them with the best way to jump-start their campaigns, attract media attention, generate campaign funds, and get voters to notice them.

The leaders of interest groups also have incentives to inform their members (and perhaps citizens more generally) about legislators' actions in office. Interest group leaders are themselves politicians who need to maintain the support of their members and attract the support of new members. By focusing citizens' attention on the errors of government and the actions of specific legislators, interest group leaders attempt to mobilize their members to support continued group action. Single-issue groups may publicize legislators' votes on specific issues, whereas broader based groups often compile and publish ratings of all legislators to show how friendly or unfriendly individual legislators have been to their group's interests.

Individual citizens have fewer incentives to become actively involved in monitoring legislators' performance in office. A single citizen can do so little to reward or punish an individual legislator that it hardly makes sense for that citizen to invest a lot of time and energy in acquiring information about legislators' actions in office. Even passive citizens, however, can acquire a great deal of politically relevant information when interest group leaders and challengers slip messages about legislators' performances in office into the daily diet of news stories, advertisements, and direct mail. Citizens are capable of learning a great deal when they are presented with information indirectly; they simply have little incentive to acquire it directly.

The alternative control model conceives of legislators as controlled agents rather than as instructed delegates. Legislators do not simply follow the preferences of those few citizens who already have policy preferences. Instead, legislators anticipate what policy preferences might exist at the time of the next election—including preferences that citizens already hold and preferences that might be generated by challengers and interest groups working to tarnish their reputations. According to this model of representation, legislators must pay attention to both the preferences of attentive publics and the potential preferences of inattentive citizens.

Uncertainty abounds in a system like this. Legislators cannot possibly know for sure what policy effects will follow from specific governmental actions, how challengers or interest group leaders might use governmental actions or inactions to stir up citizens, or whether citizens might blame or absolve legislators for their connections with specific actions. What is certain is that legislators will do their best to anticipate citizens' preferences, to avoid the most dangerous mine fields, and to chart as safe a course as possible through the treacherous territory before them.

Legislators are most fearful of electoral retribution when they consider proposals that would impose large and direct costs on their constituents. Few legislators are willing to consider doubling the gasoline tax, cutting Social Security benefits, eliminating the tax deduction for mortgage interest, closing military bases in their districts, or eliminating food stamps because they know that their roll call votes on these issues can be used against them in future elections. The costs are so great and the connections to their own actions are so obvious that legislators feel certain that journalists, challengers, and interest group leaders will inform citizens of their votes and that some citizens will come to believe that their representatives are not serving their interests.

Legislators have much less fear of electoral retribution when they consider proposals that would impose only small costs on individual citizens or when the issues are sufficiently narrow or technical that it would be difficult for citizens to understand exactly what was at stake. Issues relating to the depreciation of capital assets in the defense industry, the formula for calculating dairy price supports, or the sale of licenses for radio stations are examples. Although these three issues are readily understandable to defense contractors, dairy farmers, and broadcasters—and as a consequence legislators need to weigh carefully the preferences of these three groups—the issues are so obscure to most citizens that it is difficult to imagine challengers making them into big campaign issues.

The vast majority of policy questions lie between these two extremes, where electoral retribution is neither certain nor highly unlikely. A vote on a technical issue relating to air pollution might appear harmless, but it could become politically dangerous if a powerful environmental group used it as a litmus test for whether legislators were friendly or hostile to the environment. A vote on the details of a formula for distributing grants for urban redevelopment might appear benign, but it could become politically dangerous if a challenger showed that an incumbent voted for a formula that cost her district millions of dollars. To guarantee that a seemingly easy issue today does not come back to haunt them in a subsequent campaign, legislators need to think about every issue that comes their way.

Exactly how legislators estimate the electoral consequences of their decisions in office is a complicated matter—one that goes well beyond the scope of this essay.[19] It helps that legislators handle many of the same issues year after year. It also helps that legislators are not alone. They learn from interest groups, committee hearings, staff members, and other legislators about the policy consequences and the political consequences of specific decisions.

When legislators adjust their voting decisions to avoid generating preferences among inattentive citizens, is it fair to suggest that legislators are controlled by those inattentive citizens? It is indeed. I have already argued that citizens are considered influential (or in control) to the extent that legislators' decisions reflect citizens' preferences about policy issues. It makes little difference whether legislators are responding to citizens' existing policy preferences or to the preferences they believe would arise if they voted carelessly. The essence of citizens' control is for legislators to satisfy citizens' wants and interests. If legislators can manage to satisfy citizens' wants before they become transformed into detailed policy preferences, more power to them.

Notice how similar this kind of political control is to the economic control exercised by consumers in the marketplace. Movie producers do not survey movie audiences to discover their exact preferences about scripts, locales, and special effects; nevertheless, producers attempt to anticipate and satisfy the public's preferences so that their films will make money. When we say "the consumer is king," we do not mean that the consumer directs the design and production of movies, automobiles, or town houses. We mean that movie makers, auto makers, and real estate developers attempt to anticipate and satisfy consumers' preferences. Those who fail to satisfy consumers' tastes are eventually driven out of business, just as legislators who fail to anticipate citizens' policy preferences are eventually driven out of office.

This conception of legislators as controlled agents is very similar to the way agents in other areas are controlled. Corporate stockholders are largely unaware of what corporate managers are doing day by day, but managers still attempt to serve stockholders' interests in order to forestall negative evaluations by stock analysts and declines in stock prices, both of which stockholders would notice. Legislators are equally unaware of what bureaucratic officials are doing day by day, but bureaucrats still attempt to serve legislators' political interests in order to keep interest groups and citizens from complaining to legislators.

The comparison of citizens' oversight of legislators' decisions with that of stockholders over managers (or legislators over bureaucrats) is a useful reminder that these control relationships are imperfect. Although corporate managers may be controlled agents, they also have ample freedom to serve their own interests. The current uproar over executive salaries, in which compensation seems to increase as corporate profits decline, is a good example. Similarly, legislators have ample discretion in some policy areas; they know that their constituents will never notice the decisions they have made since the decisions will have only tiny effects on individual citizens.

The power of occasional audits to induce people to keep their behavior within the bounds of what those in control find acceptable is most compelling if we consider how the Internal Revenue Service monitors and controls 110 million taxpayers. Essentially, the IRS allows taxpayers to write their own tax bills and pay what they believe they owe the government. The IRS then audits about 1 percent of the tax returns, looking for income that taxpayers failed to report or deductions that they invented or exaggerated. Despite the infrequency of audits, the American system has an enviable record of collecting taxes. The best available research suggests that 96 percent of all households with tax liability file tax returns. Individual taxpayers report between 91 and 95 percent of their true taxable incomes, and the overreporting of itemized deductions, personal exemptions, and business expenses is only about 2 percent of total personal income.[20]

Most taxpayers report most of their income most of the time because the IRS has other sources of information and because it can impose heavy fines and criminal sanctions on those who cheat the government of its lawful share of income. The other sources of information include reports of wages and salaries from employers, reports of interest and dividends from financial institutions and corporations, reports of real estate transactions from closing agents, and reports of stock transactions from stockbrokers. The results of extensive compliance audits by the IRS demonstrate that taxpayers are most accurate in reporting items for which the IRS has alternative sources of information (for example, wages, salaries, interest, and dividends) and least accurate in reporting items for which the IRS has no good alternative sources (for example, capital gains or income from small businesses).[21] The government also encourages taxpayers to be relatively honest by imposing heavy fines on those it finds cheating and by prosecuting for criminal fraud those who seriously flout the law. A single visible prosecution, such as the conviction of Leona Helmsley for tax fraud, can help to deter many others from practicing similar deceits.

This account of how the Internal Revenue Service monitors and controls American taxpayers helps to reveal how citizens can monitor and control elected legislators without knowing much about what legislators are doing day by day. First, it shows the importance of auditable records. Although legislators may feel free to vote as they please on voice votes, they must be far more cautious when they face roll call votes because these actions are permanently and publicly recorded. Second, it shows the efficiency of having others collect and process raw information. Challengers and interest group leaders monitor what legislators have been doing and then inform citizens of legislators' misdeeds, much as employers, banks, and brokers monitor taxpayers' behavior and send summary accounts to the IRS. Third, it shows the deterrent power of heavy sanctions. Legislators anticipate and respond to citizens' preferences and potential preferences because they fear electoral defeat, much as taxpayers anticipate and respond to the rulings of the IRS because they do not wish to risk fines, public humiliation, or imprisonment.

One virtue of the alternative control model is that it avoids the four basic mistakes in identifying control relationships that were outlined in the previous section. It does not confuse the frequency with which citizens monitor legislators' behavior with the extent of their control over legislators' actions, for it allows other people to do most of the day-to-day monitoring. It does not assume that if citizens are to be influential they must have well-established policy preferences in advance of legislative action, for such preferences are required only before the next election (and only then if legislators have failed to anticipate what preferences citizens would form at that time). It does not confuse the frequency of electoral defeat with the extent of control, for such defeats are evidence of the breakdown of control. Finally, it does not assume that legislators play the electoral game only once and therefore are willing to take small risks on any given issue; instead, it assumes that legislators' aspirations for long political careers give them incentives to anticipate citizens' future preferences on every issue put before them for fear that small risks will cumulate over time and threaten their continuance in office.

The Extent of Citizens' Control

The logic of the alternative control model is simple. Legislators adjust their behavior in office to avoid electoral problems, and they do this by paying careful attention to the known preferences of attentive publics and the potential preferences of inattentive citizens. Although the logic is simple, testing the empirical validity of the model is extraordinarily difficult. How can one know that legislators are anticipating and responding to the potential preferences of inattentive citizens when by doing so they remove the stimulus (a careless vote) that would have transformed those potential preferences into real and measurable preferences?

John Kingdon offers the most persuasive evidence that legislators anticipate the preferences of citizens who are not attentive to legislative action. Kingdon interviewed House members in 1969, just after they had made decisions on fifteen important roll call votes. His extensive questioning was designed to uncover the kinds of factors legislators considered and the way they balanced conflicting forces. One of his principal findings was that legislators attempt to consider how roll call votes could be used against them, and they anticipate the reaction of inattentive citizens.[22]

In a recent book, I offer a different kind of evidence. One of the questions I examined was why would Congress first deliver narrowly concentrated benefits to some group in society and then suddenly switch sides, imposing costs on the previously favored group and delivering benefits to those whom it had long neglected? Why, in other words, would legislators enact policies that were opposed by organized, attentive publics and about which inattentive citizens had no obvious preferences? The only satisfying answer was that legislators were behaving as the alternative control model would predict—anticipating and responding to citizens' potential preferences.[23]

We know far less about the empirical validity of the alternative control model than we do about the standard control model because few scholars have taken seriously the notion of legislators as controlled agents rather than legislators as instructed delegates. What is known suggests that the alternative control model is empirically plausible. What is known also suggests that those who find little support for the standard control model and then speak of "the myth of constituency control" are confusing necessary conditions with sufficient conditions. The standard control model is not the only way in which citizens can control elected officials. The notion of legislators as controlled agents is a powerful alternative to the notion of legislators as instructed delegates.

Notes

I am indebted to Richard F. Fenno, Jr., and Fred Greenstein for their helpful comments and suggestions.

1. CBS News/*New York Times* poll "Does America Really Want to Throw the Rascals Out?" (Press release from CBS News dated Oct. 11, 1990, based on telephone survey conducted Oct. 8-10, 1990). Excerpts from the poll were published in Robin Toner, "In a Survey, Americans Wish a Pox on Both Congress and the President," *New York Times,* Oct. 12, 1990, A21.
2. Warren E. Miller and Donald E. Stokes, "Constituency Influence in Congress," *American Political Science Review* 57 (March 1963): 45-56.
3. Robert A. Bernstein, *Elections, Representation, and Congressional Voting Behavior: The Myth of Constituency Control* (Englewood Cliffs, N.J.: Prentice Hall, 1989), 98.
4. Gary C. Jacobson, *The Politics of Congressional Elections,* 3d ed. (New York: HarperCollins, 1992), 137.
5. Ibid., 140.
6. Ibid., 137.
7. Bernstein, *Elections, Representation, and Congressional Voting Behavior,* 21-22.
8. Miller and Stokes, "Constituency Influence in Congress." For a discussion of the measurement problems, see Robert S. Erikson, "Constituency Opinion and Congressional Behavior: A Reexamination of the Miller-Stokes Representation Data," *American Journal of Political Science* 22 (August 1978): 513-517.
9. Robert A. Bernstein and William W. Anthony, "The ABM Issue in the Senate, 1968-1970: The Importance of Ideology," *American Political Science Review* 68 (September 1974): 1198-1206.
10. See the citations in Bernstein, *Elections, Representation, and Congressional Voting Behavior,* 69-93.
11. It is equally odd to assume that citizens' preferences have exclusively economic roots, whereas legislators' preferences have ideological roots.

12. Larry M. Bartels, "Constituency Opinion and Congressional Policy Making: The Reagan Defense Buildup," *American Political Science Review* 85 (June 1991): 457-474.

13. Bernstein, *Elections, Representation, and Congressional Voting Behavior,* 104.

14. Although some authors find shades of difference between the three concepts of power, influence, and control, these subtleties are not crucial for my analysis of the relationship between citizens and their elected representatives. The three concepts are close enough to being synonyms that I use them interchangeably throughout this essay.

15. Mathew D. McCubbins and Thomas Schwartz, "Congressional Oversight Overlooked: Police Patrols Versus Fire Alarms," *American Journal of Political Science* 28 (February 1984): 165-179.

16. *Webster's Ninth New Collegiate Dictionary* (Springfield, Mass.: Merriam-Webster, 1983), 285, 274.

17. Alternatively, influence is "the causation of outcomes by preferences." See Jack H. Nagel, *The Descriptive Analysis of Power* (New Haven: Yale University Press, 1975), 24, 29.

18. Kenneth Prewitt, "Political Ambitions, Volunteerism, and Electoral Accountability," *American Political Science Review* 64 (March 1970): 5-17.

19. On this matter, see R. Douglas Arnold, *The Logic of Congressional Action* (New Haven: Yale University Press, 1990).

20. These estimates are from Jeffrey A. Roth, John T. Scholz, and Ann Dryden Witte, eds., *Taxpayer Compliance: An Agenda for Research* (Philadelphia: University of Pennsylvania Press, 1989), 25, 30, 42, 43.

21. Robert A. Kagan, "On the Visibility of Income Tax Law Violations," in *Taxpayer Compliance: Social Science Perspectives,* ed. Jeffrey A. Roth and John T. Scholz (Philadelphia: University of Pennsylvania Press, 1989), 83-84.

22. John W. Kingdon, *Congressmen's Voting Decisions,* 3d ed. (Ann Arbor: University of Michigan Press, 1989), 60-67.

23. Arnold, *Logic of Congressional Action.*

18

Congress and the Politics of Renewal: Redressing the Crisis of Legitimation

Lawrence C. Dodd

For two hundred years Congress has served as the touchstone of American democracy. Always a very human institution, Congress has reflected citizens' base aspirations as well as their noble ones, their calculating natures as well as their capacities for mutual regard. Yet the strength of the nation's democracy ultimately has derived from Congress's ability to identify the common concerns and shared interests of the citizenry amidst the disparate claims for personal advantage and thereby to discover shared principles for collective governance. The discovery of new collective principles of governance has allowed the nation to address the extraordinary challenges that two centuries of societal change have posed: from the struggle over slavery to the rise of industrialization to the coming of global depression and world war. The search for new and broadly acceptable governing principles has enabled Congress to maintain the support of the people and to sustain a sense of governing legitimacy, even in the midst of crises that its shortsighted policies helped induce.[1]

Today the nation faces a new set of governing challenges, posed by the coming of a postindustrial world of expanding service demands and limited resources, and it looks to Congress to chart a new course of common action.[2] Again the public sees a very human institution caught in the clash of opposing interests and shortsighted commitments. Yet as the nation enters its third century, there is another dimension to its governing concerns: a growing apprehension about the capacity of Congress to acknowledge and address the policy dilemmas of the contemporary era.

The public sees a Congress floundering in a policy deadlock unprecedented in modern times. This immobilism is symbolized by the quadrupling of the national debt to four trillion dollars in twelve years and by the emergence of our country as one of the world's largest debtor nations. The immobilism is felt daily in the homelessness, joblessness, or underemployment of much of our citizenry and in the soaring costs of health care that affect us all. It is experienced, most fundamentally, in the absence of the sense of shared community and national purpose that a vibrant legislature would provide. In the face of policy disarray and a lost sense of common identity the public's disillusionment with the government, particularly with Congress, is mounting.[3] For the first time in American history serious efforts to limit the budgetary power of Congress and to impose term limits on its members have received widespread popular support. In the past two elections incumbent reelection margins have fallen after a sustained period of steady increase. And opinion polls report that only 16 percent of the public approve of the job Congress is doing; 69 percent disapprove.[4]

Political analysts generally attribute the nation's disarray and the public's disillusionment with Congress to the divided party government of the Reagan-Bush years; they expect greater policy activism with the coming of united government under President Bill Clinton and a Democratic Congress.[5] I agree that party government matters in American politics. The coming of united party government almost certainly will generate expanded political activism in Washington and on Capitol Hill. I doubt, however, that united party government alone will reverse the long-term policy drift and institutional crisis engulfing contemporary American politics. The policy immobilism of the modern era and the public's disaffection with Congress have much deeper roots than divided party government.[6]

The source of policy immobilism in American politics, I suggest, lies embedded in the character of contemporary legislative politics. More so than at any other time in the nation's history, Congress is elected and organized to serve the disparate elements of a self-interested public rather than to identify and foster the shared concerns of a public-spirited citizenry. Congress increasingly lacks the ability to recognize the mutual concerns and shared interests of the public and the ability to discover new governing principles that could resolve our policy dilemmas and renew public faith in government. This magnified politics of self-interest came to predominance with the creation of the service state during the advanced industrialism of the twentieth century. In its wake has come a Congress bereft of its representative and deliberative capacities and virtually unable to acknowledge or address the new governing demands of a postindustrial society.

With Congress immobilized and the nation adrift, the public necessarily must doubt the legitimacy of Congress as a policymaking institution and the legitimacy of its members as true representatives of the public interest. This crisis of congressional legitimation, moreover, will fester regardless of united or divided party government as long as it is left unaddressed. Policy change and institutional reform, aided by united party government, together can redress the erosion in representative and deliberative government that gives rise to the crisis of legitimation. With a revitalization of Congress can come a renewed spirit of shared purpose and national community. But first the nation must recognize the deep-seated character of our policy immobilism and the consequent severity of the legitimation crisis that Congress faces.

I first developed this argument in the late 1970s, just before the first election of Ronald Reagan.[7] Writing now in the days immediately following the election of Bill Clinton, as the nation embraces united party government, let me reaffirm and expand the original legitimation thesis and consider its implications for political action.

I

The legitimation thesis rests on a simple assumption: to sustain the long-term support of the public, Congress and its members must demonstrate a reasonable capacity to recognize the fundamental problems of a historical era, deliberate over the proper solutions to these problems, and enact legislation that addresses them in a credible manner.[8] The public does not expect miracles from Congress: people understand that policy solutions will have drawbacks, trade-offs, and unforeseen consequences so that there are limits to what Congress can accomplish. Likewise, the public is aware that Congress alone does not control public policy, that its handiwork may be undercut by a hostile president or a recalcitrant Court. But the public does look to Congress to grapple with the serious issues of the day and to fashion reasonable strategies for addressing them. Insofar as Congress approximates these baseline goals, citizens will give it broad latitude in its policy processes and solid support as a governing institution.[9]

Throughout most of American history, Congress has been "good enough" at problem solving that it has sustained public belief in its legitimate role in national policymaking. Historically, there have been no concerted attacks by the public on its fundamental constitutional powers or decision-making authority. This is not to say that congressional authority has not been seriously tested. The growth of executive power has challenged congressional dominance of policy-making, particularly in foreign affairs and budgetary policy, and judicial activism at times has encroached on its domestic policy prerogatives. But through most of American history Congress has been seen as a valuable and legitimate participant in national policymaking. More often than not citizens, scholars, journalists, and politicians have considered how to protect and increase the power of Congress in the face of executive imperialism or judicial incursions.[10]

Public support for Congress has derived from two attributes of the institution that citizens value intrinsically and that together allow it to address policy problems in credible ways.[11] First, however imperfectly, Congress has served as our nation's primary *representative* institution—as the central decision-making body whose membership is selected by the enfranchised citizens of a historical era and which reflects in some reasonable manner the citizens' disparate sentiments on the major policy issues of the day. The representative nature of Congress has meant that citizens would have spokespersons in Washington who reflected their broad policy concerns and could speak for them in government. In touch with the central issues preoccupying the citizens, the government could stay abreast of emerging societal problems and reflect the broad range of citizens' concerns about those problems. Moreover, the representative character of Congress, its attentiveness to a broad range of popular sentiment on issues, has lent a special authority to its policy solutions.[12] Policy failures generally have been seen as resulting from an insufficiently inclusive representation of citizens and thereby from a failure to recognize fully the severity of policy problems or the range of policy concerns in society. The most popular reform of Congress thus has been the expansion of voting rights, first to all white males, then to northern blacks, then to women, then to the young, and finally to racial and ethnic minorities.

Second, Congress has served as the nation's primary *deliberative* body—the only institution that addresses national policy questions through open debate and collective policy choice. The deliberative character of Congress has meant that, when faced with severe national problems, citizens could look to Congress to clarify the problems and devise broadly acceptable solutions. Much of the internal history of Congress has been a search to find rules and norms that facilitate deliberative problem solving. Success in this endeavor has been limited at best.[13] In creating rules that allow for virtually unlimited debate, the Senate created the opportunity for filibusters, which can make a mockery of efforts at deliberation. The House, in seeking to find mechanisms for regulating debate, created a Rules Committee, which often merely forecloses debate on controversial issues.[14] Nevertheless, throughout most of American history, the House and Senate succeeded well enough in devising workable rules and norms that Congress eventually could address critical policy problems, seek to reconcile the conflicting policy views of a disparate citizenry, and enact credible legislation.

Because Congress has demonstrated a reasonable capacity to act—and to act in a way that reflected both representative and deliberative problem solving—the public has supported it even in the midst of severe crises. In the first half of the nineteenth century, for example, as westward expansion and regional conflicts raised the issue of slavery to the forefront of national consciousness, it was Congress that reflected the diverse regional concerns of the enfranchised public, debated the moral and political issues, and fashioned the great compromises of the era. Ultimately, congressional efforts at forging compromises over the expansion of slavery failed, in some real degree because the Supreme Court intervened with the *Dred Scott* decision and poisoned the atmosphere of deliberation on Capitol Hill. The issue of slavery thus was decided on the battlefields of the Civil War. Yet the coming of the war did not lead to a loss of faith in legislative decision making but to widespread doubts about the Supreme Court (as a result of the *Dred Scott* decision), the presidency (as a result of tepid leadership before the war), and state government (as a result of the southern secession). Congress emerged from the war with its legitimacy intact and even strengthened. It also won greater legislative powers as a result of the Thirteenth, Fourteenth, and Fifteenth amendments.[15]

During the late nineteenth century, faced with the corporate corruption and collusion associated with rapid industrialization, Congress again became the center of national policymaking. At issue was the national government's ability to regulate the worst abuses associated with early industrialization, including corporate trusts, child labor, environmental degradation, and consumer exploitation. Tackling these problems ultimately required that the reformers of the Progressive era attack the power of party bosses, implement extensive new election procedures, and decentralize power within Congress. From these and related efforts came an activist bureaucracy focused on regulating corporate power. Congressional efforts to regulate business had many inadequacies, including the continued and unrestrained power of the stock exchanges, so the end results were mixed. But Congress addressed the general issues of early industrialism and acted in ways that the American public found sufficient for the times. It was not Congress that the public found wanting but the political parties. Congress emerged from the reform era by the 1920s with its power enhanced by the

Sixteenth Amendment, which legalized the income tax, and with its representational base expanded through the granting of woman suffrage and the move to an elective Senate.[16]

Finally, with the coming of the Great Depression, Congress confronted the vital issue of ensuring economic stability and individual security during the advanced stages of industrialization. The strategy of choice among industrial nations was to create an extensive government bureaucracy to deliver needed social services and manage the economy. Facing the crisis of the depression and then a world war, Congress embraced bureaucratic service delivery and institutionalized the foundations of the modern service state through a wide range of programs—from farm price supports to Social Security to the Tennessee Valley Authority. Then, with the advent of World War II and the Cold War it embraced a huge military-industrial complex that provided the nation with an economic and research backbone while sustaining a widespread military commitment throughout much of Europe and Asia. Again the congressional response to the central domestic problems of the period had many limitations, including inadequate protection for ethnic and racial minorities. Furthermore, with the waning of the depression Congress became more divided about its general commitment to social programs. But it acknowledged and responded to the depression and did so earlier than the president or the Supreme Court; the election of Franklin Roosevelt in 1932 found a Congress that had already drafted many of the basic statutes of the New Deal's first hundred days. Rather than Congress being seen as the obstacle to change, that stigma fell first to President Herbert Hoover and then to a conservative Court. Out of the Great Depression and World War II, in fact, came not a call for a weakened Congress but for a stronger institution, with larger staffs and more resources, that would be able to restrain the expanding executive branch and oversee the service state. Congress also was given expanded constitutional authority, this time not through constitutional amendments but through the Supreme Court's reinterpretation of the Constitution's interstate commerce clause strengthening the regulatory authority of the legislative branch.[17]

As this brief history suggests, throughout American history Congress has sustained its public support in the face of extraordinary societal crises. In each instance, the nation relegitimated Congress through widespread popular acceptance of constitutional amendments and Supreme Court decisions that expanded its policymaking authority in ways appropriate to the distinctive policy demands of the era. The nation did so, moreover, not because Congress had performed in exemplary ways or even because it had solved the problems of an era. In each era Congress's performance included serious inadequacies and in the midnineteenth century proved insufficient to divert the nation from a devastating civil war. But Congress did well enough in its distinctive problem-solving efforts during each era to sustain the support of the public and emerge from each crisis with its formal power increased and its policymaking legitimacy renewed.

Why, then, the disrepute of the contemporary Congress? If Congress could survive a civil war, the coming of industrialization, a global depression, and a world war with its legitimacy intact, why after two hundred years of such resilience has the public begun to forsake it?[18] Instead of calls to expand the power of Congress to control public policy, there are serious efforts to limit its taxing and spending power by imposing a constitutional amendment requiring a balanced budget. Instead of efforts to increase the institutional resources of its members or to ensure adequate pay, we see attempts to oppose salary increases and to strip away perquisites. Instead of efforts to expand the capacity of citizens to select the representatives they prefer, we find initiatives passed now in fifteen states to limit legislators' terms and thereby to limit citizens' choice of representation. Why?

The answer could lie in the unique severity, perhaps even the insolubility, of postindustrial problems. After all, the technological revolutions of postindustrialism are producing a historic shift away from widespread public employment in industrial production and toward a reliance on a knowledge-based economy geared toward scientific innovations, information processing, and systems management. This shift is producing a cruel paradox. The technological advances of postindustrialism are increasing the quality of life to which citizens can aspire, with extraordinary improvements possible in health and longevity, education and self-development, and communication and transportation. Yet these same innovations reduce reliance on a large blue-collar work force involved in industrial production, thus leaving a large class of citizens bereft of the job security, union contracts, and purchasing power that would allow them access to that expanded quality of life. At the same time citizens must cope with the severe social and ecological costs produced by advanced industrialism, including urban decay and violence, the breakdown of the extended (and now the nuclear) family, and the threat to the world's ecological system.[19]

Furthermore, postindustrialism forces the nation to confront severe collective policy problems at a time when the fiscal resources of the nation-state are increasingly limited.[20] On the one hand, because there is fairly broad agreement that a free market economy alone will not redress these collective difficulties, the nation must respond to economic, social, and ecological challenges of postindustrialism through government action. Yet insofar as the government does intervene, the primary strategy that it inherits from the industrial era is reliance on direct bureaucratic provision of necessary services, whether they be jobs, health care benefits, or environmental cleanup. A reliance on bureaucracy, which brings with it management inefficiencies and patronage pressures, magnifies the costs of service delivery immeasurably. Expanding government service delivery in response to postindustrialism thus will greatly increase the fiscal pressures on a service state already burdened by the service programs of the industrial era. It will do so, moreover, at a time when the nation's fiscal resources are increasingly limited because of the depletion of its natural resources, the growing expense of foreign resources, the economic competition from Japan and Europe, and the dislocation costs of the postindustrial transition within the economy.

Perhaps the fiscal limits of the state are so severe that it is impossible for Congress to redress the collective policy problems of postindustrialism. From this perspective, Congress is simply the unwitting victim of the public's growing fury over the inevitability of societal decay and governmental breakdown. As the fury mounts, the public turns against government, particularly against the policymaking institution citizens have most consistently trusted throughout American history. Perhaps representative and deliberative government will simply collapse in the face of an insolvable policy dilemma: expanding collective problems amidst declining fiscal resources.

In truth, the policy problems of postindustrialism are almost certainly not as insolvable as they appear. It is possible, for example, that postindustrial innovations in communications will build cultural awareness and linkages across nation-states and foster the spread of democratic principles in ways that could reduce international military tensions. Reductions in global tensions (seen in the end of the Cold War) then could release the nation from devoting such an extraordinary portion of its national budget to defense spending. Likewise, the economic productivity and quality of life made possible by the technological innovations and knowledge revolution of postindustrialism could create an expanded international demand for high-tech goods and services (particularly for scientific innovations); the resulting employment in scientific and service industries could provide the public with quality jobs, sustain the growth of the nation's economy, and secure resources for the state. Finally, it might be possible for government to move away from reliance on bureaucracy and create cost-effective strategies for ensuring service delivery. Over the past decade, for example, various state and local governments have experimented successfully with the managed use of market competition among private companies and public institutions to ensure collective benefits (city sanitation, economic redevelopment, elementary and secondary education, environmental cleanup) normally considered the primary responsibility of government. Governments, for example, could provide families with vouchers to send children to schools of their choice, thereby bringing competitive pressures on schools to improve their performance and hold down costs. Such experiments have produced collective services with less expense and more efficiency while maintaining or even improving upon levels of quality.[21]

In essence, fundamental restructuring of the national government in ways that could resolve the policy dilemmas of postindustrialism is possible. This restructuring would involve a downsizing of the military-industrial complex, a lessening of the nation's dependence on military spending to sustain the economy, and the freeing of defense funds to be used in programs that help induce a competitive economy and competitive service delivery. It would provide support for educational retraining and high-tech research to help make the nation more competitive in the new global economy. Most critically, government restructuring would shift state activism away from government bureaucracy toward managed competition in the delivery of expanded services. We can refer to this restructured government as an *entrepreneurial state*—that is, a government that acknowledges its responsibility to address that nation's critical collective problems but seeks to do so by creating incentive structures that encourage publicly managed competition among private as well as public service delivery institutions. The broad goal of the entrepreneurial state would be to ensure the collective goods that a postindustrial society requires without undue dependence on direct government provision of services. The entrepreneurial state would seek to make the problems of postindustrialism manageable and to make possible the vast human opportunities that it offers.[22]

The possibilities afforded by the development of an entrepreneurial state make it difficult to argue that the policy dilemmas of postindustrialism are more severe than those posed by slavery in the early nineteenth century, by the corporate abuses of early industrialization, or by the economic dislocations of advanced industrialism. Each of these policy challenges had a viable solution: the creation of a strong national state to protect each citizen's equal right as a free laborer, the movement to a regulatory state to manage the abuses of laissez faire capitalism, the implementation of a service state to provide for the economic and social security of individuals caught in the economic dislocations of advanced industrialism. So too, it appears, do the policy challenges of postindustrialism: the creation of an entrepreneurial state to ensure the service needs of society while respecting its fiscal limits.[23] The public's disaffection with Congress thus does not appear to result from the inherent insolubility of the policy problems that it faces.

Again I ask: why the growing public disaffection with the contemporary Congress? Why now the moves to restrict its policymaking authority and punish its members collectively through the imposition of term limits? Why now forsake the one governing institution that most empowers the citizenry?

II

The public questions the legitimacy of Congress as a policymaking institution, I suggest, not because it doubts that postindustrial problems can be solved but because it doubts the problem-solving capacities of the contemporary Congress. This perception is an increasingly accurate assessment.

The problem-solving capacities of the modern Congress *are* eroding. Historically, Congress has recognized and addressed the central policy problems of the day, and thereby has sustained its popular support, through reasonably faithful representation and deliberative consideration of the public's general policy concerns. As long as Congress reflected the major policy issues troubling the public and sought to reconcile disagreement through reasoned discussion, the public could forgive the institution's shortcomings and support its continued policymaking power. But what the citizens cannot forgive is a breakdown in the representative and deliberative consideration of their general policy concerns; when that happens the institution loses touch with the people's real-life problems and with the real-life issues that a solution to their problems must address. Yet this is precisely what has happened in contemporary America.

Both the representativeness and the deliberativeness of the modern Congress are in decline. This decline, moreover, is particularly difficult to recognize and address. It is difficult to recognize because it is occurring despite objective appearances suggesting that Congress is doing better rather than worse as a representative and deliberative institution. It is difficult to address because it results from deeply ingrained alterations in the electoral and organizational politics of Congress that occurred during the industrial era and that impede institutional reform and government restructuring. Yet the demonstrable results are a Congress increasingly out of touch with the nation's critical policy problems.

Consider first the changes that are occurring in Congress as a representative institution.[24] When most of us think of political representation, we consider how easy it is for diverse groups in society to gain entrée to our governing institutions; we think about how inclusive an institution is. In terms of inclusiveness the modern Congress is certainly more representative than it was in the past and probably is the most representative institution in American government of the past two centuries. Today the right of all groups in society to vote in congressional elections is essentially assured, and virtually all major ethnic, gender, and class groups in society have at least some presence (if not leadership positions) in Congress. If inclusiveness alone were sufficient to ensure representative problem solving by Congress, the modern Congress, with its record number of women and minorities, should be the most representative in American history. As such, it should be a widely supported, legitimate, and effective participant in policymaking. There is, however, another critical dimension to representation.

To serve as an effective representative of the public, not only must Congress ensure that its members reflect the group diversity of society, but it must ensure that its members speak for a diverse public on the major policy issues of the day. In other words, to be an effective representative institution, Congress must ensure a broadly focused, issue-oriented representation. Insofar as a diverse range of voters can select legislators who are sensitive to their broad issue concerns, Congress can stay attuned to new problems as they arise in society, reflect the intense views of citizens on these problems, and have some chance of finding commonly accepted policy solutions. By contrast, if the voters are constrained in their ability to select legislators based on broad issue concerns, Congress is likely to overlook emerging societal problems and lose its distinctive capacities as a representative problem-solving institution.

The modern Congress's dilemma is that during the industrial era the selection of legislators came to focus not on the broad issue positions of candidates but on their capacity to deliver particular service benefits to constituents.[25] With the coming of the modern service state, we have had a shift away from broadly focused *issue representation* and toward narrowly focused *interest representation*. With this shift, legislators have come to build broadly inclusive electoral coalitions within their districts by servicing the particularized interests of all constituent groups—farmers, bankers, union members, students, the elderly, and so forth. Although such groups may disagree on the broad issues of the day, and would support opposing candidates in an issue-oriented campaign, they agree on the importance of maintaining in office an incumbent who has the power to serve their immediate individual and group interests. Incumbents thus win reelection by large and secure margins, as John Alford and David Brady demonstrate,[26] while their constituents receive the assistance with their service needs that an experienced and powerful incumbent can provide. Such assistance can include the improved processing of Social Security checks and veterans' benefits, intervention with regulatory agencies in behalf of farm price supports or savings and loan negotiations, the building of a local post office or dam, and the awarding of government grants for scientific research and the enactment of defense contracts critical to a local economy.

Over the long run, however, both incumbents and citizens can become so dependent on the politics of service delivery that they overlook the emerging policy problems of a new era. The voters may see the decay of urban infrastructures, sense the declining educational and job opportunities of their children, acknowledge the ecological damage of industrial pollution, and worry about the long-term effects of a mounting deficit. But as they consider their vote for senator and representative, the citizens override any broad concerns they may have with collective issues and vote in accord with ensuring immediate benefits; they do so by voting for the powerful local incumbent who can assist with a desired local defense contract or who can help them with their veterans claims or Medicare benefits. They do so because of the immediate influence that a powerful incumbent legislator can have on their particularized interests. Likewise, the legislators may share a growing concern with collective societal and economic reversals. But their efforts to maintain electoral security and exercise personal influence in Congress are best served by focusing on those particularized programs that mobilize group support, that help them build a solid reputation as effective legislators, and that ensure reelection. The emerging collective problems of the new era thus go unacknowledged and tear away at the fabric of society.

Even when mounting societal problems become so severe that they can no longer be ignored, the politics of the service state can continue to hamstring Congress. Even as societal crises confront the voters with the possibility of serious life reversals, the electorate may demand increased attention to particularized social and economic programs that shield them against personal misfortune. And politicians, faced with rising public discontent, may well increase their emphasis on the strategies of interest representation that shore up their electoral base. Neither the citizens nor the politicians may easily end their obsession with particularized interests and focus on collective issues, such as urban decay, the decline in the nation's economic productivity, environmental pollution, and the deficit. Only with the creation of a "new logic of politics" that helps participants find ways to foster their collective good without unduly harming particularized interests are they likely to face these general issues.[27] The creation of a new and shared logic of collective action generally must come through a process of political deliberation. Yet, as with political representation, the politics of the industrial era crippled the congressional capacity for deliberation.

Consider the effect of the service state on Congress as a deliberative institution.[28] Most of us think of political deliberation in fairly simple terms. In particular, we tend to think that deliberative policymaking occurs when legislators vote on policy decisions after a formal discussion of policy alternatives. If policy discussion and formal votes are our measure of political deliberation, the modern Congress is a deliberative institution par excellence. The modern Congress has created innumerable opportunities for its members to speak about policy matters in committees and subcommittees and on the floor of the House and Senate, with much of their discussion televised; in addition, the right of legislators to initiate formal votes on their bills and amendments is heavily protected in both houses and across subcommittees, committees, and floor action. Judged solely in terms of discussion and formal votes, the modern Congress probably would be the most deliberative in history and, again, should enjoy strong support from the public. Like political representation, however, political deliberation is a complex phenomenon.

To be a truly deliberative institution, Congress must not only ensure debates and votes on policy questions, but it also must facilitate the reasoned search for broadly understood and acceptable policy solutions. The primary emphasis in a deliberative body is not on debate per se, or on majoritarian imposition of policy solutions, but on a dialogue among participants that seeks to find principled agreement on how best to address policy problems. In other words, deliberation is not primarily a strategic game of calculation and maneuvering among supporters of mutually exclusive policy positions, each seeking to impose a preferred policy solution on the other—though such moments may come in the heat of political conflict. Rather, deliberation is a process of learning and discovery in which legislators of vastly different backgrounds and perspectives share concerns about common policy problems and design collective solutions based on principles that virtually all participants can accept.[29] The resulting policies then seek to resolve as many of the separate concerns of participants as possible.

Such deliberative efforts require a broad conversation among all relevant participants; they also require rules and norms that facilitate the collective crafting of commonly acceptable principles of policy action. From such broad conversations and collective choice, it is hoped, will come a clarification of common concerns and principles of action that none of the participants may originally have seen; with such clarification then may come the discovery—the learning—of new and viable policy approaches that virtually all participants can embrace. A deliberative discussion of the problems of postindustrialism might start, for example, with a sense of unresolvable conflict between the service demands of society and the fiscal limits of the state. Rather than revolving around strategic debates and votes designed to force members to choose between services and fiscal restraint, however, a deliberative process would involve shared acknowledgment of the need for both and a common search for new approaches to governance satisfying both criteria. Participants then might discover the principles of state entrepreneurship. In the process they could create a new collective logic of politics that would influence their specific consideration of a range of policy issues.

Unfortunately, seen not just in terms of strategic debates and formal votes but as reasoned dialogue and collective choice, the deliberative capacities of the modern Congress have eroded at least as much as have its representational

capacities. This erosion in deliberative capacities began in the late nineteenth
and early twentieth centuries with the internal organization and procedures Congress created to guide the development and implementation of the activist state.
Thus Congress expanded the fledgling committee system of the early nineteenth
century as a way of marshaling and focusing specialized attention on regulatory
and service delivery programs across a wide range of policy domains, from agriculture to education to banking to labor. Likewise, it created an extensive body
of rules and norms to help ensure that the work of these committees could
proceed in a systematic manner and that the House and Senate could debate the
committee proposals in an orderly fashion. As Congress used the industrial-era
committee system and policy processes to address the issues of service delivery, a
subtle shift took place away from general *dialogic deliberation* over the broad
agenda issues and governing principles and toward *strategic deliberation*. Congress
designed committee and floor rules and procedures not to facilitate collective
conversation and choice but, as the work of Douglas Arnold demonstrates, to
foster instrumental manipulation of debating and voting processes in ways that
would benefit the passage or defeat of particular policy preferences within a
preestablished programmatic agenda.[30]

The move from dialogic to strategic deliberation was heavily shaped and
reinforced by the shifting calculus of voters and politicians.[31] Citizens and interest groups wanted the particularized benefits to be derived from the service
state and thus came to value members' committee work on service delivery
programs and to oppose structures, such as political parties, that would interfere with committee or floor efforts in behalf of particularized interests; they
also came to oppose such processes as secret votes that might limit their ability
to evaluate legislators' support for major programs. For their part, the legislators, seeking long-term power in government, came to realize that advocating
particularized programs in congressional committees, subcommittees, and floor
debates could help their reelection and career-advancement efforts while giving
them direct personal influence on policy development and agency implementation. Thus they came to support norms such as seniority, which would protect
their investment in committee service, and to oppose the power of leaders, who
might interfere with their pursuit of particularized interests in the committees
or on the floor.

In essence, the voters and the politicians came to assume that the bureaucratic governing principles of the industrial era were a permanent commitment
that would not require broad deliberation or review so that congressional attention could shift to the management and implementation of that commitment.[32]
As this assumption took hold, Congress weakened the organizational structures
concerned with debating and pursuing broad governing principles, such as the
political parties and party leaders, and institutionalized the power of committees
and subcommittees focused on specific programs. Congress limited open and
inclusive debate which could address the broad problems of the nation and the
general principles of governance. In its place, as the work of Richard Hall and of
George Connor and Bruce Oppenheimer demonstrates, Congress came to rely

on narrow specialized debate in committees and subcommittees and time-constrained debate on the House floor.[33] Finally, Congress moved away from rules, norms, and structures that would facilitate the flexible voting processes necessary for fashioning near consensual agreements (as made possible, for example, by extensive closed door meetings or by the "straw polls" that come with voice votes and unrecorded tallies). It moved toward voting arrangements that would allow the processing of a large body of programmatic decisions; that would facilitate members' strategic selection among programmatic alternatives, particularly the increase or decrease in spending commitments and revenue collection; and that would protect members' rights to express their views openly and record their votes so that constituents and lobby groups could gauge their faithfulness to programmatic promises.[34]

The consequent destruction of the structures, rules, and norms that facilitate broad-gauged deliberative dialogue produced a Congress unable to engage in a reasoned and collective consideration of emerging national problems. In other words, Congress so "adapted" its organizational structure and procedures to the strategic processing of an industrial-era agenda that it weakened or lost those institutional mechanisms necessary for a broad discussion of policy problems and governing principles.[35] Lacking such mechanisms, Congress now finds it difficult to discover a new logic of politics that would enable its members to break out of the politics of interest representation and embrace collective solutions to postindustrial policy dilemmas. The irony is that if the legislators were able to focus on such a broad-gauged discussion, they might well move toward a politics of state entrepreneurship that would make it possible to satisfy the concerns of constituents for particularized services while allowing enhanced attention to long-neglected collective problems, such as the nation's infrastructure, environment, and deficit. Such a move could both solidify public support for Congress and protect members' long-term career interests.

In terms of its representational and deliberative capacities, then, the modern Congress is less prepared to address new and general policy issues than perhaps it was at any time in its history. This development is not simply a random and transitory occurrence but is a result of Congress's response to the growth of an activist government, particularly the creation and growth of the service state during the past sixty years. With the coming of the service state, congressional representation has shifted from a broadly focused issue spokesmanship to a more narrowly focused interest servantship; likewise, congressional deliberation has shifted from broad, collegial dialogue over governing principles to a more narrow strategic choice among existing programmatic preferences within the bureaucratic governing principle created by the service state. In identifying these shifts, I do not mean to imply that the historical Congress never engaged in interest representation and strategic choice; the politics of regional interest was a major aspect of nineteenth century policymaking. Nor do I suggest that the contemporary Congress never acknowledges general issues and never engages in deliberative dialogue; Congress undertook an extensive discussion of the nation's collective interests in the Persian Gulf before declaring war in

1991.[36] What I do maintain is that decisive movement has occurred in the dominant nature of representation and deliberation.

The result is a *technocratic* Congress devoted to processing incremental and particularized policy choices within the policy agenda of the service state, not a *democratic* Congress in touch with its representational and deliberative roots and capable of restructuring its governing principles and policy commitments.[37] We have a Congress that can manage, oversee, expand, and even contract the service state through strategic response to the shifting demands of interest representation. It is not, however, a Congress that can easily transform the service state through deliberative response to those broad issue concerns of citizens that might require new governing principles and state structures. Congress's disconnection from citizens' emerging issue concerns and its inability to learn new ways of governing in response to these issues has necessarily put in question its value as a problem-solving institution.

Seen from this perspective, the public's loss of faith in Congress may reflect an astute reading on the part of citizens that however well Congress manages the service state and addresses their immediate narrow interests, it is not attentive to the general issues shaping their collective well-being or their long-term future. In the first half of the nineteenth century Congress at least recognized the problems associated with slavery and deliberated their resolution in great debates. In the late nineteenth and early twentieth centuries Congress at least recognized the worst abuses of early industrialization and sought to regulate them. In the midtwentieth century Congress at least recognized the emerging service needs of an advanced industrial nation and created a bureaucracy to address the most basic public concerns. But as the nation enters the postindustrial era of the twenty-first century, Congress seems oblivious to the limits of the service state as a viable governing approach and to the consequent need for a re-creation of government.

In the face of congressional inaction, the citizens are taking matters into their own hands. Not knowing how else to protect their pocketbooks, much less the fiscal integrity of the state, they support budgetary restraints on Congress. Not knowing how better to produce a more representative and deliberative Congress, they mandate term limits to break the collective dependence on powerful incumbents. And in the interim, faced with a growing economic crisis, they toy with massive rejection of incumbents in general, despite the costs of such rejection to their pursuit of immediate particularized interests.

The public's intervention can have counterproductive consequences that may only make matters worse. Mandatory balanced budgets could cripple the service state and the nation's economy without addressing the service needs of citizens. Term limits deprive citizens even of those seasoned legislators who may truly address the real issues of the day, while leaving lobbyists and bureaucrats as the powers in Washington. And throwing the rascals out may only replace a set of legislators who have valuable experience and knowledge, as John Hibbing demonstrates, with an inexperienced group that lack a genuine understanding of national policy processes.[38]

But what are the citizens to do? They no longer have a truly representative and deliberative Congress that is attentive to their broad issue concerns and presents them with credible solutions to the nation's policy dilemmas. They choose to send a signal—early warning shots—and hope they are heard.

III

So what is to be done? First, the nation must recognize that the crisis of legitimation is real. The public's deep disaffection with Congress is not just a momentary fad to be acknowledged in the midst of the election-year anxiety of incumbents and then ignored as a new administration and united party government make policy activism the topic of the day. Beneath the short-term fluctuations in policy activism in contemporary America is a deep-seated erosion of Congress's representational and deliberative capacities that is crippling its ability to address and resolve the collective policy dilemmas raised by postindustrialism. With the problems of postindustrialism mounting, and with Congress so clearly failing to acknowledge the broad and collective issues and deliberate their resolution, the public must increasingly lose faith in Congress no matter how much particularized legislation it debates and enacts or how diverse a range of particularized interests it reflects and serves.

If the nation can acknowledge the existence of the legitimation crisis, perhaps a strategy can be devised for addressing it. I say perhaps because it is not immediately obvious how Congress can best proceed. On the one hand, it seems that the immediate need is for Congress to become a more representative and deliberative institution in order to recognize and address the general policy issues of postindustrialism. Yet if Congress moves to reform its representative and deliberative capacities without first restructuring government, the politics of the service state almost certainly will sabotage the reform efforts. Moving first to implement entrepreneurial government, thereby fostering conditions that might yield a more deliberative and representative Congress, thus seems the best strategy. But how is Congress to design effective entrepreneurial programs without a truly representative and deliberative policy process? How can it recognize the range of public concerns that such programs need to address or fashion an entrepreneurial agenda that the public can understand and accept? Congress truly seems caught in a bind. But maybe not.

Congress could attempt simultaneously to address the critical issue of postindustrialism—the restructuring of government—and to revitalize its own representational and deliberative capacities. A variety of such strategies might be possible, but consider a direct and simple approach. Congress could acknowledge that it and the nation are in the midst of what is becoming a constitutional crisis. In response, Congress could create an emergency joint committee on government restructuring, co-chaired by the Speaker of the House and the majority leader of the Senate, which would meet periodically in televised evening sessions to assess and approve the viable approaches to restructuring and refinancing the service delivery strategies of the federal government.[39] The purpose of the committee would be the creative transition of the government to state entrepreneurship across policy domains and the conversion of government from the wartime programs of the Cold War to peacetime programs. The intent of the committee would be to highlight the issues of government restructuring and state entrepreneurship, thereby making them the central focus of national policy debate. The concerns of the committee would be particularly compelling to the public if such restructuring were tied to the capacity of the government to balance the budget, restimulate long-term economic productivity, and create an expanded and universal health care system.

In creating an emergency joint committee, Congress could move to modernize the nature of representative deliberation on Capitol Hill through the example of the committee itself. The committee could be composed of a small number of members able to undertake collegial discussion and yet include a diversity of members, across ethnic, gender, and ideological lines, reflecting the heterogeneous concerns of all the citizens. Second, the committee could orchestrate the televised discussion of state entrepreneurship to maximize public as well as congressional interest and to generate understanding of programmatic principles and choices. It could even embrace the opportunities opened by the 1992 presidential campaign and engage in public televised town hall meetings around the country. Third, the committee could appear once every four to six weeks in a televised "question hour" before a joint session of the House and Senate to present its findings and propose actions. Such meetings would necessarily be large and would require creative planning. But if the British House of Commons, with more than 600 members, can find ways to meet in collective session and conduct informative and engaging debates between government and opposition leaders, surely American ingenuity can find a way to bring 535 members of Congress together to engage in meaningful joint deliberation. Alternatively, or additionally, the House and Senate could each meet in full session.

This proposal would require a dramatic break with politics as usual and a bold willingness of congressional leaders to acknowledge the severity of the legitimation crisis and pursue creative and innovative solutions to resolve it. During the Civil War and Reconstruction, the greatest previous threat to representative democracy in America, Congress embraced first a Joint Committee on the Conduct of the War and then a Joint Committee of Fifteen on Reconstruction.[40] During the Watergate crisis, perhaps the greatest modern threat to the legitimacy of the presidency as an institution, Congress authorized highly visible televised investigations into potentially criminal misconduct on the part of the president and his subordinates. It is not unthinkable for Congress to combine these strategies and create a televised joint committee to address what may be the greatest threat to Congress and representative government in the nation's history.

Less dramatic approaches are also possible. The most traditional would be for the leaders of the House and Senate to nudge members toward incremental experimentation with state entrepreneurship and toward gradualist reforms in congressional organization and procedure. With short-term improvements in the nation's economy and a lessening of the sense of national crisis, this strategy would be tempting and yet would be hard to sustain. The politics of the service state—that is, the pressures on legislators to service particularized interests and their desire to do so in order to ensure reelection and consolidate personal power—will likely undercut any such incremental and gradualist efforts outside an atmosphere of national crisis. A highly visible joint committee could dominate and shape the national debate even if the momentary atmosphere of crisis should ebb. Lacking such a highly visible strategy, congressional leaders would have to demonstrate extraordinary leadership skills to sustain incremental congressional activism on government restructuring, and they would become susceptible to cooption by the new president in behalf of strategies that might more nearly reflect the interests of executive dominance. Ideally, Congress would adopt a bold and innovative approach that would solidify its role in policymaking, as illustrated by the joint committee, and then would cooperate with the new president from a position of institutional strength.

Whatever strategy Congress adopts, the strategy should be designed to alter decisively the logic of politics that dominates American public life. It should shift the public debate away from a focus on the nature and extent of bureaucratic service delivery, and the role of legislators in facilitating that process, and toward an emphasis on government restructuring. It should do so, moreover, through visible efforts of Congress itself that would demonstrate the value and viability of representative deliberation. Congress must demonstrate that representative and deliberative government is not the problem but the solution.

In shifting the logic of politics, Congress and its leaders would change the electoral calculus of voters and thus the political strategies of politicians. By highlighting issues of government restructuring, and the ability of legislators to play a meaningful role in such restructuring, Congress would give the voters a constructive standard by which to evaluate candidates beyond their value in servicing particularized interests. And in creating this standard, Congress would give its members a constructive platform on which to campaign and by which to explain their pursuit of collective rather than (or as well as) particularized interests. The resulting alteration in the logic of politics would not end particularized programmatic concerns or ensure the long-term predominance of collective policy solutions; bureaucratic service delivery would remain a considerable dimension of government even in an entrepreneurial state because there will remain major aspects of collective service delivery that only direct government action can ensure. But a serious congressional focus on governmental restructuring and state entrepreneurship would release such policy concerns to become the central defining and realigning issue of postindustrial politics, rather than the realigning issue being support of or hostility toward representative government.

A change in the logic of politics could set in motion constructive alterations in the government and in Congress. A major issue, for example, might be how best to ensure the effective processing of service delivery within the mix of bureaucratic and entrepreneurial programs that would emerge with government restructuring. Now the role of bureaucratic ombudsman falls primarily to Congress, with each member's office organized to process the casework complaints of constituents. Members of Congress have embraced this role with relish in order to build personal support from constituents—to ensure, as Bruce Cain, John Ferejohn, and Morris Fiorina argue, a personal vote—based not on issue compatibility but on service gratitude.[41] The personal vote then increases legislators' electoral advantage by giving a diverse range of individuals and groups reasons to vote for the incumbent and to contribute massively to campaign war chests. It also creates incentives for members to forgo meaningful reforms of the bureaucracy lest they reduce bureaucratic red tape and lose their personal vote advantage as incumbents.

A public discussion of government restructuring could raise the broad issue of bureaucratic performance to the forefront of national debate and generate consideration of the single reform of government and Congress that might most immediately improve Congress's capacity to focus on issue representation and dialogic deliberation: the creation of a national ombudsman agency empowered to oversee the micromanagement of agency services. European nations have experimented with various ombudsman strategies that bypass or limit legislative involvement in casework management. These strategies leave the legislature free to represent constituents on the broad policy issues of government and to focus on broad policy deliberation and government oversight.[42] Likewise, it is possible in the United States to shift the ombudsman role from Congress into a "fourth branch" of government, with that new branch structured to perform its role according to entrepreneurial principles that might involve intra-agency competition.

The implementation of an ombudsman agency could come if the voters saw it as an integral part of government restructuring and evaluated legislators according to their support of it. For their part, legislators might see a loss of casework responsibilities and a decline in their personal vote advantage as preferable to the constitutional imposition of term limits that is likely to occur unless Congress resolves its governing crisis. In conjunction with the creation of a national ombudsman agency, Congress could downsize its own bureaucracy and make it a violation of federal law for any member to intervene on behalf of a constituent with the executive branch. Aside from improving bureaucratic service delivery, such a governmental and congressional restructuring would be intended to free the legislators, organizationally and politically, to focus on issue representation and deliberation.

Were an emergency joint committee able to focus public debate on governmental restructuring and were Congress to let go of its casework responsibilities, a new logic of politics could solidify. This logic would center on the politics of state entrepreneurship—that is, on designing and managing government programs to ensure service delivery through managed use of competitive incentives among and within private and public service institutions. Insofar as a new logic of politics could emerge, and could do so through a process that legitimized congressional policymaking rather than reliance on executive intervention, conditions would exist to support additional reforms and adjustments within Congress itself.

For example, as long as the politics of the service state remain the primary focus of the political agenda, it is doubtful that any campaign finance reform can be devised to reduce significantly the special advantage that interest representation gives to incumbents Organized groups are simply too dependent on the assistance of powerful incumbents (and there are simply too many strategies aside from direct financial contributions by which they can assist incumbents) for campaign finance reforms alone to neutralize incumbents' electoral advantage. In addition, it is extremely difficult to draft finance reform measures that successfully remove the influence of group money from politics; thus political action committee money still plays a vital role in presidential elections (through financial contributions to the political parties and through media campaigns for particular policy positions that aid individual candidates) despite public funding of presidential campaigns. Aside from the difficulty of determining what kind of campaign finance reform might conceivably work, the difficulty of drafting meaningful reform is reinforced by the effort of entrenched incumbents to design reforms that leave them protected and by the pressures of lobby groups to enact reforms in ways that sustain their leverage over politicians.[43]

By contrast, a move toward entrepreneurial government and the ending of casework responsibilities could create an environment that would support meaningful campaign finance reform and help level the electoral playing field. It could do so by lessening the obsession of specialized groups with powerful legislators who intervene with the bureaucracy on their behalf. In fact, a move toward entrepreneurial government could create an incentive for many organized groups to support new legislators with business, scientific, or state government backgrounds who are aware of and experienced with the latest entrepreneurial experiments in a policy arena. Such a shift in the incentives of interest groups could lead to increased support for serious campaign finance reform that would reduce the advantages of longstanding incumbents out of touch with entrepreneurial strategies. A change in the incentives of interest groups, reinforced by serious campaign finance reform, could also help revitalize the Republican congressional party or third-party conservative movements. It could do so, first, by lessening the special advantage that the politics of the service state gives to Democrats who support (and thereby claim credit for) bureaucratic service delivery. It could do so, second, by highlighting the value of candidates with experience in the entrepreneurial world of business, an experience designed to give them insights into the creation of state entrepreneurship. Government restructuring and state entrepreneurship, in other words, could help revitalize a competitive congressional party system while helping to sustain a sufficiently strong Congress that the spoils of electoral victory would be worthwhile.

A new logic of politics could also help direct the organizational reform of Congress along more constructive paths. My concern at present is that highly publicized reform efforts, without a clear focus on the broad agenda issues whose consideration they are designed to facilitate and without participants having a meaningful grasp of the historical context and implications of reform, are largely a shell game played by professional politicians to gain short-term publicity and career advantage. Such reforms might produce organizational and procedural changes whose ineffectiveness convinces the public that Congress is truly unredeemable.[44] By contrast, if the spotlight of congressional deliberation is placed on the great historic issues of the day, so that the reinvention of government comes clearly into focus, reform efforts in Congress may proceed more productively.[45]

Ultimately, a Congress concerned with the creation of an entrepreneurial state would have to consider how to design its internal organization to manage a restructured government; in the process it could strengthen its representative and deliberative character. A redesign of its internal organization, for example, probably would emphasize the need for a more fluid and yet well-coordinated and collective decision structure capable of responding to creative and unpredictable technological innovations and to consequent economic and social restructurings of a postindustrial society.[46] The creation of a more fluid decision structure might come through a reduction in permanent committees and subcommittees accompanied by greater use of special committees with clear policy objectives and limited terms of operation. Such an organizational rearrangement could increase the capacities of Congress to respond to a shifting policy environment. It could also limit members' incentives to build committee power bases and the consequent sweetheart relations with executive agencies and lobbyists that lock existing programs into statutory permanence. Concomitant with such changes, Congress could strengthen the authority of its party leaders, caucuses, and budgetary committees so that they could provide coordination and continuity within a more fluid policy structure; Congress and the nation could then hold them accountable for a lack of institutional responsiveness. Such strengthening could occur through greater leadership authority in the appointment of committee members and leaders and in the creation of special committees. Congress also could experiment with televised question hours attended by all members and with televised town hall meetings. It could hold special deliberation days, when committee and subcommittee meetings would be prohibited, that would be devoted solely to collective debate and votes on critical policy issues. Such organizational changes, if reinforced by the coming of state entrepreneurship, could move Congress a long way toward issue representation and broad-gauged policy deliberation.

Finally, in the effort to solidify a new logic of politics, Congress should take one major dramatic step: it should seek a formal constitutional reassertion of its legitimacy as the nation's premier democratic institution. For too long now Congress has ceded the public debate over its future—a debate currently framed by the constitutional efforts to limit terms, to restrain its taxing and spending powers, and to give the president a line item veto—to those who question the value of a strong and independent Congress. In so doing, it has adopted a defensive stance, seeking to defeat or limit constitutional moves against its legislative authority and prerogatives, rather than an assertive stance offering a vision of a revitalized Congress that the public could embrace. To regain the support of the American people, Congress must forthrightly make the case for its legitimate authority and trust the public to understand through open deliberation the current institutional dilemmas and support credible and productive efforts to address those dilemmas.

Congress could make its case by introducing and actively pursuing constitutional amendments that reframe the public debate in ways designed to stress its representational and deliberative roles and strengthen its policymaking capacities. Such amendments might seek to institutionalize the various proposals made in this essay. Amendments could include granting the special policymaking authority that a national legislature in a postindustrial era will need (for example, the creation of a legislative veto power, particularly in the area of international trade agreements negotiated by the executive).[47] And, perhaps most critically, such efforts could include an amendment protecting the right of citizens to vote for representatives of their choice, without regard to prior legislative service. In other words, Congress should directly confront the term-limit movement and reframe the issue in a way that emphasizes the special stake that individual citizens have in sustaining unfettered representative government.[48]

In short, Congress must be willing to engage with the citizens in a national reassessment of the nature and structure of our representative democracy. Such a reassessment is already underway in the court of public opinion and in the polling booth. But the reassessment is occurring in a deliberative vacuum, with the supporters of Congress failing to join the debate in an aggressive and visible manner—failing to move out of the halls of Congress and offer directly to the citizens and their state representatives a credible set of constitutional choices that the nation could embrace to help solve its governing crisis. For the public to understand the true nature of the current crisis and to engage in a collective process of learning how best to redress the crisis, meaningful public deliberation is necessary. Congress would be well advised to trust the American public, join the constitutional debate over its future, and seek constitutional reaffirmation of its legitimacy as our most representative and deliberative policymaking institution.

IV

This, then, is my assessment of where Congress and the nation are today as we end the Reagan-Bush years and proceed into a new administration. The past twelve years highlighted the drawbacks of divided government. But even more critically, they demonstrated just how vulnerable Congress and American legislatures in general are to a loss of public faith in their capacities for reasoned and responsive policymaking. United party government should produce a short-term surge in policy activism; under skillful leadership it might even generate innovative experimentation with state entrepreneurship and thereby reshape and revitalize the government and Congress. Much depends on how well Congress heeds the early warning signals sent by the voters during the early 1990s.

Should Congress remain frozen in the politics of the past, however, almost certainly we face even greater doubts about its legitimacy as a policymaking institution, and the prospects for continued erosion in our democratic processes of governance will increase. Consider, after all, the bind that will confront both citizens and legislators if Congress as an institution fails to respond to the opportunity for fundamental change that united government and the current atmosphere of crisis together provide.

Left enmeshed in a service state and deprived of a revitalized public agenda, citizens will have an unenviable choice. They can vote for incumbent legislators who serve particularized interests, thereby losing the chance to focus attention on collective issues of state entrepreneurship and institutional renewal. Or they can vote on the broad issues of the day, demanding that candidates look beyond interest representation and speak to diffuse general issues, thereby risking the loss of secure and powerful incumbents who can serve their immediate particularized needs. Caught in such a bind, we should not be surprised if the voters again rebel and turn with more sustained fury against incumbent legislators. Nor should we dismiss the possibility that citizens will continue to support movements against the policymaking power of Congress and the constitutional tenure of members, even at the risk of destroying the very avenue through which they could most directly exercise long-term influence on public policy. Such upheavals would seem most likely in periods of divided party government or institutional conflict, when the president can most aggressively lead public attacks against the legislature. This prospect is illustrated most vividly by the experience of the California state government during the past quarter-century, where Republican governors from Ronald Reagan to Pete Wilson have led direct assaults on the power, resources, and tenure of the Democratic state legislature.[49]

The continued reliance on the service state also gives elected politicians untenable choices. They can speak to the general issues of the day, attempting to redress the nation's collective and long-term problems, and thereby risk the guaranteed electoral support of particularized interests tied to a service bureaucracy, or they can serve citizens' particularized interests, seeking to maintain immediate power but risking eventual repudiation of themselves and of representative government. With politicians caught in this peculiar bind, we should not be surprised to see them yet again blame the institution, their leaders, and each other for the general and collective policy failures of government. At the same time they would reinforce the public's belief that Congress is an unworkable institution.[50] In the grip of severe crisis, and propelled by their own logic of institutional blame, the legislators themselves could become agents of congressional abdication and executive dominance. Such developments may be most likely in periods of united party government, when the president's congressional party, attempting to resolve the national crisis and thereby maintain its short-term electoral viability, chooses to give the president far-reaching authority that Congress subsequently is unable to control or reclaim.

If citizens and legislators see no way out of their political bind except through reliance on the president, the nation's response to the crisis of postindustrialism likely will activate executive control of our national government. Executive control could come through the use of vetoes and political intimidation to force a weakened Congress to accept executive budgetary priorities, through assertive control of international trade negotiations and the use of the resulting trade agreements to abrogate the domestic politics of Congress, and through the increased autonomy of executive agencies that would come with a Congress of inexperienced legislators. Executive dominance would be particularly potent if it were to include a presidential alliance with the conservative business groups that seek to weaken Congress in order to avoid its regulatory power and if it were supported by a conservative Supreme Court. Any moves to consolidate and institutionalize executive power would almost certainly prompt Congress and the public to constrain executive power (such a constraint occurred in the early 1970s after Richard Nixon's impoundment efforts and the Watergate crisis). It is always possible that out of such deep institutional confrontation could come a renewed public commitment to Congress and a renewed effort for it to reassert its authority. Yet one should not discount the possibility that a continued and deepening disaffection with Congress could solidify widespread support for executive government.

The fear is that a loss of faith in Congress might both support the rise of executive government at the national level and reinforce a loss of faith in representative government at the state and local level. Already, because of the development of service bureaucracies akin to those of the national government, many, if not most, state and local assemblies face policy dilemmas and public disaffection analogous to those facing Congress. With these bureaucracies have come a legislative politics characterized by interest representation and strategic deliberation similar to that of Congress. Thus it is not too much to say that a crisis of legislative legitimation is inherent in the coming of postindustrialism at the state and local level as well as the national level. The additional dilemma for subnational assemblies is that Congress's continued reliance on a service state mentality leads it to mandate state and local service delivery programs and to shift fiscal responsibilities to state and local governments, thus further overloading their governing capacities. Congress does so to sustain and expand programs that the federal government cannot fund and in the process to claim credit for the programs. The result is to reduce the autonomy of state and local assemblies, to limit their flexibility in resolving their own governing crises through experiments with state entrepreneurship, and to interconnect local, state, and national legislatures in a combined governing crisis that could lead—is leading—to general public rejection of the authority of legislatures.

Congress's inability to resolve its own legitimation crisis fuels citizens' general disillusionment with struggling state and local assemblies and reinforces reliance on executive government throughout the system. Thus Congress contributes to the legitimation crisis of subnational systems not only by shifting its policy dilemmas to them but by creating a national atmosphere of hostility toward legislative power which then affects the subnational systems as well. When such developments are combined with serious postindustrial problems endemic to the subnational governments, the result can be a lethal reduction in legislative power. A decline in legislative authority is seen clearly in

California, our most postindustrial state. Twenty years ago the California legislature was considered a model institution, but progressively it is being stripped of its policymaking authority, its organizational resources, and its experienced leadership. These developments have come through constitutional initiatives (supported by the governors) mandating limits to the taxing powers of the legislature, to its spending prerogatives, to its staff and operating resources (which were substantially reduced), and to the terms of its members. With the decline in the authority of the legislature has come a shift of power to the executive. Gov. Pete Wilson essentially brought the California legislature to its knees during a 1992 state fiscal crisis by forcing it to accept the bulk of his budgetary priorities despite broad and intense legislative opposition. The California experience should give pause to any observers of Congress who dismiss the severity of the congressional legitimation crisis and discount the possibility of a general breakdown in representative government.

Members of Congress must act before a general crisis of legislative legitimation overwhelms representative institutions throughout the political system. One of the few benefits of the term-limit movement is that, in threatening a near-term end to the career of all members unless they collectively regain the public trust, it may make clear to legislators the linkage between their short-term career interests and the long-term governing capacity of the institution. The message to be gleaned from public support for term limits, however, is not the need for policy activism in behalf of long-neglected particularized interests, but the need for Congress and subnational legislatures to address the collective problems of society in a way that makes possible the long-term availability of particularized services. Short-term activism focused on particularized interests may create a sense of policy movement that dispels public unease for the moment. But if short-term activism leaves unaddressed the deeper institutional and policy dilemmas of postindustrialism, it will set the stage for even greater policy crises in the future and a more dangerous public disillusionment with representative government.

If members of Congress will not act, the public must. Congress, after all, is not the property of its temporary occupants but of the American people. Our investment in representative and deliberative government is a two-hundred-year legacy not to be cast away lightly or allowed to slide silently away in the gradual erosion of congressional policymaking authority. The public has every right to intervene and save Congress, even if its current members, entrapped in the outmoded logic of a passing era, fail to do so. Yet activism by the American public must come in a collective, thoughtful, and deliberative manner that allows for reflective understanding and learning, not through the reactive and angry politics of isolated state initiatives. The Constitution gives us such a collective outlet: the right of the citizenry to demand and participate in a national constitutional convention.

It is arguable that the erosion of the representative and deliberative capacities of Congress during the industrial era occurred because there was no formal and deliberative national reconsideration of how best to restructure the institution with the coming of the service state. Instead, this responsibility was left to Congress. Congress's adaptation to the industrial era more nearly served the reelection and power concerns of its members than the representational and deliberative interests of the nation at large. Political activists, myself included, shy away from proposing formal reassessment of our constitutional arrangements, as represented by a national constitutional convention, for fear of the popular passions and uncontrolled assaults on democratic values that such a public reassessment might unleash. But such passions and assaults are already unleashed in our nation and could within two or three decades, and across several cycles of public disaffection, emasculate representative government piecemeal.

In the face of sustained congressional inaction, the nation must trust to a deliberative assembly of citizens to reassess our commitment to a truly representative and deliberative Congress. Only with deliberative reassessment and relegitimation, coming either as a result of congressional leadership or from a constitutional convention, is Congress likely to survive as a vital and democratic policymaking institution. With an open and forthright reassessment, the American people could rediscover the value of representative and deliberative policymaking. They could reassert their desire for those institutional processes that identify our shared purpose amidst a diversity of interests and that thereby bond us together as a nation. Congress then could not only survive but flourish. A revitalization of Congress could activate, as I wrote twelve years ago, "a great renewal and expansion of democratic government in America." [51]

Notes

For their assistance at various stages in the preparation of this essay, my thanks to Leslie Anderson, Ann Davies, Joan Fiore, Sean Kelly, Carolyn Mohr-Hennefeld, Calvin Jillson, Robert Lopez, Vince McGuire, and David Van Mill. A very special note of appreciation to Cris and Meredith Dodd for their patience and understanding.

1. The argument in this essay was originally presented in Lawrence C. Dodd, "Congress, the Constitution, and the Crisis of Legitimation," in *Congress Reconsidered*, 2d ed., ed. Lawrence C. Dodd and Bruce I. Oppenheimer (Washington, D.C.: CQ Press, 1981). This earlier essay, completed in the summer of 1980, was influenced significantly by Jurgen Habermas, *Legitimation Crisis* (Boston: Beacon Press, 1973). For a recent discussion of the current crisis of congressional legitimacy, see Richard F. Fenno, Jr., "Some Thoughts on Renewing Congress" (Paper presented at the Brookings Institution/American Enterprise Institute Conference on Congressional Reform, Washington, D.C., June 30, 1992).

2. On the coming of postindustrialism, see, for example, Samuel P. Huntington, "Postindustrial Politics: How Benign Will It Be?" *Comparative Politics* (January 1974): 163-191; and Lester Thurow, *The Zero-Sum Society: Distribution and the Possibilities for Economic Change* (New York: Basic Books, 1980).

3. See, for example, E. J. Dionne, Jr., *Why Americans Hate Politics* (New York: Simon and Schuster, 1991).

4. David S. Broder, "Post-Election News Is Good and Bad for Republicans," Syndicated column, Boulder *Sunday Camera*, Dec. 6, 1992, 3E.

5. Among journalists the most consistent emphasis on the role of divided government comes from David Broder. See, for example, David S. Broder, "Wreckage of Divided

Government," *Washington Post*, Aug. 30, 1992, C7; see also Broder, *The Party's Over* (New York: Harper, 1972). Among political scientists emphasizing the role of divided government see, for example, Catherine E. Rudder, "Can Congress Govern?" in this book; David E. Price, *The Congressional Experience* (Boulder: Westview Press, 1992), 108-112; and David W. Rohde, *Parties and Leaders in the Postreform House* (Chicago: University of Chicago Press, 1991). The scholarly debate over the statistical effects of divided government on policy activism is a growth industry. For the most vivid contrast in views, see the debate between Sean Kelly and David Mayhew: Sean Q. Kelly, "Divided We Govern? A Reassessment," and David R. Mayhew, "Commentary," in *Polity* (forthcoming). See also *The Politics of Divided Government*, ed. Gary Cox and Samuel Kernell (Boulder: Westview Press, 1991); Morris P. Fiorina, *Divided Government* (New York: Macmillan, 1992); David R. Mayhew, *Divided We Govern: Party Control, Lawmaking, and Investigations, 1946-1990* (New Haven: Yale University Press, 1991); James A. Thurber, "Representation, Accountability, and Efficiency in Divided Party Control of Government," in *PS: Political Science and Politics* 24 (December 1991): 653-657. My own view is that divided government helped fuel the policy gridlock of the Reagan-Bush years but was not the primary source of policy immobilism and the declining public confidence in government. Immobilism and loss of confidence were already apparent during the united government of the Carter years. See James L. Sundquist, "Congress, the President, and the Crisis of Competence in Government," in *Congress Reconsidered*, 2d ed.; Mark A. Peterson, *Legislating Together: The White House and Capitol Hill from Eisenhower to Reagan* (Cambridge: Harvard University Press, 1990), 253-260.

6. For a discussion of the coming of united government, see the essay by Lawrence C. Dodd and Bruce I. Oppenheimer in this volume.

7. Aside from "Congress, the Constitution, and the Crisis of Legitimation," see my arguments in "Congress and the Quest for Power," in *Congress Reconsidered*, 1st ed., ed. Lawrence C. Dodd and Bruce I. Oppenheimer (New York: Praeger, 1977); and "The Presidency, Congress, and the Cycles of Power," in *The Post-Imperial Presidency*, ed. Vincent David (New Brunswick, N.J.: Transaction Books, 1979). For a recent effort to develop a broader theory of political change to account for the periods of immobilism, within which to place the role of Congress and the presidency, see Lawrence C. Dodd, "Congress, the Presidency, and the American Experience: A Transformational Perspective," in James A. Thurber, *Divided Democracy: Cooperation and Conflict Between the President and Congress* (Washington, D.C.: CQ Press, 1991).

8. For a general discussion of Congress that I find useful as an underpinning to my argument, see Arthur Maass, *Congress and the Common Good* (New York: Basic Books, 1983). I shall focus on Congress as a single institution, though of course many of the arguments apply differentially to the House and Senate. For an earlier attempt to elaborate the contrasting effects of postindustrialism on the House and Senate (arguing that the House would suffer considerably more than the Senate), see Edward R. Carmines and Lawrence C. Dodd, "Bicameralism in Congress: The Changing Partnership," in *Congress Reconsidered*, 3d ed., ed. Lawrence C. Dodd and Bruce I. Oppenheimer (Washington, D.C.: CQ Press, 1985).

9. For a discussion of the ups and downs of popular support for Congress, see Roger H. Davidson, David M. Kovenock, and Michael J. O'Leary, *Congress in Crisis* (North Scituate, Mass.: Duxbury Press, 1966); Richard F. Fenno, Jr., "If, As Ralph Nader Says, Congress Is 'the Broken Branch,' How Come We Love Our Congressmen So Much?" in *Congress in Change*, ed. Norman J. Ornstein (New York: Praeger, 1975); Glenn R. Parker and Roger H. Davidson, "Why Do Americans Love Their Congressmen So Much More than Their Congress?" *Legislative Studies Quarterly* 4 (February 1979): 53-61; and Glenn R. Parker, "Some Themes in Congressional Unpopularity," *American Journal of Political Science* 21 (February 1977): 93-109.

10. See, for example, Louis Fisher, *Constitutional Conflicts Between Congress and the Presi-*

dent (Princeton: Princeton University Press, 1985); Michael L. Mezey, *Congress, the President, and Public Policy* (Boulder: Westview Press, 1989); Arthur M. Schlesinger, Jr., *The Imperial Presidency* (New York: Popular Library, 1974); Robert Scigliano, *The Supreme Court and the Presidency* (New York: Free Press, 1971); James L. Sundquist, *The Decline and Resurgence of Congress* (Washington, D.C.: Brookings Institution, 1981).

11. For an earlier discussion of the distinction between the representational (or electoral) and the deliberative (or governing) dimensions of congressional politics, see Lawrence C. Dodd, "The Rise of the Technocratic Congress," in *Remaking American Politics,* ed. Richard A. Harris and Sidney M. Milkis (Boulder: Westview Press, 1989); see also Fenno, "Renewing Congress"; and James Q. Wilson, "Comments on Congressional Reform" (Paper presented at the Brookings Institution/American Enterprise Institute Conference on Congressional Reform, June 30, 1992). For a discussion of the historical origins of representative and deliberative government, see Paul A. Rahe, *Republics Ancient and Modern: Classical Republicanism and the American Revolution* (Chapel Hill: University of North Carolina Press, 1992).

12. Richard F. Fenno, Jr., "Strengthening a Congressional Strength," in *Congress Reconsidered,* 1st ed.; see also Walter J. Stone, *Republic at Risk* (Pacific Grove, Calif.: Brooks/Cole, 1990).

13. Nelson W. Polsby, "The Institutionalization of the U.S. House of Representatives," *American Political Science Review* 74 (1980): 697-708; Donald R. Matthews, *U.S. Senators and Their World* (New York: Vintage, 1960).

14. Bruce I. Oppenheimer, "Changing Time Constraints on Congress: Historical Perspectives on the Use of Cloture," in *Congress Reconsidered,* 2d ed.; and Bruce I. Oppenheimer, "The Rules Committee: New Arm of Leadership in a Decentralized House," in *Congress Reconsidered,* 1st ed.

15. For background discussion of the three historical eras outlined here, see particularly Bruce Ackerman, *We the People: Foundations* (Cambridge: Harvard University Press, 1991); David W. Brady, *Critical Elections and Congressional Policy Making* (Stanford: Stanford University Press, 1988); Edward S. Greenberg, *Capitalism and the American Political Ideal* (New York: M. E. Sharpe, 1985); and Calvin Jillson, "Patterns of American Political Development," in *The Dynamics of American Politics: Approaches and Interpretations,* ed. Lawrence C. Dodd and Calvin Jillson (Boulder: Westview Press, 1993). On the period leading up to and including the Civil War and Reconstruction, see William W. Freehling, *The Road to Disunion: Secessionists at Bay, 1776-1854* (New York: Oxford University Press, 1990); Merrill D. Peterson, *The Great Triumvirate: Webster, Clay, and Calhoun* (New York: Oxford University Press, 1987); Allan G. Bogue, *The Congressman's Civil War* (New York: Cambridge University Press, 1989); and J. G. Randall, *The Civil War and Reconstruction* (New York: D. C. Heath, 1937). See also Woodrow Wilson's assessment of Congress in the early and midnineteenth century in Woodrow Wilson, *Congressional Government* (Gloucester, Mass.: Peter Smith, 1885, 1973).

16. George R. Brown, *The Leadership of Congress* (Indianapolis: Bobbs-Merrill, 1922); and David J. Rothman, *Politics and Power* (New York: Atheneum, 1969).

17. See the discussion in Lawrence C. Dodd, "Congress and the Rise of the Activist State, 1933-1964," in *The Encyclopedia of the United States Congress,* ed. Donald C. Bacon, Roger H. Davidson, and Morton Keller (New York: Simon and Schuster, forthcoming).

18. For an argument that the current public disaffection is but a continuation of historic patterns of "Congress bashing," see Nelson W. Polsby, "Congress Bashing for Beginners," *Public Interest* 100 (Summer 1990): 15-23.

19. Robert B. Reich, *The Work of Nations* (New York: Vintage, 1991); Alice M. Rivlin, *Reviving the American Dream* (Washington, D.C.: Brookings Institution, 1992).

20. Thurow, *Zero-Sum Society;* Paul Krugman, *The Age of Diminished Expectations: U.S.*

Economic Policy in the 1990s (Cambridge, Mass.: MIT Press, 1990).

21. Peter K. Eisenger, *The Rise of the Entrepreneurial State: State and Local Economic Development Policy in the United States* (Madison: University of Wisconsin Press, 1988); David Osborne and Ted Gaebler, *Reinventing Government: How the Entrepreneurial Spirit Is Transforming the Public Sector* (Reading, Mass.: Addison-Wesley, 1992); and John Chubb and Terry Moe, *Politics, Markets, and America's Schools* (Washington, D.C.: Brookings Institution, 1990).

22. Restructuring the national government to create an entrepreneurial state could come through a variety of strategies and across a wide range of policy areas. Such experiments are occurring not only in American state and local governments but at the national level in foreign governments as well, from the conservative Britain of the Thatcher era to Social Democratic experiments in Sweden. Aside from the area of school choice, such experiments involve the restructuring of national health systems to force competitiveness among health providers and insurers to hold costs down while making health benefits universally available. The socialist Labor party of New Zealand has even gone so far as to overhaul its entire welfare state, restructuring it according to entrepreneurial principles of competition among private and public sector units. Such restructuring also tends to bring changes in revenue systems and budgetary strategies (including multiyear budgets) designed to foster fiscal responsibility and cost containment. In the best of circumstances, with concerted planning and effective leadership, such restructuring efforts have supported service expansion combined with fiscal realism, they have received broad public support, and they have produced renewed belief in government. See Osborne and Gaebler, *Reinventing Government*, esp. 328-330.

23. Congress may need, however, some expansion of constitutional powers to address its role in the new politics of international trade that is emerging with a global economy. See Lester Thurow, *Head to Head: The Coming Economic Battle Among Japan, Europe, and America* (New York: Morrow, 1992); and Walter Russell Mead, "Bushism, Found: A Second-Term Agenda Hidden in Trade Agreements," *Harper's*, September 1992, 37-45.

24. This discussion of representation relies particularly on Hannah Pitkin, *The Concept of Representation* (Berkeley: University of California Press, 1972). See also Heinz Eulau and Paul Karps, "The Puzzle of Representation," *Legislative Studies Quarterly* 2 (1977): 233-254; Richard F. Fenno, Jr., *Home Style* (Boston: Little, Brown, 1978); and Kenneth A. Shepsle, "Representation and Governance: The Great Trade-off," *Political Science Quarterly* 103 (Fall 1988): 461-484.

25. See, for example, Samuel P. Huntington, "Congressional Responses to the Twentieth Century," in *The Congress and America's Future*, ed. David Truman (Englewood Cliffs, N.J.: Prentice-Hall, 1973); Morris P. Fiorina, *Congress: Keystone of the Washington Establishment* (New Haven: Yale University Press, 1977).

26. See the essay by John R. Alford and David W. Brady in this volume.

27. See Dodd, "Congress, the Presidency, and the American Experience."

28. See Bernard Manin, "On Legitimacy and Political Deliberation," *Political Theory* 15 (August 1987): 368; James S. Fishkin, *Democracy and Deliberation: New Directions for Democratic Reform* (New Haven: Yale University Press, 1991); Jane Mansbridge, *Beyond Adversary Democracy* (New York: Basic Books, 1980); Paul Quirk, "The Cooperative Resolution of Policy Conflict," *American Political Science Review* 83 (September 1989): 905-921.

29. See Lawrence C. Dodd, "Political Learning and Political Change: Understanding Development Across Time," in *Dynamics of American Politics*.

30. R. Douglas Arnold, *The Logic of Congressional Action* (New Haven: Yale University Press, 1990); see also Arnold's essay in this book. For a discussion of deliberative versus electoral approaches to congressional policymaking somewhat analogous to the distinction here between dialogic and strategic deliberation, see John A. Ferejohn and

Charles R. Shipan, "Congressional Influence on Administrative Agencies: A Case Study of Telecommunications Policy," in *Congress Reconsidered*, 3d ed. See also Kenneth Shepsle and Barry R. Weingast, "The Institutional Foundations of Committee Power," *American Political Science Review* (March 1987): 85-104.

31. David R. Mayhew, *Congress; The Electoral Connection* (New Haven: Yale University Press, 1973); Fiorina, *Congress: Keystone of the Washington Establishment;* Lawrence C. Dodd, "Congress and the Quest for Power," in *Congress Reconsidered*, 1st ed.; and Morris P. Fiorina, "The Decline of Collective Responsibility in American Politics," *Daedalus* 109 (Summer 1980).

32. Theodore J. Lowi, *The End of Liberalism* (New York: Norton, 1969, 1979); and Lawrence C. Dodd and Richard L. Schott, *Congress and the Administrative State* (New York: Wiley, 1979).

33. See the essays by Richard L. Hall and by George E. Connor and Bruce I. Oppenheimer in this book.

34. Aside from Arnold, *Logic of Congressional Action*, see Stanley Bach and Steven S. Smith, *Managing Uncertainty in the House of Representatives: Adaptation and Innovation in Special Rules* (Washington, D.C.: Brookings Institution, 1988); and Steven S. Smith, *Call to Order: Floor Politics in the House and Senate* (Washington, D.C.: Brookings Institution, 1989).

35. For a discussion of the adaptation problems of Congress with the coming of industrialization, see Joseph Cooper and David W. Brady, "Organization Theory and Congressional Structure (Paper presented at the annual meeting of the American Political Science Association, New Orleans, September 1973). See also Cooper, "Congress in Organizational Perspective," in *Congress Reconsidered*, 1st ed.; and Huntington, "Congressional Responses to the Twentieth Century."

36. James S. Young, *The Washington Community, 1880-1828* (New York: Columbia University Press, 1966); and Richard Franklin Bensel, *Sectionalism and American Political Development, 1880-1980* (Madison: University of Wisconsin Press, 1984). See also Elaine Swift, "The Electoral Connection Meets the Past: Lessons from Congressional History, 1789-1899," *Political Science Quarterly* 102 (Winter 1987): 625-645; and Barry Balleck, *Preparing the United States for War: The Rhetoric of the Persian Gulf Debates* (Ph.D. diss. in progress, University of Colorado, Boulder).

37. See Dodd, "Rise of the Technocratic Congress"; Edward Weisband, "Congress, Codetermination, and Arms Control," and Hugh Heclo, "The Emerging Regime," in *Remaking American Politics*.

38. See John R. Hibbing's essay in this book.

39. One of the most successful state efforts in pursuing an entrepreneurial agenda has been in Florida, where the lower house of the state legislature created the Florida Speaker's Advisory Committee on the Future in 1985, composed of forty-five citizens and seven House members. This committee devised significant restructuring proposals that later passed the legislature "despite the political environment" because the Speaker, Jon Mills, "led the effort." See Osborne and Gaebler, *Reinventing Government*, 232-236. One should expect no less political courage and boldness from congressional leaders.

40. See W. R. Brock, *An American Crisis: Congress and Reconstruction, 1865-67* (New York: St. Martin's, 1963); see also Sundquist, *Decline and Resurgence of Congress*, 26-27.

41. Bruce Cain, John Ferejohn, and Morris Fiorina, *The Personal Vote: Constituency Service and Electoral Independence* (Cambridge: Harvard University Press, 1967). On the localization of congressional elections, and a prescient discussion of the implications of this phenomenon for the politics of the early 1990s, see Thomas E. Mann, *Unsafe at Any Margin: Interpreting Congressional Elections* (Washington, D.C.: American Enterprise Institute, 1978); and R. Douglas Arnold, "The Local Roots of Domestic Policy," in *The New Congress*, ed. Thomas E. Mann and Norman J. Ornstein (Washington, D.C.: American Enterprise Institute, 1981), 250-287. For a broader discussion

of the consequent breakdown of political parties and the process of party realignment that is historically so critical to political transformation, see Walter Dean Burnham, "Revitalization and Decay," *Journal of Politics* 38 (August 1976): 146-172.

42. See, for example, Osborne and Gaebler's discussion of the British Audit Commission in *Reinventing Government,* 328.

43. Gary Jacobson, "Parties and PACs in Congressional Elections," in *Congress Reconsidered,* 4th ed., and Frank J. Sorauf, *Money in American Elections* (Glenview, Ill: Scott, Foresman, 1988).

44. Dodd, "Congress and the Quest for Power"; see also Leroy Rieselbach, *Congressional Reform* (Washington, D.C.: CQ Press, 1986); and Roger H. Davidson and Walter J. Oleszek, *Congress Against Itself* (Bloomington: Indiana University Press, 1977).

45. On the importance of an agenda shift to transformative restructuring of Congress, see Lawrence C. Dodd, "The Cycles of Congressional Change," in *Congress and Policy Change,* ed. Gerald Wright, Leroy Rieselbach, and Lawrence C. Dodd (New York: Agathon, 1986); see also Roger H. Davidson, "How Congress Changes: Organizational Engineering Versus Political Adaptation" (Paper presented at the Brookings Institution/American Enterprise Institute Conference on Congressional Reform, June 1992).

46. There is already evidence that Congress is becoming a more fluid organization. See, for example, Lawrence C. Dodd and Bruce I. Oppenheimer, "The New Congress: Fluidity and Oscillation," in *Congress Reconsidered,* 4th ed. The multiple referral process and the Speaker's task forces are also evidence of innovative efforts to create a more responsive structure in the House. For discussions, see the essays by Garry Young and Joseph Cooper and Barbara Sinclair in this book. See also Thomas E. Mann and Norman J. Ornstein, *Renewing Congress: A First Report* (Washington, D.C.: American Enterprise Institute, 1992).

47. On the nature of legislative vetoes and their role in foreign affairs, see Martha Gibson, *Weapons of Influence* (Boulder: Westview Press, 1992).

48. This proposal thus is in opposition to the position of columnist George Will, who argues that Congress should submit to the states a constitutional amendment imposing term limits. See George F. Will, *Restoration* (New York: Free Press, 1992).

49. See, for an illustrative discussion, Robert A. Jones, "California's Bitter Season," *Los Angeles Times Magazine,* Sept. 27, 1992, 14-18, 40-41.

50. On the politics of blame, see Ken Weaver, "The Politics of Blame Avoidance," *Journal of Public Policy* 6 (October-December 1986): 371-398; on the general decline in comity that the modern environment has produced, see Eric Uslaner, *The Decline of Comity in Congress* (Ann Arbor: University of Michigan Press, 1993).

51. Dodd, "Congress, the Constitution, and the Crisis of Legitimation," 418. See also Hugh Heclo, "The Emerging Regime," 317-318.

Suggested Readings

◆◆◆

Aberbach, Joel D. "Changes in Congressional Oversight." *American Behavioral Scientist* 22 (1979): 493-515.

——. *Keeping a Watchful Eye.* Washington, D.C.: Brookings Institution, 1990.

Abramowitz, Alan I. "A Comparison of Voting for U.S. Senators and Representatives in 1978." *American Political Science Review* 74 (1980): 637-640.

——. "Explaining Senate Election Outcomes." *American Political Science Review* 82 (1988): 385-404.

——. "Incumbency, Campaign Spending, and the Decline of Competition in U.S. House Elections." *Journal of Politics* 53 (1991): 34-56.

Abramson, Paul, John H. Aldrich, and David W. Rohde. "Progressive Ambition Among United States Senators: 1972-1988." *Journal of Politics* 49 (1987): 3-35.

Alesina, Alberto, and Howard Rosenthal. "Partisan Cycles in Congressional Elections and the Macroeconomy." *American Political Science Review* 83 (1989): 373-398.

Arnold, R. Douglas. *Congress and the Bureaucracy.* New Haven: Yale University Press, 1979.

——. *The Logic of Congressional Action.* New Haven: Yale University Press, 1990.

Asher, Herbert B. "The Learning of Legislative Norms." *American Political Science Review* 67 (1973): 499-513.

Asher, Herbert B., and Herbert F. Weisberg. "Voting Change in Congress: Some Dynamic Perspectives on an Evolutionary Process." *American Journal of Political Science* 22 (1978): 391-425.

Bach, Stanley, and Steven S. Smith. *Managing Uncertainty in the House: Adaptation and Innovation in Special Rules.* Washington, D.C.: Brookings Institution, 1988.

Bacheller, J. M. "Lobbyists and the Legislative Process: The Impact of Environmental Constraints." *American Political Science Review* 71 (1977): 252-263.

Baker, Ross K. *House and Senate.* New York: Norton, 1989.

Bauer, Raymond A., Ithiel de Sola Pool, and Lewis A. Dexter. *American Business and Public Policy.* New York: Atherton, 1963.

Bibby, John F., and Roger H. Davidson. *On Capitol Hill.* 2d ed. Hinsdale, Ill.: Dryden Press, 1972.

Bolling, Richard. *House Out of Order.* New York: Dutton, 1965.

——. *Power in the House.* New York: Dutton, 1965.

Bond, Jon R., Cary Covington, and Richard Fleisher. "Explaining Challenger Quality in Congressional Elections." *Journal of Politics* 47 (1985): 510-529.

Bond, Jon R., and Richard Fleisher. *The President in the Legislative Arena.* Chicago: University of Chicago Press, 1990.

Born, Richard. "Changes in the Competitiveness of House Primary Elections, 1956-1976." *American Politics Quarterly* 8 (1980): 495-506.

Brady, David W. *Congressional Voting in a Partisan Era: A Study of the McKinley Houses.* Lawrence: University of Kansas Press, 1973.

———. *Critical Elections and Congressional Policy Making.* Stanford: Stanford University Press, 1988.

Brady, David W., Joseph Cooper, and Patricia A. Hurley. "The Decline of Party in the U.S. House of Representatives, 1887-1968." *Legislative Studies Quarterly* 4 (1979): 381-407.

Bullock, Charles S., III. "House Careerists: Changing Patterns of Longevity and Attrition." *American Political Science Review* 66 (1972): 1295-1305.

———. "Redistricting and Congressional Stability, 1962-1972." *Journal of Politics* 37 (1975): 569-575.

———. "House Committee Assignments." In *The Congressional System: Notes and Readings.* 2d ed. Edited by Leroy N. Rieselbach. North Scituate, Mass.: Duxbury Press, 1979.

Cain, Bruce, John Ferejohn, and Morris Fiorina. *The Personal Vote: Constituency Service and Electoral Independence.* Cambridge: Harvard University Press, 1967.

Canon, David T. *Actors, Athletes, and Astronauts: Political Amateurs in the United States Congress.* Chicago: University of Chicago Press, 1990.

Clausen, Aage R. *How Congressmen Decide.* New York: St. Martin's, 1973.

Clem, Alan L., ed. *The Making of Congressmen: Seven Campaigns of 1974.* North Scituate, Mass.: Duxbury Press, 1976.

Collie, Melissa. "Incumbency, Electoral Safety and Turnover in the House of Representatives, 1952-1976." *American Political Science Review* 75 (1981).

Cooper, Joseph. *The Origins of the Standing Committees and the Development of the Modern House.* Houston: Rice University Studies, 1971.

———. "Strengthening the Congress: An Organizational Analysis." *Harvard Journal on Legislation* 2 (1975): 301-368.

Cooper, Joseph, and David W. Brady. "Institutional Context and Leadership Style: The House from Cannon to Rayburn." *American Political Science Review* 75 (1981).

———. "Toward a Diachronic Analysis of Congress." *American Political Science Review* 75 (1981).

Cooper, Joseph, and G. Calvin Mackenzie. *The House at Work.* Austin: University of Texas Press, 1981.

Cover, Albert D. "One Good Term Deserves Another: The Advantage of Incumbency in Congressional Elections." *American Journal of Political Science* 21 (1977): 523-541.

___ . "Contacting Congressional Constituents: Some Patterns of Perquisite Use." *American Journal of Political Science* 24 (1980): 125-134.

Cover, Albert D., and David R. Mayhew. "Congressional Dynamics and the Decline of Competitive Congressional Elections." In *Congress Reconsidered.* 2d ed. Edited by Lawrence C. Dodd and Bruce I. Oppenheimer. Washington, D.C.: CQ Press, 1981.

Cox, Gary, and Mathew McCubbins. *Parties and Committees in the U.S. House of Representatives.* Berkeley: University of California Press, 1990.

Davidson, Roger H., ed. *The Postreform Congress.* New York: St. Martin's, 1992.

Davidson, Roger H., David M. Kovenock, and Michael K. O'Leary. *Congress in Crisis: Politics and Congressional Reform.* Belmont, Calif.: Wadsworth, 1966.

Davidson, Roger H., and Walter J. Oleszek. *Congress Against Itself.* Bloomington: Indiana University Press, 1977.

___ . *Congress and Its Members.* 3d ed. Washington, D.C.: CQ Press, 1989.

Davidson, Roger H., Walter J. Oleszek, and Thomas Kephart. "One Bill, Many Referrals: Multiple Referrals in the U.S. House of Representatives." *Legislative Studies Quarterly* 13 (1988): 3-28.

Deering, Christopher J. *Congressional Politics.* Chicago: Dorsey, 1989.

Dexter, Lewis A. *How Organizations Are Represented in Washington.* Indianapolis: Bobbs-Merrill, 1969.

___ . *The Sociology and Politics of Congress.* Chicago: Rand McNally, 1969.

Dodd, Lawrence C. "Congress and the Quest for Power." In *Congress Reconsidered.* 1st ed. Edited by Lawrence C. Dodd and Bruce I. Oppenheimer. New York: Praeger, 1977.

___ . "The Expanded Roles of the House Democratic Whip System." *Congressional Studies* 6 (1979).

Dodd, Lawrence C., and Richard L. Schott. *Congress and the Administrative State.* New York: Wiley, 1979.

Eckhardt, Bob, and Charles L. Black, Jr. *The Titles of Power: Conversations on the American Constitution.* New Haven: Yale University Press, 1976.

Edwards, George C., III. *Presidential Influence in Congress.* San Francisco: Freeman, 1980.

Erikson, Robert S. "The Advantage of Incumbency in Congressional Elections." *Polity* 3 (1971).

___ . "Is There Such a Thing as a Safe Seat?" *Polity* 8 (1976): 623-632.

___ . "The Puzzle of Midterm Loss." *Journal of Politics* 50 (1988): 1011-1029.

Eulau, Heinz, and Paul Karps. "The Puzzle of Representation." *Legislative Studies Quarterly* 2 (1977): 233-254.

Evans, C. Lawrence. *Leadership in Committee.* Ann Arbor: University of Michigan Press, 1991.

Fenno, Richard F., Jr. *The Power of the Purse.* Boston: Little, Brown, 1966.

___ . *Congressmen in Committees.* Boston: Little, Brown, 1973.

___ . "If, as Ralph Nader Says, Congress Is 'the Broken Branch,' How Come We Love Our Congressmen So Much?" In *Congress in Change.* Edited by Norman J. Ornstein. New York: Praeger, 1975.

_____ . *Home Style: House Members in Their Districts.* Boston: Little, Brown, 1978.

_____ . *The United States Senate: A Bicameral Perspective.* Washington, D.C.: American Enterprise Institute, 1982.

Ferejohn, John A. *Pork Barrel Politics.* Stanford, Calif.: Stanford University Press, 1974.

Fiorina, Morris P. *Representatives, Roll Calls, and Constituencies.* Lexington, Mass.: Lexington Books, 1974.

_____ . *Congress: Keystone of the Washington Establishment.* New Haven: Yale University Press, 1977.

Fiorina, Morris P., David W. Rohde, and Peter Wissel. "Historical Change in House Turnover." In *Congress in Change.* Edited by Norman J. Ornstein. New York: Praeger, 1975.

Fishel, Jeff. *Party and Opposition.* New York: David McKay, 1973.

Fisher, Louis. *President and Congress: Power and Policy.* New York: Free Press, 1972.

_____ . *The Constitution Between Friends: Congress, the President, and the Law.* New York: St. Martin's, 1978.

Fowler, Linda. "Candidates' Perceptions of Electoral Coalitions." *American Politics Quarterly* 8 (1980): 483-494.

Fowler, Linda L., and Robert D. McClure. *Political Ambition: Who Decides to Run for Congress?* New Haven: Yale University Press, 1989.

Fox, Harrison W., Jr., and Susan Webb Hammond. *Congressional Staffs: The Invisible Force in American Lawmaking.* New York: Free Press, 1977.

Frantzich, Stephen E. "Computerized Information Technology in the U.S. House of Representatives." *Legislative Studies Quarterly* 4 (1979): 255-280.

Freeman, J. Leiper. *The Political Process.* New York: Random House, 1955.

Froman, Lewis A., Jr. *The Congressional Process: Strategies, Rules and Procedures.* Boston: Little, Brown, 1967.

Gilmour, John B. *Reconcilable Differences.* Berkeley: University of California Press, 1990.

Glazer, Amihai, and Bernard Grofman. "Two Plus Two Plus Two Equals Six: Tenure of Office of Senators and Representatives, 1953-1983." *Legislative Studies Quarterly* 12 (1987): 555-563.

Goehlert, Robert U., and John R. Sayre. *The United States Congress: A Bibliography.* New York: Free Press, 1982.

Goldenberg, Edie N., and Michael W. Traugott. *Campaigning for Congress.* Washington, D.C.: CQ Press, 1984.

Goodwin, George, Jr. *The Little Legislatures.* Amherst: University of Massachusetts Press, 1970.

Hall, Richard L. "Participation and Purpose in Committee Decision Making." *American Political Science Review* 81 (1987): 105-127.

_____ . *Participation in Congress.* New Haven: Yale University Press, 1993.

Harris, Joseph. *Congressional Control of Administration.* Washington, D.C.: Brookings Institution, 1964.

Hayes, Michael I. "Interest Groups and Congress: Toward a Transactional Theory." In *The Congressional System: Notes and Readings.* 2d ed. Edited by Leroy N. Rieselbach. North Scituate, Mass.: Duxbury Press, 1979.

Henry, Charles P. "Legitimizing Race in Congressional Politics." *American Politics Quarterly* 5 (1977): 149-176.

Herrnson, Paul S. *Party Campaigning in the 1980s.* Cambridge: Harvard University Press, 1988.

Hershey, Marjorie R. *The Making of Campaign Strategy.* Lexington, Mass.: Lexington Books, 1974.

Hibbing, John R. "Ambition in the House: Behavioral Consequences of Higher Office Goals Among U.S. Representatives." *American Journal of Political Science* 30 (1986): 651-665.

———. *Congressional Careers.* Chapel Hill: University of North Carolina Press, 1991.

Hibbing, John R., and John R. Alford. "Economic Conditions and the Forgotten Side of Congress: A Foray into U.S. Senate Elections." *British Journal of Political Science* 12 (1982): 505-513.

Hinckley, Barbara. *The Seniority System in Congress.* Bloomington: Indiana University Press, 1971.

———. *Stability and Change in Congress.* New York: Harper, 1971.

———. "The American Voter in Congressional Elections." *American Political Science Review* 74 (1980): 641-650.

Hoadly, John F. "The Emergence of Political Parties in Congress, 1789-1803." *American Political Science Review* 74 (1980): 757-779.

Holtzman, Abraham. *Legislative Liaison.* Chicago: Rand McNally, 1970.

Huitt, Ralph K., and Robert L. Peabody. *Congress: Two Decades of Analysis.* New York: Harper, 1969.

Huntington, Samuel P. "Congressional Responses to the Twentieth Century." In *The Congress and America's Future.* 2d ed. Edited by David B. Truman. Englewood Cliffs, N.J.: Prentice-Hall, 1973.

Hurley, Patricia, and Kim Quarle Hill. "The Prospects for Issue-Voting in Contemporary Congressional Elections." *American Politics Quarterly* 8 (1980): 425-448.

Jackson, John. *Constituencies and Leaders in Congress.* Cambridge: Harvard University Press, 1974.

Jacobson, Gary C. *Money in Congressional Elections.* New Haven: Yale University Press, 1980.

———. "The Marginals Never Vanished: Incumbency and Competition in Elections to the U.S. House of Representatives, 1952-81." *American Journal of Political Science* 31 (1987): 126-141.

———. *The Politics of Congressional Elections.* 2d ed. Boston: Little, Brown, 1987.

———. *The Electoral Origins of Divided Government.* Boulder: Westview Press, 1990.

Jacobson, Gary C., and Samuel Kernell. *Strategy and Choice in Congressional Elections.* New Haven: Yale University Press, 1983.

Jewell, Malcolm E. *Senatorial Politics and Foreign Policy.* Lexington: University of Kentucky Press, 1962.

Jewell, Malcolm E., and Samuel C. Patterson. *The Legislative Process in the United States.* 3d ed. New York: Random House, 1977.

Johannes, John R. *Policy Innovation in Congress.* Morristown, N.J.: General Learning Press, 1972.

Jones, Charles O. "Representation in Congress: The Case of the House Agricultural Committee." *American Political Science Review* 55 (1961): 358-367.

——. "The Role of the Congressional Subcommittee." *Midwest Journal of Political Science* 6 (1962): 327-344.

——. *The Minority Party in Congress.* Boston: Little, Brown, 1970.

——. "Will Reform Change Congress?" In *Congress Reconsidered.* 1st ed. Edited by Lawrence C. Dodd and Bruce I. Oppenheimer. New York: Praeger, 1977.

Kazee, Thomas. "The Decision to Run for the U.S. Congress: Challenger Attitudes in the 1970s." *Legislative Studies Quarterly* 5 (1980): 79-100.

Keefe, William J. *Congress and the American People.* Englewood Cliffs, N. J.: Prentice-Hall, 1980.

Keefe, William J., and Morris S. Ogul. *The American Legislative Process.* 4th ed. Englewood Cliffs, N.J.: Prentice-Hall, 1977.

Kiewiet, Roderick, and Mathew D. McCubbins. *The Spending Power.* Berkeley: University of California Press, 1991.

Kingdon, John W. *Candidates for Office.* New York: Random House, 1968.

——. *Congressmen's Voting Decisions.* New York: Harper, 1973.

Krehbiel, Keith. "Are Congressional Committees Composed of Preference Outliers?" *American Political Science Review* 84 (1990): 149-164.

——. *Information and Legislative Organization.* Ann Arbor: University of Michigan Press, 1990.

Krehbiel, Keith, Kenneth A. Shepsle, and Barry R. Weingast. "Why Are Congressional Committees Powerful?" *American Political Science Review* 81 (1987): 929-948.

Kuklinski, James H. "District Competitiveness and Legislative Roll Call Behavior: A Reassessment of the Marginality Hypothesis." *American Journal of Political Science* 21 (1977): 627-638.

LeLoup, Lance T. *Budgetary Politics.* Brunswick, Ohio: Kings Court Press, 1977.

LeLoup, Lance T., and Steven Shull. "Congress Versus the Executive: The 'Two Presidencies' Reconsidered." *Social Science Quarterly* 59 (1979): 704-719.

Loewenberg, Gerhard, and Samuel Patterson. *Comparing Legislatures.* Boston: Little, Brown, 1979.

Longley, Lawrence D., and Walter J. Oleszek. *Bicameral Politics: Conference Committees in Congress.* New Haven: Yale University Press, 1989.

Lowi, Theodore J. *The End of Liberalism.* New York: Norton, 1969, 1979.

Maass, Arthur. *Congress and the Common Good.* New York: Basic Books, 1983.

McAdams, John C., and John R. Johannes. "Congressmen, Perquisites, and Elections." *Journal of Politics* 50 (1988): 412-439.

Maisel, Louis S. *From Obscurity to Oblivion: Running in the Congressional Primary.* Knoxville: University of Tennessee Press, 1982.

Manley, John F. *The Politics of Finance.* Boston: Little, Brown, 1970.

Mann, Thomas E., *Unsafe at Any Margin: Interpreting Congressional Elections.* Washington, D.C.: American Enterprise Institute, 1978.

____. ed. *A Question of Balance: The President, the Congress, and Foreign Policy.* Washington, D.C.: Brookings Institution, 1990.

Mann, Thomas E., and Norman J. Ornstein. *The New Congress.* Washington, D.C.: American Enterprise Institute, 1981.

Mann, Thomas E., and Raymond E. Wolfinger. "Candidates and Parties in Congressional Elections." *American Political Science Review* 74 (1980): 617-632.

Matthews, Donald R. *U.S. Senators and Their World.* New York: Vintage Books, 1960.

Mayhew, David R. *Party Loyalty Among Congressmen.* Cambridge: Harvard University Press, 1966.

____. *Congress: The Electoral Connection.* New Haven: Yale University Press, 1974.

Mezey, Michael L. *Congress, the President, and Public Policy.* Boulder: Westview Press, 1989.

Moe, Terry M. "An Assessment of the Positive Theory of Congressional Dominance." *Legislative Studies Quarterly* 12 (1987): 475-520.

Nelson, Garrison. "Partisan Patterns of House Leadership Change, 1789-1977." *American Political Science Review* 71 (1977): 918-939.

Norpoth, Helmut. "Explaining Party Cohesion in Congress: The Case of Shared Party Attributes." *American Political Science Review* 70 (1976): 1157-1171.

Ogul, Morris S. *Congress Oversees the Bureaucracy.* Pittsburgh: University of Pittsburgh Press, 1976.

Oleszek, Walter J. *Congressional Procedures and the Policy Process.* 3d ed. Washington, D.C.: CQ Press, 1988.

Oppenheimer, Bruce I. *Oil and the Congressional Process: The Limits of Symbolic Politics.* Lexington, Mass.: Lexington Books, 1974.

____. "The Rules Committee: New Arm of Leadership in a Decentralized House." In *Congress Reconsidered.* 1st ed. Edited by Lawrence C. Dodd and Bruce I. Oppenheimer. New York: Praeger, 1977.

____. "Changing Time Constraints on Congress: Historical Perspectives on the Use of Cloture." In *Congress Reconsidered.* 3d ed. Edited by Lawrence C. Dodd and Bruce I. Oppenheimer. Washington, D.C.: CQ Press, 1985.

____. "Split-Party Control of Congress, 1981-1986: Exploring Electoral and Apportionment Explanations." *American Journal of Political Science* 33 (1989): 653-669.

Orfield, Gary. *Congressional Power: Congress and Social Change.* New York: Harcourt, 1975.

Ornstein, Norman J. *Congress in Change: Evolution and Reform.* New York: Praeger, 1975.

Ornstein, Norman J., and Shirley Elder. *Interest Groups, Lobbying and Policymaking.* Washington, D.C.: CQ Press, 1978.

Ornstein, Norman J., Thomas E. Mann, and Michael J. Malbin. *Vital Statistics on Congress, 1991-1992.* Washington, D.C.: Congressional Quarterly, 1991.

Ornstein, Norman J., and David W. Rohde. "Shifting Forces, Changing Rules, and Political Outcomes: The Impact of Congressional Change on Four House Committees." In *New Perspectives on the House of Representatives.* Edited by Robert L. Peabody and Nelson W. Polsby. Chicago: Rand McNally, 1977.

Parker, Glenn R. "Some Themes in Congressional Unpopularity." *American Journal of Political Science* 21 (1977): 93-110.

——. "The Advantage of Incumbency in House Elections." *American Politics Quarterly* 8 (1980): 449-464.

——. *Studies of Congress.* Washington, D.C.: CQ Press, 1984.

——. *Homeward Bound: Explaining Changes in Congressional Behavior.* Pittsburgh: University of Pittsburgh Press, 1986.

Parker, Glenn R., and S. L. Parker. "Factions in Committees: The U.S. House of Representatives." *American Political Science Review* 73 (1979): 85-102.

Payne, James L. "The Personal Electoral Advantage of House Incumbents, 1936-1976." *American Politics Quarterly* 8 (1980): 465-482.

Peabody, Robert L. *Leadership in Congress: Stability, Succession, and Change.* Boston: Little, Brown, 1976.

Peabody, Robert L., and Nelson W. Polsby, eds. *New Perspectives on the House of Representatives.* 3d ed. Chicago: Rand McNally, 1977.

Peters, John G., and Susan Welch. "The Effects of Charges of Corruption on Voting Behavior in Congressional Elections." *American Political Science Review* 74 (1980): 697-708.

Peters, Ronald M., Jr. *The American Speakership.* Baltimore: Johns Hopkins University Press, 1990.

Peterson, Mark A. *Legislating Together: The White House and Capitol Hill from Eisenhower to Reagan.* Cambridge: Harvard University Press, 1990.

Pierce, John C., and John L. Sullivan. *The Electorate Reconsidered.* Beverly Hills, Calif.: Sage, 1980.

Polsby, Nelson W. "Institutionalization in the U.S. House of Representatives." *American Political Science Review* 62 (1968): 144-168.

——. *Congress and the Presidency.* 3d ed. Englewood Cliffs, N.J.: Prentice-Hall, 1976.

Polsby, Nelson W., Miriam Gallagher, and Barry Rundquist. "The Growth of the Seniority System in the House of Representatives." *American Political Science Review* 63 (1969): 787-807.

Powell, Lynda W. "Issue Representation in Congress." *Journal of Politics* (1982).

Price, David E. *Who Makes the Laws?* Cambridge, Mass.: Schenkman, 1972.

Price, H. Douglas. "Congress and the Evolution of Legislative Professionalism."

In *Congress in Change.* Edited by Norman J. Ornstein. New York: Praeger, 1975.

Ragsdale, Lyn. "The Fiction of Congressional Elections as Presidential Events." *American Politics Quarterly* 8 (1980): 395-398.

Ragsdale, Lyn, and Timothy E. Cook. "Representatives' Actions and Challengers' Reactions: Limits to Candidate Connections in the House." *American Journal of Political Science* 31 (1987): 45-81.

Reid, T. R. *Congressional Odyssey: The Saga of a Senate Bill.* San Francisco: Freeman, 1980.

Rieselbach, Leroy N. *The Roots of Isolationism.* Indianapolis: Bobbs-Merrill, 1966.

____. *Congressional Politics.* New York: McGraw-Hill, 1973.

____. *Congressional Reform in the Seventies.* Morristown, N.J.: General Learning Press, 1977.

____. ed. *Legislative Reform: The Policy Impact.* Lexington, Mass.: Lexington Books, 1978.

Ripley, Randall B. *Party Leaders in the House of Representatives.* Washington, D.C.: Brookings Institution, 1967.

____. *Majority Party Leadership in Congress.* Boston: Little, Brown, 1969.

____. *Power in the Senate.* New York: St. Martin's, 1969.

Ripley, Randall B., and Grace N. Franklin. *Congress, the Bureaucracy, and Public Policy.* Homewood, Ill.: Dorsey, 1980.

Rohde, David W. *Parties and Leaders in the Postreform House.* Chicago: University of Chicago Press, 1991.

Rohde, David W., and Kenneth A. Shepsle. "Democratic Committee Assignments in the U.S. House of Representatives." *American Political Science Review* 67 (1973): 889-905.

Rothman, David J. *Politics and Power.* New York: Atheneum, 1969.

Rudder, Catherine E. "Committee Reform and the Revenue Process." In *Congress Reconsidered.* 1st ed. Edited by Lawrence C. Dodd and Bruce I. Oppenheimer. New York: Praeger, 1977.

Saloma, John S., III. *Congress and the New Politics.* Boston: Little, Brown, 1969.

Schick, Allen. *Making Economic Policy in Congress.* Washington, D.C.: American Enterprise Institute, 1983.

Schneider, Jerrold E. *Ideological Coalitions in Congress.* Greenwood, Conn.: Greenwood Press, 1979.

Schwarz, John E., and L. Earl Shaw. *The United States Congress in Comparative Perspective.* Hinsdale, Ill.: Dryden Press, 1976.

Seidman, Harold. *Politics, Position, and Power.* 2d ed. London: Oxford University Press, 1975.

Shepsle, Kenneth A. *The Giant Jigsaw Puzzle.* Chicago: University of Chicago Press, 1978.

Sinclair, Barbara Deckard. "Determinants of Aggregate Party Cohesion in the U.S. House of Representatives." *Legislative Studies Quarterly* 2 (1977): 155-175.

——— . *Majority Leadership in the U.S. House.* Baltimore: Johns Hopkins University Press, 1983.

——— . *The Transformation of the U.S. Senate.* Baltimore: Johns Hopkins University Press, 1989.

Smith, Steven S. *Call to Order: Floor Politics in the House and Senate.* Washington, D.C.: Brookings Institution, 1989.

Smith, Steven S., and Christopher J. Deering. *Committees in Congress.* Washington, D.C.: CQ Press, 1984.

Stone, Walter J. "The Dynamics of Constituency: Electoral Control in the House." *American Politics Quarterly* 8 (1980): 399-424.

Strahan, Randall. *New Ways and Means: Reform and Change in a Congressional Committee.* Chapel Hill: University of North Carolina Press, 1990.

Sundquist, James L. *Politics and Policy.* Washington, D.C.: Brookings Institution, 1968.

——— . *The Decline and Resurgence of Congress.* Washington, D.C.: Brookings Institution, 1981.

Thurber, James A. *Divided Democracy: Cooperation and Conflict Between the President and Congress.* Washington, D.C.: CQ Press, 1991.

Truman, David B. *The Governmental Process.* New York: Knopf, 1951.

Turner, Julius. *Party and Constituency: Pressures on Congress.* Rev. ed. Edited by Edward V. Schneier, Jr. Baltimore: Johns Hopkins University Press, 1970.

Unekis, Joseph, and Leroy N. Rieselbach. *Congressional Committee Politics: Continuity and Change.* New York: Praeger, 1984.

Uslaner, Eric M. "Policy Entrepreneurs and Amateur Democrats in the House of Representatives." In *Legislative Reform: The Policy Impact.* Edited by Leroy N. Rieselbach. Lexington, Mass.: Lexington Books, 1978.

Vogler, David J. *The Third House.* Evanston, Ill.: Northwestern University Press, 1971.

——— . *The Politics of Congress.* Boston: Allyn and Bacon, 1974.

Wahlke, John C., Heinz H. Eulau, W. Buchanan, and L. C. Ferguson. *The Legislative System: Explorations in Legislative Behavior.* New York: Wiley, 1962.

Wayne, S. J. *The Legislative Presidency.* New York: Harper, 1978.

Weingast, Barry. "Floor Behavior in the U.S. Congress: Committee Power Under the Open Rule." *American Political Science Review* 83 (1989): 795-815.

Weisberg, Herbert F. "Evaluating Theories of Congressional Roll Call Voting." *American Journal of Political Science* 22 (1978): 554-577.

Westefield, L. P. "Majority Party Leadership and the Committee System in the House of Representatives." *American Political Science Review* 68 (1974): 1593-1604.

Wildavsky, Aaron. *The Politics of the Budgetary Process.* Boston: Little, Brown, 1964.

Wilson, Rick. "Forward and Backward Agenda Procedures: Committee Experience and Structurally Induced Equilibrium." *Journal of Politics* 48 (1986): 390-409.

Wilson, Woodrow. *Congressional Government.* Gloucester, Mass.: Peter Smith, 1885, 1973.

Wolfinger, Raymond E., and Joan Heifetz Hollinger. "Safe Seats, Seniority, and Power in Congress." *American Political Science Review* 59 (1965): 337-349.

Wright, Gerald C., and Michael B. Berkman. "Candidates and Policy in United States Senate Elections." *American Political Science Review* 80 (1986): 567-588.

Wright, John. "PACs, Contributions, and Roll Calls: An Organizational Perspective." *American Political Science Review* 75 (1985): 400-414.

Young, James S. *The Washington Community, 1880-1828.* New York: Columbia University Press, 1966.

Index